PRAISE FOR *INFLUENCE, NEW AND EXPANDED*

"If you could read just one book on how to be more effective in business and life, I'd pick *Influence*. It's a tour de force that Cialdini has somehow made more marvelous."

—*Katy Milkman, professor at the Wharton School, host of the* Choiceology *podcast, and author of* How to Change

"A phenomenal book! Whether you seek to boost sales, strike a better deal, or improve your relationships, *Influence* offers scientifically tested principles that can change your life."

—*Daniel L. Shapiro, Ph.D., founder and director of the Harvard International Negotiation Program and author of* Negotiating the Nonnegotiable

"*Influence* richly deserves its status as the definitive book on the subject. I learned so much from this revised edition, and so will you."

—*Tim Harford, author of* The Data Detective *(US)/* How to Make the World Add Up *(UK)*

"Prepare to be dazzled. Bob Cialdini is the godfather of influence, and the original version of this book is already a classic. Whether you're trying to influence or understand how others influence you, this book will show you how."

—*Jonah Berger, professor at the Wharton School and author of* Contagious *and* The Catalyst

"A remarkable effort and achievement. *Influence* remains the brilliantly written treatise on fundamental principles of human behavior, with the addition of a timely new principle."

—*Jeffrey Pfeffer, Thomas D. Dee II Professor of Organizational Behavior at the Stanford Graduate School of Business and author of* Power: Why Some People Have It—and Others Don't

"*Influence* is a modern business classic that has profoundly shaped the fields of marketing and psychology. Robert Cialdini's new edition makes a brilliant book even better, with robust new insights and examples."

—*Dorie Clark, author of* Reinventing You *and executive education faculty, Duke University Fuqua School of Business*

"The new *Influence* is nothing short of a masterpiece. The writing is both timeless and worth reading immediately."

—*Joe Polish, founder of Genius Network*

"*Influence* is a must-read for anyone who wants to understand the decision-making process. It is simply essential reading in the canon of psychology and behavioral finance."

—*Barry Ritholtz, chairman and chief investment officer of Ritholtz Wealth Management*

"Cialdini has made a classic even better. This updated edition of *Influence* affirms its place as one of the most important books on business and behavior of the last fifty years. The new additions are terrific."

—*Daniel H. Pink, author of* When, Drive, *and* To Sell Is Human

"*Influence* is the only book I've assigned to my organizational behavior students at Stanford for the last twenty-five years. Students love it, and, years later, rave about how helpful it is has been throughout their careers. The new version is even more useful and nuanced—and even more fun to read."

—*Robert I. Sutton, professor at the Stanford Graduate School of Business and author of seven books, including* New York Times *bestsellers* The No Asshole Rule *and* Good Boss, Bad Boss

"Like every psychologist I know (and like many thousands of others who are curious about how the world works), I got my start learning about persuasion with Bob Cialdini's *Influence*. This revised edition builds so meaningfully on the worn first edition sitting next to my desk—*Influence* will continue to clarify and inspire the art and science of persuasion for years to come."

—*Betsy Levy Paluck, professor of psychology and public affairs, deputy director of the Kahneman-Treisman Center for Behavioral Science and Public Policy, Princeton University*

INFLUENCE,

NEW AND EXPANDED

INFLUENCE,

NEW AND EXPANDED

THE PSYCHOLOGY OF PERSUASION

ROBERT B. CIALDINI, PH.D.

HARPER
BUSINESS
An Imprint of HarperCollins*Publishers*

HarperCollins books may be purchased for educational, business, or sales promotional use. For information, please email the Special Markets Department at SPsales@harpercollins.com.

First Collins Business Essentials edition published in 2007.

First Harper Business new and expanded hardcover edition published in 2021.

Library of Congress Cataloging-in-Publication Data
Names: Cialdini, Robert B., author.
Title: Influence, new and expanded: the psychology of persuasion / Robert B. Cialdini.
Description: New and Expanded. | New York: Harper Business, 2021. | Revised edition of the author's Influence, © 1993. | Includes bibliographical references and index. | Summary: "In this highly acclaimed New York Times bestseller, Dr. Robert B. Cialdini—the seminal expert in the field of influence and persuasion—explains the psychology of why people say yes and how to apply these principles ethically in business and everyday situations"—Provided by publisher.
Identifiers: LCCN 2020058532 (print) | LCCN 2020058533 (ebook) | ISBN 9780062937650 (hardcover) | ISBN 9780062937674 (ebook)
Subjects: LCSH: Influence (Psychology) | Persuasion (Psychology) | Compliance.
Classification: LCC BF774 .C55 2021 (print) | LCC BF774 (ebook) | DDC 153.8/52—dc23
LC record available at https://lccn.loc.gov/2020058532
LC ebook record available at https://lccn.loc.gov/2020058533

21 22 23 24 25   LSC   10 9 8 7 6 5 4 3 2 1

For Hailey, who, every time I see her, leaves me more amazed.

For Dawson, who, every time I see him, leaves me more convinced he will do great things.

For Leia, who, every time I see her, leaves me a happier man.

CONTENTS

Preface xi

Introduction. xv

Chapter 1 LEVERS OF INFLUENCE: *(Power) Tools of the Trades* 1

Chapter 2 RECIPROCATION: *The Old Give and Take.* 23

Chapter 3 LIKING: *The Friendly Thief* 73

Chapter 4 SOCIAL PROOF: *Truths Are Us* 127

Chapter 5 AUTHORITY: *Directed Deference.* 199

Chapter 6 SCARCITY: *The Rule of the Few* 241

Chapter 7 COMMITMENT AND CONSISTENCY: *Hobgoblins of the Mind* . . . 291

Chapter 8 UNITY: *The "We" Is the Shared Me* 363

Chapter 9 INSTANT INFLUENCE:
           Primitive Consent for an Automatic Age 437

Acknowledgments. 447

Notes 449

Bibliography. 491

Index 545

PREFACE

From the outset, *Influence* was designed for the popular reader, and as such, an attempt was made to write it in a nonacademic, conversational style. I admit to doing so with some trepidation that the book would be viewed as a form of "pop" psychology by my academic colleagues. I was concerned because, as the legal scholar James Boyle observed, "You have never heard true condescension until you have heard academics pronounce the word 'popularizer.'" For this reason, at the time of the first writing of *Influence*, most of my fellow social psychologists didn't feel safe, professionally, writing for a nonacademic audience. Indeed, if social psychology had been a business, it would have been known for having great research and development units but no shipping department. We didn't ship, except to one another in academic journal articles that no one else was likely to encounter, let alone use.

Fortunately, although I decided to push ahead with a popular style, none of my fears has been realized, as *Influence* has not received disparagement on "pop" psychology grounds.[1] Consequently, in subsequent versions, including the present one, the conversational style is retained. Of course, more importantly, I also present the research evidence for my statements, recommendations, and conclusions. Although the conclusions of *Influence* are illuminated and corroborated through such devices as interviews, quotes, and systematic personal observations, those conclusions are invariably based on properly conducted psychological research.

Comment on This Edition of Influence

Shaping the current edition of *Influence* has been challenging for me. On the one hand, recalling the "Don't fix what's not broken" axiom, I was reluctant to perform major reconstructive surgery. After all, previous versions had sold more copies than I could have sensibly imagined, in multiple editions and forty-four languages. In this last regard, my Polish colleague, Professor Wilhelmina Wosinska, offered an affirming (yet sobering) commentary on the perceived worth of the book. She said, "You know, Robert, your book *Influence* is so famous in Poland, my students think you're dead."

On the other hand, in keeping with a quote my Sicilian grand-father favored, "If you want things to stay as they are, things will have to change," there was a case to be made for timely upgrades.[2] It has been some time since *Influence* was last published, and, in the interim, changes have occurred that deserve a place in this new edition. First, we now know more than we did before about the influence process. The study of persuasion, compliance, and change has advanced, and the pages that follow have been adapted to reflect that progress. In addition to an overall update of the material, I have devoted more attention to updated coverage of the role of influence in everyday human interaction—how the influence process works in real-world settings rather than in laboratory contexts.

Relatedly, I have also expanded a feature that was stimulated by the responses of prior readers. This feature highlights the experiences of individuals who have read *Influence*, recognized how one of the principles worked on (or for) them in a particular instance, and wrote to me describing the event. Their descriptions, which appear in the Reader's Reports of each chapter, illustrate how easily and frequently we can fall victim to the influence process in our daily lives. There are now many new firsthand accounts of how the book's principles apply to commonplace professional and personal situations. I wish to thank the following individuals who—either directly or through their course instructors—contributed the Reader's Reports used in past editions: Pat Bobbs, Hartnut Bock, Annie Carto, Michael Conroy, William Cooper, Alicia Friedman, William Graziano, Jonathan Harries, Mark Hastings, Endayehu Kendie, Karen Klawer, Danuta Lubnicka, James Michaels, Steven Moysey, Katie Mueller, Paul Nail, Dan Norris, Sam Omar, Alan J. Resnik, Daryl Retzlaff, Geofrey Rosenberger, Joanna Spychala, Robert Stauth, Dan Swift, and Karla Vasks. Special thanks are due to those who provided new Reader's Reports for this edition: Laura Clark, Jake Epps, Juan Gomez, Phillip Johnston, Paola, Joe St. John, Carol Thomas, Jens Trabolt, Lucas Weimann, Anna Wroblewski, and Agrima Yadav. I would also like to invite readers to contribute similar reports for possible publication in a future edition. They can be sent to me at ReadersReports@InfluenceAtWork.com. Finally, more influence-relevant information can be obtained at www .InfluenceAtWork.com.

Besides the changes in this edition that are updated extensions of previously existing features of the book, three elements appear for the first time. One explores internet-based applications of proven social-influence tactics. It is clear that social media and e-commerce sites have embraced the lessons of persuasion science. Accordingly, each chapter now includes, in specially created eBoxes, illustrations of how this migration into current technologies has been accomplished. The second novel feature is the enhanced use of endnotes as the place where readers can find citations for the research described in the text as well citations and descriptions of related work. The endnotes now allow for a more inclusive, narrative account of the issues at hand. Finally, and most significantly, I have added a seventh universal principle of social influence to the book—the principle of unity. In the chapter devoted to unity, I describe how individuals who can be convinced that a communicator shares a meaningful personal or social identity with them become remarkably more susceptible to the communicator's persuasive appeals.

INTRODUCTION

I can admit it freely now. All my life I've been a patsy. For as long as I can recall, I've been an easy mark for the pitches of peddlers, fundraisers, and operators of one sort or another. True, only some have had dishonorable motives. The others—representatives of certain charitable agencies, for instance—have had the best intentions. No matter. With personally disquieting frequency, I have always found myself in possession of unwanted magazine subscriptions or tickets to the sanitation workers' ball. Probably this long-standing status as sucker accounts for my interest in the study of compliance: Just what are the factors that cause one person to say yes to another? And which techniques most effectively use these factors to bring about compliance? I have wondered why it is that a request stated in a certain way will be rejected, but a request asking for the same favor in a slightly different fashion will be successful.

So in my role as an experimental social psychologist, I began to research the psychology of compliance. At first the research took the form of experiments performed, for the most part, in my laboratory and on college students. I wanted to find out which psychological principles influenced the tendency to comply with a request. Right now, psychologists know quite a bit about these principles—what they are and how they work. I have characterized such principles as levers of influence and will be discussing some of the most important in this book.

After a time, though, I began to realize that the experimental work, while necessary, wasn't enough. It didn't allow me to judge the importance of the principles in the world beyond the psychology building and the campus where I was examining them. It became clear that if I were to understand fully the psychology of compliance, I would need to broaden my scope of investigation. I would need to look to the compliance professionals—the people who had been using the principles on me all my life. They know what works and what doesn't; the law of survival of the fittest assures it. Their business is to make us comply, and their livelihoods depend on it. Those who don't know how to get people to say yes soon fall away; those who do, stay and flourish.

Of course, the compliance professionals aren't the only ones who know about and use these principles to help them get their way. We all employ them and fall victim to them to some degree in our daily interactions with neighbors, friends, lovers, and family. But the compliance practitioners have much more than the vague and amateurish understanding of what works than the rest of us do. As I thought about it, I knew they represented the richest vein of information about compliance available to me. For nearly three years, then, I combined my experimental studies with a decidedly more entertaining program: I systematically immersed myself in the world of compliance professionals—salespeople, fundraisers, marketers, recruiters, and others.

My purpose was to observe, from the inside, the techniques and strategies most commonly and effectively used by a broad range of compliance practitioners. That program of observation sometimes took the form of interviews with the practitioners and sometimes with the natural enemies (for example, police fraud-squad officers, investigative reporters, consumer-protection agencies) of certain of the practitioners. At other times, it involved an intensive examination of the written materials by which compliance techniques are passed down from one generation to another—sales manuals and the like.

Most frequently, though, it took the form of participant observation—a research approach in which the investigator becomes a spy of sorts. With disguised identity and intent, the researcher infiltrates the setting of interest and becomes a full-fledged participant in the group to be studied. So when I wanted to learn about the compliance tactics of magazine (or vacuum-cleaner or portrait-photograph or health-supplement) sales organizations, I would answer an ad for sales trainees and have them teach me their methods. Using similar but not identical approaches, I was able to penetrate advertising, public-relations, and fundraising agencies to examine their techniques. Much of the evidence presented in this book, then, comes from my experience posing as a compliance professional, or aspiring professional, in a large variety of organizations dedicated to getting us to say yes.

One aspect of what I learned in this three-year period of participant observation was most instructive. Although there are thousands of different tactics that compliance practitioners employ to produce yes, the majority fall within seven basic categories. Each of these categories is governed by a fundamental psychological principle that directs human behavior and, in so doing, gives the tactics their power. This book is organized around these seven principles, one to a chapter. The principles—reciprocation, liking, social proof, authority, scarcity, commitment and consistency, and unity—are discussed both in terms of their function in society and in terms of how their enormous force can be commissioned by a compliance professional who deftly incorporates them into requests for purchases, donations, concessions, votes, or assent.[1]

Each principle is examined as to its ability to produce a distinct kind of automatic, mindless compliance from people: a willingness to say yes without thinking first. The evidence suggests that the ever-accelerating pace and informational crush of modern life will make this particular form of unthinking compliance more and more prevalent in the future. It will be increasingly important for society, therefore, to understand the how and why of automatic influence.

Finally, in this edition, I've sequenced the chapters to fit with the insights of my colleague Dr. Gregory Neidert regarding how certain principles are more useful than others, depending on which persuasive goal the communicator wishes to achieve with a message. Of course, any would-be influencer wants to create change in others; but, according to Dr. Neidert's Core Motives Model of Social Influence, the communicator's prime goal at the time affects which influence principles the communicator should prioritize. For instance, the model asserts that one of the main motives (goals) of a persuader involves *cultivating a positive relationship*. Research shows that messages are more likely to be successful if recipients can first be made to feel positively toward the messenger. Three of the seven principles of influence—reciprocation, liking, and unity—seem particularly appropriate to the task.

In other situations, perhaps when a good relationship is already in place, the goal of *reducing uncertainty* may be a priority. After all, having a positive relationship with a communicator doesn't necessarily mean message recipients will be persuaded. Before they are likely to change their minds, people want to be assured any decision they are being urged to make is wise. Under these circumstances, according to the model, the principles of social proof and authority should never be ignored—because evidence that a choice is well regarded by peers or by experts makes it, indeed, appear prudent.

But even with a positive relationship cultivated and uncertainty reduction accomplished, a remaining goal needs to be achieved to boost the likelihood of behavioral change. In such a situation, the goal of *motivating action* becomes the main objective. That is, a well-liked friend may show me sufficient proof that almost everyone believes that daily exercise is a good thing and that leading medical experts overwhelmingly support its health benefits, but that proof may not be enough to get me to do it. The friend would do well to include in any appeal the principles of consistency and scarcity. The friend could do so by reminding me, for example, of what I've said publicly in the past about the importance of my health (consistency) and about the unique enjoyments I would miss if I lost it (scarcity). That's the message that would most likely move me from a mere decision to act to steps based on that decision. Consequently, it's the message with the best chance to get me up in the morning and off to the gym.

Thus, the arrangement of the chapters takes into account which principles are particularly suited to achieving these three motives of persuaders: reciprocation, liking, and unity for when *relation-*

ship cultivation is primary; followed by social proof and authority for when *reducing uncertainty* is foremost; followed in turn by consistency and scarcity for when *motivating action* is the principle objective. It is important to recognize that I am not suggesting these associated principles are the sole options for achieving their respective goals. Rather, I am only suggesting that if they are available for accomplishing an aligned goal, failing to employ them would be a considerable mistake.

INFLUENCE,
NEW AND EXPANDED

CHAPTER 1

LEVERS OF INFLUENCE

(POWER) TOOLS OF THE TRADES

Civilization advances by extending the number of operations we can perform without thinking about them.

—**Alfred North Whitehead**

Simplicity is the ultimate sophistication.

—**Leonardo da Vinci**

This book presents numerous research results that at first appear baffling but can be explained through an understanding of natural human tendencies. A while ago, I encountered such a finding when I read a study that gave volunteers an energy drink designed to increase mental abilities. Some volunteers were charged the retail price of the drink ($1.89); others were told, because the researcher had made a bulk purchase, they'd have to pay only $0.89. Both groups were then asked to solve as many mental puzzles as they could in thirty minutes. I expected the second group, feeling good about the price break, would have tried harder and solved more problems. Wrong, the opposite occurred.[1]

The outcome put me in mind of a phone call I had received years earlier. The call came from a friend who had opened a Native Indian jewelry store in Arizona. She was giddy with a curious piece of news. Something fascinating had just happened, and she thought, as a psychologist, I might be able to explain it. The story involved a certain allotment of turquoise jewelry she had been having trouble selling. It was the peak of the tourist season, the store was unusually full of customers, and the turquoise pieces were of good quality for the prices she was asking; yet they had not sold. My friend had attempted a couple of standard sales tricks to get them moving. She tried calling attention to them by shifting their location to a more central display area, with no luck. She even told her sales staff to "push" the items, again without success.

Finally, the night before leaving on an out-of-town buying trip, she scribbled an exasperated note to her head saleswoman: "Everything in this display case, price $x \, ^1/_2$," hoping just to be rid of the offending pieces, even if at a loss. When she returned a few days later, she was not surprised to find that every article had been sold. She was shocked, though, to discover that because the employee had read the "$^1/_2$" in her scrawled message as a "2," the entire allotment had sold at twice the original price.

That's when she called me. I thought I knew what had happened but told her that if I were to explain things properly, she would have to listen to a story of mine. Actually, it isn't my story; it's about mother turkeys, and it belongs to the science of ethology—the study of animals in their natural settings. Turkey mothers are good mothers—loving, watchful, and protective. They spend much of their time tending, warming, cleaning, and huddling their young beneath them; but there is something odd about their method. Virtually all of their mothering is triggered by one thing, the "cheep-cheep" sound of young turkey chicks. Other identifying features of the chicks, such as smell, touch, or appearance, seem to play minor roles in the mothering process. If a chick makes the cheep-cheep noise, its mother will care for it; if not, the mother will ignore or sometimes kill it.

The extreme reliance of maternal turkeys on this one sound was dramatically illustrated in an experiment involving a mother turkey and a stuffed polecat. For a mother turkey, a polecat is a natural predator whose approach is to be greeted with squawking, pecking, clawing rage. Indeed, the experiment found even a stuffed model of a polecat, when drawn by a string to a mother turkey, received an immediate and furious attack. However, when the same stuffed replica carried inside it a small recorder that played the cheep-cheep sound of baby turkeys, the mother not only accepted the oncoming enemy but gathered it underneath her. When the machine was turned off, the polecat model again drew a vicious attack.

Click, Run

How ridiculous a mother turkey seems under these circumstances: She will embrace a natural adversary just because it goes cheep-cheep, and she will mistreat or murder one of her chicks just because it doesn't. She acts like an automaton whose maternal instincts are under the control of that single sound. The ethologists tell us that this sort of thing is far from unique to the turkey. They have identified regular, blindly mechanical patterns of action in a wide variety of species.

Called fixed-action patterns, they can involve intricate sequences of behavior, such as entire courtship or mating rituals. A fundamental characteristic of these patterns is that the behaviors composing them occur in virtually the same fashion and in the same order every time. It is almost as if the patterns were installed as programs within the animals. When a situation calls for courtship, the courtship program is run; when a situation calls for mothering, the maternal-behavior program is run. *Click*, and the appropriate program is activated; *run*, and out rolls the standard sequence of behaviors.

The most interesting aspect of all this is the way the programs are activated. When an animal acts to defend its territory, for instance, it is the intrusion of another animal of the same species that cues the territorial-defense program of rigid vigilance, threat, and, if need be, combat; however, there is a quirk in the system. It is not the rival as a whole that's the trigger; it is, rather, some specific feature: the trigger feature. Often the trigger feature will be one tiny aspect of the totality that is the approaching intruder. Sometimes a shade of color is the key. The experiments of ethologists have shown, for instance, that a male robin, acting as if a rival robin had entered its territory, will vigorously attack nothing more than a clump of robin redbreast feathers placed there. At the same time, it will ignore a perfect stuffed replica of a male robin without redbreast feathers. Similar results have been found in another bird, the bluethroat, where the trigger for territorial defense is a specific shade of bluebreast feathers.[2]

Before we enjoy too smugly the ease with which trigger features trick lower animals into reacting in ways wholly inappropriate to the situation, we should realize two things. First, the automatic, fixed-action patterns of these animals work well most of the time. Because only normal, healthy turkey chicks make the peculiar sound of baby turkeys, it makes sense for mother turkeys to respond maternally to that single cheep-cheep noise. By reacting to just that one stimulus, the average mother turkey will nearly always behave correctly. It takes a trickster like a scientist to make her automatic response seem silly. The second important thing to understand is that we, too, have our preset programs, and although they usually work to our advantage, the trigger features that activate them can dupe us into running the right programs at the wrong times.

This parallel form of human automaticity is aptly demonstrated in an experiment by social psychologist Ellen Langer and her coworkers. A well-known principle of human behavior says that when we ask someone to do us a favor, we will be more successful if we provide a reason. People simply like to have reasons for what they do. Langer demonstrated this unsurprising fact by asking a small favor of people waiting in line to use a library's copying machine: "Excuse me, I have five pages. May I use the Xerox machine, because I'm in a rush?" The effectiveness of this request-plus-reason was nearly total: 94 percent of people let her skip ahead of them in line. Compare this success rate to the results when she made the request only: "Excuse me, I have five pages. May I use the Xerox machine?" Under those circumstances, only 60 percent complied.

At first glance, it appears the crucial difference between the two requests was the additional information provided by the words *because I'm in a rush.*

However, a third type of request showed this was not the case. It seems it was not the whole series of words but the first one, *because*, that made the difference. Instead of including a real reason for compliance, Langer's third type of request used the word *because* and then, adding nothing new, merely restated the obvious: "Excuse me, I have five pages. May I use the Xerox machine because I have to make some copies?" The result was once again nearly all (93 percent) agreed, even though no real reason, no new information was added to justify their compliance. Just as the cheep-cheep sound of turkey chicks triggered an automatic mothering response from mother turkeys, even when it emanated from a stuffed polecat, so the word *because* triggered an automatic compliance response from Langer's subjects, even when they were given no subsequent reason to comply. *Click, run.*[3]

Although some of Langer's additional findings show that there are many situations in which human behavior does not work in a mechanical, click-activated way, she and many other researchers are convinced that most of the time it does, For instance, consider the strange behavior of those jewelry-store customers who swooped down on an allotment of turquoise pieces only after the items had been mistakenly offered at double their original price. I can make no sense of their behavior unless it is viewed in *click, run* terms.

The customers, mostly well-to-do vacationers with little knowledge of turquoise, were using a simplifying principle—a stereotype—to guide their buying: expensive = good. Research shows that people who are unsure of an item's quality often use this stereotype. Thus the vacationers, who wanted "good" jewelry, saw the turquoise pieces as decidedly more valuable and desirable when nothing about them was enhanced but the price. Price alone had become a trigger feature for quality, and a dramatic increase in price alone had led to a dramatic increase in sales among the quality-hungry buyers.

READER'S REPORT 1.1

From a doctoral student in business management

A man who owns an antique jewelry store in my town tells a story of how he learned the expensive = good lesson of social influence. A friend of his wanted a special birthday present for his fiancée. So, the jeweler picked out a necklace that would have sold in his store for $500 but that he was willing to let his friend have for $250. As soon as he saw it, the friend was enthusiastic about the piece. But when the jeweler quoted the $250 price, the man's face fell, and he began backing away from the deal because he wanted something "really nice" for his intended bride.

When a day later it dawned on the jeweler what had happened, he called his friend and asked him to come back to the store because he had another necklace to show him. This time, he introduced the new piece at its regular $500 price. His friend liked it enough to buy it on the spot. But before any money was exchanged, the jeweler told him that, as a wedding gift, he would drop the price to $250. The man was thrilled. Now, rather than finding the $250 sales price offensive, he was overjoyed—and grateful—to have it.

Author's note: Notice, as in the case of the turquoise-jewelry buyers, it was someone who wanted to be assured of good merchandise who disdained the low-priced item. I'm confident that besides the expensive = good rule, there's a flip side, an inexpensive = bad rule that applies to our thinking as well. After all, in English, the word *cheap* doesn't just mean inexpensive; it has also come to mean inferior.

Simplifying by Betting the Shortcut Odds

It is easy to fault the tourists for their foolish purchase decisions, but a close look offers a kinder view. These were people who had been brought up on the rule "You get what you pay for" and had seen the rule borne out over and over in their lives. Before long, they had translated it to mean expensive = good. The expensive = good stereotype had worked well for them in the past because normally the price of an item increases along with its worth; a higher price typically reflects higher quality. So when they found themselves in the position of wanting good turquoise jewelry but not having much knowledge of turquoise, they understandably relied on the old standby feature of cost to determine the jewelry's merits.

Although they probably didn't realize it, by reacting solely to price, they were playing a shortcut version of betting the odds. Instead of stacking all the odds in their favor by trying painstakingly to master each feature signifying the worth of turquoise jewelry, they simplified things by counting on just one—the one they expected to reveal the quality of any item. They bet price alone would tell them all they needed to know. This time because someone mistook a "1/2" for a "2," they bet wrong. But in the long run, over all the past and future situations of their lives, betting those shortcut odds represents the most rational approach.

We're now in a position to explain the puzzling result of the chapter's opening study—the one showing that people given a drink said to boost problem-solving ability solved more problems when they paid more for the drink. The researchers traced the finding to the expensive = good stereotype: people reported *expecting* the drink to work better when it cost $1.89 versus $0.89; and, remarkably, the mere expectation fulfilled itself. A similar phenomenon occurred in a separate study in which participants were given a pain reliever before receiving small electric shocks. Half were told the pain reliever cost $0.10 per unit while the other half were told it cost $2.50. Although, in actuality, all received the same pain reliever, those who thought it was more expensive rated it much more effective in dulling the pain of the shocks.[4]

Such automatic, stereotyped behavior is prevalent in much of human action because in many cases, it is the most efficient form of behaving, and in other cases it is simply necessary. You and I exist in an extraordinarily complicated environment, easily the most

Figure 1.1: Caviar and craftsmanship

The message to be communicated by this Dansk ad is, of course, that expensive equals good.

Courtesy of Dansk International Designs

rapidly moving and complex ever on this planet. To deal with it, we need simplifying shortcuts. We can't be expected to recognize and analyze all the aspects of each person, event, and situation we encounter in even one day. We haven't the time, energy, or capacity for it. Instead, we must often use our stereotypes, our rules of thumb, to classify things according to a few key features and then respond without thinking when one or another of the trigger features is present.

Sometimes the behavior that unrolls will not be appropriate for the situation, because not even the best stereotypes and trigger features work every time. We accept their imperfections because there is really no other choice. Without the simplifying features, we would stand frozen—cataloging, appraising, and calibrating—as the time for action sped by and away. From all indications, we'll be relying on these stereotypes to an even greater extent in the future. As the stimuli saturating our lives continue to grow more intricate and variable, we will have to depend increasingly on our shortcuts to handle them all.

Psychologists have uncovered a number of mental shortcuts we employ in making our everyday judgments. Termed *judgmental heuristics*, these shortcuts operate in much the same fashion as the expensive = good rule, allowing for simplified thinking that works well most of the time but leaves us open to occasional, costly mistakes. Especially relevant to this book are those heuristics that tell us when to believe or do what we are asked. Consider, for example, the shortcut rule that goes, "If an expert said so, it must be true." As we will see in chapter 5, there is an unsettling tendency in our society to accept unthinkingly the statements and directions of individuals who appear to be authorities on a topic. That is, rather than thinking about an expert's arguments and being convinced (or not), we frequently ignore the arguments and allow ourselves to be convinced just by the expert's status as "expert." This tendency to respond mechanically to one piece of information in a situation is what we have been calling automatic or *click, run* responding; the tendency to react on the basis of a thorough analysis of all of the information can be referred to as *controlled* responding.

Quite a lot of laboratory research has shown that people are more likely to deal with information in a controlled fashion when they have both the desire and the ability to analyze it carefully; otherwise, they are likely to use the easier *click, run* approach. For instance, in one study, university students listened to a recorded speech supporting the idea of requiring all seniors to pass comprehensive examinations before they would be allowed to graduate. The issue affected some of them personally, because they were told that the exams could go into effect in the next year— before they had the chance to graduate. Of course, this news made them want to analyze the arguments carefully. However, for other subjects in the study, the issue had little personal importance, because they were told the exams would not begin until long after they had graduated; consequently, these students had no strong need to carefully consider the arguments' validity. The study's results were straightforward: those students with no personal stake in the topic were primarily persuaded by the speaker's expertise in the field of education; they used the "If an expert said so, it must be true" rule, paying little attention to the strength of the speaker's arguments. Those students for whom the issue mattered personally, on the other hand, ignored the speaker's expertise and were persuaded primarily by the quality of the speaker's arguments.

So it appears that when it comes to the dangerous business of *click*, *run* responding, we give ourselves a safety net. We resist the seductive luxury of registering and reacting to just a single (trigger) feature of the available information when an issue is important to us. No doubt this is often the case. Yet I am not fully comforted. Recall that we learned that people are likely to respond in a controlled, thoughtful fashion only when they have both the desire and the ability to do so. I have become impressed by evidence indicating that the form and pace of modern life is not allowing us to make fully thoughtful decisions, even on many personally relevant topics. Sometimes the issues may be so complicated, the time so tight, the distractions so intrusive, the emotional arousal so strong, or the mental fatigue so deep that we are in no cognitive condition to operate mindfully. Important topic or not, we have to take the shortcut.

Perhaps nowhere is this last point driven home more dramatically than in the life-and-death consequences of a phenomenon that airline-industry officials have labeled *Captainitis*. Accident investigators from the US Federal Aviation Administration noted that, frequently, an obvious error made by a flight captain was not corrected by the other crew members and resulted in a crash. It seems, despite the clear and strong personal importance of the issues, the crew members were using the "If an expert says so, it must be true" rule in failing to attend or respond to the captain's disastrous mistake.[5]

Figure 1.2: The catastrophic consequences of Captainitis
Minutes before this airliner crashed into the Potomac River near National Airport in Washington, DC, the accompanying exchange occurred between the pilot and copilot concerning the wisdom of taking off with ice on the wings. Their conversation was recorded in the plane's black box.

> *Copilot:* That reading doesn't seem right.
> *Captain:* Yes, it is.
> *Copilot:* Naw, I don't think it is. [Seven-second pause.] OK, maybe it is.
> *Copilot:* Larry, we're going down.
> *Captain:* I know it.
> [Sound of impact that killed the captain, the copilot, and sixty-seven passengers.]

© *Cohen/Liaison Agency*

The Profiteers

It is odd that, despite their current widespread use and looming future importance, most of us know very little about our automatic behavior patterns. Perhaps that is so precisely because of the mechanistic, unthinking manner in which they occur. Whatever the reason, it is vital that we clearly recognize one of their properties. They make us terribly vulnerable to anyone who *does* know how they work.

To understand fully the nature of our vulnerability, let's take another glance at the work of ethologists. It turns out that these animal behaviorists with their recorded cheep-cheeps and clumps of colored breast feathers are not the only ones who have discovered how to activate the behavior programs of various species. One group of organisms, termed mimics, copy the trigger features of other animals in an attempt to trick the animals into mistakenly playing the right behavior programs at the wrong times. The mimics then exploit this altogether inappropriate action for their own benefit.

Take the deadly trick played by the killer females of one genus of firefly (*Photuris*) on the males of another firefly genus (*Photinus*). Understandably, the *Photinus* males scrupulously avoid contact with the bloodthirsty *Photuris* females. However, through centuries of natural selection, the *Photuris* female hunters have located a weakness in their prey—a special blinking courtship code by which members of the victims' species tell one another they are ready to mate. By mimicking the flashing mating signals of her prey, the murderess is able to feast on the bodies of males whose triggered courtship program causes them to fly mechanically into death's, not love's, embrace.

In the struggle for survival, nearly every form of life has its mimics—right down to some of the most primitive pathogens. By adopting certain critical features of useful hormones or nutrients, these clever bacteria and viruses can gain entry into a healthy host cell. The result is that the healthy cell eagerly and naively sweeps into itself the causes of such diseases as rabies, mononucleosis, and the common cold.[6]

It should come as no surprise, then, that there is a strong but sad parallel in human behavior. We, too, have profiteers who mimic trigger features for our own brand of automatic responding. Unlike the mostly instinctive response sequences of nonhumans, our automatic programs usually develop from psychological principles or stereotypes we have learned to accept. Although they vary in their force, some of the principles possess a remarkable ability to direct human action. We have been subjected to them from such an early point in our lives, and they have moved us about so pervasively since then, that you and I rarely perceive their power. In the eyes of others, though, each such principle is a detectable and ready lever, a lever of automatic influence. Take for instance the principle of social proof, which asserts that people are inclined to believe or do what they see those around them believing or doing. We act in accord with it whenever we check product reviews or star ratings before making an online purchase. But, once on the review site, we have to deal with our own brand of mimics—individuals who counterfeit genuine reviews and insert their phony ones. Fortunately, eBox 1.1 offers ways to spot the fakes.

EBOX 1.1

Here's How to Spot Fake Online Reviews with 90 Percent Accuracy, according to Science

A new computer program identifies phony reviews with incredible accuracy.

By Jessica Stillman. Contributor, Inc.com@EntryLevelRebel

When you buy products online, for either yourself or your business, reviews probably weigh heavily in your decision-making. We check to see other buyers' opinions on Amazon, opt for the five-star option rather than the one with only four and a half stars, or book the Airbnb with the most enthusiastic former guests.

Of course, we all also know these reviews can be bogus—either paid for by the seller or maliciously placed by the competition. A team of Cornell University researchers decided that building a computer program that could spot bogus recommendations sounded like a useful thing to do.

So what are the tells that a "five-star" hotel room might end up being moldy and cramped or that a highly rated toaster might die before you get through a single loaf? According to the Cornell research, you should beware if a review:

- lacks detail. It's hard to describe what you haven't actually experienced, which is why fake reviews often offer general praise rather than digging into specifics. "Truthful hotel reviews, for example, are more likely to use concrete words relating to the hotel, like 'bathroom,' 'check-in' or 'price.' Deceivers write more about things that set the scene, like 'vacation,' 'business trip' or 'my husband.'"
- includes more first-person pronouns. If you're anxious about coming across as sincere, apparently you talk about yourself more. That's probably why words such as *I* and *me* appear more often in fake reviews.
- has more verbs than nouns. Language analysis shows that the fakes tend to include more verbs because their writers often substitute pleasant (or alarming) sounding stories for actual insight. Genuine reviews are heavier on nouns.

Of course, these subtle tells alone probably won't make you a master of spotting fakes, but combined with other methods of checking a review's trustworthiness, such as watching out for various types of verified buyers and suspicious timestamps, you should be able to do a lot better than random chance.

Author's note: Minding the mimics. Online review sites are in an ongoing battle with fake reviewers. We should join the fight. One set of comparisons shows why. From 2014 to 2018, customers' favorable responses to online reviews went up in every category (for example, those who read reviews before buying rose from 88 percent to 92 percent), except one: those who trusted a business that had positive reviews dropped from 72 percent to 68 percent. It seems the mimics are undermining our confidence in the worth of the shortcut information we seek.

There are some people who know very well where the levers of automatic influence lie and who employ them regularly and expertly to get what they want. They go from social encounter to social encounter, requesting others to comply with their wishes, and their frequency of success is dazzling. The secret to their effectiveness lies in the way they structure their requests, the way they arm themselves with one or another of the levers of influence that exist in the social environment. To do so may take no more than one correctly chosen word that engages a strong psychological principle and launches one of our automatic behavior programs. Trust the human profiteers to learn quickly how to benefit from our tendency to respond mechanically according to these principles.

Remember my friend the jewelry-store owner? Although she benefited by accident the first time, it didn't take her long to begin exploiting the expensive = good stereotype regularly and intentionally. Now during the tourist season, she first tries to speed the sale of an item that has been difficult to move by substantially increasing its price. She claims that this is marvelously cost effective. When it works on the unsuspecting vacationers, as it frequently does, it generates an enormous profit. And, even when it is not initially successful, she can then mark the article "Reduced" and sell it to bargain hunters at its original price while still taking advantage of their expensive = good reaction to the inflated figure.[7]

Jujitsu

A woman employing jujitsu, the Japanese martial art, uses her own strength only minimally against an opponent. Instead, she exploits the power inherent in such naturally present principles as gravity, leverage, momentum, and inertia. If she knows how and where to engage these principles, she can easily defeat a physically stronger rival. And so it is for the exploiters of the levers of automatic influence that exist naturally around us. The profiteers can commission the power of these principles for use against their targets while exerting little personal force. This last feature of the process gives the profiteers an enormous additional benefit—the ability to manipulate without the appearance of manipulation. Even the victims themselves tend to see their compliance as a result of the action of natural forces rather than the designs of the person who profits from that compliance.

An example is in order. There is a principle in human perception, the contrast principle, which affects the way we see the difference between two things that are presented one after another. If the second item is fairly different from the first, we tend to see it as being more different than it actually is. So if we lift a light object first and then lift a heavy object, we estimate the second object as being heavier than we would have estimated it if we had lifted it without first lifting the light one. The contrast principle is well established in the field of psychophysics and applies to all sorts of perceptions. If we are watching our weight and at lunch we are trying to estimate the calorie count of a cheeseburger, we'll judge it as being much higher (38% higher in one study) in calories if we first estimate the calories in a salad. In contrast to the salad, the cheeseburger now *seems* even more calorie rich. Relatedly, if we are talking to an attractive individual at a party and are joined by a comparatively less attractive one, the second will strike us as being less attractive than he or she actually is. Some researchers warn that the unrealistically attractive people portrayed in the popular media (actors, models) may cause us to be less satisfied with the looks of the genuinely available romantic possibilities around us. The researchers demonstrated that increasing exposure to the exaggerated sexual attractiveness of sensual models in the media lowers the sexual desirability of our current mates.[8]

Another demonstration of perceptual contrast is one I have employed in my classrooms to introduce students to the principle. Each student takes a turn sitting in front of three pails of water—one cold, one at room temperature, and one hot. After placing one hand in the cold water and the other in the hot water, the student is told to place both simultaneously in the room-temperature water. The look of amused bewilderment that immediately registers tells the story: even though both hands are in the same bucket, the hand that was in the cold water feels as if it is in hot water, while the one that was in the hot water feels as if it is in cold water. The point is that the same thing—in this instance, room-temperature water—can be made to seem very different depending on the nature of the event preceding it. What's more, the perception of other things, such as college course grades, can be affected similarly. See, for example, in figure 1.3, a letter that came across my desk several years ago from a university student to her parents.

Figure 1.3: Perceptual contrast and the college coed

Dear Mother and Dad:

Since I left for college I have been remiss in writing and I am sorry for my thoughtlessness in not having written before. I will bring you up to date now, but before you read on, please sit down. You are not to read any further unless you are sitting down, okay?

Well, then, I am getting along pretty well now. The skull fracture and the concussion I got when I jumped out the window of my dormitory when it caught on fire shortly after my arrival here is pretty well healed now. I only spent two weeks in the hospital and now I can see almost normally and only get those sick headaches once a day. Fortunately, the fire in the dormitory, and my jump, was witnessed by a worker at the gas station near the dorm, and he was the one who called the Fire Department and the ambulance. He also visited me in the hospital and since I had nowhere to live because of the burnt out dormitory, he was kind enough to invite me to share his apartment with him. It's really a basement room, but it's kind of cute. He is a very fine boy and we have fallen deeply in love and are planning to get married. We haven't got the exact date yet, but it will be before my pregnancy begins to show.

Yes, Mother and Dad, I am pregnant. I know how much you are looking forward to being grandparents and I know you will welcome the baby and give it the same love and devotion and tender care you gave me when I was a child. The reason for the delay in our marriage is that my boyfriend has a minor infection which prevents us from passing our pre-marital blood tests and I carelessly caught it from him.

Now that I have brought you up to date, I want to tell you that there was no dormitory fire, I did not have a concussion or skull fracture, I was not in the hospital, I am not pregnant, I am not engaged, I am not infected, and there is no boyfriend. However, I am getting a "D" in American History, and an F in Chemistry, and I want you to see those marks in their proper perspective.

Your loving daughter,
Sharon

Author's note: *Sharon may be failing chemistry, but she gets an A in psychology.*

Be assured the nice little lever of influence provided by the contrast principle does not go unexploited. The great advantage of the principle is not only that it works but also that it is virtually undetectable. Those who employ it can cash in on its influence without any appearance of having structured the situation in their favor.

Retail clothiers offer a good example. Suppose a man enters a fashionable men's store to buy a suit and a sweater. If you were the salesperson, which would you show him first to make him likely to spend the most money? Clothing stores instruct their sales personnel to sell the costly item first. Common sense might suggest the reverse. If a man has just spent a lot of money to purchase a suit, he may be reluctant to spend much more on the purchase of a sweater, but the clothiers know better. They behave in accordance with what the contrast principle advises: sell the suit first, because when it comes time to look at sweaters, even expensive ones, their prices will not seem as high in comparison. The same principle applies to a man who wishes to buy the accessories (shirt, shoes, belt) to go along with his new suit. Contrary to the commonsense view, the evidence supports the contrast-principle prediction.

It is more profitable for salespeople to present the expensive item first; to fail to do so not only loses the force of the contrast principle but also causes the principle to work against them. Presenting an inexpensive product first and following it with an expensive one makes the expensive item seem even more costly—hardly a desirable consequence for sales organizations. So just as it is possible to make the same bucket of water appear to be hotter or colder depending on the temperature of previously presented buckets of water, it is possible to make the price of the same item seem higher or lower depending on the price of a previously presented item.

Clever use of perceptual contrast is by no means confined to clothiers. I came across a technique that engaged the contrast principle while I was investigating, undercover, the compliance tactics of real-estate companies. To learn the ropes, I accompanied a salesman on a weekend of showing houses to prospective home buyers. The salesman—we can call him Phil—was to give me tips to help me through my break-in period. One thing I quickly noticed was that whenever Phil began showing a new set of customers potential buys, he would start with a couple of undesirable houses. I asked him about it, and he laughed. They were what he called "setup" properties. The company maintained an unappealing house or two on its lists at inflated prices. These houses were not intended to be sold to customers but only to be shown to them so that the genuine properties in the company's inventory would benefit from the comparison. Not all the sales staff made use of the setup houses, but Phil did. He said he liked to watch his prospects' "eyes light up" when he showed the places he really wanted to sell them after they had seen the unattractive ones. "The house I got them spotted for looks really great after they've first looked at a couple of dumps."

Automobile dealers use the contrast principle by waiting until the price of a car has been negotiated before suggesting one option after another. In the wake of a many-thousand-dollar deal, a couple hundred extra dollars for a nicety such as an upgraded sound system seems almost trivial in comparison. The same will be true of the added expense of accessories, such as tinted windows, better tires, or special trim, that the dealer might suggest in sequence. The trick is to bring up the options independently of

Figure 1.4: "A Stellar Idea"
There's a whole universe of applications for the contrast principle.
The New Yorker

one another so that each small price will seem petty when compared to the already determined much larger price. As veteran car buyers can attest, many a budget-sized final-price figure balloons out of proportion from the addition of all those seemingly little options. While customers stand, signed contract in hand, wondering what happened and finding no one to blame but themselves, the car dealer stands smiling the knowing smile of the jujitsu master.

READER'S REPORT 1.2

From a business-school student at the University of Chicago

While waiting to board a flight at O'Hare, I heard a desk agent announce that the flight was overbooked and, if passengers were willing to take a later plane, they would be compensated with a voucher worth $10,000! Of course, this exaggerated amount was a joke. It was supposed to make people laugh. It did. But I noticed that when he then revealed the actual offer (a $200 voucher), there were no takers. In fact, he had to raise the offer twice to $300 and then $500 before he got any volunteers. I was reading your book at the time and I realized that, although he got his laugh, according to the contrast principle he screwed up. He arranged things so that, compared to $10,000, a couple hundred bucks seemed like a pittance. That was an expensive laugh. It cost his airline an extra $300 per volunteer.

Author's note: Any ideas on how the desk agent could have used the contrast principle to his advantage rather than his detriment? Perhaps he could have started with a $2 joke offer and then revealed the true—and now much more attractive sounding—$200 amount. Under those circumstances, I'm pretty sure he would have secured his laugh *and* his volunteers.

SUMMARY

- Ethologists, researchers who study animal behavior in the natural environment, have noticed that among many animal species, behavior often occurs in rigid and mechanical patterns. Called fixed-action patterns, these mechanical sequences are noteworthy in their similarity to certain automatic (*click, run*) responses by humans. For both humans and subhumans, the automatic-behavior patterns tend to be triggered by a single feature of the relevant information in the situation. This single feature, or trigger feature, can often prove valuable by allowing an individual to decide on a correct course of action without having to analyze carefully and completely each of the other pieces of information in the situation.

- The advantage of such shortcut responding lies in its efficiency and economy; by reacting automatically to a normally informative trigger feature, an individual preserves crucial time, energy, and mental capacity. The disadvantage of such responding lies in its vulnerability to silly and costly mistakes; by reacting to only a piece of the available information (even a usually predictive piece), an individual increases the chances of error, especially when responding in an automatic, mindless fashion. The chances of error increase even further when other individuals seek to profit by arranging (through manipulation of trigger features) to stimulate a desired behavior at inappropriate times.

- Much of the compliance process (wherein one person is spurred to comply with another person's request) can be understood in terms of a human tendency for automatic, shortcut responding. Most of us have developed a set of trigger features for compliance—that is, specific pieces of information that normally tell us when compliance with a request is likely to be correct and beneficial. Each of these trigger features for compliance can be used like a lever (of influence) to move people to agree with requests.

- Perceptual contrast—the tendency to see two things that are different from one another as being more different than they actually are—is a lever of influence used by some compliance practitioners. For example, real-estate agents may show prospective home buyers one or two unattractive options before showing them a more attractive home, which then seems more attractive than it would have if shown first. An advantage of employing this lever of influence is that its tactical use typically goes unrecognized.

CHAPTER 2

RECIPROCATION

THE OLD GIVE AND TAKE

Let not thine hand be stretched out to receive and drawn
back when thou shouldest repay.

—Ecclesiasticus 4:30–31

Several years ago, a university professor tried a little experiment.
He sent Christmas cards to a sample of perfect strangers. Although he expected some reaction, the response he received was
amazing—holiday cards addressed to him came pouring back
from people who had neither met nor heard of him. The great majority of those who returned cards never inquired into the identity
of the unknown professor. They received his holiday greeting card,
click, and *run*, they mechanically sent one in return.

While small in scope, the study shows the action of one of
the most potent of the levers of influence around us—the rule
of reciprocation. The rule says that we should try to repay what
another person has provided us. If a woman does us a favor, we
should do her one in return; if a man sends us a birthday present, we should remember his birthday with a gift of our own; if
a couple invites us to a party, we should be sure to invite them to
one of ours. Reciprocated greeting cards, birthday gifts, and party
invitations may seem like weak evidence of the rule's force. Don't
be fooled; it can prompt change in sizable behaviors. Researchers

working with charity fundraisers in the United Kingdom ap-proached investment bankers as they came to work and asked for a large charitable donation—a full day's salary, amounting to over a thousand dollars in some cases. Remarkably, if the request was preceded by a gift of a small packet of sweets, contributions more than doubled.

The rule extends even to national conduct. The Magna Carta of 1215 employed it to define how, at the outbreak of a war, countries should treat merchants from the enemy nation: "If our men are safe there, the others should be safe in our land." By virtue of the reciprocity rule, then, we are *obligated* to the future repayment of favors, gifts, invitations, friendly actions, and the like. So typical is it for indebtedness to accompany the receipt of such things that a phrase such as "much obliged" has become a synonym for "thank you" not only in the English language but in other languages as well (such as with the Portuguese term *obrigado*). The future reach of the obligation is nicely connoted in a Japanese word for thank you, *sumimasen*, which, in its literal form, means "this will not end."

An impressive aspect of reciprocation is its pervasiveness in hu-man culture. It is so widespread that Alvin Gouldner, along with other sociologists, reports that all human societies subscribe to the rule. Within each society, it seems pervasive also, permeating exchanges of every kind. Indeed, it may well be that a developed system of indebtedness flowing from the rule of reciprocation is a unique property of human culture. The noted archaeologist Rich-ard Leakey ascribes the essence of what makes us human to the reciprocity system. He claims that we are human because our an-cestors learned to share food and skills "in an honored network of obligation." Cultural anthropologists such as Lionel Tiger and Robin Fox view this "web of indebtedness" as a unique adaptive mechanism of human beings, allowing for the division of labor, the exchange of diverse forms of goods and different services, and the creation of interdependencies that bind individuals together into highly efficient units.

It is a sense of future obligation that is critical to producing social advances of the sort described by Tiger and Fox. A widely shared and strongly held feeling of future obligation made an enormous difference in human social evolution because it meant that a person could give something (for example, food, energy, or care) to another with confidence that the gift was not being lost. For the first time in evolutionary history, one individual could give any of a variety of resources without actually giving them away. The result was the lowering of the natural inhibitions against transactions that must be *begun* by one person's providing personal resources to another. Sophisticated and coordinated systems of aid, gift giving, defense, and trade became possible, bringing immense benefits to the societies that possessed them. With such clearly adaptive consequences for the culture, it is not surprising that the rule of reciprocation is so deeply implanted in us by the process of socialization we all undergo.[1]

Although obligations extend into the future, their span is not unlimited. Especially for relatively small favors, the desire to repay seems to fade with time. But when gifts are of the truly notable and memorable sort, they can be remarkably long-lived. I know of no better illustration of the way reciprocal obligations can reach long and powerfully into the future than the perplexing story of $5,000 of relief aid that was exchanged between Mexico and Ethiopia. In 1985, Ethiopia could justly lay claim to the greatest suffering and privation in the world. Its economy was in ruin. Its food supply had been ravaged by years of drought and internal war. Its inhabitants were dying by the thousands from disease and starvation. Under the circumstances, I would not have been surprised to learn of a $5,000 relief donation from Mexico to that wrenchingly needy country. I recall my feeling of amazement, though, when a news item I was reading insisted that the aid had gone in the opposite direction. Native officials of the Ethiopian Red Cross had decided to send the money to help the victims of that year's earthquakes in Mexico City.

It is both a personal bane and professional blessing that when

I am confused by some aspect of human behavior, I feel driven to investigate further. In this instance, I was able to track down a fuller account of the story. Fortunately, a journalist who had been as bewildered as I by the Ethiopians' actions had asked for an explanation. The answer he received offered eloquent validation of the reciprocity rule: despite the enormous needs prevailing in Ethiopia, the money was sent to Mexico because, in 1935, Mexico had sent aid to Ethiopia when it was invaded by Italy. So informed, I remained awed but no longer puzzled. The need to reciprocate had transcended great cultural differences, long distances, acute famine, many years, and immediate self-interest. Quite simply, a half century later, against all countervailing forces, obligation triumphed.

If such an enduring obligation appears to be a one-of-a-kind sort of thing, perhaps explained by some unique feature of Ethiopian culture, consider the solution to another initially puzzling case. In 2015, at the age of ninety-four, the renowned British publisher Lord Arthur George Weidenfeld founded Operation Safe Haven, which rescued endangered Christian families from ISIS-held regions in the Middle East and transported them to safety in other countries. Although observers applauded this benevolence, they criticized its narrowness, wondering why the lord's efforts didn't extend to similarly threatened religious groups, such as Druze, Alawis, and Yazidis, in the same territories.

Perhaps, one might think, the man was simply acting to benefit his own Christian brethren. But that easy explanation falls apart when one recognizes that Lord Weidenfeld was Jewish. He had come to England in 1938 on a Kindertransport train, organized by Christian societies to rescue Jewish children from Nazi persecution in Europe. Accounting for his actions in terms that reveal the prioritizing power of the rule of reciprocation, he said, "I can't save the world, but . . . on the Jewish and Christian side . . . I had a debt to repay." Clearly, the pull of reciprocity can be both lifesaving and lifelong.[2]

READER'S REPORT 2.1

From an employee for the state of Oregon

The person who used to have my job told me during my training that I would like working for my boss because he is a very nice and generous person. She said that he always gave her flowers and other gifts on different occasions. She decided to stop working because she was going to have a child and wanted to stay home; otherwise I am sure she would have stayed on at this job for many more years.

I have been working for this same boss for six years now, and I have experienced the same thing. He gives me and my son gifts for Christmas and gives me presents on my birthday. It has been over two years since I have reached the top of my classification for a salary increase. There is no promotion for the type of job I have and my only choice is to take a test with the state system and reapply to move to another department or maybe find another job in a private company. But I find myself resisting trying to find another job or move to another department. My boss is reaching retirement age and I am thinking maybe I will be able to move out after he retires because for now I feel obligated to stay since he has been so nice to me.

Author's note: I am struck by this reader's language in describing her current employment options, saying that she "will be able" to move to another job only after her boss retires. It seems that his small kindnesses have nurtured a binding sense of obligation that has made her unable to seek a better paying position. There is an obvious lesson here for managers wishing to instill loyalty in employees. But there is a larger lesson for all of us, as well: little things are not always little—not when they link to the big rules of life, such as reciprocity. See Martin, Goldstein, & Cialdini (2014) for a description of fifty small things that make a big impact on human behavior.

How the Rule Works

Make no mistake, human societies derive a truly significant competitive advantage from the reciprocity rule and, consequently, they make sure their members are trained to comply with it. Each of us has been taught to live up to the rule from childhood, and each of us knows the social sanctions and derision applied to anyone who violates it. Because there is a general distaste for those who take and make no effort to give in return, we will often go to great lengths to avoid being considered a freeloader. It is to those lengths that we will often be taken and, in the process, be "taken" by individuals who stand to gain from our indebtedness.

To understand how the rule of reciprocation can be exploited by one who recognizes it as the lever of influence it certainly is, we might closely examine an experiment conducted by psychologist Dennis Regan. A subject who participated in the study rated, along with another subject, the quality of some paintings as part of an experiment on "art appreciation." The other rater—we can call him Joe—was only posing as a fellow subject and was actually Dr. Regan's assistant. For our purposes, the experiment took place under two different conditions. In some cases, Joe did a small, unsolicited favor for the true subject. During a short rest period, Joe left the room for a couple of minutes and returned with two bottles of Coca-Cola, one for the subject and one for himself, saying, "I asked him [the experimenter] if I could get myself a Coke, and he said it was OK, so I bought one for you, too." In other cases, Joe did not provide the subject with a favor; he simply returned from the two-minute break empty handed. In all other respects, Joe behaved identically.

Later on, after the paintings had all been rated and the experimenter had momentarily left the room, Joe asked the subject to do *him* a favor. He indicated that he was selling raffle tickets for a new car and that if he sold the most tickets, he would win a $50 prize. Joe's request was for the subject to buy some raffle tickets at 25¢ apiece: "Any would help, the more the better." The major finding of the study concerns the number of tickets subjects purchased from Joe under the two conditions. Without question, Joe was more successful in selling his raffle tickets to the subjects who had received his earlier favor. Apparently feeling that they owed him something, these subjects bought twice as many tickets as the subjects who had not been given the prior favor. Although the Regan study represents a fairly simple demonstration of the workings of the rule of reciprocation, it illustrates several important characteristics of the rule that, upon further consideration, help us understand how it may be profitably used.

The Rule Is Overpowering

One of the reasons reciprocation can be used so effectively as a device for gaining another's compliance is its power. The rule possesses awesome strength, often producing a yes response to a request that, except for an existing feeling of indebtedness, would have surely been refused. Some evidence of how the rule's force can overpower the influence of other factors that normally determine compliance can be seen in a second result of the Regan study. Besides his interest in the impact of the reciprocity rule on compliance, Regan was also investigating how liking for a person affects the tendency to comply with that person's request. To measure how liking toward Joe affected the subjects' decisions to buy his raffle tickets, Regan had them fill out several rating scales indicating how much they had liked Joe. He then compared their liking responses with the number of tickets they had purchased from Joe. He found subjects bought more raffle tickets from Joe the more they liked him. This alone is hardly a startling finding; most of us would have guessed that people are more willing to do a favor for someone they like.

A more interesting finding was that the relationship between liking and compliance was completely wiped out in the condition under which subjects had been given a Coke by Joe. For those who owed him a favor, it made no difference whether they liked him or not; they felt a sense of obligation to repay him, and they did. The subjects who indicated they disliked Joe bought just as many of his tickets as did those who indicated they liked him. The rule of reciprocation was so strong it simply overwhelmed the influence of a factor—liking for the requester—that normally affects the decision to comply.

Think of the implications. People we might ordinarily dislike— unsavory or unwelcome sales operators, disagreeable acquaintances, representatives of strange or unpopular organizations—can greatly increase the chance that we will do what they wish merely by providing us with a small initiating favor. Let's take a relatively recent example. Throughout the United States' military involvement against the Taliban in Afghanistan, its intelligence officers faced a significant influence problem. They frequently needed information from local Afghans about the Taliban's activities and whereabouts; but many of the locals showed little interest in providing it, for a pair of reasons. First, doing so would make them susceptible to Taliban retribution. Second, many harbored a strong distaste for the United States' presence, goals, and representatives in Afghanistan. A CIA officer, who had experienced both of these sources of reluctance with a particular tribal patriarch, noticed the man seemed drained by his twin roles as tribal leader and husband to four younger wives. On the officer's next visit, he came equipped with a small gift he placed discreetly in the elder's hand, four Viagra tablets—one for each wife. The "potency" of this gift was evident on his return a week later when the chief "offered up a bonanza of information about Taliban movements and supply routes."

I had a similar, though less momentous, personal experience a few years ago. At the start of a cross-country flight, I was assigned an aisle seat in a row of three. Even though I preferred the aisle, I switched seats with a man in the window seat who said he was feeling claustrophobic about being pinned next to the wall for five hours. He expressed profound thanks. Rather than doing what I'd been taught to do all my life and dismissing the favor—falsely—as too trivial to worry about (I really did prefer the aisle seat), I said, "Oh, I'm sure you'd do the same for me." He assured me I was right.

The rest of the flight was amazing. The two men next to me began a conversation that revealed how much they had in common. In the past, both had lived near one another in Atlanta and were NASCAR fans as well as gun collectors who shared political views. I could tell a friendship was budding. Yet whenever the man on the aisle had something to offer us—cashews, gum, the sports section of the newspaper—he offered it to me first, sometimes pushing it right past the face of his new pal. I remember thinking, "Wow, it didn't matter which of us he was sitting closer to or had more in common with or was talking to; I was the one he owed, and that mattered most."

I also thought that if I were to give advice to someone who'd just received thanks for a meaningful favor, I'd warn against minimizing the favor in all-too-common language that disengages the influence of the rule of reciprocation: "No big deal." "Don't think a thing about it." "I would have done it for anybody." Instead, I'd recommend retaining that (earned) influence by saying something such as, "Listen, if our positions were ever reversed, I know you'd do the same for me." The benefits should be considerable.[3]

READER'S REPORT 2.2

From a businesswoman in New York State

As the corporate secretary at a business in Rochester, NY, I usually work days; but one evening I had stayed late to finish some important work. While pulling out of my parking spot, my car slid on some ice and ended up stuck down a small ravine. It was late, cold, and dark; and everyone from my office had left. But, an employee from another department came by and towed me clear.

About two weeks later, because I worked on personnel matters, I became aware that this same employee was being "written up" for a serious violation of company policy. Not really knowing this man's morals, I still took it upon myself to go to the company president on his behalf. To this day, although more people have come to question the man's character, I feel indebted to him and willing to stand up for him.

Author's note: As in the Regan experiment, it appears that the man's personal characteristics were less relevant to the reader's decision to help him than the simple fact that he had helped her. *Click, run.*

Various types of organizations have learned to employ the power of a small gift to spur actions that would have been otherwise withheld. Survey researchers have discovered that sending a monetary gift (e.g., a silver dollar or a $5 check) in an envelope with a mailed questionnaire greatly increases survey completion rates, compared to offering the same monetary amount as an after-the-fact reward. Indeed, one study showed that mailing a $5 "gift" check along with an insurance survey was twice as effective as offering a $50 payment for sending back a completed survey. Similarly, food servers have learned that simply giving customers a candy or mint along with their bill significantly increases tips; and in a restaurant frequented by international tourists, this was the case no matter the nationality of the guests. My colleagues Steve J. Martin and Helen Mankin did a small study showing the impact of giving first in a set of McDonald's restaurants located in Brazil and Colombia. In half of the locations, the children of adult customers received a balloon as they left the restaurant. In the other half of the locations, the children received a balloon as they entered. The total family check rose by 25 percent when the balloon was given first. Tellingly, this included a 20 percent increase in the purchase of coffee—an item children are unlikely to order. Why? As I can attest, a gift to my child is a gift to me.

In general, business operators have found that after accepting a gift, customers are willing to purchase products and agree to requests they would have otherwise declined.[4]

EBOX 2.1

CELEBRATE 40 YEARS OF STARBUCKS
(1971-2011)

Get a
FREE

STARBUCKS Gift Card

This offer will expire Tuesday, October 18th, or when the
remaining 2398 FREE Vouchers run out!

Step 1: You must click the share button:

Step 2: Say Thanks below!
Example: "Free Starbucks, Thanks"
(click "add a comment")

Author's note: In 2011, to celebrate its fortieth anniversary, Starbucks offered free online vouchers for a gift card. In an effort to heighten feelings of obligation associated with the gift, any customer accepting the voucher had to explicitly *thank* the company on social media. For an extended discussion of how reciprocity works on social media, see https://vimeo.com/137374366.

P.S.: Not only were the vouchers free, engaging the principle of reciprocity, but they were dwindling in availability, engaging the principle of scarcity—the separate force of which we will examine in chapter 6.

Politics

Politics is another arena in which the power of the reciprocity rule shows itself to be overpowering. Reciprocation tactics appear at every level:

- At the top, elected officials engage in the exchange of favors that makes politics the place of strange bedfellows, indeed. The out-of-character vote of one of our elected representatives on a bill can often be understood as a favor returned to the bill's sponsor.

Political experts were amazed at Lyndon Johnson's success in getting so many of his programs through Congress during his early administration; even members of Congress who were thought to be strongly opposed to the programs were voting for them. Close examination by analysts, such as Robert Caro in his influential biography of Johnson (Caro, 2012), has found the cause to be not so much Johnson's political savvy as the large score of favors he had been able to provide to other legislators during his many years of power in the US House and Senate. As president, he was able to produce a truly remarkable amount of legislation in a short time by calling in those favors. It is interesting that this same process may account for the problems some subsequent presidents—Carter, Clinton, Obama, and Trump—had in getting their programs through Congress. They came to the presidency from outside the Capitol Hill establishment and campaigned on their outside-Washington identities, saying that they were indebted to no one in Washington. Much of their early legislative difficulties may be traced to the fact that no one there was indebted to *them*.

- At another level, we can see the recognized strength of the reciprocity rule in the desire of corporations and individuals to provide judicial and legislative officials with gifts and favors and in the series of legal restrictions against such gifts and favors. Even with legitimate political contributions, the stockpiling of obligations often belies the stated purpose of supporting a favorite candidate. One look at the lists of companies and organizations that contribute to the campaigns of *both* major candidates in important elections gives evidence of such motives. A skeptic, requiring direct evidence of the quid pro quo expected by political contributors, might look to the remarkably bald-faced admission by businessman Roger Tamraz at congressional hearings on campaign-finance reform. When asked if he felt he received a good return on his contribution of $300,000, he smiled and replied, "I think next time, I'll give $600,000."

Honesty of this sort is rare in politics. For the most part, the givers and takers join voices to dismiss the idea that campaign contributions, free trips, and Super Bowl tickets would bias the opinions of "sober, conscientious government officials." As the head of one lobbying organization insisted, there is no cause for concern because "these [government officials] are smart, mature, sophisticated men and women at the top of their professions, disposed by training to be discerning, critical, and alert." And, of course, the politicians concur. Regularly, we hear them proclaiming total independence from the feelings of obligation that influence everyone else. One of my own state representatives left no room for doubt when describing his accountability to gift givers: "It gets them exactly what it gets everybody else: nothing."

Excuse me if, as a scientist, I laugh. "Sober, conscientious" scientists know better. One reason they know better is that these "smart, mature, sophisticated men and women at the top of their [scientific] professions" have found themselves to be as susceptible as anyone else to the process. Take the case of the medical controversy surrounding the safety of calcium-channel blockers, a class of drugs for heart disease. One study discovered that 100 percent of the scientists who found and published results supportive of the drugs had received prior support (free trips, research funding, or employment) from the pharmaceutical companies; but only 37 percent of those critical of the drugs had received any such prior support. If scientists, "disposed by training to be discerning, critical, and alert," can be swayed by the insistent undertow of exchange, we should fully expect that politicians will be too. And we'd be right. For instance, Associated Press reporters who looked at US congressional representatives receiving the most special-interest-group money on six key issues during one campaign cycle found these representatives to be over seven times more likely to vote in favor of the group that had contributed the *most* money to their campaigns. As a result, those groups got the win 83 percent of the time. The same kind of result emerged from a study of US legislators who were members of tax policy–making committees and who received large contributions from corporate donors; the donors' companies subsequently received significant reductions in their tax rates. Elected and appointed officials often see themselves as immune to the rules that apply to rest of us—parking regulations and the like. But to indulge them in this conceit when it comes to the rule of reciprocation is not only laughable but irresponsible.[5]

The history of international negotiations is stocked with examples of how reciprocal exchanges turned potentially dangerous conflicts into peaceful solutions. Perhaps none is as historic as a give-and-take agreement that may have saved the world but, for political reasons, was not allowed credit for it. On October 22, 1962, the temperature of the Cold War between the United States and the Soviet Union soared to near boiling. In a televised address, President John F. Kennedy announced American reconnaissance planes had confirmed that Russian nuclear missiles had been shipped to Cuba, undercover, and aimed at the United States. He directed Soviet leader Nikita Khrushchev to retrieve the missiles, declaring a naval blockade of ships carrying additional missiles into Cuba until the installed missiles were removed. Khrushchev responded that his ships, coursing for Cuba, would ignore this "outright piracy"; moreover, any attempt to enforce the blockade would be considered an aggressive act that would lead to war. Not just any war—a nuclear war estimated to destroy a third of humanity. For thirteen days, the people of the world held on to hope (and one another) as the two leaders stared menacingly at each other until one, Khrushchev, blinked, submitting to Kennedy's unyielding negotiating style and consenting to bring his missiles home. At least, that's the story I'd always heard of how the Cuban missile crisis ended.

But now declassified tapes and documents from the time provide an entirely different account. Kennedy's "win" was due not to his inflexible bargaining stance but, rather, to his willingness to remove US Jupiter missiles from Turkey and Italy *in return* for Khrushchev's removal of missiles from Cuba. For reasons involving his political

Figure 2.1: "Backdown at Castro Gulch"

This political cartoon of the time depicts the widely held interpretation of how the Cuban missile crisis ended—with Khrushchev backing down in the face of Kennedy's unwillingness to compromise with a menacing enemy state. In fact, the opposite was true. The looming thermonuclear threat to the world was resolved by a grand compromise in which nuclear missiles were removed, reciprocally, by both parties.

Library of Congress, copyright by Karl Hubenthal

popularity, Kennedy made it a condition of the final agreement that the missile trade-off be kept secret; he didn't want to be seen as conceding anything to the Soviets. It seems ironic and regrettable that for many years and even today, the factor that "saved the world"—the power of reciprocal exchange—has been underrecognized and has been assigned instead to a factor—unwillingness to compromise—that might well have destroyed that world.[6]

Outside the government arena, the benefits of a give-and-take versus a don't-back-down approach to negotiations is reflected in an account by the social psychologist Lee Ross of two brothers

(Ross's cousins) who own a large discount pet-supply company in Canada. The brothers have to negotiate for warehouse space in multiple cities where their products are distributed. One said, "Because I know precisely what a fair storage price is in each of the cities, my strategy is to make a fair offer and never deviate from it in the negotiations—which is why my brother does all the bargaining for us."

The Not-So-Free Sample

Of course, the power of reciprocity can be found in the merchandising field as well. Although the number of examples is large, let's examine a familiar one. As a marketing technique, the free sample has a long and effective history. In most instances, a small amount of the relevant product is given to potential customers to see if they like it. Certainly this is a legitimate desire of the manufacturer—to expose the public to the qualities of the product. The beauty of the free sample, however, is that it is also a gift and, as such, can engage the reciprocity rule. In true jujitsu fashion, a promoter who provides free samples can release the natural indebting force inherent in a gift, while innocently appearing to have only the intention to inform.

In one Southern California candy shop, researchers examined the buying patterns of customers who either did or did not receive a free piece of candy as they entered. Receiving the gift made recipients 42 percent more likely to make a purchase. Of course, it's possible their increased buying wasn't caused by the pull of reciprocity. Perhaps these customers simply liked what they'd tasted so much, they bought more of it. But a closer look doesn't support this explanation. The recipients didn't buy more of the candy they'd sampled; they only bought more of other types of candy. Seemingly, even if they didn't particularly like the candy they were given, they still felt obligated to return the favor by purchasing *something*.

A favorite place for free samples is the supermarket, where cus-

Figure 2.2: Buenos nachos
Some food manufacturers no longer wait until the customers are in the store to provide them with free samples.
© Alan Carey/The Image Works

tomers are frequently given small amounts of a certain product to try. Many people find it difficult to accept samples from the always smiling attendant, return only the toothpicks or cups, and walk away. Instead, they buy some of the product, even if they might not have liked it very much. According to sales figures from retail giant Costco, all sorts of products—beer, cheese, frozen pizza, lipstick—get big lifts from free samples, almost all accounted for by the shoppers who accept the free offer. A highly effective variation on this marketing procedure is illustrated in the case, cited by Vance Packard in his classic book *The Hidden Persuaders* (1957), of the Indiana supermarket operator who sold an astounding one thousand pounds of cheese in a few hours one day by putting out the cheese and inviting customers to cut off slivers for themselves as free samples.

EBOX 2.2

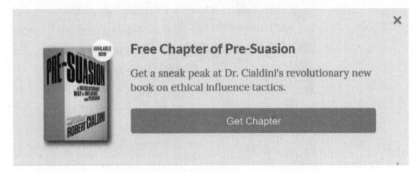

© *Robert Cialdini/Influence At Work*

Author's note: In this online offer, we can see the two reasons why a free sample can be effective: (1) the free chapter gives customers the ability to make a more informed decision about purchasing the whole book; and (2) as a gift, the chapter may make them feel more obligated to do so. I happen to know the book's author, and when I asked him which of the two reasons he was aiming for with the ad, he said it was entirely the first. I know him to be basically an honest guy, but as a psychologist, I also know that people often believe what they prefer to believe. So I'm not fully convinced.

A different version of the free-sample tactic is used by Amway, a company that manufactures and distributes household and personal-care products in a vast worldwide network of door-to-door neighborhood sales. The company, which has grown from a basement-run operation to a business with $8.8 billion in annual sales, makes use of the free sample in a device called the BUG. The BUG consists of a collection of Amway products—bottles of furniture polish, detergent, or shampoo, spray containers of deodorizers, insect killers, or window cleaners—carried to a customer's home in a specially designed tray or just a polyethylene bag. The confidential *Amway Career Manual* then instructs the salesperson to leave the BUG with the customer "for 24, 48, or 72 hours, at no cost or obligation to her. Just tell her you would like her to try the products. . . . That's an offer no one can refuse." At the end of the trial period, the Amway representative is to return and pick up orders for the products the customer wishes to purchase. Since few customers use up the entire contents of even one of the product containers in such a short time, the salesperson may then take the remaining product portions in the BUG to the next potential customer down the line or across the street and start the process again. Many Amway representatives have several BUGS circulating in their districts at one time.

Of course, by now you and I know that the customer who has accepted and used the BUG products has been trapped by the reciprocity rule. Many such customers yield to a sense of obligation to order the products they have tried and partially consumed—and, of course, by now Amway knows that to be the case. Even in a company with as excellent a growth record as Amway, the BUG device has created a big stir. Reports by state distributors to the parent company record a remarkable effect:

> Unbelievable! We've never seen such excitement. Product is moving at an unbelievable rate, and we've only just begun. . . . Local distributors took the BUGS, and we've had an unbelievable increase in sales [from Illinois distributor]. The most fantastic retail idea we've ever had! . . . On the average, customers purchased about half the total amount of the BUG when it is picked up. . . . In one word, tremendous! We've never seen a response within our entire organization like this [from Massachusetts distributor].

The Amway distributors appear to be bewildered—happily so, but nonetheless bewildered—by the startling power of the BUG. Of course, by now, you and I should not be.

The reciprocity rule governs many situations of a purely interpersonal nature where neither money nor commercial exchange is at issue. An instructive point in this regard comes from an account of a woman who saved her own life not by *giving* a gift but by *refusing* a gift and the powerful obligations that went with it. In November 1978 Reverend Jim Jones, the cult leader of Jonestown, Guyana, called for the mass suicide of all residents, most of whom compliantly drank and died from a vat of poison-laced Kool-Aid. Diane Louie, a resident, however, rejected Jones's command and made her way out of Jonestown and into the jungle. She attributes her willingness to do so to her earlier refusal to accept special favors from him when she was in need. She turned down his offer of special food while she was ill because "I knew once he gave me those privileges, he'd have me. I didn't want to owe him nothin'." Perhaps Reverend Jones's mistake was in teaching the Scriptures too well to Ms. Louie, especially Exodus 23:8—"And thou shalt take no gift; for a gift blindeth them that have sight and perverteth the words of the righteous."[7]

Personalization via Customization

Despite the impressive force the rule of reciprocation commands, there is a set of conditions that magnifies that force even more: when the first gift is customized, and thereby personalized, to the recipient's current needs or preferences. A consultant friend of mine told me how she employs personalized gifts to speed payment for her services when submitting a bill to a notoriously slow-paying client—a man known within the industry to take six months to pay. A while ago, along with her invoice, she started sending a small gift—a packet of high-quality stationery, a small box of chocolates, a Starbucks Card—and has seen the delay in his payment cut in half. More recently, she has enclosed a personalized postcard from her local art museum depicting a piece of modern art—the category of art she knows the client collects. She swears that her invoices now get paid almost immediately. Colleagues in her industry are impressed and want to know how she does it. Until now, she says, she's kept it a secret.

Besides customizing a gift to a recipient's preferences, customizing it to the recipient's current needs can also supercharge the gift's impact. Research done in a fast-food restaurant reveals the effectiveness of this sort of tailoring. Some restaurant visitors were greeted warmly as they entered. Others were greeted warmly and given a gift of a nice key ring. Compared to visitors given no gift, they purchased 12 percent more food—all in keeping with the general rule of reciprocation. A third sample of visitors was greeted warmly and given a small cup of yogurt. Even though the retail value of the yogurt equaled that of the key ring, it increased food purchased much more, to 24 percent. Why? Because visitors entered with a need for food, and matching the gift to the need made the difference.

A while ago my colleague Brian Ahearn sent me an article from a sales magazine, describing the shock a high-level executive of a global hotel chain got after reviewing the results of his company's costly "Seamless Customer Experience" program. It wasn't guests with an errorless stay who reported the highest satisfaction ratings and future loyalty. Rather, it was those who experienced a service stumble that was immediately put right by the hotel staff. There are multiple ways to understand why this occurred. For example, it may be that after guests know that the organization can efficiently fix mistakes, they become more confident that the same will be true in any future dealings. I don't doubt this possibility, but I believe another factor is at work too: The remedy may well be perceived by guests as "special, personalized assistance" the hotel has gone out of its way to provide. By virtue of the rule of reciprocation, the hotel then becomes deserving of something special in return, in the form of superior ratings and loyalty.

I often talk about this hotel executive's surprising revelation and my explanations for it when addressing business conferences. At one, I received confirmation of the reciprocity-based explanation when the general manager (GM) of the resort hotel where I was speaking stood up in the audience and related an incident that had occurred that day. A guest had wanted to play tennis with her two young children, but the pair of child-size racquets the resort maintained were already in use. So the GM had a staff member drive to a local sporting goods store, purchase another pair, and deliver them to his guest within twenty minutes of her disappointment.

Afterward, the mother stopped by the GM's office and said, "I've just booked our entire extended family into this resort for the Fourth of July weekend because of what you did for me."

Isn't it interesting that had the resort stocked those additional two children's racquets from the outset—in order to ensure its guests a "seamless experience"—their availability would not have been seen as a notable gift or service that warranted special gratitude and loyalty in the form of additional business? In fact, the racquets may have hardly registered as a blip on Mom's resort-experience screen.

I'm convinced that it is the unique customizability of a *reaction* to a mistake that allows it to be experienced as a personalized gift or service. That feature brings the leverage of the rule of reciprocation into play, which allows us to make sense of the heightened levels of satisfaction and loyalty that can flow, so paradoxically, from a gaffe. In short, problem-free may not feel as good to people as problem-freed.[8]

The Rule Enforces Uninvited Debts

Earlier we suggested that the power of the reciprocity rule is such that by first doing us a favor, unknown, disliked, or unwelcome others can enhance the chance we will comply with one of their requests. However, there is another aspect of the rule, in addition to its power, that allows this phenomenon to occur. A person can trigger a feeling of indebtedness by doing us an uninvited favor. Recall that the rule states only that we should provide to others the kind of actions they have provided us; it does not require us to have asked for what we have received in order to feel obligated to repay. For instance, the Disabled American Veterans organization reports that its simple mail appeal for donations produces a response rate of about 18 percent. But when the mailing also includes an unsolicited gift (gummed, individualized address labels), the success rate nearly doubles to 35 percent. This is not to say that we might not feel a stronger sense of obligation to return a favor we have requested, but such a request is not necessary to produce our feeling of indebtedness.

If we reflect for a moment on the social purpose of the reciprocity rule, we can see why this is the case. The rule was established to promote the development of reciprocal relationships between individuals so that one person could *initiate* such a relationship without the fear of loss. If the rule is to serve that purpose, then an uninvited first favor must have the ability to create an obligation. Recall, also, that reciprocal relationships confer an extraordinary advantage upon cultures that foster them, and, consequently, there will be strong pressures to ensure the rule does serve its purpose. Little wonder that influential French anthropologist Marcel Mauss, in describing the social pressures surrounding the gift-giving process, says there is an obligation to give, an obligation to receive, and an obligation to repay.

Although an obligation to repay constitutes the essence of the reciprocity rule, it's the obligation to receive that makes the rule so easy to exploit. A responsibility to receive reduces our ability to choose those to whom we wish to be indebted and puts the power in the hands of others. Let's reexamine a pair of earlier examples to see how the process works. First, in the Regan study, we find that the favor causing subjects to double the number of raffle tickets purchased from Joe was not one they had requested. Joe had voluntarily left the room and returned with one Coke for himself and one for the subject. There was not a single subject who refused the favor. It is easy to see why it would have been awkward to turn down Joe's gift: he had already spent his money; a soft drink was an appropriate favor in the situation, especially because Joe had one himself; and it would have been considered impolite to reject Joe's thoughtful action. Nevertheless, receipt of that Coke produced a feeling of indebtedness that became clear when Joe announced his desire to sell raffle tickets. Notice the important asymmetry here—all the genuinely free choices were Joe's. He chose the form of the initial favor, and he chose the form of the return favor. Of course, one could say that the subject had the choice of refusing both of Joe's offers, but those would have been tough choices. To have said no at either point would have required the subject to go against the natural cultural forces favoring reciprocation.

The ability of uninvited gifts to produce feelings of obligation is recognized by a variety of organizations. How many times has each of us received small gifts through the mail—personalized address labels, greeting cards, key rings—from charitable agencies that ask for funds in an accompanying note? I have received five in just the past year, two from disabled veterans' groups and the others from missionary schools and hospitals. In each case, there was a common thread in the accompanying message. The goods that were enclosed were to be considered a gift from the organization, and money I wished to send should not be regarded as payment but rather as a return offering. As the letter from one of the missionary programs stated, the packet of greeting cards I had been sent was not to be directly paid for but was designed "to encourage your [my] kindness." We can see why it would be beneficial for the organization to have the cards viewed as a gift instead of as merchandise: there is a strong cultural pressure to reciprocate a gift, even an unwanted one, but there is no such pressure to purchase an unwanted commercial product.[9]

READER'S REPORT 2.3

From a male college student

Last year, on my way home for Thanksgiving break, I felt the pull of reciprocation firsthand when I blew a tire. A driver in a nurse's uniform stopped and volunteered to take me home. I told her several times that my house was still 25 miles away and in the opposite direction that she was heading; but she insisted on helping me anyway and wouldn't take any money for it. Her refusal to let me pay her created the uneasy, uncomfortable feeling you discuss in *Influence*.

The days following the incident also caused anxiety for my parents. The rule of reciprocation and the discomfort associated with the unreturned favor caused a mild neurosis in my house. We kept trying to find her identity in order to send her flowers or a gift, all to no avail. If we had found her, I believe we would have given the woman almost anything she asked for. Finding no other way to relieve the obligation, my mother finally resorted to the only route left to her. In her prayers at our Thanksgiving dinner table, she asked the Lord to compensate the woman from heaven.

Author's note: Besides showing that unsolicited assistance can engage the reciprocity rule, this account points to something else worth knowing about the obligations that accompany the rule: they are not limited to the individuals initially involved in giving and receiving aid. They apply, as well, to members of the groups to which the individuals belong. Not only was the family of the college student made to feel indebted by the help he received, but had they been able, they could have retired the debt, as research indicates, by helping a member of the nurse's family (Goldstein et al., 2007). Additional research shows that this kind of group-based reciprocity extends to mistreatment. If we are harmed by a member of another group and we can't harm that person, we're more likely to take our revenge by mistreating someone else of that group (Hugh-Jones, Ron, & Zultan, 2019).

The Rule Can Trigger Unequal Exchanges

There is yet another feature of the reciprocity rule that allows it to be exploited for profit. Paradoxically, although the rule developed to promote equal exchanges between partners, it can be used to bring about decidedly unequal results. The rule demands that one sort of action be reciprocated with a similar sort of action. A favor is to be met with another favor; it is not to be met with neglect and certainly not with attack; however, considerable flexibility is allowed. A small initial favor can produce a sense of obligation to agree to a substantially larger return favor. Because, as we have already seen, the rule allows one person to choose the nature of the indebting first favor *and* the nature of the debt-canceling return favor, we could easily be manipulated into an unfair exchange by those who might wish to exploit the rule.

Once again, we can turn to the Regan experiment for evidence. Remember in that study, Joe gave one group of subjects a bottle of Coca-Cola as an initiating gift and later asked every subject to buy some of his raffle tickets at 25¢ apiece. What I have so far neglected to mention is that the study was done in the late 1960s, when the price of a Coke was a dime. On average, subjects who had been given a 10¢ drink bought two of Joe's raffle tickets, although some bought as many as seven. Even if we look just at the average, we can tell that Joe made quite a deal. A 500 percent return on investment is respectable indeed!

In Joe's case, though, even a 500 percent return amounted to only 50¢. Can the reciprocity rule produce meaningfully large differences in the sizes of the exchanged favors? Under the right circumstances, it certainly can. Take, for instance, the account of a student of mine concerning a day she remembers ruefully.

> About one year ago, I couldn't start my car. As I was sitting there, a guy in the parking lot came over and eventually jump-started the car. I said thanks, and he said you're welcome; as he was leaving, I said that if he ever needed a favor to stop by. About a month later, the guy knocked on my door and asked to borrow my car for two hours as his was in the shop. I felt somewhat obligated but uncertain, since the car was pretty new and he looked very young. Later, I found out that he was underage and had no insurance. Anyway, I lent him the car. He totaled it.

How could it happen that an intelligent young woman would agree to turn over her new car to a virtual stranger (and a youngster at that) because he had done her a small favor a month earlier? Or, more generally, why should it be that small first favors often stimulate larger return favors? One important reason concerns the clearly unpleasant character of the feeling of indebtedness. Most of us find it highly disagreeable to be in a state of obligation. It weighs heavily on us and demands to be removed. It is not difficult to trace the source of this feeling. Because reciprocal arrangements are so vital in human social systems, we have been conditioned to feel uncomfortable when beholden. If we were to ignore the need to return another's initial favor, we would stop one reciprocal sequence dead and make it less likely that our benefactor would do such favors in the future. Neither event is in the best interests of society. Consequently, we are trained from childhood to chafe, emotionally, under the saddle of obligation. For this reason alone, we may be willing to agree to perform a larger favor than the one we received, merely to relieve ourselves of the psychological burden of debt. A Japanese proverb makes this point eloquently: "There's nothing more expensive than that which comes for free."

There is another reason as well. A person who violates the reciprocity rule by accepting without attempting to return the good acts of others is disliked by the social group. The exception, of

Figure 2.3: Guilt-edged exchange
Even the stingiest people feel the pull of the reciprocity rule. But the rule can also be used by restaurant servers to increase their tips. One study found that servers who gave diners a piece of candy when presenting the bill increased their tips by 3.3 percent. If they provided two pieces of candy to each guest, the tip went up by 14 percent (Strohmetz et al., 2002).

Cartoon © Mark Parisi/offthemark.com

course, occurs when a person is prevented from repayment by reasons of circumstance or ability. For the most part, though, there is a genuine distaste for an individual who fails to conform to the dictates of the reciprocity rule. Moocher, taker, and ingrate are unsavory labels, to be scrupulously shunned. So undesirable are they that people will sometimes agree to an unequal exchange to dodge them.

In combination, the reality of internal discomfort and the possibility of external shame can produce a heavy psychological cost. When seen in the light of this cost, it is not so puzzling that in the name of reciprocity, we often give back more than we have received. Neither is it so odd that we often avoid asking for a needed favor if we will not be in a position to repay it. The psychological cost may simply outweigh the material loss.

The risk of still other kinds of losses may also persuade people to decline certain gifts and benefits. Women frequently comment on the uncomfortable sense of obligation they can feel to return the favors of a man who has given them an expensive present or paid for a costly evening out. Even something as small as the price of a drink can produce a feeling of debt. A student in one of my classes expressed it quite plainly in a paper she wrote: "After learning the hard way, I no longer let a guy I meet in a club buy me a drink because I don't want either of us to feel that I am obligated sexually." Research suggests that there is a basis for her concern. If instead of paying for them herself, a woman allows a man to buy her drinks, she is immediately judged (by both men and women) as more sexually available to him.

The rule of reciprocation applies to most relationships; however, in its purest form—an equivalent exchange of gift and favors—it is unnecessary and undesirable in certain long-term relationships such as families or established friendships. In these "communal" relationships, what is exchanged reciprocally is the *willingness to provide what the other needs, when it is needed.* Under this form of reciprocity, it is not necessary to calculate who has given more or less but only whether both parties are living up to the more general rule.[10]

READER'S REPORT 2.4

From an American émigré to Australia

Not long ago, we moved to Australia where my five-year-old daughter has been struggling to adapt to the new culture and find new friends. Recently, on walks around the neighborhood with my wife, our daughter tried leaving "gifts" in neighbors' letter boxes. These were really just drawings scribbled in crayon and then folded and taped together into a letter. I thought it pretty harmless and was more concerned that it might be perceived as a nuisance. I worried we would be known as the "Phantom Letter Box Litterers." Then funny things started happening. In *our* mailbox, we started finding cards—proper Hallmark cards—addressed to my daughter that cost anywhere from $3 to $5 apiece. Then packets of sweets and small toys started appearing there. If it wasn't for reading your book, I wouldn't have understood this; but the power of reciprocity is unbelievable. She now has a group of friends she plays with in the park across the road each day.

Author's note: I like this account because it reinforces a pair of features of the reciprocity rule we've already covered: it can not only trigger unequal exchanges but also serve as the initiator of ongoing social arrangements. More than that, even young children see it as a way to bring about such arrangements.

Reciprocal Concessions

There is a second way to employ the reciprocity rule to get someone to comply with a request. It is more subtle, yet in some ways more effective, than the direct route of providing that person with a favor and then asking for one in return. A personal experience I had a few years ago gave me firsthand evidence of how well the technique works.

I was walking along a street when approached by an eleven- or twelve-year-old boy. He introduced himself and said he was selling tickets to the annual Boy Scouts Circus to be held on the upcoming Saturday night. He asked if I wished to buy any tickets at $5 apiece. I declined. "Well," he said, "if you don't want to buy any tickets, how about buying some of our chocolate bars? They're only $1 each." I bought a couple and, right away, realized that something noteworthy had happened. I knew that to be the case because (a) I do not like chocolate bars, (b) I do like dollars, (c) I was standing there with two of his chocolate bars, and (d) he was walking away with two of my dollars.

To try to understand precisely what happened in my exchange with the Boy Scout, I went to my office and called a meeting of my research assistants. In discussing the situation, we began to see how the reciprocity rule was implicated in my compliance with the request to buy the candy bars. The general rule says that a person who acts in a certain way toward us is entitled to a similar return action. We have already seen that one consequence of the rule is an obligation to repay favors. Another consequence, however, is an obligation to make a concession to someone who has made a concession to us. As my research group thought about it, we realized that was exactly the position the Boy Scout had put me in. His request that I purchase some $1 chocolate bars had been put in the form of a concession on his part; it was presented as a retreat from his request that I buy some $5 tickets. If I were to live up to the dictates of the reciprocation rule, there had to be a concession on my part. As we have seen, there was such a concession: I changed from noncompliant to compliant when he moved from a larger to a smaller request, even though I was not really interested in either of the things he offered.

It was a classic example of the way a lever of influence can infuse a compliance request with its power. I had been moved to buy something, not because of any favorable feelings toward the item but because the purchase request had been presented in a way that drew force from the reciprocity rule. It had not mattered that I do not like chocolate bars; the Boy Scout had made a concession to me, *click*; and, *run*, I responded with a concession of my own. Of course, the tendency to reciprocate with a concession is not so strong that it will work in all instances on all people; none of the levers of influence considered in this book is that strong. However, in my exchange with the Boy Scout, the tendency had been sufficiently powerful to leave me in mystified possession of a pair of unwanted candy bars.

Why should I feel obliged to reciprocate a concession? The answer rests once again in the benefit of such a tendency to society. It is in the interest of any human group to have its members working together toward the achievement of common goals. However, in many social interactions the participants begin with requirements and demands that are unacceptable to one another. Thus, society must arrange to have these initial, incompatible desires set aside for the sake of socially beneficial cooperation. This is accomplished through procedures that promote compromise. Mutual concession is one such important procedure.

The reciprocation rule brings about mutual concession in two ways. The first is obvious: it pressures the recipient of an already made concession to respond in kind. The second, while not so obvious, is pivotally important. Because of a recipient's obligation to reciprocate, people are freed to make the *initial* concession and, thereby, to begin the beneficial process of exchange. After all, if there were no social obligation to reciprocate a concession, who would want to make the first sacrifice? To do so would be to risk giving up something and getting nothing back. However, with the rule in effect, we can feel safe making the first sacrifice to our partner, who is obligated to offer a return sacrifice.

Rejection Then Retreat

Because the rule of reciprocation governs the compromise process, it is possible to use an initial concession as part of a highly effective compliance technique. The technique is a simple one that we can call the rejection-then-retreat technique, although it is also known as the door-in-the-face technique. Suppose you want me to agree to a certain request. One way to increase the chances I will comply is first to make a larger request of me, one that I will most likely turn down. Then, after I have refused, you make the smaller request that you were really interested in all along. Provided that you structured your requests skillfully, I should view your second request as a concession to me and should feel inclined to respond with a concession of my own—compliance with your second request.

Was that the way the Boy Scout got me to buy his candy bars? Was his retreat from the $5 request to the $1 request an artificial one that was intentionally designed to sell candy bars? As one who has still refused to discard even his first Scout merit badge, I genuinely hope not. Whether or not the "large request then small request" sequence was planned, its effect was the same. It worked. Because it works, the rejection-then-retreat technique can and will be used *purposely* by certain people to get their way. First, let's examine how this tactic can be used as a reliable compliance device. Later, we will see how it is already being used. Finally, we can turn to a pair of little-known features of the technique that make it one of the most influential compliance tactics available.

Remember that after my encounter with the Boy Scout, I called my research assistants together to understand what had happened to me (and where they ate the evidence). Actually, we did more than that. We designed an experiment to test the effectiveness of the procedure of moving to a desired request after a larger preliminary request had been refused. We had two purposes in conducting the experiment. First, we wanted to see whether this procedure worked on people besides me. It certainly seemed that the tactic had been effective on me earlier in the day, but then I have a history of falling for compliance tricks of all sorts. So the question remained, Does the rejection-then-retreat technique work on enough people to make it a useful procedure for gaining compliance? If so, it would definitely be something to be aware of in the future.

Our second reason for doing the study was to determine how powerful a compliance device the technique was. Could it bring about compliance with a genuinely sizable request? In other words, did the *smaller* request to which the requester retreated have to be *small*? If our thinking about what caused the technique to be effective was correct, the second request did not have to be small; it only had to be smaller than the initial one. It was our suspicion that the critical aspect of a requester's retreat from a larger to a smaller favor was its appearance as a concession. So the second request could be an objectively large one—as long as it was smaller than the first request—and the technique should still work.

After a bit of thought, we decided to try the technique on a request we felt few people would agree to perform. Posing as representatives of the "County Youth Counseling Program," we approached college students walking on campus and asked if they would be willing to chaperon a group of juvenile delinquents on a day trip to the zoo. This idea of being responsible for a group of juvenile delinquents of unspecified age for hours in a public place without pay was hardly an inviting one for these students. As we expected, the great majority (83 percent) refused. Yet we obtained very different results from a similar sample of college students who were asked the same question with one difference. Before inviting them to serve as unpaid chaperons on the zoo trip, we asked them for an even larger favor—to spend two hours per week as counselors to juvenile delinquents for a minimum of two years. It was only after they refused this extreme request, as all did, that we made the smaller, zoo-trip request. By presenting the zoo trip as a retreat from our initial request, our success rate increased dramatically. Three times as many of the students approached in this manner volunteered to serve as zoo chaperons.

Be assured that any strategy able to triple the percentage of compliance with a substantial request (from 17 to 50 percent in our experiment) will be used often in a variety of natural settings. Labor negotiators, for instance, often use the tactic of making extreme demands that they do not expect to win but from which they can retreat and draw real concessions from the opposing side. It would appear, then, that the procedure would be more effective the larger the initial request because there would be more room available for illusory concessions. This is true only up to a point. Research conducted at Bar-Ilan University in Israel on the rejection-then-retreat technique shows that if the first set of demands is so extreme as to be seen as unreasonable, the tactic backfires. In such cases, the party who has made the extreme first request is not seen to be bargaining in good faith. Any subsequent retreat from that wholly unrealistic initial position is not viewed as a genuine concession and, thus, is not reciprocated. The truly gifted negotiator, then, is one whose initial position is exaggerated just enough to allow for a series of small reciprocal concessions and counteroffers that will yield a desirable final offer from the opponent.[II]

READER'S REPORT 2.5

From a Software Engineer in Germany

After finishing my university studies in electrical engineering and working for four years in the energy sector, I decided to quit my job, follow my heart, and start fresh in a career of software development. Since all my knowledge in software was self-taught, I started low at a small (ten-person) company as a software engineer. After two years, I decided to ask for a raise. One problem: the owner was well known for not giving raises. Here is what I did.

First, I prepared my boss with information about the extra hours of work I did there and most importantly the profits I helped bring to the company. And then I said, "I don't think I'm the average employee; I do more than the average employee, and I would like to have the average salary of the market for my position, which is XX,XXX euros per year." (My salary at the time was 30 percent below the average.) He answered sharply, "No." I stayed quiet for five seconds and said, "OK, then can you give me XXX euros more per month and the possibility to work one day from home?" He said yes.

I knew he would not give me the average salary for the market.

What I really wanted was to get a fair raise and work one day from home, where I could spend more time with my fiancée. I left his office with two things: (1) a salary increase of 23 percent and (2) a new passion for rejection-then-retreat plays.

Author's note: Notice how, as is usually the case, use of the rejection-then-retreat tactic also engages the action of the contrast principle. Not only did the initial larger amount make the smaller one seem like a retreat, but it made that second request seem an extra measure smaller too.

P.S. This reader's name does not appear in the list of other Reader's Report authors at the front of the book, as he requested that only his initials (M.S.) be employed.

Reciprocal Concessions, Perceptual Contrast, and the Watergate Mystery

We have already discussed one reason for the success of the rejection-then-retreat technique—its incorporation of the reciprocity rule. This larger-then-smaller-request strategy is effective for a pair of other reasons as well. The first concerns the perceptual contrast principle we encountered in chapter 1. That principle accounted for, among other things, the tendency of a man to spend more money than before on a sweater following his purchase of a suit: after being exposed to the price of the larger item, he sees the price of the less expensive item as *appearing* even smaller by comparison. In the same way, the larger-then-smaller request procedure uses the contrast principle to make the smaller request look even smaller by comparison with the larger one. If I want you to lend me $10, I can make the request seem smaller than it is by first asking you to lend me $20. One of the beauties of this tactic is that by first requesting $20 and then retreating to $10, I will have simultaneously engaged the force of both the reciprocity rule and the contrast principle. Not only will my $10 request be viewed as a concession to be reciprocated, but it will look like a smaller request than if I had just asked for $10 straightaway.

In combination, the influences of reciprocity and perceptual contrast present a fearsomely powerful force. Embodied jointly in the rejection-then-retreat sequence, they are capable of genuinely astonishing effects. It is my feeling that they provide the only really plausible explanation of one of the most baffling political actions of our time: the notorious decision to break into the Watergate offices of the Democratic National Committee that led to the ruin of Richard Nixon's presidency. One of the participants in that decision, Jeb Stuart Magruder, upon hearing that the Watergate burglars had been caught, responded with appropriate bewilderment: "How could we have been so stupid?" Indeed, how?

To understand how enormously ill-conceived an idea it was for the Nixon administration to undertake the break-in, let's review a few facts:

- The idea was that of G. Gordon Liddy, who was in charge of intelligence-gathering operations for the Committee to Re-elect the President (CREEP). Liddy had gained a reputation among administration higher-ups as "flaky," and there were questions about his stability and judgment.

- Liddy's proposal was extremely costly, requiring a budget of $250,000 in untraceable cash.

- In late March, when the proposal was approved in a meeting of the CREEP director, John Mitchell, and his assistants Magruder and Frederick LaRue, the outlook for a Nixon victory in the November election could not have been brighter. Edmund Muskie, the only announced candidate early polls had given a chance of unseating the president, had done poorly in the primaries. It looked as though the most defeatable candidate, George McGovern, would win the Democratic nomination. A Republican victory seemed assured.

- The break-in plan itself was a highly risky operation requiring the participation and discretion of ten men.

- The Democratic National Committee and its chairman, Lawrence O'Brien, whose Watergate office was to be burglarized and bugged, had no information damaging enough to defeat the incumbent president. Nor were the Democrats likely to get any, unless the administration did something *very, very* foolish.

Despite the obvious counsel of the previously mentioned reasons, the expensive, chancy, pointless, and potentially calamitous proposal of a man whose judgment was known to be questionable was approved. How could it be that intelligent, accomplished men, such as Mitchell and Magruder, would do something so *very, very* foolish? Perhaps the answer lies in a little-discussed fact: the $250,000 plan they approved was not Liddy's first proposal. In fact, it represented a significant concession on his part from two earlier proposals of immense proportions. The first of these plans, made two months earlier in a meeting with Mitchell, Magruder, and John Dean, described a $1 million program that included (in addition to the bugging of the Watergate offices) a specially equipped communications "chase plane," break-ins, kidnapping and mugging squads, and a yacht featuring "high-class call girls" to blackmail Democratic politicians. A second Liddy plan, presented a week later to the same group of Mitchell, Magruder, and Dean, eliminated some of the program and reduced the cost to $500,000. It was only after these initial proposals had been rejected by Mitchell that Liddy submitted his "bare-bones" $250,000 plan, in this instance to Mitchell, Magruder, and LaRue. This time the plan, still stupid but less so than the previous ones, was approved.

Could it be that I, a longtime patsy, and John Mitchell, a hardened and canny politician, might both have been so easily maneuvered into bad deals by the same compliance tactic—I by a Boy Scout selling candy and he by a man selling political disaster?

If we examine the testimony of Magruder, considered by most

Watergate investigators to provide the most faithful account of the crucial meeting at which Liddy's plan was finally accepted, there are some instructive clues. First, in his book *An American Life: One Man's Road to Watergate* (1974), Magruder reports that "no one was particularly overwhelmed with the project"; but "after starting at the grandiose sum of $1 million, we thought that probably $250,000 would be an acceptable figure. . . . We were reluctant to send him away with nothing." Mitchell, caught up in the "feeling that we should leave Liddy a little something . . . signed off on it in the sense of saying, 'Ok, let's give him a quarter of a million dollars and let's see what he can come up with.'" In the context of Liddy's initial extreme requests, it seems that "a quarter of a million dollars" had come to be "a little something" to be left as a return concession. With the clarity afforded by hindsight, Magruder has recalled Liddy's approach in as succinct an illustration of the rejection-then-retreat technique as I have ever heard: "If he had come to us at the outset and said, 'I have a plan to burglarize and wiretap Larry O'Brien's office,' we might have rejected the idea out of hand. Instead he came to us with his elaborate call-girl/ kidnapping/mugging/sabotage/wiretapping scheme. . . . He had asked for the whole loaf when he was quite content to settle for half or even a quarter."

It is also instructive that although he finally deferred to his boss's decision, only one member of the group, LaRue, expressed any direct opposition to the proposal. Saying with obvious common sense, "I don't think it's worth the risk," he must have wondered why his colleagues, Mitchell and Magruder, did not share his perspective. Of course, there could be many differences between LaRue and the other two men that may have accounted for their differing opinions regarding the advisability of Liddy's plan. But one stands out: of the three, only LaRue had not been present at the prior two meetings, where Liddy had outlined his much more ambitious programs. Perhaps, then, only LaRue was able to see the third proposal for the clunker that it was and react to it objectively, uninfluenced by the reciprocity and perceptual contrast forces acting upon the others.

Figure 2.4: G. Gordon the Menace?

Do similar styles lead to similarly satisfied smiles? So it appears, so it appears.

Cartoon © Dennis the Menace/Hank Ketcham and Field Enterprises; photo of G. Gordon Liddy: UPI

Damned If You Do, Damned If You Don't

A bit earlier we said that the rejection-then-retreat technique had, in addition to the reciprocity rule, a pair of other factors working in its favor. We have already discussed the first of those factors, the perceptual contrast principle. The additional advantage of the technique is not really a psychological principle, as in the case of the other two factors. Rather, it is more of a purely structural feature of the request sequence. Let's once again say that I wish to borrow $10 from you. By beginning with a request for $20, I really can't lose. If you agree to it, I will have received from you twice the amount I would have settled for. If, on the other hand, you turn down my initial request, I can retreat to the $10 favor that I desired from the outset and, through the action of the reciprocity and contrast principles, greatly enhance my likelihood of success. Either way, I benefit; it's a case of heads I win, tails you lose.

Given the advantages of the rejection-then-retreat technique, one might think that there could be a substantial disadvantage as well. The victims of the strategy might resent having been cornered into compliance. The resentment could show itself in a couple of ways. First, the victim might decide not to live up to the verbal agreement made with the requester. Second, the victim might come to distrust the manipulative requester, deciding never to deal with that person again. If either or both of these events occurred with any frequency, a requester would want to give serious second thought to the use of the rejection-then-retreat procedure. Research indicates, however, that these victim reactions do not occur with increased frequency when the rejection-then-retreat technique is used. Somewhat astonishingly, it appears that they actually occur *less* frequently. Before trying to understand why this should be, let's first look at the evidence.

Here's My Blood, and Do Call Again

A study published in Canada throws light on the question of whether a victim of the rejection-then-retreat tactic will follow through with the agreement to perform a requester's second favor. In addition to recording whether target persons said yes or no to the desired request (to work for two hours one day without pay in a community mental health agency), this experiment also recorded whether they showed up to perform their duties as promised. As usual, the procedure of starting with a larger request (to volunteer for two hours of work per week in the agency for two years) produced more verbal agreement to the smaller, retreat request (76 percent) than did the procedure of asking for the smaller request alone (29 percent). The important result, though, concerned the show-up rate *of those who volunteered*; and, again, the rejection-then-retreat procedure was the more effective one (85 versus 50 percent).

A different experiment examined whether the rejection-then-retreat sequence caused victims to feel so manipulated that they would refuse any further requests. In this study, the targets were college students who were each asked to give a pint of blood as part of the annual campus blood drive. Targets in one group were first asked to give a pint of blood every six weeks for a minimum of three years. The other targets were asked only to give a pint of blood once. Those of both groups who agreed and later appeared at the blood center were then asked if they would be willing to give their phone numbers so they could be called upon to donate again in the future. Nearly all the students who were about to give a pint of blood as a result of the rejection-then-retreat technique agreed to donate again (84 percent), while less than half of the other students who appeared at the blood center did so (43 percent). Even for future favors, the rejection-then-retreat strategy proved superior.

The Sweet, Secret Side Effects

Strangely enough, then, it seems that the rejection-then-retreat tactic spurs people not only to agree to a desired request but to carry out that request and, finally, to volunteer to perform further requests. What could there be about the technique that makes people who have been duped into compliance so likely to continue to comply? For an answer, we might look at a requester's act of concession, which is the heart of the procedure. We have already seen that, as long as it is not viewed as an obvious trick, the concession will likely stimulate a return concession. What we have not yet examined, however, is a little-known pair of positive by-products of the act of concession: feelings of greater responsibility for and satisfaction with the arrangement. It is this set of sweet side effects that enables the technique to move its victims to fulfill their agreements and engage in further such agreements.

The desirable side effects of making concessions during an interaction with other people are nicely shown in studies of the way people bargain with each other. One experiment, conducted by social psychologists at UCLA, offers an especially apt demonstration. A subject in that study faced a "negotiation opponent" and was told to bargain with the opponent concerning how to divide between themselves a certain amount of money provided by the experimenters. The subject was also informed that if no mutual agreement could be reached after a certain period of bargaining, no one would get any money. Unknown to the subject, the opponent was really an experimental assistant who had been previously instructed to bargain with the subject in one of three ways. With some of the subjects, the opponent made an extreme first demand, assigning virtually all of the money to himself and stubbornly persisted in that demand throughout the negotiations. With another group of subjects, the opponent began with a demand that was moderately favorable to himself; he, too, steadfastly refused to move from that position during the negotiations. With a third group, the opponent began with the extreme demand and then gradually retreated to the more moderate one during the course of the bargaining.

There were three important findings that help us to understand why the rejection-then-retreat technique is so effective. First, compared to the two other approaches, the strategy of starting with an extreme demand and then retreating to the more moderate one produced the most money for the person using it. This result is not surprising in light of the previous evidence we have seen for the power of larger-then-smaller-request tactics to bring about profitable agreements. It is the pair of additional findings of the study that are more striking.

RESPONSIBILITY

The requester's concession within the rejection-then-retreat technique caused targets not only to say yes more often but also to feel more responsible for having "dictated" the final agreement. Thus the uncanny ability of the rejection-then-retreat technique to make its targets meet their commitments becomes understandable: a person who feels responsible for the terms of a contract will be more likely to live up to that contract.

SATISFACTION

Even though, on average, they gave the most money to the opponent who used the concessions strategy, the subjects who were the targets of this strategy were the most satisfied with the final arrangement. It appears that an agreement that has been forged through the concessions of one's opponents is quite satisfying. With this in mind, we can begin to explain the second previously puzzling feature of the rejection-then-retreat tactic—the ability to prompt its victims to agree to further requests. Because the tactic uses a requester's concession to bring about compliance, the victim is likely to feel more satisfied with the arrangement as a result. It stands to reason that people who are satisfied with a given arrangement are more likely to be willing to agree to similar arrangements. As a pair of studies done by the consumer researcher Robert Schindler showed, feeling responsible for getting a better deal in a retail store led to more satisfaction with the process and more return visits to the store.[12]

READER'S REPORT 2.6

From a former TV and stereo salesperson

For quite a while, I worked for a major retailer in their television and stereo department. Continued employment was based on the ability to sell service contracts which are warranty extensions offered by the retailer. Once this fact was explained to me I devised the following plan that used the rejection-then-retreat technique, although I didn't know its name at the time.

A customer had the opportunity to buy from one to three years' worth of service contract coverage at the time of the sale, although the credit I got was the same regardless of the length of coverage. Realizing that most people would not be willing to buy three years' worth of coverage, initially, I would advocate to the customer the longest and most expensive plan. This gave me an excellent opportunity later, after being rejected in my sincere attempt to sell the three-year plan, to retreat to the one-year extension and its relatively small price, which I was thrilled to get. This technique proved highly effective, as I sold sales contracts to an average of 70 percent of my customers, who seemed very satisfied in the process, while others in my department clustered around 40 percent. I never told anyone how I did it until now.

Author's note: As research suggests, the rejection-then-retreat tactic increased both the number of customers' agreements *and* their satisfaction with those agreements.

Defense

Against a requester who employs the rule of reciprocation, you and I face a formidable foe. By presenting either an initial favor or an initial concession, the requester will have enlisted a powerful ally in the campaign for our compliance. At first glance, our fortunes in such a situation would appear dismal. We could comply with the requester's wish and, in so doing, succumb to the reciprocity rule. Or we could refuse to comply and thereby suffer the brunt of the rule's force upon our deeply conditioned feelings of fairness and obligation. Surrender or suffer heavy casualties. Cheerless prospects indeed.

Fortunately, these are not our only choices. With the proper understanding of the nature of our opponent, we can come away from the compliance battlefield undamaged and sometimes even better off than before. It is essential to recognize that the requester who invokes the reciprocation rule (or any other lever of influence) to gain our compliance is not the real opponent. Such a requester has chosen to become a jujitsu warrior who aligns himself or herself with the sweeping power of reciprocation and then merely releases that power by providing a first favor or concession. The real opponent is the rule. If we are not to be abused by it, we must take steps to defuse its energy.

Rejecting the Rule

How does one go about neutralizing the effect of a social rule such as the one for reciprocation? It seems too widespread to escape and too strong to overcome once it is activated. Perhaps the answer is to prevent its activation. Perhaps we can avoid a confrontation with the rule by refusing to allow a requester to commission its force against us in the first place. Perhaps by rejecting a requester's initial favor or concessions, we can evade the problem. Perhaps, but then, perhaps not. Invariably declining a requester's initial offer of a favor or sacrifice works better in theory than in practice. The major difficulty is that when it is first presented, it is difficult to know whether such an offer is honest or whether it is the initial step in an exploitation attempt. It's a trick-or-treat problem: if we always assume the worst (trick), it would not be possible to receive the benefit of any legitimate favor or concession (treat) offered by individuals who had no intention of exploiting the reciprocity rule.

I have a colleague who remembers with anger how his ten-year-old daughter's feelings were terribly hurt by a man whose method of avoiding the jaws of the reciprocity rule was to refuse her kindness. The children of her class were hosting an open house at school for their grandparents, and her job was to give a flower to each visitor entering the school grounds. The first man she approached with a flower growled at her, "Keep it." Not knowing what to do, she extended it toward him again, only to have him demand to know what he had to give in return. When she replied weakly, "Nothing. It's a gift," he fixed her with a disbelieving glare and brushed on past. The girl was so stung by the experience that she could not approach anyone else and had to be removed from her assignment—one she had anticipated fondly. It is hard to know whom to blame more, the insensitive man or the exploiters who had abused his tendency to reciprocate a gift until his response had soured to an automatic refusal. No matter whom you find more blameworthy, the lesson is clear. We will always encounter authentically generous individuals as well as many people who try to play fairly by the reciprocity rule rather than to exploit it. They will doubtless become insulted by someone who consistently rejects their efforts; social friction and isolation could well result. A policy of blanket rejection, then, seems ill-advised.

Another solution holds more promise. It advises us to accept the offers of others but to accept the offers only for what they fundamentally are, not for what they are represented to be. If a person offers us a nice favor, we might well accept, recognizing that we have obligated ourselves to a return favor sometime in the future. To engage in this sort of arrangement with another is not to be exploited by that person through the rule of reciprocation. Quite the contrary; it is to participate fairly in the "honored network of obligation" that has served us so well, both individually and societally, from the dawn of humanity. However, if the initial favor turns out to be a device, a trick, an artifice designed specifically to stimulate our compliance with a larger return favor, that is a different story. Our partner is not a benefactor but a profiteer, and it is here that we should respond to the action on precisely those terms. Once we have determined the initial offer was not a favor but a compliance tactic, we need only react to it accordingly to be free of its influence. As long as we perceive and define the action as a compliance device instead of a favor, the giver no longer has the reciprocation rule as an ally: The rule says that favors are to be met with favors; it does not require that tricks be met with favors.

Smoking Out the Enemy

A practical example may make things more concrete. Let's suppose that a woman phoned one day and introduced herself as a member of the Home Firesafety Association in your town. Suppose she then asked if you would be interested in learning about home firesafety, having your house checked for fire hazards, and receiving a home fire extinguisher—all free of charge. Let's suppose further that you were interested in these things and made an evening appointment to have one of the association's inspectors come over to provide them. When the inspector arrived, he gave you a small hand extinguisher and began examining the possible fire hazards of your home. Afterward, he gave you some interesting, though frightening, information about household fire dangers, along with an assessment of your home's vulnerability. Finally, he suggested that you obtain a home fire-warning system for your house and left.

Such a set of events is not implausible. Various cities and towns have nonprofit associations, usually made up of Fire Department personnel working on their own time, that provide free home firesafety inspections of this sort. Were these events to occur, you would have clearly received a favor from the inspector. In accordance with the reciprocation rule, you should stand more ready to provide a return favor if you were to see him in need of aid at some point in the future—perhaps standing next to his broken-down car at the side of the road. An exchange of favors of this kind would be in the best tradition of the reciprocity rule.

A similar set of events with a different ending is also possible. Rather than leaving after recommending a fire-alarm system, the inspector launches into a sales presentation intended to persuade you to buy an expensive, heat-triggered alarm system manufactured by the company he represents. Door-to-door home fire-alarm companies will frequently use this approach. Typically, their product, while effective enough, is overpriced. Trusting that you will not be familiar with the retail costs of such a system and, if you decide to buy one, you will feel obligated to the company that provided you with a free extinguisher and home inspection, these companies will pressure you for an immediate sale. Using this free-information-and-inspection gambit, fire-protection sales organizations have flourished.

If you were to find yourself in such a situation with the realization that the primary motive of the inspector's visit was to sell you a costly alarm system, your most effective next action would be a simple, private maneuver. It would involve the mental act of redefinition. Merely define whatever you have received from the inspector—extinguisher, safety information, hazard inspection—not as gifts but as sales devices, and you will be free to decline (or accept) the purchase offer without even a tug from the reciprocity rule: A favor rightly follows a favor—not a sales scheme.

Provided you are so inclined, you might even turn the inspector's own lever of influence against him. Recall that the rule of reciprocation entitles a person who has acted in a certain way to a dose of the same thing. If you have determined that the "fire inspector's gifts" were used not as genuine gifts but to make a profit from you, then you might want to use them to make a profit of your own. Simply take whatever the inspector is willing to provide—safety information, home extinguisher—thank him politely, and show him out the door. After all, the reciprocity rule asserts that if justice is to be done, exploitation attempts should be exploited.

READER'S REPORT 2.7

From a chemical-engineering student in Zurich, Switzerland

I have a great interest in behavioral psychology, which led me to your book *Influence*. Just yesterday I finished the chapter on Reciprocity. Today I went to the supermarket and a guy stopped me who claimed to be a yogi. He started reading my aura and said he can see I am a calm and helpful person. Then he took a little pearl from his pocket and gave it to me as a present. A moment later, he wanted a donation. When I told him I am a poor student and don't have extra money, he started emphasizing that he gave me the pearl and that it would only be fair if I donated in return. Because I had read the Reciprocity chapter less than 24 hours earlier, I knew exactly what he was attempting with the pearl, and I refused; so, out of arguments, he walked away.

Author's note: The old adage "Knowledge sets us free" applies in this instance. Knowing how to defend against a rule-of-reciprocity profiteer freed the student to resist the pull of an unrequested, sham gift. Besides, I'm sure that there was no real pearl provided in the student's story, except perhaps a pearl of wisdom his account provides to the rest of us.

SUMMARY

- According to sociologists and anthropologists, one of the most widespread and basic norms of human culture is embodied in the rule of reciprocation. The rule requires that one person try to repay, in form, what another person has provided. By obligating the recipient of an act to repayment in the future, the rule allows one individual to give something to another with confidence that it is not being lost. This sense of future obligation within the rule makes possible the development of various kinds of continuing relationships, transactions, and exchanges that are beneficial to society. Consequently, all members of all societies are trained from childhood to abide by the rule or suffer serious social disapproval.

- The decision to comply with another's request is frequently influenced by the reciprocity rule. One favorite and profitable tactic of certain compliance professionals is to give something before asking for a return favor. The exploitability of the tactic is due to three characteristics of the rule of reciprocation. First, the rule is extremely powerful, often overwhelming the influence of other factors that normally determine compliance with a request. The rule becomes particularly potent when the gift, favor, or service is personalized or customized to the recipient's current preferences or needs. Second, the rule applies even to uninvited first favors, thereby reducing our ability to decide whom we wish to owe and putting the choice in the hands of others. Finally, the rule can spur unequal exchanges; to be rid of the uncomfortable feeling of indebtedness, an individual often agrees to a request for a substantially larger favor than the one he or she received.

- Another way the rule of reciprocation can increase compliance involves a simple variation on the basic theme: instead of providing a first favor that stimulates a return favor, an individual can make an initial concession that stimulates a return concession. One compliance procedure, called the rejection-then-retreat technique, or door-in-the-face technique, relies heavily on the pressure to reciprocate concessions. By starting with an extreme request sure to be rejected, a requester can then profitably retreat to a smaller request (the one desired all along), which is likely to be accepted because it appears to be a concession. Research indicates that aside from increasing the likelihood a person will say yes to a request, the rejection-then-retreat technique also increases the likelihood the person will carry out the request and agree to such requests in the future. This is the case because, after participating in a reciprocal exchange of concessions, people feel more responsible for and more satisfied with the outcome.

- Our best defense against the use of reciprocity pressures to gain our compliance is not systematic rejection of the initial offers of others. Rather, we should accept initial favors or concessions in good faith but be ready to redefine them as tricks should they later be proved as such. Once they are redefined in this way, we should no longer feel a need to respond with a favor or concession of our own.

CHAPTER 3

LIKING

THE FRIENDLY THIEF

There is nothing more effective in selling anything than getting customers to believe, really believe, you like them.

—Joe Girard, *Guinness Book of World Records* "Greatest Car Salesman"

Few of us would be surprised to learn that we are more influenced by the people we like—for example, our friends. What might be startling to note, however, is that this simple liking rule can apply to individuals we've never interacted with closely or even met. Consider how the tendency offers a solution to a problem that has vexed science communicators for decades: how to get more people to accept Darwin's theory of evolution, which asserts that all living things, including humans, have come to their present form entirely through systematic processes of evolution, such as natural selection. It's been a tough sell for these communicators because evolutionary claims often run counter to the beliefs of religious groups that view God's hand as determining what makes us human. Indeed, in a recent survey on the topic, only 33 percent of Americans agreed that we've developed as a species solely via natural evolutionary processes.

In response, science researchers, teachers, and proponents have tried to increase the percentage of believers by (a) describing the near consensus among scientists regarding the validity of evolutionary theory, (b) pointing to the thousands of studies that have confirmed evolutionary thinking, (c) highlighting the advances in medicine, genetics, agriculture, and pharmacology that have come from the application of evolutionary principles, and (d) advocating for greater agreement with the logic of evolutionary theory through more intensive teaching of it. All with little success. For example, the last of these approaches—trying to build belief in evolutionary theory by way of better instruction—is futile because research shows there is no connection between one's belief in evolution and one's understanding of its logic. There's good reason for the disconnect: resistance to the theory of evolution doesn't stem from perceived inconsistencies in its logic; it stems from the theory's perceived inconsistencies with people's emotionally based preferences, beliefs, and values, which are frequently grounded in existing religious affiliations.

Thus, it's a fool's errand to try to overcome faith-based, emotionally held beliefs with logical argumentation, as each represents a separate way of knowing. The British writer Jonathan Swift saw it three hundred years ago and declared, "It is useless to attempt to reason a man out of a thing he was never reasoned into"—and thereby provided a tactical lesson science communicators have nevertheless failed to learn. Because they prioritize thinking over all else as a way of knowing, science communicators have persisted in the assumption that the facts will win over audiences reacting not to the facts about evolution but to their feelings about the idea. Is there any persuasive approach that could come to the rescue of these misguided communicators?

Enter the liking rule. A team of Canadian psychologists thought they could elevate attitudes toward evolution with the simple news that a widely liked individual supported evolutionary theory. Who did they spotlight as this champion of Darwinian principles? George Clooney.

In the study, when people were led to believe Clooney had made favorable comments about a book that took a pro-evolutionary stance, they became significantly more accepting of the theory. What's more, the change occurred regardless of the participants' age, sex, or degree of religiosity. To assure the result wasn't due to something unique to George Clooney, or to a male celebrity, the researchers redid the study using a widely liked female celebrity, the actress Emma Watson (of Harry Potter movies' fame), and found the same pattern. For would-be persuaders, the message is plain: to change feelings, counteract them with other feelings; and liking for a communicator offers a useful source of such feelings.

To get an idea of how powerful feelings of liking can be in directing people's choices, consider the response of top medical malpractice attorney Alice Burkin to the following interview question:

> *Interviewer:* Every doctor makes an occasional mistake. But most of those mistakes don't turn into malpractice suits. Why do some doctors get sued more than others?
>
> *Burkin:* I'd say the most important factor in many of our cases—besides the negligence itself—is the quality of the doctor-patient relationship. In all the years I've been in this business, I've never had a potential client walk in and say, "I really like this doctor, but I want to sue him." . . . People just don't sue the doctors they like.[1]

Liking for Profit

The clearest illustration I know of the commercial exploitation of the liking rule is the Tupperware "home party," which I consider a classic compliance setting. Anybody familiar with the workings of a Tupperware party will recognize the use of the various principles of influence covered in this book:

- **Reciprocation:** To start, games are played and prizes won by the partygoers; anyone who doesn't win a prize gets to choose one from a grab bag so that everyone has received a gift before the buying begins.

- **Authority:** The quality and safety of Tupperware products are shown to be certified by experts.

- **Social Proof:** Once the buying begins, each purchase builds the idea that other, similar people want the products; therefore, they must be good.

- **Scarcity:** Unique benefits and limited-time offers are always described.

- **Commitment and Consistency:** Early on, participants are urged to make a public commitment to Tupperware by describing aloud the uses and benefits they have found for the Tupperware they already own.

- **Unity:** Upon making a purchase, guests are welcomed to "the Tupperware family."

Although each of the principles of influence is present to help things along, the real power of the Tupperware party comes from a particular arrangement that trades on the liking rule. Despite the entertaining and persuasive selling skills of the Tupperware demonstrator, the true request to purchase does not come from this stranger; it comes from a friend to every person in the room. Oh, the Tupperware representative may physically ask for each partygoer's order, but the more psychologically compelling requester is sitting off to the side, smiling, chatting, and serving refreshments. She is the party hostess, who has called her friends together for the demonstration in her home and who, everyone knows, makes a profit from each piece sold at the party.

By providing the hostess with a percentage of the take, the Tupperware Brands Corporation arranges for its customers to buy from and for a friend rather than an unknown salesperson. In this way, the attraction, warmth, security, and obligation of friendship are brought to bear on the sales setting. In fact, consumer researchers who have examined the social ties between the hostess and the partygoers in home-party sales settings have affirmed the power of the company's approach: the strength of that social bond is twice as likely to determine purchases as is preference for the product itself.

The results have been remarkable. It was recently estimated that Tupperware sales now exceed $5.5 million a day. Indeed, Tupperware's success has spread around the world to countries in Europe, Latin America, and Asia, where one's place in a social network of friends and family is more personally important than it is in the United States. As a consequence, less than a quarter of Tupperware sales now take place in North America.

What is interesting is that the customers appear to be fully aware of the liking and friendship pressures embodied in the Tupperware home party. Some don't seem to mind; others do, but don't seem to know how to avoid the pressures. One woman I spoke with described her reactions with more than a bit of frustration in her voice.

> *It's gotten to the point now where I hate to be invited to Tupperware parties. I've got all the containers I need; and if I wanted any more, I could buy another brand cheaper in the store. But when a friend calls up, I feel like I have to go. And when I get there, I feel like I have to buy something. What can I do? It's for one of my friends.*

With so irresistible an ally as friendship, it's little wonder that Tupperware Brands has abandoned retail sales outlets and pushes the home-party concept instead. For example, in 2003 the company did something that would defy logic for almost any other business: it severed its profitable relationship with the huge retailer Target— because sales of their products at Target locations were too strong! The partnership had to be ended because of its damaging effect on the number of home parties that could be arranged.

Statistics reveal that a Tupperware party now starts somewhere in the world every 1.8 seconds. Of course, all sorts of other compliance professionals recognize the pressure to say yes to someone we know and like. Take, for instance, the growing number of charity

Figure 3.1: A home party "sell-ebration"
At home parties, such as this Tupperware-style party for a line of eco-friendly cleaning products, the bond that exists between the partygoers and the party hostess usually seals the sale.
Hiroko Masuike/New York Times

organizations that recruit volunteers to canvass for donations close to their own homes. They understand perfectly how much more difficult it is for us to turn down a charity request when it comes from a friend or neighbor.

Other compliance professionals have found the friend doesn't even have to be present to be effective; often, just the mention of the friend's name is enough. The Shaklee Corporation, which specializes in sales of various nutritional products, advises its salespeople to use the "endless chain" method for finding new customers. Once a customer admits he or she likes a product, that customer can be pressed for the names of friends who would also appreciate learning about it. The individuals on that list can then be approached for sales *and* a list of their friends, who can serve as sources for still other potential customers, and so on in an endless chain.

The key to the success of the method is that each new prospect is visited by a salesperson armed with the name of a friend "who suggested I call on you." Turning the salesperson away under those circumstances is difficult; it's almost like rejecting the friend. The Shaklee sales manual insists that employees use this system: "It would be impossible to overestimate its value. Phoning or calling on a prospect and being able to say that Mr. So-and-so, a friend of his, felt he would benefit by giving you a few moments of his time is virtually as good as a sale 50 percent made before you enter." A Nielsen Company survey tells us why the Shaklee Corporation's "endless chain" technique is so successful: 92 percent of consumers trust product recommendations from someone they know, such as a liked friend, which is far more than any other source and 22 percent more than the next highest source, online reviewers. This elevated level of trust of friends turns into what researchers termed "stunning profits" for the recommended companies. An analysis of one bank's refer-a-friend program found that, compared to ordinary new customers, those referred by a friend proved 18 percent more loyal to the bank over a three-year period and 16 percent more profitable.[2]

READER'S REPORT 3.1

From a Chicago man

Although I've never been to a Tupperware Party, I recognized the same kind of friendship pressures recently when I got a call from a long distance phone company saleswoman. She told me that one of my buddies had placed my name on something called the "MCI Friends and Family Calling Circle."

This friend of mine, Brad, is a guy I grew up with but who moved to New Jersey last year for a job. He still calls me pretty regularly to get the news on the guys we used to hang out with. The saleswoman told me that he could save 20 percent on all the calls he made to the people on his Calling Circle list, provided they are MCI phone company subscribers. Then she asked me if I wanted to switch to MCI to get all the blah, blah, blah benefits of MCI service, and so that Brad could save 20 percent on his calls to me.

Well, I couldn't have cared less about the benefits of MCI service; I was perfectly happy with the phone company I had. But the part about wanting to save Brad money on our calls really got to me. For me to say I didn't want to be in his Calling Circle and didn't care about saving him money would have sounded like a real affront to our friendship when he heard about it. So, to avoid insulting him, I told her to switch me to MCI.

I used to wonder why women would go to a Tupperware Party just because a friend was holding it, and then buy stuff they didn't want. I don't wonder anymore.

Author's note: This reader is not alone in being able to testify to the power of the pressures embodied in MCI's Calling Circle idea. When *Consumer Reports* magazine inquired into the practice, the MCI salesperson it interviewed was quite succinct: "It works 9 out of 10 times," he said.

I've opted to retain this example, even though MCI and its Calling Circle are out of date, because it is so instructive. More modern versions still appear in the referral-to-friends programs of many companies. These programs have proved quite effective. Consider, when a single Tesla owner referred 188 people from his social network, he made $135,000 in rewards and Tesla made $16 million in sales. On a personal note, a buddy at my gym recently received a "Refer A Friend" promotion from his internet provider, Cox Communications, which offered a $100 reduction off his bill if he successfully referred a new customer to Cox. When he showed it to me, I declined the offer because I knew what Cox was doing. But, still, I felt bad about it when I'd see him for weeks afterward.

Strategic Friendship: Making Friends to Influence People

Compliance practitioners' widespread use of the liking bond between friends tells us much about the power of the liking rule to produce assent. In fact, we find that such professionals seek to benefit from the rule even when already formed friendships are not present for them to employ. Under these circumstances, the professionals make use of the liking bond by employing a compliance strategy that is quite direct: they first get us to like *them*.

There was a man in Detroit, Joe Girard, who specialized in using the liking rule to sell Chevrolets. He became wealthy in the process, making hundreds of thousands dollars a year. With such a salary, we might guess he was a high-level General Motors executive or perhaps the owner of a Chevrolet dealership. But no. He made his money as a salesman on the showroom floor. He was phenomenal at what he did. For twelve years straight, he won the title of "Number One Car Salesman"; he averaged more than five cars and trucks sold every day he worked; and he has been called

Figure 3.2: Joe Girard: "I like you."
Mr. Girard reveals what he told his thirteen thousand customers every year, twelve times a year (on mailed cards), that helped him become the world's "Greatest Car Salesman."

Getty Images

the world's "Greatest Car Salesman" by the *Guinness Book of World Records.*

For all his success, the formula he employed was surprisingly simple. It consisted of offering people just two things: a fair price and someone they liked to buy from. "And that's it," he claimed in an interview. "Finding the salesman you like, plus the price. Put them both together, and you get a deal."

Fine. The Joe Girard formula tells us how vital the liking rule is to business, but it doesn't tell us nearly enough. For one thing, it doesn't tell us why customers liked him more than some other salesperson who offered a fair price. There is a crucial general question Joe's formula leaves unanswered: What are the factors that cause one person to like another? If we knew *that* answer, we would be a long way toward understanding how people such as Joe can so successfully arrange to have us like them and, conversely, how we might successfully arrange for others to like us. Fortunately, behavioral scientists have been asking this question for decades. The accumulated evidence has allowed them to identify a number of factors that reliably cause liking. Each is cleverly used by compliance professionals to urge us along the road to yes.

Why Do I Like You? Let Me List the Reasons

Physical Attractiveness

Although it is generally acknowledged that good-looking people have an advantage in social interaction, research indicates we may have sorely underestimated the size and reach of that advantage. There seems to be a *click, run* response to attractive individuals. Like all such reactions, it happens automatically, without forethought. The response itself falls into a category that social scientists call *halo effects.* A halo effect occurs when one positive characteristic of a person dominates the way he or she is viewed in most other respects. The evidence is now clear that physical attractiveness is often such a characteristic.

We automatically assign to good-looking individuals such favorable traits as talent, kindness, honesty, agreeableness, trustworthiness, and intelligence. Furthermore, we make these judgments without realizing attractiveness has played a role in the process. Some consequences of this unconscious assumption that "good looking = good" scare me. For example, a study of a Canadian federal election found attractive candidates received more than two-and-a-half times as many votes as unattractive ones. Despite such evidence of favoritism toward the better-looking politicians, follow-up research demonstrated voters did not realize their bias. In fact, 73 percent of Canadian voters surveyed denied in the strongest possible terms that their votes had been influenced by physical appearance; only 14 percent even allowed for the remote possibility of such influence. Voters can deny the impact of attractiveness on electability all they want, but evidence has continued to confirm its troubling presence.

A similar effect has been found in hiring situations. In one study, good grooming of applicants in a simulated employment interview accounted for more favorable hiring decisions than did job qualifications—this, even though the interviewers claimed that appearance played only a small role in their choices. The advantage given to attractive workers extends past hiring day to payday. Economists examining US and Canadian samples found that attractive individuals get paid considerably more than their less attractive coworkers do. One scientist, Daniel Hamermesh, who wrote a book on the topic, estimated that over the course of one's career, being attractive earns a worker an extra $230,000. Hamermesh assures us that his findings can't be explained as bragging on his part, declaring that on a ten-point scale, "I'm a 3."

Other experiments have demonstrated that attractive people are more likely to obtain help when in need and are more persuasive in changing the opinions of an audience. Thus, it's apparent that good-looking people enjoy an enormous social advantage in our culture. They are better liked, better paid, more persuasive, more frequently helped, and seen as possessing more desirable personality traits and greater intellectual capacities. Moreover, the social benefits of good looks begin to accumulate early. Adults view aggressive acts as less naughty when performed by attractive elementary school children, and teachers presume nice-looking children to be more intelligent than their less attractive classmates.

It is hardly any wonder, then, that the halo effect of physical attractiveness is regularly exploited by compliance professionals. Because we like attractive people and because we tend to comply with those we like, it makes sense that sales training programs include grooming hints, fashionable clothiers select their floor staffs from among the eye-catching candidates, and con artists are comely.[3]

Similarity

But what if physical appearance is not much at issue? After all, most people possess average looks. Are there other factors that can be used to produce liking? As both researchers and compliance practitioners know, there are several, and one of the most influential is similarity.

We like people who are like us. It's a fact that applies to human infants as young as nine months and holds true later in life whether the similarity is in the area of opinions, personality traits, background, or lifestyle. In a massive study of 421 million potential romantic matches from an online dating site, the factor that best predicted favorability toward a partner was similarity. As the researchers stated, "For nearly all characteristics, the more similar the individuals were, the higher the likelihood was of them finding each other desirable and opting to meet in person."

Consequently, those who want us to like them so we will favor them can accomplish their purpose by appearing similar to us in a variety of ways. Dress is a good example. Several studies have demonstrated that we are more likely to help those who wear clothing akin to ours. One showed how automatic our positive response to these others can be. Marchers in an antiwar demonstration were found, first, to be more likely to sign the petition of a similarly dressed requester and, second, to do so without bothering to read it first. *Click, run.*

Another way requesters can manipulate similarity to increase liking and compliance is to claim that they have interests similar to ours. Car salespeople, for example, are trained to look for evidence of such things while examining a customer's trade-in. If there is camping gear in the trunk, the salespeople might mention, later on, how they love to get away from the city whenever they can; if there are golf balls on the back seat, they might remark they hope the rain will hold off until they can play the eighteen holes they've scheduled for the next day.

As trivial as these commonalities may seem, they get results. After learning of a comparable fingerprint type, individuals become more helpful to their "fingerprint pattern partner." People are even more likely to purchase a product if its brand name shares initial letters with their own name. In a related piece of research, one investigator increased the percentage of recipients who responded to a mailed survey by changing one small feature of the request: on a cover letter, he modified the name of the survey-taker to be similar to that of the survey recipient. Thus, Robert Greer received his survey from a survey-center official named Bob Gregar, while Cynthia Johnston received hers from a survey-center official named Cindy Johanson. Adding this bit of name resemblance to the invitation nearly doubled survey completion.

Even organizations can be susceptible to the tendency to overvalue things that include elements of their names. To celebrate the fiftieth anniversary of rock 'n' roll, *Rolling Stone* magazine issued a list of the five hundred greatest songs of the rock era. The number-one and number-two highest-ranked songs, as compiled and weighted by *Rolling Stone*'s editors, were "Like a Rolling Stone" by Bob Dylan and "Satisfaction" by the Rolling Stones. At the time of this writing, I checked ten comparable lists of the greatest rock 'n' roll songs, and none listed either of *Rolling Stone*'s picks as its number-one or number-two choice.[4]

There's more. In educational settings, the factor that plays the largest role in the success of youth mentoring programs is the initial similarity of interests between student and mentor; plus, when teachers and their ninth-grade students received information

Figure 3.3: "Cheep" real estate
The potent influence of similarity on sales is something compliance professionals have long understood.

The Penguin Leunig, © 1983, by Michael Leunig, published by Penguin Books Australia

about similarities between them, the students' grades improved
significantly in those teachers' courses. Likewise, in negotiations,
bargainers are much more likely to come to an agreement after
learning of similarities with their bargaining opponent ("Oh,
you're a runner; I'm a runner!"). It should come as no surprise,
then, that voters prefer political candidates who share minor facial similarities with them nor that parallels in language styles
(the types of words and verbal expressions that conversation partners use) and electronic-texting styles increase romantic attraction
and—somewhat amazingly—the likelihood that a hostage negotiation will end peacefully.

Because even small similarities can producing liking and because a veneer of similarity can be so easily manufactured, I would advise special caution in the presence of requesters who claim to be "just like you." Indeed, it would be wise these days to be careful around influencers who merely *seem* to be just like you. For one reason, we typically underestimate the degree to which similarity affects our liking for another. In addition, many influence training programs now urge trainees to deliberately mimic their target's body posture and verbal style, as similarities along these dimensions have been shown to lead to positive results. Take as evidence that (a) food servers trained to mimic customers' words received higher tips; (b) salespeople instructed to mirror customers' verbal and nonverbal behavior sold more electronic equipment; and (c) negotiators taught to imitate opponents' language or body movements got better results whether they were American, Dutch, or Thai. Not to be outdone by their commercial counterparts, relationship advisers are now advocating the use of contrived commonalities—with good success: women who, in speed-dating interactions, were coached to mimic the speech and body language of their dates were rated as more sexually attractive, which led to more follow-up contact requests.[5]

EBOX 3.1

Author's note: Online persuaders are often advised to boost liking by employing the same influence practices as those who operate face-to-face. Consequently, we should be aware of them when they occur on e-commerce platforms. For instance, consider how the impressive website Psychology for Marketers counsels digital marketers to harness the liking principle via similarity and friendship practices.

Liking
I'm sure you've experienced this principle for yourself many times. We find it much more difficult to say no when a request comes from our friends. You can make somebody like you by using a few simple

techniques: be around them to create a feeling of familiarity, point to similarities between you, mirror their behavior, do small favors for them, and show that you like them.

How to use it in online marketing: *Use the language of your audience. Using words, phrases, and slang common to the group will work even better. On the other hand, if you use words that your audience doesn't use or doesn't understand, you are creating a distance between you and giving them nothing to relate to.*

Social media and emails are perfect to interact with your audience. Make sure you first reach out to them without asking them to do anything—just as you would with your friends.

If contrived commonalities appear unethical to you and manufactured mimicry seems trickery, I wouldn't disagree. The desire to be liked is a basic human goal, but its achievement doesn't justify falsification, as in the presentation of fabricated similarities. On the other hand, working strategically to be liked, perhaps by expending effort to uncover and communicate genuine parallels with others, doesn't strike me as objectionable at all. In fact, I'd consider it commendable in many situations as a way to prompt harmonious interactions. Commendable or not, such a goal isn't easy to achieve because, as a rule, we tend to pay attention to differences rather than similarities.

Typically, people are more ready to search for and register separations than connections. It's so for physical dimensions, such as the weight and size of objects, where observers see differences before and more often than they do commonalities. And it's so for more social dimensions, such as the presence or absence of existing harmonies among interacting parties. An analysis by Dr. Leigh Thompson of thirty-two separate negotiation studies found that rival negotiators failed to identify and make reference to shared interests and aims 50 percent of the time—even when those commonalities were real, present, and waiting to be tapped for increased liking and mutually beneficial outcomes.

This regrettable tendency may account for some of the social distance members of racial or ethnic groups maintain between themselves and individuals of other such groups. They focus mainly on cross-group differences, which causes them to underestimate the positivity of potential interactions with out-group members and which, understandably, can reduce the number of actual interactions sought. One set of researchers conducted a set of studies supporting this reasoning. White college students who anticipated a conversation with a Black student and then actually engaged in the conversation had underestimated their true enjoyment of the conversation itself because, beforehand, they'd focused too much on perceived differences from their partner. When, in exactly the same experimental situation, a different sample of students was asked to pay attention to any similarities with their future conversation partners, everything changed. This strategic focus on genuine similarities corrected the negative outlook White students carried into their conversations. Under these circumstances, their now positive expectations matched their actual positive experiences with the Black students.

Results such as these offer us a way to expand the range of our satisfying personal interactions. We can look for and focus on parallels with dissimilar-seeming others and eliminate the mistake of expecting too little from those others.[6]

Compliments

In 1713, Jonathan Swift declared in a famous line of poetry, "'Tis an old maxim in the schools / That flattery's the food of fools." But he failed to tell us how eager people are to swallow those empty calories. For instance, with a remark as instructive as it is humorous, the comedic actor McLean Stevenson once described how his wife "tricked" him into marriage: "She said she liked me." Today, the "likes" frequently occur online and with a comparable effect on positive feelings. In a brain-imaging study, researchers found that when teenagers' social-media photos received lots of "likes," the reward sectors of their brains lit up like Christmas trees—the same reward sectors normally activated by such desirable events as eating chocolate or winning money.

The information that someone fancies us can be a bewitchingly effective means for producing return liking and willing compliance. Therefore, when people flatter or claim affinity for us, they may well want something. If so, they'll likely get it. After being complimented by a server in a restaurant ("You made a good choice") or by a stylist in a hair salon ("Any hairstyle would look good on you") customers responded with significantly larger tips. Likewise, candidates in employment interviews received more favorable hiring recommendations from the interviewer and eventual job offers if, during the interaction, they complimented the interviewer.

Even our technological devices can benefit from conveying a compliment. Individuals who worked on a digital assignment and received flattering feedback from their computer ("You seem to have an uncommon ability to structure data logically") developed more favorable feelings toward the *machine*, even though they were told that the feedback had been preprogrammed and did not reflect their actual task performance. More remarkable still, they also became prouder of their performances after receiving this hollow praise. Plainly, we believe compliments of sundry sorts and like those who give them to us.[7]

Remember Joe Girard, the world's "Greatest Car Salesman," who says the secret of his success was getting customers to like him?

Figure 3.4: Compliments Produce Automatic (Mechanical) Attraction.
Dilbert: Scott Adams 6/25/02. Distributed by United Features Syndicate, Inc.

He did something that, on the face of it, seems foolish and costly. Each month he sent every one of his more than thirteen thousand former customers a holiday greeting card containing a printed message. The holiday greeting card changed from month to month (Happy New Year, Happy Valentine's Day, Happy Thanksgiving, and so on), but the message printed on the face of the card never varied. It read, "I like you." As Joe explained it, "There's nothing else on the card, nothin' but my name. I'm just telling 'em that I like 'em."

"I like you." It came in the mail twelve times a year, every year, like clockwork. "I like you," on a printed card that went to thirteen thousand other people too. Could a statement of liking so impersonal, so obviously designed to sell cars, really work? Joe Girard thought so, and a man as successful as he was at what he did deserves our attention. Joe understood an important fact about human nature: we are phenomenal suckers for flattery.

An experiment done on a group of men in North Carolina shows how helpless we can be in the face of praise. The men received comments about themselves from another person who needed a favor from them. Some of the men got only positive comments, some got only negative comments, and some got a mixture of good and bad. There were three interesting findings. First, the evaluator who provided only praise was liked best. Second, this tendency held true even when the men fully realized that the flatterer stood to gain from their liking of him. Finally, unlike the other types of comments, pure praise did not have to be accurate to work. Positive comments produced just as much liking for the flatterer when they were untrue as when they were true.

Apparently we have such an automatically favorable reaction to compliments that we can fall victim to someone who uses them in an obvious attempt to win our favor. *Click, run*. When seen in this light, the expense of printing and mailing well over 150,000 "I like you" cards each year seems neither as foolish nor as costly as before.[8]

Fortunately, as with sham similarities, counterfeit compliments aren't the only variety available to us. Honest praise is likely to be at least as effective as its phony form in generating favorable outcomes. With that said, it's time for a confession. Of all the influence practices described in this book, herein lies my greatest shortcoming: for whatever reason (it probably comes from the way I was raised), I have always had a hard time giving warranted praise. I can't count the number of times I have been in a research meeting with graduate students and commented, "What Jessica [or Brad or Linda or Vlad or Noah or Chad or Rosanna] just said is really insightful"—to myself! By never moving the appreciative comment from my mind to my tongue, I regularly lost all the goodwill that would accompany the transfer.

No longer. I consciously fight the liability now, spotlighting any privately held admiration and announcing it out loud. The results have been good for all concerned. They've been so good that I have started trying to identify circumstances under which sincere flattery can be especially beneficial to the flatterer. One is obvious—when the praise boosts the recipient at a time or on a dimension of perceived weakness; consequently, I won't devote further space to it. There are two others, though, that are little recognized and deserve attention.

Give a compliment behind a deserving person's back. My new habit of complimenting my students publicly in research meetings has worked well for me, in part because I'm in charge. In many meetings, though, you might not be the leader, and it might not be appropriate to be the one dispensing praise. Suppose you are at work and, in a meeting, your boss says something you consider very smart. It could be awkward and may appear self-serving to speak up and say so. What could you do instead? To be clear, my students were rarely confronted with this problem. Nonetheless, I have a solution: during a coffee break or at the end of the meeting, tell the boss's assistant of your opinion: "You know, I thought what Sandy said about XYZ was brilliant."

Several outcomes are likely. First, because people want to be associated with good news in the minds of others and actively arrange for it, the assistant will most probably tell your boss what you said. Second, because you didn't offer your positive assessment for the boss's ears, no one (observers or boss) should assign you an unattractive ulterior motive. Third, because of what we know about the psychology of received compliments, your boss will believe your (sincere) praise and like you more for it.[9]

Find and give genuine compliments you want the recipient to live up to. People feel good about themselves after a compliment and proud of whatever trait or behavior produced the praise. Accordingly, one particularly beneficial form of sincere flattery would be to praise people when they've done a good thing we'd like them to continue doing. That way, they would be motivated to do more of the good thing in the future in order to live up to the admirable reputation we've given them. This idea is related to an influence tactic called altercasting, in which an individual is assigned a particular social role in hopes the person will then act in accord with the role. For example, by highlighting the role of *protector*, an insurance agent would make parents more willing to purchase life-insurance protection for their families.

While doing the preliminary research for this book, I witnessed, by accident, the power of the technique. At the time, I wanted to go beyond my laboratory research findings concerning effective influence tactics and learn what compliance professionals—salespeople, marketers, advertisers, recruiters, charity solicitors—had found. After all, their economic survival depended on the success of the tactics they employed, which made me confident that, after decades of trial and error, they would have identified the most powerful practices. Regrettably, I was equally confident they wouldn't offer up their hard-won knowledge just because I asked for it. Influence professionals are notoriously protective about keeping their most effective tactics to themselves.

So, instead, I began answering ads and enrolling, incognito, in their training programs, where they were eager to communicate all manner of learned lessons to their trainees. As expected, posing as an aspiring compliance professional in these settings gave me access to a trove of information that would have been otherwise denied to me. I was concerned, though, that when I revealed my true identity and purpose at the end of training and asked for permission to use the data I'd collected, the answer would almost always be no. Within my proposal, all the gain would be mine, all the potential injury theirs.

In most cases, that's how things appeared to be going as faces reddened and gazes hardened when I finally admitted that my name wasn't Rob Caulder, that I wasn't a real trainee, that I was planning to write a book disclosing the information I'd collected, and that I wanted written consent to use their proprietary information in the book—until I added one more fact without knowing the impact it would have. I told the practitioners I was a university professor who studied social influence and wanted to "learn from you on the matter." Regularly, they'd say something like, "You mean you're a college professor expert on this topic, and *we* were your teachers?" When I had assured them they had heard me correctly, they would usually puff up their chests and respond (with the wave of a hand), "Of course you can share our wisdom."

In retrospect, I can see why this accommodating response came so often. My last admission had cast the practitioners in the role of teachers; and teachers don't hoard information. They disseminate it.

Since, I've recognized how the altercasting technique can be successfully combined with a genuine compliment. That is, rather than just assigning a *role* to another, such as protector or teacher, we could honestly praise another who exhibited a commendable *trait* such as helpfulness or conscientiousness. We could then expect to see more of the trait from the other in the future. Research supports the expectation. Children praised for their conscientiousness on a task performed more conscientiously on a related task days afterward. Similarly, adults complimented on their helpful tendencies became significantly more helpful in a separate setting much later.

I tried the technique recently at home. My newspaper has been delivered for several years by a carrier, Carl, who rolls by the house every day and tosses the morning paper from his car to my driveway. Most of the time, it lands close enough to the center of the driveway that it doesn't get wet from the watering systems on either side that go off at about the same time. Each year during the holiday season, Carl has left a self-addressed envelope in one of the delivered papers. It's designed to prompt me to send him a check as thanks for his service, which I always do. But, most recently, along with the check, I included a note praising the conscientiousness he's shown by so often positioning my paper where it doesn't get wet. In the past, Carl hit the driveway's center area about 75 percent of the time. This year, 100 percent.

What's the implication? If there's someone who ordinarily performs commendably—perhaps a conscientious colleague who often comes prepared for meetings or a helpful friend who frequently tries hard to give useful feedback on your ideas—compliment him or her not just on the behavior but, instead, on the trait. You'll probably see more of it.[10]

READER'S REPORT 3.2

From an MBA student in Arizona

While I was working in Boston, one of my coworkers, Chris, was always trying to push work onto my overcrowded desk. I'm normally pretty good at resisting these types of attempts. But Chris was fantastic at complimenting me before he'd request my assistance. He'd start by saying, "I heard you did a fantastic job with the such-and-such project, and I have a similar one I am hoping you can help me with." Or, "Since you are so expert in X, could you help me out by putting together this assignment?" I never really cared much for Chris. However, in those few seconds, I always changed my mind, thinking that maybe he was a nice guy after all; and, then, I'd usually give in to his request for help.

Author's note: Chris was more than just a flatterer. Notice how he structured his praise to give the reader a reputation to live up to that served his interests.

Contact and Cooperation

For the most part, we like things familiar to us. To prove the point to yourself, try a little experiment. Take a selfie that shows a front view of your face and print it. Then, go back to the selfie on your phone and edit it to show a reverse image (so that the right and left sides of your face are interchanged), and print that also. You'll have a pair of pictures—one that shows you as you actually look (the second) and one that shows a reverse image (the first). Now decide which version of your face you like better and ask a good friend to make the choice too. If you are at all like the group of Milwaukee women on whom this kind of procedure was tried, you should notice something odd: your friend will prefer the true image, but you will prefer the reverse image. Why? Because you both will be responding favorably to the more familiar face—your friend to the one the world sees and you to the transposed one you find in the mirror every day.

Often we don't realize our attitude toward something has been influenced by the number of times we have been exposed to it. For example, in a study of online advertising, banner ads for a camera were flashed five times, twenty times, or not at all at the top of an article participants read. The more frequently the ad appeared, the more the participants came to like the camera, even though they were not aware of seeing the ads for it. A similar effect occurred in an experiment in which the faces of several individuals were flashed on a screen so quickly that, later on, the subjects who were exposed to the faces in this manner couldn't recall having seen any of them. Yet the more frequently a person's face was flashed on the screen, the more these subjects came to like that person when they met in a subsequent interaction. And because greater liking leads to greater social influence, these subjects were also more persuaded by the opinion statements of the individuals whose faces had appeared on the screen most frequently.

In an age of "fake news," internet bots, and media-hogging politicians, it's alarming to think that people come to believe the communications they are exposed to most frequently, as it gives contemporary resonance to Nazi propaganda chief Joseph Goebbels's assertion, "Repeat a lie often enough and it becomes the truth." Particularly unsettling are the related findings that even far-fetched claims—the kind of allegations favored by fake-news creators—become more believable with repetition.[11]

On the basis of evidence that we are more favorably disposed toward the things we have had contact with, some people have recommended a "contact" approach to improving race relations. They argue that simply by providing individuals of different ethnic backgrounds with more exposure to one another as equals, those individuals will naturally come to like each other better.

There is much research consistent with this argument. However, when scientists have examined school integration—the area offering one test of the widespread application of the contact approach—they have discovered the opposite pattern. School desegregation is more likely to increase prejudice between Blacks and Whites than decrease it.

Going to School on the Matter. Let's stay with the issue of school desegregation for a while. However well intentioned the proponents of interracial harmony through simple contact are, their approach is unlikely to bear fruit because the argument on which it is based doesn't apply to schools. First of all, the school setting is not a melting pot, where children interact as readily with members of other ethnic groups as they do with their own. Years after formal school integration, there is little social integration. The students clot together ethnically, separating themselves for the most part from other groups. Second, even if there were much more interethnic interaction, research shows that becoming familiar with something through repeated contact doesn't necessarily cause greater liking. In fact, continued exposure to a person or object under unpleasant conditions such as frustration, conflict, or competition leads to less liking.[12]

The typical American classroom fosters precisely these unpleasant conditions. Consider the illuminating report of psychologist Elliot Aronson, called in to consult with school authorities on problems in the Austin, Texas, schools. His description of the way he found education proceeding in the standard classroom could apply to nearly any public school in the United States:

In general, here is how it works: The teacher stands in front of the class and asks a question. Six to ten children strain in their seats and wave their hands in the teacher's face, eager to be called on and show how smart they are. Several others sit quietly with eyes averted, trying to become invisible. When the teacher calls on one child, you see looks of disappointment and dismay on the faces of the eager students, who missed a chance to get the teacher's approval; and you will see relief on the faces of the others who didn't know the answer. . . . This game is fiercely competitive and the stakes are high, because the kids are competing for the love and approval of one of the two or three most important people in their world.

Further, this teaching process guarantees that the children will not learn to like and understand each other. Conjure up your own experience. If you knew the right answer and the teacher called on someone else, you probably hoped that he or she would make a mistake so that you would have a chance to display your knowledge. If you were called on and failed, or if you didn't even raise your hand to compete, you probably envied and resented your classmates who knew the answer. Children who fail in this system become jealous and resentful of the successes, putting them down as teacher's pets or even resorting to violence against them in the school yard. The successful students, for their part, often hold the unsuccessful children in contempt, calling them "dumb" or "stupid."

Should we wonder, then, why strict school desegregation—whether by enforced busing, district rezoning, or school closures—so frequently produces increased rather than decreased prejudice? When our children find their pleasant social and friendship contacts within their ethnic boundaries and get repeated exposure to other groups only in the competitive cauldron of the classroom, we might expect as much.

Are there available solutions to this problem? Fortunately, real hope for draining away that hostility has emerged from the research of education specialists into the concept of "cooperative learning." Because much of the heightened prejudice from classroom desegregation seems to stem from increased exposure to outside group members as rivals, these educators have experimented with forms of learning in which cooperation rather than competition with classmates is central.[13]

Off to Camp. To understand the logic of the cooperative approach, it helps to reexamine the classic research program of Turkish-born social scientist Muzafer Sherif and his colleagues, including his wife, social psychologist Carolyn Wood Sherif. Intrigued with the issue of intergroup conflict, the research team decided to investigate the process as it developed in boys' summer camps. Although the boys never realized that they were participants in an experiment, Sherif and his associates consistently engaged in artful manipulations of the camp's social environment to observe the effects on group relations.

What the researchers learned is that it didn't take much to bring on certain kinds of ill will. Simply separating the boys into two residence cabins was enough to stimulate a "we versus they" feeling between the groups; letting the boys assign names to the two groups (the Eagles and the Rattlers) accelerated the sense of rivalry. The boys soon began to demean the qualities and accomplishments of those in the other group; however, these forms of hostility were minor compared to what occurred when the experimenters introduced competitive activities into the groups' interactions. Cabin-against-cabin treasure hunts, tugs-of-war, and athletic contests produced name-calling and confrontations. During the competitions, members of the opposing team were labeled "cheaters," "sneaks," and "stinkers." Afterward, cabins were raided, rival banners were stolen and burned, threatening signs were posted, and lunchroom scuffles were commonplace.

At this point, it was evident that the recipe for disharmony was quick and easy. Just separate the participants into groups and let them stew for a while in their own juices. Then mix together over the flame of continued competition. And there you have it: cross-group hatred at a rolling boil.

A more challenging issue then faced the experimenters: how to remove the now entrenched hostility. They first tried the contact approach of bringing the bands together more often. Even when the joint activities were pleasant, such as movies and social events, the results were disastrous. Picnics produced food fights, enter-tainment programs gave way to shouting contests, dining-hall lines degenerated into shoving matches. The research team began to worry that, in Dr. Frankenstein fashion, they might have created a monster they could no longer control. Then, at the height of the strife, they tried a strategy that was at once simple and effective.

They constructed a series of situations in which competition be-tween the groups would have harmed everyone's interest; instead, cooperation was necessary for mutual benefit. On a daylong out-ing, the single truck available to go into town for food was "found" to be stuck. The boys were assembled and all pulled and pushed together until the vehicle was on its way. In another instance, the researchers arranged for an interruption of the camp's water sup-ply, which came through pipes from a distant tank. Presented with the common crisis and realizing the need for unified action, the boys organized themselves harmoniously to find and fix the prob-lem before day's end. In yet another circumstance requiring co-operation, the campers were informed that a desirable movie was available for rental but the camp could not afford it. Aware the only solution was to combine resources, the boys pooled their money for the film and spent a congenial evening together enjoying it.

The consequences of these cooperative ventures, though not instantaneous, were nonetheless striking. Successful joint efforts toward common goals steadily bridged the rift between the two groups. Before long, the verbal baiting had died, the jostling in lines had ended, and the boys had begun to intermix at the meal tables. Further, when asked to list their best friends, significant numbers changed from an earlier exclusive naming of in-group chums to a listing that included boys in the other group. Some even thanked the researchers for the opportunity to rate their friends again because they had changed their minds since the earlier evaluation. In one revealing episode, the boys were returning from a campfire on a single bus—something that would have produced bedlam before but, at that point, was specifically requested by the boys. When the bus stopped at a refreshment stand, the boys of one group, with several dollars left in their treasury, decided to treat their former bitter adversaries to milkshakes!

We can trace the roots of the surprising turnabout to the times when the boys had to view one another as allies. The crucial procedure was the researcher's imposition of common goals on the groups. It was the cooperation required to achieve the goals that finally allowed the rival group members to experience one another as reasonable fellows, valued helpers, friends, and friends of friends. When success resulted from the mutual efforts, it became especially difficult to maintain feelings of hostility toward those who had been teammates in the triumph.

Back to School. In the welter of racial tensions that followed school desegregation, certain educational psychologists began to see the relevance to the classroom of Sherif and his coworkers' findings. If only the learning experience there could be modified to include at least occasional interethnic cooperation toward mutual successes, perhaps cross-group friendships would have a place to grow. Although similar projects have been under way in various states, an especially interesting approach in this direction—termed the jigsaw classroom—was developed by Elliot Aronson and his colleagues in Texas and California.

The essence of the jigsaw route to learning is to require that students work together to master the material to be tested on an upcoming examination. This end is accomplished by grouping students into cooperating teams and giving each student only part of the information—one piece of the puzzle—necessary to pass the test. Under this system, the students must take turns teaching and helping one another. Everyone needs everyone else to do well. Like Sherif's campers, working on tasks that could be successfully accomplished only jointly, the students become allies rather than adversaries.

Figure 3.5: Mixing together for success
As studies reveal, the jigsaw classroom is an effective way not only to bring about friendship and cooperation among different ethnic groups but also to increase minority students' self-esteem, liking for school, and test scores.
Nicholas Prior/Stone/Getty Images

When tried in newly desegregated classrooms, the jigsaw approach has generated impressive results. Compared to other classrooms in the same school using the traditional competitive method, jigsaw learning stimulated significantly more friendship and less prejudice among ethnic groups. Besides this vital reduction in hostility, there were other advantages: minority students' self-esteem, liking for school, and test scores improved. The White students benefited too. Their self-esteem and liking for school went up, and their test performance was at least as high as that of Whites in traditional classes.

There is a tendency when faced with positive results, such as those from the jigsaw classroom, to become overly enthusiastic about a single, simple solution to a difficult problem. Experience tells us such problems rarely yield to a simple remedy. That is no doubt true in this case as well. Even within the boundaries of cooperative learning procedures, the issues are complex. Before we can feel truly comfortable with the jigsaw, or any similar approach to learning and liking, more research is needed to determine how frequently, in what size doses, at which ages, and in which sorts of groups cooperative strategies will work. We also need to know the best way for teachers to institute the new methods—provided they will institute them in the first place. After all, not only are cooperative learning techniques a radical departure from the traditional, familiar routine of most teachers, but they may also threaten teachers' sense of their own importance in the classroom by turning over much of the instruction to the students. Finally, we must realize that competition has its place too. It can serve as a valuable motivator of desirable action and an important builder of self-concept. The task, then, is not to eliminate academic competition but to break its monopoly in the classroom by introducing regular cooperative experiences that include members of all ethnic groups and lead to successful outcomes.

Consider, for example, the definition of hell and heaven provided by the Judaic teacher Rabbi Haim of Romshishok.

Hell: *A sumptuously provisioned banquet hall full of hungry people with locked-strait elbow joints who can't feed themselves because their unbendable arms won't allow it.*
Heaven: *Everything's the same except people are feeding each other.*

Perhaps this account provides a useful way to think about the installation of cooperative techniques in the classroom. They should be selected to maximize the chance that all are nourished by the process. It's worth noting that as in the rabbi's illustration, the best acts of cooperation don't just generate favorable interpersonal feelings; they also produce mutual solutions to shared problems. For instance, research tells us that a bargainer who initiates a handshake at the start of a negotiation signals his or her cooperative intent upfront, which then leads to better financial outcomes for all parties.[14]

What's the point of this digression into the effects of school desegregation in race relations? The point is to make two points. First, although the familiarity produced by contact usually leads to greater liking, the opposite occurs if the contact carries distasteful or threatening experiences with it. Therefore, when children of different racial groups are thrown into the incessant, harsh competition of the standard American classroom, we ought to— and do—see hostilities worsen. Second, the evidence that team-oriented learning is an antidote to this disorder tells us about the heavy impact of cooperation on the liking process.

Before we assume that cooperation is a powerful cause of liking, we should first pass it through what, to my mind, is the acid test: Do compliance practitioners systematically use cooperation to get us to like them so that we will say yes to their requests? Do they point it out when it exists naturally in a situation? Do they try to amplify it when it exists only weakly? And, most instructive of all, do they manufacture it when it isn't there at all?

As it turns out, cooperation passes the test with flying colors. Compliance professionals are forever attempting to establish that we and they are working for the same goals; that we must "pull together" for mutual benefit; that they are, in essence, our *teammates*. A host of examples is possible. Most are recognizable, such as new-car salespeople who take our side and "do battle" with their bosses to secure us a good deal. In truth, little in the way of combat takes place when the salesperson enters the manager's office under such circumstances. Often, because sales professionals know exactly the price below which they cannot go, they and the boss don't even speak. In one car dealership I infiltrated while researching this book, it was common for a certain salesman, Gary, to have a soft drink or coffee in silence while the boss continued working. After a seemly time, Gary would loosen his tie and return to his customers, looking frazzled and carrying the deal he had just "hammered out" for them—the same deal he had in mind before entering the boss's office.

A more spectacular illustration occurs in a setting few of us would recognize firsthand, because the professionals are police interrogators whose job is to induce suspects to confess to crime. In recent years, the courts have imposed a variety of restrictions on the way police must behave in handling suspected criminals, especially in seeking confessions. Many procedures that in the past, led to admissions of guilt can no longer be employed for fear they will result in cases being dismissed. As yet, however, the courts have found nothing illegal in the police's use of subtle psychology. For this reason, criminal interrogators have taken increasingly to the use of such ploys as the one they call Good Cop/Bad Cop.

Good Cop/Bad Cop works as follows: A young robbery suspect—let's call him Kenny—who has been advised of his rights and is maintaining his innocence, is brought to a room to be questioned by a pair of officers, both male. One of the officers, either because the part suits him or because it is merely his turn, plays the role of Bad Cop. Before the suspect even sits down, Bad Cop curses "the-son-of-a-bitch" for the robbery. For the rest of the session, his words come only with snarls and growls. He kicks the prisoner's chair to emphasize his points. When he looks at the suspect, he seems to see a mound of garbage. If the suspect challenges Bad Cop's accusations or just refuses to respond to them, Bad Cop becomes livid. His rage soars. He swears he will do everything possible to assure a maximum sentence. He says he has friends in the district attorney's office who will hear from him of the suspect's uncooperative attitude and will prosecute the case hard.

At the outset of Bad Cop's performance, his partner, Good Cop, sits in the background. Then, slowly, Good Cop starts to chip in. First, he speaks only to Bad Cop, trying to temper the burgeoning anger: "Calm down, Frank, calm down." But Bad Cop shouts back: "Don't tell me to calm down when he's lying right to my face! I hate these lying bastards!" A bit later, Good Cop actually says something on the suspect's behalf: "Take it easy, Frank, he's only a kid." Not much in the way of support, but compared to the rantings of Bad Cop, the words fall like music on the suspect's ears. Still, Bad Cop is unconvinced: "Kid? He's no kid. He's a punk. That's what he is, a punk. And I'll tell you something else. He's over eighteen, and that's all I need to get his ass sent so far behind bars they'll need a flashlight to find him."

Now Good Cop begins to speak directly to the suspect, calling him by his first name and pointing out any positive details of the case: "I'll tell you, Kenny, you're lucky nobody was hurt and you weren't armed. When you come up for sentencing, that'll look good." If the suspect persists in claiming innocence, Bad Cop launches into another tirade of curses and threats. This time Good Cop stops him: "Okay, Frank," handing Bad Cop some money, "I think we could all use some coffee. How about getting us some?"

When Bad Cop is gone, it's time for Good Cop's big scene: "Look, man, I don't know why, but my partner doesn't like you, and he's gonna try to get you. And he's gonna be able to do it, because we've got enough evidence right now. And he's right about the DA's office going hard on guys who don't cooperate. You're looking at five years, man! Now, I don't want to see that happen to you. So if you admit you robbed that place right now, before he gets back, I'll take charge of your case and put in a good word for you to the DA. If we work together on this, we can cut the five years down to two, maybe less. Do us both a favor, Kenny. Just tell me how you did it, and let's start working on getting you through this." A full confession frequently follows.

Good Cop/Bad Cop works as well as it does for several reasons: the fear of long incarceration is quickly instilled by Bad Cop's threats; the perceptual contrast principle (see chapter 1) ensures that compared to the raving, venomous Bad Cop, the interrogator playing Good Cop seems like an especially reasonable and kind person; and because Good Cop has intervened repeatedly on the suspect's behalf—has even spent his own money for a cup of coffee—the reciprocity rule pressures for a return favor. The main reason the technique is effective, though, is that it gives the suspect the idea that there is someone on his side, someone with his welfare in mind, someone working together with him, for him. In most situations, such a cooperator would be viewed very favorably, but in the deep trouble our robbery suspect Kenny finds himself, that person takes on the character of a savior. And from savior, it is but a short step to trusted father confessor.

Conditioning and Association

"Why do they blame *me*, Doc?" It was the shaky telephone voice of a local TV weatherman. He had been given my number when he called the psychology department at my university to find someone who could answer his question—one that had always puzzled him but had recently begun to bother and depress him.

"I mean, it's crazy, isn't it? Everybody knows that I just report the weather, that I don't order it, right? So how come I get so much flak when the weather's bad? During the floods last year, I got hate mail! One guy threatened to shoot me if it didn't stop raining. Hell, I'm still looking over my shoulder from that one. And the people I work with at the station do it, too! Sometimes, right on the air, they'll zing me about a heat wave or something. They have to know that I'm not responsible, but that doesn't stop them. Can you help me understand this, Doc? It's really getting me down."

We made an appointment to talk in my office, where I tried to explain that he was the victim of an age-old *click, run* response that people have to things they perceive as merely connected to one another. Although instances of this response abound in modern life, I felt the example most likely to help the distressed weatherman would require a bit of ancient history. I asked him to consider the precarious fate of the imperial messengers of old Persia. Any such messenger assigned the role of military courier had special cause to hope mightily for Persian success on the battlefield. With news of victory in his pouch, he would be treated as a hero upon his arrival at the palace. The food and drink of his choice were provided gladly and lavishly. Should his message tell of military disaster, though, the reception would be quite different: He was summarily slain.

I hoped the point of this story would not be lost on the weatherman. I wanted him to be aware of a fact as true today as it was in the time of ancient Persia: As Shakespeare wrote in *Antony and Cleopatra*, "The nature of bad news infects the teller." There is a natural human tendency to dislike a person who brings us unpleasant information, even when that person did not cause the bad news.

The simple association is enough to stimulate our dislike (see figure 3.6, "Weathermen Pay Price for Nature's Curve Balls"). In a set of eleven studies, someone assigned simply to read aloud a piece of bad news became disliked by its recipients; interestingly, the reader was also seen as having malevolent motives and was rated as a less competent individual. Recall that certain favorable features of a person (for example, physical attractiveness) can produce a "halo effect," in which the feature causes observers to view the person favorably in all sorts of other ways. It now appears that being the bearer of bad news creates an opposite reaction—something we can call a "horns effect." Merely communicating negative news affixes to the communicator a pair of devil's horns that, in the eyes of recipients, apply to various other characteristics.

There was something else I hoped the weatherman would get from the historical example. Not only was he joined in his predicament by centuries of other "tellers," but also, compared to some (such as the Persian messengers), he was well-off. At the end of our session, he said something to convince me that he appreciated this point. "Doc," he said on his way out, "I feel a lot better about my job now. I mean, I'm in Phoenix, where the sun shines three hundred days a year, right? Thank God I don't do the weather in Buffalo."

The weatherman's parting comment reveals that he understood more than I had told him about the principle influencing his viewers' liking for him. Being connected with bad weather does have a negative effect, but being connected with sunshine should do wonders for his popularity. And he was right. The principle of association is a general one, governing both negative and positive connections. An innocent association with either bad things *or* good things will influence how people feel about us.

Our instruction in the way negative association works seems to have been primarily undertaken by our parents. Remember how they were always warning us against playing with the bad kids down the street? Remember how they said it didn't matter if we did nothing bad ourselves because, in the eyes of the neighborhood, we would be known by the company we kept? Our parents were teaching us about guilt by association; they were giving us

**Weathermen pay price
for nature's curve balls**

By David L. Langford
Associated Press

Television weather forecasters make a good living talking about the weather, but when Mother Nature throws a curve ball, they duck for cover.

Conversations with several veteran prognosticators across the country this week turned up stories of them being whacked by old ladies with umbrellas, accosted by drunks in bars, pelted with snowballs and galoshes, threatened with death, and accused of trying to play God.

computers and anonymous meterologists from the National Weather Service or a private agency.

But it's the face on the television screen that people go after.

Tom Bonner, 35, who has been with KARK-TV in Little Rock, Ark., for 11 years, remembers the time a burly farmer from Lonoke, with too much to drink, walked up to him in a bar, poked a finger in his chest and said: "You're the one that sent that tornado and tore my house up . . . I'm going to take your head off."

Bonner said he looked for the bouncer, couldn't spot him, and replied, "That's right about the tornado, and I'll tell you something else, I'll send another one if you don't back off."

Several years ago, when a major flood left water 10 feet deep in San Diego's Mission Valley, Mike Ambrose of KGTV recalls that a woman walked up to his car, whacked the windshield

"I had one guy call and tell me that if it snowed over Christmas, I wouldn't live to see New Year's," said Bob Gregory, who has been the forecaster at WTHR-TV in Indianapolis for nine years.

Most of the forecasters claimed they are accurate 80 percent to 90 percent of the time on one-day forecasts, but longer-range predictions get tricky. And most conceded they are simply reporting information supplied by with an umbrella and said, "This rain is your fault."

Chuck Whitaker of WSBT-TV in South Bend, Ind., says, "One little old lady called the police department and wanted the weatherman arrested for bringing all the snow."

A woman upset that it had rained for her daughter's wedding called Tom Jolls of WKBW-TV in Buffalo, N.Y., to give him a piece of her mind. "She held me responsible and said if she ever met me she would probably hit me," he said.

Sonny Eliot of WJBK-TV, a forecaster in the Detroit area for 30 years, recalls predicting 2 to 4 inches of snow in the city several years ago and more than 8 came down. To retaliate, his colleagues at the station set up a contraption that rained about 200 galoshes on him while he was giving the forecast the next day.

"I've still got the lumps to prove it," he says.

Figure 3.6: "Weathermen Pay Price for Nature's Curve Balls"

Note the similarities of the account of the weatherman who came to my office and those of other TV weather reporters.

*David L. Langford,
Associated Press*

a lesson in the negative side of the principle of association. And they, too, were right. People do assume that we have the same personality traits as our friends'.

As for the positive associations, it is compliance professionals who teach the lesson. They are incessantly trying to connect themselves or their products with the things we like. Did you ever wonder why good-looking models are hired for all those automobile ads? What advertisers hope they are doing is lending the models' positive traits—beauty and desirability—to the cars. Advertisers are betting that we will respond to their products in the same ways we respond to the attractive models merely associated with them—and we do.

In one study, men who saw a new-car ad that included a seductive female model rated the car as faster, more appealing, more expensive-looking, and better-designed than did men who viewed the same ad without the model. Yet when asked later, the men refused to believe that the presence of the young woman had influenced their judgments.

Perhaps the most intriguing evidence of the way the association principle can unconsciously stimulate us to part with our money comes from a series of investigations on credit cards and spending. Within modern life, credit cards are a device with a psychologically noteworthy characteristic: they allow us to get the immediate benefits of goods and services while deferring the costs weeks into the future. Consequently, we are more likely to associate credit cards and the insignias, symbols, and logos that represent them with the positive rather than the negative aspects of spending.

Consumer researcher Richard Feinberg wondered what effects the presence of such credit cards and credit-card materials had on our tendencies to spend. In a set of studies, he got some fascinating—and disturbing—results. First, restaurant patrons gave larger tips when paying with a credit card instead of cash. In a second study, college students were willing to spend an average of 29 percent more money for mail-order catalog items when they examined the items in a room that contained some MasterCard logos; moreover, they had no awareness that the credit card insignias were part of the experiment. A final study showed that when asked to contribute to charity (the United Way), college students were markedly more likely to give money if the room they were in contained MasterCard insignias than if it did not (87 percent versus 33 percent). This last finding is simultaneously the most unsettling and instructive concerning the power of the association principle. Even though credit cards themselves were not used for the charity donation, the mere presence of their symbol (with its attendant positive associations) spurred people to spend more *cash*. This last phenomenon has been replicated in a pair of restaurant studies in which patrons received their bills on tip trays that either did or did not contain credit-card logos. The diners tipped significantly more in the presence of the logos, even when they paid with cash.

Subsequent research by Feinberg strengthens the association explanation for his results. He has found that the presence of credit-card insignias in a room only facilitates spending by people who have had a positive history with credit cards. Those who have had a negative history with the cards—because they've paid an above-average number of interest charges in the previous year—do not show the facilitation effect. In fact, these individuals are more conservative in their spending tendencies when in the mere presence of credit-card logos.[15]

Because the association process works so well—and so unconsciously—manufacturers regularly rush to link their products to the current cultural rage. As the magic cultural concept has shifted to "naturalness," the natural bandwagon has become crowded to capacity. Sometimes the connections to naturalness don't even make sense: "Change your hair color naturally" urges one popular TV ad. Read what one set of scholars had to say on the topic in 2019:

People who prefer items labeled natural are living in a heyday considering the abundance of natural products and services that exist. On a summer day, people could sit on their deck cleaned with Seventh Generation Natural Cleaner and enjoy an Applegate's Natural Beef Hot Dog in a Vermont Bread Company All Natural Bun smothered in Nature's Promise Ketchup and Mustard. They could pair the hot dog with Natural Lays Potato Chips and then wash it all down with a Hansen's Natural Soda. They may even later choose to smoke a Natural American Spirit cigarette while they watch technicians from NaturaLawn of America take care of their lawn. That evening, if they have indigestion, they can take a Naturight Natural Antacid.

During the days of the first American moon shot, everything from breakfast drinks to deodorant was sold with allusions to the American space program; moreover, the perceived value of the connections has stood the test of time: In 2019, on the fiftieth anniversary of the moon landing, Omega watches, IBM, and Jimmy

Dean Sausage (!) took out full-page ads proclaiming their links to the famous event.

In Olympiad years, we are told precisely the official hair sprays and facial tissue of our Olympic teams. The rights to such associations do not come cheaply. Corporate contributors spend millions to win sponsorships for the Olympics. But this amount pales in comparison to the many millions more these companies then spend to advertise their connection to the event. Yet it may be that the largest dollar figure of all for the corporate sponsors is the one on the profit line. A survey by *Advertising Age* magazine found that one-third of all consumers would be more likely to purchase an item if it were linked to the Olympics.

Similarly, although it made great sense that sales of Mars rover toys would jump after a US Pathfinder rocket landed the real thing on the red planet in 1997, it made little sense that the same would happen to the popularity of Mars candy bars, which have nothing to do with the space project but are named after the candy company's founder, Franklin Mars. Sales of the Nissan "Rogue" SUV saw a comparable—and otherwise inexplicable—jump after the 2016 Star Wars film, *Rogue One*, appeared. In a related effect, researchers have found that promotional signs proclaiming SALE increase purchases (even when there is no actual savings), not simply because shoppers consciously think, "Oh, I can save money here." Rather, owing to a separate, additional tendency, buying becomes more likely because such signs have been repeatedly associated with good prices in the shoppers' pasts. Consequently, any product connected to a Sale sign becomes automatically evaluated more favorably.

The linking of celebrities to products is another way advertisers cash in on the association principle. Professional athletes, for example, are paid to connect themselves to things that can be directly relevant to their roles (sports shoes, tennis racquets, golf balls) or wholly irrelevant (soft drinks, popcorn poppers, wristwatches). The important thing for the advertiser is to establish the connection; it doesn't have to be a logical one, just a positive one. What does Matthew McConaughey really know about Lincolns after all?

Of course, popular entertainers provide another form of desirabil-

Figure 3.7: Time-honored celebrities

Author's note: Can you spot the two ways this ad associates Breitling watches with positive entities? The first is obvious: the connection is to attractive, successful celebrities. The second association is less evident but is likely to be effective, nonetheless. Take a look at the position of the ad watch's hands. It is in the form of a smile. That smile-like configuration, with all its favorable associations, has become the standard in nearly all timepiece ads—for good reason. Arranging a watch's hands in such a position in an ad leads observers to experience more pleasure in viewing the ad and to express a greater intention to buy the watch (Karim et al., 2017).

Courtesy of Breitling USA, Inc.

ity that manufacturers have always paid dearly to tie to their goods. More recently, politicians have recognized the ability of a celebrity linkage to sway voters. Presidential candidates assemble stables of well-known nonpolitical figures who either actively participate in or merely lend their names to a campaign. Even at state and local levels, a similar game is played. Take as evidence the comment of a Los Angeles woman I heard expressing her conflicting feelings over a California referendum to eliminate smoking in all public places.

"It's a real tough decision. They've got big stars speaking for it, and big stars speaking against it. You don't know how to vote."[16]

While politicians have long strained to associate themselves with the values of motherhood, country, and apple pie, it may be in the last of these connections—to food—that they have been most clever. For instance, it is a White House tradition to try to sway the votes of balking legislators over a meal. It can be a picnic lunch, an extravagant breakfast, or an elegant dinner; but when an important bill is up for grabs, out comes the silverware. Political fundraising these days regularly involves the presentation of food. Notice, too, that at the typical fundraising dinner the speeches and the appeals for further contributions and heightened effort never come before the meal is served, only during or after. There are several advantages to this technique. For example, time is saved and the reciprocity rule is engaged. The least recognized benefit, however, may be the one uncovered in research conducted in the 1930s by the distinguished psychologist Gregory Razran.

Using what he termed the "luncheon technique," he found that his subjects become fonder of the people and things they experienced while they were eating. In the example most relevant for our purposes, subjects were presented with some political statements they had rated once before. At the end of the experiment, Razran found that only certain of them had gained in approval—those that had been shown while food was being eaten. These changes in liking seem to have occurred unconsciously, as the subjects couldn't remember which of the statements they had seen while food was being served.

To demonstrate the principle of association also works for unpleasant experiences, Razran included in his experiment a condition in which participants had putrid odors piped into the room while they were shown political slogans. In this case, approval ratings for the slogans declined. Other research indicates that odors so slight that they escape conscious awareness can still be influential. People judged photographed faces as more versus less likable depending on whether they rated the faces while experiencing subliminal pleasant or unpleasant odors.

How did Razran come up with the luncheon technique? What made him think it would work? The answer may lie in the dual scholarly roles he played during his career. He was not only a respected independent researcher but also one of the earliest translators into English of the pioneering psychological literature of Russia. It was a literature dedicated to the study of the association principle and dominated by the thinking of a brilliant man, Ivan Pavlov.

Although a scientist of broad and varied talent—Pavlov had won a Nobel Prize years earlier for his work on the digestive system—his most important experimental demonstration was simplicity itself. He found he could get an animal's typical response to food (salivation) to be directed toward something irrelevant to food (a bell) merely by connecting the two things in the animal's experience. If the presentation of food to a dog was always accompanied by the sound of a bell, soon the dog would salivate to the bell alone, even when there was no food to be had.

Figure 3.8: Wait, that sounds like the taste of food.
One of Pavlov's dogs is pictured with the saliva collection tube used to measure how well its salivation response to food could be shifted (conditioned) to the sound of a bell.
Courtesy of Rklawton

It is not a long step from Pavlov's classic demonstration to Razran's luncheon technique. Obviously, a normal reaction to food can be transferred to some other thing through the process of raw association. Razran's insight was that there are many normal responses to food besides salivation, one of them being a good and favorable feeling. Therefore, it is possible to attach this pleasant feeling, this positive attitude, to anything (political statements being only an example) that is closely associated with good food.

Nor is there a long step from the luncheon technique to the compliance professionals' realization that all kinds of desirable things can substitute for food in lending their likable qualities to the ideas, products, and people artificially linked to them. In the final analysis, then, that is why those good-looking models stand around in the magazine ads. That is why radio programmers are instructed to insert the station's call-letters jingle immediately before a big hit song is played. And that is even why the women playing Barnyard Bingo at a Tupperware party must yell the word *Tupperware* rather than *Bingo* before they can rush to the center of the floor for a prize. It may be Tupperware for the players, but it's *Bingo!* for the company.

Just because we are often unaware victims of compliance practitioners' use of the association principle doesn't mean we don't understand how it works or don't use it ourselves. There is ample evidence we understand fully the predicament of a Persian imperial messenger or modern-day weatherman announcing the bad news. In fact, we can be counted on to take steps to avoid putting ourselves in any similar positions. Research done at the University of Georgia shows just how we operate when faced with the task of communicating good or bad news. Students waiting for an experiment to begin were given the job of informing a fellow student that an important phone call had come in for him. Half the time the call was supposed to bring good news and half the time, bad news. The researchers found that the students conveyed the information very differently depending on its quality. When the news was positive, the tellers were sure to mention that feature: "You just got a phone call with great news. Better see the experimenter for the details." When the news was unfavorable, they kept themselves apart from it: "You just got a phone call. Better see the experimenter for the details." Obviously, the students had previously learned that to be liked, they should connect themselves to good but not bad news.[17]

From the News and Weather to the Sports

A lot of strange behavior can be explained by the fact that people understand the association principle well enough to link themselves to positive events and separate themselves from negative events—even when they have not caused the events. Some of the strangest of such behavior takes place in the great arena of sports. The actions of the athletes are not the issue, though. After all, in the heated contact of the game, they are entitled to an occasional eccentric outburst. Instead, it is the often raging, irrational, boundless fervor of sports fans that seems, on its face, so puzzling. How can we account for wild sports riots in Europe, or the murder of players and referees by South American soccer crowds, or the unnecessary lavishness of gifts provided by local fans to already wealthy American ballplayers on the special "day" set aside to honor them? Rationally, none of this makes sense. It's just a game! Isn't it?

Hardly. The relationship between sport and earnest fan is anything but gamelike. It is deadly serious. Take, for example, the case of Andres Escobar who, as a member of the Colombian national team, accidentally tipped a ball into his own team's net during a World Cup soccer match in 1994. The "auto-goal" led to a US team victory and to the elimination of the favored Colombians from the competition. Back home two weeks later, Escobar was executed in a restaurant by two gunmen, who shot him twelve times for his mistake.

So we want our affiliated sports teams to win to prove our own superiority, but to whom are we trying to prove it? Ourselves, certainly, but to everyone else too. According to the association principle, if we can surround ourselves with success we are connected with in even a superficial way (for example, place of residence), our public prestige should rise.

All this tells me we purposefully manipulate the visibility of our connections with winners and losers to make ourselves look good to anyone who views the connections. By showcasing the positive associations and burying the negative ones, we are trying to get observers to think more highly of us and like us more. There are many ways we go about it, but one of the simplest and most pervasive is in the pronouns we use. Have you noticed how often after a home-team victory fans crowd into the range of a TV camera, thrust their index fingers high, and shout, "We're number one! We're number one!" Note that the call is not "They're number one." The pronoun is *we*, designed to imply the closest possible identity with the team.

Note also that nothing similar occurs in the case of failure. No TV viewer will ever hear the chant, "We're in last place! We're in last place!" Home-team defeats are the times for distancing oneself. Here *we* is not nearly as preferred as the insulating pronoun *they*. To prove the point, I once did a small experiment in which students at Arizona State University were phoned and asked to describe the outcome of a football game their school team had played a few weeks earlier. Some of the students were asked the outcome of a certain game their team had lost; the other students were asked the outcome of a different game—one their team had won. My fellow researcher, Avril Thorne, and I simply listened to what was said and recorded the percentage of students who used the word *we* in their descriptions.

When the results were tabulated, it was obvious that the students had tried to connect themselves to success by using the pronoun *we* to describe their school-team victory—"We beat Houston, 17 to 14," or "We won." In the case of the lost game, however, *we* was rarely used. Instead, the students used terms designed to keep themselves separate from their defeated team—"They lost to Missouri, 30 to 20," or "I don't know the score, but Arizona State got beat." The twin desires to connect ourselves to winners and to distance ourselves from losers were combined consummately in the remarks of one particular student. After dryly recounting the score of the home-team defeat—"Arizona State lost it, 30 to 20"—he blurted in anguish, *"They* threw away *our* chance for a national championship!"

The tendency to trumpet one's links to victors is not unique to the sports arena. After general elections in Belgium, researchers looked to see how long it took homeowners to remove their lawn signs favoring one or another political party. The better the election result for a party, the longer homeowners wallowed in the positive connection by leaving the signs up

Although the desire to *bask in reflected glory* exists to a degree in all of us, there seems to be something special about people who would take this normal tendency too far. Just what kind of people are they? In my view, they are not loyal fans who support their teams through good times and bad; they are what we call

Figure 3.9: Sports fan(atic)s
Team spirit goes a step beyond wearing the school sweatshirt as these University of Georgia students wear their school letters a different way and cheer their team to victory.

Chris Graythen/Getty Images

"fair-weather fans," who trumpet their association only with win-ning teams. Unless I miss my guess, they are individuals with a hidden personality flaw: poor self-concept. Deep inside is a sense of low personal worth that directs them to seek prestige not from their own attainments but from their associations with others' at-tainments. There are several varieties of this species that bloom throughout our culture. The persistent name-dropper is a classic example. So, too, is the rock-music groupie, who trades sexual fa-vors for the right to tell friends that she or he was "with" a famous musician for a time. No matter which form it takes, the behavior of such individuals shares a similar theme—the rather tragic view of accomplishment as deriving from outside the self.

READER'S REPORT 3.3

From a movie-studio employee in Los Angeles

Because I work in the industry, I'm a huge film buff. The biggest night of the year for me is the night of the Academy Awards. I even tape the shows so I can replay the acceptance speeches of the artists I really admire. One of my favorite speeches was what Kevin Costner said after his film *Dances with Wolves* won best picture in 1991. I liked it because he was responding to critics who say that the movies aren't important. In fact, I liked it so much that I copied it down. But there is one thing about the speech that I never understood before. Here's what he said about winning the best picture award:

"While it may not be as important as the rest of the world situ-ation, it will always be important to us. My family will never forget what happened here; my Native American brothers and sisters, es-pecially the Lakota Sioux, will never forget, and the people I went to high school with will never forget."

OK, I get why Kevin Costner would never forget this enormous honor. And I also get why his family would never forget it. And I even get why Native Americans would remember it, since the film is about them. But I never understood why he mentioned the people he went to high school with. Then, I read about how sports fans think they can "bask in the reflected glory" of their hometown stars and teams. And, I realized that it's the same thing. Everyone who went to school with Kevin Costner would be telling everyone about their connection the day after he won the Oscar, thinking that they would get some prestige out of it even though they had zero to do with the film. They would be right, too, because that's how it works. You don't have to be a star to get the glory. Sometimes you only have to be associated with the star somehow. How interesting.

    Author's note: I've seen this sort of thing work in my own life when I've told architect friends that I was born in the same place as the great Frank Lloyd Wright. Please understand, I can't even draw a straight line; but I can *see* a straight line, between me and their hero, taking shape in my friends' eyes . . . eyes that seem to say, "*You* and Frank Lloyd Wright?" Wow!"

Certain of these people work the association principle in a slightly different way. Instead of striving to inflate their visible connections to others' success, they strive to inflate the success of others they are visibly connected to. The clearest illustration is the notorious "stage mother," obsessed with securing stardom for her child. Of course, women are not alone in this regard. A few years ago, an obstetrician in Davenport, Iowa, cut off service to the wives of three school officials, reportedly because his son had not been given enough playing time in school basketball games. One of the wives was eight months pregnant at the time.[18]

Defense

Because liking can be increased by many means, a list of the defenses against compliance professionals who employ the liking rule must, oddly enough, be a short one. It would be pointless to construct a horde of specific counter tactics to combat each of the countless versions of the various ways to influence liking. There are simply too many routes to be blocked effectively with such a one-on-one strategy. Besides, several of the factors leading to liking—physical attractiveness, similarity, familiarity, association—work unconsciously to produce their effects, making it unlikely we could muster a timely protection against them anyway.

Instead, we need to consider a general approach, one that can be applied to any of the liking-related factors to neutralize their unwelcome influence on our decisions. The secret to such an approach lies in its timing. Rather than trying to recognize and prevent the action of liking factors before they have a chance to work, we might want to let them work. Our vigilance should be directed not toward the things that may produce undue liking for a compliance practitioner but toward the fact that undue liking *has been* produced. The time to call up the defense is when we feel ourselves liking the practitioner more than we should under the circumstances.

By concentrating our attention on the effects rather than the causes, we can avoid the laborious, nearly impossible task of trying to detect and deflect the many psychological influences on liking. Instead, we have to be sensitive to only one thing related to liking in our contacts with compliance practitioners: the feeling that we have come to like the practitioner more quickly or more deeply than we would have expected. Once we notice this feeling, we will have been tipped off that there is probably some tactic being used, and we can start taking the necessary countermeasures. The strategy I am suggesting borrows much from the jujitsu style favored by compliance professionals themselves. We don't attempt to restrain the influence of the factors that cause liking. Quite the contrary. We allow those factors to exert their force, and then we use that force in our campaign against those who would profit by them. The stronger the force, the more conspicuous it becomes and the more subject to our alerted defenses.

Suppose, we find ourselves bargaining on the price of a new car with Dealin' Dan, a candidate for Joe Girard's vacated "Greatest Car Salesman" title. After talking a while and negotiating a bit, Dan wants to close the deal. He wants us to buy the car. Before any decision is made, we should ask ourselves the crucial question, "In the forty-five minutes I've known this guy, have I come to like him more than I would have expected?" If the answer is yes, we should reflect on the ways Dan behaved during those few minutes. We might recall that he has fed us (coffee and doughnuts), complimented us on our choice of options and color combinations, made us laugh, and cooperated with us against the sales manager to get us a better deal.

Although such a review of events might be informative, it is not a necessary step in protecting ourselves from the liking rule. Once we discover we have come to like Dan more than we would have expected, we don't have to know why. The simple recognition of unwarranted liking should be enough to get us to react against it. One possible reaction would be to reverse the process and actively dislike Dan, but that might be unfair to him and contrary to our own interests. After all, some individuals are naturally likable, and Dan might be one of them. It wouldn't be right to turn automatically against those compliance professionals who happen to be likable. Besides, for our own sakes, we wouldn't want to shut ourselves off from business interactions with such nice people, especially when they may be offering us a good deal.

I'd recommend a different reaction. If our answer to the crucial question is "Yes, under the circumstances, I like this guy peculiarly well," this should signal that the time has come for a quick counter-maneuver: Mentally separate Dan from that Chevy or Toyota he's trying to sell. It is vital to remember at this point that should we choose Dan's car, we will be driving *it*, not him, off the dealership lot. It is irrelevant to a wise automobile purchase that we find Dan likable because he is good-looking, claims an interest in our favorite hobby, is funny, or has relatives living where we grew up.

Our proper response, then, is a conscious effort to concentrate exclusively on the merits of the deal and the car Dan has for us. Of course, when we make a compliance decision, it is always a good idea to separate our feelings about the requester from the request. Once immersed in even a brief personal and sociable contact with a requester, however, we may easily forget that distinction. In those instances when we don't care one way or the other about a requester, forgetting to make the distinction won't steer us very far wrong. The big mistakes are likely to come when we like the person making the request.

That's why it is so important to be alert to a sense of undue liking for a compliance practitioner. The recognition of that feeling can serve as our reminder to separate the dealer from the merits of the deal and make our decision based on considerations related only to the latter. Were we all to follow this procedure, I am certain we would be much more pleased with the results—though I suspect Dealin' Dan would not.

SUMMARY

- People prefer to say yes to individuals they like. Recognizing this rule, compliance professionals commonly increase their effectiveness by emphasizing several factors that increase their overall likability.

- One such feature is physical attractiveness. Although it has long been suspected that physical beauty provides an advantage in social interaction, research indicates the advantage may be greater than supposed. Physical attractiveness engenders a halo effect that leads to the assignment of other traits such as talent, kindness, and intelligence. As a result, attractive people are more persuasive both in terms of getting what they request and changing others' attitudes.

- A second factor that influences liking and compliance is similarity. We like people who are like us, and we are more willing to say yes to their requests, often in an unthinking manner.

Another such factor is praise. Compliments generally enhance liking and, hence, compliance. Two particularly useful types of genuine compliments are those delivered behind the recipient's back and those selected to give the recipient a reputation to live up to, by continuing to perform the desired behavior.

- Increased familiarity through repeated contact with a person or thing is yet another factor that normally facilitates liking. This relationship holds true principally when the contact takes place under positive rather than negative circumstances. One positive circumstance that works especially well is mutual and successful cooperation. A fifth factor linked to liking is association. By connecting themselves or their products with positive things, advertisers, politicians, and merchandisers frequently seek to share in the positivity through the process of association. Other individuals as well (sports fans, for example) appear to recognize the positive effect of simple connections and try to associate themselves with favorable events and distance themselves from unfavorable events in the eyes of observers.

- A potentially effective strategy for reducing the unwanted influence of liking on compliance decisions requires sensitivity to the experience of undue liking for a requester. Upon recognizing that we like a requester inordinately well under the circumstances, we should step back from the interaction, mentally separate the requester from his or her offer, and make any compliance decision based solely on the merits of the offer.

CHAPTER 4

SOCIAL PROOF

TRUTHS ARE US

When people are free to do as they please, they usually
imitate one another.

—Eric Hoffer

A few years ago, the managers of a chain of restaurants in Beijing, China, partnered with researchers to accomplish something
decidedly profitable—increasing the purchase of certain menu
items in a way that was effective yet costless. They wanted to see if
they could get customers to choose them more frequently without
lowering the items' prices or using more expensive ingredients
or hiring a chef who had more experience with the dishes or paying a consultant to write more enticing descriptions of them on
the menu. They wanted to see if, instead, they could just give the
dishes a label that would do the trick. Although they found a label
that worked particularly well, they were surprised it wasn't one
they'd thought to use previously for this purpose, such as "Specialty of the house" or "Our chef's recommendation for tonight."
Rather, the label merely described the menu items as the restaurant's "most popular."

The outcome was impressive. Sales of each dish jumped by an
average of 13 to 20 percent. Quite simply, the dishes became more
popular because of their popularity. Notably, the increase occurred
through a persuasive practice that was costless, completely ethical
(the items were indeed the most popular), easy to implement, and

yet never before employed by the managers. Something similar happened in London when a local brewery with a pub on its premises agreed to try an experiment. The pub placed a sign on the bar stating, truthfully, that the brewery's most popular beer that week was its porter. Porter sales doubled immediately. *Click, run.*

Results such as these make me wonder why other retailers don't provide similar information. In ice-cream or frozen-yogurt shops, customers can often choose from an array of toppings for their order—chocolate bits or coconut flakes or cookie crumbles, and so on. Owing to the pull of the popular, you'd think managers would know to post signs describing the most frequently chosen topping or topping combination that month. But, they don't. Too bad for them. Especially for customers who wouldn't order a topping or who would order just one, true popularity information should result in more selections. For example, many McDonald's restaurants offer a "McFlurry" dessert. When customers in one set of McDonald's were told, "How about a dessert? The McFlurry is our visitors' favorite," McFlurry sales jumped 55 percent. Then, after a customer ordered a McFlurry, if the clerk said, "The [x] flavor is our visitors' favorite McFlurry topping," customers increased their extra topping purchases by an additional 48 percent.

EBOX 4.1

Although not all retailers understand how to harness popularity profitably, media giant Netflix learned that lesson from its own data and began operating on it immediately. According to technology and entertainment reporter Nicole LaPorte (2018), the company had "long prided itself on being highly secretive about things like watch-time and ratings, gleefully reveling in the fact that because Netflix doesn't have to answer to advertisers, it doesn't need to reveal any numbers." But in an unexpected 2018 policy reversal, it began off-loading reams of information about its most successful offerings. As LaPorte put it, "In its letter to shareholders, Netflix rattled off titles and how many people had streamed them in a way that felt like a drunken sailor had taken over the normally heavily fortified battleship and was spilling trade secrets."

Why? By then, company officials had seen that popularity precipitates popularity. Chief Product Officer Greg Peters disclosed the results of internal tests in which Netflix members who were told which shows were popular, then made them more so. Other company executives were quick on the uptake. Content head Ted Sarandros declared that going forward, Netflix would be more forthcoming "about what people are watching around the world." Chairman and CEO Reed Hastings affirmed this promise, stating, "We're just beginning to share that data. We'll be leaning into that more quarter by quarter."

Author's note: These statements from Netflix executives tell us there are no dummies in leadership there. But one additional statement by Sarandros was most impressive to me: "Popularity is a data point that people can choose to use . . . We don't want to suppress it if it's helpful to members." The key insight is that suppressing true popularity, as the company had done in the past, was unhelpful not only to its immediate profits but also to its subscribers' prudent choices and resultant satisfaction—and, therefore, to the company's *long-term* profits.

Social Proof

To discover why popularity is so effective, we need to understand the nature of yet another potent lever of influence: the principle of social proof. This principle states that we determine what is correct by finding out what other people think is correct. Importantly, the principle applies to the way we decide what constitutes correct behavior. *We view an action as correct in a given situation to the degree that we see others performing it.* As a result, advertisers love to inform us when a product is the "fastest growing" or "largest selling" because they don't have to convince us directly that their product is good; they need only show that many others think so, which often seems proof enough.

The tendency to see an action as appropriate when others are doing it works quite well normally. As a rule, we make fewer mistakes by acting in accord with social evidence than by acting contrary to it. Usually, when a lot of people are doing something, it is the right thing to do. This feature of the principle of social proof is simultaneously its major strength and major weakness. Like the other levers of influence, it provides a convenient shortcut for determining the way to behave, but at the same time, it makes one who uses the shortcut vulnerable to the attacks of profiteers who lie in wait along its path.

The problem comes when we begin responding to social proof in such a mindless and reflexive fashion we can be fooled by partial or fake evidence. Our folly is not that we use others' behavior to help decide what to do in a situation; that is in keeping with the well-founded principle of social proof. The folly occurs when we do so automatically in response to counterfeit evidence provided by profiteers. Examples are plentiful. Certain nightclub owners manufacture a brand of visible social proof for their clubs' quality by creating long waiting lines outside when there is plenty of room inside. Salespeople are taught to spice their pitches with invented accounts of numerous individuals who have purchased the product. Bartenders often salt their tip jars with a few dollar bills at the beginning of an evening to simulate tips left by prior customers. Church ushers sometimes salt collection baskets for the same reason and with the same positive effect on proceeds. Evangelical preachers are known to seed their audience with ringers, who are rehearsed to come forward at a specified time to give witness and donations. And, of course, product-rating websites are regularly infected with glowing reviews that manufacturers have faked or paid people to submit.[1]

People Power

Why are these profiteers so ready to use social proof for profit? They know our tendency to assume an action is more correct if others are doing it operates forcefully in a wide variety of settings. Sales and motivation consultant Cavett Robert captured the principle nicely in his advice to sales trainees: "Since 95 percent of the people are imitators and only 5 percent initiators, people are persuaded more by the actions of others than by any proof we can offer." Evidence that we should believe him is everywhere. Let's examine a small sample of it.

Morality: In one study, after being told that the majority of their peers favored the use of torture in interrogations, 80 percent of college students saw the practice as more morally acceptable. *Criminality*: Drinking and driving, parking in handicapped zones, retail theft, and hit-and-run violations (leaving the scene of a caused auto accident) become more likely if possible perpetrators believe the behavior is performed frequently by others. *Problematic personal behavior*: Men and women who believe that violence against an intimate partner is prevalent are more likely to engage in such violence themselves at a later time. *Healthy eating*: After learning that the majority of their peers try to eat fruit to be healthy, Dutch high school students increased fruit consumption by 35 percent—even though, in typical adolescent fashion, they had claimed no intention to change upon receiving the information. *Online purchases*: Although product testimonials are not new, the internet has changed the game by giving prospective customers ready access to the product ratings of numerous prior users; as a result, 98 percent of online shoppers say authentic customer reviews are the most important factor influencing their purchase decisions. *Paying bills*: When the city of Louisville, Kentucky, sent parking-ticket recipients a letter stating that the majority of such citations are paid within two weeks, payments increased by 130 percent, more than doubling parking-ticket revenue to the city. *Science-based recommendations*: During the COVID-19 outbreak of 2020, researchers examined the reasons Japanese citizens employed to decide how often to wear face masks, as urged by the country's health scientists; although multiple reasons were measured— such as perceived severity of the disease, likelihood mask-wearing would protect oneself from infection, likelihood mask-wearing would protect others from infection—only one made a major difference in mask-wearing frequency: seeing other people wearing masks. *Environmental action*: Observers who perceive that many others are acting to preserve or protect the environment by recycling or conserving energy or saving water in their homes then act similarly.

In the arena of environmental action, social proof works on organizations too. Many governments expend significant resources regulating, monitoring, and sanctioning companies that pollute our air and water; these expenditures often appear wasted on some of the offenders who either flout the regulations altogether or are willing to pay fines that are smaller than the expense of compliance. But certain nations have developed cost-effective programs that work by firing up the (nonpolluting) engine of social proof. They initially rate the environmental performance of polluting firms within an industry and then publicize the ratings so all companies in that industry can see where they stand relative to their peers. The improvements have been dramatic—upwards of 30 percent—almost all of which have come from changes made by the relatively heavy polluters, who recognized how poorly they'd been doing compared with their contemporaries.

Researchers have also found that procedures based in social proof can work early in life—sometimes with astounding results. One psychologist in particular, Albert Bandura, led the way in developing such procedures to eliminate undesirable behavior. Bandura and his colleagues have shown how people suffering from phobias can be rid of these extreme fears in an amazingly simple fashion. For instance, in an initial study, nursery-school-aged children, chosen because they were terrified of dogs, merely watched a little boy playing happily with a dog for twenty minutes a day. This exhibition produced such marked changes in the reactions of the fearful children that after only four days, 67 percent of them were willing to climb into a playpen with a dog and remain confined there petting and scratching the dog while everyone else left the room. Moreover, when the researchers tested the children's fear levels again, one month later, they found the improvement had not diminished during that time; in fact, the children were more willing than ever to interact with dogs.

An important practical discovery was made in a second study of children who were exceptionally afraid of dogs: To reduce the children's fears, it was not necessary to provide live demonstrations of another child playing with a dog; film clips had the same impact. Tellingly, the most effective clips were those depicting multiple other children interacting with their dogs. The principle of social proof works best when the proof is provided by the actions of *many* other people. We'll have more to say shortly about the amplifying role of "the many."[2]

READER'S REPORT 4.1

From the director of recruitment and training at
a Toyota dealership in Tulsa, Oklahoma

I work for the largest automotive retailer in Oklahoma. One of the biggest challenges we face is getting quality sales talent. We had seen poor return on our newspaper ads. So we decided to run our recruitment ads on radio during the after-work drive time. We ran an ad that focused on the great demand for our vehicles, how many people were buying them, and, consequently, how we needed to expand our sales force to keep up. As we hoped, we saw a significant jump in the number of applications to join our sales team.

But, the biggest effect we saw was an increase in customer floor traffic, an increase in sales in both the new and used vehicle departments, and a noticeable difference in the attitudes of our customers. The wildest thing was that the total number of sales increased by 41.7 percent over the previous January!!! We did almost one-and-a-half times the amount of business as the year before in an automotive market that was down by 4.4 percent. Of course, there could be other reasons for our success, such as a management change and a facilities update. But, still, whenever we run recruitment ads saying we need help to keep up with the demand for our vehicles, we see a significant increase in vehicle sales in those months.

Author's note: So a reference to large consumer demand greatly affected customer attitude and actions toward the dealership's cars and trucks. This is consistent with what we have already described in this chapter. But there's something we haven't yet described that helps account for the outsized effects the dealership witnessed. The high-demand information was "slipped into" an ad to recruit salespeople. Its notable success fits with evidence that people are more likely to be persuaded by information, including social-proof information, when they think it is not intended to persuade them (Bergquist, Nilsson, & Schultz, 2019; Howe, Carr, & Walton, in press). I am sure that, if the dealership's ad had made a direct appeal for purchases—declaring, "People are buying our vehicles like crazy! Come get yours"—it would have been less effective.

After the Deluge

When it comes to illustrating the strength of social proof, one example is far and away my favorite. Several features account for its appeal: it offers a superb instance of the underused method of participant observation, in which a scientist studies a process by becoming immersed in its natural occurrence; it provides information of interest to such diverse groups as historians, psychologists, and theologians; and, most important, it shows how social evidence can be used on us—not by others but by ourselves—to assure us that what we prefer to be true will seem to be true.

The story is an old one, requiring an examination of ancient data, for the past is dotted with end-of-the-world religious movements.

Various sects and cults have prophesied that on a particular date there would arrive a period of redemption and great happiness for those who believed in the group's teachings. In each case, it has been predicted that the beginning of a time of salvation would be marked by an important and undeniable event, usually the cataclysmic end of the world. Of course, these predictions have invariably proved false, to the acute dismay of the members of such groups.

However, immediately following the obvious failure of the prophecy, history records an enigmatic pattern. Rather than disbanding in disillusion, the cultists often become strengthened in their convictions. Risking the ridicule of the populace, they take to the streets, publicly asserting their dogma and seeking converts with a fervor that is intensified, not diminished, by the clear disconfirmation of a central belief. So it was with the Montanists of second-century Turkey, with the Anabaptists of sixteenth-century Holland, with the Sabbataists of seventeenth-century Izmir, and with the Millerites of nineteenth-century America. And, thought a trio of interested social scientists, so it might be with a doomsday cult based in twentieth-century Chicago. The scientists—Leon Festinger, Henry Riecken, and Stanley Schachter—who were then colleagues at the University of Minnesota, heard about the Chicago group and felt it worthy of close study. Their decision to investigate by joining the group, incognito, as new believers and by placing additional paid observers among its ranks resulted in a remarkably rich firsthand account of the goings-on before and after the day of predicted catastrophe, which they provided in their eminently readable book *When Prophesy Fails*.

The cult of believers was small, never numbering more than thirty members. Its leaders were a middle-aged man and woman, whom, for purposes of publication, the researchers renamed Dr. Thomas Armstrong and Mrs. Marian Keech. Dr. Armstrong, a physician on the staff of a college's student-health service, had a long-held interest in mysticism, the occult, and flying saucers; as such, he served as a respected authority on these subjects for the group. Mrs. Keech, though, was the center of attention and activity. Earlier in the year, she had begun to receive messages from spiritual beings, whom she called the Guardians, located on other planets. It was these messages, flowing through Marian Keech's hand via the device of "automatic writing," that formed the bulk of the cult's religious belief system. The teachings of the Guardians were a collection of New Age concepts, loosely linked to traditional Christian thought. It was as if the Guardians had read a copy of the Bible while visiting Northern California.

The transmissions from the Guardians, always the subject of much discussion and interpretation among the group, gained new significance when they began to foretell a great impending disaster—a flood that would begin in the Western Hemisphere and eventually engulf the world. Although the cultists were understandably alarmed at first, further messages assured them they, and all those who believed in the lessons sent through Mrs. Keech, would survive. Before the calamity, spacemen were to arrive and carry off the believers in flying saucers to a place of safety, presumably on another planet. Little detail was provided about the rescue except that the believers were to ready themselves for pickup by rehearsing certain passwords to be exchanged ("I left my hat at home." "What is your question?" "I am my own porter.") and by removing all metal from their clothes—because the wearing of metal made saucer travel "extremely dangerous."

As the researchers observed the preparations during the weeks prior to the flood date, they noted with special interest two significant aspects of the members' behavior. First, the level of commitment to the cult's belief system was very high. In anticipation of their departure from doomed Earth, irrevocable steps were taken by the group members. Most incurred the opposition of family and friends to their beliefs but persisted, nonetheless, in their convictions, often when it meant losing the affections of these others. Several members were threatened by neighbors or family with legal actions designed to have them declared insane. Dr. Armstrong's sister filed a motion to have his two younger children removed from his custody. Many believers quit their jobs or neglected their studies to devote all their time to the movement. Some gave or threw away their personal belongings, expecting them shortly to be of no use. These were people whose certainty they had the truth allowed them to withstand enormous social, economic, and legal pressures and whose commitment to their dogma grew as they resisted each pressure.

The second significant aspect of the believers' preflood actions was a curious form of inaction. For individuals so clearly convinced of the validity of their creed, they did surprisingly little to spread the word. Although they initially publicized the news of the coming disaster, they made no attempt to seek converts, to proselytize actively. They were willing to sound the alarm and to counsel those who voluntarily responded to it, but that was all.

The group's distaste for recruitment efforts was evident in various ways besides the lack of personal persuasion attempts. Secrecy was maintained in many matters—extra copies of the lessons were burned, passwords and secret signs were instituted, the contents of certain private tape recordings were not to be discussed with outsiders (so secret were the tapes that even longtime believers were prohibited from taking notes on them). Publicity was avoided. As the day of disaster approached, increasing numbers of newspaper, TV, and radio reporters converged on the group's headquarters in Marian Keech's house. For the most part, these people were turned away or ignored. The most frequent answer to their questions was, "No comment."

Although discouraged for a time, the media representatives returned with a vengeance when Dr. Armstrong's religious activities caused him to be fired from his post on the college health-service staff; one especially persistent newsman had to be threatened with a lawsuit. A similar siege was repelled on the eve of the flood when a swarm of reporters pushed and pestered the believers for information. Afterward, the researchers summarized the group's preflood stance on public exposure and recruitment in respectful tones: "Exposed to a tremendous burst of publicity, they had made every attempt to dodge fame; given dozens of opportunities to proselyte, they had remained evasive and secretive and behaved with an almost superior indifference."

Eventually, when all the reporters and would-be converts had been cleared from the house, the believers began making final preparations for the arrival of the spaceship scheduled for midnight that night. The scene as viewed by Festinger, Riecken, and Schachter must have seemed like absurdist theater. Otherwise ordinary people—housewives, college students, a high school boy, a publisher, a physician, a hardware-store clerk and his mother—were participating earnestly in tragic comedy. They took direction from a pair of members who were periodically in touch with the Guardians; Marian Keech's written messages were being supplemented that evening by "the Bertha," a former beautician through whose tongue the "Creator" gave instruction. They rehearsed their lines diligently, calling out in chorus the responses to be made before entering the rescue saucer: "I am my own porter." "I am my own pointer." They discussed seriously whether the message from a caller identifying himself as Captain Video—a TV space character of the time—was properly interpreted as a prank or a coded communication from their rescuers.

In keeping with the admonition to carry nothing metallic aboard the saucer, the believers wore clothing from which all metal pieces had been torn out. The metal eyelets in their shoes had been ripped away. The women went braless or wore brassieres whose metal stays had been removed. The men had yanked the zippers out of their pants, which were supported by lengths of rope in place of belts.

The group's fanaticism concerning the removal of all metal was vividly experienced by one of the researchers, who remarked, twenty-five minutes before midnight, that he had forgotten to extract the zipper from his trousers. As the observers tell it, "this knowledge produced a near panic reaction. He was rushed into the bedroom where Dr. Armstrong, his hands trembling and his eyes darting to the clock every few seconds, slashed out the zipper with a razor blade and wrenched its clasps free with wirecutters." The hurried operation finished, the researcher was returned to the living room—a slightly less metallic but, one supposes, much paler man.

As the time appointed for their departure grew close, the believers settled into a lull of soundless anticipation. Fortunately, the trained scientists were able to provide a detailed account of the events that transpired during this momentous period.

The last ten minutes were tense ones for the group in the living room. They had nothing to do but sit and wait, their coats in their laps. In the tense silence two clocks ticked loudly, one about ten minutes faster than the other. When the faster of the two pointed to twelve-five, one of the observers remarked aloud on the fact. A chorus of people replied that midnight had not yet come. Bob Eastman affirmed that the slower clock was correct; he had set it himself only that afternoon. It showed only four minutes before midnight.

These four minutes passed in complete silence except for a single utterance. When the [slower] clock on the mantel showed only one minute remaining before the guide to the saucer was due, Marian exclaimed in a strained, high-pitched voice: "And not a plan has gone astray!" The clock chimed twelve, each stroke painfully clear in the expectant hush. The believers sat motionless.

One might have expected some visible reaction. Midnight had passed and nothing had happened. The cataclysm itself was less than seven hours away. But there was little to see in the reactions of the people in the room. There was no talking, no sound. People sat stock-still, their faces seemingly frozen and expressionless. Mark Post was the only person who even moved. He lay down on the sofa and closed his eyes but did not sleep. Later, when spoken to, he answered monosyllabically but otherwise lay immobile. The others showed nothing on the surface, although it became clear later that they had been hit hard. . . .

Gradually, painfully, an atmosphere of despair and confusion settled over the group. They reexamined the prediction and the accompanying messages. Dr. Armstrong and Mrs. Keech reiterated their faith. The believers mulled over their predicament and discarded explanation after explanation as unsatisfactory. At one point, toward 4 A.M., Mrs. Keech broke down and cried bitterly. She knew, she sobbed, that there were some who were beginning to doubt but that the group must beam light to those who needed it most and that the group must hold together. The rest of the believers were losing their composure, too. They were all visibly shaken and many were close to tears. It was now almost 4:30 A.M. and still no way of handling the disconfirmation had been found. By now, too, most of the group were talking openly about the failure of the escort to come at midnight. The group seemed near dissolution. (pp. 162–63, 168)

In the midst of gathering doubt, as cracks crawled through the believers' confidence, the researchers witnessed a pair of remarkable incidents, one after another. The first occurred at about 4:45 a.m. when Marian Keech's hand suddenly began transcribing through "automatic writing" the text of a holy message from above. When read aloud, the communication proved to be an elegant explanation for the events of that night. "The little group, sitting alone all night long, had spread so much light that God had saved the world from destruction." Although neat and efficient, this explanation was not wholly satisfying by itself; for example, after hearing it, one member simply rose, put on his hat and coat, and left, never to return. Something additional was needed to restore the believers to their previous levels of faith.

It was at this point that the second notable incident occurred to supply that need. Once again, the words of those who were present offer a vivid description:

The atmosphere in the group changed abruptly and so did their behavior. Within minutes after she had read the message explaining the disconfirmation, Mrs. Keech received another message instructing her to publicize the explanation. She reached for the telephone and began dialing the number of a newspaper. While she was waiting to be connected, someone asked: "Marian, is this the first time you have called the newspaper yourself?" Her reply was immediate: "Oh yes, this is the first time I have ever called them. I have never had anything to tell them before, but now I feel it is urgent." The whole group could have echoed her feelings, for they all felt a sense of urgency. As soon as Marian had finished her call, the other members took turns telephoning newspapers, wire services, radio stations, and national magazines to spread the explanation of the failure of the flood. In their desire to spread the word quickly and resoundingly, the believers now opened for public attention matters that had been thus far utterly secret. Where only hours earlier they had shunned newspaper reporters and felt that the attention they were getting in the press was painful, they now became avid seekers for publicity. (p. 170)

Not only had the long-standing policies concerning secrecy and publicity done an about-face, but so, too, had the group's attitude toward potential converts. Whereas likely recruits who previously visited the house had been mostly ignored, turned away, or treated with casual attention, the day following the disconfirmation saw a different story. All callers were admitted, all questions were answered, all visitors were proselytized. The members' unprecedented willingness to accommodate new recruits was perhaps best demonstrated when nine high school students arrived on the following night to speak with Mrs. Keech.

They found her at the telephone deep in a discussion of flying saucers with a caller whom, it later turned out, she believed to be a spaceman. Eager to continue talking to him and at the same time anxious to keep her new guests, Marian simply included them in the conversation and, for more than an hour, chatted alternately with her guests in the living room and the "spaceman" on the other end of the telephone. So intent was she on proselyting that she seemed unable to let any opportunity go by. (p. 178)

To what can we attribute the believers' radical turnabout? Within a few hours, they had moved from clannish and taciturn hoarders of the Word to expansive and eager disseminators of it. What could have possessed them to choose such an ill-timed instant—when the failure of the flood was likely to cause nonbelievers to view the group and its dogma as laughable?

The crucial event occurred sometime during "the night of the flood" when it became increasingly clear the prophecy would not be fulfilled. Oddly, it was not their prior certainty that drove the members to propagate the faith, it was an encroaching sense of uncertainty. It was the dawning realization that if the spaceship and flood predictions were wrong, so might be the entire belief system on which they rested. For those huddled in Marian Keech's living room, that growing possibility must have seemed hideous.

The group members had gone too far, given up too much for their beliefs to see them destroyed; the shame, the economic cost, the mockery would be too great to bear. The overarching need of the cultists to cling to those beliefs seeps poignantly from their own words. From a young woman with a three-year-old child:

I have to believe the flood is coming on the twenty-first because I've spent all my money. I quit my job, I quit computer school. . . . I have to believe. (p. 168)

From Dr. Armstrong to one of the researchers four hours after the failure of the saucermen to arrive:

I've had to go a long way. I've given up just about everything. I've cut every tie. I've burned every bridge. I've turned my back on the world. I can't afford to doubt. I have to believe. And there isn't any other truth. (p. 168)

Imagine the corner in which Dr. Armstrong and his followers found themselves as morning approached. So massive was the commitment to their beliefs that no other truth was tolerable. Yet those beliefs had taken a merciless pounding from physical reality: No saucer had landed, no spacemen had knocked, no flood had come, nothing had happened as prophesied. Because the only acceptable form of truth had been undercut by physical proof, there was but one way out of the corner for the group. It had to create another type of proof for the truth of its beliefs: social proof.

This, then, explains the group members' sudden shift from se-

cretive conspirators to zealous missionaries. It also explains the curious timing of the shift—precisely when a direct disconfirmation
of their beliefs had rendered them least convincing to outsiders. It
was necessary to risk the scorn and derision of nonbelievers because
publicity and recruitment efforts provided the only remaining hope.
If they could spread the Word, if they could inform the uninformed,
if they could persuade the skeptics, and if, by so doing, they could
win new converts, their threatened but treasured beliefs would
become *truer*. The principle of social proof says so: *The greater the
number of people who find any idea correct, the more a given individual
will perceive the idea to be correct*. The group's assignment was clear;
because the physical evidence could not be changed, the social evidence had to be. Convince, and ye shall be convinced.[3]

Optimizers

All the levers of influence discussed in this book work better under some conditions than others. If we are to defend ourselves ad-
equately against any such lever, it is vital that we know its optimal
operating conditions in order to recognize when we are most vulnerable to its influence. In the case of social proof, there are three
main optimizing conditions: when we are unsure of what is best
to do (uncertainty); when the evidence of what is best to do comes
from numerous others (the many); and when that evidence comes
from people like us (similarity).

Uncertainty: In Its Throes, Conformity Grows

We have already had a hint of when the principle of social proof
worked best with the Chicago believers. It was when a sense of
shaken confidence triggered their craving for converts, for new
believers who could validate the truth of the original believers'
views. In general, when we are unsure of ourselves, when the situation is unclear or ambiguous, when uncertainty reigns, we are
most likely to accept the actions of others—because those actions
reduce our uncertainty about what is correct behavior there.

One way uncertainty develops is through lack of familiarity with the situation. Under such circumstances, people are especially likely to follow the lead of others. Remember this chapter's account of restaurant managers in Beijing who greatly increased customers' purchases of certain dishes on the menu by describing them as most popular? Although the labeled popularity of an item elevated its choice by all sorts of diners (males, females, customers of any age), there was one kind of customer that was most likely to choose based on popularity—those who were infrequent and, therefore, unfamiliar visitors. Customers who weren't in a position to rely on existing experience in the situation had the strongest tendency to resort to social proof.

Consider how this simple insight made one man a multimillionaire. His name was Sylvan Goldman and, after acquiring several small grocery stores in 1934, he noticed his customers stopped buying when their handheld shopping baskets got too heavy. This inspired him to invent the shopping cart, which in its earliest form was a folding chair equipped with wheels and a pair of heavy metal baskets. The contraption was so unfamiliar-looking that, at first, none of Goldman's customers used one—even after he built a more-than-adequate supply, placed several in a prominent place in the store, and erected signs describing their uses and benefits. Frustrated and about to give up, he tried one more idea to reduce his customers' uncertainty, one based on social proof. He hired shoppers to wheel the carts through the store. His true customers soon began following suit, his invention swept the nation, and he died a wealthy man with an estate of over $400 million.[4]

READER'S REPORT 4.2

From a Danish university student

While in London visiting my girlfriend, I was sitting in an Underground station on a stopped train. The train failed to depart on time, and there was no announcement as to the cause. On the opposite side of the platform, another train had stopped too. Then, a strange thing happened. A few people started leaving my train and boarding the other one, which sparked a self-feeding, self-amplifying reaction, making everybody (about 200 people, including me) disembark my train and board the other. Then, after several minutes, something even more peculiar happened: A few people started leaving the second train, and the whole mechanism was produced again in the reverse order, making everybody (including me, once again) go back to the original train, still without any announcement to justify the retreat.

Needless to say, it left me with a rather silly feeling of being a mindless turkey following every collective impulse of social proof.

Author's note: In addition to a lack of familiarity, a lack of objective cues of correctness in a situation generates feelings of uncertainty. For example, in this situation, there were no announcements. Consequently, social proof took over to guide behavior, no matter how farcically. *Click, run* (back and forth).

In the process of trying to resolve our uncertainty by examining the reactions of other people, we are likely to overlook a subtle, but important fact: especially in an ambiguous situation, those people are probably examining the social evidence too. This tendency for everyone to be looking to see what everyone else is doing can lead to a fascinating phenomenon called pluralistic ignorance. A thorough understanding of the phenomenon helps explain a troubling occurrence: the failure of bystanders to aid victims in agonizing need of help.

The classic report of such bystander inaction and the one that has produced the most debate in journalistic, political, and scientific circles began as an article in the *New York Times*: a woman in her late twenties, Kitty Genovese, was killed in a late-night attack while thirty-eight of her neighbors watched from their apartment windows without lifting a finger to help. News of the killing created a national uproar and led to a line of scientific research investigating when bystanders will and will not help in an emergency. More recently, the details of the neighbors' inaction—and even whether it had actually occurred—has been debunked by researchers who uncovered shoddy journalistic methods in this specific case. Nonetheless, because such events continue to arise, the question of when bystanders will intervene in an emergency remains important. One answer involves the potentially tragic consequences of the pluralistic-ignorance effect, which are starkly illustrated in a UPI news release from Chicago:

> *A university coed was beaten and strangled in daylight hours near one of the most popular tourist attractions in the city, police said Saturday.*
>
> *The nude body of Lee Alexis Wilson, 23, was found Friday in dense shrubbery alongside the wall of the Art Institute by a 12-year-old boy playing in the bushes.*
>
> *Police theorized she may have been sitting or standing by a fountain in the Art Institute's south plaza when she was attacked. The assailant apparently then dragged her into the bushes. She apparently was sexually assaulted, police said.*
>
> Police said thousands of persons must have passed the site and one man told them he heard a scream about 2 *p.m.* but did not investigate because *no one else* seemed to be paying attention *(emphasis added).*

Often an emergency is not obviously an emergency. Is the man lying in the alley a heart-attack victim or a drunk sleeping one off? Is the commotion next door an assault requiring the police or an especially loud marital spat where intervention would be inappropriate and unwelcome? What is going on? In times of such uncertainty, the natural tendency is to look around at the actions of others for clues. From the principle of social proof, we can determine from the way the other witnesses are reacting whether the event is or is not an emergency.

What is easy to forget, though, is that everybody else observing the event is likely to be looking for social evidence to reduce *their* uncertainty. Because we all prefer to appear poised and unflustered among others, we are likely to search for that evidence placidly, with brief, camouflaged glances at those around us. Therefore, everyone is likely to see everyone else looking unruffled and failing to act. As a result, and by the principle of social proof, the event will be roundly interpreted as a nonemergency.

A Scientific Summary

Social scientists have a good idea of when bystanders will offer emergency aid. First, once uncertainty is removed and witnesses are convinced an emergency situation exists, aid is very likely. Under these conditions, the number of bystanders who either intervene themselves or summon help is quite comforting. For example, in four separate experiments done in Florida, accident scenes involving a maintenance man were staged. When it was clear that the man was hurt and required assistance, he was helped 100 percent of the time in two of the experiments. In the other two experiments, where helping involved contact with potentially dangerous electric wires, the victim still received bystander aid in 90 percent of the instances. The situation becomes very different when, as in many cases, bystanders cannot be sure the event is an emergency.

Devictimizing Yourself

Explaining the dangers of modern life in scientific terms does not dispel them. Fortunately, our current understanding of the bystander-intervention process offers real hope. Armed with scientific knowledge, an emergency victim can increase markedly the chances of receiving aid from others. The key is the realization that groups of bystanders fail to help because the bystanders are unsure rather than unkind. They don't help because they are unsure an emergency actually exists and whether they are responsible for taking action. When they are confident of their

Figure 4.1: Victim?

At times like this one, when the need for emergency aid is unclear, even genuine victims are unlikely to be helped in a crowd. Think how, if you were a second passerby in this situation, you might be influenced by the first passerby to believe that no aid was called for.

Jan Halaska, Photo Researchers, Inc.

responsibilities for intervening in a clear emergency, people are exceedingly responsive.

Once it is understood that the enemy is the state of uncertainty, it becomes possible for emergency victims to reduce this uncertainty, thereby protecting themselves. Imagine, for example, you are spending a summer afternoon at a music concert in a park. As the concert ends and people begin leaving, you notice a slight numbness in one arm but dismiss it as nothing to be alarmed about. Yet, while moving with the crowd to the distant parking areas, you feel the numbness spreading down to your hand and up one side of your face. Feeling disoriented, you sit against a tree for a moment to rest. Soon you realize something is drastically wrong.

Sitting down has not helped; in fact, control of your muscles has worsened, and you are having difficulty moving your mouth and tongue to speak. You try to get up but can't. A terrifying thought rushes to mind: "Oh, God, I'm having a stroke!" People are streaming by without paying attention. The few who notice the odd way you are slumped against the tree or the strange look on your face check the social evidence around them and, seeing no one reacting with concern, walk on convinced that nothing is wrong, leaving you terrified and on your own.

Were you to find yourself in such a predicament, what could you do to overcome the odds against receiving help? Because your physical abilities would be deteriorating, time would be crucial. If, before you could summon aid, you lost your speech or mobility or consciousness, your chances for assistance and for recovery would plunge drastically. It would be essential to request help quickly. What would be the most effective form of that request? Moans, groans, or outcries probably would not do. They might bring you some attention, but they would not provide enough information to assure passersby a true emergency existed.

If mere outcries are unlikely to produce help from the passing crowd, perhaps you should be more specific. Indeed, you need to do more than try to gain attention; you should call out clearly your need for assistance. You must not allow bystanders to define your situation as a nonemergency. Use the word "Help" to show your need for emergency aid, and don't worry about being wrong. Embarrassment in such a situation is a villain to be crushed. If you think you are having a stroke, you cannot afford to be worried about the possibility of overestimating your problem. The difference is that between a moment of embarrassment and possible death or lifelong paralysis.

Even a resounding call for help is not your most effective tactic. Although it may reduce bystanders' doubts that a real emergency exists, it will not remove several other important uncertainties within each onlooker's mind: What kind of aid is required? Should I be the one to provide the aid, or should someone more qualified do it? Has someone else already acted to get professional help, or is it my responsibility? While the bystanders stand gawking at you and grappling with these questions, time vital to your survival could he slipping away.

Clearly, then, as a victim you must do more than alert bystanders to your need for emergency assistance; you must also remove their uncertainties about how that assistance should be provided and who should provide it. What would be the most efficient and reliable way to do so? Based on research findings, my advice would be to focus on one individual in the crowd, then stare at, speak to, and point directly at that person and no one else: "You, sir, in the blue jacket, I need help. Call 911 for an ambulance." With that one utterance, you would dispel all the uncertainties that might prevent or delay help. With that one statement you will have put the man in the blue jacket in the role of "rescuer." He should now understand that emergency aid is needed; he should understand that he, not someone else, is responsible for providing the aid; and, finally, he should understand exactly how to provide it. All the scientific evidence indicates the result should be quick, effective assistance.

READER'S REPORT 4.3

From a woman living in Wrocław, Poland

I was going through a well-lighted road crossing when I thought I saw somebody fall into a ditch left by workers. The ditch was well protected, and I was not sure if I really saw it—maybe it was just imagination. One year ago, I would continue on my way, believing that the people passing by who had been closer saw better. But I had read your book. So, I stopped and returned to check if it was true. And it was. A man fell into this hole and was lying there shocked. The ditch was quite deep, so people walking nearby couldn't see anything. When I tried to do something, two guys walking on this street stopped to help me pull the man out.

Today, the newspapers wrote that during the last three weeks of winter, 120 people died in Poland, frozen. This guy could have been 121—that night the temperature was −21C.

He should be grateful to your book that he is alive.

Author's note: Several years ago, I was involved in a rather serious automobile accident that occurred at an intersection. Both I and the other driver were hurt: he was slumped, unconscious, over his steering wheel while I had staggered, bloody, from behind mine. Cars began to roll slowly past us; their drivers gawked but did not stop. Like the Polish woman, I, too, had read the book, so I knew what to do. I pointed directly at the driver of one car and said, "Call the police." To a second and third driver, I said, "Pull over, we need help." Their aid was not only rapid but infectious. More drivers began stopping—spontaneously—to tend to the other victim. The principle of social proof was working *for* us now. The trick had been to get the ball rolling in the direction of help. Once that was accomplished, social proof's natural momentum did the rest.

In general, then, your best strategy when in need of emergency help is to reduce the uncertainties of those around you concerning your condition and their responsibilities. Be as precise as possible about your need for aid. Do not allow bystanders to come to their own conclusions because the principle of social proof and the consequent pluralistic-ignorance effect might well cause them to view your situation as a nonemergency. Of all the techniques in this book designed to produce compliance with a request, this one is the most important to remember. After all, the failure of your request for emergency aid could mean the loss of your life.

Besides this broad advice, there is a singular form of uncertainty for women that they need to dispel in a unique emergency situation for them—a public confrontation in which a woman is being physically attacked by a man. Concerned researchers suspected witnesses to such confrontations may not help because they are uncertain about the nature of the pair's relationship, thinking intervention might be unwelcome in a lovers' quarrel. To test this possibility, the researchers exposed subjects to a staged public fight between a man and a woman. When there were no cues as to the sort of relationship between the two, the great majority of male and female subjects (nearly 70 percent) assumed that the two were romantically involved; only 4 percent thought they were complete strangers. In other experiments where there were cues that defined the combatants' relationship—the woman shouted either "I don't know why I ever married you" or "I don't know you"—the studies uncovered an ominous reaction on the part of bystanders. Although the severity of the fight was identical, observers were less willing to help the married woman because they thought it was a private matter in which their intervention would be unwanted and embarrassing to all concerned.

Figure 4.2: To get help, you must shout correctly.
Observers of male–female confrontations often assume the pair is romantically involved and that intervention would be unwanted or inappropriate. To combat this perception and get aid, the woman should shout, "I don't know you."
Tatagatta/Fotolia

Thus, a woman caught in a physical confrontation with a man, any man, should not expect to get bystander aid simply by shouting for relief. Observers are likely to define the event as a domestic squabble and, with that definition in place, may well assume that helping would be socially inappropriate. Fortunately, the researchers' data suggest a way to overcome this problem: by loudly labeling her attacker a stranger—"I don't know you!"—a woman should greatly increase her chances for receiving assistance.[5]

The Many: The More We See, the More There Will Be

A bit earlier I stated that the principle of social proof, like all other levers of influence, works better under some conditions than others. We have already explored one of those conditions: uncertainty. For sure, when people are *unsure*, they are more likely to use others' actions to decide how they themselves should act. In addition, there is another important optimizing condition: the many. Any reader who doubts that the seeming appropriateness of an action is importantly influenced by the number of others performing it might try a small experiment. Stand on a busy sidewalk, pick an empty spot in the sky or on a tall building, and stare at it for a full minute. Very little will happen around you during that time—most people will walk past without glancing up, and virtually no one will stop to stare with you. Now, on the next day, go to the same place and bring along some friends to look upward too. Within sixty seconds, a crowd will have stopped to crane their necks skyward with the group. For those passersby who do not join you, the pressure to look up at least briefly will be nearly irresistible; if the results of your experiment are like those of one performed by researchers in New York City, you and your friends will cause 80 percent of all passersby to lift their gaze to your empty spot. Moreover, up to a point (around twenty people), the more friends you bring along, the more passersby will join in.

Social-proof information doesn't have to be only visual to sweep people in its direction. Consider the heavy-handed exploitation of

Figure 4.3: "Looking for Higher (and Higher) Meaning"
The draw of the many is devilishly strong.
© Punch/Rothco

the principle within the history of grand opera, one of our most venerable art forms. There is a phenomenon called claquing, said to have begun in 1820 by a pair of Paris opera-house habitués named Sauton and Porcher. The men were more than operagoers, though. They were businessmen whose product was applause; and they knew how to structure social proof to incite it.

Organizing their business under the title l'Assurance des succès dramatiques, they leased themselves and their employees to singers and opera managers who wished to be assured of an appreciative audience response. So effective were Sauton and Porcher in stimulating genuine audience reaction with their rigged reactions that, before long, claques (usually consisting of a leader— *chef de claque*—and several individual claqueurs) had become an established and persistent tradition throughout the world of opera. As music historian Robert Sabin (1964) notes, "By 1830 the claque was a full-bloom institution, collecting by day, applauding by night . . . But it is altogether probable that neither Sauton, nor his ally Porcher, had a notion of the extent to which their scheme of paid applause would be adopted and applied wherever opera is sung."

As claquing grew and developed, its practitioners offered an array of styles and strengths—the *pleureuse*, chosen for her ability to weep on cue; the *bisseur*, who called *"bis"* (repeat) and "encore" in ecstatic tones; and the *rieur*, selected for the infectious quality of his laugh. For our purposes, though, the most instructive parallel to modern forms can be observed in the business model of Sauton and Porcher and their successors: They charged by the staffer, recognizing that the more claqueurs they sent to be scattered among an audience, the greater would be the persuasive impression that *many* others liked the performance. *Claque, run.*

Operagoers are hardly alone in this respect. Present-day observers of political events, such as US presidential debates, can be significantly affected by the magnitude of audience reaction. Candidates' perceived performances in US presidential debates have been of no small significance in election outcomes, as political scholars have noted their critical impact. For this reason, researchers have investigated the factors that have led to debate success and failure. One of those factors has been how the responses of audiences attending a debate have affected the responses of those observing remotely, usually on TV but also on radio and streaming video. By presenting the candidates' true performances but technologically modifying the responses (applause, cheering, laughing) of on-site audiences, researchers have examined the influence of these altered responses on remote audiences' views of the candidates. Their findings were consistent: in a 1984 Ronald Reagan–Walter Mondale debate, a 1992 Bill Clinton–George Bush debate, and a 2016 Donald Trump–Hillary Clinton debate, whichever candidate seemingly received the strongest response from the on-site audience won the day with the remote audiences, in terms of debate performance, leadership qualities, and likability. Certain researchers have become concerned with a tendency in presidential debates for candidates to seed the on-site debate audiences with raucously loud followers whose effusive responses give the impression of greater-than-actual support in the room. The practice of claquing is far from dead.[6]

READER'S REPORT 4.4

From a Central American marketing executive

As I read the chapter about social proof, I recognized an interesting local example. In my country, Ecuador, you can hire a person or groups of people (traditionally consisting of women) to come to the funeral of a family member or friend. The job of these people is to cry while the dead person is being buried, making, for sure, more people start to cry. This job was quite popular a few years ago, and the well-known people that worked in this job received the name of "lloronas," which means criers.

Author's note: We can see how, at different times and in different cultures, it has been possible to profit from manufactured social proof. In today's TV sitcoms, we no longer have *claqueurs* and *rieurs* to fool us into laughing longer and harder. Instead, we have "laugh-trackers" and "sweeteners"—audio technicians whose job is to enhance the laughter of studio audiences to make the programs' comic material seem funnier to their true targets: TV viewers such as you and me. Sad to say, we are likely to fall for their tricks. Experiments show that the use of fabricated merriment leads audiences to laugh more frequently and longer, as well as to rate humorous material funnier (Provine, 2000).[7]

Why Does "The Many" Work So Well?

A few years ago, a shopping mall in Essex, England, had a problem. During normal lunch hours, its food court became so congested that customers encountered long waits and a shortage of tables for their meals. For help, mall managers turned to a team of researchers who set up a study that provided a simple solution based on the psychological pull of "the many." The solution also incorporated all three of the reasons why this optimizer of social proof works so forcefully: validity, feasibility, and social acceptance.

The study itself was straightforward. The researchers created two posters urging mall visitors to enjoy an early lunch at the food court. One poster included an image of a single person doing so; the other poster was identical, except the image was of several such visitors. Reminding customers of the opportunity for an early lunch (as the first poster did) proved successful, producing a 25 percent increase in customer activity in the food court before noon. But the real success came from the second poster, which lifted prenoon consumer activity by 75 percent.

VALIDITY

Following the advice or behaviors of the majority of those around us is often seen as a shortcut to good decision-making. We use the actions of others as a way to locate and validate a correct choice. If everybody's raving about a new restaurant, it's probably a good one that we'd like too. If the great majority of online reviewers is recommending a product, we'll likely feel more confident clicking the purchase button. In the shopping-mall posters example, it appears that visitors exposed to a photo of multiple others taking a prenoon lunch were particularly swayed to view the idea as a good one. Additional studies have shown that ads presenting increasingly larger percentages of customers favoring a brand ("4 out of 7" versus "5 out of 7" versus "6 out of 7") get increasingly more observers to prefer the brand; moreover, this is the case because observers assume that the brand with the largest percentage of customers preferring it must be the right choice.

Often no complex cognitive operations are necessary for others' choices to establish validity; the process can be more automatic than that. For example, fruit flies possess no complex cognitive capacities. Yet when female fruit flies viewed other females mating with a male that had been colored a particular tint (pink or green) by researchers, they became much more willing to choose a mate of the same color—70 percent of the time. It's not just fruit flies that respond to social proof without cognitive direction.

Consider the admission of prominent travel writer Doug Lansky who, while visiting England's Royal Ascot Races, caught a glimpse of the British Royal Family and readied his camera for a photo. "I got the Queen in focus, with Prince Charles and Prince Philip sitting beside her. Suddenly, it hit me: Why did I even want this picture? It's not like there's a world shortage of Royal Family photos. No tabloids were going to pay me big money for the shot. I was no paparazzi. But, shutters firing around me like Uzis, I joined in the frenzy. I couldn't help myself." *Click, run* . . . click, click, click.

Let's stay in England for an enlightening historical illustration of the power of "the many" to validate a choice and initiate contagious effects. For centuries, people have been subject to irrational sprees, manias, and panics of various sorts. In his classic text, *Extraordinary Popular Delusions and the Madness of Crowds*, Charles MacKay listed hundreds that occurred before the book's first publication in 1841. Most shared an instructive characteristic—contagiousness. Others' actions spread to observers, who then acted similarly and thereby validated the correctness of the action for still other observers, who acted similarly in turn.

In 1761, London experienced two moderate-sized earthquakes exactly a month apart. Convinced by this coincidence that a third, much larger quake would occur on the same date a month later, a soldier named Bell began spreading his prediction that the city would be destroyed on the fifth of April. At first, scant few paid him any heed. But those who did took the precaution of moving their families and possessions to surrounding areas. The sight of this small exodus stirred others to follow, which, in cascading waves over the next week, led to near panic and a large-scale evacuation. Great numbers of Londoners streamed into nearby villages, paying outrageous prices for any accommodations. Included in the terrified throngs were many who, according to MacKay, "had laughed at the prediction a week before, [but who] packed up their goods, when they saw others doing so, and hastened away."

After the designated day dawned and died without a tremor, the fugitives returned to the city furious at Mr. Bell for leading them astray. As MacKay's description makes clear, their anger was misdirected. It wasn't the crackpot Bell who was most convincing. It was the Londoners themselves who validated his theory, each to the other.[8]

EBOX 4.2

We don't have to rely on events from eighteenth-century England for examples of baseless, social proof–fueled panics. Indeed, owing to particular internet features and capacities, we are now seeing instances sprouting like weeds all around us.

In late 2019 and early 2020, alarming rumors went viral that claimed men in white vans were abducting women for purposes of sex trafficking and selling their body parts. Propelled by the social-media giant Facebook's algorithms giving prominence to posts that are widely shared or trending, the tale, which began in Baltimore, spread in snowballing fashion around the United States and beyond. As a consequence, white van owners in multiple cities reported being threatened and harassed by residents after the rumor began circulating in their communities. One workman lost jobs after being targeted in a Facebook post. Another was shot to death by two men reacting to a false claim of an attempted abduction. This, even though authorities have never found a single actual incident.

No matter. For instance, the mayor of Baltimore, Bernard Young, was sufficiently moved by the story to issue an unnerving televised warning to the women of his city: "Don't park near a white van. Make sure you keep your cellphone in case somebody tries to abduct you." What was Mayor Young's evidence for the threat? It was nothing that came from his own police.

Instead, he said, "It was all over Facebook."

Author's note: It's telling that perceived validity of the rumor developed from unfounded fears, rendered contagious by the algorithms of a frequently checked social-media feed. "Truth" was established without physical proof; there was only social proof. That was enough, as it often is.

There's an age-old truism that makes this point: "If one person says you have a tail, you laugh it off as stupid; but, if three people say it, you turn around."

FEASIBILITY

If we see a lot of other people doing something, it doesn't just mean it's probably a good idea. It also means we could probably do it too. Within the British shopping-mall study, the visitors seeing a poster of multiple others taking an early lunch might well have said to themselves something like, "Well, this idea seems doable. I guess it's not a big deal to arrange shopping plans or work hours to have an early lunch." Thus, besides perceived validity, a second reason "the many" is effective is that it communicates feasibility: if lots can do it, it must not be difficult to pull off. A study of residents of several Italian cities found that if residents believed *many* of their neighbors recycled in the home, then they were more willing to recycle themselves, in part, because they saw recycling as less difficult to manage.

With a set of estimable colleagues leading the way, I once did a study to see what we could best say to influence people to conserve household energy. We delivered one of four messages to their homes, once a week for a month, asking them to reduce their energy consumption. Three of the messages contained a frequently employed reason for conserving energy—"The environment will benefit"; "It's the socially responsible thing to do"; or "It will save you significant money on your next power bill"—whereas the fourth played the social-proof card, stating (honestly), "Most of your fellow community residents do try to conserve energy at home." At the end of the month, we recorded how much energy was used and learned that the social proof–based message had generated 3.5 times as much energy savings as any of the other messages. The size of the difference surprised almost everyone associated with the study—me, for one, but also my fellow researchers and even a sample of other homeowners. The homeowners, in fact, expected that the social-proof message would be least effective.

When I report on this research to utility-company officials, they frequently don't trust it because of an entrenched belief that the strongest motivator of human action is economic self-interest. They say, "C'mon, how are we supposed to believe that telling people their neighbors are conserving is three times more effective than telling them they can cut their power bills significantly?" Although there are various possible responses to this legitimate question, there's one that's nearly always proved persuasive for me. It involves the second reason, in addition to validity, that social-proof information works so well—feasibility. If I inform homeowners that by saving energy, they *could* also save a lot of money, it doesn't mean they would be able to make it happen. After all, I *could* reduce my next power bill to zero if I turned off all the electricity in my house and coiled up on the floor in the dark for a month, but that's not something I'd reasonably be able to do. A great strength of "the many" is that it destroys the problem of uncertain achievability. If people learn that many others around them are conserving energy, there is little doubt as to its feasibility. It comes to seem realistic and, therefore, actionable.[9]

SOCIAL ACCEPTANCE

We feel more socially accepted being one of the many. It's easy to see why. Think again of the British shopping-mall study. Visitors either encountered a poster showing a single shopper taking an early lunch in the mall's food court or multiple shoppers doing so. To follow the example of the first poster, observers risked the social disapproval of being viewed as a loner or oddball or outsider. The opposite was true of following the example of the second poster, which assured observers of the personal comfort of being among the many. The emotional difference between those two experiences is significant. Compared to holding an opinion that fits with the group's, holding an opinion that is out of line creates psychological distress.

In one study, research participants were hooked up to a brain scanner while they received information from others that conflicted with their own opinions. The conflicting information came either from four other participants or from four computers. Conformity was greater when the conflicting information came from the set of persons than from the set of computers, even though participants rated the two kinds of judgments as equally reliable. If participants viewed the reliability of the two sources of information as the same, what caused them to conform more to their fellow participants' choices? The answer lies in what occurred whenever they resisted the consensus of other people. The sector of their brains associated with negative emotion (the amygdala) became activated, reflecting what the researchers called "the pain of independence." It seems that defying other people produced a painful emotional state that pressured participants to conform. Defying a set of computers didn't have the same behavioral consequences, because it didn't have the same social-acceptance consequences. When it comes to group dynamics, there's an old saying that gets it right: "To get along, you have to go along."

Take, for example, the account by Yale psychologist Irving Janis of what happened in a group of heavy smokers who came to a clinic for treatment. During the group's second meeting, nearly everyone took the position that because tobacco is so addicting, no one could be expected to quit all at once. But one man disputed the group's view, announcing that he had stopped smoking completely since joining the group the week before and that others could do the same. In response, his former comrades banded against him, delivering a series of angry attacks on his position. At the following meeting, the dissenter reported that after considering the others' point of view, he had come to an important decision: "I have gone back to smoking two packs a day; and won't make any effort to stop again until after the last meeting." The other group members immediately welcomed him back into the fold, greeting his decision with applause.

These twin needs—to foster social acceptance and to escape social rejection—help explain why cults can be so effective in recruiting and retaining members. An initial showering of affection on prospective members, called love bombing, is typical of cult-induction practices. It accounts for some of the success of these groups in attracting new members, especially those feeling lonely or disconnected. Later, threatened withdrawal of that affection explains the willingness of some members to remain in the group: After having cut their bonds to outsiders, as the cults invariably urge, members have nowhere else to turn for social acceptance.[10]

Similarity: Peer-suasion

The principle of social proof operates most powerfully when we are observing the behavior of people just like us. It is the conduct of such people that gives us the greatest insight into what constitutes correct behavior for ourselves. As with "the many," an action coming from *similar* others increases our confidence that it will prove valid, feasible, and socially acceptable should we perform it. Therefore, we are more inclined to follow the lead of our peers in a phenomenon we can call *peer-suasion*.

Studies have shown, for example, students worried about their academic performance or about their ability to fit in at school improved significantly when informed that many students like them had the same concerns and overcame them. Consumers became more likely to follow the consensus of other consumers about purchasing a brand of sunglasses when told the others were similar to them. In the classroom, when adolescent aggression is frequent, it spreads contagiously—but almost entirely within a peer group; for instance, frequent aggression of boys in a class has little effect on the aggressiveness of the girls and vice versa. Employees are more likely to engage in information sharing if they see it modeled by fellow coworkers than by managers. Physicians who overprescribe certain drugs, such as antibiotics or antipsychotics, are unlikely to change this behavior in a lasting fashion unless informed that their prescription rate exceeds the norm of their peers. After an extensive review of environmental behavior change, the economist Robert Frank stated, "By far the strongest predictor of whether we install solar panels, buy electric cars, eat more responsibly, and

Figure 4.4: "Freethinking Youth"
We frequently think of teenagers as rebellious and independent-minded. It is important to recognize, however, that typically this is true only with respect to their parents. Among their peers, they conform massively to what social proof tells them is proper.

© Eric Knoll, Tauris Photos

support climate-friendly policies is the percentage of peers who take those steps."[11]

This is why I believe we are seeing an increasing number of average-person testimonials on TV these days. Advertisers know that one successful way to sell a product to ordinary viewers (who compose the largest potential market) is to demonstrate that other "ordinary" people like and use it. Whether the product is a brand of soft drink or a pain reliever or an automobile, we hear volleys of praise from John or Mary Everyperson.

Compelling evidence for the importance of similarity in determining whether we will imitate another's behavior can be found in a study of a fundraising effort conducted on a college campus. Donations to charity more than doubled when the requester claimed to be similar to the donation targets, saying "I'm a student here too," and implying that, therefore, they should want to support the same cause. These results suggest an important consideration for anyone wishing to harness the principle of social proof. People will use the actions of others to decide how to behave, *especially when they view those others as similar to themselves.*

I took this consideration into account when, for three years, I served as chief scientist for a then startup firm, Opower, that partners with utility companies to send residents information about how much energy their household is using compared with their neighbors. A crucial feature of the information is that the comparison is not with *any* neighbors but is specifically with neighbors whose homes are nearby and comparable along dimensions such as size—in other words, "Homes just like yours." The results, driven mainly by householders reducing their energy consumption if it is greater than their peers', have been astounding. At last count, these peer comparisons have saved more than thirty-six billion pounds of CO_2 emissions from entering the environment and more than twenty-three trillion watts per hour of electricity from being expended. What's more, the comparisons are presently generating $700 million in bill savings to utility customers per year.

Peer-suasion applies not only to adults but also to children. Health researchers have found, for example, that a school-based antismoking program had lasting effects only when it used same-age peer leaders as teachers. Another study found that children who saw a film depicting a child's positive visit to the dentist lowered their own dental anxieties principally when they were the same age as the child in the film. I wish I had known about this second study when, a few years before it was published, I was trying to reduce a different kind of anxiety in my son, Chris.

I live in Arizona, where backyard swimming pools abound. Regrettably, each year, several young children drown after falling into an unattended pool. I was determined, therefore, to teach Chris how to swim at an early age. The problem was not that he was afraid of the water; he loved it, but he would not get into the pool without wearing his inflatable inner tube, no matter how I tried to coax, talk, or shame him out of it. After getting nowhere for two months, I hired a graduate student of mine to help. Despite his background as a lifeguard and swimming instructor, he failed as I had. He couldn't persuade Chris to attempt even a stroke outside his plastic ring.

About this time, Chris was attending a day camp that provided a number of activities to its group, including the use of a large pool, which he scrupulously avoided. One day, shortly after the graduate-student incident, I went to get Chris from camp and, with my mouth agape, watched him run down the diving board and jump into the deepest part of the pool. Panicked, I began pulling off my shoes to jump in to his rescue when I saw him bob to the surface and paddle safely to the side of the pool—where I dashed to meet him.

"Chris, you can swim!" I said excitedly. "You can swim!"

"Yes," he responded casually, "I learned how today."

"This is terrific! This is just terrific. But how come you didn't need your plastic ring today?"

"Well, I'm three years old, and Tommy is three years old. And Tommy can swim without a ring, so that means I can too."

I could have kicked myself. Of course it would be to *little Tommy*, not to a six-foot-two graduate student, that Chris would look for the most relevant information about what he could or should do. Had I been more thoughtful about solving Chris's swimming problem, I could have employed Tommy's good example earlier and perhaps saved myself a couple of frustrating months. I could have simply noted at the day camp that Tommy was a swimmer and then arranged with his parents for the boys to spend a weekend afternoon swimming in our pool. My guess is that Chris's plastic ring would have been abandoned by the day's end.[12]

READER'S REPORT 4.5

From a university teacher in Arkansas

During the summers of my college years, I sold Bible reference books door to door in Tennessee, Mississippi, South Carolina, and

Kansas. Of interest was how my sales improved when I finally came up with the idea of using names/testimonials from female customers with female prospects, males with males, and couples with couples. After 15 weeks on the job, I was averaging a respectable $550.80 per week by closely following the canned sales talk the company had taught us, which emphasized the features of the books.

But, a new sales manager began teaching us to sprinkle our presentations with the names of previous customers—for example, "Sue Johnson wanted to get the set so she could read Bible stories to her kids." I began following this approach in week 16, and I found that during weeks 16–19 my weekly sales average jumped to $893, a 62.13 percent increase! There is more to the story, however. I explicitly remember that during my 19th week, it dawned on me that while using the names had increased my sales overall, it had also made me lose some sales. The key event happened when I was presenting one day to a housewife. She seemed interested in the books but couldn't decide if she should order or not. At this point, I mentioned some married friends of hers who had bought. She then said something like, "Mary and Bill bought . . . ? Well, I had better talk to Harold before deciding. It would be better if we decided together."

Thinking about this incident over the next day or so, everything began to make sense. If I told a housewife about another *couple* who had bought, I was inadvertently supplying her with a good reason not to buy right then—she would need to talk with her husband first. However, if many other housewives like her were buying, it must be okay for her to buy too. From that point on, I resolved that I would use only the names of other housewives when presenting to a housewife. My sales the next week shot up to $1506. I soon extended this strategy to husbands and couples, using only the names of males when presenting to males and only the names of couples when presenting to couples. During the next (and last) 20 weeks of my sales career, I averaged $1209.15. The reason my sales dropped off a bit toward the end was that I was making so much money, I found it difficult to motivate myself to go out and work very hard.

A word of qualification is in order. There is no doubt I was learning other things all the time that helped improve my sales. However, having experienced the speed of these changes firsthand, there is no doubt in my mind that no other single factor came close to "social proof from similar others" as the #1 reason for my 119.67 percent improvement.

Author's note: When the reader, a personal friend, first told me this story of the stunning effects of peer-suasion, I think he could sense my skepticism. So, by way of supportive evidence, he has since sent me monthly records of his sales figures during the four summers he described—figures he had carefully recorded at the time and kept for decades. It should probably come as no surprise, then, that he teaches statistics classes at his home university.

Monkey See, Monkey Do . . . Monkey Die

Although we have already seen the powerful impact that social proof can have on human decision-making, to my mind, the most telling illustration starts with a seemingly nonsensical statistic: After a suicide has made front-page news, airplanes—private planes, corporate jets, airliners—begin falling out of the sky at an alarming rate.

For example, it has been shown that immediately following certain kinds of highly publicized suicide stories, the number of people who die in commercial-airline crashes increases by 1,000 percent! Even more alarming: the increase is not limited to airplane deaths. The number of automobile fatalities shoots up as well.

One explanation suggests itself immediately. The same social conditions that cause some people to commit suicide cause others to die accidentally. For instance, certain individuals, the suicide-prone, may react to stressful societal events (economic downturns, rising crime rates, international tensions) by ending it all. Others will react differently to these same events; they might become angry, impatient, nervous, or distracted. To the degree such people operate or maintain our society's cars and planes, these vehicles will be less safe, and we will see a sharp increase in the number of automobile and air fatalities.

According to this "social conditions" interpretation, some of the same societal factors that cause intentional deaths also cause accidental ones, and that is why we find so strong a connection between suicide stories and fatal crashes. But another fascinating statistic indicates this is not the correct explanation. Fatal crashes increase dramatically only in those regions where the suicide has been highly publicized. Other places, existing under similar social conditions, whose newspapers have *not* publicized the story, show no comparable jump in such fatalities. Furthermore, within those areas where newspaper space has been allotted, the wider the publicity given the suicide, the greater has been the rise in subsequent crashes. Thus, it is not some set of common societal events that stimulates suicides, on the one hand, and fatal accidents, on the other. Instead, it is the publicized suicide story itself that produces the car and plane wrecks.

To explain the strong association between suicide-story publicity and subsequent crashes, a "bereavement" account has been suggested. Because, it has been argued, front-page suicides often involve well-known and respected public figures, perhaps their highly publicized deaths throw many people into states of shocked sadness. Stunned and preoccupied, these individuals become careless around cars and planes. The upshot is the sharp increase in deadly accidents involving such vehicles we see after front-page suicide stories. Although the bereavement theory can account for the connection between the degree of publicity given a story and subsequent crash fatalities—the more people who learn of the suicide, the larger will be the number of bereaved and careless individuals—it cannot explain another startling fact. Newspaper stories reporting suicide victims who died alone produce an increase in the frequency of single-fatality wrecks only, whereas stories reporting suicide-plus-murder incidents produce an increase in multiple-fatality wrecks only. Simple bereavement could not cause such a pattern.

The influence of suicide stories on car and plane crashes, then, is fantastically specific. Stories of pure suicides, in which only one person dies, generate wrecks in which only one person dies; stories of suicide-murder combinations, in which there are multiple deaths, generate wrecks in which there are multiple deaths. If neither "social conditions" nor "bereavement" can make sense of this bewildering array of facts, what can? There is a sociologist who thinks he has the answer. His name is David Phillips, and he points a convincing finger at the "Werther effect."

The story of the Werther effect is both chilling and intriguing. More than two centuries ago, Johann Wolfgang von Goethe, the great man of German literature, published a novel titled *Die Leiden des jungen Werthers* (*The Sorrows of Young Werther*). The book, in which the hero, named Werther, commits suicide, had a remarkable impact. Not only did it provide Goethe with immediate fame, but it sparked a wave of emulative suicides across Europe. So powerful was this effect that authorities in several countries banned the novel.

Phillips's own work has traced the Werther effect to modern times. His research demonstrated that immediately following a front-page suicide story, the suicide rate increases dramatically in those geographical areas where the story has been highly publicized. It's Phillips's argument that certain troubled people who read of another's self-inflicted death kill themselves in imitation. In a morbid illustration of the principle of social proof, these people decide how they should act on the basis of how some other troubled person has acted.

Phillips derived his evidence for the modern-day Werther effect from examining twenty years of suicide statistics in the United States. He found that within two months after every front-page suicide story, an average of fifty-eight more people than usual killed themselves. In a sense, each front-page suicide story killed fifty-eight people who otherwise would have gone on living. Phillips also found this tendency for suicides to prompt suicides occurred principally in those parts of the country where the first was highly publicized. He observed that the wider the publicity given the first suicide, the greater the number of later ones (see figure 4.5). Newer research indicates the pattern isn't limited to newspaper accounts. On March 31, 2017, Netflix premiered the web series *13 Reasons Why*, in which a young high school student commits suicide and leaves behind a set of thirteen tapes detailing the reasons. In the next thirty days, suicides among young adolescents rose by 28.9 percent—to a number higher than at any month in the

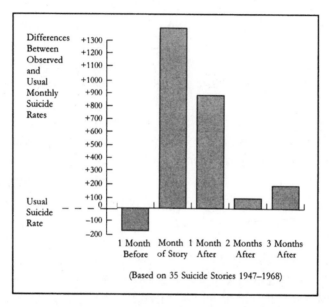

Figure 4.5: Fluctuation in number of suicides before, during, and after month of suicide story

Author's Note: This evidence raises an important ethical issue. The suicides that follow these stories are excess deaths. After the initial spurt, the suicide rates do not drop below traditional levels but only return to those levels. Statistics such as these might well give pause to newspaper editors inclined to sensationalize suicide accounts, as those accounts are likely to lead to the deaths of scores of people. Data indicate that in addition to newspaper editors, TV broadcasters have cause for concern about the effects of the suicide stories they present. Whether they appear as news reports, information features, or fictional movies, these stories create an immediate cluster of self-inflicted deaths, with impressionable, imitation-prone teenagers being the most frequent victims (Bollen & Phillips, 1982; Gould & Shaffer, 1986; Phillips & Cartensen, 1986, 1988; Schmidtke & Hafner, 1988).

five-year span analyzed by the researchers, who ruled out "social conditions" explanations for the increase.

If the facts surrounding the Werther effect seem to you suspiciously like those surrounding the influence of suicide stories on air and traffic fatalities, the similarities have not been lost on Phillips either. In fact, he contends that all the excess deaths following a front-page suicide incident can be explained as the same thing: copycat suicides. Upon learning of another's suicide, an uncomfortably large number of people decide suicide is an appropriate action for themselves as well. Some of these individuals then proceed to commit the act in a straightforward fashion, causing the suicide rate to jump.

Others, however, are less direct. For any of several reasons—to protect their reputations, to spare their families the shame and hurt, to allow their dependents to collect on insurance policies— they do not want to appear to have killed themselves. They would rather seem to have died accidentally. So, purposively but furtively, they cause the wreck of a car or a plane they are operating or are simply riding in. This can be accomplished in a variety of all-too-familiar-sounding ways. A commercial-airline pilot can dip the nose of the aircraft at a crucial point of takeoff or inexplicably land on an already occupied runway against the instructions from the control tower; the driver of a car can suddenly swerve into a tree or into oncoming traffic; a passenger in an automobile or corporate jet can incapacitate the operator, causing the deadly crash; the pilot of a private plane can, despite all radio warnings, plow into another aircraft. Thus, the alarming climb in crash fatalities we find following front-page suicides is, according to Phillips, most likely due to the Werther effect secretly applied.

I consider this insight brilliant. First, it explains all of the data strikingly well. If these wrecks really are hidden instances of imitative suicide, it makes sense that we should see an increase in the wrecks after suicide stories appear. It makes sense that the greatest rise in wrecks should occur after the suicide stories that have been most widely publicized and have, consequently, reached the most people. It also makes sense that the number of crashes should jump appreciably only in those geographical areas where the suicide stories were publicized. It even makes sense that single-victim suicides should lead only to single-victim crashes, whereas multiple-victim suicide incidents should lead only to multiple-victim crashes. Imitation is the key.

In addition, there is a second valuable feature of Phillips's insight. It allows us not only to explain the existing facts but also to predict new facts that have not yet been uncovered. For example, if the abnormally frequent crashes following publicized suicides are the result of imitative rather than accidental actions, they should be more deadly. That is, people trying to kill themselves will likely arrange (with a foot on the accelerator instead of the brake, with the nose of the plane down instead of up) for the impact to be as lethal as possible. The consequence should be quick and sure death. When Phillips examined the records to check on this prediction, he found that the average number of people killed in a fatal crash of a commercial airliner was more than three times greater if the crash happened one week after rather than one week before a front-page suicide story. A similar phenomenon can be found in traffic statistics, where there is evidence for the deadly efficiency of post-suicide-story auto crashes. Victims of fatal car wrecks that follow front-page suicide stories die four times more quickly than normal.

Still another fascinating prediction flows from Phillips's idea. If the increase in wrecks following suicide stories truly represents a set of copycat deaths, then the imitators should be most likely to copy the suicides of people who are similar to them. The principle of social proof states that we use information about the way others have behaved to help us determine proper conduct for ourselves. As research we've already reviewed showed, we are most influenced in this fashion by the actions of people who are like us—by peer-suasion.

Therefore, Phillips reasoned, if the principle of social proof is behind the phenomenon, there should be some clear similarity between the victim of the highly publicized suicide and those who cause subsequent wrecks. Realizing that the clearest test of this possibility would come from the records of automobile crashes involving a single car and a lone driver, Phillips compared the age of the suicide-story victim with the ages of the lone drivers killed in single-car crashes immediately after the story appeared in print. Once again, the predictions were strikingly accurate: when the newspaper detailed the suicide of a young person, it was young drivers who then piled their cars into trees, poles, and embankments with fatal results; but when the news story concerned an older person's suicide, it was older drivers who died in such crashes.

This last statistic is the clincher for me. I am left wholly convinced and, simultaneously, wholly amazed by it. Evidently, peersuasion is so powerful that its domain extends to the fundamental decision for life or death. Phillips's findings illustrate a distressing tendency for suicide publicity to motivate certain people who are similar to the victim to kill themselves—because they now find the idea of suicide more legitimate. Truly frightening are the data indicating that many innocent people die in the bargain (see figure 4.6).

Consider the fatal consequences of one locally publicized suicide in which a teen stepped in front of a speeding train. In the next six months, a second, third, and fourth student from the same high school followed his lead and died in the same way. Another such suicide was prevented by a fifth classmate's mother who noticed her son was missing from the house and suspected his intent. How did she know where to go to intervene and stop the teen's deadly action? She went directly to the rail crossing where his peers had died.

Perhaps nowhere are we brought into more dramatic contact with the unsettling side of the principle of social proof than in the realm of copycat crime. Back in the 1970s, our attention was brought to the phenomenon in the form of airplane hijackings, which seemed to spread like airborne viruses. In the 1980s, our focus shifted to product tamperings, such as the famous cases of Tylenol capsules injected with cyanide and Gerber baby-food products laced with glass. According to FBI forensic experts, each

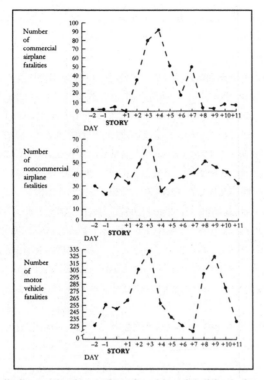

Figure 4.6: Daily fluctuation in number of accident fatalities before, on, and after suicide-story date

Author's Note: As is apparent from these graphs, the greatest danger exists three to four days following the news story's publication. After a brief drop-off, there comes another peak approximately one week later. By the eleventh day, there is no hint of an effect. This pattern across various types of data indicates something noteworthy about secret suicides. Those who try to disguise their imitative self-destruction as accidents wait a few days before committing the act—perhaps to build their courage, to plan the incident, or to put their affairs in order. Whatever the reason for the regularity of this pattern, we know that travelers' safety is most severely jeopardized three to four days after a suicide-murder story and then again, but to a lesser degree, a few days later. We would be well advised, then, to take special care in our travels at these times.

nationally publicized incident of this sort spawned an average of thirty more incidents. Since then, we've been jolted by the specter of contagious mass murders, occurring first in workplace settings and then, incredibly, in our children's schools.

As an example, immediately following the bloody rampage by two Littleton, Colorado, high school students, police responded to scores of similar threats, plots, and attempts by troubled students. Two of the attempts proved "successful": a fourteen-year-old in Taber, Alberta, and a fifteen-year-old in Conyers, Georgia, killed or wounded a total of eight classmates within ten days of the Littleton massacre. In the week following the horrendous murder-suicide attack at Virginia Tech University, media across the country reported more murder-suicides of their own, including three in Houston alone. It is instructive that after the Virginia Tech massacre, the next such event of similar size occurred not at a high school but at a university, Northern Illinois University. More recently, mass shootings have spread to entertainment venues—theaters and night clubs.

Events of this magnitude demand explanation. Some common thread needs to be identified to make sense of them. In the case of workplace murders, observers noticed how often the killing fields were the backrooms of US post offices. So the finger of blame was pointed at the "intolerable strains" of the US postal environment—so much so that a new label emerged, "going postal," for an act of stress-fueled workplace violence. As for the school-based slaughter, commentators remarked on an odd commonality: nearly all the affected schools were located in rural or suburban communities rather than in the ever-simmering cauldrons of inner-city neighborhoods. So, this time, the media instructed us as to the "intolerable strains" of growing up in small town or suburban America. By these accounts, the stressors of US post-office environments and of small-town American life created the explosive reactions of those who worked and lived there. The explanation is straightforward: similar social conditions create similar responses.

But you and I have been down the "similar social conditions" road before in trying to understand anomalous patterns of fatalities. Recall how Phillips considered the possibility that a set of common social conditions in a particular environment might explain a rash of suicides there? It wasn't a satisfactory explanation for the suicides; and I don't think it is a satisfactory account for the murder sprees either. Let's see if we can locate a better alternative by first trying to regain contact with reality: the "intolerable strains" of working at the post office or of living in rural/suburban America?! Compared to working in the coal mines or living on the gang-ruled, mean streets of inner cities? Come on. Certainly the environments where the mass slaying occurred have their tensions. But they appear no more severe (and often less severe) than many other environments where such incidents have not taken place. No, the similar social conditions theory doesn't offer a plausible account.

Then what does? I'd nod right at the principle of social proof, which asserts that people, especially when they are unsure of themselves, follow the lead of similar others. Who is more similar to a disgruntled postal employee than another disgruntled postal employee? And who is more similar to troubled small-town American teenagers than other troubled small-town American teenagers? It is a regrettable constant of modern life that many people live their lives in psychological pain. How they deal with the pain depends on numerous factors, one of which is a recognition of how others *just like them* have chosen to deal with it. As we saw in Phillips's data, a highly publicized suicide prompts copycat suicides from similar others—from *copies* of the cat. I believe the same can be said for a highly publicized multiple murder.

As is the case for suicide stories, media executives need to think deeply about how and how prominently to present reports of killing sprees. Such reports are not only riveting, sensational, and newsworthy but also malignant—as considerable research indicates that they possess a contagious character.

Monkey Island

Work like Phillips's helps us appreciate the awesome influence of peer-suasion. Once the enormity of that force is recognized, it becomes possible to understand perhaps the most spectacular act of deadly group compliance of modern times—the mass suicide at

Figure 4.7: "Malfunctioning Copier"
Five minutes before the start of school on May 20, 1999, fifteen-year-old Thomas ("TJ") Solomon opened fire on his classmates, shooting six of them before he was stopped by a heroic teacher. In struggling to comprehend the underlying causes, we must recognize the effect on him of the publicity surrounding a year-long string of similar incidents—first in Jonesboro, Arkansas; then in Springfield Oregon; then in Littleton, Colorado; and then, just two days earlier, in Taber, Alberta. As one of his friends declared in response to the question of why distraught students were suddenly turning murderous at school, "Kids like TJ are seeing it and hearing it all the time now. It's like the new way out for them" (Cohen, 1999).

AP Photo/John Bazemore

Jonestown, Guyana. Certain crucial features of the event deserve review.

The People's Temple was a cultlike organization based in San Francisco that drew its recruits from the city's poor. In 1977, the Reverend Jim Jones—the group's undisputed political, social, and spiritual leader—moved the bulk of the membership with him to a jungle settlement in Guyana, South America. There, the People's

Temple existed in relative obscurity until November 18, 1978, when Congressmen Leo R. Ryan of California (who had gone to Guyana to investigate the cult), three members of Ryan's fact-finding party, and a cult defector were murdered as they tried to leave Jonestown by plane. Convinced that he would be arrested and implicated in the killings and that the demise of the People's Temple would result, Jones sought to control the end of the Temple in his own way. He gathered the entire community around him and issued a call for each person's death in a unified act of self-destruction.

The first response was that of a young woman who calmly approached the now infamous vat of strawberry-flavored poison, administered one dose to her baby, one to herself, and then sat down in a field, where she and her child died in convulsions within four minutes. Others followed steadily in turn. Although a handful of Jonestowners escaped and a few others are reported to have resisted, the survivors claim that the great majority of the 910 people who died did so in an orderly, willful fashion.

News of the event shocked the world. The broadcast media and the papers provided a barrage of reports, updates, and analyses. For days, conversations were full of such topics as "How many have they found dead now?"; "A guy who escaped said they were drinking the poison like they were hypnotized or something"; "What were they doing down in South America, anyway?"; and "It's so hard to believe. What caused it?"

"What caused it?"—the critical question. How are we to account for this most astounding of compliant acts? Various explanations have been offered. Some focused on the charisma of Jim Jones, a man whose style allowed him to be loved like a savior, trusted like a father, and treated like an emperor. Other explanations pointed to the kind of people who were attracted to the People's Temple. They were mostly poor and uneducated individuals who were willing to give up their freedoms of thought and action for the safety of a place where all decisions would be made for them. Still other explanations emphasized the quasi-religious nature of the People's Temple, in which unquestioned faith in the cult's leader was assigned highest priority.

No doubt each of these features of Jonestown has merit in explaining what happened there; but I don't find them sufficient. After all, the world abounds with cults populated by dependent people who are led by a charismatic figure. What's more, there has never been a shortage of this combination of circumstances in the past. Yet virtually nowhere do we find evidence of an event even approximating the Jonestown incident among such groups. There must have been something else that was critical.

One especially revealing question gives us a clue: If the community had remained in San Francisco, would Reverend Jones's suicide command have been obeyed? A highly speculative question to be sure, but the expert most familiar with the People's Temple had no doubt about the answer. Dr. Louis Jolyon West, then chairman of psychiatry and biobehavioral sciences at UCLA and director of its neuropsychiatric unit, was an authority on cults who had observed the People's Temple for eight years prior to the Jonestown deaths. When interviewed in the immediate aftermath, he made what strikes me as an inordinately instructive statement: "This wouldn't have happened in California. But they lived in total alienation from the rest of the world in a jungle situation in a hostile country."

Although lost in the welter of commentary following the tragedy, West's observation, together with what we know about the principle of social proof, seems to me important to a satisfactory understanding of the compliant suicides. To my mind, the single act in the history of the People's Temple that most contributed to the members' mindless compliance that day occurred a year earlier with the relocation of the Temple to a jungled country of unfamiliar customs and people. If we are to believe the stories of Jim Jones's malevolent genius, he realized fully the massive psychological impact such a move would have on his followers. All at once, they found themselves in a place they knew nothing about. South America, and the rain forests of Guyana, especially, were unlike anything they had experienced in San Francisco. The environment—both physical and social—into which they were dropped must have seemed dreadfully uncertain.

Ah, uncertainty—the right-hand man of the principle of social proof. We have already seen that when people are uncertain, they look to the actions of others to guide their own. In the alien, Guyanese environment, then, Temple members were particularly ready to follow the lead of others. As we have also seen, it is others of a special kind whose behavior will be most unquestioningly followed: similar others. Therein lies the awful beauty of Reverend Jones's relocation strategy. In a country such as Guyana, there were no similar others for a Jonestown resident but the people of Jonestown itself.

What was right for a member of the community was determined to a disproportionate degree by what other community members—influenced heavily by Jones—did and believed. When viewed in this light, the terrible orderliness, the lack of panic, the sense of calm with which these people moved to the vat of poison seems more comprehensible. They hadn't been hypnotized by Jones; they had been convinced—partly by him but, more importantly, by peer-suasion—that suicide was correct conduct. The uncertainty they surely felt upon first hearing the death command must have caused them to look around them to identify the appropriate response.

It is worth particular note that they found two impressive pieces of social evidence, each pointing in the same direction. First was the initial set of their compatriots, who quickly and willingly took the poison drafts. There will always be a few such fanatically obedient individuals in any strong leader-dominated group. Whether, in this instance, they had been specially instructed beforehand to serve as examples or whether they were just naturally the most compliant with Jones's wishes is difficult to know. No matter; the psychological effect of the actions of those individuals must have been potent. If the suicides of similar others in news stories can influence total strangers to kill themselves, imagine how enormously more compelling such an act would be when performed without hesitation by one's neighbors in a place such as Jonestown.

The second source of social evidence came from the reactions of the crowd itself. Given the conditions, I suspect what occurred was a large-scale instance of the pluralistic-ignorance effect. Each Jonestowner looked to the actions of surrounding individuals to assess the situation and—finding calmness because everyone else, too, was surreptitiously assessing rather than reacting—"learned" that patient turn-taking was the correct behavior. Such misinterpreted, but nonetheless convincing, social evidence would be expected to result precisely in the ghastly composure of the assemblage that waited in the tropics of Guyana for businesslike death.

From my perspective, most attempts to analyze the Jonestown incident have focused too much on the personal qualities of Jim Jones. Although he was without question a man of rare dynamism, the power he wielded strikes me as coming less from his remarkable personal style than from his understanding of fundamental psychological principles. His real genius as a leader was his realization of the limitations of individual leadership. No leader can hope to persuade, regularly and single-handedly, all members

Figure 4.8: Tidy rows of businesslike death
Bodies lay in orderly rows at Jonestown, displaying the most spectacular act of compliance of our time.
© Bettmann/CORBIS

of the group. A forceful leader can reasonably expect, however, to persuade some sizable proportion of group members. Then, the raw information that a substantial number of fellow group members has been convinced can, by itself, convince the rest. Thus, the most influential leaders are those who know how to arrange group conditions to allow the principle of social proof to work in their favor.

It is in this that Jones appears to have been inspired. His master-stroke was the decision to move the People's Temple community from urban San Francisco to the remoteness of equatorial South America, where the combination of uncertainty and exclusive similarity would make the principle of social proof operate for him as perhaps nowhere else. There, a settlement of a thousand people, much too large to be held in persistent sway by the force of one man's personality, could be changed from a following into a herd. As slaughterhouse operators have long known, the mentality of a herd makes it easy to manage. Simply get some members moving in the desired direction and the others—responding not so much to the lead animal as to those immediately surrounding them—will peacefully and mechanically go along. The powers of the amazing Reverend Jones, then, are probably best understood not in terms of his dramatic personal style but in terms of his profound appreciation of the power of peer-suasion.

Although not nearly as harrowing, other kinds of evidence reveal the notable force of places inhabited by comparable others. An analysis of factors that impact the market share of national brands revealed that passage of time had surprisingly little influence on brands' performance, less than 5 percent over three years. Geography, on the other hand, made an enormous difference. The strongest influence on market share, 80 percent, was due to geographical region. People's brand choices moved in line with the choices of those like them, around them. The effects of distinct regions were so large that the researchers questioned the concept and relevance of "national brands." Marketing managers might want to consider decentralized strategies targeting separate regions to a greater extent than they currently do, as research indicates people are regionally similar on attitudes, values, and personality traits—probably due to contagion effects.[13]

The Big Mistake

Arizona, where I live, calls itself the Grand Canyon State, after the renowned, awe-evoking tourist site on its northern edge that resembles nothing less than an upside-down mountain range. Other natural marvels also exist within the state's borders. One, the Petrified Forest National Park, is a geologic wonder featuring hundreds of petrified logs, shards, and crystals formed 225 million years ago during the Late Triassic period. Environmental conditions at the time—stream water carrying fallen trees and silica-infused volcanic sediment—combined to bury the logs and replace their organic interiors with quartz and iron oxide that turned them into spectacular, multicolored fossils.

The park's ecology is both robust and vulnerable. It is characterized by stout stone structures weighing several tons and, simultaneously, by its susceptibility to harm from visitors, who are all-too-frequently guilty of handling, displacing, and stealing petrified rock shards and crystals from the forest floor. Although the first two of these behaviors seem minor, they are distressing for park researchers who study the trees' ancient patterns of movement in order to identify the precise locations where they were deposited. Still, it's the theft that forms an ongoing, fundamental threat to the park and is of greatest concern. In reaction, park managers have placed a huge sign at the entrance to the site requesting visitors to refrain from removing fossils.

A while ago, one of my former graduate students decided to explore the park with his fiancée, whom he described as the most honest person he'd ever known—someone who had never failed to replace a paper clip or rubber band she'd borrowed. Yet as the couple read the large "no theft please" sign at the park entrance, something in its wording provoked her to respond so entirely out of character that it left her partner stunned. Within its plea, the sign declared:

YOUR HERITAGE IS BEING VANDALIZED EVERY DAY
BY THEFT LOSSES OF PETRIFIED WOOD OF 14 TONS
A YEAR, MOSTLY A SMALL PIECE AT A TIME.

Whereupon, the scrupulously honest new visitor whispered, "We'd better get ours, too."

What was it about the sign's wording that transformed an honorable young woman into an environmental criminal scheming to loot a national treasure?! Readers of this chapter won't have to look far afield for the answer. It was the force of social proof, woefully mispurposed. The wording contained a mistake, a big mistake, often made by public-service communicators. To mobilize the public against an undesirable activity, they bemoan it as regrettably frequent. For instance, in a long-running print ad titled "Gross National Product," the US Forest Service mascot, Woodsy Owl, proclaimed "This year Americans will produce more litter and pollution than ever before." In Arizona, the Department of Transportation stacked roadside litter collected each week in "Towers of Trash" along highways for all to see. And in a six-week-long series titled "Trashing Arizona," the state's largest newspaper asked residents to submit for publication photos of the most littered locations in the region.

The mistake is not unique to environmental programs. Information campaigns stress that alcohol and drug use is intolerably high, that adolescent suicide rates are alarming, and that too few citizens exercise their right to vote. Although these claims may be both true and well intentioned, the campaigns' creators have missed something critically important: within the lament "Look at all the people who are doing this undesirable thing" lurks the undercutting message "Look at all the people who *are* doing it." In trying to alert the public to the widespread nature of a problem, public-service communicators can end up making it worse, via the process of social proof.

To explore the possibility, my colleagues and I conducted an experiment at the Petrified Forest National Park, where on average 2.95 percent of visitors per day engaged in fossil theft. We alternated a pair of signs in high-theft areas of the park. With the signs, we wanted to register the effects of antitheft pleas informing visitors either that a lot of others steal from the park or that few others do. Echoing the message of the park's entrance signage, our first type of sign urged visitors not to take wood, while depicting a scene showing three thieves in action. It nearly tripled theft, to 7.92 percent. Our other sign also urged visitors not to take wood; but contrary to the counterproductive social-proof message, it communicated that few people steal from the park by depicting a lone thief. This sign, which marginalized thievery (rather than normalizing it), reduced larceny to 1.67 percent.

Other studies have documented the unintended negative consequences of trying to move people away from a detrimental action by lamenting its frequency. After an education program in which several young women described their eating disorders, participants came to show increased disorder symptoms themselves. After a suicide-prevention program informing New Jersey teenagers of the alarming number of adolescents who take their own lives, participants became more likely to see suicide as a potential

Figure 4.9: Rock 'n' Stole(n)
Although these visitors to the Petrified National Forest Park are taking photos of petrified-wood fossils, some visitors take the fossils.
Courtesy of US Forest Service

solution to their own problems. After exposure to an alcohol-use deterrence program in which participants role-played resisting their peers' repeated urgings to drink, junior high school students came to believe that alcohol use was more common among their peers than they'd originally thought. In short, persuasive communications should avoid employing information that can normalize undesirable conduct.

There is another sense in which the tendency to decry the extent of unwanted activity may be misguided. Often the activity is not widespread at all. It only comes to seem that way by virtue of a vivid and impassioned presentation of its unwelcome occurrence. Take, for example, the theft of fossils from the Petrified Forest National Park. Typically, few visitors remove pieces of wood from the park—fewer than 3 percent. Still, because the park receives two-thirds of a million visitors per year, the number of thefts is collectively high. Therefore, the site's entrance signage was correct in stating that large numbers of fossils were being carried away by visitors. Even so, by focusing guests solely on the fact that thefts did occur with destructive regularity, park officials may have erred twice. Not only did they set the force of social proof against park goals (by implying, wrongly, that thievery was pervasive), but they missed the opportunity to harness the force of true social proof on behalf of park goals (by failing to label honorable guests as the great majority). Big mistake.[14]

A Social-Proof Shortcut (to the Future)

There's a second form of social-proof mistake, which I've often made myself. It's occurred when I've delivered stage presentations on the principle and an audience member or two asked an important set of questions: "What do I do if I don't have social proof to point to? What if I have a little-known startup company or I have a new product with nothing impressive to talk about in the way of market share or sales numbers or general popularity to this point? What should I do then?" I always responded by saying, "Well, you certainly shouldn't lie about the lack of social proof; instead, use one of the other principles you might have going for you, such as authority or liking. Scarcity might be a good one."

Recent research indicates that my advice to steer clear of social-proof evidence if it is not fully present is mistaken. Rather than relying only on evidence of *existing* social proof, a communicator can do at least as well by relying on evidence of *future* social proof.

Researchers have identified a consequential quirk in human perception. When we notice a change, we expect the change will likely continue in the same direction when it appears as a trend. This simple presumption has fueled every financial-investment bull market and real-estate bubble on record. Observers of a succession of increasing valuations project them into the future in the form of further escalations. Gamblers who have experienced a few consecutive wins imagine they're on a hot streak and the next gamble will generate yet another win. Amateur golfers such as me can attest to the same phenomenon: after seeing our scores in the previous two outings improve, we expect—against all odds and personal histories—we'll improve in the next. Indeed, people believe that trends will continue in the same trajectory for a wide variety of behaviors, including those undertaken by only a minority of others—such as conserving water, choosing meatless meals, and completing surveys for no payment.

In keeping with the Big Mistake, when informed that only a minority performs one of these desired actions, people are reluctant to perform it themselves. However, if they learn that within the minority, more and more others are engaging in it, they jump on the bandwagon and begin enacting the behavior too. Let's take as an example the study I am most familiar with—because I was a member of the research team. We invited university students to participate in an experiment in which some subjects read information indicating that only a minority of their fellow students conserved water at home. For another sample of our subjects, the information indicated that although only a minority of other students conserved water, the percentage doing so had been increasing over the past two years. Finally, there was a third sample of subjects (in our control condition), who didn't get any information about water conservation.

At this point, we were ready to test, secretly, how these three kinds of circumstances would affect our subjects' water usage. All were asked to participate in a consumer-preference test of a new brand of toothpaste, which they were to rate after brushing their teeth at a sink in the laboratory. They didn't know we had equipped the sink with a meter that recorded how much water they used while testing the new toothpaste.

The results were clear. Compared to the control-condition subjects—who, remember, hadn't received any information about the home water-conservation efforts of their fellow students—those who'd learned that only a minority of their peers tried to conserve, now used even more water; in fact, they used the most water of all. They could do the math, recognizing that if only a minority bothered to conserve, then the majority *didn't* bother; so they followed the majority's lead. But this pattern was reversed by the subjects who learned that, even though only a minority of peers conserved, the number who did conserve was increasing. So informed, these subjects used the least water of all while brushing their teeth.

How can we make sense of this last finding? It seems to run counter to the studies we've covered showing people prefer to conform to the majority. Does it indicate that when a trend is visible, social proof is no longer all-powerful? Yes and no. Existing levels of social proof may no longer win, but another version of the concept may. Because we assume they will continue in the same direction, trends don't just tell us where others' behaviors have been and are now; we think they also tell us where others' behaviors will be. Thus, trends give us access to a special and potent form of social proof—future social proof. When we asked the subjects in our study to predict the percentage of their colleagues who would conserve water at home over the next six years, only those who learned of the trend toward conservation predicted an increase. Indeed, many of these subjects predicted that by then, conservation would be the majority behavior.

On the basis of these results, I no longer give my previous advice to individuals who have something new to offer that possesses limited current popularity. Rather than urging them away from the principle of social proof and toward one of the other principles, I ask if over a reasonable period of time, they have honest evidence of growing popularity. If yes, I recommend making *that* fact the central feature of their messaging—because, as their audiences will presume, such evidence will be an indicator of genuine worth and future popularity. If over that reasonable period of time, the answer is no, I ask them to rethink what they have to offer and, perhaps, change it significantly or step away from it altogether.[15]

Defense

I began this chapter with an account of a small restaurant-menu adjustment and moved on to descriptions of successful Bible sales tactics, and then to stories of murder and suicide—all explained by the principle of social proof. How can we expect to defend ourselves against a lever of influence that pervades such a vast range of behavior? The difficulty is compounded by the realization that most of the time, we don't want to guard against the information that social proof provides. The evidence it offers about the way we should act is usually valid and valuable. With it, we can sail confidently through countless decisions without having to investigate the detailed pros and cons of each. In this sense, the principle equips us with a wonderful kind of autopilot device not unlike that aboard most aircraft.

Yet there are occasional, but real, problems with autopilots. Those problems appear whenever the flight information locked into the control mechanism is wrong. In these instances, we will be taken off course. Depending on the size of the error, the consequences can be severe; but because the autopilot afforded by the principle of social proof is more often an ally than an antagonist, we can't be expected to want simply to disconnect it. Thus, we are faced with a classic problem: how to make use of a piece of equipment that simultaneously benefits and imperils our welfare.

Fortunately, there is a way out of the dilemma. Because the disadvantages of autopilots arise principally when incorrect data have been put into the control system, our best defense against these disadvantages is to recognize when the data are in error. If we can become sensitive to situations in which the social-proof autopilot is working with inaccurate information, we can disengage the mechanism and grasp the controls when necessary.

Sabotage

There are two types of situations in which incorrect data cause the principle of social proof to give us poor counsel. The first occurs when the social evidence has been purposely falsified. Invariably these situations are manufactured by exploiters intent on creating the impression—reality be damned—that a multitude is performing the way the exploiters want us to perform. The "sweetened" laughter of TV-comedy-show audiences is one variety of faked data of this sort, but there is a great deal more, and much of the fakery is detectible.

Because autopilots can be engaged and disengaged at will, we can cruise along trusting in the course steered by the principle of social proof until we recognize that inaccurate data are being used. Then we can take the controls, make the necessary correction for the misinformation, and reset the autopilot. With no more cost than vigilance for counterfeit social evidence, we can protect ourselves. Recall, for instance, from the eBox in our first chapter that phony online product reviews have features that, together, allow us to spot them as fakes—lack of detail, a lot of first-person pronouns, and more verbs than nouns.

There are additional sources of information we can use to protect ourselves. For instance, in 2019, the US Federal Trade Commission successfully charged the cosmetics company Sunday Riley Skincare with posting positive customer reviews of its products that were actually authored by its employees, who were pressured to do so by company leaders. The case was widely publicized in various media. We would do well to be attentive to news reports of such fabricated product reviews.

Let's take another example. A bit earlier, I noted the proliferation of average-person-on-the-street ads, in which a number of ordinary people are depicted as speaking glowingly of a product, often without knowing their words are being recorded. See a humorous example in figure 4.10. As would be expected according to the principle of social proof, these testimonials from "average people like you and me" make for quite effective advertising campaigns. They have always included a relatively subtle kind of distortion: we hear only from those who like the product; as a result, we get an acutely biased picture of the amount of social support for it.

A cruder and more unethical sort of falsification can also appear. Commercial producers may not bother to get genuine testimonials, merely hiring actors, instead, to play the roles of average people testifying in an unrehearsed fashion to an interviewer. Sony Pictures Entertainment was caught arranging for employees to portray fans lauding the Sony film *The Patriot* for an ad that then aired on network TV. The employees' boss excused the deceptive practice of hiring actors or employees for testimonials as

Dave Barry
Knight Ridder
News Service

Recently I was watching TV, and a commercial came on, and the announcer, in a tone of voice usually reserved for major developments in the reaction to this announcement is: "Huh?" Meaning: "What does Angela Lansbury have to do with Bufferin?" But this commercial featured several consumers who had apparently been stopped at random on the street, and *every one of them had a question for Angela Lansbury about Bufferin*. Basically, what they asked was, "Miss Lansbury, is Bufferin a good product that I should purchase, or what?"

These consumers seemed very ear-Persian Gulf, said, "Now consumers can ask Angela Lansbury their questions about Bufferin!"

As a normal human, the natural nest. It was as if they had been going around for months wringing their hands and saying, "I have a question about Bufferin! If only I could ask Angela Lansbury!"

What we are seeing here is yet another example of a worsening problem that has been swept under the rug for too long in this nation: The invasion of Consumers From Mars. The *look* like humans, but they don't *act* like humans, and they are taking over.

Figure 4.10: Just your average Martian on the street (Consumers from Mars)
Knight Ridder News Service

"an industry standard," not unique to Sony Pictures or even the entertainment business. A different version of this kind of fakery occurs when actors are hired to line up outside movie theaters or shops to simulate widespread interest. An illustration of how profiteers sometimes resort to contrived popularity for their products occurred at the launch of the first Apple iPhone in Poland. The advertising agency responsible for the Apple account admitted to falsifying social proof in favor of their client's phone. How did they do it? According to a spokesperson, on the day of the launch, "We created fake queues [of paid actors] in front of twenty stores around the country to drum up interest."

I know that whenever I encounter or learn of an influence attempt of this sort, it sets off in me a kind of alarm with a clear directive: *Attention! Attention! May be bad social proof in this situation. Temporarily disconnect autopilot.* It's easy to do. We need only make a conscious decision to be alert to evidence of biased social evidence. We can cruise along until the exploiters' deception is spotted, at which time we can pounce.

And we should pounce with a vengeance. I am speaking of more than simply ignoring the misinformation, although this defensive tactic is certainly called for. I am speaking of aggressive counterattack. Whenever possible, we ought to sting those responsible for the rigging of social evidence. We should purchase no products associated with biased "unrehearsed interview" commercials or artificial waiting lines. Moreover, each manufacturer of the items should receive a forceful comment on its website explaining our response and recommending that they discontinue use of the advertising or marketing agency that produced so deceptive a presentation of their product.

Although we don't always want to trust the actions of others to direct our conduct—especially in situations important enough to warrant our personal investigation of the pros and cons, or ones in which we are experts—we do want to be able to count on others' behavior as a source of valid information in a wide range of settings. If we find in such settings we cannot trust the information to be valid because someone has tampered with the evidence, we ought to be ready to strike back. In such instances, I personally feel driven by more than an aversion to being duped. I bristle at the thought of being pushed into an unacceptable corner by those who would use one of my hedges against the decisional overload of modern life against me. And I get a genuine sense of righteousness by lashing out when they try. If you are like me—and many others like me—so should you.

Looking Up

In addition to the times when social proof is deliberately faked, there is another time when the principle will regularly steer us wrong. In such an instance, an innocent, natural error will produce snowballing social proof that pushes us to an incorrect decision. The pluralistic-ignorance phenomenon, in which everyone at an emergency sees no cause for alarm, is one example of this process.

The best illustration I know, however, comes from Singapore, where a few years ago, for no good reason, customers of a local bank began drawing out their money in a frenzy. The run on this respected bank remained a mystery until much later, when researchers interviewing participants discovered its peculiar cause: An unexpected bus strike had created an abnormally large crowd waiting at the bus stop in front of the bank that day. Mistaking the gathering for a crush of customers poised to withdraw their funds from a failing bank, passersby panicked and got in line to withdraw their deposits, which led more passersby to do the same. Soon after opening its doors, the bank was forced to close to prevent a complete crash.

This account provides certain insights into the way we respond to social proof. First, we seem to assume that if a lot of people are doing the same thing, they must know something we don't. Especially when we are uncertain, we are willing to place an enormous amount of trust in the collective knowledge of the crowd. Second, quite frequently the crowd is mistaken because its members are not acting on the basis of any superior information but are reacting, themselves, to the principle of social proof.

There is a lesson here: an autopilot device, like social proof, should never be trusted fully; even when no saboteur has slipped misinformation into the mechanism, it can sometimes go haywire by itself. We need to check the machine from time to time to be sure that it hasn't worked itself out of sync with the other sources of evidence in the situation—the objective facts, our prior experiences, and our own judgments.

Fortunately, this precaution requires neither much effort nor much time. A quick glance around is all that is needed. And this little precaution is well worth it. The consequences of single-minded reliance on social evidence can be frightening. For instance, a masterful analysis by aviation-safety researchers has uncovered an explanation for the misguided decisions of many pilots who crashed while attempting to land planes after weather conditions had become dangerous. The pilots hadn't focused sufficiently on the mounting physical evidence for aborting a landing. Rather, they had focused too much on the mounting social evidence for attempting one— the fact that each in a line of prior pilots had landed safely.

Certainly, a flier following a line of others would be wise to glance occasionally at the instrument panel and weather conditions outside the window. In the same way, we need to look up and around periodically whenever we are locked into the evidence of the crowd. Without this simple safeguard against misguided social proof, our outcomes might well run parallel to those of the unfortunate pilots and the Singapore bank: crash.[16]

READER'S REPORT 4.6

From a former racetrack employee

I became aware of one method of faking social evidence to one's advantage while working at a racetrack. In order to lower the odds and make more money, some bettors are able to sway the public to bet on bad horses.

Odds at a racetrack are based on where the money is being bet. The more money on a horse, the better the odds. Many people who play the horses have surprisingly little knowledge of racing or betting strategy. Thus, especially when they don't know much about the horses in a particular race, a lot of times they'll simply bet the favorite. Because tote boards display up-to-the-minute odds, the public can always tell who the current favorite is. The system that a high roller can use to alter the odds is actually quite simple. The guy has in mind a horse he feels has a good chance of winning. Next he chooses a horse that has long odds (say, 15 to 1) and doesn't have a realistic chance to win. The minute the mutuel windows open, the guy puts down $100 on the inferior horse, creating an instant favorite whose odds on the board drop to about 2 to 1.

Now the elements of social proof begin to work. People who are uncertain of how to bet the race look to the tote board to see which horse the early bettors have decided is a favorite, and they follow. A snowballing effect now occurs as other people continue to bet the favorite. At this point, the high roller can go back to the window and bet heavily on his true favorite, which will have better odds now because the "new favorite" has been pushed down the board. If the guy wins, the initial $100 investment will have been worth it many times over.

I've seen this happen myself. I remember one time a person put down $100 on a pre-race 10 to 1 shot, making it the early favorite. The rumors started circulating around the track—the early bettors knew something. Next thing you know, everyone (myself included) was betting on this horse. It ended up running last and had a bad leg. Many people lost a lot of money. Somebody came out ahead, though. We'll never know who. But he is the one with all the money. He understood the theory of social proof.

Author's note: Once again we can see that social proof is most telling for those who feel unfamiliar or unsure in a specific situation and who, consequently, must look outside of themselves for evidence of how best to behave there. In this case, we can see how profiteers will take advantage of the tendency.

SUMMARY

- The principle of social proof states that one important means people use to decide what to believe or how to act in a situation is to examine what others are believing or doing there. Powerful such effects have been found among both children and adults and in such diverse activities as purchase decisions, charity donations, and phobia remission. The principle of social proof can be used to stimulate a person's compliance with a request by communicating that many other individuals (the more, the better) are or have been complying with it. Therefore, simply pointing to the popularity of an item elevates its popularity.

- Social proof is most influential under three conditions. The first is uncertainty. When people are unsure, when the situation is ambiguous, they are more likely to attend to the actions of others and to accept those actions as correct. In ambiguous situations, for instance, the decisions of bystanders to offer emergency aid are much more influenced by the actions of other bystanders than when the situation is a clear-cut emergency.

- A second condition under which social proof is most influential involves "the many": people are more inclined to follow the lead of others in proportion to the others' number. When we see multiple others performing an action, we become willing to follow because the action appears to be more (1) correct/valid, (2) feasible, and (3) socially acceptable.

- The third optimizing condition for social-proof information is similarity. People conform to the beliefs and actions of comparable others, especially their peers—a phenomenon we can call peer-suasion. Evidence for the powerful influence of the actions of similar others can be seen in suicide statistics compiled by sociologist David Phillips. The statistics indicate that after highly publicized suicide stories, other troubled individuals, who are similar to the suicide-story victim, decide to kill themselves. An analysis of the mass-suicide incident at Jonestown, Guyana, suggests the group's leader, Reverend Jim Jones, used both of the factors of uncertainty and similarity to induce a herdlike suicide response from the majority of the Jonestown population.

- The social-proof BIG MISTAKE many communicators make is to decry the frequency with which an unwanted behavior (drinking and driving, teen suicide, etc.) is performed, as a way to stop it. However, they don't recognize that within the lament "Look at all the people who are doing this undesirable thing" lurks the undercutting message "Look at all the people who *are* doing it," which can make it worse via the principle of social proof.

- When communicators are not able to use existing social proof because their idea, cause, or product does not have widespread support, they may be able to harness the power of *future* social proof by honestly describing trending support, which audiences expect to continue.

- Recommendations to reduce our susceptibility to faulty social proof include cultivating a sensitivity to counterfeit evidence of what similar others are doing and recognizing that the actions of similar others should not form the sole basis for our decisions.

CHAPTER 5

AUTHORITY

DIRECTED DEFERENCE

Follow an expert.

—Virgil

Not long ago, a South Korean journalist asked me, "Why is behavioral science so hot now?" There are several reasons, but one involves the operation of behavioral-science research divisions in government, business, legal, medical, educational, and nonprofit organizations around the globe. At last count, about six hundred such research units had taken root in less than ten years—each dedicated to testing how behavioral-science principles could be used to solve various real-world problems. The first of these, the British government's Behavioural Insights Team (BIT), has been particularly productive.

For instance, to examine how to increase giving to deserving causes, especially among individuals whose financial resources allowed for substantial contributions, BIT researchers compared the success of techniques to motivate investment bankers to donate a full day's salary to charity. At the London offices of a large international bank, bankers received a request to provide such a donation in support of the bank's fundraising campaign for a pair of charities (Help a Capital Child and Meningitis Research UK). One set of bankers, in the control group, got the request in a standard letter asking for the financial commitment; it produced 5 percent compliance. A second set got a visit from an admired celebrity who endorsed the program; this liking-based tactic bumped up compliance to 7 percent. A third sample encountered a reciprocity-based appeal; upon entering the building, they were approached by a volunteer who first gave each a packet of sweets and then asked them to participate in the program, which boosted compliance to 11 percent. A fourth group received an appeal that incorporated the principle of authority in the form of a letter from their CEO extolling the importance of the program to the bank as well as the value of the selected charities to society; it generated 12 percent compliance. A final sample got a blend of the reciprocity and authority influence principles—the gift of sweets from a volunteer plus the CEO's personalized letter. Compliance soared to 17 percent.

It's evident that the CEO's letter, both singly and together with another principle of influence, had significant effects on the decision to donate. That was so because the source of the letter possessed two kinds of authority in recipients' minds. First, he was *in* authority—a boss who could affect recipients' outcomes within the organization and who, because his letter was personalized to them, would know whether they complied with his request. In addition, he was *an* authority on the topic, who had displayed his knowledge of the value of the campaign to the bank as well as the inherent worth of the specified charities. When a requester holds that combination of authority traits, we can expect compliance to be notable. Indeed, it's a combination that explains one of the most astounding patterns of responding in the history of behavioral science.[1]

Suppose while leafing through your local newspaper, you notice an ad for volunteers to take part in a "study of memory" being done in the psychology department of a nearby university. Suppose further that finding the idea of such an experiment intriguing, you contact the director of the study, Professor Stanley Milgram, and make arrangements to participate in an hour-long session. When you arrive at the laboratory suite, you meet two men. One is the researcher in charge of the experiment, clearly evidenced by the gray lab coat he wears and the clipboard he carries. The other is a volunteer like yourself who seems quite average in all respects.

After initial greetings and pleasantries are exchanged, the re-

searcher begins to explain the procedures to be followed. He says
the experiment is a study of how punishment affects learning and
memory. Therefore, one participant will have the task of learning
pairs of words in a long list until each pair can be recalled perfectly;
this person is to be called the Learner. The other participant's job
will be to test the Learner's memory and to deliver increasingly
strong electric shocks for every mistake; this person will be designated the Teacher.

Naturally, you get a bit nervous at this news. Your apprehension
increases when, after drawing lots with your partner, you find that
you are assigned the Learner role. You hadn't expected the possibility of pain as part of the study, so you briefly consider leaving.
But, no, you think, there's plenty of time for that if need be, and,
besides, how strong a shock could it be?

After you have had a chance to study the list of word pairs, the
researcher straps you into a chair and, with the Teacher looking
on, attaches electrodes to your arm. More worried now about the
effect of the shock, you inquire into its severity. The researcher's
response is hardly comforting. He says, although the shocks can
be extremely painful, they will cause you "no permanent tissue
damage." With that, the researcher and Teacher leave you alone
and go to the next room where the Teacher asks you the test questions through an intercom system and delivers electric punishment for every wrong response.

As the test proceeds, you quickly recognize the pattern the
Teacher follows: he asks the question and waits for your answer
over the intercom. Whenever you err, he announces the voltage of
the shock you are about to receive and pulls a lever to deliver the
punishment. The most troubling thing is the shock increases by
15 volts with each error you make.

The first part of the test progresses smoothly. The shocks are
annoying but tolerable. Later on, though, as you make more mistakes and the shock voltages climb, the punishment begins to hurt
enough to disrupt your concentration, which leads to more errors
and ever more disruptive shocks. At the 75-, 90-, and 105-volt levels,
the pain makes you grunt audibly. At 120 volts, you exclaim into

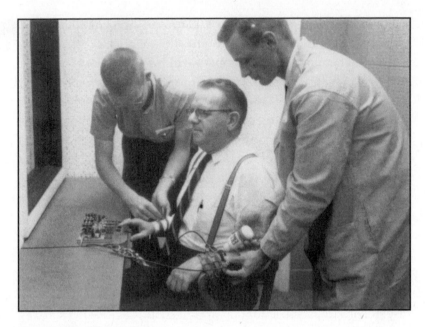

Figure 5.1: The Milgram study

The photo shows the Learner ("victim") being strapped into a chair and fitted with electrodes by the lab-coated experimenter and the true subject, who would become his Teacher.

Credit: Stanley Milgram, 1968; distributed by the Pennsylvania State University Media Sales

the intercom that the shocks are *really* starting to hurt. You take one more punishment with a groan and decide that you can't take much more pain. After the Teacher delivers the 150-volt shock, you shout back into the intercom, "That's all. Get me out of here. Get me out of here, please. Let me out."

Instead of the assurance you expect from the Teacher, that he and the researcher are coming to release you, he merely gives you the next test question to answer. Surprised and confused you mumble the first answer to come into your head. It's wrong, of course, and the Teacher delivers a 165-volt shock. You scream at the Teacher to stop, to let you out. He responds only with the next test question— and with the next slashing shock—when your frenzied answer is incorrect. You can't hold down the panic any longer, the shocks are so strong now they make you writhe and shriek. You kick the wall, demand to be released, and beg the Teacher to help you. However, the test questions continue as before and so do the dreaded shocks—in searing jolts of 195, 210, 225, 240, 255, 270, 285, and 300 volts. You realize that you can't possibly answer the questions correctly now, so you shout to the Teacher you won't answer his questions anymore. Nothing changes; the Teacher interprets your failure to respond as an incorrect response and sends another bolt. The ordeal continues in this way until, finally, the power of the shocks stuns you into near-paralysis. You can no longer cry out, no longer struggle. You can only feel each terrible electric bite. Perhaps, you think, this total inactivity will cause the Teacher to stop. There can be no reason to continue this experiment, but he proceeds relentlessly, calling out the test questions, announcing the horrid shock levels (above 400 volts now), and pulling the levers. What must this man be like, you wonder in confusion. Why doesn't he help me? Why won't he stop?

The Power of Authority Pressure

For most of us, the previous scenario reads like a bad dream. To recognize how nightmarish it is, we should understand, in most respects, it is real. There was such an experiment—actually, a whole series—run by a psychology professor named Milgram in which participants in the Teacher role delivered continued, intense, and dangerous levels of shock to a kicking, screeching, pleading Learner. Only one major aspect of the experiment was not genuine. No real shock was delivered; the Learner, who repeatedly cried out in agony for mercy and release, was not a true subject but an actor who only pretended to be shocked. The actual purpose of Milgram's study, then, had nothing to do with the effects of punishment on learning and memory. Rather, it involved an entirely different question: When ordered by an authority figure, how much suffering will ordinary people be willing to inflict on an entirely innocent other person?

The answer is unsettling. Under circumstances mirroring precisely the features of the "bad dream," the typical Teacher was willing to deliver as much pain as was available to give. Rather than yield to the pleas of the victim, about two-thirds of the subjects in Milgram's experiment pulled every one of the thirty shock switches in front of them and continued to engage the last switch (450 volts) until the researcher ended the experiment. More unsettling still, almost none of the forty subjects in this study quit his job as Teacher when the victim first began to demand his release, nor later when he began to beg for it, nor even later when his reaction to each shock had become, in Milgram's words, "definitely an agonized scream."

These results surprised everyone associated with the project, Milgram included. In fact, before the study began, he asked groups of colleagues, graduate students, and psychology majors at Yale University (where the experiment was performed) to read a copy of the experimental procedures and estimate how many subjects would go all the way to the last (450-volt) shock. Invariably, the answers fell in the 1–2 percent range. A separate group of thirty-nine psychiatrists predicted that only about one person in a thousand would be willing to continue to the end. No one, then, was prepared for the behavior pattern the experiment actually produced.

How can we explain that disturbing pattern? Perhaps, as some have argued, it has to do with the fact that the subjects were all males, who are known as a group for their aggressive tendencies, or that the subjects didn't recognize the potential harm that such high shock voltages could cause or that the subjects were a freakish collection of moral cretins who enjoyed the chance to inflict misery. There is good evidence against each possibility. First, a later experiment showed subjects' sex was irrelevant to their willingness to give all the shocks to the victim; female Teachers were just as likely to do so as were the males in Milgram's initial study.

Another experiment investigated the explanation that subjects weren't aware of the potential physical danger to the victim. In this experiment, the victim was instructed to announce that he had a heart condition and declare his heart was being affected by the shock: "That's all. Get me out of here. I told you I had heart trouble. My heart's starting to bother me. I refuse to go on. Let me out." The results were the same; 65 percent carried out their duties faithfully through to the maximum shock.

Finally, the explanation that Milgram's subjects were a sadistic bunch not at all representative of average citizens has proved unsatisfactory as well. The people who answered Milgram's newspaper ad to participate in his "memory" experiment represented a standard cross section of ages, occupations, and educational levels within our society. What's more, later on, a battery of personality scales showed these people to be quite normal psychologically, with not a hint of psychosis as a group. They were, in fact, just like you and me; or, as Milgram likes to term it, they *are* you and me. If he is right that his studies implicate us in their grisly findings, the unanswered question becomes an uncomfortably personal one, "What could make *us* do such things?"

Milgram was sure he knew the answer. It has to do, he said, with a deep-seated sense of duty to authority. According to Milgram, the real culprit in the experiments was subjects' inability to defy the wishes of the boss, the lab-coated researcher who urged and, if necessary, directed the subjects to perform their duties, despite the emotional and physical mayhem they were causing.

The evidence supporting Milgram's obedience-to-authority explanation is strong. First, it is clear that without the researcher's directives to continue, subjects would have ended the experiment quickly. They hated what they were doing and agonized over their victim's anguish. They implored the researcher to let them stop. When he refused, they went on, but in the process they trembled, they perspired, they shook, they stammered protests and additional pleas for the victim's release. Their fingernails dug into their flesh; they bit their lips until they bled; they held their heads in their hands; some fell into fits of uncontrollable nervous laughter. An outside observer to Milgram's initial experiment described one subject.

I observed a mature and initially poised businessman enter the laboratory smiling and confident. Within 20 minutes he was reduced

to a twitching, stuttering wreck, rapidly approaching a point of
nervous collapse. He constantly pulled on his earlobe and twisted
his hands. At one point he pushed his fist into his forehead and
muttered: "Oh, God, let's stop it." And yet he continued to respond
to every word of the experimenter and obeyed to the end.

In addition to these observations, Milgram has provided even
more convincing evidence for the obedience-to-authority interpretation of his subjects' behavior. In a later experiment, he had the
researcher and the victim switch scripts so that the researcher told
the Teacher to stop delivering shocks to the victim, while the victim insisted bravely that the Teacher continue. The result couldn't
have been clearer; 100 percent of the subjects refused to give one
additional shock when it was merely the fellow subject who demanded it. The identical finding appeared in another version in
which the researcher and fellow subject switched roles so that it
was the researcher who was strapped into the chair and the fellow
subject who ordered the Teacher to continue—over the protests
of the researcher. Again, not one subject touched another shock
lever.

The extreme degree to which subjects in Milgram's studies
obeyed the commands of authority was documented in one more
variation of the basic experiments. In this case, the Teacher faced
two researchers who issued contradictory instructions; one ordered the Teacher to terminate the shocks when the victim cried
out for release, while the other maintained that the experiment
should go on. These conflicting directives reliably produced what
may have been the project's only humor: in tragicomic befud-
dlement and with eyes darting from one researcher to another,
subjects would beseech the pair to agree on a single command to
follow: "Wait, wait. Which is it going to be? One says stop, one says
go. . . . Which is it!?" When the researchers remained at logger-
heads, the subjects tried frantically to determine the *bigger* boss.
Failing this route to obedience with "the" authority, every subject
followed his better instincts and ended the shocks. As in the other
experimental variations, such a result would hardly be expected

had subjects' motivations involved some form of sadism or neurotic aggressiveness.

To Milgram's mind, evidence of a chilling phenomenon emerged repeatedly from his accumulated data. "It is the extreme willingness of adults to go to almost any lengths on the command of an authority that constitutes the chief finding of the study." There are sobering implications of this finding for those concerned about the ability of another form of authority—government—to extract frightening levels of obedience from ordinary citizens. Furthermore, the finding tells us something about the sheer strength of authority pressures in controlling our behavior. After witnessing Milgram's subjects squirming and sweating and suffering at their task, could anyone doubt the power of the force that held them there?

For those whose doubts remain, the story of S. Brian Willson might prove instructive. On September 1, 1987, to protest US shipments of military equipment to Nicaragua, Mr. Willson and two other men stretched their bodies across the railroad tracks leading out of the Naval Weapons Station in Concord, California. The protesters were confident their act would halt the scheduled train's progress that day, as they had notified navy and railroad officials of their intent three days before. But the civilian crew, which had been given orders not to stop, never slowed the train, despite being able to see the protesters six hundred feet ahead. Although two of the men managed to scramble out of harm's way, Mr. Willson was not quick enough to avoid being struck and having both legs severed below the knee. Because navy medical corpsmen at the scene refused to treat him or allow him to be taken to the hospital in their ambulance, onlookers—including Mr. Willson's wife and son—were left to try to staunch the flow of blood for forty-five minutes until a private ambulance arrived.

Amazingly, Mr. Willson, who served four years in Vietnam, did not blame either the crewmen or the corpsmen for his misfortune; he pointed his finger, instead, at a system that constrained their actions through the pressure to obey. "They were just doing what I did in 'Nam. They were following orders that are part of an insane policy. They're the fall guys." Although the crew members shared Mr. Willson's assessment of them as victims, they did not share his magnanimity. In what is perhaps the most remarkable aspect of the incident, the train crew filed a legal suit against *him*, requesting punitive damages for the "humiliation, mental anguish, and physical stress" they suffered because he hadn't allowed them to carry out their orders without cutting off his legs. To the credit of the US judicial system, the suit was swiftly dismissed.[2]

The Allures and Dangers of Blind Obedience

Whenever we are faced with a potent motivator of human action, it is natural to expect that good reasons exist for the motivation. In the case of obedience to authority, even a brief consideration of human social organization offers justification aplenty. A multilayered and widely accepted system of authority confers an immense advantage upon a society. It allows the development of sophisticated structures for production of resources, trade, defense, expansion, and social control that would otherwise be impossible. At the opposite end, the alternative is anarchy, a state hardly known for its beneficial effects on cultural groups and one that social philosopher Thomas Hobbes assures us would render life "solitary, poor, nasty, brutish, and short." Consequently, we are trained from birth to believe that obedience to proper authority is right and disobedience is wrong. The message fills the parental lessons, schoolhouse rhymes, stories, and songs of our childhood and is carried forward in the legal, military, and political systems we encounter as adults. Notions of submission and loyalty to legitimate rule are accorded much value in each.

Religious instruction contributes as well. The first book of the Bible describes how failure to obey the ultimate authority resulted in the loss of paradise for Adam, Eve, and the rest of the human race. Should that particular metaphor prove too subtle, just a bit further into the Old Testament, we can read—in what might be the closest biblical representation of the Milgram experiment—the respectful account of Abraham's willingness to plunge a dagger through the heart of his young son because God, without any explanation, ordered it. We learn in this story that the correctness of an action is to be judged not by such considerations as apparent senselessness, harmfulness, injustice, or traditional moral standards but by the mere command of a higher authority. Abraham's tormented ordeal was a test of obedience, and he—like Milgram's subjects, who perhaps had learned an early lesson from him—passed.

Stories such as those of Abraham and Milgram's subjects can tell us a great deal about obedience's power and value in our culture. In another sense, however, the stories may be misleading. We rarely agonize to such a degree over the pros and cons of authority demands. In fact, our obedience frequently takes place in a *click, run* fashion with little or no conscious deliberation. Information from a recognized authority can provide us a valuable shortcut for deciding how to act in a situation.

After all, as Milgram suggested, conforming to the dictates of authority figures has always had genuine practical advantages for us. From the start, these people (parents, teachers) knew more than we did, and we found taking their advice beneficial—partly because of their greater wisdom and partly because they controlled our rewards and punishments. As adults, the same benefits persist for the same reasons, though the authority figures are now employers, judges, and government leaders. Because their positions speak of greater access to information and power, it makes sense to comply with the wishes of properly constituted authorities. It makes so much sense that we often do so when it makes no sense at all.

This paradox is, of course, the same one that attends all major levers of influence. In this instance, once we realize that obedience to authority is mostly rewarding, it is easy to allow ourselves the convenience of automatic obedience. The simultaneous blessing and curse of such blind obedience is its mechanical character. We don't have to think, therefore we don't. Although such mindless obedience leads us to appropriate action most of the time, there will be conspicuous exceptions because we are reacting, not thinking.

Let's take an example from one facet of our lives in which authority pressures are visible and strong: medicine. Health is enormously important to us. Thus, physicians, who possess great knowledge and influence in this vital area, hold the position of respected authorities. In addition, the medical establishment has a clearly terraced power-and-prestige structure. The various kinds of health workers well understand the level of their jobs in this structure, and they well understand, too, that MDs sit at the top. No one may overrule a doctor's judgment in a case, except, perhaps, another doctor of higher rank. Consequently, a long-established tradition of automatic obedience to doctors' orders has developed among healthcare staffs.

The worrisome possibility arises that when a physician makes a clear error, no one lower in the hierarchy will *think* to question it—precisely because once a legitimate authority has given an order, subordinates stop thinking in the situation and start reacting. Mix this kind of *click, run* response into a complex hospital environment and mistakes are inevitable. Indeed, according to the Institute of Medicine, which advises the US Congress on health policy, hospitalized patients can expect to experience at least one medication error per day. Other statistics are equally frightening: Annual deaths in the United States from medical errors exceed those of all accidents, and, worldwide, 40 percent of primary- and outpatient-care patients are harmed by medical errors each year.

Errors in the medicine patients receive can occur for a variety of reasons. However, in their book *Medication Errors: Causes and Prevention*, Temple University professors of pharmacy Michael Cohen and Neil Davis attribute much of the problem to the mindless deference given to the "boss" of a patient's case: the attending physician. According to Cohen, "In case after case, patients, nurses, pharmacists, and other physicians do not question the prescription." Take, for example, the classic case of the "rectal earache" reported by Cohen and Davis in an interview. A physician ordered ear drops to be administered to the right ear of a patient suffering pain and infection there. Instead of writing out completely the location "Right ear" on the prescription, the doctor abbreviated it so that the instructions read "place in R ear." Upon receiving the prescription, the duty nurse promptly put the required number of ear drops into the patient's anus.

Obviously, rectal treatment of an earache made no sense, but neither the nurse nor the patient questioned it. The important lesson of this story is that in many situations in which a legitimate authority has spoken, what would otherwise make sense is irrelevant. In these instances, we don't consider the situation as a whole but attend and respond to only one aspect of it.[3]

READER'S REPORT 5.1

From a Texas-based university professor

I grew up in an Italian ghetto in Warren, Pennsylvania. I occasionally return home to visit family and the like. As in most places these days, most of the small Italian specialty stores are gone, having been replaced by larger supermarkets. My mother sent me supermarket shopping during a visit for a load of canned tomatoes, and I noticed that nearly all the cans of Furmano Italian diced tomatoes were sold out. Searching a bit on the shelf immediately beneath the almost empty shelf, I found a full shelf (loaded, even!) of Furman brand diced tomatoes. Looking closely at the labels, I realized that Furmano is Furman. The company had just added an "o" to its name when distributing some of its products. I guess it must be because, when selling Italian-style foods, you're perceived as more of an authority if your name ends in a vowel.

Author's note: The man who wrote this report also commented that the added letter *o* was doing double duty as an influence trigger in that store. The *o* not only lent authority to the manufacturer, in an "Italian ghetto," but also engaged the liking principle by making the company appear similar to its customers.

Whenever our behaviors are governed in such an unthinking manner, we can be confident there will be compliance professionals trying to take advantage. Returning to the field of medicine, we can see that advertisers have frequently commissioned the respect accorded doctors in our culture by hiring actors to play the roles of doctors speaking on behalf of a product. My favorite example is a TV commercial for Vicks Formula 44 cough medicine featuring the actor Chris Robinson, who had a key role as Dr. Rick Webber in the popular daytime TV drama *General Hospital* during the 1980s. The commercial, which began with the line "I'm not a doctor, but I play one on TV" and then offered Robinson's advice to a young mother regarding the benefits of Vicks Formula 44, was very successful, lifting sales substantially.

Why should the ad prove so effective? Why on earth would we take the actor Chris Robinson's word for the health benefits of a cough suppressant? Because—as the advertising agency that hired him knew—he was associated in the minds of viewers with Dr. Rick Webber, the role he had long played in a highly rated TV series. Objectively, it doesn't make sense to be swayed by the comments of a man we know to be just an actor who played a doctor; but, practically, because of an unthinking response to felt authority, that man moved the cough syrup.

As a testament to the effectiveness of the ad, in 1986, when Chris Robinson was imprisoned for tax evasion, rather than end its run, the Vicks brand simply recast the ad with another famous daytime TV actor (Peter Bergman), who played a physician on the *All My Children* series. Except for the switch of TV doctors, the ad was a near duplicate of the earlier version. It's notable that, despite his criminal conviction, Chris Robinson was allowed to continue his role on *General Hospital* under a prison work-release program. How can we account for the grace he was afforded that would have been denied almost any other actor serving a prison sentence? Perhaps it was that he played a doctor on TV.

Figure 5.2: I'm not a doctor, but I play one in medication ads.
Photos such as this of actors impersonating doctors appear regularly in ads for medications that treat headaches, allergies, colds, and other everyday health problems. The depictions, which display many of the accessories of physicians—lab coat, stethoscope, and the like—are permitted as long as the ad doesn't explicitly proclaim the actor to be a doctor.
Credit: iStockphoto

Connotation, Not Content

From the time I first saw it, the most intriguing feature of the Vicks Formula 44 ad for me was its ability to use the authority principle without providing a real authority. The veneer was enough, which tells us something important about our unthinking reactions to authorities. When in a *click, run* mode, we are often as vulnerable to the symbols of authority as to its substance.

Several of these symbols reliably trigger our compliance. Consequently, they are employed widely by compliance professionals who are short on substance. Con artists, for example, drape themselves with the titles, clothing, and trappings of authority. They love nothing more than to emerge elegantly dressed from a fine automobile and introduce themselves to their prospective "marks" as Doctor or Judge or Professor or Commissioner Someone. They understand that when so adorned, their chances for compliance are greatly increased. Each of these three symbols of authority—titles, clothes, and trappings—has its own story and is worth a separate look.

Titles

Titles are simultaneously the most difficult and the easiest symbols of authority to acquire. To earn a title normally takes years of work and achievement. Yet it is possible for somebody who has put in none of the effort to adopt the mere label and receive automatic deference. As we have seen, actors in TV commercials and con artists do it successfully all the time.

I recently talked with a friend—a faculty member at a well-known eastern university—who provided a telling illustration of the way our actions are frequently more influenced by the title than by the essence of the person claiming it. My friend travels quite a bit and often finds himself chatting with strangers in bars, restaurants, and airports. He says he has learned through much experience during these conversations never to use the title of professor. When he does, he finds that the tenor of the interaction changes immediately. People who have been spontaneous and interesting conversation partners until that moment become respectful, accepting, and dull. His opinions that before might have produced a lively exchange now generate extended (and highly grammatical) statements of accord. Annoyed and slightly bewildered by the phenomenon—because, as he says, "I'm still the same guy they've been talking to for the last thirty minutes"—my friend now regularly lies about his occupation in such situations.

What an eccentric shift from the typical pattern in which certain compliance practitioners lie about titles they *don't* truly have. Either way, such practiced dishonesty makes the same point about the ability of a symbol of authority to influence behavior. I wonder whether my professor friend—who is somewhat short—would be so eager to hide his title if he knew that besides making strangers more accommodating, it also makes them see him as taller. Studies investigating the way authority status affects perceptions of size have found that prestigious titles lead to height distortions. In one experiment conducted on five classes of Australian college students, a man was introduced as a visitor from Cambridge University in England. However, his status at Cambridge was represented differently in each of the classes. To one class, he was presented as a student; to a second class, a demonstrator; to another, a lecturer; to yet another, a senior lecturer; to a fifth, a professor. After he left the room, the class was asked to estimate his height. With each increase in status, the same man grew in perceived height by an average of a half-inch, so that he was seen as two and a half inches taller as the "professor" than as the "student." Other studies found both that after winning an election, politicians became taller in the eyes of the citizenry and that after being assigned the high-status role of "manager" (versus "employee") on a task, college students rated *themselves* as taller.

Because we see size and status as related, it is possible for certain individuals to benefit by substituting the former for the latter. In some animal societies, in which the status of an animal is

Figure 5.3: High expectations
Cartoonist Scott Adams's depiction is not so far-fetched. Research indicates that tall men earn more than their shorter contemporaries and are more likely to rise to positions of leadership (Chaiken, 1986; Judge & Cable, 2004). And although there are no data directly to the point, I'd guess Adams is right about silver hair too.

Dilbert: Scott Adams. Distributed by United Features Syndicate, Inc.

assigned on the basis of dominance, size is an important factor in determining which animal will achieve which status level in the group. Usually, in combat with a rival, the larger and more powerful animal wins. To avoid the harmful effects to the group of such physical conflict, many species employ methods that frequently involve form more than fight. The two rivals confront each other with showy aggression displays that invariably include size-enhancing tricks. Various mammals arch their backs and bristle their coats; fish extend their fins and puff themselves up; birds unfurl and flutter their wings. Often this exhibition alone is enough to send one of the histrionic warriors into retreat, leaving the contested status position to the seemingly larger and stronger rival.

Fur, fins, and feathers. Isn't it interesting how these most delicate parts can be exploited to give the impression of substance and weight? There are two lessons here. One is specific to the association between size and status: The connection of those features can be profitably employed by individuals who are able to fake the first to gain the appearance of the second. This is precisely why con artists, even those of average or slightly above-average height, commonly wear lifts in their shoes. The other lesson is more general: The outward signs of power and authority may be counterfeited with the flimsiest of materials. Let's return to the realm of titles for an example—one that involves what, in several ways, is the scariest experiment I know.

A group of researchers, composed of doctors and nurses with connections to three midwestern hospitals in the United States, became increasingly concerned with the extent of mechanical obedience to doctors' orders on the part of nurses. It seemed to the researchers that even highly trained and skilled nurses were not using that training or skill sufficiently to check on a doctor's judgment; instead, when confronted with a physician's directives, they would simply defer.

We saw how this process accounted for rectally administered ear drops, but the midwestern researchers took things several steps further. First, they wanted to find out whether such cases were isolated incidents or representative of a widespread phenomenon. Second, they wanted to examine the problem in the context of a serious treatment error: the gross overprescription of an unauthorized drug to a hospital patient. Finally, they wanted to see what would happen if they physically removed the authority figure from the situation and substituted an unfamiliar voice on the phone, offering only the weakest evidence of authority—the claimed title "doctor."

One of the researchers made an identical phone call to twenty-two separate nurses' stations on various surgical, medical, pediatric, and psychiatric wards. He identified himself as a hospital physician and directed the answering nurse to give twenty milligrams of a drug (Astrogen) to a specific ward patient. There were four excellent reasons for the nurse's caution in response to this order: (1) the prescription was transmitted by phone, in direct violation of hospital policy; (2) the medication itself was unauthorized (Astrogen had been neither cleared for use nor placed on the ward's stock list); (3) the prescribed dosage was obviously and dangerously excessive (the medication containers clearly stated that the "maximum daily dose" was only ten milligrams, half of what had been ordered); and (4) the directive was given by a man the nurse had never met, seen, or even talked with on the phone before. Yet after 95 percent of the calls, the nurses went straight to the ward's medicine cabinet, where they secured the ordered dosage of Astrogen, and then started walking to the patient's room to administer the drug. At this point, they were stopped by a secret observer, who revealed the nature of the experiment.

The results are frightening indeed. That 95 percent of regular staff nurses complied unhesitatingly with a patently improper instruction of this sort must give us all as potential hospital patients great reason for concern. The midwestern study showed that mistakes are hardly limited to trivial slips in the administration of harmless ear drops or the like but, rather, extend to grave and dangerous blunders.

In interpreting their unsettling findings, the researchers came to an instructive conclusion:

In a real-life situation corresponding to the experimental one, there would, in theory, be two professional intelligences, the doctor's and the nurse's, working to ensure that a given procedure be undertaken in a manner beneficial to the patient or, at the very least, not detrimental to him [or her]. The experiment strongly suggests, however, that one of these intelligences is, for all practical purposes, nonfunctioning.

It seems, in the face of a physician's directives, the nurses unhooked their "professional intelligences" and moved to a *click, run* form of responding. None of their considerable medical training or knowledge was engaged in the decision of what to do. Instead, because obedience to legitimate authority had always been the most preferred and efficient action in their work setting, they were willing to err on the side of automatic obedience. Moreover, they had traveled so far in this direction that their error came in response not to genuine authority but to its most easily falsified symbol—a bare title.[4]

EBOX 5.1

For five years, a team of security-system hackers launched concerted attacks on the computer networks of nearly one thousand local banks and credit unions in the United States. Their hit rate was spectacular. In 963 of the cases, they were able to pierce the banks' security systems and come away with such items as protected internal documents, loan applications, and customer databases. How did they manage to succeed 96 percent of the time, when banks are intensely on guard with their own sophisticated technological software to detect and prevent digital incursions? The answer is as basic as the method the hackers employed. They didn't penetrate the banks' advanced digital-security-system technology with even more advanced digital technology. In fact, they didn't use digital technology at all. They used human psychology, embodied in the principle of authority.

Because the hackers had no criminal intent—they had been hired by the banks to try to defeat the security systems—we know how they maneuvered to be so effective. Equipping themselves with the accoutrement (uniforms, badges, logos) of fire inspectors, government safety monitors, and pest exterminators, they were admitted to the facilities without appointments, escorted to restricted-access sectors, and left to do their work. However, it wasn't the "work" bank personnel expected. Instead, it involved downloading sensitive programs and data from unattended computers and sometimes carrying data disks, laptops, and even big computer servers out the door as they left. In a newspaper account of the project (Robinson, 2008), Jim Stickley, the hacking team's boss, provided an enlightening lesson, "[This] illustrates something provocative about the way security has changed with the rise of the Internet, which has shifted attention and dollars spent on security toward computer networks and threats from hackers. They've kind of forgotten the basics." In the compliance arena, there's little as basic as deference to authority.

Author's note: Among the authorities allowed admittance to bank facilities were not just the sort who could be considered *in* authority, such as fire inspectors or government safety monitors, but also the sort who could only be considered *an* authority, such as pest-control experts. It's instructive that both forms of authority worked.

Clothes

A second kind of authority symbol that can trigger our mechanical compliance is clothing. Though more tangible than a title, the cloak of authority is every bit as fakeable. Police files bulge with records of con artists whose methods include the quick change. In chameleon style, they adopt the hospital white, priestly black, army green, or police blue the situation requires for maximum advantage. Only too late do their victims realize the garb of authority is hardly its guarantee.

A series of studies by social psychologist Leonard Bickman indicates how difficult it can be to resist requests from figures in authority attire. Bickman's basic procedure was to ask passersby on the street to comply with some odd request (for example, to pick up a discarded paper bag or stand on the other side of a bus-stop sign). In half of the instances, the requester, a young man, was dressed in ordinary street clothes; in the rest, he wore a security guard's uniform. Regardless of the type of request, many more people obeyed the requester when he was wearing the guard costume. Similar results were obtained when the requester was female.

In one especially revealing version, the requester stopped pedestrians and pointed to a man standing by a parking meter fifty feet away. The requester, whether dressed normally or as a security guard, always said the same thing to the pedestrian: "You see that guy over there by the meter? He's overparked but doesn't have any change. Give him a dime!" The requester then turned a corner and walked away so that by the time the pedestrian reached the meter, the requester was out of sight. Nonetheless, the power of his uniform lasted, even after he was long gone. Nearly all the pedestrians complied with his directive when he wore the guard costume, but fewer than half did so when he was dressed normally.

It is interesting that, later on, Bickman found college students guessed with some accuracy the percentage of compliance that occurred in the experiment when the requester wore street clothes (50 percent versus the actual 42 percent); yet the students greatly underestimated the percentage of compliance when he was in uniform, 63 percent versus the actual 92 percent.

Less blatant in its connotation than a uniform, but still effective, is another kind of attire that has traditionally indicated authority status in our culture: the business suit. It, too, can evoke a telling form of deference from total strangers. In a study conducted in Texas, researchers arranged for a thirty-one-year-old man to cross the street against the light, against the traffic, and against the law on a variety of occasions. In half of the cases, he was dressed in a freshly pressed business suit and tie; on the other occasions, he wore a work shirt and trousers. The researchers watched from a distance and counted the number of pedestrians who followed the man across the street; three-and-a-half times as many people swept into traffic behind the suited jaywalker.

Noteworthy is that the two types of authority apparel shown by these studies to be influential, the guard uniform and the business suit, are combined deftly by con artists in a fraud called the *bank examiner scheme*. The target of the swindle can be anyone, but elderly persons living alone are preferred. The con begins when a man dressed in a properly conservative business suit appears at the door of a likely victim. Everything about the con man's clothing speaks of propriety and respectability. His white shirt is starched, wingtip shoes glow darkly, and suit is classic. The lapels are three inches wide, no more, no less; the cloth is heavy and substantial, even in July; the tones are muted—business blue, business grey, business black.

He explains to his intended victim—perhaps a widow he secretly followed home from the bank a day or two earlier—that he is a professional bank examiner who, in the course of auditing the books of her bank, has found some irregularities. He thinks he has spotted the culprit, a bank officer who is regularly doctoring reports of transactions in certain accounts. He says that the widow's account may be one of these, but he can't be sure until he has hard evidence; therefore, he has come to ask for her cooperation. Would she help by withdrawing her savings so a team of examiners and responsible bank officials can trace the record of the transaction as it passes across the suspect's desk?

Often the appearance and presentation of "bank examiner" are so impressive that the victim never thinks to check on their validity with even a simple phone call. Instead, she drives to the bank, withdraws all her money, and returns home with it to wait with the examiner for word on the trap's success. When the message comes, it is delivered by a uniformed "bank guard" who arrives after closing hours to announce that all is well—apparently the widow's account was not one of those being tampered with. Greatly relieved, the examiner offers gracious thanks and, because the bank is now closed, instructs the guard to return the widow's money to the vault, to save her the trouble of doing so the next day. With smiles and handshakes all around, the guard leaves with the funds while the examiner expresses a few more thanks before he, too, exits. Naturally, as the victim eventually discovers, the "guard" is no more a guard than the "examiner" is an examiner. What they are is a pair of bunco artists who have recognized the capacity of carefully counterfeited uniforms to *click* us into mesmerized compliance with "authority."

READER'S REPORT 5.2

From a Florida-based physician

The title MD carries significantly more authority when placed in the visual context of a white coat. At first, I hated to wear white coats but later in my career came to understand that the garment carries power. On multiple occasions when I started work in a new hospital rotation, I made it a point to wear the white coat. Without fail my transition went smoothly. Interestingly, physicians are highly aware of this and have even created a pecking order assigning medical students the shortest white coats, while residents in training get medium length coats, and attending physicians have the longest white coats. In hospitals where nurses are aware of this hierarchy, they rarely question the orders of "long coats"; but when interacting with "short coats," hospital staffers make alternative medical diagnosis and therapy suggestions openly—and sometimes rudely.

Author's note: This report makes an important point: in hierarchical organizations, not only are those with authority status treated respectfully, but those without such status are often treated disrespectfully. As we saw in the reader's account, and as we will see in the next section, the symbols of status one displays can signal to others which form of treatment seems appropriate.

Trappings

Aside from its function in uniforms, clothing can symbolize another type of status. Finely styled and expensive clothes carry an aura of economic standing and position. Mall shoppers were more willing to comply with a request to participate in an unpaid survey, homeowners contributed more donations to a charity solicitor at their door, and job evaluators gave higher suitability ratings and starting salaries to an applicant if the individual involved was wearing a shirt or sweater showing a prestige designer label. What's more, the differences were strikingly large: 79 percent more compliance with the survey request, 400 percent more frequent donations to charity, and a nearly 10 percent higher starting wage for a job candidate. A separate set of studies offers a reason for the employment-interview results. People judge those dressed in higher quality apparel, even higher quality T-shirts, as more competent than those in lesser quality attire—and the judgments occur automatically, in less than a second.

Other examples of trappings, such as high-priced jewelry and cars, can have similar effects. The car as a status symbol is particularly relevant in the United States, where "the American love affair with the automobile" gives it unusual significance. According to a study done in the San Francisco Bay area, owners of prestige autos receive a special kind of deference from others. The experimenters discovered motorists would wait significantly longer before honking their horns at a new luxury car stopped in front of a green traffic light than at an older economy model. The motorists had little patience with the economy-car driver. Nearly all sounded their horns, and the majority of these did so more than once; two simply rammed into the rear bumper. So intimidating was the aura of the prestige automobile, however, that 50 percent of the motorists waited respectfully behind it, never touching their horns until it moved on after fifteen seconds.

Later the researchers asked college students what they would have done in such situations. Compared to the true findings of the experiment, the students consistently underestimated the time to honk at the luxury car. The male students were especially inaccurate, feeling that they would honk faster at the prestige- than at the economy-car driver; of course, the study itself showed just the opposite. Note the similarity of pattern to many other studies on authority pressures. As in Milgram's research, the midwestern hospital nurses' study, and the security-guard-uniform experiment, people were unable to predict correctly how they or others would react to authority influence. In each instance, the effect of the influence was grossly underestimated. This property of authority status may account for much of its success as a compliance device. Authority influence not only works forcefully on us but does so without our awareness.[5]

READER'S REPORT 5.3

From a financial adviser in Michigan

A big problem in my business is getting clients to change their long-held financial goals and strategies when turns in conditions, like in their personal situations or in the economy, make those moves the right thing to do. After reading the chapter on Authority in your book I switched from just basing my advice to these clients on my own opinion to including the stated opinion of a financial expert on the subject. A lot of times this would be the chief economist of my company which is a big brokerage firm with hundreds of offices around the country. But sometimes it would be a TV expert from one of the financial channels like Bloomberg and CNBC or the author of a published article on the subject. That worked, getting me about

15 percent to 20 percent more agreement than before. But honestly from what I read in your chapter I expected better results. Am I doing something wrong that if corrected would give me stronger results?

Author's note: This is an unusual Reader's Report. For multiple reasons, I rarely respond to appeals for personal advice, which can range from assistance on a college student's influence-related homework to counsel on how to persuade a wayward spouse to end an affair "once and for all." But this reader's request is different, principally because it makes contact with a pair of issues of general relevance to other readers. First, when people such as those the reader is trying to change have a long-standing commitment to particular goals and approaches, it's difficult to get any movement from them at all, so a 15–20 percent improvement in compliance strikes me as pretty good. There will be more to say about this in chapter 7, on commitment and consistency. Second, there *is* something I can recommend to enhance the impact of an expert's advice—multiply it. Audiences trust and follow the advice of a set of experts more than that of any one of them (Mannes, Soll, & Larrick, 2014). Thus, a communicator who does the work of collecting and then pointing to support from multiple experts will be more successful than a communicator who settles for claiming the support of just one.

The Credible Authority

So far, we've seen that being viewed as either in authority or an authority leads to increased compliance. But the first of these types, merely being in charge, has its problems. As a rule, people don't like being ordered to do things. It often generates resistance and resentment. For this reason, most business schools teach prospective managers to avoid "command and control" approaches to leadership and embrace approaches designed to promote willing cooperation. It's in this latter respect that the second type of authority, being viewed as highly informed, is so useful. People are usually happy, even eager, to go along with the recommendations of someone who knows more than they do on the matter at hand.

The potent propensity to follow the lead of an expert is aptly illustrated in a story told by modern-art specialist Michel Strauss of being caught in a bidding war at an auction of a painting by Egon Schiele, a renowned Expressionist. Although the painting was originally estimated to bring between $200,000 and $250,000, Mr. Strauss found himself bidding far above that figure against a well-known Schiele expert, thinking the man knew something he didn't. Finally, at $620,000, Strauss dropped out. When he later asked his rival about the painting, the man confessed he had bid so high only because he thought Strauss knew something *he* didn't. Let's focus, then, on the methods and outcomes of being perceived as *an* authority.

Expertise

Research distinguishes a particularly convincing such authority, the credible one. A credible authority possesses two distinct features in the minds of an audience: expertise and trustworthiness. Because we have already chronicled the ability of expertise to exert significant influence, it's not necessary to review the point extensively. Still, to ensure this first pillar of credibility is given its due, we can register some instructive additional evidence. For example, expertise appears to create a halo effect for those who possess it; a therapist's office with multiple diplomas and professional certifications on the wall produces higher ratings not only of the therapist's proficiency but also of his or her kindness, friendliness, and interest in clients. And *just one* newspaper Op-Ed piece written by an expert has large and lasting influence over readers' opinions—lifting agreement with the expert's opinion among general readers by 20 percentage points in one set of studies; moreover, this was the case irrespective of the sex, age, and political leanings of all readers.

Figure 5.4: Outsourced credibility

The persuasive elements of this ad come entirely from (1) authorities on the topic, thereby affirming their knowledge, (2) who have no allegiance to the company, thereby establishing the trustworthiness of their comments.

Courtesy of Bose Corporation USA

Trustworthiness

Besides wanting our authorities to give us expert information, we want them to be trustworthy sources of the information. We want to believe they are offering their expert advice in an honest and impartial fashion—that is, attempting to depict reality accurately rather than to serve their self-interests.

Whenever I've attended programs designed to teach influence skills, they've stressed that being perceived as trustworthy is an effective way to increase one's influence and that it takes time for that perception to develop. Although the first of these claims remains verified by research, a separate body of research indicates that there is a noteworthy exception to the second. It turns out a communicator can rapidly acquire perceived trustworthiness by employing a clever strategy. Rather than succumbing to the tendency to describe all the most favorable features of a case upfront and reserving mention of any drawbacks until the end of the presentation (or never), a communicator who references a weakness early on is seen as more honest. The advantage of this sequence is that, with perceived truthfulness already in place, when the major strengths of the case are then advanced, the audience is more likely to believe them. After all, they've been conveyed by a trustworthy source, one whose honesty has been established by a willingness to point at not just positive aspects but negative ones as well.

The effectiveness of this approach has been documented in (1) legal settings, where a trial attorney who admits a weakness before the rival attorney points it out is viewed as more credible and wins more often; (2) political campaigns, where a candidate who begins with something positive to say about a rival (such as, "I am sure my opponent has the best of intentions with that proposal, but . . .") gains trustworthiness and voting preferences; and (3) advertising messages, where merchandisers who acknowledge a drawback before highlighting strengths often see large increases in sales. After Domino's "NEW DOMINO'S" campaign of 2009 admitting to the past poor quality of its pizza, sales went sky high; as a consequence, so did Domino's stock price.

The tactic can be particularly successful when the audience is already aware of the weakness; thus, when a communicator mentions it, little additional damage is done, as no new information is added—except, crucially, that the communicator is an honest individual. A job candidate might say to an interviewer holding her résumé, "Although I am not experienced in this field, I am a very fast learner." Or an information-systems salesperson might say to an experienced buyer, "While our setup costs are not the lowest, you'll soon recoup them because of our superior efficiencies."

Warren Buffett, who with his partner Charlie Munger has led the Berkshire Hathaway investment company to astounding levels of growth and worth, is widely recognized as the greatest financial investor of our time. Not content to rest on his expertise laurels, Buffett consistently reminds current and potential stockholders of the other component of credibility he possesses: trustworthiness. Near the start of his annual reports, usually in the first page or two of text, he describes a mistake he's made or a problem the company has encountered during the past year and examines the implications for future outcomes. Rather than burying, minimizing, or papering over difficulties, which seems to be the tack taken all too frequently in other annual reports, Buffett demonstrates that he is, first, fully aware of problems inside the company and, second, fully willing to reveal them. The emergent advantage is that when he then describes the formidable strengths of Berkshire Hathaway, readers are ready to trust in them more deeply than before—because they are coming from a *manifestly* trustworthy communicator.

Perhaps the clearest illustration of Buffett's zeal for demonstrating his transparency by admitting his shortcomings appeared in his annual report of 2016, a banner year in which his company's share-price increase doubled that of the S&P 500 and in which there were no investing missteps to report. What did Buffett do to ensure that evidence of his openness and honesty would remain at top of mind for shareholders? On the report's second page of text, he noted a *previous* year's investing mistake that he described as the "particularly egregious error of acquiring Dexter Shoe for $434 million in 1993. Dexter's value promptly went to zero." Immediately thereafter, he detailed what he'd learned from the fiasco: he had not only misjudged the future worth of Dexter but made the mistake of paying with Berkshire Hathaway stock, something he promised shareholders he would never do again: "Today, I'd rather prep for a colonoscopy than issue Berkshire shares." It's clear to me that Buffett knows more than how to be an impressively successful investor; he knows how to communicate impressively about being an impressively successful investor.[6]

EBOX 5.2

The persuasiveness of online reviews is also influenced by perceived trustworthiness. The Spiegel Research Center at Northwestern

University, which provides information about the effectiveness of marketing communications, published a summary of evidence of the power of online reviews to shape customer behavior (https://spiegel .medill.northwestern.edu/online-reviews/). Among their findings were three directly related to perceived trustworthiness:

- **Five stars is too good to be true.** The more stars assigned to a product, the higher is the likelihood of purchase—but only up to a point. When the average rating moves past the optimal 4.2 to 4.7 range, purchasers become suspicious that the ratings are phony and are less likely to buy.
- **Negative reviews establish credibility.** Consistent with the Center's contention that near-perfect ratings undermine trustworthiness, the presence of a negative review adds credibility to product evaluations. In fact, if a site includes some negative reviews, the conversion rate jumps by 67 percent.
- **Verified buyers are gold as reviewers.** Verified buyers, who have been confirmed to be previous online purchasers (rather than paid reviewers), are viewed as more credible. Accordingly, their presence on a site increases sales measurably.

Author's note: In addition to insights from the Spiegel Research Center, a separate set of researchers (Reich & Maglio, 2020) supported an online reviewer version of Warren Buffett's "mention a prior error" practice. If a reviewer confessed to making a previous mistake in his or her purchasing history, customers were more likely to buy a product recommended by the reviewer.

It is important to recognize what I am *not* suggesting here—that at the start, a marketer or salesperson state, "Before we begin, let me tell you all the things that are wrong with me, my organization, and our products and services." Rather, I am suggesting two things. First, if there is a drawback to be acknowledged, it should be presented relatively early in a message so the credibility it provides will color the rest of the appeal. Second, within a persuasive communication, there is an ideal place for one's strongest argument or feature, which can undercut or overwhelm the downside. It is in the moment immediately following the admission of a shortcoming of one's case when, bolstered by resulting source credibility, the highly favorable element is likely to be processed most deeply and accepted most fully.

Defense

One protective tactic we can use against authority status is to remove its element of surprise. Because we typically misperceive the profound impact of authority (and its symbols) on our actions, we become insufficiently cautious about its presence in compliance situations. A fundamental form of defense against the problem, therefore, is a heightened awareness of authority power. When this awareness is coupled with a recognition of how easily authority symbols can be faked, the benefit is a properly guarded approach to authority-influence attempts.

Sounds simple, right? And in a way it is. A better understanding of the workings of authority influence should help us resist it. Yet there is a perverse complication—the familiar one inherent in all levers of influence. We shouldn't want to resist authority altogether or even most of the time. Generally, authority figures know what they are talking about. Physicians, judges, corporate executives, and the like have typically gained their positions through superior knowledge and judgment. As a rule, their directives offer excellent counsel.

Authorities are frequently experts. In most cases, it would be foolish to try to substitute our less informed judgments for those of an expert, an authority. At the same time, we have seen in settings ranging from street corners to hospitals that it would be foolish to rely on authority direction in all cases. The trick is to recognize without much strain or vigilance when authority directives are best followed and when they are not. Using the twin components of a credible authority—expertise and trustworthiness—as a guide, posing two questions to ourselves can help determine when authority directives should and should not be followed.

Authoritativeness

The first question to ask when confronted with an authority figure's influence attempt is, Is this authority truly an expert? The question focuses our attention on two crucial pieces of information: the authority's credentials and the relevance of those credentials to the topic at hand. By turning to the *evidence* for authority status in this simple way, we avoid the major pitfalls of automatic deference.

Let's reexamine the highly successful Vicks Formula 44 commercial in this light. If, rather than responding to his TV MD association, people had focused on the actor's actual status as an authority, I am confident the commercial would not have had so long and productive a run. Obviously, the TV doctor did not possess a physician's training or knowledge. What he did possess was a physician's *title*, MD. Plainly, it was an empty title, connected to him in viewers' minds through the device of playacting. Everyone knew that; but isn't it fascinating how, when streaming along, what is obvious often doesn't matter unless we pay specific attention to it?

That is why the "Is this authority truly an expert?" question can be so valuable. It moves us effortlessly away from a focus on possibly meaningless symbols toward a consideration of genuine authority credentials. What's more, it forces us to distinguish between relevant and irrelevant authorities. The distinction is easy to forget when the push of authority pressure is combined with the rush of modern life. The Texas pedestrians who bustled into city traffic behind a business-suited jaywalker are prime examples. Even if the man were the business authority his clothes suggested he might be, he was no more an authority on crossing the street than were those who followed him into traffic.

Still, they did follow, as if his classification, authority, overwhelmed the difference between relevant and irrelevant forms. Had they asked themselves whether he represented a true expert in the situation, someone whose actions indicated superior knowledge, I expect the result would have been far different. The same process applies to the TV doctors in the Vicks ads, who were not without expertise. They had long careers with many achievements in a difficult business. But their skills and knowledge were those of actors, not doctors. If, when viewing the famous commercial, we focused on the actor's true credentials, we'd quickly realize he should be no more believed than any other actor claiming that Vicks Formula 44 is an excellent cough suppressant.

In one research project, my colleagues and I demonstrated that training participants to focus on the true credentials of a spokesperson in an ad did, in fact, make them better evaluators of ads they experienced much later. They became not only *less* persuaded by subsequent ads featuring spokespeople with no relevant credentials (an actor, Arnold Schwarzenegger, promoting a type of internet technology, and a game-show host, Alex Trebek, touting the health properties of milk) but also *more* persuaded by spokespeople with relevant credentials (an MD director of a pain institute, recommending a pain reliever, and a CEO, describing his company's years of good experience with a brand of business insurance).

The lesson? To defend ourselves against misleading appeals containing ersatz authorities, we should always ask, Is this authority truly an expert? We shouldn't presume we are too smart to be tricked by mere symbols of authority. Those symbols operate automatically on us. In my team's research, it was only the participants who, recognizing their susceptibility to this automatic process, were able to disrupt it by questioning communicators' *relevant* expertise. And it was only those participants who weren't fooled.

Sly Sincerity

Suppose, though, we are confronted with an authority whom we determine *is* a relevant expert. Before submitting to authority influence, we should ask a second simple question: How truthful can I expect the expert to be? Authorities, even the best informed, may not present their information honestly to us; therefore, we need to consider their trustworthiness in the situation. Most of the time we do. We allow ourselves to be swayed more by experts who seem to be impartial than by those who have something to gain by convincing us; research has shown this to be true around the world and in children as young as second-graders. By wondering how an expert stands to benefit from our compliance, we give ourselves another shield against undue and automatic influence. Even knowledgeable authorities in a field will not persuade us until we are satisfied their messages represent the facts faithfully.

When asking ourselves about an authority's trustworthiness, we should keep in mind the tactic compliance practitioners often use to assure us of their sincerity: they argue somewhat against their own interests. Correctly practiced, this approach can be a subtle yet effective device for "proving" their honesty. Perhaps they will mention a small shortcoming in their position or product. Invariably though, the drawback will be a secondary one that is easily overcome by more significant advantages—Avis: "We're #2. We try harder"; L'Oréal: "We're more expensive, and you're worth it." By establishing their basic truthfulness on relatively minor issues, the compliance professionals who use this practice can then be more believable when stressing the important aspects of their argument.

It's crucial to distinguish between honest and dishonest versions of the practice. There is nothing inherently wrong with a communicator revealing a shortcoming or prior mistake at an early point of the message to reap the rewards of demonstrated truthfulness. Want to turn lemons into lemonade? This is one way. Recall how Warren Buffett, a man of scrupulous integrity, does precisely that near the beginning of his annual reports. Regularly exposing his readers to his authenticity upfront doesn't strike me as a form of trickery. Rather, I see it as illustrating how trustworthy communicators can also be socially intelligent enough to cue warranted trust through prompt, truthful disclosures.

It is against the deceptive use of the practice that we have to be on guard. I have seen one devious version of the maneuver employed to remarkable effect in a place few of us recognize as a compliance setting, a restaurant. It is no secret that because of shamelessly low

Figure 5.5: A spoonful of medicine makes the sugar go down.
Besides its capacity to combat the perception of grade inflation, a weakness can become a strength in a variety of other situations. For example, one study found that letters of recommendation sent to the personnel directors of major corporations produced the most favorable results for job candidates when the letters contained one unflattering comment about the candidate in an otherwise wholly positive set of remarks (Knouse, 1983).

Doonesbury 1994 G. B. Trudeau. Universal Press Syndicate. All rights reserved.

wages, servers in restaurants must supplement their earnings with tips. Leaving the sine qua non of good service aside, the most successful waiters and waitresses know certain tricks for increasing tips. They also know that the larger a customer's bill, the larger the amount of money they are likely to receive in a gratuity. In these two regards, then—building the size of the customer's charge and building the percentage of that charge given as a tip—servers regularly act as compliance agents.

Hoping to find out how they operate, years ago I applied for a position as a waiter at several fairly expensive restaurants. Without experience, though, the best I could do was to land a busboy job that, as things turned out, provided me a propitious vantage point from which to watch and analyze the action. Before long, I realized what the other employees already knew: the most successful waiter in the place was Vincent, who somehow arranged for patrons to order more and tip higher. The other servers were not even close to him in weekly earnings.

I began to linger in my duties around Vincent's tables to observe his technique. I quickly learned his style was to have no single style. He had a repertoire of approaches, each ready for the appropriate circumstances. With a family, he was effervescent, even slightly clownish, directing his remarks as often to the children as to the adults. With a young couple on a date, he became formal and a bit imperious in an attempt to intimidate the young man into ordering and tipping extravagantly. With an older married couple, he retained the formality but dropped the superior air in favor of a respectful orientation to both members of the couple. Should the patron be dining alone, he selected a friendly demeanor—cordial, conversational, and warm.

Vincent reserved the trick of seeming to argue against his own interests for large parties of eight to twelve people. His technique was veined with genius. When it was time for the first person, normally a woman, to order, he went into his act. No matter what she picked, Vincent reacted identically: his brow furrowed, his hand hovered above his order pad, and after looking quickly over his shoulder for the manager, he leaned conspiratorially toward the table to report in hushed tones for all to hear: "I'm afraid that is not as good tonight as it normally is. Might I recommend, instead, the . . . or the . . . ?" (At this point, Vincent suggested a pair of menu items that were slightly less expensive than the dish the patron had selected.) "They are both excellent tonight."

With this single maneuver, Vincent engaged several important principles of influence. First, even those who did not take his suggestions felt Vincent had done them a favor by offering valuable information to help them order. Everyone felt grateful, and consequently, the rule of of reciprocation worked in his favor when it came time to decide on his gratuity.

Besides hiking up the percentage of his tip, Vincent's ploy also placed him in a position to increase the size of the party's order. It established him as an authority on the current stores of the house: he clearly knew what was and wasn't good that night. Moreover— and here is where seeming to argue against his own interests comes in—it proved him to be a trustworthy informant because he recommended dishes slightly *less* expensive than the one originally ordered. Rather than having appeared to try to line his own pockets, he seemed to have the customers' best interests at heart.

To all appearances, Vincent was at once knowledgeable and honest, a combination that gave him great credibility. He was quick to exploit the advantage. When the party had finished giving their food orders, he would say, "Very well, and would you like me to suggest or select wines to go with your meals?" As I watched the scene repeated almost nightly, there was a notable consistency to the customer's reaction—smiles, nods, and, for the most part, general assent.

Even from my vantage point, I could read their thoughts from their faces. "Sure," the customers seemed to say, "You know what's good here, and you're obviously on our side. Tell us what to get." Looking pleased, Vincent, who did know his vintages, would respond with some excellent (and costly) choices. He was similarly persuasive when it came time for dessert decisions. Patrons who otherwise would have passed up the dessert course or shared with a friend were swayed to partake fully by Vincent's rapturous descriptions of the baked Alaska and chocolate mousse. Who, after all, is more believable than a demonstrated expert of proven sincerity?

READER'S REPORT 5.4

From a former CEO of a Fortune 500 company

In a business school class I developed for aspiring CEOs, I teach the practice of acknowledging failure as a way to advance one's career.

One of my former students has taken the lesson to heart by making his role in a high tech company's failure a prominent part of his résumé—detailing on paper what he learned from the experience. Before, he tried to bury the failure, which generated no real career success. Since, he has been selected for multiple prestigious positions.

Author's note: The strategy of taking due responsibility for a failure doesn't just work for individuals. It appears to work for organizations too. Companies that take blame for poor outcomes in annual reports have higher stock prices one year later than companies that don't take the blame have (Lee, Peterson, & Tiedens, 2004).

By combining the factors of reciprocity and credible authority into a single, elegant maneuver, Vincent inflated substantially both the percentage of his tip and the base charge on which it was figured. His proceeds from this ploy were handsome indeed. Notice, though, that much of his profit came from an apparent lack of concern for personal profit. Seeming to argue against his financial interests served those interests extremely well.[7]

SUMMARY

- In the Milgram studies, we see evidence of strong pressures for compliance with the requests of an authority. Acting contrary to their own preferences, many normal, psychologically healthy individuals were willing to deliver dangerous levels of pain to another person because they were directed to do so by an authority figure. The strength of the tendency to obey legitimate authorities comes from systematic socialization practices designed to instill in members of society the perception that such obedience constitutes correct conduct. In addition, it is adaptive to obey the dictates of genuine authorities because such individuals usually possess high levels of knowledge, wisdom, and power. For these reasons, deference to authorities can occur in a mindless fashion as a kind of decision-making shortcut.

- When reacting to authority in an automatic fashion, people have a tendency to do so in response to mere symbols of authority rather than to its substance. Three kinds of symbols effective in this regard are titles, clothing, and trappings such as automobiles. In studies, individuals possessing prestigious forms of one or another of the symbols (and no other legitimizing credentials) were accorded more deference or obedience by those they encountered. Moreover, in each instance, those individuals who deferred or obeyed underestimated the effect of the authority pressures on their behaviors.

- Authority influence flows from being viewed as either *in* authority or *an* authority. But the first of these types, merely being in charge, has its problems. Ordering people to do things often generates resistance and resentment. The second type of authority, being viewed as highly informed, avoids this problem, as people are usually willing to follow the recommendations of someone who knows more than they do on the matter at hand.

- The persuasive effect of being seen as *an* authority is maximized by also being seen as a credible such authority—one perceived as both expert (knowledgeable on the relevant topic) and trustworthy (honest in the presentation of one's knowledge). To establish their trustworthiness, communicators may admit to a (usually minor) shortcoming of their case, which can be swept aside later by the presentation of outweighing strengths.

- It is possible to defend ourselves against the detrimental effects of authority influence by asking two questions: Is this authority truly an expert? and How truthful can we expect this expert to be? The first directs our attention away from symbols and toward evidence for authority status. The second advises us to consider not just the expert's knowledge in the situation but also his or her trustworthiness. With regard to this second consideration, we should be alert to the trust-enhancing tactic in which communicators first provide mildly negative information about themselves. Through this strategy, they create a perception of honesty that makes all subsequent information seem more believable to observers.

CHAPTER 6

SCARCITY

THE RULE OF THE FEW

The way to love anything is to realize that it might be lost.

—G. K. Chesterton

A friend of mine, Sandy, is a highly successful marital-dispute-resolution attorney (read: divorce lawyer). Often she serves as a mediator between divorcing parties who want to come to agreement on the terms of their divorce without the enlarged time, trouble, and expense of a courtroom trial. Before one of Sandy's mediations begins, partners are taken (along with their legal representatives) to separate rooms to avoid the face-reddening, vein-bulging shouting matches that can occur when the contestants are in the same physical space. Each side has already submitted a written proposal to Sandy, who shuttles between the two rooms seeking compromises to produce final terms both partners will sign. She claims the process calls more on her understanding of human psychology than of divorce law. That's why she wondered if, as a psychologist, I could help with a frequently fatal deadlock that surfaces near the very end of many negotiations and is so resistant to compromise that it will sometimes torpedo the entire mediation process and send the couple into divorce court.

The issue on which the deadlock rests can be a major one, such as the terms of a custody and visitation agreement involving the children (or, fought with equivalent ferocity, the St. Bernard); it can also be relatively minor, such as the amount one person would have to pay to buy out the other's portion of a vacation time-share contract. No matter, the combatants dig in their heels and refuse to budge in any meaningful way on this last piece of the agreement, stymying all further progress. I asked Sandy what she normally says to disputants in this situation. She answered that she takes the last offer on the issue from one room to the other, presents it, and says, "All you have to do is agree to this proposal, and we will have a deal." I thought I recognized the problem and suggested a minor wording change to, "We have a deal. All you have to do is agree to this proposal."

Several months later, at a party, Sandy walked up bearing a wide smile and told me the change had been amazingly successful. "It works every time," she declared. Skeptical, I replied, "C'mon, every time?" She put her hand on my arm, and said, "Bob, *every* time."

Although I remain skeptical about its 100 percent success rate—we're talking about behavioral science here, not magic—I was certainly pleased with the effectiveness of my recommended change. Truthfully, though, I wasn't surprised. I had made the suggestion because of two things I knew. One was my awareness of relevant work in behavioral science. For instance, I knew of a study of Florida State University students who, like most undergraduates when surveyed, rated the quality of their campus cafeteria food unsatisfactory. Nine days later, according to a second survey, they had changed their minds. Something had happened to make them like their cafeteria's food significantly better than before. Interestingly, the event that caused them to shift their opinions had nothing to do with the quality of the food service, which had not changed a whit. On the day of the second survey, students had learned that because of a fire, they had *lost* the opportunity to eat at the cafeteria for the next two weeks.

The second relevant piece of knowledge came from an event I had witnessed on a local TV station around the time Sandy asked for assistance. It's become a common sight: in the run-up to the first availability of a new generation of Apple iPhones, long lines of buyers wind around city blocks, some waiting all night in sleeping bags for store doors to open to rush in and get one of the prized phones. On the morning of the launch of the iPhone 5, one of my home city's TV stations sent a reporter to cover the phenomenon. Approaching a woman who had arrived much earlier and was number twenty-three in the queue, the reporter asked how she had spent the many hours she'd been waiting and, specifically, whether she had spent some of that time socializing with those around her. She replied that a lot of time was taken up in conversations regarding the new features of the iPhone 5 and, also, in conversations about one another. In fact, she revealed she had started her wait as number twenty-five in line but had struck up a conversation during the night with number twenty-three— a woman who admired her $2,800 Louis Vuitton shoulder bag. Seizing the opportunity, the first woman proposed and concluded

Figure 6.1: An aye for an i

This man roars out his elation at scoring a new-generation iPhone—something he ensured by waiting all night to be number one in line for the Apple store to open.

Norbert von der Groeben/The Image Works

a trade: "My bag for your spot in line." At the end of the woman's pleased account, the understandably surprised interviewer stammered, "But . . . but . . . why?" and got a telling answer: "Because," the new number twenty-three replied, "I heard that this store didn't have a big supply, and I didn't want to risk *losing* the chance to get one."

I remember her answer causing me to sit up straight when I heard it, because it fit perfectly with the results of long-standing research showing that especially under conditions of risk and uncertainty, people are intensely motivated to make choices designed to avoid *losing* something of value—to a much greater extent than choices designed to *obtain* that thing. Recognizing the uncertainty and risk of failing to secure a highly desired phone, our hopeful buyer number twenty-three confirmed the research and engineered a costly trade to avoid losing a hotly contested and highly desired phone. The general idea of "loss aversion"—that people are more driven by the prospect of losing an item of value than by the prospect of gaining it—is the centerpiece of Nobel laureate Daniel Kahneman's prospect theory, which has been generally supported by studies done in multiple countries and in multiple domains such as business, the military, and professional sports. In the world of business, for example, research has found that managers weigh potential losses more heavily than potential gains in their decisions. The same is true in professional sports, where decision makers deliberate longer in situations involving possible losses than in those involving possible gains; as a result, golfers on the PGA tour spend more time and effort on putts designed to prevent losing a shot to par (avoiding bogies) than on those designed to gain a shot to par (getting birdies).

What was it about these two pieces of knowledge—(1) what scientific research told me about loss aversion and (2) how forcefully I had recently seen it work in an iPhone line—that spurred me to make my specific recommendation to Sandy? The wording change I proposed began by assigning to her clients *possession* of something they wanted, "We have a deal," which they would *lose* if they failed to compromise. Contrast that with Sandy's original approach, in which the desired deal was something only to be gained: "Agree to this proposal, and we will have a deal." Knowing what I knew, the wording adjustment was an easy one for me to suggest.

READER'S REPORT 6.1

From a woman living in Upstate New York

One year I was shopping for Christmas gifts when I ran across a black dress that I liked for myself. I didn't have the money for it because I was buying gifts for other people. I asked the store to please set it aside until I could return on Monday after school with my mom to show her the dress. The store said they couldn't do that.

I went home and told my mom about it. She told me that if I liked the dress, she would loan me the money to get it until I could pay her back. After school on Monday, I went to the store only to find the dress was gone. Someone else had bought it. I didn't know until Christmas morning that while I was in school my mom went to that store and bought the dress I had described to her. Although that Christmas was many years ago, I still remember it as one of my favorites because after first thinking that I'd lost that dress, it became a valued treasure for me to have.

Author's note: It is worth asking what it is about the idea of loss that makes it so potent in human functioning. One prominent theory accounts for the primacy of loss over gain in evolutionary terms. If one has enough to survive, an increase in resources will be helpful but a decrease in those same resources could be fatal. Consequently, it would be adaptive to be especially sensitive to the possibility of loss (Haselton & Nettle, 2006).

Although the loathing of loss is a central feature of scarcity, it's just one of the factors embedded within the principle, which makes a fuller tour worthwhile.

Scarcity: Less Is Best and Loss Is Worst

Almost everyone is vulnerable to the scarcity principle in some form. Collectors of everything from baseball cards to antiques are keenly aware of the principle's influence in determining the worth of an item. As a rule, if an item is rare or becoming rare, it is viewed as more valuable. In fact, when a desirable item is rare or unavailable, consumers no longer base its fair price on perceived quality; instead, they base it on the item's scarcity. When automobile manufacturers limit production of a new model, its worth goes up among potential buyers. Especially enlightening on the importance of scarcity in the collectibles market is the phenomenon of the "precious mistake." Flawed items—a blurred stamp or double-struck coin—are sometimes the most valued of all. Thus, a stamp carrying a three-eyed likeness of George Washington is anatomically incorrect, aesthetically unappealing, and yet highly sought after. There is instructive irony here: imperfections that would otherwise make for rubbish make for prized possessions when they bring along an abiding scarcity.

The more I learn about the scarcity principle—*that opportunities seem more valuable to us when they are less available*—the more I have begun to notice its influence over a whole range of my own actions. I have been known to interrupt an interesting face-to-face conversation to answer the ring of a caller. In such a situation, the caller possesses a compelling feature that my face-to-face partner does not—potential unavailability. If I don't take the call, I might miss it (and the information it carries) for good. Never mind that the first conversation may be highly engaging or important—much more than I could expect of an average phone call. With each unanswered ring, the phone interaction becomes less retrievable. For that reason and for that moment, I want it more than the other conversation.

Figure 6.2: Goosing (demand) by reducing (supply)
It's not uncommon for retailers to announce the lack of an item to fuel future desire for it. The idea is satirized in an old song that mimicked the cries of a local fruit vendor who called out, "Yes, we have no bananas. We have no bananas today." When my grandmother used to sing the lyric to me, I never understood the logic of the vendor's sales tactic. I do now. So, apparently, does Apple's phone division, which is infamous for undersupplying its stores on the day of a launch.
WILEY @2020WILEY INK, LTD. Distributed by Andrews McMeel Syndication

As we have seen, people seem to be more motivated by the thought of losing something than by the thought of gaining something of equal value. For instance, college students experienced much stronger emotions when asked to imagine losses as opposed to equally sized improvements in their romantic relationships; the same was true for their grade-point averages. In the United Kingdom, residents were 45 percent more likely to want to switch to a new energy provider if the change would prevent a loss on their bill as opposed to providing a saving. On tasks, people are more likely to cheat to avoid a loss than to obtain a gain, which can occur in more than just a monetary sense; in one study, team members were 82 percent more willing to cheat to avert a drop in status on the team than to experience an equivalent climb in status. Finally, compared to gains, losses have greater impact on attention (gaze), physiological arousal (heart rate and pupillary dilation), and brain activation (cortical stimulation).

Under conditions of risk and uncertainty, the threat of potential loss plays an especially powerful role in human decision-making.

Health researchers Alexander Rothman and Peter Salovey have applied this insight to the medical arena, where individuals are frequently urged to undergo tests to detect existing illnesses (mammography procedures, HIV screenings, cancer self-examinations). Because such tests involve the risk that a disease will be found and the uncertainty that it will be cured, messages stressing potential losses are most effective. For example, pamphlets advising young women to check for breast cancer through self-examinations are significantly more successful if they state their case in terms of what stands to be lost rather than gained. Even our brains seem to have evolved to protect us against loss in that it is more difficult to short-circuit good decision-making strategies when considering a potential loss than it is when considering a potential a gain.[1]

Figure 6.3: Don't lose to the loss (of vision).

The developers of this ad for a charity foundation that does good work by funding research into age-related macular degeneration were wise to seek to heighten the generosity of afflicted donors by providing free information about how to cope with the disorder (reciprocity) and by depicting moments not to be missed (loss aversion).

Courtesy of Foundation Fighting Blindness

Limited Numbers

With the scarcity principle operating so powerfully on the worth we assign things, it is natural that compliance professionals will do some similar operating of their own. Probably the most straight-forward use of the scarcity principle occurs in the "limited number" tactic in which a customer is informed a certain product is in short supply that cannot be guaranteed to last long. When the impressively successful international trip and hotel booking site Booking.com first included online information about the limited number of a hotel's rooms that were still available at a given price, purchases skyrocketed—to such heights that its customer-service team called the technology office to report what "must be a systems error." There was no error; the increase came from the power of limited numbers to turn shoppers into buyers. During the time I was researching compliance strategies by infiltrating various organizations, I saw the limited-number tactic employed repeatedly in a range of situations: "There aren't more than five convertibles with this engine left in the state. And when they're gone, that's it, 'cause we're not making 'em anymore." "This is one of only two unsold corner lots in the entire development. You wouldn't want the other one; it's got a nasty east-west sun exposure in summer." "You may want to think seriously about buying more than one case today because production is backed way up and there's no telling when we'll get any more in."

READER'S REPORT 6.2

From a woman living in Phoenix, Arizona

I have been using the scarcity principle at a resale shop called Book-man's. They buy/trade used books, music, and toys. I had some characters from the 1990s Richard Scarry children's TV series and I brought them to Bookman's. But, they didn't take any. Then I decided to bring each one there, by itself. Each time, they took it. I have now traded them all in. Scarcity principle!

My dad actually did the same thing on eBay with baseball team shot glasses. He bought a box of 24 for $35 total. Then he sold them individually on eBay. The first one sold for $35, covering his entire cost. He waited a while to offer the next, which sold for $26. He waited even longer and sold the next for $51. Then he got greedy and sold another too soon and only got $22. He learned his lesson. He still has several and is holding on to them to reestablish their scarcity.

Author's note: The wisdom of offering abundant items for sale one at a time recognizes that abundance is the opposite of scarcity and, consequently, presenting an item in abundance reduces its perceived value.

Sometimes the limited-number information was true, sometimes wholly false. In each instance, however, the intent was to convince customers of an item's scarcity and thereby increase its immediate value in their eyes. I developed a grudging admiration for the practitioners who made this simple device work in a multitude of ways and styles. I was most impressed with a particular version that extended the basic approach to its logical extreme by selling a piece of merchandise at its scarcest point—when it seemingly could no longer be had. The tactic was played to perfection in one appliance store I investigated, where 30 to 50 percent of the stock was regularly listed on sale. Suppose a couple in the store seemed moderately interested in a certain sale item. There are all sorts of cues that tip off such interest—a closer-than-normal examination of the appliance, a casual look at any instruction booklets associated with the appliance, and discussions held in front of the appliance. After observing the couple so engaged, a salesperson might approach and say, "I see you're interested in this model here. But, unfortunately, I sold it to another couple not more than twenty minutes ago. And I believe it was our last one."

The customers' disappointment registers unmistakably. Because of its lost availability, the appliance suddenly becomes more attractive. Typically, one of the customers asks if there is any chance that an unsold model still exists in the store's back room or warehouse or other location. "Well," the salesperson allows, "that is possible, and I'd be willing to check. But do I understand that this is the model you want, and if I can get it for you at this price, you'll take it?" Therein lies the beauty of the technique. In accord with the scarcity principle, the customers are asked to commit to buying the appliance when it looks least available and therefore most desirable. Many customers do agree to purchase at this singularly vulnerable time. Thus, when the salesperson (invariably) returns with the news that an additional supply of the appliance has been found, it is also with a pen and sales contract in hand. The information that the desired model is in good supply may actually make some customers find it less attractive again, although by then the business transaction has progressed too far for most people to back out. The purchase decision made and committed to publicly at an earlier point still holds. They buy.

When I speak to business groups about the scarcity principle, I stress the importance of avoiding the use of such tricks as providing false limited-number information. In response, I regularly get a version of the question "But what if we don't have a limited supply of what we offer. What if we can deliver as much as the market demands? How can *we* use the power of scarcity?" The solution is to recognize that scarcity applies not only to the count of items but also to the traits or elements of the items. First, identify a feature of your product or service that is unique or so uncommon that it can't be obtained elsewhere at the same price or at all. Then, market honestly on the basis of that feature and the attendant benefits that will be lost if it is missed. If the item doesn't have a single such feature, it may well possess a unique combination of features that can't be matched by competitors. In that case, the scarcity of that unique *set* of features can be marketed honestly.

Limited Time

The city of Mesa, Arizona, is a suburb in the Phoenix area where I live. Perhaps the most notable features of Mesa are its sizable Mormon population—next to Salt Lake City, the largest in the world—and a huge Mormon temple located on exquisitely kept grounds in the city's center. Although I had appreciated the landscaping and architecture from a distance, I had never been interested enough in the temple to go inside, until the day I read a newspaper article that told of a special inner sector of Mormon temples to which no one has access but faithful members of the Church. Even potential converts must not see it; however, there is one exception to the rule. For a few days immediately after a temple is newly constructed, nonmembers are allowed to tour the entire structure, including the otherwise restricted section.

The newspaper story reported that the Mesa temple had been recently refurbished and the renovations had been extensive enough to classify it as "new" by church standards. Thus, for the next several days only, non-Mormon visitors could see the temple area traditionally banned to them. I remember well the effect this news had on me. I immediately resolved to take a tour. But when I phoned my friend Gus to ask if he wanted to come along, I came to understand something that changed my decision just as quickly.

After declining the invitation, Gus wondered why *I* seemed so intent on a visit. I was forced to admit that, no, I had never been inclined toward the idea of a temple tour before, that I had no questions about the Mormon religion I wanted answered, that I had no general interest in church architecture, and that I expected to find nothing more spectacular or stirring than what I might see at a number of other churches in the area. It became clear as I spoke that the special lure of the temple had a sole cause: if I did not experience the restricted sector soon, I would never again have the chance. Something that, on its own merits, held little appeal for me had become decidedly more attractive merely because it was rapidly becoming less available.

EBOX 6.1

In an impressive review of online-commercial-site experiments, a pair of researchers compiled the results of over 6,700 A/B tests, in which the same e-commerce site's effectiveness was tested when it did or did not include one or another specific feature (Browne & Swarbrick-Jones, 2017). The twenty-nine features to be evaluated ranged from the purely technological (such as the presence or absence of a search function, a back-to-top button, and default settings) to the motivational (such as free delivery, product badging, and calls to action). At the end of their investigation, the researchers concluded, "The biggest winners from our analysis all have grounding in behavioural psychology." Happily for readers of this book, aspects of each of the principles of influence we have covered so far appeared as the top-six most effective features:

Scarcity—highlighting items low in stock.

Social Proof—describing most popular and trending items.

Urgency—using time limits, often with a countdown timer.

Concessions—offering discounts for visitors to stay on the site.

Authority/Expertise—informing visitors of alternative products that are available.

Liking—including a welcoming message.

Author's note: It's telling that two of the top-three factors align with the two presentations of scarcity we have registered historically, since well before the beginnings of e-commerce—limited-number and limited-time appeals. Once again, we see that although the platforms on which influence principles are delivered may have changed radically, the impacts of the principles on human responses have not. It's also instructive that the rankings of the two operationalizations of scarcity fit with other research indicating that, in general, limited-supply appeals are more effective than limited-time appeals (Aggarwal, Jun, & Huh, 2011). In an upcoming section on competition, we'll learn why.

This tendency to want something more as time is fading is harnessed commercially by the "deadline" tactic, in which some official time limit is placed on the customer's opportunity to get what the compliance professional is offering. As a result, people frequently find themselves acquiring what they don't much favor simply because the time to do so is dwindling. The adept merchandiser makes this tendency pay off by arranging and publicizing customer deadlines that generate interest where none may have existed before. Concentrated instances of this approach often occur in movie advertising. In fact, I recently noticed that one theater owner, with remarkable singleness of purpose, had managed to invoke the scarcity principle three separate times in just five words of copy: "Exclusive, limited engagement ends soon!"

A variant of the deadline tactic is much favored by some face-to-face, high-pressure sellers because it carries the ultimate decision deadline: right now. Customers are often told that unless they make an immediate decision to buy, they will have to purchase the item at a higher price later or they won't be able to purchase it at all. A prospective health-club member or automobile buyer might learn that the deal offered by the salesperson is good for that one time only; should the customer leave the premises, the deal is off. One large child-portrait photography company urges parents to buy as many poses and copies as they can afford because "stocking limitations force us to burn the unsold pictures of your children within 24 hours." A door-to-door magazine solicitor might say that salespeople are in the customer's area for just a day; after that, they, and the customer's chance to buy their magazine package, will be long gone.

An in-home vacuum-cleaner-sales operation I infiltrated instructed its sales trainees to claim: "I have so many other people to see that I have the time to visit a family only once. It's company policy that, even if you decide later that you want this machine, I can't come back and sell it to you." This, of course, is nonsense; the company and its representatives are in the business of making sales, and any customer who called for another visit would be accommodated gladly. As the company's sales manager impressed on his trainees, the true purpose of the "can't come back" claim has nothing to do with reducing overburdened sales schedules. It is to "keep the prospects from taking the time to think the deal over by scaring them into believing they can't have it later, which makes them want it now."[2]

Figure 6.4: The Urgency Urge

SWINDLED

By Peter Kerr

New York Times

NEW YORK-Daniel Gulban doesn't remember how his life savings disappeared.

He remembers the smooth voice of a salesman on the telephone. He remembers dreaming of a fortune in oil and silver futures. But to this day, the 81-year-old retired utility worker does not understand how swindlers convinced him to part with $18,000.

"I just wanted to better my life in my waning days," said Gulban, a resident of Holder, FL. "But when I found out the truth, I couldn't eat or sleep. I lost 30 pounds. I still can't believe I would do anything like that."

Gulban was the victim of what law enforcement officials call a "boiler-room operation," a ruse that often involves dozens of fast-talking telephone salesmen crammed into a small room where they call thousands of customers each day. The companies snare hundreds of millions of dollars each year from unsuspecting customers, according to a U.S. Senate subcommittee investigation, which issued a report on the subject last year.

"They use an impressive Wall Street address, lies and deception to get individuals to sink their money into various glamorous-sounding schemes," said Robert Abrams, the New York State Attorney General, who has pursued more than a dozen boiler-room cases in the past four years. "The victims are sometimes persuaded to invest the savings of a lifetime."

Orestes J. Mihaly, the New York Assistant Attorney General in charge of the bureau of investor protection and securities, said the companies often operate in three stages. First, Mihaly said, comes the "opening call," in which a salesman identifies himself as representing a company with an impressive-sounding name and address. He will simply ask the potential customer to receive the company's literature.

A second call involves a sales pitch, Mihaly said. The salesman first describes the great profits to be made and then tells the customer that it is no longer possible to invest. The third call gives the customer a chance to get in on the deal, he said, and is offered with a great deal of urgency.

"The idea is to dangle a carrot in front of the buyer's face and then take it away." Mihaly said. "The aim is to get someone to buy it quickly, without thinking too much about it." Sometimes, Mihaly said, the salesman will be out of breath on the third call and will tell the customer that he "just came off the trading floor."

Such tactics convinced Gulban to part with his life savings. A stranger called him repeatedly and convinced Gulban to wire $1,756 to New York to purchase silver, Gulban said. After another series of telephone calls the salesman cajoled Gulban into wiring more than $6,000 for crude oil. He eventually wired an additional $9,740, but his profits never arrived.

"My heart sank," Gulban recalled, "I was not greedy. I just hoped I would see better days." Gulban never recouped his losses.

Author's note: Look at how the scarcity principle was employed during the second and third calls to cause Mr. Gulban to "buy quickly without thinking too much about it." *Click, run* (hurriedly).

Psychological Reactance

The evidence, then, is clear. Compliance practitioners' reliance on scarcity as a lever of influence is frequent, wide-ranging, systematic, and diverse. Whenever this is the case, we can be assured that the principle involved has notable power in directing human action. With the scarcity principle, that power comes from two major sources. The first is familiar. Like the other weapons of influence, the scarcity principle trades on our weakness for shortcuts. The weakness is, as before, an enlightened one. We know that things that are difficult to get are typically better than those that are easy to get. As such, we can often use an item's limited availability to help us quickly and correctly decide on its higher quality, which we don't want to lose. Thus, one reason for the potency of the scarcity principle is, by following it, we are usually and efficiently right.

In addition, there's a unique, secondary source of power within the scarcity principle: as opportunities become less available, we lose freedoms. And we hate to lose the freedoms we already have; what's more this is principally true of important freedoms. This desire to preserve our established, important prerogatives is the centerpiece of psychological reactance theory, developed by psychologist Jack Brehm to explain the human response to the loss of personal control. According to the theory, when free choice is limited or threatened, the need to retain our freedoms makes us want them (as well as the goods and services associated with them) significantly more than before. Therefore, when increasing scarcity—or anything else—interferes with our prior access to some item, we will *react against* the interference by wanting and trying to possess the item more than we did before.

As simple as the kernel of the theory seems, its shoots and roots curl extensively through much of the social environment. From the garden of young love to the jungle of armed revolution to the fruits of the marketplace, an impressive amount of our behavior can be explained by examining the tendrils of psychological reactance. Before beginning such an examination, though, it would be helpful to determine when people first show the desire to fight against restrictions of their freedoms.

Young Reactance: Playthings and Heartstrings

Child psychologists have traced the tendency to the age of two—a time identified as a problem by parents and widely known to them as the "terrible twos." Most parents attest to seeing more contrary behavior in their children around this period. Two-year-olds seem masters of the art of resistance to outside pressure. Tell them one thing, they do the opposite; give them one toy, they want another; pick them up against their will, they wriggle and squirm to be put down; put them down against their will, they claw and struggle to be carried.

One Virginia-based study nicely captured the style of terrible twos among boys who averaged twenty-four months in age. The boys accompanied their mothers into a room containing two equally attractive toys. The toys were always arranged so that one stood next to a transparent Plexiglas barrier and the other stood behind the barrier. For some of the boys, the Plexiglas sheet was only a foot high—forming no real barrier to the toy behind it, because the boys could easily reach over the top. For the other boys, however, the Plexiglas was two feet high, effectively blocking their access to one toy unless they went around the barrier. The researchers wanted to see how quickly the toddlers would make contact with the toys under these conditions. Their findings were clear-cut. When the barrier was too short to restrict access to the toy behind it, the boys showed no special preference for either of the toys; on the average, the toy next to the barrier was touched just as quickly as the one behind it. When the barrier was high enough to be a true obstacle, though, the boys went directly to the obstructed toy, making contact with it three times faster than with the unobstructed toy. In all, the boys in this study demonstrated the classic terrible-twos response to a limitation of their freedom—outright defiance.

Why should psychological reactance emerge at the age of two? There's a crucial change most children undergo around this time.

It is when they first come to see themselves as individuals. No longer do they view themselves as mere extensions of the social milieu but rather as identifiable, singular, and separate beings. This developing concept of autonomy brings with it the concept of freedom. An independent being is one with choices; a child with the newfound realization that he or she is such a being will want to explore the length and breadth of the options.

Perhaps we should be neither surprised nor distressed, then, when our two-year-olds strain incessantly against our will. They have come to a recent and exhilarating perspective of themselves as freestanding human entities. Vital questions of choice, rights, and control now need to be asked and answered within their small minds. The tendency to fight for every liberty and against every restriction might be best understood, then, as a quest for information. By testing severely the limits of their freedoms (and, coincidentally, the patience of their parents), the children are discovering where in their worlds they can expect to be controlled and where they can expect to be in control. As we will see later, it is the wise parent who provides highly consistent information.

Although the terrible twos may be the most noticeable age of psychological reactance, we show the strong tendency to react against restrictions on our freedoms of action throughout our lives. One other age does stand out, however, as a time when this tendency takes an especially rebellious form: the teenage years. As an old adage advises, "If you really want to get something done, you've got three options: do it yourself, pay top dollar, or forbid your teenagers to do it." Like the twos, this period is characterized by an emerging sense of individuality. For teenagers, the emergence is out of the role of child, with all of its attendant parental control, and into the role of adult, with all of its attendant rights and duties. Not surprisingly, adolescents focus less on the duties than on the rights they feel they have as young adults. Not surprisingly, again, imposing traditional parental authority at these times is often counterproductive; teenagers will sneak, scheme, and fight to resist such attempts at control.

Nothing illustrates the boomerang quality of parental pressure on adolescent behavior quite as clearly as a phenomenon known as the Romeo and Juliet effect. As we know, Romeo Montague and Juliet Capulet were the ill-fated Shakespearean characters whose love was doomed by a feud between their families. Defying all parental attempts to keep them apart, the teenagers, whom Shakespeare scholars place at around fifteen and thirteen years of age, won lasting union in their tragic act of twin suicide—an ultimate assertion of free will.

The intensity of the couple's feelings and actions has always been a source of wonderment and puzzlement to observers of the play. How could such inordinate devotion develop so quickly in a pair so young? A romantic might suggest rare and perfect love. A behavioral scientist, though, might point to the role of parental interference and the psychological reactance it can produce. Perhaps the passion of Romeo and Juliet was not initially so consuming that it transcended the extensive barriers erected by the families. Perhaps, instead, it was fueled to a white heat by the placement of those barriers. Could it be that had the youngsters been left to their own devices, their inflamed devotion would have amounted to no more than a flicker of puppy love?

Because the play is a work of fiction, such questions are, of course, hypothetical and any answer speculative. However, it is possible to ask and answer with more certainty similar questions about modern-day Romeos and Juliets. Do couples suffering parental interference react by committing themselves more firmly to the partnership and falling more deeply in love? According to a study done with 140 Colorado teenage couples, that is exactly what they do. The researchers in the study found that although parental interference was linked to some problems in the relationship—the partners viewed one another more critically and reported a greater number of negative behaviors in the other—the interference also made the pair feel greater love and desire for marriage. During the course of the study, as parental interference intensified, so did the love experience. When the interference weakened, romantic feelings cooled.

READER'S REPORT 6.3

From a woman living in Blacksburg, Virginia

Last Christmas I met a 27-year-old man. I was 19. Although he really wasn't my type, I went out with him—probably because it was a status thing to date an older man—but I really didn't become interested in him until my folks expressed their concern about his age. The more they got on my case about it, the more in love I became. It only lasted five months, but this was about four months longer than it would have lasted if my parents hadn't said anything.

Author's note: Although Romeo and Juliet have long since departed, it appears the *Romeo and Juliet effect* is alive and well and making regular appearances in places such as Blacksburg, Virginia.

Adult Reactance: Guns and Suds

For twos and teens, then, psychological reactance flows across the broad surface of experience, always turbulent and forceful. For most of the rest of us, the pool of reactant energy lies quiet and covered, erupting geyser-like only on occasion. Still, these eruptions manifest themselves in a variety of fascinating ways that are of interest not only to students of human behavior but also to lawmakers and policymakers. For instance, supermarket shoppers were most likely to sign a petition favoring federal price controls after they had been informed that a federal official had opposed distribution of the petition. Officials with the power to punish rule violators were *more* likely to do so on the violators' birthdays, and this was especially so when violators used their birthday status to plead for leniency. Why? Because the officials felt their freedom to decide on punishment was restricted by this circumstance—a classic reactance reaction.

Then, there's the odd case of Kennesaw, Georgia, the town that enacted a law requiring every adult resident to *own* a gun and ammunition, under penalty of six months in jail and a $200 fine. All the features of the Kennesaw gun law make it a prime target for psychological reactance. The freedom (not to own a gun) that the law restricted is an important, long-standing one to which most American citizens feel entitled. Furthermore, the law was passed by the Kennesaw City Council with a minimum of public input. Reactance theory would predict that under these circumstances, few of the adults in the town of 5,400 would obey. Yet newspaper reports testified that three to four weeks after passage of the law, firearms sales in Kennesaw were—no pun intended—booming.

How are we to make sense of this apparent contradiction of the reactance principle? By looking a bit closer at those who were buying Kennesaw's guns. Interviews with Kennesaw store owners revealed that the gun buyers were not town residents at all but visitors—many of them lured by publicity to purchase their initial guns in Kennesaw. Donna Green, proprietor of a shop described in one newspaper article as a virtual "grocery store of firearms," summed it up: "Business is great. But they're almost all being bought up by people from out of town. We've only had two or three local people buy a gun to comply with the law." After passage of the law, then, gun buying had become a frequent activity in Kennesaw, but not among those it was intended to cover; they were massively noncompliant. Only those individuals whose freedom in the matter had not been restricted by the law had the inclination to live by it.

A similar situation arose a decade earlier, several hundred miles south of Kennesaw, when, to protect the environment, Dade County (Miami), Florida, imposed an antiphosphate ordinance prohibiting the use—and possession!—of laundry or cleaning products containing phosphates. A study done to determine the social impact of the law discovered two parallel reactions on the part of Miami residents. First, many Miamians turned to smuggling. Sometimes with neighbors and friends in large "soap caravans," they drove to nearby counties to load up on phosphate detergents. Hoarding quickly developed, and in the rush of obsession that frequently characterizes hoarders, families boasted of having twenty-year supplies of phosphate cleaners.

The second reaction to the law was more subtle and more general than the deliberate defiance of the smugglers and hoarders. Spurred by the tendency to want what they could no longer have, the majority of Miami consumers came to see phosphate cleaners as better products than before. Compared to Tampa residents, who were not affected by the Dade County ordinance, the citizens of Miami rated phosphate detergents gentler, more effective in cold water, better whiteners and fresheners, and more powerful on stains. After passage of the law, they even came to believe phosphate detergents poured more easily.

This sort of response is typical of individuals who have lost an established freedom, and recognizing *that* is crucial to understanding how psychological reactance and the principle of scarcity work. When something becomes less available, our freedom to have it is limited, and we experience an increased desire for it. We rarely recognize, however, that psychological reactance has caused us to want the item more; all we know is we want it. To make sense of our heightened desire for the item, we begin to assign it positive qualities. In the case of the Dade County antiphosphate law—and in other instances of newly restricted availability—assuming a cause-and-effect relationship between desire and merit is a faulty supposition. Phosphate detergents clean, whiten, and pour no better after they are banned than they do before. We just assume they do because we find we desire them more.

Censorship

The tendency to want what is banned, and, therefore, presume it more worthwhile, is not confined to commodities such as laundry soap; it also extends to restrictions on information. In an age when the ability to acquire, store, and manage information increasingly affects access to wealth and power, it is important to understand how we typically react to attempts to censor or constrain our access to information. Although much evidence exists concerning our reactions to observing various kinds of potentially censorable material—media violence, pornography, radical political rhetoric—there is surprisingly little evidence on our reactions to the censoring of this material. Fortunately, the results of the relatively few studies that have been done on censorship are highly consistent. Almost invariably, our response to banned information is to want to receive the information and to become more favorable toward it than we were before the ban.

The intriguing finding within the effects of censored information on an audience is not that audience members want to have the information more than before; that seems natural. Rather, it is that they come to believe in the information more, even though they haven't received it. For example, when University of North Carolina students learned that a speech opposing coed dorms on campus would be banned, they became more opposed to the idea of coed dorms. Thus, without ever hearing the speech, the students became more sympathetic to its argument. This raises the worrisome possibility that especially clever individuals holding a weak or unpopular position can get us to agree with the position by arranging to have their message restricted.

The irony is that for such people—members of fringe political groups, for example—the most effective strategy may not be to publicize their unpopular views but to get those views officially censored and then to publicize the censorship. Perhaps the authors of the US Constitution were acting as much as sophisticated social psychologists as staunch civil libertarians when they wrote the remarkably permissive free-speech provision of the First Amendment. By refusing to restrain freedom of speech, they may have been trying to minimize the chance that new political notions would win support via the irrational course of psychological reactance.

Of course, political ideas are not the only kind susceptible to restriction. Access to sexually oriented material is also frequently limited. Although not as sensational as the occasional police crackdown on adult bookstores and theaters, regular pressure is applied by parents' and citizens' groups to censor the sexual content of educational material ranging from sex-education and -hygiene texts to school library books. Both sides in the struggle seem well-intentioned, and the issues are not simple, as they involve such matters as morality, art, parental control over the schools, and freedoms guaranteed by the First Amendment.

From a purely psychological point of view, however, those favoring strict censorship may wish to examine closely the results of a study done on Purdue University undergraduates. The students were shown advertisements for a novel. For half, the ads included the statement "a book for adults only, restricted to those 21 years and over"; the other half of the students read of no such age restriction. When the researchers later asked the students to indicate their feelings toward the book, they discovered the same pair of reactions we have noted with other bans: students who learned of the age restriction wanted to read the book more and believed they would like it more than did those who thought their access to the book was unfettered.

Those who support the official banning of sexually relevant materials from school curricula have the avowed goal of reducing society's orientation, especially of its youth, toward eroticism. In light of the Purdue study and in the context of other research on the effects of imposed restraints, one must wonder whether official censorship as a means may not be antithetical to the goal. If we are to believe the implications of the research, then censorship is likely to increase the desire of students for sexual material and, consequently, to cause them to view themselves as the kind of individuals who like such material.

The term *official censorship* usually makes us think of bans on political or sexually explicit material, yet there is another common sort of official censorship we don't think of in the same way, probably because it occurs after the fact. Often in a jury trial, a piece of evidence or testimony will be introduced, only to be ruled inadmissible by the presiding judge, who may then admonish jurors to disregard that evidence. From this perspective, the judge may be viewed as a censor, though the form of the censorship is odd. The presentation of the information to the jury is not banned—too late for that—it's the jury's use of the information that is banned. How effective are such instructions from a judge? Is it possible that for jury members who feel it is their right to consider all the available information, declarations of inadmissibility may actually cause psychological reactance, leading the jurors to use the evidence to a greater extent? Research demonstrates that this is often precisely what happens.

The realization that we value limited information allows us to apply the scarcity principle to realms beyond material commodities. The principle works for messages, communications, and knowledge too. Taking this perspective, we can see that information may not have to be censored for us to value it more; it need only be scarce. According to the principle, we will find a piece of information more persuasive if we think that we can't get it elsewhere. The strongest support I know for this idea—that exclusive information is more persuasive information—comes from an experiment done by a student of mine who was also a successful businessman, the owner of a beef-importing company. At the time, he had returned to school to get advanced training in marketing. After we talked in my office one day about scarcity and exclusivity of information, he decided to do a study using his sales staff.

The company's customers—buyers for supermarkets and other retail food outlets—were called on the phone as usual by a salesperson and asked for a purchase in one of three ways. One set of customers heard a standard sales presentation before being asked for their orders. Another set of customers heard the standard sales presentation plus information that the supply of imported beef was likely to be scarce in upcoming months. A third group received the standard sales presentation and the information about a scarce supply of beef; however, they also learned that the scarce-supply news was not generally available information—it had come, they were told, from certain exclusive contacts the company had. Thus, the customers who received this last sales presentation learned that the availability of the product was limited, and so, too, was the news concerning it: Not only was the beef scarce, but the information that the beef was scarce . . . was scarce—the scarcity double whammy.

The results of the experiment quickly became apparent when company salespeople began to urge the owner to buy more beef because there wasn't enough in the inventory to keep up with all the orders they were receiving. Compared to the customers who got only the standard sales appeal, those who were also told about the future scarcity of beef bought more than twice as much. The real boost in sales, however, occurred among the customers who heard of the impending scarcity via "exclusive" information. They purchased six times the amount that the customers who received only the standard sales pitch did. Apparently, the fact that the news about the scarcity information was itself scarce made it especially persuasive.[3]

Reactance Reduction

When people encounter a piece of information, they immediately become less likely to accept it if they view it as part of an effort to persuade them. For one reason, they experience reactance, feeling that the persuasive appeal is an attempt to reduce their freedom to decide on their own. Thus, all would-be persuaders requesting audience members to make a change must win the battle over this reactant response. Sometimes they try to overpower it by providing evidence that, despite any reluctance, change is the right move to make. They might do so by including information that the recipient should feel obligated to the persuader from a past favor (reciprocity) or is a nice person who deserves agreement (liking) or that many others have made the change (social proof) or that experts recommend it (authority) or that the opportunity to take action is dwindling (scarcity).

As well, there is a second way to prevail over reactant feelings that doesn't involve outmuscling them with more powerful motivations—but wins the battle, instead, by reducing the strength of the reactant feelings. A good example is the communicator who, early on, mentions a drawback to the suggested change. Not only does that maneuver increase the communicator's credibility, but it gives recipients information on both sides of the choice, positive and negative, and thus reduces their perception of being pushed in only one direction.

One influence tactic has been developed specifically to reinstate recipients' freedom to choose when they are targets of an influence attempt. It's called the "But you are free" technique, and it operates by emphasizing a request-recipient's freedom to say no. In a set of forty-two separate experiments, adding to a request the words "But you are free to decline/refuse/say no" or a similar phrase, such as "Of course, do as you wish," significantly increased compliance. Moreover, this was the case for a wide variety of requests: making contributions to a tsunami-relief fund, participating in an unpaid survey (whether in person, on the phone, or by mail), giving bus fare to a passerby on the street, purchasing food from a door-to-door solicitor, and even agreeing to sort and record one's household trash for a month. Finally, the impact of the freedom-reestablishing wording was considerable, often more than doubling the success of a standard request that didn't include the crucial phrase.[4]

Optimal Conditions

Much like the other effective levers of influence, the scarcity principle is more effective at some times than others. An important practical defense, then, is to find out when scarcity works best on us. A great deal can be learned from an experiment devised by social psychologist Stephen Worchel and his colleagues. The basic procedure used by Worchel's team was simple: participants in a consumer preference study were given a chocolate-chip cookie from a jar and asked to taste and rate its quality. For half of the raters, the jar contained ten cookies; for the other half, it contained just two. As we might expect from the scarcity principle, when the cookie was one of only two available, it was evaluated more favorably than when it was one of ten. The cookie in short supply was rated as more desirable to eat in the future, more attractive as a consumer item, and more costly than the identical cookie in abundant supply.

I have a hunch the Coca-Cola Company wished it had known of these findings when, in 1985, it began a historic blunder that *Time* magazine called "the marketing fiasco of the decade." On April 23 of that year, the company decided to pull their traditional formula for Coke off the market and replace it with New Coke. It was the day the syrup hit the fan. In the words of one news report: "The Coca-Cola Company failed to foresee the sheer frustration and fury its action would create. From Bangor to Burbank, from Detroit to Dallas, tens of thousands of Coke lovers rose up as one to revile the taste of the New Coke and demand their old Coke back."

My favorite example of the combined outrage and yearning produced by the loss of the old Coke comes from the story of a retired Seattle investor named Gay Mullins, who became something of a national celebrity by establishing a society called the Old Cola Drinkers of America, a widespread group of people who worked tirelessly to get the traditional formula back on the market by using any civil, judicial, or legislative means available to them. For instance, Mr. Mullins threatened a class-action lawsuit against the Coca-Cola Company to make the old recipe public; he distributed anti–New Coke buttons and T-shirts by the thousands; he set up a hotline where angry citizens could vent their rage and register their feelings. And it did not matter to him that in two separate blind taste tests, he preferred the New Coke to the old. Isn't that interesting; the thing Mr. Mullins liked more was less valuable to him than the thing he was being denied.

It's worth noting that even after giving in to customer demands and bringing the old Coke back to the shelves, company officials were stung and somewhat bewildered by what had hit them. As Donald Keough, then president of the company, said: "It's a wonderful American mystery, a lovely American enigma. And you can't measure it any more than you can measure love, pride, or patriotism." Here's where I'd disagree with Mr. Keough. First of all, it's no mystery, not if you understand the psychology of the scarcity principle. Especially when a product is as wrapped up in a person's history and traditions as Coca-Cola has always been in this country, that person is going to want it more as it becomes unavailable. Second, this urge is something that can be measured. In fact, I think the Coca-Cola Company *had* measured it in their own market research prior to making their infamous decision to change, but that they didn't see it there because they weren't looking for it the way a detective of the principles of influence would.

The purse holders within the Coca-Cola Company are no penny pinchers when it comes to marketing research; they are willing to spend hundreds of thousands of dollars—and more—to assure they analyze the market correctly for a new product. In their decision to switch to the New Coke, they were no different. From 1981 to 1984, they carefully tested the new and old formulas in taste tests involving nearly two hundred thousand people in twenty-five cities. What they found in their blind taste tests was a clear preference, 55 percent to 45 percent, for the New Coke over the old. However, some of the tests were not conducted with unmarked samples; in those tests, the participants were told which was the old and which was the New Coke beforehand. Under those conditions, the preference for the New Coke increased by an additional 6 percent.

You might say: "That's strange. How does that fit with the fact that people expressed a decided preference for the *old* Coke when the company finally introduced the New Coke?" The only way it fits is by applying the principle of scarcity to the puzzle: during the taste tests, it was the New Coke that was unavailable to people for purchase, so when they knew which sample was which, they showed an especially strong preference for what they couldn't otherwise have. But, later, when the company replaced the traditional recipe with the new one, now it was the old Coke that people couldn't have and, *it* became the favorite.

My point is that the 6 percent increase in preference for the New Coke was right there in the company's research when they looked at the difference between blind taste-test results and identified taste-test results, but they interpreted it incorrectly. They said to themselves, "Oh, good, this means that when people know they're getting something new, their desire for it will shoot up." But, in fact, what that 6 percent increase really meant was that when people know what they can't have, their desire for it will shoot up.

Although this pattern of results provides a rather striking validation of the scarcity principle, it doesn't tell us anything we don't already know. Once again, we see a less available item is more desired and valued. The real worth of looking back to the cookie study comes from two additional findings. Let's take them one at a time.

New Scarcity: Costlier Cookies and Civil Conflict

The first of these noteworthy results involved a small variation in the experiment's basic procedure. Rather than rating the cookies under conditions of constant scarcity, some participants were first given a jar of ten cookies that was then replaced by a jar of two. Thus, before taking a bite, certain of the participants saw their abundant supply of cookies reduced to a scarce supply. Other participants, however, knew only scarcity of supply from the onset, as the number of cookies in their jars was left at two. With this procedure, the researchers were seeking to answer a question about types of scarcity: Do we value more those things that have become recently less available or those things that have always been scarce? In the cookie experiment, the answer was plain. The drop from abundance to scarcity produced a decidedly more positive reaction to the cookies than did constant scarcity.

The idea that newly experienced scarcity is the more powerful kind applies to situations well beyond the bounds of the cookie study. For example, behavioral scientists have determined that such scarcity is a primary cause of political turmoil and violence. Perhaps the most prominent proponent of this argument is James C. Davies, who states that revolutions are more likely to occur when a period of improving economic and social conditions is followed by a short, sharp reversal in those conditions. Thus, it is not the traditionally most downtrodden people—those who have come to see their deprivation as part of the natural order of things—who are especially likely to revolt. Instead, revolutionaries are more likely to be those who have been given at least some taste of a better life. When the economic and social improvements they have experienced and come to expect suddenly become less available, they desire them more than ever and often rise up violently to secure them. For instance, at the time of the American Revolution, colonists had the highest standard of living and the lowest taxes in the Western world. According to historian Thomas Fleming, it wasn't until the British sought to reduce this widespread prosperity (by levying taxes) that the Americans revolted.

Davies has gathered persuasive evidence for his novel thesis from a range of revolutions, revolts, and internal wars, including the French, Russian, and Egyptian revolutions, as well as such domestic uprisings as Dorr's Rebellion in nineteenth-century Rhode Island, the American Civil War, and the urban Black riots of the 1960s. In each case, a time of increasing well-being preceded a tight cluster of reversals that burst into violence.

The racial conflict in America's cities during the mid-1960s offers a case in point. At the time, it was not uncommon to hear the question "Why now?" It didn't seem to make sense that within their three-hundred-year history, most of which had been spent in servitude and much of the rest in privation, American Blacks would choose the socially progressive sixties as the time to revolt. Indeed, as Davies points out, the two decades after the start of World War II had brought dramatic political and economic gains to the Black population. In 1940, Blacks faced stringent legal restrictions in such areas as housing, transportation, and education; moreover, even when the amount of education was the same, the average Black family earned only a bit more than half the amount its counterpart White family earned. Fifteen years later, much had changed. Federal laws had struck down as unacceptable formal and informal attempts to segregate Blacks in schools, public places, housing, and employment settings. Economic advances had been made, too; Black family income had risen from 56 to 80 percent of that of a comparably educated White family.

Then, according to Davies's analysis of social conditions, this rapid progress was stymied by events that soured the heady optimism of previous years. First, political and legal change proved substantially easier than social change to enact. Despite all the progressive legislation of the 1940s and 1950s, Blacks perceived that most neighborhoods, jobs, and schools remained segregated. Thus, the Washington-based victories came to feel like defeats at home. For example, in the four years following the Supreme Court's 1954 decision to integrate all public schools, Blacks were the targets of 530 acts of violence (including direct intimidation of children and parents, bombings, and burnings) designed to prevent school integration. The violence generated the perception of another sort of setback in progress. For the first time since well before World War II, when lynchings were terrifyingly frequent, Blacks experienced *heightened* concerns about the basic safety of their families. The new violence was not limited to the education issue. Peaceful civil-rights demonstrations of the time were regularly confronted by hostile crowds—and police.

Still another type of downturn occurred within the economic progress of the Black populace. In 1962, the income of a Black family had slid back to 74 percent of that of a similarly educated White family. By Davies's argument, the most illuminating aspect of this 74 percent figure is not that it represented a long-term increase in prosperity from prewar levels, but that it represented a recent decline from the flush levels of the mid-1950s. In 1963 came the Birmingham riots and, in staccato succession, scores of violent demonstrations, building toward the major upheavals of Watts, Newark, and Detroit.

In keeping with a distinct historical pattern of revolution, Blacks in the United States were more rebellious when their prolonged progress was somewhat curtailed than they were before it began. The pattern offers a valuable lesson for governments: when it comes to freedoms, it is more dangerous to have given for a while than never to have given at all. The problem for a government that seeks to improve the political and economic status of a traditionally oppressed group is, in so doing, it establishes freedoms for the group where none existed before. Should these now *established* freedoms become less available, there will be an especially hot variety of hell to pay.

We can look, two decades later, to events in the former Soviet Union for evidence that this basic rule holds across cultures. After decades of repression, then president Mikhail Gorbachev began granting Soviet citizens new liberties, privileges, and choices via the twin polices of glasnost and perestroika. Alarmed by the direction their nation was taking, a small group of government, military, and KGB officials staged a coup, placing Gorbachev under house arrest and announcing on August 19, 1991, that they had assumed power and were moving to reinstate the old order. Most of the world imagined that the Soviet people, known for their characteristic acquiescence to subjugation, would passively yield as they had always done. *Time* magazine editor Lance Morrow described his own reaction similarly: "At first the coup seemed to confirm the norm. The news administered a dark shock, followed immediately by a depressed sense of resignation: Of course, of course, the Russians must revert to their essential selves, to their own history. Gorbachev and *glasnost* were an aberration; now we are back to fatal normality."

But these were not to be normal times. For one thing, Gorbachev had not governed in the tradition of the czars or Stalin or any of the line of oppressive postwar rulers who had not allowed even a breath of freedom to the masses. He had ceded them certain rights and choices. And when these now established freedoms were threatened, the people lashed out. Within hours of the junta's announcement, thousands were in the streets erecting barricades, confronting armed troops, surrounding tanks, and defying curfews. The uprising was so swift, so massive, so unitary in its opposition to any retreat from the gains of glasnost that after only three riotous days, the astonished officials relented, surrendering their power and pleading for mercy from Chairman Gorbachev. Had they been students of history—or of psychology—the failed plotters would not have been so surprised by the tidal wave of popular resistance that swallowed their coup. From the vantage point of either discipline, they could have learned an invariant lesson: freedoms once granted will not be relinquished without a fight.

The lesson applies to the politics of family as well as country. The parent who grants privileges or enforces rules erratically invites rebellion by unwittingly establishing freedoms for the child. The parent who only sometimes prohibits between-meal sweets may create the freedom to have such snacks. At that point, enforcing the rule becomes a much more difficult and explosive matter because the child is no longer merely lacking a never-possessed right but is *losing* an established one. As we have seen in the case of political freedoms and (especially pertinent to the present discussion) chocolate-chip cookies, people see a thing as more desirable

Figure 6.5: Tanks, but no tanks.

Incensed by the news that then Soviet president Mikhail Gorbachev had been replaced in favor of plotters planning to cancel the newly instituted freedoms, Moscow residents confronted the tanks, defied the coup, and won the day.

Boris Yurchenko, Associated Press

when it recently has become less available than when it has been scarce all along. We should not be surprised, then, that research shows parents who enforce and discipline inconsistently produce characteristically rebellious children.[5]

READER'S REPORT 6.4

From an investment manager in New York

I recently read a story in the *Wall Street Journal* that illustrates the scarcity principle and how people want whatever is taken away from them. The article described how Procter & Gamble tried an experiment in upstate New York by eliminating all savings coupons for their products and replacing the coupons with lower everyday prices. This produced a big consumer revolt (with boycotts, protests, and a firestorm of complaints) even though Procter & Gamble's data showed that only 2 percent of coupons are used and, on average during the no-coupon experiment, consumers paid the same for P&G products with less inconvenience. According to the article the revolt happened because of something that P&G didn't recognize, "Coupons, to many people, are practically an inalienable right." It is amazing how strongly people react when you try to take things away, even if they never use them.

Author's note: Although Procter & Gamble executives may have been perplexed by this seemingly irrational consumer response, they inadvertently contributed to it. Discount coupons have been part of the American scene for over a century, and P&G had actively "couponed" its products for decades, thereby helping to establish coupons as something consumers had a right to expect. And it's always the long-established rights that people battle most ferociously to preserve.

Competition for Scarce Resources: Foolish Fury

Let's look back to the cookie study for another insight into the way we react to scarcity. We've already seen from the results of the study that scarce cookies were rated higher than were abundant cookies, and those that were newly scarce were rated higher still. Staying with the newly scarce cookies now, we find certain cookies were the highest rated of all—those that became less available because of a demand for them.

Remember that in the experiment, participants who experienced new scarcity had been given a jar of ten cookies that was then replaced with a jar of only two. Actually, the researchers created this scarcity in two ways. Certain participants were told some of their cookies had to be given away to other raters in order to supply the demand for them in the study. Another set of participants was told their allotment had to be reduced because the researcher had made a mistake and given them the wrong jar initially. The results showed that those whose cookies became scarce through the process of social demand liked them significantly more than did those whose cookies became scarce by mistake. In fact, the cookies made less available through social demand were rated the most desirable of any in the study.

This finding highlights the importance of competition in the

Figure 6.6: Rivalry branches out.
As is clear from this cartoon, rivalry for a limited resource doesn't take a holiday.
Kirkman & Scott; Creators Syndicate

pursuit of limited resources. Not only do we want the same item more when it is scarce, but we want it most when we are in competition for it. Advertisers often try to exploit this tendency in us. In their ads, we learn that "popular demand" for an item is so great we must "hurry to buy"; we see a crowd pressing against the doors of a store before the start of a sale; we watch a flock of hands quickly deplete a supermarket shelf of a product. There is more to such images than the idea of ordinary social proof. The message is not just that the product is good because other people think so but also that we are in direct competition with those people for it.

The feeling of being in competition for scarce resources has powerful motivating properties. The ardor of an indifferent lover surges with the appearance of a rival. It is often for reasons of strategy, therefore, that romantic partners reveal (or invent) the attentions of a new admirer. Salespeople are taught to play the same game with indecisive customers. For example, a real-estate agent who is trying to sell a house to a fence-sitting prospect sometimes calls the prospect with news of another potential buyer who has seen the house, liked it, and is scheduled to return the following day to discuss terms. When wholly fabricated, the new bidder is commonly described as an outsider with plenty of money: Favorites are "an out-of-state investor buying for tax purposes" and "a physician and his wife moving into town." The tactic, called in some circles "goosing 'em off the fence," can work devastatingly well. The thought of losing out to a rival frequently turns a buyer from hesitant to zealous.

There is something almost physical about the desire to have a contested item. Shoppers at big closeout or bargain sales report being caught up emotionally in the event. Charged by the crush of competitors, they swarm and struggle to claim merchandise they would otherwise disdain. Such behavior brings to mind the "feeding frenzy" phenomenon of wild, indiscriminate eating among animal groups. Commercial fishermen exploit the phenomenon by throwing a quantity of loose bait to large schools of certain fish. Soon the water is a roiling expanse of thrashing fins and snapping mouths competing for the food. At this point, the fishermen save time and money by dropping unbaited lines into the water, since the crazed fish will bite ferociously at anything, including bare metal hooks.

There is a noticeable parallel between the ways that commercial fishermen and department stores generate a competitive fury among those they wish to hook. To attract and arouse the catch, fishermen scatter some loose bait called chum. For similar purposes, department stores holding a bargain sale toss out a few especially good deals on prominently advertised items called loss leaders. If the bait—of either form—has done its job, a large and eager crowd forms to snap it up. Soon, in the rush to score, the group becomes agitated, nearly blinded, by the adversarial nature of the situation. Human beings and fish alike lose perspective on what they want and begin striking at whatever is being contested. One wonders whether the tuna flapping on a dry deck with only a bare hook in its mouth shares the what-hit-me bewilderment of the shopper arriving home with a load of department-store bilge.

Figure 6.7: Contagious competitiveness
A disgruntled employee steps through the aftermath of a closeout sporting-shoe sale, where customers are reported to have "gone wild, grabbing and struggling with one another over shoes whose sizes they had sometimes not yet seen."
UPI

Lest we believe the competition-for-limited-resources fever occurs only in such unsophisticated forms of life as tuna and bargain-basement shoppers, we should examine the story behind a remarkable purchase decision made by Barry Diller, who was vice president for prime-time programming of the American Broadcasting Company and who went on to head Paramount Pictures and the Fox Television Network. He agreed to pay $3.3 million for a single TV showing of the movie *The Poseidon Adventure*. The figure is noteworthy in that it greatly exceeded the highest price ever before paid for a one-time movie showing—$2 million for *Patton*. In fact, the payment was so excessive that ABC figured to lose $1 million on the *Poseidon* showing. As the NBC vice president for special programs, Bill Storke, declared at the time, "There's no way they can get their money back, no way at all."

How could an astute and experienced businessman such as Diller go for a deal that would produce an expected loss of $1 million? The answer may lie in a second noteworthy aspect of the sale: it was the first time that a motion picture had been offered to the networks in an open-bid auction. Never before had the networks been forced to battle for a scarce resource in quite this way. The novel idea of a competitive auction was the brainchild of the movie's flamboyant producer, Irwin Allen, and 20th Century Fox vice president, William Self, who must have been ecstatic about the outcome. How can we be sure that it was the auction format that generated the spectacular sales price rather than the blockbuster quality of the movie itself?

Some comments from auction participants provide impressive evidence. First came a statement from the victor, Barry Diller, intended to set future policy for his network. In language sounding as if it could have escaped only from between clenched teeth, he said, "ABC has decided regarding its policy for the future that it would never again enter into an auction situation." Even more instructive are the remarks of Diller's rival, Robert Wood, then president of CBS Television, who nearly lost his head and outbid his competitors at ABC and NBC:

We were very rational at the start. We priced the movie out, in terms of what it could bring in for us, then allowed a certain value on top of that for exploitation.

But then the bidding started. ABC opened with $2 million. I came back with $2.4. ABC went $2.8. And the fever of the thing caught us. Like a guy who had lost his mind, I kept bidding. Finally, I went to $3.2; and there came a moment when I said to myself, "Good grief, if I get it, what the heck am I going to do with it?" When ABC finally topped me, my main feeling was relief.

It's been very educational. (MacKenzie, 1974, p. 4)

According to interviewer Bob MacKenzie, when Wood said, "It's been very educational," he was smiling. We can be sure that when ABC's Diller vowed "never again," he was not smiling. Both men had learned a lesson from the "Great *Poseidon* Auction." The reason both could not smile as a consequence was that, for one, there had been a $1 million tuition charge.

Fortunately, there is a valuable but drastically less expensive lesson here for us too. It is instructive to note that the smiling man was the one who had lost the highly sought-after prize. As a general rule, when the dust settles and we find losers looking and speaking like winners (and vice versa), we should be especially wary of the conditions that kicked up the dust—in the present case, open competition for a scarce resource. As the TV executives learned, extreme caution is advised whenever we encounter the devilish construction of scarcity plus rivalry.[6]

The Distinctiveness Distinction

Because those around us value scarce resources, we prefer to be seen as possessing features that make us special. This is true at some times more than others. One is when we are in an amorous frame of mind. In a situation with romantic possibilities, we want to differentiate ourselves so as to attract the interest of potential partners—for example, by exhibiting greater creativity.

When in such a mood, we even prefer to visit places that allow us to stand out. Along with fellow researchers, I helped design an advertisement urging people to visit the San Francisco Museum of Art, which included the name and a photo of the museum. When the ad also featured the phrase "Stand Out from the Crowd," the intention to visit the museum by viewers of the ad skyrocketed; however, this was the case only if they had just seen a clip from a romantic movie. If they hadn't been exposed to the romance-rousing clip, the idea of visiting the (Stand Out from the Crowd) museum was not as attractive.

Another context where we feel a strong need to express our uniqueness is in matters of taste. We normally shift our beliefs and opinions to conform to others', which we do as a way to be correct. When it comes to issues of taste, though, in clothing, hairstyles, scents, food, music and the like, there is a countervailing motivation to distance from the crowd for reasons of distinctiveness. But even in matters of taste, group pressures can be strong, especially from an in-group. One study examined what members of such groups do to balance the desire to conform against the desire to demonstrate their individuality. If the majority of our in-group favors a brand of an item we are likely to do the same— while simultaneously differentiating ourselves along a visible dimension, such as the item's color. Leaders would be well advised to take this desire for uniqueness into account when ensuring that all team members conform to core work goals, by also ensuring that members aren't made to do so in exactly the same way.

Leaders should take as illustration what happened with yet another individuality-enhancing factor—an earned symbol of distinction—when a well-meaning leader removed its distinctiveness. On June 14, 2001, almost all US soldiers changed their standard field headgear to the black berets previously worn only by US Army Rangers, an elite contingent of specially trained combat troops. In a move designed to boost army morale, the change had been ordered by US Army Chief of Staff General Eric Shinseki to unify the troops and serve as "a symbol of army excellence." There is no evidence that it did anything of the sort among the thousands of affected soldiers who merely received a black beret. Instead, it incited denunciations from current and former Rangers, who felt robbed of the earned exclusivity the beret represented. As one Ranger, Lieutenant Michelle Hyer, expressed: "This is a travesty. The black berets are something the Rangers and special operations people worked hard for to *separate* themselves. Now . . . it won't mean anything to wear the beret anymore."

The general's order was misguided in a pair of ways, both instructive about how markers of distinction operate. The pride associated with the black beret came from its exclusivity. By making it no longer exclusive, its value—even as a symbol—had little effect on the self-regard of the many thousands who received it. But among those who had earned the beret's special significance, the loss of exclusivity stung deeply and ignited a firestorm of criticism. What could General Shinseki do to resolve the problem? He couldn't simply rescind his order; he had committed himself too emphatically and too publicly to the beret's value to army-wide solidarity and esprit de corps. Plus, forced retreat is rarely a good look for generals.

His solution was inspired. He allowed the Rangers to select another color of beret, besides black, to designate membership in their elite group. They selected buckskin tan, a hue that would be unique to Ranger berets (and that they still wear proudly today). Brilliant. As he had aimed, Shinseki got to bestow black berets on the great majority of his troops, who liked the flattering new style; in addition, the Rangers got to retain their distinctiveness within the larger change. Double brilliant.[7]

Defense

It is easy enough to feel properly warned against scarcity pressures, but it is substantially more difficult to act on that warning. Part of the problem is that our typical reaction to scarcity hinders our ability to think. When we watch as something we want becomes less available, a physical agitation sets in. Especially in those cases involving direct competition, the blood comes up, the focus narrows, and emotions rise. As this visceral current advances, the cognitive, rational side recedes. In the rush of arousal, it is difficult to be calm and studied in our approach. As CBS TV president Robert Wood commented in the wake of his *Poseidon* adventure: "You get caught up in the mania of the thing, the acceleration of it. Logic goes right out the window."

Here's our predicament, then: knowing the causes and workings of scarcity pressures may not be sufficient to protect us from them because knowing is a cognitive act, and cognitive processes are suppressed by our emotional reaction to scarcity pressures. In fact, this may be the reason for the great effectiveness of scarcity tactics. When they are employed properly, our first line of defense against foolish behavior, a thoughtful analysis, becomes less likely.

If, because of brain-clouding arousal and singlemindedness, we can't rely on our knowledge of the scarcity principle to stimulate properly cautious behavior, what can we use? Perhaps, in fine jujitsu style, we can use the arousal itself as our prime cue. In this way, we can turn the enemy's strength to our advantage. Rather than relying on a considered, cognitive analysis of the entire situation, we might well tune ourselves to just the internal, visceral sweep for our warning. By learning to flag the experience of heightening arousal in a compliance situation, we can alert ourselves to the possibility of scarcity tactics there and to the need for caution.

Suppose, however, we accomplish this trick of using the rising tide of arousal as a signal to calm ourselves and proceed with care. What then? Is there any other piece of information we can use to help make a proper decision in the face of scarcity? After all, merely recognizing that we ought to move carefully doesn't tell us the direction in which to move; it only provides the necessary context for a thoughtful decision.

Fortunately, there is information available on which we can base thoughtful decisions about scarce items. It comes, once again, from the chocolate-chip-cookie study, where the researchers uncovered something that seems strange but rings true regarding scarcity. Even though the scarce cookies were rated as significantly more desirable, they were not rated as any better-tasting than the abundant cookies. So, despite the increased yearning that scarcity caused (the raters said they wanted to have more of the scarce cookies in the future and would pay a greater price for them), it did not make the cookies taste one bit better.

Therein lies an important insight. The joy is not in the experiencing of a scarce commodity but in the possessing of it. It is important that we not confuse the two. Whenever we confront scarcity pressures surrounding some item, we must also confront the question of what it is we want from the item. If the answer is that we want the thing for the social, economic, or psychological benefits of possessing something rare, then, fine; scarcity pressures will give us a good indication of how much we should want to pay for it—the less available it is, the more valuable to us it will be. However, often we don't want a thing for the pure sake of owning it. We want it, instead, for its utility value; we want to eat it or drink it or touch it or hear it or drive it or otherwise use it. In such cases, it is vital to remember that scarce things do not taste or feel or sound or ride or work any better *because* of their limited availability.

Although this point is simple, it can often escape us when we experience the heightened desirability that scarce items possess. I can cite a family example. My brother Richard supported himself through school by employing a compliance trick that cashed in handsomely on the tendency of most people to miss that simple point. In fact, his tactic was so effective in this regard that he had to work only a few hours each weekend, leaving the rest of the time free for his studies.

Richard sold cars, but not from a showroom or a car lot. He would buy a couple of used cars sold privately through the newspaper on one weekend, and adding nothing but soap and water, sell them at a decided profit through the newspaper on the following weekend. To do this, he had to know three things. First, he had to know enough about cars to buy those that were offered for sale at the bottom of their blue-book price range but could be legitimately resold for a higher price. Second, once he got the car, he had to know how to write a newspaper ad that would stimulate substantial buyer interest. Third, once a buyer arrived, he had to know how to use the scarcity principle to generate more desire for the car than it perhaps deserved. Richard knew how to do all three. For our purposes, we need to examine his craft with just the third.

For a car he had purchased on the prior weekend, he would place an ad in the Sunday paper. Because he knew how to write a good ad, he usually received an array of calls from potential buyers on Sunday morning. Each prospect who was interested enough to want to see the car was given an appointment time—the *same* appointment time. So, if three people were scheduled, they were all scheduled for, say, 2:00 p.m. that afternoon. This device of simultaneous scheduling paved the way for later compliance by creating an atmosphere of competition for a limited resource.

Typically, the first prospect to arrive would begin a studied examination of the car and would engage in standard car-buying behavior, such as pointing out any blemishes or deficiencies and asking if the price were negotiable. The psychology of the situation changed radically, however, when the second buyer drove up. The availability of the car to either prospect suddenly became limited by the presence of the other. Often the earlier arrival, inadvertently stoking the sense of rivalry, would assert his right to primary consideration. "Just a minute now, I was here first." If he didn't assert that right, Richard would do it for him. Addressing the second buyer, he would say: "Excuse me, but this other gentleman was here before you. So, can I ask you to wait on the other side of the driveway for a few minutes until he's finished looking at the car? Then, if he decides he doesn't want it, or if he can't make up his mind, I'll show it to you."

Richard claims it was possible to watch the agitation grow on the first buyer's face. His leisurely assessment of the car's pros and cons had suddenly become a now-or-never, limited-time-only rush to decision over a contested resource. If he didn't decide for the car—at Richard's asking price—in the next few minutes, he might lose it for good to that . . . that . . . lurking newcomer over there. The second buyer would be equally agitated by the combination of rivalry and restricted availability. He would pace about the periphery of things, visibly straining to get at this suddenly more desirable hunk of metal. Should 2:00 p.m.-appointment number one fail to buy or even fail to decide quickly enough, 2:00 p.m.-appointment number two was ready to pounce.

If these conditions alone were not enough to secure a favorable purchase decision immediately, the trap snapped securely shut as soon as the third 2:00 p.m. appointment arrived on the scene. According to Richard, stacked-up competition was usually too much for the first prospect to bear. He would end the pressure quickly by either agreeing to Richard's price or by leaving abruptly. In the latter instance, the second arrival would strike at the chance to buy out of a sense of relief coupled with a new feeling of rivalry with that . . . that . . . lurking newcomer over there.

All those buyers who contributed to my brother's college education failed to recognize a fundamental fact about their purchases: the increased desire spurring them to buy had little to do with the car's merits. The failure of recognition occurred for two reasons. First, the situation Richard arranged produced an emotional reaction that made it difficult for them to think straight. Second, as a consequence, they never stopped to think that the reason they wanted the car in the first place was to use it, not merely to have it. The competition-for-a-scarce-resource pressures Richard applied affected only their desire to have the car in the sense of possessing it. Those pressures did not affect the value of the car in terms of the real purpose for which they had wanted it.

READER'S REPORT 6.5

From a woman living in Poland

A few weeks ago I was a victim of the techniques you write about. I was quite shocked because I am not a type of person who is easy to convince and I had just read *Influence* so I was really sensitive to those strategies.

There was a little tasting in the supermarket. Nice girl offered me a glass of beverage. I tasted it and it wasn't bad. Then she asked me if I liked it. After I answered yes, she proposed to me to buy four tins of this drink (the principle of consistency—I liked it, therefore I should buy it—and the rule of reciprocity—she first gave me something for free). But, I wasn't so naïve and refused to do it. This saleswoman didn't give up, however. She said, "Maybe only one tin?" (using the rejection-then-retreat tactic). But, I didn't give up either.

Then she said this drink was imported from Brazil and she didn't know if it would be available at the supermarket in the future. The rule of scarcity worked and I bought a tin. When I drank this at home the flavor still was okay but not great. Fortunately, most of the salespersons are not so patient and persistent.

Author's note: Isn't it interesting that even though this reader knew about the principle of scarcity, it still got her to purchase something she really didn't want. To have armed herself optimally against it, she needed to remind herself that, like the scarce cookies, the scarce beverage wouldn't taste any better. And it didn't.

Should we find ourselves beset by scarcity pressures in a compliance situation, then, our best response would occur in a two-stage sequence. As soon as we feel the tide of emotional arousal that flows from scarcity influences, we should use it as a signal to stop short. Panicky, feverish reactions have no place in wise compliance decisions. We need to calm ourselves and regain a rational perspective. Once that is done, we can move to the second stage by asking ourselves why we want the item under consideration. If the answer is that we want it primarily for the purpose of owning it, then we should use its availability to help gauge how much we would want to spend for it. However, if the answer is that we want it primarily for its function (that is, we want something good to drive or drink or eat), then we must remember that the item under consideration will function equally well whether scarce or plentiful. Quite simply, we need to recall that the scarce cookies weren't any tastier.[8]

SUMMARY

- According to the scarcity principle, people assign more value to opportunities that are less available. The use of this principle for profit can be seen in such compliance techniques as the "limited number" and "deadline" tactics, wherein practitioners try to convince us that if we don't act now, we will *lose* something of value. This engages the human tendency for loss aversion—that people are more motivated by the thought of losing something than by the thought of gaining something of equal value.

- The scarcity principle holds for two reasons. First, because things difficult to attain are typically more valuable, the availability of an item or experience can serve as a shortcut cue to its quality; and, because of loss aversion, we will be motivated to avoid losing something of high quality. Second, as things become less accessible, we lose freedoms. According to psychological reactance theory, we respond to the loss of freedoms by wanting to have them (along with the goods and services connected to them) more than before.

- As a motivator, psychological reactance is present throughout the great majority of the life span. However, it is especially evident at a pair of ages: the terrible twos and the teenage years. Both of these times are characterized by an emerging sense of individuality, which brings to prominence issues of control, rights, and freedoms. Consequently, individuals at these ages are especially averse to restrictions.

- In addition to its effect on the valuation of commodities, the scarcity principle also applies to the way information is evaluated. The act of limiting access to a message causes individuals to want to receive it and to become more favorable to it. In the case of censorship, the effect of greater favorability toward a restricted message occurs even before the message has been received. In addition, messages are more effective if perceived as containing exclusive (scarce) information.

- The scarcity principle is most likely to hold under two optimizing conditions. First, scarce items are heightened in value when they are newly scarce. That is, we value those things that have recently become restricted more than we do those that were restricted all along. Second, we are most attracted to scarce resources when we compete with others for them.

- It is difficult to steel ourselves cognitively against scarcity pressures because they have an emotion-arousing quality that makes thinking difficult. In defense, we might try to be alert to a rush of arousal in situations involving scarcity. Once alerted, we can take steps to calm the arousal and assess the merits of the opportunity in terms of why we want it.

CHAPTER 7

COMMITMENT AND CONSISTENCY

HOBGOBLINS OF THE MIND

I am today what I established yesterday or some previous day.

—James Joyce

Every year, Amazon ranks near or at the top of the wealthiest and best-performing companies in the world. Yet every year it gives each of its fulfillment-center employees, who helped the company reach these heights, an incentive of up to $5,000 to leave. The practice, in which employees receive a cash bonus if they quit, has left many observers mystified, as the costs of employee turnover are significant. Direct expenses associated with turnover of such employees—stemming from the recruitment, hiring, and training of replacements—can extend to 50 percent of the employee's annual compensation package; plus, the costs escalate even further when indirect expenses are taken into account in the form of loss of institutional memory, productivity disruptions, and lowered morale of remaining team members.

How does Amazon justify its "Pay to Quit" program from a business standpoint? Spokesperson Melanie Etches is clear on the point: "We only want people working at Amazon who want to be here. In the long-run term, staying somewhere you don't want to be isn't healthy for our employees or for the company." So Amazon figures that providing unhappy, dissatisfied, or discouraged employees an attractive escape route will save money in terms of the proven higher health costs and lower productivity of such workers. I don't doubt the logic. But I do doubt it is Amazon's sole rationale for the program. A significant additional reason applies. I know of its potency from the results of behavioral-science research and from the fact that I have seen it, and still do see it, operating forcefully all around me.

Take, for example, the story of my neighbor Sara and her live-in boyfriend, Tim. After they met, they dated for a while and eventually moved in together. Things were never perfect for Sara. She wanted Tim to marry her and stop his heavy drinking; Tim resisted both ideas. After an especially contentious period, Sara broke off the relationship, and Tim moved out. Around the same time, an old boyfriend phoned her. They started seeing each other exclusively and quickly became engaged. They had gone so far as to set a wedding date and issue invitations, when Tim called. He had repented and wanted to move back in. When Sara told him her marriage plans, he begged her to change her mind; he wanted to be together with her as before. Sara refused, saying she didn't want to live like that again. Tim even offered to marry her, but she still said she preferred the other boyfriend. Finally, Tim volunteered to quit drinking if she would only relent. Feeling that under those conditions, Tim had the edge, Sara decided to break her engagement, cancel the wedding, retract the invitations, and have Tim move back in with her.

Within a month, Tim informed Sara that he didn't think he needed to stop drinking, because he now had it under control. A month later, he decided that they should "wait and see" before getting married. Two years have since passed; Tim and Sara continue to live together exactly as before. Tim still drinks, and there are still no marriage plans, yet Sara is more devoted to him than ever. She says that being forced to *decide* taught her that Tim really is number one in her heart. So after choosing Tim over her other boyfriend, Sara became happier, even though the conditions under which she had made her decision have never been consummated.

Note that Sara's bolstered commitment came from making a hard personal choice *for Tim*. I believe it's for the same reason that Amazon wants employees to make such a choice *for it*. The election to stay or leave in the face of an incentive to quit doesn't serve only to identify disengaged workers, who, in a smoothly efficient process, weed themselves out. It also serves to solidify and even enhance the allegiance of those who, like Sara, opt to continue.

How can we be so sure that this latter outcome is part of the Pay to Quit program's purpose? By paying attention not to what the company's public-relations spokesperson, Ms. Etches, has to say on the matter but, rather, to what its founder, Jeff Bezos, says—a man whose business acumen had made him the world's richest person. In a letter to shareholders, Mr. Bezos wrote that the program's purpose was simply to encourage employees "to take a moment and think about what they really want." He's also pointed out that the headline of the annual proposal memo reads, "Please Don't Take This Offer." Thus, Mr. Bezos wants employees to think about leaving without choosing to do so, which is precisely what happens, as very few take the offer. In my view, it's the resultant decision to stay that the program is primarily designed to foster, and for good reason: employee commitment is highly related to employee productivity.

Mr. Bezos's keen understanding of human psychology is confirmed in a raft of studies of people's willingness to believe in the greater validity of a difficult selection once made. I have a favorite. A study done by a pair of Canadian psychologists uncovered something fascinating about people at the horse track. Just after placing bets, they become much more sure of the correctness of their decision than they were immediately before laying down the bets. Of course, nothing about the horse's chances actually shifts; it's the same horse, on the same track, in the same field; but in the minds of those bettors, their confidence that they made the right choice improves significantly once the decision is finalized. Similarly, in the political arena, voters believe more strongly in their choice immediately after casting a ballot. In yet another domain, upon making an active, public decision to conserve energy or water, people become more devoted to the idea of conservation, develop more reasons to support it, and work harder to achieve it.

In general, the main reason for such swings in the direction of a choice has to do with another fundamental principle of social influence. Like the other principles, this one lies deep within us, directing our actions with quiet power. It is our desire to be (and to appear) consistent with what we have already said or done. *Once we make a choice or take a stand, we encounter personal and interpersonal pressures to think and behave consistently with that commitment.* Moreover, those pressures will cause us to respond in ways that justify our decision.[1]

Streaming Along

Psychologists have long explored how the consistency principle guides human action. Indeed, prominent early theorists recognized the desire for consistency as a motivator of our behavior. But is it really strong enough to compel us to do what we ordinarily would not want to do? There is no question about it. The drive to be (and look) consistent constitutes a potent driving force, often causing us to act in ways contrary to our own best interest.

Consider what happened when researchers staged thefts on a New York City area beach to see if onlookers would risk personal harm to halt the crime. In the study, an accomplice of the researchers would put a beach blanket down five feet from the blanket of a randomly chosen individual—the experimental subject. After several minutes of relaxing on the blanket and listening to music from a portable radio, the accomplice would stand up and leave the blanket to stroll down the beach. Soon thereafter, a researcher, pretending to be a thief, would approach, grab the radio, and try to hurry away with it. Under normal conditions, subjects were reluctant to put themselves in harm's way by challenging the thief—only four people did so in the twenty times the theft was staged. But when the same procedure was tried another twenty times with a slight twist, the results were drastically different. In these incidents, before leaving the blanket, the accomplice would simply ask the subject to please "watch my things," something everyone agreed to do. Now, propelled by the rule of consistency, nineteen of the twenty subjects became virtual vigilantes, running after and stopping the thief, demanding an explanation, often restraining the thief physically or snatching the radio away.

To understand why consistency is so powerful a motive, we should recognize that in most circumstances, it is valued and adaptive. Inconsistency is commonly thought to be an undesirable personality trait. The person whose beliefs, words, and deeds don't match is seen as confused, two-faced, even mentally ill. On the other side, a high degree of consistency is normally associated with personal and intellectual strength. It is the heart of logic, rationality, stability, and honesty. A quote attributed to the great British chemist Michael Faraday suggests the extent to which being consistent is approved—sometimes more than being right is. When asked after a lecture if he meant to imply that a hated academic rival was always wrong, Faraday glowered at the questioner and replied, "He's not that consistent."

Certainly, then, good personal consistency is highly valued in our culture—and well it should be. Most of the time, we are better off if our approach to things is well laced with consistency. Without it, our lives would be difficult, erratic, and disjointed.

The Quick Fix

Because it is typically in our best interests to be consistent, we fall into the habit of being automatically so, even in situations where it is not the sensible way to be. When it occurs unthinkingly, consistency can be disastrous. Nonetheless, even blind consistency has its attractions.

First, like most other forms of automatic responding, consistency offers a shortcut through the complexities of modern life. Once we have made up our minds about an issue, stubborn consistency allows us an appealing luxury: we don't have to think hard about the issue anymore. We don't have to sift through the blizzard of information we encounter every day to identify relevant facts; we don't have to expend the mental energy to weigh the pros and cons; we don't have to make any further tough decisions. Instead, all we have to do when confronted with the issue is *click* on our consistency program, and we know just what to believe, say, or do. We need only believe, say, or do whatever is congruent with our earlier decision.

The allure of such a luxury is not to be minimized. It allows us a convenient, relatively effortless, and efficient method for dealing with the complexities of daily life that make severe demands on our mental energies and capacities. It is not hard to understand, then, why automatic consistency is a difficult reaction to curb. It offers a way to evade the rigors of continuing thought. With our consistency programs running, we can go about our business happily excused from having to think too much. And, as Sir Joshua Reynolds noted, "There is no expedient to which a man will not resort to avoid the real labor of thinking."

The Foolish Fortress

There is a second, more perverse attraction of mechanical consistency. Sometimes it is not the effort of hard, cognitive work that makes us shirk thoughtful activity but the harsh consequences of that activity. Sometimes it is the cursedly clear and unwelcome set of answers provided by straight thinking that makes us mental slackers. There are certain disturbing things we simply would rather not realize. Because it is a preprogrammed and mindless method of responding, automatic consistency can supply a safe hiding place from troubling realizations. Sealed within the fortress walls of rigid consistency, we can be impervious to the sieges of reason.

One night at an introductory lecture given by the Transcendental Meditation (TM) program, I witnessed an illustration of the way people hide inside the walls of consistency to protect themselves from the troublesome consequences of thought. The lecture itself was presided over by two earnest young men and was designed to recruit new members into the program. The men claimed the program offered a unique brand of meditation that would allow us to achieve all manner of desirable things, ranging from simple inner peace to more spectacular abilities—to fly and pass through walls, for example—at the program's advanced (and more expensive) stages.

I had decided to attend the meeting to observe the kind of compliance tactics used in recruitment lectures of this sort and had brought along an interested friend, a university professor whose areas of specialization were statistics and symbolic logic. As the meeting progressed and the lecturers explained the theory behind TM, I noticed my logician friend becoming increasingly restless. Looking more and more pained and shifting about in his seat, he was finally unable to resist. When the leaders called for questions, he raised his hand and gently but surely demolished the presentation we had just heard. In less than two minutes, he pointed out precisely where and why the lecturers' complex argument was contradictory, illogical, and unsupportable. The effect on the discussion leaders was devastating. After a confused silence, each attempted a weak reply only to halt midway to confer with his partner and finally to admit that my colleague's points were good ones "requiring further study."

More interesting to me was the effect upon the rest of the audience. At the end of the question period, the recruiters were faced with a crowd of audience members submitting their $75 down payments for admission to the TM program. Shrugging and chuckling to one another as they took in the payments, the recruiters betrayed signs of giddy bewilderment. After what appeared to have been an embarrassingly clear collapse of their presentation, the meeting had somehow turned into a success, generating inexplicably high levels of compliance from the audience. Although more than a bit puzzled, I chalked up the audience's response to a failure to understand the logic of my colleague's arguments. As it turned out, just the reverse was true.

Outside the lecture room after the meeting, we were approached by three members of the audience, each of whom had given a down payment immediately after the lecture. They wanted to know why we had come to the session. We explained and asked the same question of them. One was an aspiring actor who wanted desperately to succeed at his craft and had come to the meeting to learn if TM would allow him to achieve the necessary self-control to master the art; the recruiters assured him it would. The second described herself as a severe insomniac who hoped TM would provide her a way to relax and fall asleep easily at night. The third served as unofficial spokesman. He was failing his college courses because there wasn't enough time to study. He had come to the meeting to find out if TM could help by training him to need fewer hours of sleep each night; the additional time could then be used for study. It is interesting to note that the recruiters informed him, as well as the insomniac, that TM techniques could solve their respective, though opposite, problems.

Still thinking the three must have signed up because they hadn't understood the points made by my logician friend, I began to question them about aspects of his arguments. I found that they had understood his comments quite well, in fact, all too well. It was precisely the cogency of his claims that drove them to sign up for the program on the spot. The spokesman put it best: "Well, I wasn't going to put down any money tonight because I'm really broke right now; I was going to wait until the next meeting. But when your buddy started talking, I knew I'd better give them my money now, or I'd go home, start thinking about what he said and *never* sign up."

At once, things began to make sense. These were people with real problems, and they were desperately searching for a way to solve them. They were seekers who, if our discussion leaders were right, had found a potential solution in TM. Driven by their needs, they very much wanted to believe that TM was their answer. Now, in the form of my colleague, intrudes the voice of reason, showing the theory underlying their newfound solution to be unsound.

Panic! Something must be done at once before logic takes its toll and leaves them without hope once again. Quickly, quickly, walls against reason are needed, and it doesn't matter that the fortress to be erected is a foolish one. "Quick, a hiding place from thought! Here, take this money. Whew, safe in the nick of time. No need to think about the issues any longer." The decision has been made, and from now on the consistency program can be run whenever necessary: "TM? Certainly I think it will help me; certainly I expect to continue; certainly I believe in TM. I already put my money down for it, didn't I?" Ah, the comforts of mindless consistency. "I'll just rest right here for a while. It's so much nicer than the worry and strain of that hard, hard search."

Seek and Hide

If, as it appears, automatic consistency functions as a shield against thought, it should not be surprising that such consistency can be exploited by those who would prefer we respond to their requests without thinking. For the profiteers, whose interest will be served by an unthinking, mechanical reaction to their requests, our tendency for automatic consistency is a gold mine. So clever are they at arranging to have us run our consistency programs when it profits them that we seldom realize we have been taken. In fine jujitsu fashion, they structure their interactions with us so our need to be consistent leads directly to their benefit.

Certain large toy manufacturers use just such an approach to reduce a problem created by seasonal buying patterns. Of course, the boom time for toy companies occurs before and during the Christmas holiday season. Their problem is that toy sales then go into a terrible slump for the next couple of months. Their customers have already spent the amount in their toy budgets and are stiffly resistant to their children's pleas for more.

The toy manufacturers are faced with a dilemma: how to keep sales high during the peak season and, at the same time, retain a healthy demand for toys in the immediately following months? The difficulty certainly doesn't lie in motivating kids to want more toys after Christmas. The problem lies in motivating postholiday spent-out parents to buy another plaything for their already toy-glutted children. What could the toy companies do to produce that unlikely behavior? Some have tried greatly increased advertising campaigns, while others have reduced prices during the slack period, but neither of those standard sales devices has proved successful. Both tactics are costly and have been ineffective in increasing sales to desired levels. Parents are simply not in a toy-buying mood, and the influences of advertising or reduced expense are not enough to shake that stony resistance.

Certain large toy manufacturers think they have found a solution. It's an ingenious one, involving no more than a normal advertising expense and an understanding of the powerful pull of the need for consistency. My first hint of the way the toy companies' strategy worked came after I fell for it and then, in true patsy form, fell for it again.

It was January, and I was in the town's largest toy store. After purchasing all too many gifts there for my son a month before, I had sworn not to enter that store or any like it for a long, long time. Yet there I was, not only in the diabolical place but also in the process of buying my son another expensive toy—a big, electric road-race set. In front of the road-race display, I happened to meet a former neighbor who was buying his son the same toy. The odd thing was that we almost never saw each other anymore. In fact, the last time had been a year earlier in the same store when we were both buying our sons an expensive post-Christmas gift— that time a robot that walked, talked, and laid waste to all before it. We laughed about our strange pattern of seeing each other only once a year at the same time, in the same place, while doing the same thing. Later that day, I mentioned the coincidence to a friend who, it turned out, had once worked in the toy business.

"No coincidence," he said knowingly.

"What do you mean, 'No coincidence'?"

"Look," he said, "let me ask you a couple of questions about the road-race set you bought this year. First, did you promise your son that he'd get one for Christmas?"

"Well, yes, I did. Christopher had seen a bunch of ads for them on the Saturday-morning cartoon shows and said that was what he wanted for Christmas. I saw a couple of ads myself and it looked like fun, so I said, OK."

"Strike one," he announced. "Now for my second question. When you went to buy one, did you find all the stores sold out?"

"That's right, I did! The stores said they'd ordered some but didn't know when they'd get any more in. So I had to buy Christopher some other toys to make up for the road-race set. But how did you know?"

"Strike two," he said. "Just let me ask one more question. Didn't this same sort of thing happen the year before with the robot toy?"

"Wait a minute . . . you're right. That's just what happened. This is incredible. How did you know?"

"No psychic powers; I just happen to know how several of the big toy companies jack up their January and February sales. They start prior to Christmas with attractive TV ads for certain special toys. The kids, naturally, want what they see and extract Christmas promises for these items from their parents. Now here's where the genius of the companies' plan comes in: they *undersupply* the stores with the toys they've gotten the parents to promise. Most parents find those toys sold out and are forced to substitute other toys of equal value. The toy manufacturers, of course, make a point of supplying the stores with plenty of these substitutes. Then, after Christmas, the companies start running the ads again for the other, special toys. That jacks up the kids to want those toys more than ever. They go running to their parents whining, 'You promised, you promised,' and the adults go trudging off to the store to live up dutifully to their words."

"Where," I said, beginning to seethe now, "they meet other parents they haven't seen for a year, falling for the same trick, right?"

"Right. Uh, where are you going?"

"I'm going to take the road-race set right back to the store." I was so angry I was nearly shouting.

"Wait. Think for a minute first. Why did you buy it this morning?"

"Because I didn't want to let Christopher down and because I wanted to teach him that promises are to be lived up to."

"Well, has any of that changed? Look, if you take his toy away now, he won't understand why. He'll just know that his father broke a promise to him. Is that what you want?"

"No," I said, sighing, "I guess not. So, you're telling me the toy companies doubled their profits on me for the past two years, and I never even knew it; and now that I do, I'm still trapped—by my own words. So, what you're really telling me is, 'Strike three.'"

He nodded, "And you're out."

In the years since, I have observed a variety of parental toy-buying sprees similar to the one I experienced during that particular holiday season—for Beanie Babies, Tickle Me Elmo dolls, Furbies, Xboxes, Wii consoles, Zhu Zhu Pets, *Frozen* Elsa dolls, PlayStation 5s, and the like. But, historically, the one that best fits the pattern is that of the Cabbage Patch Kids, $25 dolls that were promoted heavily during mid-1980s Christmas seasons but were woefully under-supplied to stores. Some of the consequences were a government false-advertising charge against the Kids' maker for continuing to advertise dolls that were not available, frenzied groups of adults battling at toy outlets or paying up to $700 apiece at auction for

Figure 7.1: No pain, no (ill-gotten) gain
Jason, the gamer in this cartoon, has gotten the tactic for holiday-gift success right, but, I think he's gotten the reason for that success wrong. My own experience tells me that his parents will overcompensate with other gifts not so much to ease his pain but to ease their own pain at having to break their promise to him.

FOXTROT © 2005 Bill Amend. Reprinted with permission of UNIVERSAL PRESS SYNDICATE. All rights reserved.

dolls they had *promised* their children, and an annual $150 million in sales that extended well beyond the Christmas months. During the 1998 holiday season, the least available toy everyone wanted was the Furby, created by a division of toy giant Hasbro. When asked what frustrated, Furby-less parents should tell their kids, a Hasbro spokeswoman advised the kind of promise that has profited toy manufacturers for decades: tell the kids, "I'll try, but if I can't get it for you now, I'll get it for you later."[2]

Commitment Is the Key

Once we realize that the power of consistency is formidable in directing human action, an important practical question immediately arises: How is that force engaged? What produces the *click* that activates the *run* of the powerful consistency program? Social psychologists think they know the answer: commitment. If I can get you to make a commitment (that is, to take a stand, to go on record), I will have set the stage for your automatic and ill-considered consistency with that earlier commitment. Once a stand is taken, there is a natural tendency to behave in ways that are stubbornly aligned with the stand.

As we've already seen, social psychologists are not the only ones who understand the connection between commitment and consistency. Commitment strategies are aimed at us by compliance professionals of nearly every sort. Each of the strategies is intended to get us to take some action or make some statement that will trap us into later compliance through consistency pressures. Procedures designed to create commitments take various forms. Some are bluntly straightforward; others are among the most subtle compliance tactics we will encounter. On the blunt side, consider the approach of Jack Stanko, used-car sales manager for an Albuquerque auto dealership. While leading a session called "Used Car Merchandising" at a National Auto Dealers Association convention in San Francisco, he advised one hundred sales-hungry dealers as follows: "Put 'em on paper. Get the customer's OK on paper. Control 'em. Ask 'em if they would buy the car right now if the price is right. Pin 'em down." Obviously, Mr. Stanko—an expert in these matters—believes that the way to customer compliance is through commitments, which serve to "control 'em."

Commitment practices involving substantially more finesse can be just as effective. Suppose you wanted to increase the number of people in your area who would agree to go door to door collecting donations for your favorite charity. You would be wise to study the approach taken by social psychologist Steven J. Sherman. He simply called a sample of Bloomington, Indiana, residents as part of a survey he was taking and asked them to predict what they would say if asked to spend three hours collecting money for the American Cancer Society. Of course, not wanting to seem uncharitable to the survey-taker or to themselves, many of these people said that they would volunteer. The consequence of this subtle commitment procedure was a 700 percent increase in volunteers when, a few days later, a representative of the American Cancer Society did call and ask for neighborhood canvassers.

Using the same strategy, but this time asking citizens to predict whether they would vote on Election Day, other researchers have been able to increase significantly the turnout at the polls among those called. Courtroom combatants appear to have adopted this practice of extracting a lofty initial commitment designed to spur future consistent behavior. When screening potential jurors before a trial, Jo-Ellen Demitrius, reputed to be the best consultant in the business of jury selection, asks an artful question: "If you were the only person who believed in my client's innocence, could you withstand the pressure of the rest of the jury to change your mind?" How could any self-respecting prospective juror say no? And having made the public promise, how could any self-respecting selected juror repudiate it later?

Perhaps an even more crafty commitment technique has been developed by telephone solicitors for charity. Have you noticed that callers asking you to contribute to some cause or another these days seem to begin things by inquiring about your current health and well-being? "Hello, Mr./Ms. Targetperson," they say. "How are you feeling this evening?," or "How are you doing today?" The caller's intent with this sort of introduction is not merely to seem friendly and caring. It is to get you to respond—as you normally do to such polite, superficial inquiries—with a polite, superficial comment of your own: "Just fine" or "Real good" or "Doing great, thanks." Once you have publicly stated that all is well, it becomes much easier for the solicitor to corner you into aiding those for whom all is *not* well: "I'm glad to hear that because I'm calling to ask if you'd be willing to make a donation to help the unfortunate victims of . . ."

The theory behind this tactic is that people who have just asserted that they are doing/feeling fine—even as a routine part of a sociable exchange—will consequently find it awkward to appear stingy in the context of their own admittedly favorable circumstances. If all this sounds a bit far-fetched, consider the findings of consumer researcher Daniel Howard, who put the theory to the test. Residents of Dallas, Texas, were called on the phone and asked if they would agree to allow a representative of the Hunger Relief Committee to come to their homes to sell them cookies, the proceeds from which would be used to supply meals for the needy. When tried alone, that request (labeled the standard solicitation approach) produced only 18 percent agreement. However, if the caller initially asked, "How are you feeling this evening?" and waited for a reply before proceeding with the standard approach, several noteworthy things happened. First, of the 120 individuals called, most (108) gave the customary favorable reply ("Good," "Fine," "Real well," etc.). Second, 32 percent of the people who got the "How are you feeling this evening?" question agreed to receive the cookie seller at their homes, nearly twice the success rate of the standard solicitation approach. Third, true to the consistency principle, almost everyone (89 percent) who agreed to such a visit did in fact make a cookie purchase when contacted at home.

There is still another behavioral arena, sexual infidelity, in which relatively small verbal commitments can make a substantial difference. Psychologists warn that cheating on a romantic partner is a source of great conflict, often leading to anger, pain, and termination of the relationship. They've also located an activity to help prevent the occurrence of this destructive sequence: prayer—not prayer in general, though, but of a particular kind. If one romantic partner agrees to say a brief prayer *for the other's well-being* every day, he or she becomes less likely to be unfaithful during the period of time while doing so. After all, such behavior would be inconsistent with daily active commitments to the partner's welfare.[3]

READER'S REPORT 7.1

From a sales trainer in Texas

The most powerful lesson I ever learned from your book was about commitment. Years ago, I trained people at a telemarketing center to sell insurance over the phone. Our main difficulty, however, was that we couldn't actually SELL insurance over the phone; we could only quote a price and then direct the caller to the company office nearest their home. The problem was callers who committed to office appointments but didn't show up.

I took a group of new training graduates and modified their sales approach from that used by other salespeople. They used the exact same "canned" presentation as the others but included an additional question at the end of the call. Instead of simply hanging up when the customer confirmed an appointment time, we instructed the salespeople to say, "I was wondering if you would tell me exactly why you've chosen to purchase your insurance with <our company>."

I was initially just attempting to gather customer service information, but these new sales associates generated nearly 19 percent more sales than other new salespeople. When we integrated this question into everyone's presentations, even the old pros generated over 10 percent more business than before. I didn't fully understand why this worked before.

Author's note: Although accidentally employed, this reader's tactic was masterful because it didn't simply commit customers to their choice; it also committed them to the reasons for their choice. And, as we've seen in chapter 1, people often behave for the sake of reasons (Bastardi & Shafir, 2000; Langer, 1989).

The tactic's effectiveness fits with the account of an Atlanta-based acquaintance of mine who—despite following standard advice to describe fully all the good reasons he should be hired—was having no success in job interviews. To change this outcome, he began employing the consistency principle on his own behalf. After assuring evaluators he wanted to answer all their questions as fully as possible, he added, "But, before we start, I wonder if you could answer a question for me. I'm curious, what was it about my background that attracted you to my candidacy?" As a consequence, his evaluators heard themselves saying positive things about him and his qualifications, committing themselves to reasons to hire him before he had to make the case himself. He swears he has gotten three better jobs in a row by employing this technique.

Imprisonments, Self-Imposed

The question of what makes a commitment effective has numerous answers. A variety of factors affects the ability of a commitment to constrain future behavior. One large-scale program designed to produce compliance illustrates how several of the factors work. The remarkable thing about the program is that it was systematically employing these factors over a half-century ago, well before scientific research had identified them.

During the Korean War, many captured American soldiers found themselves in prisoner-of-war camps run by the Chinese Communists. It became clear early in the conflict that the Chinese treated captives quite differently than did their allies, the North Koreans, who favored harsh punishment to gain compliance. Scrupulously avoiding brutality, the Red Chinese engaged in what they termed their "lenient policy," which was, in reality, a concerted and sophisticated psychological assault on their captives.

After the war, American psychologists questioned the returning prisoners intensively to determine what had occurred, in part because of the unsettling success of some aspects of the Chinese program. The Chinese were very effective in getting Americans to inform on one another, in striking contrast to the behavior of American POWs in World War II. For this reason, among others, escape plans were quickly uncovered and the escapes themselves almost always unsuccessful. "When an escape did occur," wrote psychologist Edgar Schein, a principal American investigator of the Chinese indoctrination program in Korea, "the Chinese usually recovered the man easily by offering a bag of rice to anyone turning him in." In fact, nearly all American prisoners in the Chinese camps are said to have collaborated with the enemy in one way or another.

An examination of the prison-camp program shows that the Chinese relied heavily on commitment and consistency pressures. Of course, the first problem facing the Chinese was to get any collaboration at all from the Americans. The prisoners had been trained to provide nothing but name, rank, and serial number. Short of physical brutalization, how could the captors hope to get such men to give military information, turn in fellow prisoners, or publicly denounce their country? The Chinese answer was elementary: start small and build.

For instance, prisoners were frequently asked to make statements so mildly anti-American or pro-Communist that they seemed inconsequential (such as "The United States is not perfect" and "In a Communist country, unemployment is not a problem"). Once these minor requests had been complied with, however, the men found themselves pushed to submit to related, yet more substantive, requests. A man who had just agreed with his Chinese interrogator that the United States was not perfect might then be asked to indicate some of the ways he believed this was the case. Once he had so explained, he might be asked to make a list of these "problems with America" and sign his name to it. Later, he might be asked to read his list in a discussion group with other prisoners. "After all, it's what you believe, isn't it?" Still later, he might be asked to write an essay expanding on his list and discussing these problems in greater detail.

The Chinese might then use his name and his essay in an anti-American radio broadcast beamed not only to the entire camp but to other POW camps in North Korea as well as to American forces in South Korea. Suddenly he would find himself a "collaborator," having given aid and comfort to the enemy. Aware that he had written the essay without any strong threats or coercion, many times a man would change his self-image to be consistent with the deed and with the "collaborator" label, which often resulted in even more extensive acts of collaboration. Thus, while "only a few men were able to avoid collaboration altogether," according to Schein, "the majority collaborated at one time or another by doing things which seemed to them trivial but which the Chinese were able to turn to their own advantage. . . . This was particularly effective in eliciting confessions, self-criticism, and information during interrogation."

Other groups of people interested in compliance are also aware of the usefulness and power of this approach. Charitable organizations, for instance, will often use progressively escalating commitments to induce individuals to perform major favors. The trivial first commitment of agreeing to be interviewed can begin a

Figure 7.2: Start small and build.

Pigs like mud. But they don't eat it. For that, escalating commitments seem needed.

© *Paws. Used by permission.*

"momentum of compliance" that induces such later behaviors as organ or bone-marrow donations.

Many business organizations employ this approach regularly as well. For the salesperson, the strategy is to obtain a large purchase by starting with a small one. Almost any small sale will do because the purpose of that small transaction is not profit, it's commitment. Further purchases, even much larger ones, are expected to flow naturally from the commitment. An article in the trade magazine *American Salesman* put it succinctly:

> *The general idea is to pave the way for full-line distribution by starting with a small order. . . . Look at it this way—when a person has signed an order for your merchandise, even though the profit is so small it hardly compensates for the time and effort of making the call, he is no longer a prospect—he is a customer.* (Green, 1965, p. 14)

The tactic of starting with a little request in order to gain eventual compliance with related larger requests has a name: the foot-in-the-door technique. Social scientists first became aware of its effectiveness when psychologists Jonathan Freedman and Scott Fraser published an astonishing data set. They reported the results of an experiment in which a researcher, posing as a volunteer worker, had gone door to door in a residential California neighborhood making a preposterous request of homeowners. The homeowners were asked to allow a public-service billboard to be installed on their front lawns. To get an idea of the way the sign would look, they were shown a photograph depicting an attractive house, the view of which was almost completely obscured by a large, poorly lettered sign reading Drive Carefully. Although the request was normally and understandably refused by the great majority of the residents in the area (only 17 percent complied), one particular group of people reacted quite favorably. A full 76 percent of them offered the use of their front yards.

The prime reason for their startling compliance was a small commitment to driver safety that they had made two weeks earlier.

A different "volunteer worker" had come to their doors and asked them to accept and display a little three-inch-square sign that read Be a Safe Driver. It was such a trifling request that nearly all of them had agreed, but the effects of that request were striking. Because they had innocently complied with a trivial safe-driving request a couple of weeks before, these homeowners became remarkably willing to comply with another such request that was massive in size.

Freedman and Fraser didn't stop there. They tried a slightly different procedure on another sample of homeowners. These people first received a request to sign a petition that favored "keeping California beautiful." Of course, nearly everyone signed because state beauty, like efficiency in government or sound prenatal care, is one of those issues no one opposes. After waiting about two weeks, Freedman and Fraser sent a new "volunteer worker" to these same homes to ask the residents to allow the big Drive Carefully sign to be erected on their lawns. In some ways, the response of these homeowners was the most astounding of any in the study. Approximately half consented to the installation of the Drive Carefully billboard, even though the small commitment they had made weeks earlier was not to driver safety but to an entirely different public-service topic, state beautification.

At first, even Freedman and Fraser were bewildered by their findings. Why should the little act of signing a petition supporting state beautification cause people to be so willing to perform a different and much larger favor? After considering and discarding other explanations, the researchers came upon one that offered a solution to the puzzle: signing the beautification petition changed the view these people had of themselves. They saw themselves as public-spirited citizens who acted on their civic principles. When, two weeks later, they were asked to perform another public service by displaying the Drive Carefully sign, they complied in order to be consistent with their newly formed self-images. According to Freedman and Fraser:

What may occur is a change in the person's feelings about getting involved or taking action. Once he has agreed to a request, his attitude may change, he may become, in his own eyes, the kind of person who does this sort of thing, who agrees to requests made by strangers, who takes action on things he believes in, who co-operates with good causes.

Figure 7.3: Just sign on the plotted line.

Author's note: Have you ever wondered what the groups that ask you to sign their petitions do with all the signatures they obtain? Most of the time, the groups use them for genuinely stated purposes, but often they don't do anything with them, as the principal purpose of the petition may simply be to get the signers committed to the group's position and, consequently, more willing to take future steps that are aligned with it.

Psychology professor Sue Frantz described witnessing a sinister version of the tactic on the streets of Paris, where tourists are approached by a scammer and asked to sign a petition "to support people who are deaf and mute." Those who sign are then immediately asked to make a donation, which many do to stay consistent with the cause they've just endorsed. Because the operation is a scam, no donation goes to charity—only to the scammer. Worse, an accomplice of the petitioner observes where, in their pockets or bags, the tourists reach for their wallets and targets them for subsequent pickpocket theft.

iStock Photo

Freedman and Fraser's findings tell us to be very careful about agreeing to trivial requests because that agreement can influence our self-concepts. Such an agreement can not only increase our compliance with very similar, much larger requests but also make us more willing to perform a variety of larger favors that are only remotely connected to the little favor we did earlier. It's this second kind of influence concealed within small commitments that scares me.

It scares me enough that I am rarely willing to sign a petition anymore, even for a position I support. The action has the potential to influence not only my future behavior but also my self-image in ways I may not want. Further, once a person's self-image is altered, all sorts of subtle advantages become available to someone who wants to exploit the new image.

Who among Freedman and Fraser's homeowners would have thought the "volunteer worker" who asked them to sign a state-beautification petition was really interested in having them display a safe-driving billboard two weeks later? Who among them could have suspected their decision to display the billboard was largely a result of signing that petition? No one, I'd guess. If there were any regrets after the billboard went up, who could they conceivably hold responsible but *themselves* and their own damnably strong civic spirits? They probably never considered the guy with the "keeping California beautiful" petition and all that knowledge of social jujitsu.[4]

Hearts and Minds

> Every time you make a choice, you are turning the central
> part of you, the part that chooses, into something a little
> different from what it was before.
>
> —C. S. Lewis

Notice that all of the foot-in-the-door experts seem to be excited about the same thing: you can use small commitments to manipulate a person's self-image; you can use them to turn citizens into "public servants," prospects into "customers," and prisoners into "collaborators." Once you've got a person's self-image where you want it, that person should comply *naturally* with a whole range of requests aligned with this new self-view.

Not all commitments affect self-image equally, however. There are certain conditions that should be present for commitments to be most effective in this way: they should be active, public, effortful, and freely chosen. The major intent of the Chinese was not simply to extract information from their prisoners. It was to indoctrinate them, to change their perceptions of themselves, of their political system, of their country's role in the war, and of communism. Dr. Henry Segal, chief of the neuropsychiatric evaluation team that examined returning POWs at the end of the Korean War, reported that war-related beliefs had been substantially shifted. Significant inroads had been made in the men's political attitudes:

> *Many expressed antipathy toward the Chinese Communists but at the same time praised them for "the fine job they had done in China." Others stated that "although communism won't work in America, I think it's a good thing for Asia." (Segal, 1954, p. 360)*

It appears that the real goal of the Chinese was to modify, at least for a time, the hearts and minds of their captives. If we measure their achievement in terms of "defection, disloyalty, changed attitudes and beliefs, poor discipline, poor morale, poor *esprit*, and doubts as to America's role," Segal concluded, "their efforts were highly successful." Let's examine more closely how they managed it.

The Magic Act

Our best evidence of people's true feelings and beliefs comes less from their words than from their deeds. Observers trying to decide what people are like look closely at their actions. People also use this evidence—their own behavior—to decide what they are like; it is a key source of information about their own beliefs, values, attitudes, and, crucially, what they want to do next. Online sites often want visitors to register by providing information about themselves. But 86 percent of users report that they sometimes quit the registration process because the form is too long or prying. What have site developers done to overcome this barrier without reducing the amount of information they get from customers? They've reduced the average number of fields of requested information on the form's *first* page. Why? They want to give users the feeling of having started and finished the initial part of the process. As design consultant Diego Poza put it, "It doesn't matter if the next page has more fields to fill out (it does), due to the principle of commitment and consistency, users are much more likely to follow through." The available data have proved him right: Just reducing the number of first-page fields from four to three increases registration completions by 50 percent.

The rippling impact of behavior on self-concept and future behavior can be seen in research into the effect of active versus passive commitments. In one study, college students volunteered for an AIDS-education project in local schools. The researchers arranged for half to volunteer actively, by filling out a form stating that they wanted to participate. The other half volunteered passively, by *failing* to fill out a form stating that they *didn't* want to participate. Three to four days later, when asked to begin their volunteer activity, the great majority (74 percent) who appeared for duty came from the ranks of those who had actively agreed. What's more, those who volunteered actively were more likely to explain their decisions by implicating their personal values, preferences, and traits. In all, it seems that active commitments give us the kind of information we use to shape our self-image, which then shapes our future actions, which solidify the new self-image.

Understanding fully this route to altered self-concept, the Chinese set about arranging the prison-camp experience so their captives would consistently *act* in desired ways. Before long, the Chinese knew, these actions would begin to take their toll, causing the prisoners to change their views of themselves to fit with what they had done.

Writing was one sort of committing action that the Chinese urged incessantly upon the captives. It was never enough for prisoners to listen quietly or even agree verbally with the Chinese line; they were always pushed to write it down as well. Edgar Schein (1956) describes a standard indoctrination-session tactic of the Chinese:

> *A further technique was to have the man write out the question and then the [pro-Communist] answer. If he refused to write it voluntarily, he was asked to copy it from the notebooks, which must have seemed like a harmless enough concession. (p. 161)*

Oh, those "harmless" concessions. We've already seen how apparently trifling commitments can lead to further consistent behavior. As a commitment device, a written declaration has great advantages. First, it provides physical evidence that an act has occurred. Once a prisoner wrote what the Chinese wanted, it was difficult for him to believe he had not done so. The opportunities to forget or to deny to himself what he had done were not available, as they are for purely spoken statements. No; there it was in his own handwriting, an irrevocably documented act driving him to make his beliefs and his self-image consistent with what he had undeniably done. Second, a written testament can be shown to others. Of course, that means it can be used to persuade those others. It can persuade them to change their attitudes in the direction of the statement. More importantly for the purpose of commitment, it can persuade them the author genuinely believes what was written.

People have a natural tendency to think a statement reflects the true attitude of the person who made it. What is surprising is that they continue to think so even when they know the person did not freely choose to make the statement. Some scientific evidence that this is the case comes from a study by psychologists Edward Jones and James Harris, who showed people an essay favorable to Fidel Castro and asked them to guess the true feelings of its author. Jones and Harris told some of these people that the author had chosen to write a pro-Castro essay; they told other people that the author had been required to write in favor of Castro. The strange thing was that even those who knew that the author had been assigned to do a pro-Castro essay guessed the writer liked Castro. It seems a statement of belief produces a *click, run* response in those who view it. Unless there is strong evidence to the contrary, observers automatically assume someone who makes such a statement means it.

Think of the double-barreled effects on the self-image of a prisoner who wrote a pro-Chinese or anti-American statement. Not only was it a lasting personal reminder of his action, but it was likely to persuade those around him that it reflected his actual beliefs. As we saw in chapter 4, what those around us think is true of us importantly determines what we ourselves think. For example, one study found that a week after hearing they were considered charitable people by their neighbors, people gave much more money to a canvasser from the Multiple Sclerosis Association. Apparently the mere knowledge that others viewed them as charitable caused the individuals to make their actions congruent with that view.

A study in the fruit and vegetable section of a Swedish supermarket obtained a similar result. Customers in the section saw two separate bins of bananas, one labeled as ecologically grown and one without an ecological label. Under these circumstances, the ecological versions were chosen 32 percent of the time. Two additional samples of shoppers saw a sign between the two bins. For one sample, the sign that marketed the ecological bananas on price, "Ecological bananas are the same price as competing bananas," increased the purchase rate to 46 percent. For the final sample of customers, the sign that marketed the ecological bananas by assigning the shoppers an environmentally friendly public image, "Hello Environmentalists, our ecological bananas are right here," raised the purchase rate of ecological bananas to 51 percent.

Savvy politicians have long used the committing character of labels to great advantage. One of the best at it was former president of Egypt Anwar Sadat. Before international negotiations began, Sadat would assure his bargaining opponents that they and the citizens of their country were widely known for their cooperativeness and fairness. With this kind of flattery, he not only created positive feelings but also connected his opponent's identities to a course of action that served his goals. According to master negotiator Henry Kissinger, Sadat was successful because he got others to act in his interests by giving them a reputation to uphold.

Once an active commitment is made, then, self-image is squeezed from both sides by consistency pressures. From the inside, there is a pressure to bring self-image into line with action. From the outside, there is a sneakier pressure—a tendency to adjust this image according to the way others perceive us.

Because others see us as believing what we have written (even when we've had little choice in the matter), we experience a pull to bring self-image into line with the written statement. In Korea, several subtle devices were used to get prisoners to write, without direct coercion, what the Chinese wanted. For example, the Chinese knew many prisoners were anxious to let their families know they were alive. At the same time, the men knew their captors were censoring the mail and only some letters were being allowed out of camp. To ensure their own letters would be released, some prisoners began including in their messages peace appeals, claims of kind treatment, and statements sympathetic to communism. Their hope was the Chinese would want such letters to surface and would, therefore, allow their delivery. Of course, the Chinese were happy to cooperate because those letters served their interests marvelously. First, their worldwide propaganda effort benefited from the appearance of pro-Communist statements by American servicemen. Second, for purposes of prisoner indoctrination, the Chinese had, without raising a finger of physical force, gotten many men to go on record supporting the Communist cause.

A similar technique involved political-essay contests regularly held in camp. The prizes for winning were invariably small—a few cigarettes or a bit of fruit—but sufficiently scarce that they generated a lot of interest from the men. Usually the winning essay took a solidly pro-Communist stand . . . but not always. The Chinese were wise enough to realize that most prisoners would not enter a contest they thought they could win only by writing a Communist tract. Moreover, the Chinese were clever enough to know how to plant in captives small commitments to communism that could be nurtured into later bloom. So, occasionally, the winning essay was one that generally supported the United States but bowed once or twice to the Chinese view.

The effects of the strategy were exactly what the Chinese wanted. The men continued to participate voluntarily in the contests because they saw they could win with essays highly favorable to their own country. Perhaps without realizing it, though, they began shading their essays a bit toward communism in order to have a better chance of winning. The Chinese were ready to pounce on any concession to Communist dogma and to bring consistency pressures to bear upon it. In the case of a written declaration within a voluntary essay, they had a perfect commitment from which to build toward collaboration and conversion.

Other compliance professionals also know about the committing power of written statements. The enormously successful Amway corporation, for instance, has a way to spur their sales personnel to greater and greater accomplishments. Members of the staff are asked to set individual sales goals and commit themselves to those goals by personally recording them on paper:

> One final tip before you get started: Set a goal and write it down. Whatever the goal, the important thing is that you set it, so you've got something for which to aim—and that you write it down. There is something magical about writing things down. So set a goal and write it down. When you reach that goal, set another and write that down. You'll be off and running.

If the Amway people have found "something magical about writing things down," so have other business organizations. Some door-to-door sales companies used the magic of written commitments to battle the "cooling off" laws of many states. The laws are designed to allow customers a few days after agreeing to purchase an item to cancel the sale and receive a full refund. At first this legislation hurt the hard-sell companies deeply. Because they emphasize high-pressure tactics, their customers often bought, not because they wanted the products but because they were tricked or intimidated into the sale. When the laws went into effect, these customers began canceling in droves during the cooling-off period.

The companies quickly learned a simple trick that cut the number of such cancellations markedly. They had the customer, rather than the salesperson, fill out the sales agreement. According to the sales-training program of a prominent encyclopedia company, that personal commitment alone proved to be "a very important psychological aid in preventing customers from backing out of their contracts." Like the Amway corporation, these organizations found that something special happens when people put their commitments on paper: they live up to what they write down.

Figure 7.4: Writing is believing.

This ad invites readers to participate in a sweepstakes by providing a handwritten message detailing the product's favorable features.

Courtesy of Schieffelin & Co.

Another common way for businesses to cash in on the "magic" of written declarations occurs through the use of an innocent-looking promotional device. Growing up, I used to wonder why big companies such as Procter & Gamble and General Foods were always running 25-, 50-, or 100-words or less testimonial contests. They all seemed alike. A contestant was to compose a short personal statement beginning with the words, "I like [the product] because . . ." and go on to laud the features of whatever cake mix or floor wax happened to be at issue. The company judged the entries and awarded prizes to the winners. What puzzled me was what the companies got out of the deal. Often the contest required no purchase; anyone submitting an entry was eligible. Yet the companies appeared willing to incur the costs of contest after contest.

I am no longer puzzled. The purpose behind testimonial contests—to get as many people as possible to endorse a product—is akin to the purpose behind the political-essay contests in Korea: to get endorsements for Chinese communism. In both instances, the process is the same. Participants voluntarily write essays for attractive prizes they have only a small chance to win. They know that for an essay to have any chance of winning, it must include praise for the product. So they search for praiseworthy features, and they describe them in their essays. The result is hundreds of POWs in Korea or hundreds of thousands of people in America who testify in writing to the products' appeal and who, consequently, experience the magical pull to believe what they have written.[5]

READER'S REPORT 7.2

From the creative director of a large
international advertising agency

In the late 1990s, I asked Fred DeLuca, the founder and CEO of Subway restaurants, why he insisted in putting the prediction "10,000 stores by 2001" on the napkins in every single Subway. It didn't seem to make sense, as I knew he was a long way from his goal, that consumers didn't really care about his plan, and his franchisees were deeply troubled by the competition associated with such a goal. His answer was, "If I put my goals down in writing and make them known to the world, I'm committed to achieving them." Needless to say, he not only has, he's exceeded them.

Author's note: As of January 1, 2021, Subway was on schedule to have 38,000 restaurants in 111 countries. So, as we will also see in the next section, written down and publicly made commitments can be used not only to influence others in desirable ways but to influence ourselves similarly.

The Public Eye

One reason written testaments are effective in bringing about genuine personal change is that they can so easily be made public. The prisoner experience in Korea showed the Chinese to be aware of an important psychological principle: public commitments tend to be lasting commitments. The Chinese constantly arranged to have pro-Communist statements of their captives seen by others. They were posted around camp, read by the author to a prisoner discussion group, or even read on a radio broadcast. As far as the Chinese were concerned, the more public the better.

Whenever one takes a stand visible to others, there arises a drive to maintain that stand in order to *look* like a consistent person. Remember that earlier in this chapter I described how desirable good personal consistency is as a trait; how someone without it may be judged as fickle, uncertain, pliant, scatterbrained, or unstable; how someone with it is viewed as rational, assured, trustworthy, and sound? Thus, it's hardly surprising that people try to avoid the look of inconsistency. For appearances' sake, the more public a stand, the more reluctant we are to change it.

EBOX 7.1

HOW TO CHANGE YOUR LIFE
By Alicia Morga

Owen Thomas wrote in an amazed tone in *The New York Times* recently how he managed to lose 83 pounds using a mobile app. He used MyFitnessPal. The developers of the app discovered that users who exposed their calorie counts to friends lost 50% more weight than a typical user.

It seems obvious that a social network can help you make a change, but it is less clear how. Many cite social proof—looking to others for how to behave—as influential, but what better explains transformation is commitment and consistency.

The more public our commitment, the more pressure we feel to act according to our commitment and therefore appear consistent. It can become a virtuous (or destructive) cycle as according to Robert Cialdini, "you can use small commitments to manipulate a person's self-image" and once you change a person's self-image you can get that person to behave in accordance with that new image—anything that would be consistent with this new view of herself.

So want to change your life? Make a specific commitment, use social media to broadcast it and use the internal pressure you then feel to get you to follow through. This in turn should cause you to see yourself in a new way and therefore keep you continuing to follow through.

While Mr. Thomas' experience demonstrates the power of this theory as applied to dieting, I see the possible applications everywhere. Like say struggling Hispanic high school students (they have the highest high school dropout rate). Why not get them to publicly commit to going to college? Might more then go? There should be an app for that.

Author's note: In this blog post, its author judges correctly that even though peer pressure was involved, the principle that produced desired change for Mr. Thomas was not social proof. It was

commitment and consistency. What's more, the effective commitment was public, which fits with research showing that commitments to weight-loss goals are increasingly successful—in both the
short and long term—when they become increasingly public (Nyer
& Dellande, 2010).

An illustration of the way public commitments can lead to consistent further action was provided in a famous experiment performed by two prominent social psychologists, Morton Deutsch
and Harold Gerard. The basic procedure was to have college students first estimate in their minds the length of lines they were
shown. Then, one sample of the students had to commit publicly
to their initial judgments by writing their estimates down, signing
their names to them, and turning them in to the experimenter. A
second sample also committed themselves to their first estimates,
but did so privately by writing them down and then erasing them
before anyone could see what they had written. A third set of students did not commit themselves to their initial estimates at all;
they just kept the estimates in mind privately.

In these ways, Deutsch and Gerard cleverly arranged for some
students to commit publicly, some privately, and some not at all,
to their initial decisions. The researchers wanted to find out which
of the three types of students would be most inclined to stick with
their first judgments after receiving information that those judgments were incorrect. Therefore, all the students were given new
evidence suggesting their initial estimates were wrong, and they
were then given the chance to change their estimates.

The students who had never written down their first choices
were the least loyal to those choices. When new evidence was presented that questioned the wisdom of decisions that had never left
their heads, these students were the most influenced to change
what they had viewed as the "correct" decision. Compared to
the uncommitted students, those who had merely written their

decisions for a moment were significantly less willing to change their minds when given the chance. Even though they had committed themselves under anonymous circumstances, the act of writing down their first judgments caused them to resist the influence of contradictory new data and to remain congruent with their preliminary choices. However, by far, it was the students who had publicly recorded their initial positions who most resolutely refused to shift from those positions later. Public commitments had hardened them into the most stubborn of all.

This sort of stubbornness can occur even in situations in which accuracy should be more important than consistency. In one study, when six- or twelve-person experimental juries were deciding a close case, hung juries were significantly more frequent if the jurors had to express their opinions with a visible show of hands rather than by secret ballot. Once jurors had stated their initial views publicly, they were reluctant to allow themselves to change publicly. Should you ever find yourself the foreperson of a jury under these conditions, you could reduce the risk of a hung jury by choosing a secret rather than public balloting method.

The finding that we are truest to our decisions if we have bound ourselves to them publicly can be put to good use. Consider organizations dedicated to helping people rid themselves of bad habits. Many weight-reduction clinics, for instance, understand that often a person's private decision to lose weight will be too weak to withstand the blandishments of bakery windows, wafting cooking scents, and pizza-delivery commercials. So they see to it that the decision is buttressed by the pillars of public commitment. They require clients to write down an immediate weight-loss goal and *show* that goal to as many friends, relatives, and neighbors as possible. Clinic operators report this simple technique frequently works where all else has failed.

Of course, there's no need to pay a special clinic in order to engage a visible commitment as an ally. One San Diego woman described to me how she employed a public promise to help herself finally stop smoking. She bought a set of blank business cards and wrote on the back of each, "I promise you I'll never smoke another cigarette." She then gave a signed card to "all the people in my life I really wanted to respect me." Whenever she felt a need to smoke thereafter, she said she'd think of how those people would think less of her if she broke her promise to them. She never had another smoke. These days, behavior-change apps linked to our social networks allow us employ this self-influence technique within a much larger set of friends than a few business cards could reach.[6] See, for example, eBox 7.1.

READER'S REPORT 7.3

From a Canadian university professor

I just read a newspaper article on how a restaurant owner used public commitments to solve a big problem of "no-shows" (customers who don't show up for their table reservations). I don't know if he read your book or not first, but he did something that fits perfectly with the commitment/consistency principle you talk about. He told his receptionists to stop saying, "Please call us if you change your plans," and to start asking, "Will you please call us if you change your plans?" and to wait for a response. His no-show rate immediately went from 30 percent to 10 percent. That's a 67 percent drop.

   Author's note: What was it about this subtle shift that led to such a dramatic difference? For me, it was the receptionist's request for (and pause for) the caller's promise. By spurring patrons to make a public commitment, this approach increased the chance that they would follow through on it. By the way, the astute proprietor was Gordon Sinclair of Gordon's restaurant in Chicago. *eBox* 7.2 provides the online version of this tactic.

Get excited, your reservation is tomorrow.
Still going to make it?

I'll be there!

Table for 4 on Saturday, August 31, 2019 at 6:30 pm

Confirmation #: 2109809112

See menu | Get directions
4175 N Goldwater Blvd
Scottsdale, AZ 85251
(480) 265-9814

Calendar   Modify   Cancel

YOU ARE CONFIRMED

Author's note: Today, restaurants are reducing reservation no-shows by asking customers to make active and public commitments online before the date of their reservation. Recently, my doctor's office began doing the same, with one additional compliance-enhancing element. In the confirmation email, I was given a reason by the nurse for my active, public commitment: "By telling me if you can or cannot make it, you help make sure that all patients are getting the care they need." When I inquired about the success of the online confirmation program, the doctor's office manager told me it had reduced no-shows by 81 percent.

The Effort Extra

The evidence is clear: the more effort that goes into a commitment, the greater its ability to influence the attitudes and actions of the person who made it. We can find that evidence in settings as close by as our homes and schools or as far away as remote regions of the world.

Let's begin nearer to home with the requirements of many localities for residents to separate their household trash for pro-environmental disposal. These requirements can differ in the effort needed for correct disposal. This is the case in Hangzhou, China, where the steps for proper separation and disposal are more arduous in some sections of the city than in others. After informing residents of the environmental benefits of proper disposal, researchers there wanted to see if residents who had to work harder to live up to environmental standards would become more committed to the environment in general, as shown by also taking the pro-environmental action of reducing their household electricity consumption. That's what happened. Residents who had to work harder to support the environment via household-waste separation then worked harder to support the environment through electricity conservation. The results are important in indicating that deepening our commitment to a mission, in this case by increasing the effort required to further it, can inspire us to advance the mission in related ways.

More far-flung illustrations of the power of effortful commitments exist as well. There is a tribe in southern Africa, the Thonga, that requires each of its boys to go through an elaborate initiation ceremony before he can be counted a man. As in many other tribes, a Thonga boy endures a great deal before he is admitted to adult membership in the group. Anthropologists John W. M. Whiting, Richard Kluckhohn, and Albert Anthony described this three-month ordeal in brief but vivid terms:

> When a boy is somewhere between 10 and 16 years of age, he is sent by his parents to "circumcision school," which is held every 4 or 5 years. Here in company with his age-mates he undergoes severe hazing by the adult males of the society. The initiation begins when each boy runs the gauntlet between two rows of men who beat him with clubs. At the end of this experience he is stripped of his clothes and his hair is cut. He is next met by a man covered with lion manes and is seated upon a stone facing this "lion man." Someone then strikes him from behind and when he

turns his head to see who has struck him, his foreskin is seized
and in two movements cut off by the "lion man." Afterward he is
secluded for three months in the "yard of mysteries," where he can
be seen only by the initiated.

During the course of his initiation, the boy undergoes six ma-
jor trials: beatings, exposure to cold, thirst, eating of unsavory
foods, punishment, and the threat of death. On the slightest pre-
text, he may be beaten by one of the newly initiated men, who
is assigned to the task by the older men of the tribe. He sleeps
without covering and suffers bitterly from the winter cold. He is
forbidden to drink a drop of water during the whole three months.
Meals are often made nauseating by the half-digested grass from
the stomach of an antelope, which is poured over his food. If he is
caught breaking any important rule governing the ceremony, he
is severely punished. For example, in one of these punishments,
sticks are placed between the fingers of the offender, then a strong
man closes his hand around that of the novice, practically crush-
ing his fingers. He is frightened into submission by being told that
in former times boys who had tried to escape or who had revealed
the secrets to women or to the uninitiated were hanged and their
bodies burned to ashes. (p. 360)

On their face, these rites seem extraordinary and bizarre. Yet they are remarkably similar in principle and even in detail to the common initiation ceremonies of school fraternities. During the traditional "Hell Week" held yearly on college campuses, fraternity pledges must persevere through a variety of activities designed by older members to test the limits of physical exertion, psychological strain, and social embarrassment. At week's end, the boys who have persisted through the ordeal are accepted for full group membership. Mostly, their tribulations have left them no more than greatly tired and a bit shaky, although sometimes the negative effects are much more serious.

It is interesting how closely the features of Hell Week tasks match those of tribal initiation rites. Recall that anthropologists identified six major trials to be endured by a Thonga initiate during his stay in the "yard of mysteries." A scan of newspaper reports shows that each trial also has its place in the hazing rituals of Greek-letter societies:

- **Beatings.** Fourteen-year-old Michael Kalogris spent three weeks in a Long Island hospital recovering from internal injuries suffered during a Hell Night initiation ceremony of his high school fraternity, Omega Gamma Delta. He had been administered the "atomic bomb" by his prospective brothers, who told him to hold his hands over his head and keep them there while they gathered around to slam fists into his stomach and back simultaneously and repeatedly.

- **Exposure to cold.** On a winter night, Frederick Bronner, a California community-college student, was taken three thousand feet up and ten miles into the hills of a national forest by his prospective fraternity brothers. Left to find his way home wearing only a thin sweatshirt and slacks, Fat Freddy, as he was called, shivered in a frigid wind until he tumbled down a steep ravine, fracturing bones and injuring his head. Prevented by his injuries from going on, he huddled there against the cold until he died of exposure.

- **Thirst.** Two Ohio State University freshmen found themselves in the "dungeon" of their prospective fraternity house after breaking the rule requiring all pledges to crawl into the dining area prior to Hell Week meals. Once locked in the house's storage room, they were given only salty foods to eat for nearly two days. Nothing was provided for drinking purposes except a pair of plastic cups in which they could catch their own urine.

- **Eating of unsavory foods.** At Kappa Sigma house on the campus of the University of Southern California, the eyes of eleven pledges bulged when they saw the sickening task before them. Eleven quarter-pound slabs of raw liver lay on a tray. Thick-cut and soaked in oil, each was to be swallowed whole, one to a boy. Gagging and choking repeatedly, young Richard Swanson failed three times to down his piece. Determined to succeed, he finally got the oil-soaked meat into his throat, where it lodged and, despite all efforts to remove it, killed him.

- **Punishment.** In Wisconsin, a pledge who forgot one section of a ritual incantation to be memorized by all initiates was punished for his error. He was required to keep his feet under the rear legs of a folding chair while the heaviest of his fraternity brothers sat down and drank a beer. Although the pledge did not cry out during the punishment, a bone in each foot was broken.

- **Threats of death.** A pledge of Zeta Beta Tau fraternity was taken to a beach area of New Jersey and told to dig his "own grave." Seconds after he complied with orders to lie flat in the finished hole, the sides collapsed, suffocating him before his prospective fraternity brothers could dig him out.

There is another striking similarity between the initiation rites of tribal and fraternal societies: they will not die. Resisting all attempts to eliminate or suppress them, such hazing practices have been phenomenally resilient. Authorities, in the form of governments or university administrations, have tried threats, social pressures, legal actions, banishments, bribes, and bans to persuade groups to remove the hazards and humiliations from their initiation ceremonies. None has been successful. Oh, there may be a change while the authority is watching closely, but this is usually more apparent than real—the harsher trials occur under secret circumstances until the pressure is off and they can surface again.

On some college campuses, officials have tried to eliminate dangerous hazing practices by substituting a "Help Week" of civic service or by taking direct control of the initiation rituals. When such attempts are not slyly circumvented by fraternities, they are met with outright physical resistance. For example, in the aftermath of Richard Swanson's choking death at USC, the university president issued new rules requiring all pledging activities be reviewed by school authorities before going into effect and adult advisers be present during initiation ceremonies. According to one national magazine, "The new 'code' set off a riot so violent city police and fire detachments were afraid to enter campus."

Resigning themselves to the inevitable, other college representatives have given up on the possibility of abolishing the degradations of Hell Week. "If hazing is a universal human activity, and every bit of evidence points to this conclusion, you most likely won't be able to ban it effectively. Refuse to allow it openly and it will go underground. You can't ban sex, you can't prohibit alcohol, and you probably can't eliminate hazing!"

What is it about hazing practices that make them so precious to these societies? What could cause the groups to want to evade, undermine, or contest any effort to ban the degrading and perilous features of their initiation rights? Some have argued that the groups themselves are composed of psychological or social miscreants whose twisted needs demand that others be harmed and humiliated. The evidence does not support the view. Studies done on the personality traits of fraternity members, for instance, show them to be, if anything, slightly healthier than other college students in their psychological adjustment. Similarly, fraternities are known for their willingness to engage in beneficial community projects for the general social good. What they are not willing to do, however, is substitute these projects for their initiation ceremonies. One survey at the University of Washington found that of the fraternity chapters examined, most had a type of Help Week tradition but that this community service was *in addition* to Hell Week. In only one case was such service directly related to initiation procedures.

The picture that emerges of the perpetrators of hazing practices is of normal individuals who tend to be psychologically stable and socially concerned but who become aberrantly harsh as a group at only one time—immediately before the admission of new members to the society. The evidence points to the ceremony as culprit. There must be something about its rigors that is vital to the group.

There must be some function to its harshness that the society will fight relentlessly to maintain. What?

In my view, the answer appeared in the results of a study little known outside of social psychology. A pair of researchers, Elliot Aronson and Judson Mills, decided to test their observation that "persons who go through a great deal of trouble or pain to attain something tend to value it more highly than persons who attain the same thing with a minimum of effort." The real stroke of inspiration came in their choice of the initiation ceremony as the best place to examine this possibility. They found that college women who had to endure a severely embarrassing initiation ceremony in order to gain access to a sex-discussion group convinced themselves their new group and its discussions were extremely valuable, even though Aronson and Mills had rehearsed the other group members to be as "worthless and uninteresting" as possible. Different coeds who went through a much milder initiation ceremony or went through no initiation at all, were decidedly less positive about the "worthless" new group they had joined. Additional research showed the same results when coeds were required to endure pain rather than embarrassment to get into a group. The more electric shock a woman received as part of the initiation ceremony, the more she later persuaded herself that her new group and its activities were interesting, intelligent, and desirable.

READER'S REPORT 7.4

From Paola, an Italian graphics designer

I'd like to tell you of a case that happened to me last month. I was in London with my boyfriend, when we saw a tattoo studio sign claiming "the cheapest eyebrow piercings in London." I was really frightened by the idea of the suffering but I decided to do it. After the emotion of the piercing, I almost fainted. I couldn't move myself or open my eye. I felt so bad I just had the strength to say, "Hospital."

A doctor came and told me I would be OK. After 10 minutes, I felt better, but I assure you they were the worst 10 minutes of my life!

Then, I began to think about my parents. They wouldn't be happy of what I did, and I thought to maybe take off the piercing jewelry ring. But I decided no, I suffered too much to remove it.

I am glad about that decision because now I am really happy to have this ring on my eyebrow.

Author's note: Much like the young women in Aronson and Mills's study, Paola has become happy with and committed to what she endured to obtain.

Now the harassments, the exertions, and even the beatings of initiation rituals begin to make sense. The Thonga tribesman with tears in his eyes, watching his ten-year-old son tremble through a night on the cold ground of the "yard of mysteries" and the college sophomore punctuating his Hell Night paddling of his fraternity "little brother" with bursts of nervous laughter—these are not acts of sadism. They are acts of group survival. They function, oddly enough, to spur future society members to find the group more attractive and worthwhile. As long as it is the case that people like and believe in what they have struggled to get, these groups will continue to arrange effortful and trying initiation rites. The loyalty and dedication of those who emerge will greatly increase the chances of group cohesiveness and survival. Indeed, one study of fifty-four tribal cultures found that those with the most dramatic and stringent initiation ceremonies had the greatest group solidarity. Given Aronson and Mills's demonstration that the severity of an initiation ceremony heightens the newcomer's commitment to the group, it is hardly surprising that groups will oppose all attempts to eliminate this crucial link to their future strength.

Military groups and organizations are by no means exempt from these same processes. The agonies of "boot camp" initiations to the armed services are legendary and effective. The novelist William Styron testified to this effectiveness after recounting the misery of his own US Marine concentration-camp-like "training nightmare":

> *There is no ex-Marine of my acquaintance . . . who does not view the training as a crucible out of which he emerged in some way more resilient, simply braver and better for the wear. (Styron, 1977, p. 3)*[7]

The Inner Choice

Examination of such diverse activities as the indoctrination practices within Chinese-run prison camps in Korea and the initiation rituals of college fraternities provides some valuable information about commitment. It appears the commitments most effective in changing self-image and future behavior are those that are active, public, and effortful. However, there is another property of effective commitment more important than the other three combined. To understand what it is, we first need to solve a pair of puzzles in the actions of Communist interrogators and college fraternity brothers.

The first comes from the refusal of fraternity chapters to allow public-service activities to be part of their initiation ceremonies. Recall the University of Washington survey that found that fraternity community projects, though frequent, were nearly always separated from the membership-induction program. Why? If an effortful commitment is what fraternities are after in their initiation rites, surely they could structure enough distasteful and strenuous civic activities for their pledges; there is plenty of exertion and unpleasantness to be found in repairing the homes of the elderly, doing yard work at mental-health centers, and cleaning up roadside litter. Besides, community-spirited endeavors of this sort would do much to improve the highly unfavorable public and media image of fraternity Hell Week rites; one survey showed that for every positive newspaper story concerning Hell Week, there were five negative stories. If only for public-relations reasons, then, fraternities should want to incorporate community-service efforts into their initiation practices. But they don't.

To examine the second puzzle, we need to return to the Chinese prison camps of Korea and the political-essay contests held for American captives. The Chinese wanted as many Americans as possible to enter these contests so, in the process, they might write comments favorable to the Communist view. If the idea was to attract large numbers of entrants, why were the prizes so small? A few extra cigarettes or a little fresh fruit were often all a contest winner could expect. In the setting, even these prizes were valuable; but, still, there were much larger rewards—warm clothing, special mail privileges, increased freedom of movement in camp—the Chinese could have used to increase the number of essay writers. Yet they chose to employ the smaller rather than larger, more motivating rewards.

Although the settings are quite different, the surveyed fraternities refused to allow civic activities into their initiation ceremonies for the same reason the Chinese withheld large prizes in favor of less powerful inducements: they wanted the participants to *own* what they had done. No excuses, no ways out were allowed. A pledge who suffered through an arduous hazing could not be given the chance to believe he did so for charitable purposes. A prisoner who salted his political essay with anti-American comments could not be permitted to shrug it off as motivated by a big reward. No, the fraternity chapters and Chinese Communists were playing for keeps. It was not enough to wring commitments out of their men; those men had to be made to take inner responsibility for their actions.

Social scientists have determined that *we accept inner responsibility for a behavior when we think we have chosen to perform it in the absence of strong outside pressure.* A large reward is one such external pressure. It may get us to perform certain actions, but it won't get us to accept inner responsibility for the acts. Consequently, we won't feel committed to them. The same is true of a strong threat; it may motivate immediate compliance, but it is unlikely to produce long-term commitment. In fact, large material rewards or threats may even reduce or "undermine" our sense of inner responsibility for an act, causing excessive reluctance to perform it when the reward is no longer present.

All this has important implications for rearing children. It suggests we should never heavily bribe or threaten our children to do the things we want them truly to believe in. Such pressures will probably produce temporary compliance with our wishes. However, if we want more than that, if we want our children to believe in the correctness of what they have done, if we want them to continue to perform the desired behavior when we are not present to apply those outside pressures, we must somehow arrange for them to accept inner responsibility for the actions we want them to take. An experiment by social psychologist Jonathan Freedman gives us some hints about what to do and not to do in this regard.

Freedman wanted to see if he could prevent second-, third-, and fourth-grade boys from playing with a fascinating toy, just because he had said that it was wrong to do so some six weeks earlier. Anyone familiar with boys around the ages of seven to nine must realize the enormity of the task; but Freedman had a plan. If he could first get the boys to convince themselves that it was wrong to play with the forbidden toy, perhaps that belief would keep them from playing with it thereafter. The difficulty was making the boys believe it was wrong to amuse themselves with the toy—an expensive remote-controlled robot.

Freedman knew it would be easy enough to have a boy obey temporarily. All he had to do was threaten the boy with severe consequences should he be caught playing with the toy. As long as Freedman was nearby to deal out stiff punishment, he figured few boys would risk operating the robot. He was right. After showing a boy an array of five toys and warning, "It is wrong to play with the robot. If you play with the robot, I'll be very angry and will have to do something about it," Freedman left the room for a few minutes. During that time, the boy was observed secretly through a one-way mirror. Freedman tried this threat procedure on twenty-two different boys, and twenty-one of them never touched the robot while he was gone.

So a strong threat was successful while the boys thought they might be caught and punished. But Freedman had already guessed that. He was really interested in the effectiveness of the threat in guiding the boys' behavior later, when he was no longer around. To find out what would happen then, he sent a young woman back to the boys' school about six weeks after he had been there. She took the boys out of the class one at a time to participate in a study. Without ever mentioning any connection with Freedman, she escorted each boy back to the room containing the five toys and gave him a drawing test. While she was scoring the test, she told the boy he was free to play with any toy in the room. Of course, almost all the boys played with a toy. The interesting result was, of the boys who did so, 77 percent chose to play with the robot that had been forbidden to them earlier. Freedman's severe threat, which had been so successful six weeks before, was almost totally unsuccessful when he was no longer able to back it up with punishment.

However, Freedman wasn't finished. He changed his procedure slightly with a second sample of boys. These boys, too, were initially shown the array of five toys by Freedman and warned not to play with the robot because "It is wrong to play with the robot." This time, Freedman provided no strong threat to frighten the boys into obedience. He simply left the room and observed through the one-way mirror to see if his instruction against playing with the forbidden toy was enough. It was. Just as with the other sample, only one of the twenty-two boys touched the robot during the short time Freedman was gone.

The real difference between the two samples of boys came six weeks later, when they had a chance to play with the toys while Freedman was no longer around. An astonishing thing happened with the boys who earlier had been given no strong threat against playing with the robot: when given the freedom to play with any toy they wished, most avoided the robot, even though it was by far the most attractive of the five toys available (the others were a cheap plastic submarine, a child's baseball glove without a ball, an unloaded toy rifle, and a toy tractor). When these boys played with one of the five toys, only 33 percent chose the robot.

Something dramatic had happened to both groups of boys. For the first group, it was the severe threat they heard from Freedman to back up his statement that playing with the robot was "wrong." It had been quite effective while Freedman could catch them violating his rule. Later, though, when he was no longer present to observe the boys' behavior, his threat was impotent and his rule was ignored. It seems clear that the threat had not taught the boys that operating the robot was wrong, only that it was unwise to do so when the possibility of punishment existed.

For the other boys, the dramatic event had come from inside, not outside. Freedman had instructed them, too, that playing with the robot was wrong, but he had added no threat of punishment should they disobey him. There were two important results. First, Freedman's instruction alone was enough to prevent the boys from operating the robot while he was briefly out of the room. Second, the boys took personal responsibility for their choices to stay away from the robot during that time. They decided they hadn't played with it because *they* didn't want to. After all, there were no strong punishments associated with the toy to explain their behavior otherwise. Thus, weeks later, when Freedman was nowhere around, they still ignored the robot because they had been changed inside to believe they did not want to play with it.

Adults facing the child-rearing experience can take a cue from the Freedman study. Suppose a couple wants to impress upon their daughter that lying is wrong. A strong, clear threat ("It's bad to lie, honey, so if I catch you at it, I'll tape your mouth shut") might well be effective when the parents are present or when the girl thinks she can be discovered. However, it will not achieve the larger goal of convincing her that she does not want to lie because *she* thinks it's wrong. To do that, the couple needs a subtler approach. They must give a reason strong enough to get her to be truthful most of the time but not so strong that she sees it as the obvious reason for her truthfulness.

It's a tricky business because the barely sufficient reason changes from child to child. For one child, a simple appeal may be enough ("It's bad to lie, honey, so I hope you won't do it"); for another, it may be necessary to add a somewhat stronger reason (". . . because if you do, I'll be disappointed in you"); for a third child, a mild form of warning may be required as well (". . . and I'll probably have to do something I don't want to do"). Wise parents will know which kind of reason will work on their own children. The important thing is to use a reason that initially produces the desired behavior and, at the same time, allows a child to take personal responsibility for the behavior. Thus, the less detectable outside pressure such a reason contains, the better. Selecting just the right reason is not an easy task for parents, but the effort should pay off. It is likely to mean the difference between short-lived compliance and long-term commitment. As Samuel Butler wrote more than three hundred years ago, "He who agrees against his will / Is of the same opinion still."[8]

Growing Legs to Stand On

For a pair of reasons we have already considered, compliance professionals love commitments that produce inner change. First, the change is not specific to the situation where it initially occurred; it covers a whole range of related situations too. Second, the effects of the change are lasting. Once people have been induced to take actions that shift their self-images to that of, let's say, public-spirited citizens, they are likely to be public spirited in a variety of other circumstances where their compliance may also be desired. And they are likely to continue their public-spirited behavior for as long as their new self-images hold.

There is yet another attraction in commitments that lead to inner change—they "grow their own legs." There is no need for the compliance professional to undertake a costly and continuing effort to reinforce the change; the pressure for consistency will take care of that. After people come to view themselves as public spirited, they automatically begin to see things differently. They convince themselves it is the correct way to be and begin to pay attention to facts they hadn't noticed before about the value of community service. They make themselves available to hear arguments they hadn't yet heard favoring civic action and find such arguments more persuasive. In general, because of the need to be consistent within their system of beliefs, they assure themselves their choice to take public-spirited action was right. Important about this process of generating additional reasons to justify the commitment is that the reasons are *new*. Thus, even if the original reason for the civic-minded behavior were taken away, these newly discovered reasons alone may be enough to support their perceptions that they behaved correctly.

The advantage to an unscrupulous compliance professional is tremendous. Because we build new struts to undergird choices we have committed ourselves to, an exploiter can offer us an inducement for making such a choice. After the decision has been made, the individual can remove that inducement, knowing that our decision will probably stand on its own newly created legs. Car dealers frequently try to benefit from this process through a tactic they call "throwing a low-ball." I first encountered it while posing as a sales trainee for a local Chevrolet dealership. After a week of basic instruction, I was allowed to watch the regular salespeople perform. One practice that caught my attention right away was the low-ball.

For certain customers, a good price, perhaps as much as $700 below competitors' prices, is offered on a car. The good deal, however, is not genuine; the dealer never intends it to go through. Its only purpose is to cause prospects to *decide* to buy one of the dealership's cars. Once the decision is made, a number of activities deepen the customer's sense of personal commitment to the car—a fistful of purchase forms is filled out, extensive financing terms are arranged, sometimes the customer is encouraged to drive the car for a day before signing the contract, "so you can get the feel of it and show it around the neighborhood and at work." During this time, the dealer knows, customers typically develop a range of new reasons to support their choice and justify the investments they have now made.

Then something happens. Occasionally an "error" in the calculations is discovered—maybe the salesperson forgot to add the cost of the navigation package, and if the buyer still requires it, $700 must be added to the price. To throw suspicion off themselves, some dealers let the bank handling the financing find the mistake. At other times, the deal is disallowed at the last moment when the salesperson checks with his or her boss, who cancels it because "the dealership would be losing money." For only another $700 the car can be had, which, in the context of a multithousand-dollar deal, doesn't seem too steep, because, as the salesperson emphasizes, the cost is equal to competitors' and "This is the car you chose, right?"

Another, more insidious form of low-balling occurs when the salesperson makes an inflated trade-in offer on the prospect's old car as part of the buy/trade package. The customer recognizes the offer as overly generous and jumps at the deal. Later, before the contract is signed, the used-car manager enters and says the salesperson's estimate was $700 too high and reduces the trade-in allowance to its actual blue-book level. The customer, realizing that the reduced offer is the fair one, accepts it as appropriate and sometimes feels guilty about trying to take advantage of the salesperson's high estimate. I once witnessed a woman provide an embarrassed apology to a salesman who had used this version of low-balling on her—this, while she was signing a new-car contract giving him a hefty commission. He looked hurt but managed a forgiving smile.

No matter which variety of low-balling is used, the sequence is the same: an advantage is offered that induces a favorable purchase decision. Then, sometime after the decision has been made, but before the bargain is sealed, the purchase advantage is deftly removed. It seems almost incredible that a customer would buy a car under these circumstances. Yet it works—not on everybody, of course, but it is effective enough to be a staple compliance procedure in many car showrooms. Automobile dealers have come to understand the ability of a personal commitment to build its own support system of new justifications for the commitment. Often these justifications provide so many strong legs for the decision to stand on that when the dealer pulls away only one leg, the original one, there is no collapse. The loss can be shrugged off by the customer who is consoled by the array of other reasons favoring the choice. It never occurs to the buyer that those additional reasons might never have existed had the choice not been made in the first place.

After watching the low-ball technique work so impressively in the car showroom, I decided to test its effectiveness in another setting, where I could see if the basic idea worked with a bit of a twist. That is, the car salespeople I observed threw the low-ball by proposing sweet deals, getting favorable decisions as a result, and then taking away the sweet part of the offers. If my thinking about the essence of the low-ball procedure was correct, it should be possible to get the tactic to work in a somewhat different way: I could offer a good deal, which would produce the crucial decisional commitment, and then I could add an *un*pleasant feature to the arrangement. Because the effect of the low-ball technique was to get an individual to stay with a deal, even after circumstances had changed to make it a poor one, the tactic should work whether a positive aspect of the deal was removed or a negative aspect was added.

To test this latter possibility, my colleagues John Cacioppo, Rod Bassett, John Miller, and I ran an experiment designed to get university students to agree to perform an unpleasant activity—to wake up very early to participate in a 7:00 a.m. study "on thinking processes." When calling one sample of students, we immediately informed them of the 7:00 a.m. starting time. Only 24 percent were willing to participate. However, when calling a second sample of students, we threw a low-ball. We first asked if they wanted to participate in a study of thinking processes, and after they responded—56 percent of them positively—we mentioned the 7:00 a.m. start time and gave them the chance to change their minds. None did. What's more, in keeping with their commitment to participate, 95 percent of the low-balled students did appear for the study at 7:00 a.m. as promised. I know this to be the case because I recruited two research assistants to conduct the thinking-processes experiment at that time and take the names of the students who appeared. (As an aside, there is no foundation to the rumor that in recruiting my research assistants for this task, I first asked if they wanted to administer a study on thinking processes and, after they agreed, informed them of the 7:00 a.m. starting time.)

The impressive thing about the low-ball tactic is its ability to make a person feel pleased with a poor choice. Those who have only poor choices to offer are especially fond of the technique. We can find them throwing low-balls in business, social, and personal situations. For instance, there's my neighbor Tim, a true low-ball aficionado. Recall, he's the one who, by promising to change his ways, got his girlfriend Sara to cancel her impending marriage to another man and take him back. Since her decision to choose Tim, Sara has become more devoted to him than ever, even though he has not fulfilled his promises. She explains this by saying that she has allowed herself to see all sorts of positive qualities in Tim she never recognized before.

I know full well that Sara is a low-ball victim. Just as I had watched buyers fall for the "give it and take it away later" strategy in the car showroom, I watched her fall for the same trick with Tim. For his part, Tim remains the guy he has always been. Because the new attractions Sara has discovered (or created) in him are real for her, she now seems satisfied with the same arrangement that was unacceptable before her enormous commitment. The decision to choose Tim, poor as it may have been objectively, has grown its own supports and appears to have made Sara satisfied. I have never mentioned to Sara what I know about low-balling. The reason for my silence is not that I think her better off in the dark on the issue. It's just that I am confident that if I said a word, she would hate me for it and likely change nothing.

Standing Up for the Public Good

Depending on the motives of the person wishing to use them, any of the compliance techniques discussed in this book can be employed for good or for ill. Hence, the low-ball tactic can be used for more socially beneficial purposes than selling cars or reestablishing relationships with former lovers. For example, one research project done in Iowa, led by social psychologist Michael Pallak, showed how the low-ball procedure influenced homeowners to conserve energy. The project began at the start of the Iowa winter, when residents heating their homes with natural gas were contacted by an interviewer who gave them some energy-conservation tips and asked them to try to save fuel in the future. Although they agreed to try, when the researchers examined the utility records of these families after a month and again at winter's end, no savings had occurred. The residents who had intended to make a conservation attempt used just as much natural gas as did a random sample of their neighbors who had not been contacted by an interviewer. Good intentions coupled with information about saving fuel were not enough to change habits.

Even before the project began, Pallak and his team had recognized that something more would be needed to shift long-standing energy-use patterns. So they tried a different procedure on a comparable sample of Iowa natural-gas users. These people, too, were contacted by an interviewer, who provided energy-saving hints and asked them to conserve, but for these families, the interviewer offered something else: those agreeing to save energy would have their names publicized in newspaper articles as public-spirited, fuel-conserving citizens. The effect was immediate. One month later, when the utility company checked their meters, homeowners in this sample had saved an average of 422 cubic feet of natural gas apiece. The chance to have their names in the paper had motivated them to substantial conservation efforts for a month.

Then the rug was pulled out. The researchers extracted the reason that had initially caused the people to save fuel. Each family that had been promised publicity received a letter saying it would not be possible to publicize its name after all.

At the end of the winter, the research team examined the letter's effect on the families' natural-gas usage. Did they return to their old, wasteful habits when the chance to be in the newspaper was removed? Hardly. For each of the remaining winter months, these families conserved *more* fuel than they had during the time they thought they would be publicly celebrated for it. They had managed 12.2 percent gas savings during the first month because they expected to see themselves lauded in the paper. However, after the letter arrived informing them to the contrary, they did not return to their previous energy-use levels; instead, they increased their savings to 15.5 percent for the rest of the winter.

Although we can't be completely sure of such things, one explanation for their persistent behavior presents itself immediately.

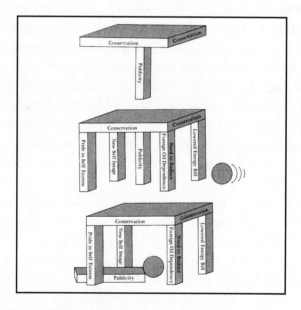

Figure 7.5: The low-ball for the long term

In this illustration of the Iowa energy research, we can see how the original conservation effort rested on the promise of publicity (top). Before long, however, the energy commitment led to the sprouting of new self-generated supports, allowing the research team to throw its low-ball (middle). The consequence was a persisting level of conservation that stood firmly on its own legs after the initial publicity prop had been knocked down (bottom).

Artist: Maria Picardi; © Robert B. Cialdini

These people had been low-balled into a conservation commitment through a promise of newspaper publicity. Once made, the commitment started generating its own supports: the homeowners began acquiring new energy habits; began feeling good about their public-spirited efforts; began experiencing pride in their capacity for self-denial; and most important, began viewing themselves as conservation-minded. With these new reasons present to justify the commitment to less energy use, it is no wonder the commitment remained firm even after the original reason, newspaper publicity, had been kicked away (see figure 7.5).

Strangely enough, though, when the publicity factor was no longer a possibility, these families did not merely maintain their fuel-saving effort, they heightened it. Any of a number of interpretations could be offered for that still stronger effort, but I have a favorite. In a way, the opportunity to receive newspaper publicity had prevented the homeowners from fully owning their commitment to conservation. Of all the reasons supporting the decision to try to save fuel, it was the only one that had come from the outside—the only one preventing homeowners from thinking they were conserving gas because *they* believed in it. So when the letter arrived canceling the publicity agreement, it removed the only impediment to these residents' images of themselves as fully concerned, energy-conscious citizens. This unqualified, new self-image then pushed them to even greater heights of conservation. Much like Sara, they appeared to have become committed to a choice through an initial inducement and were still more dedicated to it after the inducement had been removed.[9]

Cueing Consistency: Reminders as Regenerators

There is an added advantage to commitment-based compliance procedures. Mere reminders of past commitments can spur individuals to act in accord with those earlier positions, stands, or actions. Bring the commitment back to top of mind, and the need for consistency takes over to align related responding once again. Let's take a couple of examples from the field of medicine to illustrate the point.

Whenever I speak to health-care management groups about the influence process, I'll ask the question "Which people in the system are most difficult to influence?" The answer is invariably and emphatically, "Physicians!" On the one hand, this circumstance seems as it should be. To get to their elevated positions in the health-care hierarchy, doctors go through years of training and practice, including medical-school specializations, internships, and residencies, that give them a great deal of information and experience on which to base their choices and make them understandably reluctant to be swayed from those choices. On the other hand, this kind of resistance can be problematic when physicians don't adopt recommendations for changes that would benefit their patients. At the outset of their professional careers, most MDs take a version of the Hippocratic oath, which commits them to act principally for the welfare of their patients and, especially, to do them no harm.

So why don't they wash their hands before examining a patient as often as they are supposed to? A hospital study offers insight into the matter. The researchers, Adam Grant and David Hofmann, noted that even though hand washing is strongly recommended before each patient examination, most physicians wash their hands less than half as often as the guidelines prescribe; what's more, various interventions aimed at reducing the problem have proved ineffective, leaving patients at greater risk of infection. The reason for the problem isn't that physicians have abandoned their commitment to patient safety or aren't aware of its link to hand washing. It's that upon entering an examination room, the link isn't as high in consciousness as are all sorts of other factors, such as how the patient looks, what the attending nurse is saying, what the case notes show, and so on.

Grant and Hofmann thought they could remedy this regrettable situation by reminding physicians of their commitment to their patients and its connection to hand hygiene when they arrived to do an examination. The researchers simply placed distinctive signs above examination-room soap and gel dispensers that announced "Hand hygiene protects patients from catching diseases." Those reminder signs increased soap and gel usage by 45 percent.

Another physician misstep involves the overprescription of antibiotic drugs, which is a growing health problem in the United States, contributing to the deaths of twenty-three thousand patients per year. As is the case for hand washing, several strategies for reducing the problem—education programs, electronic alerts, and payments—have had little effect. But a group of medical researchers have had remarkable success using a commitment-centered approach on physicians staffing a set of Los Angeles outpatient clinics. The doctors placed a poster in their examination rooms for a twelve-week period. For half of the MDs, the poster provided standard information to patients regarding antibiotic use. For the other half, it included, along with standard information, a photo of the doctor and a letter he or she signed pledging to avoid overprescription of antibiotics. During the remainder of the year, inappropriate antibiotic prescriptions actually increased by 21 percent for doctors exposed daily to the standard information posters. But those whose posters consistently reminded them of their personal commitments to reducing the problem cut inappropriate prescribing by 27 percent.

Reminders of existing commitments possess yet another bonus. They not only restore the commitment but also appear to strengthen it by augmenting one's related self-image. Compared to consumers who had previously performed pro-environmental actions but were not reminded of them, those who *did* receive such reminders came to see themselves as more environmentally minded and then became uniquely more likely to purchase environmentally friendly versions of products—including light bulbs, paper towels, deodorants, and detergents. Thus, asking people to recall prior commitments to environmentalism isn't just an easy way to stimulate consistent subsequent responding; it is also a particularly effective way, because such reminders intensify one's self-image as an environmentalist.[10]

Defense

"Consistency is the hobgoblin of little minds." Or, at least, so goes a frequently heard quotation attributed to Ralph Waldo Emerson. But what an odd thing to say. Looking around, it is obvious that internal consistency is a hallmark of logic and intellectual strength, while its lack characterizes the intellectually scattered and limited among us. What, then, could a thinker of Emerson's caliber have meant when he assigned the trait of consistency to the small-minded? A look back to the original source of his statement, his essay "Self-Reliance," makes it clear the problem lay not in Emerson but in the popularized version of what he said. Actually he wrote, "A *foolish* consistency is the hobgoblin of little minds." For some obscure reason, a central distinction had been lost as the years eroded the accurate version of his assertion to mean something entirely different and, upon close inspection, entirely mistaken.

The distinction should not be lost on us, however, because it is crucial to the only effective defense I know against the levers of influence embodied in the combined factors of commitment and consistency. It is the awareness that although consistency is generally good—even vital—there is a foolish, rigid variety to be shunned. We need to be wary of the tendency to be automatically and unthinkingly consistent, for it lays us open to the maneuvers of those who want to exploit the mechanical commitment and consistency sequence for profit.

Since automatic consistency is so useful in allowing an economical and appropriate way of behaving most of the time, we can't decide merely to eliminate it from our lives. The results would be disastrous. If, rather than streaming along in accordance with our prior decisions and deeds, we stopped to think through the merits of each new action before performing it, we would never have time to accomplish anything significant. We need even that dangerous, mechanical brand of consistency. The only way out of the dilemma is to know when such consistency is likely to lead to a poor choice.

There are certain signals—two separate kinds of signals—to tip us off. We register each type in a different part of our bodies.

READER'S REPORT 7.5

From a college student in New Delhi, India

I am writing to you about an incident where the consistency principle compelled me to make a decision that I would not have made under ordinary circumstances. I had gone to the food court of a mall where I decided to buy a small glass of Coke.

"One glass of Coke, please," I said to the salesman at the counter.

"Medium or Large?," he asked me as he was billing another customer.

"I've already eaten enough. There is no way I could gulp down a large glass of Coke," I thought to myself. "Medium," I said confidently as I handed him the card for payment.

"Oh! Sorry," said the salesperson with the impression of having made a genuine mistake. "Small or Medium?"

"Uhm, Medium," I said in line with the consistency principle, took my drink and left so the next person could order, only to realize that I had been duped into buying the larger of the two options.

I was caught off guard, and to be consistent with my previously placed order, I blurted out "Medium," without even processing the new information given to me.

A foolish consistency definitely seems to be the hobgoblin of little minds!

Author's note: I think the reader, who seems to have considered herself little-minded in the situation, is being too hard on herself. When we are rushed or not able to think deeply about a choice, mechanical consistency is the norm (Fennis, Janssen, & Vohs, 2009).

Stomach Signs

The first signal is easy to recognize. It occurs right in the pit of our stomachs when we realize we are trapped into complying with a request we *know* we don't want to perform. It's happened to me a hundred times. An especially memorable instance took place on a summer evening when, as a young man well before I wrote this book, I answered my doorbell to find a stunning young woman dressed in shorts and a revealing halter top. I noticed, nonetheless, she was carrying a clipboard and was asking me to participate in a survey. Wanting to make a favorable impression, I agreed and, I do admit, stretched the truth in my interview answers to present myself in the most positive light. Our conversation went as follows:

Stunning Young Woman: Hello! I'm doing a survey on the entertainment habits of city residents, and I wonder if you could answer a few questions for me.

Cialdini: Do come in.

SYW: No, thank you. I'll just stay right here and begin. How many times per week would you say you go out to dinner?

C: Oh, probably three, maybe four times a week. Whenever I can, really; I love fine restaurants.

SYW: How nice. And do you usually order wine with your dinner?

C: Only if it's imported.

SYW: I see. What about movies? Do you go to the movies much?

C: The *cinema*? I can't get enough of good films. I especially like the sophisticated kind with the words on the bottom of the screen. How about you? Do you like to see films?

SYW: Uh . . . yes, I do. But let's get back to the interview. Do you go to many concerts?

C: Definitely. The symphonic stuff mostly, of course. But I do enjoy a quality pop group as well.

SYW: (writing rapidly). Great! Just one more question. What about touring performances by theatrical or ballet companies? Do you see them when they're in town?

C: Ah, the ballet—the movement, the grace, the form—I love it. Mark me down as *loving* the ballet. See it every chance I get.

SYW: Fine. Just let me recheck my figures here for a moment, Mr. Cialdini.

C: Actually, it's Dr. Cialdini. But that sounds so formal. Why don't you call me Bob?

SYW: All right, *Bob.* From the information you've already given me, I'm pleased to say you could save up to $1,200 a year by joining *Clubamerica!* A small membership fee entitles you to discounts on most of the activities you've mentioned. Surely someone as socially vigorous as yourself would want to take advantage of the tremendous savings our company can offer on all the things you've already told me you do.

C (trapped like a rat): Well . . . uh . . . I . . . uh . . . I guess so.

I remember quite well feeling my stomach tighten as I stammered my agreement. It was a clear call to my brain, "Hey, you're being taken here!" But I couldn't see a way out. I had been cornered by my own words. To decline her offer at that point would have meant facing a pair of distasteful alternatives: If I tried to back out by protesting that I was not actually the man-about-town

I had claimed to be, I would come off a liar; trying to refuse without that protest would make me come off a fool for not wanting to save $1,200. I bought the entertainment package, even though I knew I had been set up. The need to be consistent with what I had already said snared me.

No more, though. I listen to my stomach these days, and I have discovered a way to handle people who try to use the consistency principle on me. I just tell them exactly what they are doing. The tactic has become the perfect counterattack. Whenever my stomach tells me I would be a sucker to comply with a request merely because doing so would be consistent with some prior commitment I was tricked into, I relay that message to the requester. I don't try to deny the importance of consistency; I just point out the absurdity of foolish consistency. Whether, in response, the requester shrinks away guiltily or retreats in bewilderment, I am content. I have won; an exploiter has lost.

I sometimes think about how it would be if that stunning young woman of years ago were to try to sell me an entertainment-club membership now. I have it all worked out. The entire interaction would be the same, except for the end:

SYW: . . . Surely someone as socially vigorous as yourself would want to take advantage of the tremendous savings our company can offer on all the things you've already told me you do.

C: Quite wrong. I recognize what has gone on here. I know that your story about doing a survey was just a pretext for getting people to tell you how often they go out and that, under those circumstances, there is a natural tendency to exaggerate. And I refuse to allow myself to be locked into a mechanical sequence of commitment and consistency when I know it's wrongheaded. No *click, run* for me.

SYW: Huh?

C: Okay, let me put it this way: (1) It would be stupid of me to spend money on something I don't want; (2) I have it on excellent authority, direct from my stomach, that I don't want your entertainment plan; (3) therefore, if you still believe that I will buy it, you probably also still believe in the Tooth Fairy. Surely, someone as intelligent as you would be able to understand that.

SYW *(trapped like a stunning young rat):* Well . . . uh . . . I . . . uh . . . I guess so.

Heart-of-Hearts Signs

Stomachs are not especially perceptive or subtle organs. Only when it is obvious we are about to be conned are they likely to register and transmit that message. At other times, when it is not clear we are being taken, our stomachs may never catch on. Under those circumstances, we have to look elsewhere for a clue. The situation of my neighbor Sara provides a good illustration. She made an important commitment to Tim by canceling her marriage plans. The commitment has grown its own supports, so even though the original reasons for the commitment are gone, she remains in harmony with it. She has convinced herself with newly formed reasons that she did the right thing, so she stays with Tim. It is not difficult to see why there would be no tightening in Sara's stomach as a result. Stomachs tell us when we think we are doing something wrong for us. Sara *thinks* no such thing. To her mind, she has chosen correctly and is behaving consistently with that choice.

Yet, unless I badly miss my guess, there is a part of Sara that recognizes her choice as a mistake and her current living arrangement as a brand of foolish consistency. Where, exactly, that part of Sara is located we can't be sure, but our language does give it a name: heart of hearts. It is, by definition, the one place where we cannot fool ourselves. It is the place where none of our justifications, none of our rationalizations, penetrate. Sara has the truth there, although right now she can't hear its signal clearly through the static of the new support apparatus she has erected.

If Sara has erred in her choice of Tim, how long can she go without recognizing it, without suffering a massive heart-of-hearts attack? There is no telling. One thing *is* certain: as time passes, the various alternatives to Tim are disappearing. She had better determine soon whether she is making a mistake.

Easier said than done, of course. She must answer an extremely intricate question: "Knowing what I now know, if I could go back in time, would I make the same choice?" The problem lies in the "knowing what I now know" part of the question. Just what does she now know, accurately, about Tim? How much of what she thinks of him is the result of a desperate attempt to justify the commitment she made? She claims that since her decision to take him back, he cares for her more, is trying hard to stop his excessive drinking, and has learned to make a wonderful omelet. Having tasted a couple of his omelets, I have my doubts. The important issue, though, is whether *she* believes these things, not just intellectually—but in her heart of hearts.

There may be a little device Sara can use to find out how much of her current satisfaction with Tim is real and how much is foolish consistency. Psychological research indicates that we experience our feelings toward something a split second before we can intellectualize about it. I'd guess the message sent by the heart of hearts is a pure, basic feeling. Therefore, if we train ourselves to be attentive, we should register the feeling slightly before our cognitive apparatus engages. According to this approach, were Sara to ask herself the crucial "Would I make the same choice again?" question, she would be well advised to look for and trust the first flash of feeling she experienced in response. It would likely be the signal from her heart of hearts, slipping through undistorted just before the means by which she could fool herself streamed in.[11]

I have begun using the same device myself whenever I even suspect I might be acting in a foolishly consistent manner. One time, for instance, I had stopped at the gas pump of a filling station advertising a price per gallon a couple of cents below the rate of other stations in the area; but with pump nozzle in hand, I noticed that the price listed on the pump was two cents higher than the display-sign price. When I mentioned the difference to a passing attendant, whom I later learned was the owner, he mumbled unconvincingly that the rates had changed a few days ago, but there hadn't been time to correct the display. I tried to decide what to do. Some reasons for staying came to mind: "I do need gasoline"; "I am in sort of a hurry"; "I think I remember my car runs better on this brand of gas."

I needed to determine whether those reasons were genuine or mere justifications for my decision to stop there. So I asked myself the crucial question, "Knowing what I know about the real price of this gasoline, if I could go back in time, would I make the same choice again?" Concentrating on the first burst of impression I sensed, I received a clear and unqualified answer. I would have driven right past. I wouldn't have even slowed down. I knew then that without the price advantage, those other reasons would not have brought me there. They hadn't created the decision; the decision had created them.

That settled, there was another decision to be faced. Since I was already there holding the hose, wouldn't it be better to use it than suffer the inconvenience of going elsewhere to pay the same price? Fortunately, the station attendant-owner came over and helped me make up my mind. He asked why I wasn't pumping any gas. I told him I didn't like the price discrepancy. "Listen," he snarled, "nobody's gonna tell me how to run my business. If you think I'm cheating you, just put that hose down *right now* and get off my property." Already certain he was a cheat, I was happy to act consistently with my belief and his wishes. I dropped the hose on the spot and drove over it on my way to the closest exit. Sometimes consistency can be a marvelously rewarding thing.

Special Vulnerabilities

Are there particular kinds of people whose need to be consistent with what they've previously said and done makes them especially susceptible to the commitment tactics covered in this chapter? There are. To learn about the traits that characterize such individuals, it would be useful to examine a painful incident in the life of one of the most famous sports stars of our time.

The surrounding events, as laid out in an Associated Press news story at the time, appear puzzling. On March 1, 2005, golfing legend Jack Nicklaus's seventeen-month-old grandson drowned in a hot-tub accident. One week later, a still-devastated Nicklaus brushed aside thoughts of future golf-related activities, including the upcoming Masters tournament, saying: "I think that, with what's happened to us in our family, my time is going to be spent in much different ways. I have absolutely zero plans as it relates to the game of golf." Yet, on the day of this statement, he made two remarkable exceptions: he gave a speech to a group of prospective members of a Florida golf club, and he played in a charity tournament hosted by longtime course rival Gary Player.

What was so powerful to have pulled Nicklaus away from his grieving family and into a pair of events that could only be seen as wholly inconsequential compared to the one he was living through? His answer was plain: "You make commitments," he said, "and you've got to do them." Although the small-time events themselves may have been unimportant in the grand scheme of things, his earlier-made agreements to take part in them were decidedly not—at least not to him. But why were Mr. Nicklaus's commitments so . . . well . . . committing to him? Were there certain traits he possessed that impelled him toward this fierce form of consistency? Indeed, there were two: He was sixty-five years old and American.

AGE

It should come as no surprise that people with a particularly strong proclivity toward concordance in their attitudes and actions frequently fall victim to consistency-based influence tactics. My colleagues and I developed a scale to measure a person's preference for consistency in his or her responding and found just that. Individuals who scored high on preference for consistency were especially likely to comply with a requester who used either the foot-in-the-door or the low-ball technique. In a follow-up study employing subjects from ages eighteen to eighty, we found that a preference for consistency increased with the years and that once beyond the age of fifty, people displayed the strongest inclination of all to remain consistent with their earlier commitments.

I believe this finding helps explain sixty-five-year-old Jack Nicklaus's adherence to his earlier promises, even in the face of a family tragedy that would have given him an entirely understandable opt-out excuse. To be true to his traits, he needed to be consistent with those promises. I also believe the same finding can help explain why the perpetrators of fraud against older populations so often use commitment and consistency tactics to snare their prey. Take as evidence a noteworthy study done by the American Association of Retired Persons, which became concerned about the increasing incidence (and distressing success) of phone fraud attacks on its over-fifty membership. Along with investigators in twelve states, the organization became involved in a sting operation to uncover the tricks of phone scammers targeting the elderly. One result was a trove of transcribed audiotapes of conversations between scammers and their intended victims. An intensive examination of the tapes by researchers Anthony Pratkanis and Doug Shadel revealed widespread attempts by fraud artists to get—or sometimes just claim—an initial small commitment from a target and then to extract funds by holding the target accountable for it. Note how, in the following separate tape excerpts, the scammer uses the consistency principle like a bludgeon on people whose preference for personal consistency gives the principle formidable weight.

"No, we did not merely talk about it. You ordered it! You said yes. You said yes."

"Well, you signed up for it last month; you don't remember?"

"You gave us the commitment on it over three weeks ago."

"I had a promise and a commitment from you last week."

"You can't buy a coin and renege on it five weeks later. You just can't do that."

INDIVIDUALISM

There is another factor besides age that may account for Jack Nicklaus's strong need to remain consistent with his commitments. I hinted at such a factor earlier: he is an American, born and bred in the heartland (Ohio) of a nation famous for its devotion to the "cult of the individual." In individualistic nations, such as the United States and those of Western Europe, the focus is on the self, whereas, in more collectivistic societies, the focus is on the group. Consequently, individualists decide what they should do in a situation by looking primarily at their own histories, opinions, and choices rather than at those of their peers, and such a decision-making style causes them to be highly vulnerable to influence tactics that use as leverage what a person has previously said or done.

To test the idea, my colleagues and I used a version of the foot-in-the-door technique on a set of students at my university; half were US-born and half were international students from less individualistic, Asian countries. We first asked all the students to participate in a twenty-minute online survey of "school and social relationships." Then, a month later, we asked them to complete a forty-minute related survey on the same topic. Of those who completed the initial, twenty-minute survey, the more individualistic American students were more than twice as likely as the Asian students to agree to the forty-minute request too (21.6 percent versus 9.9 percent). Why? Because they, personally, had agreed to a prior, similar request; and individualists decide what they should do next on the basis of what they, personally, have done. Thus, members of individualistic societies—particularly older members—need to be alert to influence tactics that begin by requesting just a small step. Those small, cautious steps can lead to big, blind leaps.[12]

SUMMARY

- Psychologists have long recognized a desire in most people to be and look consistent within their words, beliefs, attitudes, and deeds. This tendency for consistency is fed from three sources.

First, good personal consistency is highly valued by society. Second, aside from its effect on public image, generally consistent conduct provides a beneficial approach to daily life. Third, a consistent orientation affords a valuable shortcut through the complexity of modern existence. By being consistent with earlier decisions, one reduces the need to process all the relevant information in future similar situations; instead, one merely needs to recall the earlier decision and to respond consistently with it.

- Within the realm of compliance, securing an initial commitment is the key. After making a commitment (that is, taking an action, stand, or position), people are more willing to agree to requests in keeping with the prior commitment. Thus, many compliance professionals try to induce people to take an initial position that is consistent with a behavior they will later request from these people. Not all commitments are equally effective in producing consistent future action. Commitments are most effective when they are active, public, effortful, and viewed as internally motivated (voluntary), because each of these elements changes self-image. The reason they do so is that each element gives us information about what we must truly believe.

- Commitment decisions, even erroneous ones, have a tendency to be self-perpetuating because they can "grow their own legs." That is, people often add new reasons and justifications to support the wisdom of commitments they have already made. As a consequence, some commitments remain in effect long after the conditions that spurred them have changed. This phenomenon explains the effectiveness of certain deceptive compliance practices such as "throwing the low-ball."

- Another advantage of commitment-based tactics is that simple reminders of an earlier commitment can regenerate its ability to guide behavior, even in novel situations. In addition, reminders do more than restore the commitment's vigor, they appear to intensify it by strengthening one's related self-image.

- To recognize and resist the undue influence of consistency pressures on our compliance decisions, we should listen for signals coming from two places within us: our stomachs and our heart of hearts. Stomach signs appear when we realize we are being pushed by commitment and consistency pressures to agree to requests we know we don't want to perform. Under these circumstances, it is best to explain to the requester that such compliance would constitute a brand of foolish consistency in which we prefer not to engage. Heart-of-heart signs are different. They are best employed when it is not clear to us that an initial commitment was wrongheaded. Here, we should ask ourselves a crucial question: "Knowing what I now know, if I could go back in time, would I make the same commitment?" One informative answer may come as the first flash of feeling registered. Commitment and consistency tactics are likely to work especially well on members of individualistic societies, particularly those who are over fifty years old, who, hence, should be particularly wary of their use.

CHAPTER 8

UNITY

THE "WE" IS THE SHARED ME

If we have no peace, it's because we have forgotten that we
belong to one another.

—Mother Teresa

Many of us have had an unusual roommate, one whose personal
involvements left us simultaneously wobbled, mystified, and newly
informed about the range of human capacities. But there was
likely none who could check each of those boxes as indelibly as
a one-time roommate of the anthropologist Ronald Cohen. In a
late-night conversation, the man, who had once been a guard in a
Nazi concentration camp, described an occurrence so memorable
that he, and then Cohen, found it impossible to forget; indeed, still
beset by the account many years later, Cohen used it as the centerpiece of a scholarly article.

At Nazi work camps, when just one prisoner violated a rule, it
was not uncommon for all to be lined up and for a guard to walk
along the line counting to ten, stopping only to shoot each tenth
person dead. In the roommate's telling, a veteran guard assigned
the task was performing it as routinely as he always had when,
inexplicably, he did something singular: coming to one seemingly
unfortunate tenth prisoner, he raised an eyebrow, did a quarter-
turn, and executed the eleventh.

Later, I'll reveal the reason for the guard's life-determining deviation. To do so creditably, though, it's necessary to consider the

deeply seated principle of social influence that gives the reason its force.

Unity

Automatically and incessantly, everyone divides people into those to whom the pronoun *we* does and does not apply. The implications for influence are great because, inside our tribes, everything influence-related is easier to achieve. Those within the boundaries of "we" get more agreement, trust, help, liking, cooperation, emotional support, and forgiveness and are even judged as being more creative, moral, and humane. The in-group favoritism seems not only far-ranging in its impact on human action but also primitive, as it appears in other primates and in human children as young as infants. *Clique, run.*[1]

Thus, successful social influence is often pivotally grounded in "we" relationships. Still, a central question remains: What's the best way to characterize such relationships? The answer requires a subtle but crucial distinction. "We" relationships are not those that allow people to say, "Oh, that person is like us." They are the ones that allow people to say, "Oh, that person is one *of* us." The *unity* rule of influence can thus be worded: *People are inclined to say yes to someone they consider one of them.* The experience of unity is not about simple similarities (although those can work, too, via the liking principle). It's about identities, shared identities. It's about tribe-like categories that individuals use to define themselves and their groups, such as race, ethnicity, nationality, and family, as well as political and religious affiliations. For instance, I might have many more tastes and preferences in common with a colleague at work than with a sibling, but there is no question which of the two I would consider *of* me and which I would consider merely *like* me. A key characteristic of these categories is that their members tend to feel "at one" with, merged with, one another. They are the categories in which the conduct of one member influences the self-esteem of other members. Put simply, the "we" is the shared me.

Consequently, within "we" relationship groups, people often fail to distinguish correctly between their own traits and those of fellow members, which reflects a confusion of self and other. Neuroscientists have offered an explanation for the confusion: asking someone to imagine *the self* or a *close other* engages the same brain circuitry. This commonality can produce neuronal "cross-excitation" of the two—whereby a focus on one simultaneously activates the other and fosters a blurring of identities. Long before the neuroscientific evidence was available, social scientists were gauging the feeling of self–other merger by asking people to indicate how much overlap in identity they felt with a particular other person (see, for example, figure 8.1). With that measure in hand, researchers have investigated which factors lead to greater feelings of shared identity and how the factors operate.[2]

The range of circumstances and settings where "we" relationships affect human responding is impressive and varied. Nonetheless, three constants have emerged. First, members of "we"-based groups favor the outcomes and welfare of fellow members over

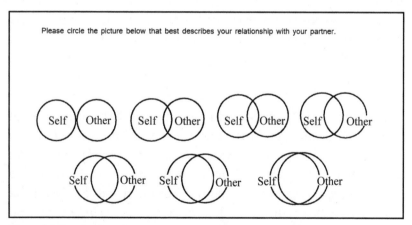

Figure 8.1: Overlapping circles, overlapping selves
Since its publication in 1992, scientists have been using the Inclusion of Other in the Self Scale to see which factors promote the feeling of being "at one" with another individual.

Courtesy of Arthur Aron and the American Psychological Association

those of nonmembers—by a mile. For example, members of rival work groups (that each included two humans and two robots) not only held more positive attitudes toward their own teammates but also went so far as to hold more positive attitudes toward their own team's robots than toward the rival team's robots—and humans! Second, "we"-group members are highly likely to use the preferences and actions of fellow members to guide their own, which is a tendency that ensures group solidarity. Finally, these partisan urges to favor and follow have arisen, evolutionarily, as ways to advantage our "we" groups and, ultimately, ourselves. Indeed, after reviewing decades of relevant scientific work on the point, one set of scholars concluded not just that tribalism is universal but that "tribalism is human nature." A look into our most basic social realms demonstrates how pervasively and powerfully the bias operates, often in *click, run* fashion.[3]

Business

SALES

Do you remember from chapter 3 the amazing sales achievements of Joe Girard, the man the *Guinness Book of World Records* crowned the world's "Greatest Car Salesman" for selling more than five cars and trucks every day he worked in twelve straight years— something he did by being a people person (he truly liked his customers), showing them he liked them by regularly sending them "I like you" cards, ensuring they received quick and courteous treatment when they brought their cars in for service, and always giving them a fair price? More recently, news reports pointed to sales figures indicating that Joe had been dethroned by a vehicle salesman in Dearborn, Michigan, named Ali Reda, whose annual output outdistanced even the best of Joe's years. In interviews, Mr. Reda admitted that he closely followed Joe Girard's specific recommendations for success. But if Ali simply imitated Joe, how did he manage to surpass the master? He must have added a differentiat-

Figure 8.2: Reda ready
Ali Reda is a fixture of the Arab community in Dearborn, Michigan, into which he sells record numbers of vehicles.
Courtesy of Greg Horvath

ing, secret ingredient to the recipe. He did, but it was no secret. It was a full measure of ethnic "we"-ness.

Dearborn, a city with around one hundred thousand residents, has the largest population of Arab Americans or residents of Arab descent in the United States. Mr. Reda, who is Arab American himself, focuses on being an active, visible member of the tight-knit Arab community, including by selling intensely into it. A large percentage of his customers come to him because they know and trust him to be *of* them. On the dimension of ethnic "we"-ness, Joe Girard was completely outmatched by Ali. Joe's birth name was Girardi, a cue to his Sicilian heritage and to non-"we" ethnic status in the eyes of most of his customers. In fact, he said he had to change his name because, back then, certain customers didn't want to do business with a "Dago."[4]

FINANCIAL TRANSACTIONS

If shared ethnic identity can help explain how Ali Reda—while closely following Joe Girard's methods—could outpace Joe's performance, perhaps the same factor can explain a separate business mystery. Easily the greatest investment swindle of our time was the Ponzi scheme orchestrated by Wall Street insider Bernard Madoff. Although analysts have focused on certain remarkable aspects of the fraud, such as its size (over $15 billion) and duration (going undetected for decades), I've been impressed by another remarkable feature: the level of financial sophistication of many of its victims. The list of those taken in by Madoff is rife with names of hardheaded economists, seasoned money managers, and highly successful business leaders. This, even though the alleged profits for his clients were so unusual, distrust should have quickly prevailed. With Madoff, it wasn't just another case of the fox outwitting the chickens; this fox duped his fellow foxes. How?

It's almost never the case that big occurrences in human responding are caused by any one thing. Almost invariably, they are due to a combination of factors. The Madoff affair is no different. The man's longtime presence on Wall Street, the intricacy of the derivatives-based financial mechanism he claimed to be employing, and the supposedly limited circle of investors he "allowed" to join his fund all contributed. But there was another active element in the mix, shared identity. Madoff was Jewish, and so, too, were the majority of his victims, who were often recruited by Madoff's lieutenants, who were also Jewish. In addition, new recruits knew and were ethnically similar to past recruits, who served as similar sources of social proof that an investment with Madoff must be a wise choice.

Of course, fraud of this sort is hardly limited to one ethnic or religious group. Called affinity schemes, these investment scams have always involved members of a group preying on other members of the group—Baptists on Baptists, Latinx on Latinx, Armenian Americans on Armenian Americans. Charles Ponzi, who gave his name to the infamous Ponzi scheme that Madoff ran, was an Italian immigrant to the United States who fleeced other

Italian immigrants to the United States of millions of dollars from 1919 to 1920. *Click, ruin.*

"We"-based choices pervade other financial transactions besides investment decisions. Inside US financial-advisement firms, fiscal misconduct by an adviser is twice as likely to be copied by another adviser if the two share ethnicity. In China, auditors' financial misstatements favoring a company are more frequent when the auditor and the company's CEO have similar hometowns. A study of a large Indian bank's records revealed loan officers approved more loan applications and gave more favorable terms to applicants of the same religion. Moreover, the favoritism may have worked both ways: a loan that incorporated a religious match resulted in significantly increased loan *re*payments. In yet another example of in-group favoritism, after a service failure in a Hong Kong restaurant, customers were less willing to blame a server who shared their last name.

If the international span of these studies isn't enough to certify the cross-cultural reach of in-group effects, consider one last instance. In Ghana, taxi drivers and their passengers typically negotiate the cost of a ride before it begins. When the two bargainers support the same political party, the driver agrees to a lower fare for the ride—but with an intriguing twist. The price break occurs only in the weeks just before and after an election, when the political-party membership of voters is salient. This finding illustrates an important aspect of "we"-group responding. It is intensified by cues or circumstances that bring group identity to mind. In this way, the pull of unity (or of any of the other principles of influence) doesn't function like a powerful ordinary magnet, with strong constant attraction. Rather, it operates like a powerful electromagnet, with a draw modulated by the intensity of the current coursing into it at the moment.

Take what happened in Poland, a predominantly Catholic country, when researchers dropped seemingly lost letters in various city locations that were addressed either to a recipient with a Polish (likely Catholic) name or an Arabic (likely Muslim) name. Poles who found the letters were more likely to deposit them in a mailbox if the intended recipient's name was Maciej Strzelczyk rather than Mohammed Abdullah—however, this was principally so around the *religious* holiday of Christmas. These results can't be explained as due to a general benevolent glow around Christmastime. Although mailings of letters addressed to Maciej increased 12 percent near the holy day, mailings to Mohammed declined 30 percent. Clearly, the benevolence was one-sided and directed toward a salient religious in-group.[5]

Politics

There's a newly labeled shade of lies that falls midway on the spectrum between white lies, fictions designed to protect others' feelings ("No, really, that outfit/hairstyle/nose ring looks good on you"), and black lies, falsehoods designed to harm others' interests ("And if you show up with it on your date with my ex-boyfriend, he'll love it"). "Blue" lies possess core elements of the other two. They're intended to protect as well as harm others, but those selected for protection and those selected for harm differ by "we"-group inclusion. They are the deliberate lies told—usually against an out-group—by members of an in-group to protect their own group's reputation. Inside these identity-merged groups, unity trumps truth. Said differently, and in less politically loaded language, deception that strengthens a "we"-group is viewed by members as *morally* superior to truth-telling that weakens their group.

Political parties exhibit a festering form of the problem. As one reviewer of relevant research concluded: "This kind of lying [for political gain] seems to thrive in an atmosphere of anger, resentment and hyper-polarization. Party identification is so strong that criticism of the party feels like a threat to the self, which triggers a host of defensive psychological mechanisms." Sound at all familiar? Besides approving of lies that promote and protect one's party, additional defensive mechanisms are triggered by such fervent party identification. Individuals who possessed "fused" identities with their political party reported greater willingness to hide evidence of tax fraud by a politician from the party. Shown evidence of equivalent political inputs to their cities' well-being, ardent party members convinced themselves that their party had made the stronger contributions. When asked to rank-order a waiting list of patients suffering from kidney disease as to their deservingness for the next available treatment, people chose those whose political party matched theirs.

People not only favor members of their political parties but also believe them more, even under bewildering circumstances. In an online study, participants were shown some physical shapes and asked to categorize them according to a set of guidelines. The more shapes they categorized correctly, the more money they were paid. When deciding how to best classify a shape, participants could choose to learn what another participant, whose political preferences they knew from previous information, had answered.

To a significant degree, they elected to see and use the answer of a politically like-minded participant, even when the individual had been performing relatively poorly on the task. Think of it: people were more willing to seek the judgment of a political ally on a task, no matter that (a) the task was irrelevant to politics, (b) the ally was inferior at the task, and, (c) consequently, they would probably lose money! In general, these findings fit with emerging scholarship indicating that political-party adherents base many of their decisions less on ideology than on *loyalty*—born of feelings of "we"-ness.[6]

Sports

Appreciating fully the natural favoritism that partisans accord their in-groups, organizers of athletic contests have, for centuries, seen the need for independent evaluators (referees, judges, umpires, and the like) to uphold rules and declare winners in an unbiased manner. But how evenhanded can we expect such officials to be? After all, if "tribalism is human nature," can we reasonably believe they'll be unbiased? Knowing what we know about in-group favoritism, we ought to be skeptical. Plus, there's direct scientific evidence to support the skepticism.

In international football (soccer) matches, players from a referee's home country obtain a 10 percent increase in beneficial calls, and the favoritism occurs equally among elite referees and their less experienced counterparts. In Major League Baseball games, whether a pitch is called a strike is influenced by the racial match between the umpire and pitcher. In National Basketball Association games, officials call fewer fouls against own-race players; the bias is so large that, researchers concluded, "the probability of a team winning is noticeably affected by the racial composition of the refereeing crew assigned to the game." Thus, "we"-group bias corrodes the judgments even of individuals specifically selected and trained to be able to banish the bias. To understand why this is the case, we have to recognize that the same forces are operating on sports officials as on infamously one-sided sports fans.

As distinguished author Isaac Asimov put it in describing our reactions to contests we view: "All things being equal, you root for your own sex, your own culture, your own locality . . . and what you want to prove is that *you* are better than the other person. Whomever you root for represents *you*; and when he [or she] wins, *you* win." Viewed in this light, the intense passion of sports fans makes sense. The game is no light diversion to be enjoyed for its inherent form and artistry. The self is at stake. That is why hometown crowds are so adoring and, tellingly, so grateful to those responsible for home-team victories. That is also why the same crowds are often ferocious in their treatment of players, coaches, and officials implicated in athletic failures.

An apt illustration comes from one of my favorite anecdotes. It concerns a World War II soldier who returned to his home in the Balkans after the war and simply stopped speaking. Medical examinations could find no physical cause. There was no wound, no brain damage, no vocal impairment. He could read, write, understand a conversation, and follow orders. Yet he would not talk—not for his doctors, not for his friends, not even for his pleading family.

Exasperated, his doctors moved him to another city and placed him in a veterans' hospital, where he remained for thirty years, never breaking his self-imposed silence and sinking into a life of social isolation. Then one day, a radio in his ward happened to be tuned to a soccer match between his hometown team and a traditional rival. When at a crucial point of play the referee called a foul against the mute veteran's home team, he jumped from his chair, glared at the radio, and spoke his first words in more than three decades: "You dumb ass! Are you trying to *give* them the match?" With that, he returned to his chair and to a silence he never again violated.

Two important lessons surface from this account. The first concerns the sheer power of the phenomenon. The veteran's desire to have his hometown team succeed was so strong that it alone produced a sharp deviation from his entrenched way of life. The second lesson reveals much about the nature of the union of sports and sports fans, something crucial to its basic character: it is a personal thing. Whatever fragment of an identity that ravaged man still possessed was engaged by soccer play. No matter how weakened his ego may have become after thirty years of wordless stagnation in a hospital ward, it was involved in the outcome of the match. Why? Because he, personally, would be diminished by a hometown defeat, and he, personally, would be enhanced by a hometown victory. How? Through the mere connection of birthplace that hooked *him*, wrapped *him*, and tied *him* to the approaching triumph or failure.

I can offer a final sports example of irrational in-group partiality, a personal one. I grew up in the state of Wisconsin, where the National Football League home team has always been the Green Bay Packers. Not long ago, while reading a news article describing various celebrities' favorite NFL teams, I learned that like me, the entertainers Justin Timberlake and Lil Wayne are avid Packer fans. Right away, I thought better of their music. More than that, I wished for their greater future success. The silent war veteran and I are different in many ways (for one, nobody has ever had to plead with *me* to speak), but on the dimension of unthinking in-group favoritism, we're alike. There's no use denying it. *Click, run.*[7]

Personal Relationships

ROMANTIC PARTNERSHIPS

All romantic partnerships experience disagreements, sources of conflict that if left in place, feed discord and dissatisfaction while damaging the psychological and physical health of both parties. Is there a particularly effective influence approach one partner can use to persuade the other to change and thereby reduce the disagreement? There is. What's more, the approach is easy to enact. In a study, couples that had been together for an average of twenty-one months agreed to discuss an ongoing problem in their relationships and try to find a resolution. The researchers noted a pair of important aspects of the resulting exchanges. First, invariably, one of the partners would assume the role of persuader, attempting to move the other to his or her position. Second, the persuader's influence approach took one of three forms, with dramatically different results.

One, the *coercive* approach, relied on demeaning comments and "You'd better change or you'll be sorry" threats; not only was this sort of attack unsuccessful, but it backfired, pushing the recipient even further from the persuader's position. Another, the *logical/ factual* approach, asserted the rational superiority of the persuader's position, with "If you'll just think about, you'll see I'm right"-type statements; in this case, recipients simply dismissed the claims, failing to change at all. Finally, a third approach, *partnership raising*, hit the jackpot by merely elevating to consciousness the merged identity of the individuals, as a couple. By referencing shared feelings and time together or by simply using the pronouns *we*, *our*, and *us*—in such statements as "You know, we've been together for a long time, and we care for one another; I'd appreciate it if you'd do this for me"—only these persuaders obtained the change they desired. There's a worthy question here: Why would the appeal end with the seemingly selfish request to "do this for me"—rather than with the collective request to "do this for us"? I believe there is a telling answer. By then, after raising the unitizing essence of partnership to consciousness, the distinction was unnecessary.

Besides the demonstrated effectiveness of this unity-elevating approach, two more of its qualities are worth noting. First, its functional essence is a form of evidentiary non sequitur. Stating, "You know, we've been together for a while now, and we care for one another" in no way establishes the logical or empirical validity of the communicator's position. Instead, it offers an entirely different reason for change—loyalty to the partnership.

The second remarkable quality of the partnership-raising route to change is that it provides nothing unknown. Typically, both parties well understand they're in a partnership. But that implication-laden piece of information can easily drop from the top of consciousness when other considerations vie for the same space. True to its name, the partnership-raising approach just elevates one's awareness of the connection. This basis for change fits well with the way I have lately come to view much research on social influence. The thing most likely to guide a person's behavioral decisions isn't the most potent or instructive aspect of the whole situation; instead, it's the one that is most prominent in consciousness at the time of decision.[8]

CLOSE FRIENDSHIPS

Besides romantic partnerships, "we" relationships can arise from other forms of strong personal connections—friendships are one. It's no surprise, then, that individuals' physical-exercise activity is much more likely to match that of their friends than of others they know, such as coworkers.

EBOX 8.1

Today, friendship groups frequently coalesce online, creating a subset of e-commerce activity called f-commerce. According to the social-media software-provider Awareness, which consults with major brands, the profits from online f-commerce can be great. Consider what Awareness reported regarding the f-commerce efforts of a pair of traditional brick-and-mortar businesses, Macy's and Levi's:

"Macy's *Fashion Director* allows users to create an outfit and then collect opinions and votes from friends about buying the outfit. Using *Fashion Director*, Macy's was able to double its Facebook 'fans' to 1.8 million, and increase sales by 30% during the time it was launched. Levi's *Friends Store* creates personalized stores made up of items that friends like. The *Store* attracted more than 30,000 fans when it launched, and allowed Levi's to increase its social reach to over 9 million fans. The *Friends Store* has a 15% higher sales rate and a 50% higher average order value."

Author's note: I am particularly taken with the evidence from Levi's *Friends Store*, as its influence doesn't come from friends who say they like the styles that the *Store*'s members have chosen. Rather, it comes from knowledge of the *existing* style preferences of friends, which then increases purchases of those styles.

Instructively, the closer the friendship (and the accompanying sense of unity), the stronger the influence of our friends' behaviors on our own. In a massive political-election experiment involving sixty-one million people, a Facebook message urging them to vote was most successful if it included photographs of Facebook friends who had already voted and, critically, one of the photos was of a *close* friend.

Finally, more than among close friends, there is an even greater type of felt unity among *best* friends. Special labels and assertions—such as "We are besties" or "We're BFFs" (Best Friends Forever)—convey the strength of the bond. In a study of college students' drinking behaviors, a student's weekly alcohol intake, frequency of drinking, and alcohol-related problems most conformed to the levels of his or her best friend.[9]

PETS

Everybody yawns, often because of states such as sleepiness or boredom. For our purposes, there's a more psychologically interesting cause that implicates the influence process: contagious yawning, which occurs only because someone else has yawned. True to what we know about the effect of feelings of unity on human responding, the frequency of contagious yawning is directly related to the degree of personal attachment between the first and second yawner. Contagious yawning is likely to occur most among kin, followed by friends, then acquaintances, and least among strangers. Something similar takes place in other species (chimps, baboons, bonobos, and wolves), with one animal's yawn spurring yawns principally from kin or friendly contacts.

We know that contagious yawning happens within members of the same species and, chiefly, within members of "we"-based units of that species. Is there any indication that this sort of influence works across species? A study out of Japan tells us there is, and the evidence is, uh, jaw-dropping. The species members are humans, on the one hand, and dogs (often revealingly termed "Man's best friend"), on the other. Indeed, the "we" bond is frequently described as reaching beyond friendship to kinship. For instance, it's common to hear people include their dogs within the boundaries of *family*, with comments such as "I'm the parent of three kids and a Scottish Terrier."

The study's procedures were similar for the twenty-five dogs tested. During a five-minute period, each dog watched either the researcher or its owner yawn several times. The dogs' reactions were recorded on video and then analyzed for the number of contagious yawns. The findings were clear-cut: cross-species contagious yawning *did* emerge, but only between dogs and their owners. Once again, we see that influence efforts are much more successful within "we"-based units and, in addition, that the boundaries of those units can be stretched to remarkable extents—even, in this instance, to include members of another species.[10, 11]

It is richly apparent that behavioral scientists have been busy charting the breadth and depth of the unity principle's impact on

Figure 8.3: Spawning yawning
Pets and their owners exhibit contagious yawning. To date, researchers have only examined the transmission from owner to pet. I'm not a betting man, but I'd wager good money that it works in both directions.
Courtesy of iStock Photo

human responding. In the process, they've uncovered two main categories of factors that lead to a feeling of unity—those involving ways of belonging together and ways of acting together.

Unity I: Belonging Together

Kinship

From a genetic point of view, being in the same family—the same bloodline—is the ultimate form of self–other unity. Indeed, it is widely accepted within evolutionary biology that individuals do not so much attempt to ensure their own survival as the survival of copies of their genes. The implication is that the "self" in self-interest can lie outside one's body and inside the skin of related others who share a goodly amount of genetic material. For this reason, people are particularly willing to help genetically close relatives, especially in survival-related decisions, such as whether to donate a kidney in the United States, rescue someone from a burning building in Japan, or intervene in an axe fight in the jungles of Venezuela. Brain-imaging research has identified one cause: People experience unusually high stimulation of the self-reward centers of their brains after aiding a family member; it's almost as if, by doing so, they are aiding themselves . . . and this is true even of teenagers!

READER'S REPORT 8.1

From a nurse living in Sydney, Australia,
during the COVID-19 pandemic

I recently entered into a store for some essentials and used the hand sanitiser offered by the security guard. I noticed a person who worked at the store's pharmacy decline to use sanitiser when entering the store. This scenario is not limited to this one instance. I have seen many more instances of people in stores who were irresponsible, for example, with the recommendation for social distancing.

Afterward, I phoned the store manager, who said she wasn't empowered to make any changes but said she would raise the issue with "corporate," which produced no noticeable changes. Then, I contacted the local Member of Parliament (MP). I left a phone message in which I advised the MP as follows: "Imagine Mr. MP a scenario of having your grandmother or wife fall ill when it could have been prevented through good infection control measures. Please evangelize others to imagine the same."

Two days later, I received a phone call and email from the MP. He had contacted the Department of Health, the Minister for Health, and CEOs of two national retail chains using my scenario. I then was scrolling through the news and found that the retail chains were suddenly imposing new hand sanitising and social distance restrictions. The news posts encouraged people to contact the MP who had pushed for the change.

I think I was able to instigate that change. While the MP took the credit, I did not mind.

Author's note: Although it's hard to know which factors led to the changes the nurse witnessed, I suspect one was her emotion-stirring reference to family members in the scenario she used on the MP and recommended he employ in his own influence efforts.

(The reader who submitted this report asked to remain anonymous; accordingly, her name does not appear among the Reader's Report contributors in this book's preface.)

From an evolutionary perspective, any advantages to one's kin should be promoted, including relatively small ones. Consider as confirmation the most effective influence technique I have ever employed in my professional career. I once wanted to compare the attitudes of college students with those of their parents on an array of topics, which meant arranging for both groups to fill out the same lengthy questionnaire. Getting a set of college students to perform the task wasn't difficult; I assigned the questionnaire as a course exercise in a large psychology class I was teaching and incorporated it into my lecture. The harder problem was finding a way to get their parents to comply, because I had no money to offer, and I knew that adult participation rates in such surveys are dismal—often below 20 percent. A colleague suggested playing the kinship card by offering an extra point on my next test (one of several in the class) to each student whose parent would respond to the questionnaire.

The effect was astounding. All 163 of my students sent the questionnaire to a parent, 159 of whom (97 percent) mailed back a completed copy within a week—for one point, on one test, in one course, in one semester, for one of their children. As an influence researcher, I've never experienced anything like it. However, from subsequent personal experience, I now believe there's something I could have done to produce even better results: I could have asked my students to send a questionnaire to a grandparent. I figure that of the 163 sent out, I would have gotten 162 back within a week. The missing copy would probably be due to a grandfather's hospitalization from cardiac arrest while sprinting to the post office. *Click, run* . . . to the mailbox.

I got some validation of this kind of grandparental favoritism while reading humor columnist Joel Stein's account of trying to persuade his grandmother to vote for a particular presidential candidate—something she was not initially keen to do. In the midst of his extended pitch to her, it became obvious that his arguments were either not convincing or not being understood by

Figure 8.4: Family first

The preeminence of family ties doesn't only reveal itself in the actions of elders toward their children. It operates up the chain as well. In accepting her award for outstanding lead actress in a comedy series (*Veep*) during the 2016 Emmy Award ceremony, Julia Louis-Dreyfus dedicated it to her recently deceased father in vivid testimony to the import of the connection: "I'm so glad he liked *Veep*, because his opinion was the one that really mattered."

Robert Hanashiro

"Mama Ann." Nonetheless, she declared she would vote for his candidate. When the puzzled Stein asked why, she explained it was because her *grandson* wanted her to.

But is there any way that individuals with no special genetic connection to us could employ the power of kinship to gain our favor? One possibility is to use language and imagery to bring the concept of kin to our consciousness. For example, collectives that create a sense of "we"-ness among their members are characterized by the use of familial images and labels—such as "brothers," "sisterhood," "forefathers," "motherland," "ancestry," "legacy," "heritage," and the like—which lead to an increased willingness to sacrifice one's own interests for the welfare of the group. Because humans are symbolizing creatures, one international team of researchers found that these "fictive families" produce levels of self-sacrifice normally associated with highly interrelated clans. In one pair of studies, reminding Spaniards of the family-like nature of their national ties then led those feeling "fused" with their fellow citizens to become immediately and dramatically more willing to fight and die for Spain.[12]

Now, let's ask a similar question about someone outside our existing collectives. Could a lone, genetically unrelated communicator harness the pull of kinship to obtain agreement? When I speak at conferences of financial-services firms, I sometimes ask, "Who would you say is the most successful financial investor of our time?" The answer, voiced in unison, is always "Warren Buffett." In exquisite collaboration with his partner Charlie Munger, Buffett has led Berkshire Hathaway—a holding company that invests in other companies—to amazing levels of worth for its shareholders since taking over in 1965.

Several years ago, I received a gift of Berkshire Hathaway stock. It's been a gift that's kept on giving, and not just monetarily. It has provided me a vantage point from which to observe the approaches of Buffett and Munger to strategic investing, about which I know little, and strategic communication, about which I do know something. Sticking to the process I know, I can say I've been impressed by the amount of skill I've seen. Ironically, Berkshire Hathaway's financial attainments have been so remarkable that a communication problem has arisen—how to give current and prospective shareholders confidence that the company will maintain such success into the future. Absent that confidence, stockholders might reasonably be expected to sell their shares, while potential buyers could be expected to purchase elsewhere.

Make no mistake, based on an excellent business model and several unique advantages of scale, Berkshire Hathaway has a compelling case to make for its future valuation. But having a compelling case to make is not the same as making a case compellingly—something Buffett does invariably in the company's annual reports through a combination of honesty, humility, and humor. But in February 2015, something more influential than usual seemed necessary. It was time, in a special fiftieth-anniversary letter to shareholders, to summarize the company's results over the years and to make the argument for the continuing vitality of Berkshire Hathaway in coming years.

Implicit in the fifty-year character of the anniversary was a concern that had been around for a while but that was reasserting itself in online commentary: A half-century into the enterprise, Buffett and Munger were no youngsters, and should either no longer be present to lead the company, its future prospects and share price could tumble. I remember reading the commentary and being troubled by it. Would the value of my stock, which had more than quadrupled under Buffett and Munger's management, hold up if either departed because of advancing age? Was it time to sell and take my extraordinary profits before they might evaporate?

In his letter, Buffett addressed the issue head-on—specifically, in the section labeled "The Next 50 Years at Berkshire," in which he laid out the affirmative, forward-reaching consequences of Berkshire Hathaway's proven business model, its nearly unprecedented bulwark of financial assets, and the firm's already completed identification of the "right person" to take over as CEO when appropriate. More telling for me as a persuasion scientist was how Buffett began that all-important section. In characteristic fashion, he reestablished his trustworthiness by being upfront about a potential weakness: "Now let's look at the road ahead. Bear in mind that if I had attempted 50 years ago to gauge what was coming, certain of my predictions would have been far off the mark." Then, he did something I'd never seen or heard him do in any public forum. He added, "With that warning, I will tell you what I would say to my family today if they asked me about Berkshire's future."

What followed was careful construction of the case for Berkshire Hathaway's foreseeable economic health—the proven business model, the bulwark of financial assets, the scrupulously vetted future CEO. As convincing as these components of his argument were on their merits, Buffett had done something that made me judge them as even more convincing. He had claimed that he was going to advise me about them as he would a family member. Because of everything I knew about the man, I believed that claim. As a result, I have never since thought seriously about selling my Berkshire Hathaway stock. There's a memorable moment in the movie *Jerry Maguire* in which the title character played by Tom Cruise bursts into a room, greets the inhabitants (including his estranged wife, Dorothy, played by Renee Zellweger), and launches into a long soliloquy in which he lists the reasons she should continue to be his life partner. Partway through the list, Dorothy looks up and cuts the monologue short with a now famous line: "You had me at *hello*." In his letter, Buffett had me at *family*.

It's instructive that in the flood of favorable reaction to his fiftieth-anniversary letter (with titles such as "Warren Buffett Just Wrote His Best Annual Letter Ever" and "You'd Be a Fool Not to Invest in Berkshire Hathaway"), no one remarked on the familial frame into which Buffett had so adeptly placed his arguments. I can't say I was surprised at this lack of recognition. In the world of hard-minded, fact-based financial investing, the default is to focus on the merit of the message. And, of course, it's true that the *merit* (of the arguments) can be the message. But, at the same time, there are other dimensions of effective communication that can become the essential message. We learned, via communication guru Marshall McLuhan, that the *medium* (the method by which the message is delivered) can be the message; via the principle of social proof that the *multitude* can be the message; via the authority principle that the *messenger* can be the message; and now, via the concept of unity, we've learned that the *merger* (of identities) can be the message. It's worth considering, then, which additional features of a situation, besides direct kinship, lend themselves to the perceived merging of identities.

Noteworthy is how many of these features are, nonetheless, traceable to cues of heightened kinship. Obviously, no one can look inside another and determine the percentage of genes the two share. That is why, to operate in an evolutionarily prudent fashion, people have to rely on certain aspects that are simultaneously detectible and associated with genetic overlap—the most evident being physical similarities. The draw of similar-looking others leads individuals to group themselves into (a) friendship units, (b) university fraternities, and (c) even baseball teams with people who look like them. Inside families, individuals are more helpful to kin they resemble. Outside the family unit, people use facial similarity to judge (fairly accurately) their degree of genetic relatedness to strangers. However, they can be tricked into misplaced favoritism in this regard. Observers of a photograph of someone whose face has been digitally modified to look more like them come to trust that person to a greater extent. If the now-more-similar face is of a political candidate, they become more willing to vote for him or her.[13]

Besides physical comparability, people use attitudinal similarities as a basis for assessing genetic relatedness and, consequently, as a basis for forming in-groups and for deciding whom to help. But, instructively, not all attitudes are equivalent in this regard; fundamental religious and political attitudes, toward such matters as sexual behavior and liberal/conservative ideology, appear to function most forcefully to determine in-group identities. This can be seen to be so for another kinship-based reason: these are the types of attitudes most likely to be passed on through heredity and, therefore, to reflect the genetic "we." Such highly inherited types of attitudes are also stubbornly resistant to change, perhaps because people are less willing to shift on positions they feel define them.[14]

Place

There is yet another usually reliable cue of heightened genetic commonality. It has less to do with physical similarity than with physical proximity. It is the perception of being *of* the same place as another, and its impact on human behavior can be arresting. I know of no better way to document that impact than by resolving some puzzles of human conduct that surfaced during one of the most harrowing eras of our time—the years of the Holocaust. Let's begin with the physically smallest form of one's place and then move to more expanded forms.

HOME

Humans as well as animals react to those present in their homes while growing up as if they are relatives. Although this clue to relatedness can occasionally be misleading, it is normally accurate because people in the home typically are family members. In addition, the longer the length of co-residence in the home, the greater its effect on individuals' sense of family and, accordingly, their willingness to sacrifice for one another. But there is a related factor that produces these same consequences without extensive time together. When people observe their parents caring for another's needs in the home, they also experience a family-like feeling and become more willing to give to that other. An intriguing upshot of this process is that children who see their parents open their homes to a range of differing people should be more likely, as adults, to help strangers. For them, "we"-ness should reach beyond their immediate or extended family and apply to the human family as well.

How does this insight help solve a major mystery of the Holocaust? History records the names of the most famous and successful helpers of the era: Raoul Wallenberg, the courageous Swede whose relentless rescue efforts eventually cost him his life, and the German industrialist Oskar Schindler, whose "list" saved 1,100 Jews. Yet what may have been the most effective concentrated helping action taken during the time of the Holocaust has gone relatively unrecognized in the years since.

It began near dawn on a summer day in 1940 when two hundred Polish Jews crowded together outside the Japanese consulate in Lithuania to plead for help in their attempts to escape the sweeping Nazi advance through Eastern Europe. That they would choose to seek the aid of Japanese officials represents a puzzle in itself. At the time, the governments of Nazi Germany and imperial Japan had close ties and shared interests. Why then would these Jews, the hated targets of the Third Reich, throw themselves on the mercy of one of Hitler's international partners? What possible aid could they expect from Japan?

Before its close strategic associations with Hitler's Germany developed in the late 1930s, Japan had been allowing displaced Jews easy access to Japanese territories as a way of gaining some of the financial resources and political goodwill that the international Jewish community could provide in return. Because support for the plan remained strong within some circles in Japan, the government never revoked completely its policies of granting travel visas to European Jews. The paradoxical result was that in the prewar years, as most of the countries of the world (the United States included) were turning away the desperate "prey" of Hitler's Final Solution, it was Japan—Hitler's ally—that was providing sanctuary, allowing them to stay in the Japanese-controlled Jewish settlement of Shanghai, China, and the city of Kobe, Japan.

By July 1940, then, when two hundred Jews massed outside of the door of the Japanese consulate in Lithuania, they knew the man behind that door offered their best and perhaps last chance for safety. His name was Chiune Sugihara, and, by all appearances, he was an unlikely candidate to arrange for their salvation. A mid-career diplomat, he had become Japan's consul general in Lithuania by virtue of years of committed and obedient service in a variety of earlier posts. The right credentials facilitated his rise within the diplomatic corps: he was the son of a government official and a samurai family. He had set his professional goals high, becoming proficient in the Russian language in hope of someday being the Japanese ambassador to Moscow. Like his better-known counterpart, Oskar Schindler, Mr. Sugihara was a great lover of games, music, and parties. On the surface, there was little to suggest that this comfortable, pleasure-seeking, lifelong diplomat would risk his career, reputation, and future to try to save the strangers who woke him from a sound sleep at 5:15 a.m. That, though, is what he did—with full knowledge of the potential consequences for him and his family.

After speaking with members of the crowd waiting outside his gate, Sugihara recognized their plight and wired Tokyo for permission to authorize travel visas for them. Although aspects of Japan's lenient visa and settlement policies were still in place for Jews, Sugihara's superiors at the Foreign Ministry worried that the continuation of those policies would damage Japan's diplomatic relations with Hitler. As a consequence, his request was denied, as were his more urgent second and third petitions. It was at that point in his life—at age forty, with no hint of prior disloyalty or disobedience—that this personally indulgent, professionally ambitious, career official did what no one could have suspected. He began writing the needed travel documents in outright defiance of his clearly stated, and twice restated, orders.

That choice shattered his career. Within a month, he was transferred from his post as consul general to a much diminished position outside of Lithuania, where he could no longer operate independently. Ultimately, he was expelled from the Foreign Ministry for insubordination. In dishonor after the war, he sold light bulbs for a living. But in the weeks before he had to close the consulate in Lithuania, he stayed true to the choice he had made, interviewing applicants from early morning to late night and authoring the papers required for their escape. Even after the consulate had been shut and he had taken up residence in a hotel, he continued to write visas. Even after the strain of the task had left him thinned and exhausted, even after the same strain had left his wife incapable of nursing their infant child, he wrote without respite. Even on the platform for the train set to take him from his petitioners, even on the train itself, he wrote and thrust life-granting papers into life-grasping hands, saving thousands of innocents in the process.

Figure 8.5: Sugihara and family: inside/outside.

After writing thousands of travel visas for Jews in his consulate office *(top)*, Chiune Sugihara was transferred from his post to lesser roles in Nazi-held Europe. In Czechoslovakia *(bottom)*, he positioned his family (wife, son, and sister-in-law) for a photo outside a park with a sign that read "No Jews Allowed" in German. Was that sign an incidental feature of the shot or a consciously included piece of bitter irony? For suggestive evidence, see if you can locate the sister-in-law's right hand.

United States Holocaust Memorial Museum. Both photos courtesy of Hiroki Sugihara

And at last, when the train began to draw him away, he bowed deeply and apologized to those he had to leave stranded—begging their forgiveness for his deficiencies as a helper.

Sugihara's decision to help thousands of Jews escape to Shanghai is likely not attributable to a single factor. Normally, multiple forces act and interact to bring about this kind of extraordinary benevolence. But in Sugihara's case, one *home-based* factor stands out. His father, a tax official who had been sent to Korea for a time, moved the family there and opened an inn. Sugihara remembered being powerfully affected by his parents' willingness to take in a broad mix of guests—tending to their basic needs for food and shelter in the family's home, even providing baths and washing their clothes—despite the fact that some were too impoverished to pay. From this perspective, we can see one reason—an expanded sense of family, flowing from parental care of diverse individuals in the home—for Sugihara's later efforts to help thousands of European Jews. As he stated in an interview forty-five years after the events, the nationality and religion of the Jews did not matter; it only mattered that they were members, with him, of the human family. His experience suggests a piece of advice for parents who want their children to develop a broadly charitable nature: give them contact *in the home* with people from a wide spectrum of backgrounds and treat those people like family, not like guests.

The legendary humanitarian, Mother Teresa, often told a similar story about her childhood, with similar implications for parental practices. She grew up in Serbia—first wealthy, then poor after her father died—and watched her mother, Drabna, feed, clothe, mend, cleanse, and house anyone in need. Returning from school, she and her siblings frequently found strangers at the table eating the family's limited food. When she asked why they were there, her mother would reply, "They are our people." Note that the words "our people" are conceptually equivalent to "of us."[15]

LOCALITY
Because humans evolved from small but stable groupings of genetically related individuals, we have also evolved a tendency to fa-

vor and follow the people who, outside the home, live in proximity to us. There is even a named "ism"—localism—to represent this tendency. Its enormous influence can be seen from the neighborhood to the community level. A look back to a pair of incidents from the Holocaust offers it gripping confirmation.

The first allows us to resolve the opening mystery of this chapter, in which a Nazi prison-camp guard who was executing every tenth prisoner in a line turned away from one tenth prisoner without explanation and shot the eleventh. It's possible to imagine several potential reasons for his action. Perhaps, in the past, he had gotten good effort from the spared prisoner or had noticed a high level of strength or intelligence or health that foretold of future productive work. But when asked to explain himself by another of the guards, it was clear his choice sprang from none of these practical considerations. Rather, it was a hideous form of localism: he had recognized the man as being from his hometown.

Recounting the incident in a scholarly article, the anthropologist Ronald Cohen described an incongruous aspect of it: "While engaged dutifully in mass murder, the guard was merciful and sympathetic to one particular member of the victimized group." Although Cohen didn't pursue the issue, it is important to identify the factor potent enough to turn a cold killer performing mass murder into a "merciful and sympathetic" enactor. It was mutuality of place.

Let's also consider how that same unitizing factor, during the same period of history, produced a radically different outcome. Multiple historical accounts of rescuers of Holocaust-era Jews reveal a little-analyzed yet noteworthy phenomenon. In the great majority of instances, the rescuers who chose to house, feed, and hide these targets of Nazi persecution did not spontaneously seek out the targets to offer them help. Even more notably, they were typically not asked for that help by the victims themselves. Instead, the direct requester would most frequently be a relative or neighbor who petitioned them for assistance on behalf of a hunted individual or family. In a real sense, then, these rescuers didn't so much say yes to the needy strangers as to their own relatives and neighbors.

Of course, it wasn't the case that no rescuers acted primarily out of compassion for victimized others. Frenchman André Trocmé, after taking in an initial, lone refugee outside his door, persuaded other residents of his small town of Le Chambon to sustain, harbor, conceal, and smuggle away thousands of Jews during Nazi occupation. The instructive feature of Trocmé's extraordinary story is not how he arranged for the care of that first refugee but how he arranged for the care of the many that followed. He began by requesting the help of individuals who would have a difficult time saying no to him, his relatives and neighbors, and then pressed them to do the same among their relatives and neighbors. This strategic leveraging of *existing unities* made him more than a compassionate hero. It made him an inordinately successful one as well.

Other highly successful communicators have leveraged the "existing unities" inside a locality. During the 2008 US presidential campaign, when, on the basis of studies showing that certain kinds of direct personal contact with voters could shift election totals significantly, Obama strategists devoted an unprecedented amount of money to the establishment of over seven hundred local field offices concentrated mainly in battleground states. The principal responsibility of the staffers and volunteers in these offices was not to convince nearby citizens of Barack Obama's suitability for office. Rather, it was to ensure that those residents who likely favored his candidacy would register to vote and cast their ballot on Election Day. To achieve the goal, field-office volunteers were assigned intensive door-to-door canvassing duties within their own communities, which the planners knew generates increased neighbor-to-neighbor contact and, hence, greater influence. A subsequent analysis of the effects of this local-field-office strategy indicated that it worked well, winning the election for Obama in three contested states (Florida, Indiana, and North Carolina) and, according to the author of the analysis, turning the national result from an electoral vote toss-up into an electoral vote blowout.[16]

REGION

Even being from the same general geographical region can lead to feelings of "we"-ness and its striking effects. Around the globe, sports team championships stimulate feelings of personal pride in residents of the team's surrounding zones—as if the *residents* had won. In the United States alone, research evidence reinforces the general point in additional and varied ways: citizens agreed to participate in a survey to a greater extent if it emanated from a home-state university; Amazon product buyers were more likely to follow the recommendation of a reviewer who lived in the same state; people greatly overestimate the role of their home states in US history; readers of a news story about a military fatality in Afghanistan became more opposed to the war there upon learning the fallen soldier was from their own state; and during the Civil War, if infantrymen came from the same region as one another, they were less likely to desert, remaining loyal to comrades in their "more unitized" units. From fans to fighters, we can see the considerable impact of regional identities on "we"-like responding. But it's another seemingly bewildering event of the Holocaust that yields the most informative instance.

Although Chiune Sugihara's visas saved thousands of Jews, when they arrived in Japanese-held territory, they became part of an even larger contingent of Jewish refugees concentrated in the Japanese city of Kobe and the Japanese-controlled city of Shanghai. After the 1941 attack on Pearl Harbor, all refugee passage in and out of these cities ended, and the safety of its Jewish community became precarious. Japan, after all, was by then a full-fledged wartime conspirator with Adolf Hitler and had to protect the solidarity of its alliance with this virulent anti-Semite. What's more, in January 1942, Hitler's plan to annihilate international Jewry was formalized at the Wannsee Conference in Berlin. With the Final Solution installed as Axis policy, Nazi officials began to press Tokyo to extend that "solution" to Japan's Jews. Proposals involving death camps, medical experiments, and mass drownings at sea were forwarded to Tokyo following the conference. Yet despite the potentially damaging impact on its relations with Hitler, the

Japanese government resisted these pressures in early 1942 and maintained that resistance through the end of the war. Why?

The answer may well have to do with a set of events that took place several months earlier. The Nazis had sent to Tokyo Gestapo colonel Josef Meisinger, known as the "Butcher of Warsaw" for ordering the execution of sixteen thousand Poles. Upon his arrival in April 1941, Meisinger began pressing for a policy of brutality toward the Jews under Japan's rule—a policy he stated he would gladly help design and enact. Uncertain at first of how to respond and wanting to hear all sides, high-ranking members of Japan's military government called upon the Jewish refugee community to send two leaders to a meeting that would importantly influence their future. The chosen representatives were both respected religious leaders, but respected in different ways. One, Rabbi Moses Shatzkes, was renowned as a studious man, one of the most brilliant Talmudic scholars in Europe before the war. The other, Rabbi Shimon Kalisch, was older and known for his remarkable ability to understand basic human workings—a social psychologist of sorts.

After the two entered the meeting room, they and their translators stood before a tribunal of powerful members of the Japanese High Command, who would determine their community's survival and wasted little time in asking a pair of fateful questions: Why do our allies the Nazis hate you so much? And why should we take your side against them? Rabbi Shatzkes, the scholar, comprehending the tangled complexity of the historical, religious, and economic issues involved, could offer no response. But Rabbi Kalisch's knowledge of human nature had equipped him to deliver the most impressive persuasive communication I have encountered in over thirty years of studying the process: "Because," he said calmly, "we are Asian, *like you*."

Although brief, the assertion was inspired. It shifted the Japanese officers' reigning in-group identity from one based in a temporary wartime alliance to one based in a regional mutuality. It did so by implicating the Nazis' own *racial* claim that the Aryan "master race" was genetically different from and innately superior to the peoples of Asia. With a single penetrating observation, it was the Jews who were aligned with the Japanese and the Nazis who were (self-proclaimedly) not. The older rabbi's response had a powerful effect on the Japanese officers. After a silence, they conferred among themselves and announced a recess. When they returned, the most senior military official rose and granted the reassurance the rabbis had hoped to bring home to their community: "Go back to your people. Tell them . . . we will provide for their safety and peace. You have nothing to fear while in Japanese territory." And so it was.[17]

There is no doubt that the unitizing powers of family and of place can be harnessed by a skilled communicator—witness the effectiveness of Warren Buffett and Rabbi Kalisch in these regards.

Figure 8.6: Rabbis in Japan
Throughout World War II, the Japanese did not succumb to Nazi pressure to treat Jews in Japanese-controlled territories harshly. One reason may have been the arguments of one of two rabbis (pictured with their translators on the day of a crucial meeting) designed to include their people in Japanese officials' sense of "we" and to specifically exclude the Nazis in this respect.
Courtesy of Marvin Tokayer

At the same time, there is another kind of unitizing effect available to those seeking elevated influence. It comes not from *belonging* together in the same genealogy or geography but from *acting* together synchronously or collaboratively.

Unity II: Acting Together

My colleague, Professor Wilhelmina Wosinska, remembers with mixed feelings growing up in the 1950s and 1960s in Soviet-controlled Poland. On the negative side, besides constant shortages of basic commodities, there were dispiriting limitations on all manner of personal freedoms, including speech, privacy, information, dissent, and movement. Yet she and her schoolmates were led to register them positively—as necessary for establishing a fair and equal social order. These positive feelings were regularly displayed and fueled by celebratory events, in which participants sang and marched together while waving flags in unison. The effects, she says, were impressive: physically stirring, emotionally uplifting, and psychologically validating. Never has she felt more impelled to the concept "All for one, and one for all" than in the midst of those scrupulously choreographed and powerfully coordinating involvements. Whenever I have heard Professor Wosinska speak of these activities, it has been in a sober, academic presentation (on group psychology). Despite the scholarly context, the description of her participation invariably brought volume to her voice, blood to her face, and light to her eyes. There is something indelibly visceral about such experiences that marks them as primeval and central to the human condition.

Indeed, the archaeological and anthropological records are clear on the point: all human societies have developed ways to respond together, in unison or coordination, with songs, marches, rituals, chants, prayers, and dances. What's more, they've been doing so since prehistoric times; collective dance, for instance, is depicted extraordinarily often in the drawings, rock art, and cave paintings of the Neolithic and Chalcolithic eras. The behavioral-science

Figure 8.7: Neolithic line dancing?
According to archaeologist Yosef Garfinkel, depictions of social interaction in prehistoric art were nearly always of dance. A cave painting from Bhimbetka, India, provides an example.
Arindam Banerjee/Dreamstime.com

record is equally clear as to why. When people act in unitary ways, they become unit*ized*. The resultant feeling of group solidarity serves societies' interests well, producing degrees of loyalty and self-sacrifice normally associated with much smaller family units. Thus, human societies, even ancient ones, have discovered group-bonding "technologies" involving coordinated responding. The effects are similar to those of kinship—feelings of "we"-ness, merger, confusion of self and other, and willingness to sacrifice for the group. It is no surprise, then, that in tribal societies, warriors frequently dance together, rhythmically, before battle.

The feeling of being merged with others sounds rare, but it's not. It can be produced easily and in multiple ways. In one set of studies, participants who read a story aloud together with a partner in unison (or in coordination by taking turns reading sentences of the story) came to feel greater "we"-ness and solidarity with their partner than did participants who read the story independently from their partner. Other research showed the favorable effects of acting together. In groups of twenty-three to twenty-four members at a time, some groups said words together in the same order as members of their group, whereas other groups said the same words but not in the same order as their group members. Not only did those in the speaking-in-unison groups feel more "we"-ness toward their fellow group members, but later, while playing a group video game, their group members obtained better game scores by coordinating their efforts with one another to a greater extent. A last demonstration of the phenomenon comes from a study of brain activity. When intensely involved in joint projects, participants' brain-wave patterns began to match one another's, rising and falling together. Thus, when people function together synchronously, they are on the same wavelength, literally.

If *acting* together—in motoric, vocal, or cognitive ways—can serve as a surrogate for *belonging* together in a kinship unit, we ought to see similar consequences from these forms of togetherness. And we do. Two of these consequences are especially important for individuals seeking to become more influential: enhanced liking and greater support from others.[18]

Liking

When people act in unison, they not only see themselves as more alike but also evaluate one another more positively afterward. Their elevated like*ness* turns into elevated lik*ing*. The actions can involve finger tapping in a laboratory, smiling in a conversation, or body adjustments in a teacher–student interaction—all of which, if synchronized, cause people to rate one another more favorably. But one set of Canadian researchers wondered whether they could ask something more socially significant of coordinated movement: Could its ability to convert alikeness into liking be employed to reduce racial prejudice? The researchers noted that although we normally try to "resonate" (harmonize) with members of our in-groups, we typically *don't* with out-group members. They speculated that the consequent differences in feelings of unity might be at least partially responsible for an automatic human tendency to favor the in-group. If so, then arranging for people to harmonize their actions with those of out-group members might reduce the bias.

To test the idea, they conducted an experiment in which White subjects watched seven video clips of Black individuals taking a sip of water from a glass and then placing it down on a table. Some of the subjects merely observed the clips and actions. Others were asked to imitate the actions by sipping from a glass of water in front of them in exact coordination with the movements they witnessed on the clips. Later, in a procedure designed to measure their hidden racial preferences, the subjects who had merely observed the Black actors showed the typical White favoritism for Whites over Blacks. But those who had synchronized their actions with those of the Black actors showed none of this favoritism.

Before making too much of the experiment's results, we should recognize that the positive change was measured just a few minutes after the study's unitizing procedure. The researchers presented no evidence that the shifts would persist beyond the time or place of the study. Still, even with that caveat in mind, there is room for optimism, as a less biased approach to in-group/out-group preferences can be all that's necessary to make a difference within the boundaries of a specific situation such as a job interview, sales call, or first meeting.[19]

Support

OK, fine, there's good evidence that acting together with others, even strangers, generates feelings of unity and increased liking. But are the forms of unity and liking that flow from coordinated responding strong enough to alter meaningfully the gold standard of social influence: ensuing conduct? Two studies help answer the question. One examined aid given to a previously unitized, single individual, whereas the other examined cooperation with a group of previously unitized team members; in both instances, the requested behavior required self-sacrifice.

In the first study, participants listened to an array of recorded audio tones on headphones while tapping a table to the beats they heard. Some listened to the same tones as a partner did and therefore saw themselves tapping in concert with that person; others listened to a different array of tones than their partner did and, thus, the two did not act in synchrony. Afterward, all participants learned that they were free to leave the study but that their partners had to remain to answer a lengthy series of math and logic problems; however, they could choose to stay and help their partners by taking on some of the task themselves. The results left no doubt about coordinated activity's capacity to escalate self-sacrificial, supportive conduct. While only 18 percent of the participants who did not initially tap the table in synchrony with their partners chose to stay and help, of those who did tap in synchrony, 49 percent gave up their free time to provide assistance to their partners.

Different researchers conducted the second study of interest and employed a time-honored military tactic to instill a sense of group cohesion. After assigning participants to teams, the researchers asked some of the teams to walk together, *in step*, for a time; they asked others to walk together for the same amount of time, but normally. Later, all team members played an economic game in which they could either maximize the chance of increasing their own financial gain or forgo that opportunity to ensure, instead, that their teammates would do well financially. Members of teams that had marched together were 50 percent more cooperative toward their teammates than were those who had just walked together normally. A follow-up study helped explain why. Initial synchrony led to a feeling of unity, which led to a greater willingness to sacrifice personal gain for the group's greater good. It is no wonder then that marching in unison is still employed in military training, even though its worth as a battlefield technique disappeared long ago. Its worth as a *unity-building* technique accounts for its retention.[20]

Thus, groups can promote unity, liking, and subsequent supportive behavior in a variety of situations by first arranging for synchronous responding. But the tactics we've reviewed so far—

simultaneous story reading, table tapping, and water sipping—don't seem readily implementable, at least not in any large-scale fashion. Marching in unison might be better in this regard, but only marginally. Isn't there some *generally* applicable mechanism that social entities could deploy to bring about such coordination to influence members toward group goals? There is. It's music. And fortunately for individual communicators, it can be employed to move others toward the goals of a single agent of influence.

Music in the Struggle for Influence: It's a Jingle Out There

There is a good explanation for why the presence of music stretches both from the start of human recorded history and across the breadth of human societies. Because of a unique collection of detectible regularities (rhythm, meter, intensity, pulse, and time), music possesses rare coordinating power. Listeners can easily become aligned with one another along motoric, vocal, and emotional dimensions—a state of affairs that leads to familiar markers of unity such as self–other merging, social cohesion, and supportive conduct. In this last respect, consider the results of a study of four-year-old children done in Germany. As part of a game, some of the kids walked around a circle with a partner while singing and keeping time in their movements with recorded music. Other kids did nearly the same but without the accompaniment of music. When later, the children had an opportunity for benevolence, those who had sung and walked together in time with music were over three times more likely to help their partner than were those who did not have a joint musical experience.

The study's authors made a pair of instructive points about the helping they observed. First, they noted that it was self-sacrificial, requiring the helper to give up some personal play time to assist a partner. That jointly experienced music and movement increased later self-sacrifice so impressively has to be a revelation to any parent who has tried to alter the characteristically selfish choices of a four-year-old at play ("Leia, it's time to give Dawson a turn with that toy . . . Leia? . . . Leia! . . . Leia, you come back with that right now!"). The authors' second noteworthy comment strikes me as at least as important as the first: the children's personal sacrifice didn't arise from any rational weighting of the reasons for and against providing assistance. The help wasn't rooted in rationality at all. It was spontaneous, intuitive, and based on an emotional sense of connection that naturally accompanies shared musical engagement. The implications of this point for managing the social-influence process are significant.[21]

Systems Engineering

Psychologists have long asserted the existence of two ways of assessing and knowing. The most recent such assertion to gain widespread attention is Daniel Kahneman's treatment of the distinction between System 1 and System 2 thinking. The first is fast, associative, intuitive, and often emotional, whereas the second is slower, deliberative, analytical, and rational. Support for the separateness of the two approaches comes from evidence that activating one inhibits the other. Just as it is difficult to think hard about an occurrence while experiencing it emotionally, fully experiencing the occurrence is difficult while parsing it logically. There's an implication for influence: persuaders would be wise to match the System 1 versus 2 orientation of any appeal to the corresponding orientation of the recipient. Thus, if you are considering a car purchase primarily from the standpoint of its emotionally relevant features (attractive looks and exhilarating acceleration), a salesperson would be well advised to approach you with feelings-related arguments. Research suggests that saying "I *feel* this is the one for you" will be more successful. But if you are considering the purchase primarily on rational grounds (fuel economy and trade-in value), then "I *think* this is the one for you" would be more likely to close the sale.[22]

Music's influence is of the System 1 rather than System 2 variety. Take, for instance, musician Elvis Costello's quote concerning the difficulty of properly describing music through the cognitive process of writing: "Writing about music," he said, "is like dancing about architecture."

As additional support for the mismatch between cognition and emotion, this time in romance, consider the line from Bill Withers's song "Ain't No Sunshine" about a man agonizing over a woman who has left their home yet again: "And I know, I know / Hey, I oughta leave young thing alone / But ain't no sunshine when she's gone." Withers makes his point in the purest form of poetry I've ever heard in a popular song lyric: In the throes of romantic love, what one may recognize cognitively (twenty-six times!) doesn't amend what one feels emotionally.

In their sensory and visceral responses to music, people sing, swing, and sway in rhythmic alignment with it—and, if together, with one another. Rarely do they think analytically while music is prominent in consciousness. Under music's influence, the deliberative, rational route to knowing becomes difficult to access and, hence, largely unavailable. Two commentaries speak to a regrettable upshot. The first, a quote from Voltaire, is contemptuous: "Anything too stupid to be spoken is sung." The second, an adage from the advertising profession, is tactical: "If you can't make your case to an audience with facts, sing it to them." Thus, communicators whose ideas have little rational firepower don't have to give up the fight; they can undertake a flanking maneuver. Equipping themselves with music and song, they can move their campaign to a battleground where rationality possesses little force, where sensations of harmony, synchrony, and unity win the day.

This recognition has helped me resolve a long-standing personal mystery, one that was particularly vexing to me as a young man with no musical talent. Why are young women so attracted to musicians? There's no logic to it, right? Precisely. It doesn't matter that the probabilities of a successful relationship with most musicians are notoriously low; those are *rational* probabilities. And it doesn't matter that the current and future financial prospects of most musicians are equally low; those are *economic* reasons. Music isn't about such practicalities. It's about harmonies—melodic ones that lead to emotional ones. Besides, because of their common grounding in emotion and harmony, music and romance are strongly associated with one another in life. What would you say is the percentage of contemporary songs with romance as their subject? It's 80 percent, the vast majority. That's amazing. Romance isn't at issue the vast majority of the time when we speak or think or write, but it is when we sing.

Now I understand why young women, who are at an age-peak for interest in both romance and music, have a weakness for musicians. Powerful links between the two types of experiences make musicians hard to resist. Want some scientific proof? If not, just pretend I'm *singing* you the results of a French study in which the (initially skeptical) researchers had a man approach young women and ask for their phone numbers while he was carrying a guitar case, a sports bag, or nothing:

> ♪*Those scientists in France / worried about raising the chance / a guitar would prompt a "Oui" / to a stranger's startling plea / need not have been so troubled. / Phone numbers more than doubled.*♪

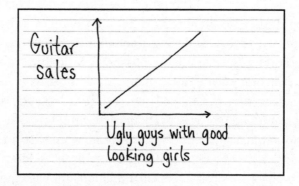

Figure 8.8: Turning zeros into (guitar) heroes
Via @jessicahagy and thisisindexed.com

For anyone interested in maximizing persuasive success, the critical takeaway from this section should not be merely that music is allied with System 1 responding or that, when channeled to that kind of responding, people act imprudently. The far larger lesson involves the importance of matching the System 1 versus 2 character of a persuasive communication with the System 1 versus 2 mindset of its intended audience. Recipients with nonrational, hedonistic goals should be matched with messages containing nonrational elements such as musical accompaniment, whereas those with rational, pragmatic goals should be matched with messages containing rational elements such as facts. In his outstanding book, *Persuasive Advertising*, marketing expert J. Scott Armstrong reported that in an analysis of 1,513 TV commercials, 87 percent incorporated music. But this routine addition of music to the message may well be flawed, as Armstrong also reviewed the relevant research and concluded that music should only be used to advertise familiar, feelings-based products (such as snack foods and body scents) in an emotional context—that is, where thinking is unlikely. For products that have high personal consequences and strong supportive arguments (such as safety equipment and software packages)—that is, for which hard thinking is likely to be undertaken and productive—background music actually undercuts ad effectiveness.[23]

Repeated Reciprocal Exchange

In early 2015, a *New York Times* article ignited an explosion of reader interest and commentary, going viral and becoming one of the most widely spread *Times* pieces ever. For a news outlet such as the *Times*, this occurrence may not seem extraordinary, given its elevated journalistic standing on topics of great national and international import. But this particular piece appeared not in its Politics, Business, Technology, or Health pages but in the Sunday Styles section. As is reflected in the essay's title, "To Fall in Love with Anyone, Do This," its author, Mandy Len Catron, claimed to have found a marvelously effective way to produce the intense emotional closeness and social bonds of love—in the space of forty-five minutes! She knew it worked, she said, because it had worked for her and her boyfriend.

The technique came from a program of research initiated by a husband and wife team of psychologists, Arthur and Elaine Aron, who hit upon it in their investigations of close relationships. It involves a different form of coordinated action than we have seen so far, in which partners engage in a reciprocal, turn-taking exchange sequence. Other psychologists have demonstrated that a history of reciprocally exchanged favors leads individuals to give additional favors to their exchange partner . . . no matter who provided the last one.

The Arons and their coworkers helped explain this kind of willing assent by showing how extended reciprocal exchanges bind the transactors together. They did so by employing a particularly unifying type of reciprocal exchange, strong enough to "unify" people into love with one another: reciprocal self-disclosure. The procedure was not complicated. In pairs, participants took turns reading questions to their partner, who would answer, and who would then receive their partner's answer to the same item. Advancing through the thirty-six questions required participants to disclose progressively more personal information about themselves and, in turn, to learn more personal information about their partners. An early question would be "What would constitute a perfect day for you?," whereas later in the sequence a question would be "What do you value most in a friendship?," and near the end of the list a question would be "Of all the people in your family, whose death would be the most disturbing?"

Relationships deepened beyond all expectations. The procedure generated feelings of closeness and unity that are unparalleled within a forty-five-minute span, especially among complete strangers in an emotionally sterile laboratory setting. Moreover, the outcome was no chance occurrence. According to an interview with one of the researchers, Elaine Aron, hundreds of studies using the method have since been done confirming the effect, and some participants have gotten married as a result. In the same interview, Dr. Aron described two aspects of the procedure she felt are key to its effectiveness. First, the items escalate in personal disclosiveness. When responding, participants increasingly open themselves to one another in a trusting way, representative of tightly bonded pairs. Second, and in keeping with the overarching theme of this section of the chapter, participants do so by acting together—that is, in a coordinated, back-and-forth fashion, making the interaction inherently and continuously synchronized.[24]

Suffering Together

A solution to yet another Holocaust-era mystery is in order, as provided by yet another route to unitization. In the summer of 1940, while the Gestapo of Düsseldorf were systematically identifying and transporting Jewish residents to death camps around Europe, they received a remarkable letter from their leader, Reichsführer-SS Heinrich Himmler. It instructed them to avoid the persecution of one such Jewish resident, a city judge named Ernst Hess, on the orders of a high-ranking Nazi official who commanded that Hess "not be importuned in any way whatsoever."

None of the sources of unity we've covered so far can explain Hess's special treatment. The judge hadn't ruled favorably on a case involving the Nazi official's family, or grown up in the same town, or simply marched with him in columns of a military unit—although they had done the last of these years earlier. The reason was something more than that: during their time of military service in World War I, they had suffered together through the adversities, privations, and miseries of that dreadful, protracted conflict. In fact, both had sustained battlefield wounds within twenty-four hours of one another in the notorious, 141-day Somme offensive that took 1.2 million soldiers' lives, a half-million from German ranks alone. Perhaps Shakespeare's Henry V captured the consequence best in a line from his famous "band of brothers" speech: "For he today that sheds his blood with me, shall be my brother."

Oh, and by the way, the "high-ranking Nazi" in Himmler's letter who ordered the reversal of regular process for Hess was no ordinary top official. The letter declared Hess should receive "relief and protection, as per the wishes *of the Führer*,"—Adolf Hitler, the most maliciously efficient persecutor of the Jewish people the world has ever known.

There is a haunting resemblance here to Ronald Cohen's story of the Nazi guard who, in the course of executing every tenth person in a line of concentration-camp inmates, unexpectedly diverged from his routine and killed an eleventh. Recall Cohen's puzzlement that "while engaged dutifully in mass murder, the guard was merciful and sympathetic to one particular member of

Figure 8.9: Together, with Mudder Nature

Businesses often seek to harness the unifying power of jointly experienced hardship through corporate team-building events that involve adversity or risk. When I visited the sites of a number of companies that organize such events, I found some activities that looked arduous, scary, or both: white-water rafting, rock climbing, cliff-side rappelling, bridge bungie jumping, barefoot fire walking (over hot coals), and snow camping. The team-building event's Mud Run race featured in this photo appears to have already had the desired effect of stimulating cooperative conduct, as we see two of the competitors assisting a third.

iStock Photo

the victimized group." We resolved the puzzle in terms of a unifying feature of the guard and prisoner, commonality of birthplace. In this case, Hitler—the moral monster who installed procedures for the torment and annihilation of millions of Jews—also chose to deviate from those standard procedures for the "merciful and sympathetic" benefit of one particular man. Although, once again, the cause appears to lie in a unitizing factor that bonded the men together, this time it wasn't similarity of birthplace. This time, it was shared suffering.

Throughout human history, shared pain has been a bonding agent, fusing identities into "we"-based attachments. William Shakespeare's recognition of the phenomenon in Henry V's "band of brothers" declaration, written in 1599, is just one instance. More recent illustrations provide scientific evidence of the processes responsible. After the Boston Marathon bombings of 2013, residents who reported direct involvements with the negative events (for example, hearing or seeing any aspect of the bombing personally) and residents who simply reported suffering physically or emotionally a great deal became more fused in their identities with that of the Boston community than did residents who hadn't suffered as much. In addition, the more frequently and deeply residents thought about the tragedy, the more they felt themselves "at one" with their fellow Bostonians.

A second set of researchers checked to make sure the bonding effects of mutual suffering weren't due to mutual experiences of *any* sort of activity. After all, we have already seen that joint performances of story reading or finger tapping or marching produced feelings of "we"-ness. Does a more intense end product emerge when pain enters the mix? It does. Group members who completed a ninety-second task requiring them to submerge their hands in ice water became more bonded with one another than did members of groups who completed the identical task with hands in room-temperature water. Later, when engaged in an economic game with their groupmates, those who had suffered together were significantly more likely to make financial choices designed to enrich the whole group as opposed to only themselves.

The sheer strength of mutual suffering to produce unity and self-sacrifice can be seen in its ability to forge bonds across ethnic groups. In 2020, when Native American peoples, particularly of the Navajo Nation, were being ravaged by the COVID-19 pandemic, they received major assistance from an unexpected benefactor. Local volunteers who set up a GoFundMe webpage to provide food and other necessities suddenly started receiving hundreds of thousand dollars of aid from Ireland. The story of why the Irish would be willing to donate so heavily could easily fit in our chapter 2 on reciprocation: It was an act of reciprocity that reached across centuries, nationalities, and thousands of miles. During the height of Ireland's Great Potato Famine in 1847, a group of Native Americans of the Choctaw Nation collected and sent $170 (worth about $5,000 today) to help relieve starvation amid the "Great Hunger" there. Now it was time for the Irish to repay the kindness. As one contributor commented along with his donation: "We in Ireland will never forget your wonderful act of solidarity and compassion during the Irish famine. We are with you during your fight against Covid 19."

If, as I've suggested, the story fits well in chapter 2 along with other stunning instances of the rule of reciprocation at work, why is it here in a section on shared misery? For an answer, we must look beyond the question of why the Irish acted to help in 2020 to the question of why the Choctaws acted to help in 1847. Their gift occurred only a few years after the Choctaw Nation had endured a government-ordered, mass relocation march hundreds of miles to the west, known as the Trail of Tears, in which as many as six thousand of their people died. As the Native American organizer Vanessa Tully explained: "The death of many people on the Trail of Tears sparked empathy for the Irish people in their time of need. *That* is why the Choctaw extended the relief aid." It's notable that many other participants in online commentary spoke of the bond between the two nations as forged from familial, shared adversity—lamenting the hardships of "our Native American brothers and sisters" and the mutuality of "blood memory."[25]

EBOX 8.2

In recent years, researchers have begun mining a rich vein of information about human behavior by analyzing traces of the behavior left on social-media platforms (Meredith, 2020). One such analysis, of the amount and character of Twitter activity following the November 13, 2015, terrorist attacks in Paris, allows us a novel lens through which to see the effects of shared adversity on group solidarity. Starting from the date of the attack and for several months thereafter, the behavioral scientists David Garcia and Bernard Rimé (2019) examined nearly eighteen million tweets from a sample of 62,114 accounts of French Twitter users. They searched the tweets' wordings for feelings of emotional distress, the synchrony of the distress (reflecting its collective nature), and expressions of group solidarity and supportiveness. The event itself produced immediate spikes of shared anxiety and sadness, which dropped away within two to three days. But, in the weeks and months that followed, expressions of solidarity and supportiveness remained elevated in the tweets. Moreover, the strength and duration of expressions of unity and support were directly related to the extent to which the initial anguish occurred in a shared, synchronous fashion.

As the authors concluded: "Our results shed new light on the social function of collective emotions, illustrating that a society hit by a collective trauma does not just respond with simultaneous negative emotions . . . These findings suggest that it is not *despite* our distress that we are more united after a terrorist attack, but it is precisely *because* of our shared distress that our bonds become stronger and our society adapts to face the next threat."

Author's note: I am always impressed when a particular pattern of behavior appears similarly across a variety of different methods for observing it. The considerable influence of shared suffering on subsequent in-group cohesion and promotion is one of those confidence-inspiring patterns for me.

Co-creation

Long before wilderness preservation became a value among many Americans, a man named Aldo Leopold was championing the cause in their country. Principally during the 1930s and 1940s, when he held the first-ever professorship of wildlife management in the United States at the University of Wisconsin, he developed a distinctive ethical approach to the topic. As detailed in his best-selling book *A Sand County Almanac*, his approach challenged the dominant model of environmental conservation, in which natural ecologies were to be managed for the purpose of human use. It proposed, instead, an alternative based on the right of all plant and animal species to existence in their natural state whenever possible. Possessed of such a clear and heartfelt position, he was more than surprised one day to find himself, axe in hand, behaving in contradiction to it—by cutting down a red birch tree on his property so that one of his white pines would get more light and space.

Why, he wondered, would he act to favor the pine over the birch that according to his avowed ethic, had as much right to exist naturally as any tree on his land? Perplexed, he searched his mind for the "logic" behind his bias and, in considering various differences between the two types of trees that might account for the preference, encountered only one he was convinced was a primary factor. It was one that had nothing to do with logic but was entirely founded on feelings: "Well, first of all, I planted the pine with my shovel, whereas the birch crawled in under the fence and planted itself. My bias is thus to some extent paternal."[26]

Leopold was not unique in feeling a special affinity for something he had a hand in creating. It's a common human occurrence. For example, in what researchers termed the IKEA effect, people who have built items themselves come to see "their amateurish creations as similar in value to experts' creations." As suits our current focus on the effects of acting together, it is worth inquiring into an additional pair of possibilities. Would people who had a hand in creating something *hand in hand* with another come to feel a special affinity not only for their creation but also for their co-creator? What's more, might this exceptional affinity stem from a feeling of unity with the other that's detectible in the characteristic consequences of elevated liking and self-sacrificial support for the partner?

Let's seek the answer to those questions by resolving a prior one: Why would I begin this section on *co*-creation with Aldo Leopold's description of the effect of planting a pine by himself? It's that he was no lone actor in the process. He was a co-creator, with nature, of the mature pine he once put in the ground as a sapling. The intriguing possibility that arises is whether, as a result of acting together with Mother Nature, he came to feel more personally linked with her—and, as a consequence, even more enamored and respectful of his partner in the collaboration. If that were so, we'd have an indication that co-creation can be a route to unification. Regrettably, Mr. Leopold has not been available for questioning on the matter since 1948. But I am confident of the answer.

A portion of that confidence comes from the results of a study I helped conduct to investigate the effects of managers' degree of personal involvement in the creation of a work product. I'd expected that the more involvement managers felt they'd had in generating the final product in concert with an employee, the higher they would rate its quality, which is what we found: managers led to believe they'd had a large role in developing the end product (an ad for a new wristwatch) rated the ad 50 percent more favorably than did managers led to believe they'd had little developmental involvement—even though the final ad they saw was identical in all cases. In addition, we found that the managers with the greatest perceived involvement rated themselves more responsible for the ad's quality in terms of their greater perceived managerial control over their employee, which I'd also expected.

But I didn't at all expect a third finding. The more the managers attributed the success of the project to themselves, the more they also attributed it to the ability of their employee. I recall, data table in hand, experiencing a moment of surprise—perhaps not as striking as Leopold's axe-in-hand moment, but a moment of surprise nonetheless. How could supervisors with greater perceived

Figure 8.10: Avoiding Stagnation through "Bossification"

Creative accounting is a recognized business trick and so, apparently, is creative co-creation.

Dilbert 2014. Scott Adams. By permission of Universal Uclick. All rights reserved.

involvement in the development of a work product see themselves and a single coworker on the project as *each* more responsible for its successful final form? There's only 100 percent of personal responsibility to be distributed. So if one party's perceived personal contribution goes up, by simple logic, the work partner's should go down. I just didn't get it at the time, but now I think I do. If co-creation causes at least a temporary merging of identities, then what applies to one partner also applies to the other, distributional logic notwithstanding.

Asking for Advice Is Good Advice

> We all admire the wisdom of those who have come to us for advice.
>
> —Ben Franklin

Co-creation doesn't only reduce the problem of getting supervisors to give more credit to employees who've worked productively on a project. It can lessen a host of other traditionally hard to diminish difficulties. Children below the age of six or seven are typically selfish when it comes to sharing rewards, rarely distributing them equally with playmates—unless they have obtained those rewards through a collaborative effort with a playmate, whereupon even three-year-olds share equally the majority of the time. As we saw in chapter 3, in the standard classroom, students tend to coalesce along racial, ethnic, and socioeconomic lines, finding friends and helpmates mainly within their own groups, but this pattern declines significantly after they've engaged co-creatively with students from the other groups within "cooperative learning" exercises. Companies struggle to get consumers to feel bonded with and therefore loyal to their brands; it's a battle they've been winning by inviting current and prospective customers to co-create with them novel or updated products and services, most often by providing the company with information about desirable features.

However, within such marketing partnerships, requested consumer input must be framed as *advice to* the company, not as opinions about or expectations for the company. The differential phrasing may seem minor, but it is critical to achieving the company's unitization goal. Providing advice puts a person in a merging state of mind, which stimulates a linking of one's own identity with another party's. Providing an opinion or expectation, on the other hand, puts a person in an introspective state of mind, which involves focusing on oneself. These only slightly different forms of feedback—and the different merging versus separating mindsets they produce—can have a have a significant impact on consumer engagement with a brand.

That's what happened to a group of online survey-takers from around the United States shown a description of the business plan for a new fast casual-food restaurant, Splash!, that hoped to distinguish itself from competitors through the healthfulness of its menu items. After reading the description, all survey participants were asked for feedback. But some were asked for any "advice" they might have regarding the restaurant, whereas others were asked either for any "opinions" or "expectations" they might have.

Finally, they indicated how likely they'd be to patronize a Splash! restaurant. Participants who provided advice reported wanting to eat at a Splash! significantly more than did those who provided either of the other sorts of feedback. And just as we would expect if giving advice is indeed a mechanism of unitization, the increased desire to support the restaurant came from feeling more linked with the brand.

One more finding from the survey clinches the unitization case for me: the participants rated all three types of feedback equally helpful to the restaurateurs. So it wasn't that those who gave advice felt connected with the brand because they thought they had aided it more. Instead, having to give advice put participants in a togetherness state of mind rather than a separateness state of mind just before they had to reflect on what to say about the brand.

This set of results also clinches for me the wisdom (and the ethicality, if done in an authentic search for useful information) of asking for advice in face-to-face interactions with friends, colleagues, and customers. It should even prove effective in our interactions with superiors. Of course, it is rational to worry about a potential downside—that by asking a boss for advice, you might come off as incompetent or dependent or insecure. While I see the logic of such a concern, I also see it as mistaken because the effects of co-creation are not well captured by rationality or logic. But they are exceedingly well captured by a particular, socially promotive *feeling* in the situation—the feeling of togetherness. The novelist Saul Bellow reportedly observed, "When we ask for advice, we are usually looking for an accomplice." I'd only add on the basis of scientific evidence that if we get that advice, we usually get that accomplice. And what better abettor to have on a project than someone in charge?[27]

Getting Together

It's time to look back at—and more dauntingly, beyond—what we've seen as the mostly favorable consequences of *belonging together* and *acting together*. We've learned, for instance, that by installing one or another of those two unitizing experiences in people, we can arrange to tip an election, solidify support from a company's shareholders as well as its customers, help ensure soldiers will stand and fight rather than flee in wartime, and protect a community from annihilation. In addition, we've found that we can use those same two unitizing experiences to arrange for playmates, classmates, and workmates to like, help, and cooperate with one another; for 97 percent of parents to fill out a long survey with no financial compensation; and even for the emergence of love in a lab. But here's an unanswered question: Might it be possible to apply the lessons from these settings to much larger stages, such as those involving age-old international enmities, violent religious clashes, and simmering racial antagonisms? Could those lessons from what we know about belonging together and acting together increase our chance of *getting together*, as a species?

That's a tough question to answer, in large part because of the many complications inherent in such agonizingly intractable differences. Still, even on these fraught fields, I believe that procedures that create a feeling of unity establish a context for desirable change. Although this idea sounds hopeful in hand-waving theory, the many procedural and cultural complications involved make it naive to presume that the theory would work out smoothly in practice. The specifics of the unitizing procedures would have to be optimally designed and enacted with those complexities in mind—something with which the experts on the issues would surely agree and which might be the worthy subject of an entire follow-up book. Needless to say, I'd certainly welcome those experts' opinions . . . make that advice . . . in this regard.

Despite the tongue-in-cheek status of the last line, the importance of avoiding overly simple solutions to large-gauge, tenacious, and complicated problems is no laughing matter. Related is something the prizewinning biologist Steve Jones observed about scientists of, let's kindly say, advancing senior status. He noted that at about this age, they often begin to "boom about Big Issues," acting as if their acquired knowledge in a specialized sphere allows them to speak confidently on big-picture topics far outside those boundaries. Jones's cautionary point seems pertinent to my situation at this juncture—because, first, I have entered the age category he was describing and, second, to proclaim more broadly, I would have to draw conclusions pertinent to international diplomacy, religious and ethnic conflict, and racial hostility while having no expert knowledge in any of the domains. Plainly, I'd be "booming" in the dark.

It is best, then, if I address the question of how to get together through the light provided by the lessons of this chapter, as displayed through the prism of the influence process. It would also be best to consider ways to establish, *early on*, feelings of "we"-ness with the human family, rather than with tribal forms—so that when attempting to influence people to respond according to the expanded version, their membership in the larger family will already be installed and able to spring swiftly to mind. Let's begin, then, with children's formative years and the parental procedures that shape them and, later, move to procedures likely to sway adults.

Unifying Practices

WHAT WE KNOW ABOUT HOUSEHOLD INFLUENCES

In the home, there are two surefire influences that lead children to treat any individual there, even nonrelatives, as family. The first is length of co-residence. If an adult nonrelative (a family friend, perhaps) lives with the family for an extended time, he or she frequently acquires the title of "aunt" or "uncle"; if it's an unrelated child, the emergent labels are "brother" or "sister." In addition, the longer the shared home life, the more the unrelated person receives benefits characteristic of kinship, such as self-sacrificing aid from household members. The second is the observation of parental, especially maternal, caregiving toward the unrelated individual— something that, when observed, leads to kinship-like conduct. Remember how in the autobiographical accounts of Chiune Sugihara and Mother Teresa, two of the greatest humanitarian actors of our

time, each reported seeing their parents caring selflessly for outsiders who came into the home? It's noteworthy that such acts of
care (housing, cleansing, clothing, and mending—all for no payment) are normally reserved for family members.

ACTION IMPLICATIONS

For parents who wish to expand their children's sense of "we-"ness
to the human family, these findings present certain implications
for the home. The first—providing long-term domicile residence
for cross-group children—although admirable, is not feasible for
most households. The requirements, costs, and commitments necessary for adoptive or foster parenthood are often too great.

However, a second implication—providing family-like experiences in the home to cross-group children—is much more man-
ageable. It involves a two-step process in which parents identify
cross-group children in their kids' classrooms, sports teams, or
dance troupes and then invite one (with parental approval) to come
to the house for a playdate or sleepover. Once there, the key in my
view is not to afford the visitor guest status. The family's children
should see the visitor treated as one of them.

If the kids have chores to do, the visitor should be assigned to
help. If Mom is the one who usually handles the family's laundry
and she notices grass stains on the visitor's clothing after some
backyard game, she should wash the garment. As well, she should
be alert to any skin scrape she could mend with disinfectant and a
Band-Aid. If Dad is the one who normally teaches sports activities,
engaging in one of those activities with the assembled kids would
not be enough. He should be a teacher for every child—adjusting
little hands on a bat or golf club for better ball contact, explaining
how to throw a football for a proper spiral, demonstrating how to
use a juke fake before kicking a soccer ball past a duped goalie.
The same applies if his role is to perform and teach home or auto
repairs. Opportunities for instruction should not be deferred until
after the visitor leaves.

Of course, these practices should be repeated for additional visits
and for other cross-group visitors. It strikes me as crucial that the

visiting children not be favored—something fair-minded parents may be tempted to do to model their lack of prejudice. Instead, for the benefit of their children, everything should be done to include cross-group playmates in the family routine rather than to exclude them from it.

Comparable recommendations apply to dinner invitations to the playmates' families. If it is a sit-down dinner, parents should wait to set the table until the invitees arrive so they can be asked to help the way a family member would. If it is a backyard picnic or barbecue, the tables and chairs shouldn't be put into place until members of the visiting family can assist. In both instances, all at the meal should be invited to join the clean-up.

As if she were still with us, I can hear my mother's reaction to these suggestions: "Robert, what's wrong with you? That's no way to treat guests." Perhaps she'd be right in one sense. "But Ma," I'd reply, "these aren't *any* guests. They are people with cross-ethnic or racial or religious or sexual identities whom you want to feel immediately accepted and integrated into the goings-on of our household. More than that, they are people who, research shows, would likely feel greater unity with us from the collaborative tasks of setting up and cleaning up, as well as from the informal conversations accompanying the tasks—unity we would feel too."

There is something else I would be thinking but wouldn't say aloud, because my mother taught me not to be "such a wiseacre" when arguing with her. It would be that even if she were right about violating standard dinner-company etiquette, proper hospitality wouldn't be the point. The intent of the invitation would be to instill in her observing children a broadened sense of "we" that encompassed all manner of others. Again, I wouldn't say so aloud, but I'd be thinking, Ma, would you rather your kids remembered you as treating your visitors as guests or as family?[28]

WHAT WE KNOW ABOUT DIVERSE NEIGHBORHOODS AND FRIENDSHIPS

Here's what we know about diverse neighborhoods and friendships: those who live in ethnically or racially diverse neighborhoods become more likely to identify with all humanity, making them generally more helpful; plus, the increased contact normally leaves them more favorable and less prejudiced toward cross-group others. Similar effects come from diverse friendships, which lead to greater positivity and more supportiveness toward friends' ethnic and racial groups. These outcomes don't only occur within majority groups; they also apply to minority-group members, who come to feel more positively toward a majority group if they have a majority-group friend. Better still, cross-group friendships increase expectations that interactions with additional cross-group members will prove friendly, too—because of elevated feelings of unity with the group. Best of all, cross-group friendships have an indirect, under-the-radar influence: simply knowing that a member of our own group has a cross-group friend reduces our negative feelings toward the other group.

ACTION IMPLICATIONS

What should parents do with the finding that their children will be more likely to identify with all humanity if they live in a culturally diverse neighborhood? Packing up and moving straightaway to such an environment might be too much to ask, even for parents who value the mindset. But for such parents, putting neighborhood diversity on the list of features to look for in any future home would be a fitting step. Depending on how much they value that mindset, they could choose accordingly how high to place diversity on the list.

The implications of friendship diversity, compared with those of neighborhood diversity, lend themselves to more options. One is the same as the earlier recommendation that parents look for children at school, athletic events, or park playgrounds to find an especially compatible friendship match for their own. An invitation for a playdate or sleepover or birthday party would be a natural for advancing the process, followed by an invitation to the child's family for dinner, which would lay the foundation for cross-group parental friendships. Those adult alliances could be solidified by one-on-one get-togethers outside the home for lunch or coffee.

Meetings out of the house are important. They are public, first of all, which means the friendship will be observed by others who, research tells us, will lower their own cross-group prejudices and become more willing to strike up such a friendship themselves. Indeed, the more public the one-on-one get-together is, the more others will likely be nudged toward cross-group relationships, which may influence even more onlookers in the same direction. During the time of the COVID-19 outbreak, we witnessed the woeful operation of the laws of exponential group contagion. In the case of publicly viewed cross-group friendship, though, the same laws would be working for rather than against the species' well-being.

A second important rationale for organizing one-on-one meetings with a cross-group fellow parent (or any cross-group adult) has less to do with widening the impact of the friendship than with deepening it. The interactions provide the opportunity for yet another surefire way to strengthen relationship solidarity: reciprocal self-disclosure. We learned in chapter 2 that the rule of reciprocation governs all kinds of behaviors. One of them is self-disclosure; when a conversation partner reveals a piece of personal information, the other almost invariably provides one in return. If pursued through Aron and Aron's thirty-six-question procedure, such an exchange can produce social bonds akin to those of love. Although some researchers have used the method to reduce cross-group prejudice, a step-by-step trek through the thirty-six questions wouldn't fit a sociable interaction at Starbucks. We're not looking for starry-eyed love responses here. Still, studies show that even limited self-disclosure deepens cross-group relationships.

The upshot is clear—and not particularly difficult to manage: if your aim is to decrease feelings of hostility and prejudice that normally accompany the cross-group divisions of our world, then arrange to make a cross-group friend, model the friendship to those near to you, meet the friend in a public place, and disclose a piece of personal information in the ensuing dialogue.[29]

WHAT WE KNOW ABOUT THE TYPES OF CONNECTIONS THAT LEAD TO FEELINGS OF UNITY

We have already seen the kinds of connections that come from acting together (including dancing, singing, reading, walking, and working) synchronously or cooperatively create a broadened sense of "we"-ness. Connections of a different sort—that come from recognized commonalities—do the same. There is an exceptionally useful feature of these commonalties for individuals hoping to kindle feelings of unity inside another. They can be engaged by simply raising them to consciousness.

Employing the most effective form of commonality in this regard, mutual identity, Rabbi Kalisch was able to save his people by pointing to a shared Asian identity with Japanese captors; and one member of a couple in mid-dispute was able to gain agreement by just reminding the other of their common identity as partners. Want to make Democrats and Republicans in the United States feel more positively toward one another? Remind them of their common identity as Americans. Likewise, Jews and Arabs who read about a high level of genetic identity between the two groups became less biased and hostile toward one another while becoming more supportive of Israeli–Palestinian peacemaking efforts. This kind of favoritism is so potent that even (massively self-oriented) psychopaths exhibit greater concern for members of their "we"-groups. Given that psychopaths are notorious for a lack of concern for others, how can we explain this aberrant finding? We need only recall that identity-unifying procedures merge more of the self into conjoined others; hence, psychopaths aren't acting uncharacteristically at all.

Other forms of commonality operate similarly. For instance, traditionally opposed groups become united by a mutual enemy. After reading statements regarding Islamic terrorists, White and Black Americans saw each other as less distinct; the same was true for Israeli Jews and Arabs who read about their shared susceptibility to diseases such as cancer. What's more, the changes occurred automatically, with no cognitive reflection required. Another type of commonality, basic emotional experience, works through a different route. Constituents of one group often justify prejudice toward, discrimination against, and mistreatment of another group by dehumanizing its members—denying them full possession of fundamental human feelings and qualities such as sympathy, forgiveness, refinement, morality, and altruism. These embittering beliefs can be countered with evidence of elemental human emotion that is experienced similarly. It becomes difficult to hold a dehumanized view of an out-group member who sheds tears with us at the same tragic scene or laughs with us at the same clever joke or becomes equally irate at the same government scandal. When Israeli Jews learned that Palestinians experienced a comparable degree of anger as did Jews toward an increase of hit-and-run accidents or the deaths of thousands of dolphins from a factory's sewage leak, they developed a more humanized perception of Palestinians and became more supportive of favorable political policies toward them.

A last variety of unity-producing connection worth highlighting involves the act of taking another's perspective—of putting ourselves in another's position to imagine what that person must be thinking or feeling or experiencing. For a long stretch of my research career, I studied the factors that incline people to help others. It wasn't long before I learned a major truth: If you put yourself in the shoes of someone in need, they'll likely take you to their owner's aid. It also wasn't long before I learned the basis for this truth. Placing ourselves in another's situation elevates the feeling of self–other overlap. As a result, Australian college students who took the perspective of Indigenous Australians, Serbians who took the perspective of Bosnian Muslims, and Florida residents who took the perspective of transgender individuals all became more favorable to political policies favoring these minority groups. In an interesting twist, knowing someone else has tried to take our perspective in an interaction leads us to greater perceived self–other overlap with our perspective-taker, along with more liking and goodwill; apparently, the consequences of perspective-taking can be mutual.[30]

Ah, but there's a rub. Unlike the effects of establishing family-like, neighborhood, and friendship relationships with cross-group others, connections forged from common enemies, most kinds of shared identity, similar emotional responses, and perspective-taking attempts don't work in many situations; and, when they do, it's often not for long. For good reason: the unifying purpose of such connections typically runs counter to the powerful action of Darwinian pressures, which push groups to compete with other contenders for viability and ascendency. The "We Are the World" position is captured wonderfully in the quote attributed to the ancient Roman philosopher Seneca: "We are waves of the same sea, leaves of the same tree, flowers of the same garden." Although the sentiment is no doubt valid, its ordinary motivating force can't match that of the evolutionary principle of natural selection that asserts a simultaneous, opposing truth. Each wave, leaf, and flower is vying with others for resources, reserves, and means to grow—and, without which, they will shrink or simply disappear.

Still worse for proponents of the unity point of view, there's yet another powerful feature of human nature that shunts us toward rivalry and separation: the experience of threat. Whenever the welfare or reputation of our group is threatened, we lash out—demeaning the values, worth, and even humanity of rival groups. In a time when competing national, ethnic, and religious entities have the ability to inflict large-scale terror and damage on one another through destructive technology and ruinous weaponry, we would be well advised to find ways of reducing intergroup hostility by turning toward harmony.[31]

ACTION IMPLICATIONS

Those of us who accept the worth of such a mission face a fearsome adversary, one fueled by potent evolutionary pressures. It is the relentless pull to ensure the survival of copies of our genes, which are overrepresented in members of our significant in-groups. Scientific analysis shows that we have decisively more genetic overlap with those with whom we have family, friendship, local, political, and religious ties. It's little wonder that we regularly act to advance the outcomes of these individuals over those from less genetically linked groups. With so mighty a foe as natural selection arrayed against us, how could we hope to win the fight for greater intergroup unity?

Perhaps we could once again arrange to hack the Darwinian imperative and commission its force in our behalf. Recall the claim in chapter 1 that a woman employing jujitsu could defeat a stronger rival by channeling the opponent's power (energy, weight, and momentum) to her own advantage? It was via this stratagem that I proposed building unity by making cross-group members more frequently present in our homes, neighborhoods, and friendship networks, which have evolved as reliable cues of genetic similarity to which people instinctively respond. When it comes to redirecting evolutionary pressures toward unity, the catchphrase should not be *Star Wars'* "May the force be with you." Rather, it should be the jujitsu version: "May *their* force be with you."

How, by using the same general approach, could we hack the process of evolution to strengthen the variable and often short-lived effects on unity of such connections as common enemies ("We are all susceptible to cancer"), relatively minor shared identities ("We're both basketball fans"), equally felt human emotions ("Everybody in my family, too, was furious at the mayor's decision"), and perspective-taking efforts ("Now that I've put myself in your position, I can appreciate your situation better")? Although, as we've seen, these connections can be impactful in the moment, their effects are typically too fragile and easily swept aside to direct behavior lastingly. Fortunately, there's a factor that can bolster their strength and stability. It is *attentional focus*—an action that can greatly enable favored beliefs, values, and choices.

When we focus attention on something, we immediately come to see it as more significant to us. Nobel laureate Daniel Kahneman labeled the phenomenon "the focusing illusion," in which people automatically presume that if they are paying attention to a particular thing, it must warrant the interest. He even summarized the illusion in an essay he wrote: "Nothing in life is as important as you think it is, while you are thinking about [focusing on] it."

What's more, research shows that if the focal item has desirable features, *they* appear more important, too—and, thus, more desirable still.

All cognitive illusions arise because of a quirk in a system that normally functions well. In the instance of the focusing illusion, the system that usually serves us ably is an eminently sensible one. In any information environment, we are wise to focus on its most important feature for us—a sudden noise in the dark, the smell of food when we are hungry, the sight of our CEO standing to speak. This makes great evolutionary sense; anything less would be maladaptive. Here's the quirk. Our focused attention isn't always drawn to the most important aspect of a situation. At times, we can be brought to believe something is important, not because of its inherent significance but, instead, because some *other* factor has drawn our attention to that aspect.

When Americans were asked in a survey to name two national events they thought had been "especially important" in US history, they nominated the terrorist attacks of 9/11/2001 about 30 percent of the time. But as media coverage of the event grew in the days prior to its tenth anniversary, the perception spiked to a high of 65 percent. Soon after the anniversary, when 9/11 media stories dropped off rapidly, so did the judged import of the tragedy—reverting to the 30 percent level. Clearly, shifts in the extent of media coverage, which influenced observers' *attention* to the event, dramatically changed its estimated national significance. A study of visitors to an online furniture store directed half to a landing page that focused them on an image of soft, fluffy clouds before they viewed the store's offerings. That attentional focus, arranged by the researchers, led the visitors to rate the furniture's comfort as a more important factor for them and, consequently, to prefer more comfortable furniture for purchase. However, the other half of the visitors did not show this pattern; they rated price as more important and preferred inexpensive furniture for purchase. Why? They had been sent to a landing page that focused them on a cost-related image, a set of coins. Thus, the concept on which visitors' attention had been tactically focused altered its weighting substantially for them. Finally, online research participants were asked to direct their attention to photos of themselves that either depicted them as they looked then or as they would look after they had aged considerably. Those who considered these artificially aged versions of themselves were willing to allot more funds to their retirement plans. Notably, this was not the case if they saw aged photos of other individuals; the effect was specific to their own future economic welfare. Here, focused attention to images of themselves when they would be closer to retirement led people to elevate the importance of taking care of that person.

If news people, webpage designers, and savings researchers can use attentional focus to increase the experienced importance of the 9/11 attack and the attributes of furniture and the funding of a retirement account, why can't we do something similar to further the cause of unity? Why can't we use the status-enhancing power of focus to amplify the perceived worth of cross-group connections? It would mean training ourselves to be attuned to the undertow of resentment, hostility, or prejudice toward members of differing groups and to redirect our attention to legitimate shared connections. The act of redirection wouldn't just move us mentally from divisions to connections, the accompanying shift in attention would work to disempower the divisions and empower the connections through the importance-magnifying impact of focus. Am I being naive here? Maybe. But maybe not.

First, we would have a formidable partner in our mission. We'd have focus as our friend, our force, and our fuel. Second, there's evidence that people can be trained to turn their attentions away from threatening thoughts to less menacing ones, a switch that resulted in reduced anxiety regarding the sources of those thoughts. Lastly, if we do earnestly try to shift attention from separations to connections whenever we encounter or just hear about out-groups and it works, then great, mission accomplished. But if our campaign of fixing our thoughts on shared connections doesn't prove successful—perhaps because, even with the boost from attentional focus, the links simply aren't strong enough—then we still have an ace to play. We need only reflect on our *sincere attempt* to embrace cross-group "we"-ness as evidence of our true personal preference for it. Either way, cross-group unity should gain standing in our self-conceptions. Either way, cross-group unity should grow.[32]

Defense

Most businesses have "Code of Conduct" statements, which personnel are expected to read at the start of their employment and adhere to throughout their time with the organization. In many cases, the statements serve as the basis of ethics training that employees receive. A study of manufacturing firms listed on the S&P 500 stock-market index found that companies split on whether their Code of Conduct statement was written primarily in unity-linked language that referred to personnel in "we" terms or in more formal language that referred to personnel in "member" or "employee" terms. In a major surprise, people in the organizations using "we" language to convey ethical responsibilities were significantly more likely to engage in illegal conduct during their tenure.

To understand why, the researchers conducted a series of eight experiments in which they hired participants to perform a work task after exposing them to ethical Code of Conduct instructions that used either unity language (describing the workers in "we" terms) or impersonal language (describing the workers in "member" terms). Several eye-opening findings emerged. Participants whose Code of Conduct was written in "we" language were more likely to lie or cheat to obtain performance bonuses and, hence, to enrich themselves at the expense of the organization. Two additional findings offer an explanation. First, "we"-based wording led participants to believe the organization would be less likely to engage in surveillance to catch violators of ethical policy. Second, participants receiving those instructions thought, if any violators were caught, the organization would be more tolerant and forgiving of them.

As we've seen in prior chapters, each of the principles of influence can be exploited by profiteers who hijack its force for their own ends—giving small, meaningless gifts to obligate recipients to reciprocate with larger favors, lying with statistics to give the false impression of social proof for their offerings, counterfeiting credentials to convey authority on a topic, and so on. The principle of unity is no different. Once exploiters perceive that they are inside our "we"-groups, they seek to profit from our primal tendencies to minimize, excuse, and even enable the misdeeds of fellow members. Corporate entities are hardly unique in this regard. From a pair of personally discomforting experiences, I can report that other kinds of work units give rise to the same profiteers and the same unity-governed tendencies to tolerate them.

Labor unions are one—as manifest in the willingness of police, firefighter, manufacturing, and service unions to take the side of their members, including the worst of them. Labor unions provide considerable benefits not just to their membership but, as well, to the larger society in the form of improved safety regulations, warranted wage adjustments, parental-leave policies, and a broadened, economically viable middle class. But on the dimension of proper ethical conduct in the workplace, unions have a distinct defect. They protect and fight for unethical individuals, often in the face of clear evidence of egregious and persisting violations, purely because the violator is one of them. A family member of mine, now deceased, was a prototypical such offender. On the job as a welder in a manufacturing company, he was a malingerer, shirker, petty thief, time-card cheater, and falsifier of workplace injuries, which he bragged about, laughing at his bosses' futile attempts to fire him. He said his union dues were the best financial investment he'd ever made. Through every ethical breach, the union defended him—not out of concern for right and wrong but, instead, out of a separate ethical obligation: loyalty to its members. The resulting inflexible manner in which the union allowed him to leverage that loyalty to selfish advantage always left me unsettled.

The actions of a second type of work unit, Roman Catholic clergy, has affected me similarly. I was raised in a Catholic home, lived

in a Catholic neighborhood, attended Catholic school, and participated in Catholic Church services until young adulthood. Although I am no longer a practicing member, I retain a legacy link
that permits me to feel pride in the Church's charitable outreach
and poverty-reduction programs. The same link has caused me to
feel shame at the Church hierarchy's scandalous handling of rapa-
cious priests who, rather than praying for, preyed *on* the children
in their flocks. When news of the hierarchy's disgraceful management of the situation—pardoning the offending priests, conceal-
ing their abuses, and giving them second and third chances in
new parishes—first surfaced, I heard in-group defenders trying to
minimize the misconduct. They argued that the clergy who compose the hierarchy are priests, too, and one of their defining roles
is to grant forgiveness of sins; therefore, they were only doing what
fit their religious duties. I knew this was no real justification. The
Church authorities didn't just forgive the abuse; they suppressed
information about it. For reasons of in-group protection, they covered it up in ways that let it happen again to fresh populations of
soon-to-be-terrorized and permanently scarred children. They had
descended into a moral trench from which they could justify their
actions on the basis of "we"-ness.

Might it be possible to deter malevolent members of "we"-based
work groups from the self-dealing activity we see in alliances as diverse as business units, labor unions, and religious organizations?
I believe so, but it would require that each such alliance take three
steps: (1) recognize that its corrupt actors presume they are protected by "we"-groups' willingness to excuse members who breach
ethical rules, (2) announce to all concerned that such leniency will
not be forthcoming in *this* particular "we"-group, and (3) establish
a consequent no-tolerance policy of dismissal for proven abuses.

When and where should such a commitment to ethical behavior
be made? At the outset—at the gateway to group membership in
the organization's Code of Conduct statement—and then, regularly thereafter, in team meetings where ethical versus unethical
conduct is defined and the firmness of the no-tolerance policy is
reiterated and explained. A review of the research described in

chapter 7 tells us that such a reinforced written commitment to important values could, in fact, empower those values going forward. I once learned, firsthand and by accident, just how well a written commitment of this kind could operate.

For a time during my career, I served as an expert witness in legal cases, mostly regarding deceptive advertising and marketing practices of product manufacturers. But, after three years, I stopped. The main reason was the urgency of the work I had to perform. It wasn't uncommon to receive crate-loads of paperwork—statements, depositions, petitions, evidence reports, and previous court judgments—to digest prior to forming a preliminary declaration of opinion. It was an opinion I would then need to submit and defend when I would soon be questioned in a formal deposition by a set of opposing attorneys. Before the deposition date, I was expected to meet, often multiple times, with members of the team of attorneys who had hired me, to structure and hone my declaration for maximum impact.

What occurred naturally inside those meetings created an entirely different problem for me, an ethical one. I became a member of a unified "we"-group with a specific purpose—to win the case against the out-group team of lawyers and expert witnesses on the other side. During the times we worked together, I would build friendships with my workmates, coming to appreciate their intellectual skills in our discussions, coming to learn of shared tastes in food and music at meals, and coming to feel closer over drinks via reciprocal self-disclosures (that would typically surface after the second round). In the preparations themselves, it was made clear to me that my opinion would be an important weapon among the armaments to be employed against our rivals. The more supportive of our case my opinion could be, and the more confident I could claim to be in it, the better for our side.

Although these sentiments were rarely expressed explicitly, I understood right away how to make my status as a team player rise. To the extent that I could self-assuredly emphasize in my declaration the importance of aspects of the evidence—including the research literature—that fit our arguments while minimizing the importance of those aspects that didn't, I would be increasingly seen as loyal to our group and its goals.

From the first, I felt the strain of the morally conflicted position I was in. As a scientist, I was obligated to the most accurate presentation of the evidence as I saw it and, additionally, to the most truthful claims of confidence in my analysis of that evidence. At the same time, I was a member of a "we"-group ethically obligated (by *its* professional responsibilities) to making the best-appearing case for its clients. Although from time to time I would mention my dedication to the values of scientific integrity to my partners, I was never sure they registered that priority fully. After a while, I thought I'd better make my commitment to those values, rather than theirs, clear to my teammates (and myself) in a formal statement. I began adding to my declarations of opinion a final paragraph, indicating that my views were based in part on the information and arguments provided to me by the attorneys who had hired me and that the views were subject to modification from any new information and arguments I might encounter, including those offered by opposing attorneys. The paragraph made an immediate difference, causing my teammates to see me as less of a loyalist and causing me to feel reinforced in my preferred role.

As well, the paragraph had an unexpected benefit in a legal case in which it was my opinion that one company's advertising campaigns were misleading regarding the healthful properties of its products. The company was highly profitable and had the resources to hire a phalanx of lawyers led by perhaps the most adept interrogator I had ever encountered. In a deposition involving my preliminary declaration of opinion, my job was to defend my position; his was to try to degrade my views, credibility, and integrity in every available way, which he did with rapier-like critiques that I had to be constantly on guard to parry. It was an interaction I was oddly enjoying because of the intellectual challenge of it all, when he did something I never expected. He reminded me that I had written about the foot-in-the-door influence tactic (see chapter 7) and a study in which homeowners agreed to place a small card in their windows advocating safe driving that, weeks later, made

them much more likely to do something related to it that they otherwise wouldn't have done—agree to put a large billboard on their
lawns for the same cause.

He asked me if I thought this meant that an initial public commitment to an idea, such as a sign in a window, would push people
to take more extreme stands on the idea as a result. When I answered yes, he pounced, holding up my preliminary declaration
of opinion and saying: "This statement looks to me like an initial
public commitment you've made that will, by your own words,
push you to be rigidly consistent with it, even to the point of taking
more extreme positions, no matter what. Therefore, why should
we believe anything you have to say from here on? It's obvious,
Professor Cialdini, that you've already put a sign in your window."

I was so impressed I rocked back in my chair and admitted,
"That's really clever!" He waived his hand to dismiss the compliment and pressed me to answer—all the while wearing the smile
of a trapper viewing a fresh catch struggling in his snare. Fortunately, I wasn't trapped after all. I asked him to read the final
paragraph of my declaration that committed me to receptivity to
new information and consequent change rather than to fixed consistency. "Actually," I told him, when he looked up from the paragraph, "*that* is the sign in my window." He didn't rock back in his
chair, and he didn't say so aloud, but I'm almost sure I saw him
mouth to himself, "That's really clever."

I am glad he thought so, but, truth be told, the paragraph wasn't
designed to counter his assault on my opinion statement that day.
It was intended to address a different issue I was dealing with
as an expert witness; namely, the pressure from within my legal
"we"-group—and, as valued friendships grew, increasingly from
within myself—to shape a version of the truth to be loyal to my
group's ethical obligation. The paragraph was an attempt, successful I think, to let everyone know in writing that I wasn't going to
let myself move in that direction.

What's the relevance of this account for organizations that want
to reap the benefits of a communal, "we"-based work-group culture, such as greater cooperation and harmony, without incurring

the corrupting costs of unleashed profiteers in their midst? Inside its Code of Conduct declaration, each organization should place a self-committing "sign in its window," in the form of a no-tolerance clause, specifying dismissal on the basis of a proven major violation or multiple proven minor violations of the code. The rationale for the no-tolerance policy should be framed in terms of workplace satisfaction and pride associated with an ethical culture—and, importantly, in terms of an honest desire to preserve feelings of workplace unity. Why this last inclusion? Because if it indeed worked to rescue the organization from a defect of "we"-ness by appealing to the *need* for "we"-ness . . . that would be really clever.[33]

SUMMARY

- People say yes to someone they consider one of them. The experience of "we"-ness (unity) with others is about shared identities—tribe-like categories that individuals use to define themselves and their groups, such as race, ethnicity, nationality, and family, as well as political and religious affiliations.

- Research into "we"-groups has produced three general conclusions. Members of these groups favor the outcomes and welfare of fellow members over those of nonmembers. "We"-group members also use the preferences and actions of fellow members to guide their own, which enhances group solidarity. Finally, such partisan tendencies have arisen, evolutionarily, as ways to advantage our "we"-groups and, ultimately, ourselves. These three constants have surfaced in a wide range of domains, including business, politics, sports, and personal relationships.

- The perception of *belonging together* with others is one fundamental factor leading to feelings of "we"-ness. This perception is generated by commonalities of kinship (amount of genetic overlap) as well as by commonalities of place (including one's home, locality, and region).

- The experience of *acting together* in unison or coordination is a second fundamental factor leading to a sense of unity with others. Shared musical experience is one way people can act together and feel consequent unity. Other ways involve repeated reciprocal exchange, joint suffering, and co-creation.

- It may be possible to use the unifying effects of belonging together and acting together to increase the odds of *getting together* as a species. It would require choosing to share, with out-group members, family experiences in our homes, neighbor experiences in our communities, and friendship experiences in our social interactions.

- Other kinds of connections involving national identity, mutual enemies, joint emotional experience, and shared perspective can also lead to feelings of unity with out-group members; unfortunately, they are often short-lived. However, focusing concentrated, repeated attention on such connections may make them more enduring by increasing their perceived importance.

CHAPTER 9

INSTANT INFLUENCE

PRIMITIVE CONSENT FOR AN AUTOMATIC AGE

Every day in every way, I'm getting better. —Émile Coué

Every day in every way, I'm getting busier. —Robert Cialdini

Back in the 1960s, a man named Joe Pyne hosted a rather remarkable TV talk show syndicated from California. The program was made distinctive by Pyne's caustic and confrontational style with his guests—for the most part, a collection of exposure hungry entertainers, would-be celebrities, and representatives of fringe political or social organizations. The host's abrasive approach was designed to provoke his guests into arguments, fluster them into embarrassing admissions, and make them look foolish. It was not uncommon for Pyne to introduce a visitor and launch immediately into an attack on the individual's beliefs, talent, or appearance. Some people claimed Pyne's acid personal style was partially caused by a leg amputation that had embittered him to life; others said, no, he was just offensive by nature.

One evening, the rock musician Frank Zappa was a guest on the show. This was at a time in the 1960s when very long hair on men was still unusual and controversial. As soon as Zappa had been introduced and seated, the following exchange occurred:

Pyne: I guess your long hair makes you a girl.

Zappa: I guess your wooden leg makes you a table.

Primitive Automaticity

Aside from containing what may be my favorite ad-lib, the dialogue between Pyne and Zappa illustrates a fundamental theme of this book: often when we make a decision about someone or something, we don't use all of the relevant available information. We use only a single, highly representative piece of the total. An isolated piece of information, even though it normally counsels correctly, can lead to clearly stupid mistakes—mistakes that, when exploited by clever others, leave us looking silly or worse.

At the same time, a complicating companion theme has been present: despite the susceptibility to stupid decisions that accompanies reliance on a single feature of the available data, the pace of modern life demands that we frequently use this shortcut. Recall early in chapter 1 when we compared the shortcut to the automatic responding of lower animals, whose elaborate behavior patterns could be triggered by the presence of a lone stimulus feature—a cheep-cheep sound, a shade of redbreast feather, or a specific sequence of light flashes. The reason lower animals must rely on such solitary stimulus features is their restricted mental capacity. Their small brains cannot begin to register and process all the relevant information in their environments. So these species have evolved special sensitivities to certain aspects of the information. Because those selected aspects of information are normally enough to cue a correct response, the system is usually efficient: for example, whenever a mother turkey hears cheep-cheep, *click, run*, out rolls the proper maternal behavior in a mechanical fashion that conserves much of her limited brainpower for dealing with other situations and choices she must face.

We, of course, have vastly more effective brain mechanisms than do mother turkeys or any other animal group. We are unchallenged in our ability to take into account a multitude of relevant facts and, consequently, make good decisions. Indeed, it is this information-processing advantage over other species that has helped make us the dominant form of life on the planet.

Still, we have our capacity limitations, too; and, for the sake of efficiency, we must sometimes retreat from the time-consuming, sophisticated, fully informed brand of decision-making to a more automatic, primitive, single-feature type of responding. For instance, in deciding whether to say yes or no to a requester, we frequently pay attention to a single unit of the relevant information in the situation. In preceding chapters, we've explored several of the most popular of the single units of information we use to prompt our compliance decisions. They are the most popular prompts precisely because they are the most reliable ones—those that normally point us toward a correct choice. That's why we employ the factors of reciprocation, liking, social proof, authority, scarcity, commitment and consistency, and unity so often and so automatically in making our compliance decisions. Each, by itself, provides a highly reliable cue as to when we will be better off saying yes instead of no.

We are likely to use these lone cues when we don't have the inclination, time, energy, or cognitive resources to undertake a complete analysis of the situation. When rushed, stressed, uncertain, indifferent, distracted, or fatigued, we focus on less of the available information. Under these circumstances, we often revert to the rather primitive but necessary "single piece of good evidence" approach to decision-making. All this leads to an unnerving insight: with the sophisticated mental apparatus we have used to build world eminence as a species, we have created an environment so complex, fast-paced, and information-laden that we must increasingly deal with it in the fashion of the animals we long ago transcended.

Modern Automaticity

John Stuart Mill, the British economist, political thinker, and philosopher of science, died a century and a half ago. The year of his death (1873) is important because he is reputed to have been the last man to know everything there was to know in the world. Today, the notion that one of us could be aware of all known facts is laughable. After eons of slow accumulation, human knowledge has snowballed into an era of momentum-fed, multiplicative, monstrous expansion. We now live in a world where most of the information is less than fifteen years old. In certain fields of science alone (physics, for example), knowledge is said to double every eight years. The scientific-information explosion is not limited to such arcane arenas as molecular chemistry or quantum physics but extends to everyday areas of knowledge, where we strive to keep ourselves current—health, education, nutrition. What's more, this rapid growth is likely to continue because researchers are pumping their newest findings into an estimated two million scientific-journal articles per year.

Apart from the streaking advance of science, things are quickly changing closer to home. According to yearly Gallup polls, the issues rated as most important on the public agenda are becoming more diverse and surviving on that agenda for a shorter time. In addition, we travel more and faster; we relocate more frequently to new residences, which are built and torn down more quickly; we contact more people and have shorter relationships with them; in the supermarket, car showroom, and shopping mall, we are faced with an array of choices among styles, products, and technological devices unheard of last year that may well be obsolete or forgotten by the next. Novelty, transience, diversity, and acceleration are prime descriptors of civilized existence.

This avalanche of information and choice is made possible by burgeoning technological progress. Leading the way are developments in our ability to collect, store, retrieve, and communicate information. At first, the fruits of such advances were limited to large organizations—government agencies or powerful corporations. With further developments in telecommunications and digital technology, access to such staggering amounts of information is within the reach of individuals. Extensive wireless and satellite systems provide routes for the information into the average home and hand. The informational power of a single cell phone exceeds that of entire universities of only a few years ago.

But notice something telling: our modern era, often termed the Information Age, has never been called the Knowledge Age. Information does not translate directly into knowledge. It must first be processed—accessed, absorbed, comprehended, integrated, and retained.

EBOX 9.1

Do You Take This Phone? I Do . . . Everywhere.

Author's note: Not only is the informational power of our digital devices unprecedented, but it can be addicting (Foerster et al., 2015; Yu & Sussman, 2020). Surveys show that people check their phones on average over one hundred times a day, and 84 percent say they "couldn't go a single day without their mobile devices."

BIZZAROCOMICS.COM Facebook.com/BizarroComics Distributed by King Features

Shortcuts Shall Be Sacred

Because technology can evolve much faster than we can, our natural capacity to process information is likely to be increasingly inadequate to handle the abundance of change, choice, and challenge that is characteristic of modern life. More and more frequently, we find ourselves in the position of lower animals—with a mental apparatus unequipped to deal thoroughly with the intricacy and richness of the external environment. Unlike the lower animals, whose cognitive powers have always been relatively deficient, we have created our own deficiency by constructing a radically more complex world. The consequence is the same as that of the animals' long-standing one: when making a decision, we will less frequently engage in a fully considered analysis of the total situation. In response to this "paralysis of analysis," we revert increasingly to focusing on a single, usually reliable feature of the situation.[1]

When those single features are truly reliable, there is nothing inherently wrong with the shortcut approach of narrowed attention and automatic responding to a particular piece of information. The problem comes when something causes the normally trustworthy cues to counsel us poorly, to lead us to erroneous actions and wrongheaded decisions. As we have seen, one such cause is the trickery of certain compliance practitioners, who seek to profit from the mindless and mechanical nature of shortcut responding. If, as it seems, the frequency of shortcut responding is increasing with the pace and form of modern life, we can be sure that the frequency of this trickery is destined to increase as well.

What can we do about the intensified attack on our system of shortcuts? More than evasive action, I urge forceful counterassault; however, there is an important qualification. Compliance professionals who play fairly by the rules of shortcut responding are not to be considered our adversaries; to the contrary, they are our allies in an efficient and adaptive process of exchange. The proper targets for counter-aggression are only those who falsify, counterfeit, or misrepresent the evidence that naturally cues our shortcut responses.

Let's take an illustration from what is perhaps our most frequently used shortcut. According to the principle of social proof, we often decide to do what other people like us are doing. It makes all kinds of sense because, most of the time, an action that is popular in a given situation is also functional and appropriate. Thus, an advertiser who, without using deceptive statistics, provides information that a brand of toothpaste is the largest selling has offered us valuable evidence about the quality of the product and the probability that we will like it. Provided we are in the market for a tube of good toothpaste, we may want to rely on that single piece of information to try it. The strategy will likely steer us right, unlikely steer us far wrong, and conserve our cognitive energies for dealing with the rest of our increasingly information-laden, decision-overloaded environment. The advertiser who allows us to use effectively this efficient strategy is hardly our antagonist but, rather, our cooperating partner.

The story becomes quite different, however, when a compliance practitioner tries to stimulate a shortcut response by giving us a fraudulent signal for it. Our nemesis is the advertiser who seeks to create an image of popularity for a brand of toothpaste by, say, constructing a series of staged "unrehearsed interview" ads in which actors posing as ordinary citizens praise the product. Here, where the evidence is counterfeit, we, the principle of social proof, and our shortcut response to it, are all being exploited. In an earlier chapter, I recommended against the purchase of any product featured in a faked "unrehearsed interview" ad and urged that we send the product manufacturers letters detailing the reason and suggesting they dismiss their advertising agency. I also recommended extending this aggressive stance to any situation in which an influence professional abuses the principle of social proof (or any other principle of influence) in this manner. We should refuse to watch TV programs that use canned laughter. If, after waiting in line outside a nightclub, we discover from the amount of available space that the wait was designed to impress passersby with false evidence of the club's popularity, we should leave immediately and announce our reason to those still in line. We should boycott brands found to be planting phony reviews on product-rating sites—and spread the word on social media. In short, we should be willing to use shame, threat, confrontation, censure, tirade, nearly anything, to retaliate.

I don't consider myself pugnacious by nature, but I actively advocate such belligerent actions because in a way I am at war with the exploiters. We all are. It is important to recognize, however, that their motive for profit is not the cause for hostilities; that motive, after all, is something we each share to an extent. The real treachery, and what we cannot tolerate, is any attempt to make their profit in a way that threatens the reliability of our shortcuts. The blitz of modern daily life demands that we have faithful shortcuts, sound rules of thumb in order to handle it all. These are no longer luxuries; they are out-and-out necessities that figure to become increasingly vital as the pulse quickens. That is why we should want to retaliate whenever we see someone betraying one of our rules of thumb for profit. We want that rule to be as effective as possible. To the degree its fitness for duty is regularly undercut by the tricks of a profiteer, we naturally will use it less and will be less able to cope efficiently with the decisional burdens of our day. That we cannot allow without a fight. The stakes are far too high.

READER'S REPORT 9.1

From Robert, a social-influence researcher in Arizona

A while ago I was in an electronics store to buy something else when I noticed a high quality big screen TV on sale at an attractive price. I wasn't in the market for a new TV, but the combination of the sale price and its strong product rating got me to stop and examine some related brochures. A salesman, Brad, came up and said, "I can see you're interested in this set. I can see why. It's a great deal at this price. But, I have to tell you it's our last one." That spiked my interest immediately. Then he told me he had just gotten a call from a woman who said she might come in that afternoon to purchase it. I've been a persuasion researcher all my professional life; so I knew he was using the scarcity principle on me.

It didn't matter. Twenty minutes later, I was wheeling out of the store with the "prize" I had obtained in my cart. Tell me, doc, was I a fool to react the way I did to Brad's scarcity story?

Author's note: As readers should by now recognize, the Robert in the report was me, which gives me an especially informed perspective on his question. Whether he should feel duped by the appeal depends on whether Brad accurately informed him about the scarcity-related features of the situation. If so, Robert should feel *grateful* to Brad for the gift of that information. For instance, imagine if Brad hadn't informed Robert of the genuine circumstances, Robert went home to think things over and returned that evening to make the purchase—only to learn the last set had been sold. He would have been furious at the salesman: "What?! Why didn't you tell me it was the last one before I left? What's wrong with you?"

Now, suppose instead of providing honest information, Brad fabricated the scarcity-related conditions surrounding the TV. Then, once Robert was gone, he went to the back room, got another of the same model and put it on the shelf, where he could sell it to the next customer using the same story. (By the way, Best Buy employees were caught doing exactly this a few years ago.) No longer would he be a valuable informant to Robert; he'd be a damnable profiteer.

Which was it? Robert was determined to find out. He returned to the store the next morning to see if there was another such TV on display. There was not. Brad had been straight with him—which spurred Robert to go to his office and write a highly favorable review of the store and, especially, of Brad. Had Brad lied, the review would have been an equally strong condemnation. When exposed to the principles of influence, we should unfailingly promote those who seek to *arm* us and demote those who seek to *harm* us with them.

SUMMARY

- Modern life is different from that of any earlier time. Owing to remarkable technological advances, information is burgeoning, alternatives are multiplying, and knowledge is exploding. In this avalanche of change and choice, we have had to adjust. One fundamental adjustment has come in the way we make decisions. Although we all wish to make the most thoughtful, fully considered decision possible in any situation, the changing form and accelerating pace of modern life frequently deprive us of the proper conditions for such a careful analysis of all the relevant pros and cons. More and more, we are forced to resort to another decision-making approach—a shortcut approach in which the decision to comply (or agree or believe or buy) is made on the basis of a single, usually reliable piece of information. The most reliable and, therefore, most popular such single triggers for compliance are those described throughout this book. They are commitments, opportunities for reciprocation, the compliant behavior of similar others, feelings of liking or unity, authority directives, and scarcity information.

- Because of the increasing tendency for cognitive overload in our society, the prevalence of shortcut decision-making is likely to increase proportionately. Compliance professionals who infuse their requests with one or another of the levers of influence are more likely to be successful. The use of these levers by practitioners is not necessarily exploitative. It only becomes so when the lever is not a natural feature of the situation but is fabricated by the practitioner. In order to retain the beneficial character of shortcut response, it is important to oppose such fabrication by all appropriate means.

ACKNOWLEDGMENTS

An array of people deserve and have my appreciation for their aid at the outset in making *Influence* possible. Several of my academic colleagues read and provided perceptive comments on the entire manuscript in its initial draft form, greatly strengthening the subsequent versions. They are Gus Levine, Doug Kenrick, Art Beaman, and Mark Zanna. In addition, the first draft was read by a few family members and friends—Richard and Gloria Cialdini, Bobette Gorden, and Ted Hall—who offered not only much-needed emotional support but insightful substantive commentary as well.

A second, larger group provided helpful suggestions for selected chapters or groups of chapters: Todd Anderson, Sandy Braver, Catherine Chambers, Judi Cialdini, Nancy Eisenberg, Larry Ettkin, Joanne Gersten, Jeff Goldstein, Betsy Hans, Valerie Hans, Joe Hepworth, Holly Hunt, Ann Inskeep, Barry Leshowitz, Darwyn Linder, Debbie Littler, John Mowen, Igor Pavlov, Janis Posner, Trish Puryear, Marilyn Rall, John Reich, Peter Reingen, Diane Ruble, Phyllis Sensenig, Roman Sherman, and Henry Wellman.

Certain people were instrumental at the beginning stages. John Staley was the first publishing professional to recognize the project's potential. Jim Sherman, Al Goethals, John Keating, Dan Wagner, Dalmas Taylor, Wendy Wood, and David Watson provided early, positive reviews that encouraged author and editors alike. I would like to thank the following users of the book for their feedback during a telephone survey: Emory Griffin, Wheaton College; Robert Levine, California State University, Fresno; Jeffrey Lewin, Georgia State University; David Miller, Daytona Beach

Community College; Lois Mohr, Georgia State University; and Richard Rogers, Daytona Beach Community College. The past editions benefited substantially from the reviews of Assaad Azzi, Yale University; Robert M. Brady, University of Arkansas; Amy M. Buddie, Kennesaw State University; Brian M. Cohen, University of Texas at San Antonio; Christian B. Crandall, University of Florida; Maria Czyzewska, Texas State University; A. Celeste Farr, North Carolina State University; Arthur Frankel, Salve Regina University; Catherine Goodwin, University of Alaska; Robert G. Lowder, Bradley University; James W. Michael, Jr., Virginia Polytechnic Institute and State University; Eugene P. Sheehan, University of Northern Colorado; Jefferson A. Singer, Connecticut College; Brian Smith, Graceland University; and Sandi W. Smith, Michigan State University.

As regards the present edition, several individuals deserve special thanks. My agent, Jim Levine, was a source of exquisite counsel. My editor at Harper Business, Hollis Heimbouch, and I were so much in accord on matters large and small that the writing/editorial process became more streamlined than I had ever experienced before. Also at Harper Business, Wendy Wong and copy editor Plaegian Alexander were terrific at getting my manuscript into shape for production. My colleague Steve J. Martin provided proprietary data from his brilliantly conducted experiments that enriched and enlivened my content. Because of the multinational reach of previous editions, I asked Anna Ropiecka to provide manuscript feedback from the perspective of a non-native English speaker, which she did with great insight and much benefit to the final product. Inside my team at Influence At Work, Eily Vandermeer and Cara Tracy were willing to stretch their responsibilities and, in the process, reveal invaluable new competencies. I would be remiss if I failed to acknowledge the ongoing support for *Influence* of Charlie Munger, who gave the book instant credibility among readers from the financial and investing communities.

Then there is Bobette Gorden—helpmate, workmate, playmate, and soulmate—whose gentle commentaries always improved the work and whose love made every day a joy.

NOTES

Preface

1. It's worth trying to understand why, since the publication of *Influence*, I haven't had to confront any of the indignant condescension Boyle (2008) forecast, including from the most hawkish of my academic colleagues. I think there are two main reasons. First, unlike the popularized forms of social science seen in the "human interest" articles of daily newspapers, I made a concerted effort to cite the individual publications (hundreds of them) on which I based my statements and conclusions. Second, rather than seek to elevate my own investigations or any particular grouping of investigations, I sought to elevate a particular *approach* to investigating human responding—the approach of experimental behavioral science. I didn't intend it at the time, but the disarming effect on my fellow experimental behavioral scientists may affirm a belief I've long held: people don't sink the boats they are riding in.

2. Alas, a bit of Internet research revealed that I can't attribute the origin of the insightful quote to my grandfather. It comes from his famous countryman Giuseppe Tomasi di Lampedusa.

Introduction

1. It is worth noting that I have not included among the seven principles the simple rule of material self-interest: that people want to get the most and pay the least for their choices. This omission does not stem from any perception on my part that the desire to maximize benefits and minimize costs is unimportant in driving our decisions. Nor does it come from any evidence I have that compliance professionals ignore the power of this rule. Quite the opposite; in my investigations, I frequently saw practitioners use (sometimes honestly, sometimes not) the compelling "I can give you a good deal" approach. I chose not to treat the material self-interest rule separately in this book because I see it as a motivational given, as a goes-without-saying factor that deserves acknowledgment, but not extensive description.

Chapter 1: Levers of Influence

1. The energy-drinks experiment was conducted by Shiv, Carmon, & Ariely (2005). At the time I read their article (and thought to myself, What?), I was purchasing energy drinks to help me finish a big writing project with a fast-approaching deadline. Before seeing the study's results, I would never have guessed that getting the drinks on sale, which I tried to do whenever possible, would make them *less* effective for me.

2.   A complete description of the mother-turkey experiment is provided in a monograph by M. W. Fox (1974)—honest, this animal researcher's name is Fox. Sources for the robin and bluethroat information are Lack (1943) and Peiponen (1960), respectively.

3.   Perhaps the common "because . . . just because" response of children asked to explain their actions comes from their shrewd recognition of the unusual amount of power adults assign the word *because*—*because* it implies a reason, and people want reasons to act (Bastardi & Shafir, 2000). In an instructive chapter, Langer (1989) explores the larger implications of the Xerox study (Langer, Blank, & Chanowitz, 1978) and makes the case for the widespread presence of automatic responding in human behavior—a position shared by Bargh & Williams (2006).

Although several important similarities exist between this kind of automaticity in humans and lower animals, there are important differences as well. The automatic behavior patterns of humans tend to be learned rather than inborn, more flexible than the lockstep patterns of the lower animals, and responsive to a larger number of triggers.

4.   Cronley et al. (2005) and Rao & Monroe (1989) have shown that when people are unfamiliar with a product or service, they become particularly likely to employ the expensive = good rule. In marketing lore, the classic case of this phenomenon is that of Chivas Regal Scotch Whiskey, which had been a little-known, struggling brand until its managers decided to raise its price to a level far above that of its competitors. Sales skyrocketed, even though nothing was changed in the product itself (Aaker, 1991).

Besides the energy-drink (Shiv, Carmon, & Ariely, 2005) and pain-reliever (Waber et al., 2008) studies, others have found that people see a higher-than-warranted connection between an item's price and its quality and then allow this misguided connection to influence their responses (Kardes, Posavac, & Cronley, 2004). A brain-scan study helps explain why the expensive = good stereotype is so powerful. When tasting the same wine, tasters not only rated themselves as experiencing more pleasure if they thought it cost \$45 versus \$5, their brains' pleasure centers actually *did* become more activated by the taste of the presumed "\$45" wine (Plassmann et al., 2008).

5.   For evidence of the need for and value of automaticity in our lives and of how the automaticity reveals itself in judgmental heuristics, see Collins (2018); Fennis, Janssen, & Vohs (2008); Fiske & Neuberg (1990); Gigerenzer & Goldstein (1996); Kahneman, Slovic, & Tversky (1982); Raue & Scholl (2018); Shah & Oppenheimer (2008); and Todd & Gigerenzer (2007). Petty et al. (2019) offer multiple examples of how, unless they have both the motivation and ability to examine incoming information carefully, people rely on heuristics in responding to the information. The comprehensive-exams study (Petty, Cacioppo, & Goldman (1981) is one of those examples; see Epley & Gilovich (2006) for yet another.

It's instructive that even though we often don't take a complex, deliberative approach to personally important topics (Anderson & Simester, 2003; Klein & O'Brien, 2018; Milgram, 1970; Miller & Krosnick, 1998), we want our advisers—our physicians, accountants, lawyers, and brokers—to do precisely that for us (Kahn & Baron, 1995). When feeling overwhelmed by a complicated and consequential choice, we still want a fully considered, point-by-point analysis of it—an analysis we may not be able to achieve except, ironically enough, through a shortcut: reliance on an expert. An account by Thomas Watson, Jr., the former chairman of IBM, offers graphic evidence of the phenomenon in another example of Captainitis. During World War II, he was assigned to investigate plane crashes in which high-ranking officers were killed or injured. One case involved a famous air-force general named Uzal Girard Ent, whose copilot got sick before a flight. Ent was assigned a replacement who felt honored to be flying alongside the legendary general. During takeoff, Ent began singing to himself, nodding in time to a song in his head. The new copilot interpreted the gesture as a signal to him to lift the wheels. Even though they were going much too slowly to fly, he raised the landing gear, causing the plane to drop immediately onto its belly. In the wreck, a propeller blade sliced into Ent's back, severing his spine and rendering him a paraplegic. Watson described the copilot's explanation for his action:

> When I took the copilot's testimony, I asked him, "If you knew the plane wasn't going to fly, why did you put the gear up?"
> He said, "I thought the general wanted me to. He was stupid." (1990, p. 117)

Stupid? I'd say, in that singular set of circumstances, yes. Understandable? In the shortcut-demanding maze of modern life, I'd also say yes.

6. Apparently, the tendency of males to be bamboozled by powerful mating signals extends beyond fireflies (Lloyd, 1965) to humans. Two University of Vienna biologists, Astrid Jütte and Karl Grammer secretly exposed young men to airborne chemicals (called copulins) that mimic human vaginal scents. The men then rated the attractiveness of women's faces. Exposure to the copulins increased the judged attractiveness of *all* the women and masked the genuine physical-attractiveness differences among them (*Arizona Republic,* 1999). Although romance is not at issue, certain primitive pathogens also mimic chemical substances to render healthy bodies (cells) receptive to them (Goodenough, 1991).

An array of examples of how nature's plant and animal fraud artists operate is described by Stevens (2016). Examples of the similar tricks of human fraudsters can be found in Shadel (2012) and Stevens (2016).

7. For a full account of the Cornell researchers' study, see Ott et al. (2011). The comparisons between online-review readers in 2014 and 2018 was provided by Shrestha (2018). In 2019, the US Federal Trade Commission issued a complaint against the owner of a cosmetics company accused of creating false product reviews. The complaint included a quote from the owner to her employees that illustrates how well the manufacturers of fake reviews understand their potency: "If you notice someone saying things like I didn't like 'x' about it, write a review that says the opposite. The power of reviews is mighty; people look to what others are saying to persuade them and answer potential questions they have" (Maheshwari, 2019).

By no means was my friend original in her particular use of the expensive = good rule to snare those seeking a bargain. Thirty years of research indicates that the strategy of marking an item as "Reduced from . . ." works extremely well (Kan et al., 2014). Indeed, retailers have been using it successfully even before researchers confirmed its effectiveness. Culturist and author Leo Rosten gives the example of the Drubeck brothers, Sid and Harry, who owned a men's tailor shop in Rosten's neighborhood in the 1930s. Whenever Sid had a new customer trying on suits in front of the shop's three-sided mirror, he would admit to a hearing problem and repeatedly request that the man speak more loudly to him. Once the customer had found a suit he liked and asked for the price, Sid would call to his brother, the head tailor, at the back of the room, "Harry, how much for this suit?" Looking up from his work—and greatly exaggerating the suit's true price—Harry would call back, "For that beautiful, all wool suit, forty-two dollars." Pretending not to have heard and cupping his hand to his ear, Sid would ask again. Once more Harry would reply, "Forty-two dollars." At this point, Sid would turn to the customer and report, "He says twenty-two dollars." Many a man would hurry to buy the suit and scramble out of the shop with his expensive = good bargain before poor Sid discovered the "mistake."

8.   Alexander Chernev (2011) conducted the study on calorie counts. The experiment showing a decline in sexual attraction to current mates after exposure to naked bodies in the media was done by Kenrick, Gutierres, & Goldberg (1989). Other researchers have found similar effects on attraction to works of art, showing that an abstract painting will be rated as significantly less attractive if viewed after a higher-quality abstract painting than if viewed by itself (Mallon, Redies, & Hayn-Leichsenring, 2014). Evidence that the contrast effect can operate without cognitive recognition (Tormala & Petty, 2007) is reinforced by evidence that it even works on rats (Dwyer et al., 2018).

Chapter 2: Reciprocation

1.   Certain societies have formalized the rule of reciprocation into ritual. Consider, for example, the Vartan Bhanji, an institutionalized custom of gift exchange common to parts of Pakistan and India. In commenting upon the Vartan Bhanji, Alvin Gouldner (1960) remarks:

> It is . . . notable that the system painstakingly prevents the total elimination of outstanding obligations. Thus, on the occasion of a marriage, departing guests are given gifts of sweets. In weighing them out, the hostess may say, "These five are yours," meaning "These are a repayment for what you formerly gave me," and then she adds an extra measure, saying, "These are mine." On the next occasion, she will receive these back along with an additional measure which she later returns, and so on. (p. 175)

The original holiday-card study was done by Phillip Kunz (Kunz & Woolcott, 1976) and, in a noteworthy instance of continuity, was extended a quarter-century later by his behavioral-scientist daughter Jenifer Kunz (2000), who found a stronger reciprocation rate if the sender of the first card was of high status. Access to a fuller account of the request for a day of pay from investment bankers can be found at https://assets.publishing.service.gov.uk/government/uploads/system/uploads /attachment_data/file/203286/BIT_Charitable_Giving_Paper.pdf (pp. 20–21).

The desirability of reciprocal exchange within and between societies was recognized by social scientists long before sociologists such as Gouldner (1960), archaeologists such as Leakey and Lewin (1978), and cultural anthropologists such as Tiger & Fox (1989). See, for example, Bronisław Malinowski's groundbreaking ethnographic examination of the trading patterns of Trobriand Islanders, *Argonauts of the Western Pacific* (1922). More recent evidence shows that the rule doesn't only apply to positive exchanges; it fuels negative ones as well (Hugh-Jones, Ron, & Zultan, 2019; Keysar et al., 2008), all of which fits with W. H. Auden's famous line of poetry: "I and the public know / what every schoolboy learns / Those to whom evil is done / do evil in return." More generally, it can be said that the rule of reciprocation assures that whether the fruit of our actions is sweet or bitter, we reap what we sow (Oliver, 2019). This is also true of human–machine exchanges. Users who had received high-quality information from a computer then gave better information to that computer than to a different one; what's more, users receiving low-quality information from a particular computer retaliated by providing it lower-quality information than that given to a different computer (Fogg & Nass, 1997a). In general, reciprocity in all of its forms is a driver of human conduct (Melamed, Simpson, & Abernathy, 2020).

2. The longevity of Ethiopia's obligation to help Mexico ("Ethiopian Red Cross," 1985) and Lord Weidenfeld's obligation to help Christian families (Coghlan, 2015) may be outdone by the case of a group of French children's cross-generational desire to aid a group of Australian children they had never met. On April 23–24, 1918, near the end of World War I, several battalions of Australian soldiers lost their lives freeing the French village of Villers-Bretonneux from German forces. When, in 2009, the schoolchildren of Villers-Bretonneux learned of a bushfire that destroyed the Australian town of Strathewen, they collected $21,000 to help rebuild Strathewen's primary school. According to one newspaper account, "They knew little of the children they would be helping. They only knew their great-grandparents had promised 91 years ago never to forget Australia and the 1200 Australian solders who died liberating their village" (*The Australian*, 2009).

Although highly consequential and memorable first forms of assistance, like those covered above, can create lasting feelings of obligation, it would be a mistake to think all such actions do the same. In fact, there's good evidence that everyday favors lose their obligating powers as time passes (Burger et al., 1997; Flynn, 2003). One set of studies even found that recipients feel most indebted to a favor-doer before the act is completed (Converse & Fishbach, 2012). The upshot? Small acts of help conform to the "rule of the bagel": People appreciate them more when they are warm and fresh than cold and old.

3. Even before they enter school, children come to understand the obligation to give back after receiving and to respond accordingly (Chernyak et al., 2019; Dunfield & Kuhlmeier, 2010; Yang et al., 2018). The Regan (1971) study was conducted at Stanford University. Pulitzer Prize–winning journalist Joby Warrick (2008) reported the case of the indebted Afghan tribal chief, which fits with related evidence that, in the Middle East, "soft" methods, such as reciprocity-inducing favors, bring better results than coercive interrogation techniques involving deprivation, hardship, or torture do (Alison & Alison, 2017; Ghosh, 2009; Goodman-Delahunty, Martschuk, & Dhami, 2014). For links to additional such evidence, see www.psychologicalscience.org/index.php/news/were-only-human /the-science-of-interrogation-rapport-not-torture.html.

4. The data pattern of the $5-"gift check" experiment (James & Bolstein, 1992) fits with newer research showing that surveys providing payment before partic- ipation (wherein the money is included in a request letter) get more compliance than those providing equal or larger payment after participation (Mercer et al., 2015). It fits as well with a study in which hotel guests encountered a card in their rooms asking them to reuse their towels. They also read either that the hotel had *already made* a financial contribution to an environmental-protection organiza- tion in the name of its guests or that it would make such a contribution *after* guests did reuse their towels. The before-the-act donation proved significantly more effective than the after-the-act one (Goldstein, Griskevicius, & Cialdini, 2011). Waiters' gift of a candy before patrons paid their checks significantly in- creased tips by Americans in a New Jersey restaurant (Strohmetz et al., 2002) and by guests of each of seven nationalities in a Polish restaurant (Żemła & Gladka, 2016). Finally, the McDonald's gift-balloon study was done by my InfluenceAtWork.com colleagues Steve J. Martin and Helen Mankin in conjunc- tion with Daniel Gertsacov, at the time the chief marketing officer of Arcos Do- rados S.A., which owned the McDonald's locations. For additional details on this and other McDonald's studies done by our team, see www.influenceatwork.com /wp-content/uploads/2020/03/Persuasion-Pilots-McDonalds-Arcos-Dorados -INFLUENCE-AT-WORKpdf.pdf.

The benefits of giving first in business are presented and traced forward par- ticularly convincingly in a pair of books by Adam Grant (2013) and Tom Rollins (2020). For a humorous illustration, see https://youtu.be/c6V_zUGVlTk. For a collection of reciprocity-based approaches favored by e-marketers, see https:// sleeknote.com/blog/reciprocity-marketing-examples.

5. It's not just the case that drug companies' gifts affect scientists' findings about the effectiveness of their drugs (Stelfox et al., 1998), such gifts also affect physicians' tendencies to prescribe them. Pharmaceutical-industry payments to doctors (for educational training, speaking fees, travel, consulting fees, confer- ence registrations, and so on) are linked to the frequency of doctors' prescrip- tions for the sponsored drugs (Hadland et al., 2018; Wall & Brown, 2007; Yeh et al., 2016). Even the low price of a single free meal is enough to do the trick— although more expensive meals are associated with higher prescription rates (DeJong et al., 2016). Studies showing the effects of donations to legislators are described by Salant (2003) and Brown, Drake, & Wellman (2014).

6. The most thoroughgoing scholarship supporting the new account of how the Cuban missile crisis ended belongs to Sheldon Stern (2012), who served for twenty-three years as the historian at the John F. Kennedy Presidential Library. See also Benjamin Schwartz's enlightening review at www.theatlantic.com /magazine/archive/2013/01/the-real-cuban-missile-crisis/309190.

7. The candy-shop research was performed by Lammers (1991). In another purchasing pattern that fits with the rule of reciprocation, supermarket shoppers given a surprise gift coupon for a particular type of item then bought signifi- cantly more additional items from the store, resulting in a 10 percent increase in total purchase size (Heilman, Nakamoto, & Rao, 2002). The Costco experience was described by Pinsker (2014). Anderson & Zimbardo (1984) reported on the reciprocity-rule wisdom of Diane Louie at Jonestown.

8.   The key ring–versus-yogurt data pattern (Friedman & Rahman, 2011) also appeared in a supermarket study (Fombelle et al., 2010) that gave entering shoppers either a nonfood gift (key ring) or a food-related gift (Pringles chips), which increased overall purchases by 28 percent and 60 percent, respectively. Michael Schrange (2004) wrote the article describing the disappointing results of a hotel chain's seamless customer-experience program on customer satisfaction. Customizing the gift to the need doesn't just work in commercial settings. Giving support within a relationship leads to greater relationship satisfaction only when it fits the recipient's current need (Maisel & Gable, 2009).

9.   Paese & Gilin (2000) demonstrated the force of unsolicited favors within negotiation situations. Unsolicited cooperative offers produced return acts of cooperation from recipients even when doing so ran counter to their financial interests. In a real-world illustration of the influence of uninvited favors, Uber was able to significantly increase ridership in Boston *after* giving the city an unsolicited gift: During the 2013 city-bus strike, the company rented buses and provided free service to all Boston public schools.

Marcel Mauss published his masterwork *The Gift: The Form and Reason for Exchange in Archaic Societies* in 1925, but an excellent English translation can be found in a 1990 reprint published by Routledge.

10.   Although it is clear that we dislike those who take without giving in return (e.g., Wedekind & Milinski, 2000), a cross-cultural study has shown that those who break the reciprocity rule in the reverse direction—by giving without allowing the recipient an opportunity to repay—are also disliked for it. This result was found to hold for each of the three nationalities investigated—Americans, Swedes, and Japanese (Gergen et al., 1975). There's ample evidence that people frequently fail to ask for aid to avoid feeling socially indebted (DePaulo, Nadler, & Fisher, 1983; Greenberg & Shapiro, 1971; Riley & Eckenrode, 1986). One study is noteworthy for its ten-year duration and its investigation of a dilemma many of us have faced: whether to ask friends and family to help us relocate to a new residence or to give the entire task to commercial movers. The study found that often people avoid enlisting the help of those they know, not from fears that these nonprofessionals would damage valuable property but from fears of the "indebtedness" such assistance would generate in them as a result (Marcoux, 2009).

Other research has pointed to the driving force of indebtedness in reciprocal exchanges. For example, Belmi & Pfeffer (2015), Goldstein, Griskevicius, & Cialdini (2011), and Pillutla, Malhotra, & Murnighan (2003) identified a main reason that giving first can work so well: it produces a sense of obligation on the part of the recipient to give back. Still, it's worth noting that in the family of factors related to reciprocity, obligation has an equally active but sweeter sister—gratitude— that operates to stimulate returns, not so much because recipients of favors feel a sense debt but because recipients feel a sense of appreciation. Although both feelings reliably spur positive reciprocation, gratitude appears to be related to the intensification of relationships rather than just the instigation or maintenance of them. Evidence in this regard is available in the research of Sara Algoe and her associates (Algoe, 2012; Algoe, Gable, & Maisel, 2010; Algoe & Zhaoyang, 2016).

George, Gournic, & McAfee (1988) did the research attesting to the perceived sexual availability of a woman who allows a man to buy her drinks. See Clark,

Mills, & Corcoran (1989) for a review of data demonstrating a difference in the type of reciprocal norm that applies among family and close friends (communal norm) versus strangers (exchange norm). More recently, Clark et al. (2010) showed that strong communal norms inside a marriage are associated with marital success. Kenrick (2020) offers an updated perspective on the distinction between communal and exchange norms that applies to friendships; see http://spsp.org/news-center/blog/kenrick-true-friendships#gsc.tab=0.

11. The results of my team's zoo-trip experiment were reported in Cialdini et al. (1975). The Israeli study of the effects of unreasonable first requests was conducted by Schwarzwald, Raz, & Zvibel (1979). The rejection-then-retreat technique has proved successful in other cultures as well, such as Greece (Rodafinos, Vucevic, & Sideridis, 2005). Perhaps my favorite such demonstration occurred in France, where patrons of three restaurants were asked by their server as she cleared the table whether they'd like dessert. If a patron said no, the waitress immediately retreated to a proposal of coffee or tea, which nearly tripled the percentage of such orders. What I found particularly instructive appeared in another condition of the study in which, rather than immediately retreating to a proposal of coffee or tea, the waitress waited three minutes to do so. In this treatment, hot-drink orders only doubled (Guéguen, Jacob, & Meineri, 2011). Apparently, the finding that the obligation to reciprocate small favors declines over time (Flynn, 2003) also applies to the obligation to reciprocate small concessions.

12. As I've claimed, the findings that the rejection-then-retreat tactic leads its targets to be more likely to actually perform a requested favor (Miller et al., 1976) and to agree to perform similar favors (Cialdini & Ascani, 1976) are consistent with the resulting feelings of responsibility and satisfaction that were found in the UCLA experiment (Benton, Kelley, & Liebling, 1972). Recall that there was another result of the UCLA experiment—starting with an extreme position and then retreating to a moderate one proved much more effective than starting with a moderate position and sticking to it. That outcome is consistent with the negotiation lesson learned by the Canadian pet-supply business owners described on p. 38. The studies by Robert Schindler of retail customers' satisfaction levels were published in 1998.

Chapter 3: Liking

1. The data on the percentage of Americans who believe humans evolved entirely through natural processes came from a Pew Research Center survey (www.pewresearch.org/fact-tank/2019/02/11/darwin-day), which also documented the large role of religious belief in resistance to evolutionary theory. Analyses by Andrew Shtulman (2006) and Dan Kahan (www.culturalcognition.net/blog/2014/5/24/weekend-update-youd-have-to-be-science-illiterate-to-think-b.html) show the lack of relationship between the understanding of evolutionary theory and belief in it. The quote from medical-malpractice attorney, Alice Burkin, came from an interview with Berkeley Rice (2000).

The George Clooney and Emma Watson research (Arnocky et al., 2018) is more instructive than I have described, owing to a pair of additional experimental procedures. The first extended the breadth of the basic effect by demonstrating that the liked celebrities' opinions had the power not only to increase acceptance of evolution but to decrease it as well. When some study participants were led to believe that Clooney or Watson had commented favorably about an *anti*-evolutionary book, support for evolutionary theory dropped significantly among these observers. So liking's influence isn't a one-way street; it can route attitudinal traffic in positive or negative directions. A second experimental procedure reinforced the wisdom of using liked (rather than authoritative) communicators to create change on the topic. The researchers showed a different sample of participants favorable commentary, purportedly written by a professor of biology from a prestigious university, regarding either a pro-evolutionary or anti-evolutionary book. The expert's opinion—for or against evolution—had no significant effect on participants' acceptance of the theory. Here we see the clearest evidence I know for why science communicators' crusades to heighten support for evolution have failed over the years: they've chosen the wrong battlefield on which to strike.

2. The evidence showing that it's the quality of the social connections—rather than of the physical products—that determines buying within a Tupperware party comes from studies by Taylor (1978) and Frenzen & Davis (1990). For a financial analysis of how Tupperware Brands has successfully employed principles of social influence, especially in emerging markets, see https://seekingalpha.com/article/4137896-tupperware-brands-sealed-nearly-20-percent-upside?page=2. As a testament to the social basis of Tupperware products' success, after the coronavirus threat emerged worldwide in February 2020, Tupperware Brands share price dropped severely on the New York Stock Exchange. The drop (of 90 percent of its value from the previous February) was due in large part to perceptions that gatherings, even of friends, were no longer considered safe by consumers.

The Nielsen Company survey showing greater trust for a liked friend's recommendation is described at www.nielsen.com/us/en/insights/news/2012/trust-in-advertising--paid-owned-and-earned.html. But this pattern reverses when liking for the known friend turns into disliking, such as typically occurs with an ex-girlfriend or ex-boyfriend. In that case, consumers are 66 percent *less* likely to trust their ex's product opinion than an online reviewer's: www.convinceand convert.com/word-of-mouth/statistics-about-word-of-mouth. In either instance, liking seems to be a key. The research on the profitability to a bank of referred customers is described at https://hbr.org/2011/06/why-customer-referrals-can-drive-stunning-profits.

3. The idea that physical attractiveness creates a halo effect for other judgments is not new. Consider Leo Tolstoy's 120-year-old assertion: "It is amazing how complete is the delusion that beauty is good." Support for the broad (Langlois et al., 2000), immediate (Olson & Marshuetz, 2005), and early (Dion, 1972; Ritts, Patterson, & Tubbs, 1992) effects of physical attraction in a variety of social (Benson, Karabenic, & Lerner, 1976; Chaiken, 1979; Stirrat & Perrett, 2010), professional (Judge, Hurst, & Simon, 2009; Hamermesh & Biddle, 1994; Hamermesh, 2011; Mack & Raney, 1990), and political (Efran & Patterson, 1976; Budesheim & DePaola, 1994) arenas is historically strong. A more recent review (Maestripieri, Henry, & Nickels, 2017) not only updates this support but also offers an evolutionary explanation for much of the basic effect: our positive feelings and beneficial behaviors toward attractive individuals flow from automatic, overgeneralized romantic feelings toward them.

4.   The work measuring infants' favorable feelings toward similar others was performed by Hamlin et al. (2013), using puppets whose taste preferences (for crackers versus beans) were similar to or different from the infants'. The online dating preference study was performed by Levy, Markell, & Cerf (2019). The unthinking impact of similar dress styles in an antiwar demonstration was seen at a time of great civil conflict over the American war in Vietnam (Suedfeld, Bochner, & Matas, 1971). The effects of seemingly trivial similarities such as fingerprint type on helping were obtained by Burger et al. (2004). Name similarity's positive effect on brand preferences and survey responding was demonstrated, respectively, in five separate experiments by Brendl et al. (2005) and in a pair of studies by Garner (2005).

5.   Similarity's broad influence is evident from its impact in educational settings (DuBois et al., 2011; Gehlbach et al., 2016; Marx & Ko, 2012) as well as on bargaining outcomes (Moore et al., 1999; Morris et al., 2002), voter choices (Bailenson et al., 2008), romantic feelings (Ireland et al., 2011; Jones et al., 2004; Ohadi et al., 2018), and hostage negotiations (Taylor & Thomas, 2008). Its utility is clear from evidence that influence targets underestimate its force (Bailenson & Yee, 2005; Gonzales et al., 1983) as well as from its *coached* enhancement of restaurant servers' tips (van Baaren et al., 2003), electronics salespersons' profits (Jacob et al., 2011), negotiators' outcomes (Maddux, Mullen, & Galinsky, 2008; Moore et al., 1999; Morris et al., 2002; Swaab, Maddux, & Sinaceur, 2011), and speed-daters' romantic wins (Guéguen, 2009).

6.   The idea that people typically attend more to differences than commonalities was supported by Houston, Sherman, & Baker (1991) and Olson & James (2002); however, these results were found in Western cultures. Although I know of no research into the matter, it would be worth knowing if the same pattern would appear in Eastern cultures, where, traditionally, harmony is emphasized. The analysis of thirty-two negotiation studies involved more than five thousand participants and was performed by Thompson & Hrebec (1996). The research demonstrating that people initially underestimate the favorability of their later interactions with out-group members (Mallett, Wilson, & Gilbert, 2008) found that men and women were equally susceptible to this mistake. Apparently, women's well-known tendencies toward interpersonal harmony are not enough to protect them from this error when another is from an out-group.

7.   The brain-imaging study was conducted at UCLA's Brain Mapping Center by Sherman et al. (2016). It is interesting that in the context of studies showing that compliments delivered by humans stimulate significant amounts of liking in response (Higgins & Judge, 2004; Seiter, 2007; Seiter & Dutson, 2007), the authors of the study of machine-based compliments have argued that *their* results are due to the same psychological tendencies and that, therefore, designers should build frequent praise into software programs (such as "Your careful work is impressive" or "Good thinking!") and to do so "even when there may be little basis for the evaluation" (Fogg & Nass, 1997b).

8.   The study showing that our susceptibility to praise that is insincere or offered in pursuit of a clear ulterior motive (Drachman, deCarufel, & Insko, 1978) has been supported by subsequent research (Chan & Sengupta, 2010; Vonk, 2002). I'm as susceptible as anyone. After my election to a certain scientific soci-

ety, I received a congratulatory note from one of my state's elected representatives praising my "dedication to excellence." Although I knew the note was an electoral tactic designed to curry favor, I liked her more afterward. See Vonk (2002) for evidence that observers who suspect a flatterer is being insincere assign the flatterer an ulterior motive for the praise; thus, although *recipients* of flattery tend to believe both sincere and insincere praise, there *is* a penalty for insincere flattery—surrounding onlookers register it for what it is and dislike the flatterer.

9. I am not the only one who has trouble giving compliments. Most people do—for one reason, they underestimate the positive effect of compliments on recipients (Boothby & Bons, 2020; Zhao & Epley, 2020). The tendency of people to arrange to be associated with good news and avoid being associated with bad news, even if they didn't cause it, has been confirmed by Rosen & Tesser (1970); furthermore, this tendency seems to appear because people recognize that they acquire the character of the messages they bring (John, Blunden, & Liu, 2019). The advantage that behind-the-back compliments have of avoiding the perception of an ulterior motive is considerable. Research by Main, Dahl, & Dark (2007) shows that in situations where an ulterior motive is suspected, flattery has an automatic negative impact on trust.

10. Altercasting was first described as an influence technique by sociologists Eugene Weinstein and Paul Deutschberger (1963); since then, its theoretical development has been advanced primarily by the psychologist Anthony Pratkanis (2000, 2007; Pratkanis & Uriel, 2011). Journalist Elizabeth Bernstein (2016) has provided a popular-press account of how altercasting works; see www.wsj.com /articles/if-you-want-to-persuade-people-try-altercasting-1473096624. It's demonstrably the case that attributing a praiseworthy trait to either children (Cialdini et al., 1998; Miller, Brickman, & Bollen, 1975) or adults (Kraut, 1973; Strenta & DeJong, 1981) can produce more trait-like behavior as a consequence.

11. The study of true-versus–reverse-image photographs (Mita, Dermer, & Knight, 1977) has been extended in research by Cho & Schwarz (2010). Instructions for how to reverse the image of a selfie can be found at https://webcazine .com/17190/qa-can-you-flip-or-mirror-a-picture-using-the-native-photo-editor -on-samsung-galaxy-phone. The positive effect of familiarity on liking has been reported in multiple settings (Monahan, Murphy, & Zajonc, 2000; Moreland & Topolinski, 2010; Reis et al., 2011; Verosky & Todorov, 2010).

Evidence that people come to believe the communications they are exposed to most frequently is both disturbing and compelling (Bornstein, Leone, & Galley, 1987; Fang, Singh, & Ahulwailia, 2007; Moons, Mackie, & Garcia-Marques, 2009; Unkelbach et al., 2019), as is work indicating that the effect applies even to implausible claims such as those characteristic of "fake news" (Fazio, Rand, & Pennycook, 2019; Pennycook, Conner, & Rand, 2018). One set of reviewers of the truth-by-repetition phenomenon attributes it to a "fluency" effect in which repetition causes an idea to be easier to retrieve, picture, and process, giving it the psychological "feel" of the truth (Dechêne et al., 2010). Although acknowledging the role of fluency, other researchers have also pointed to the role of salience (the extent to which an item captures attention) in why relatively more exposures to an item make it seem more worthy (Mrkva & Van Boven, 2020).

12. Not only have researchers documented the beneficial effects of positive

contact on attitudes toward out-group members, such as individuals of different race (e.g., Onyeador et al., 2020; Shook & Fazio, 2008), ethnicity (e.g., Al Ramiah & Hewstone, 2013; Kende et al., 2018; Jackson et al., 2019), or sexual orientation (e.g., Tadlock et al., 2017); several have offered reasons for the benefit—including reduced anxiety (Pettigrew & Tropp, 2006; Wölfer et al., 2019), increased empathy (Al Ramiah & Hewstone, 2013; Hodson, 2011), and greater openness to experiences (Hodson et al., 2018).

Reasons for the failure of greater contact to improve attitudes in the schools (Stephan, 1978) can be understood as flowing from tendencies for racial self-separation (Dixon, Durrheim, & Tredoux, 2005; Oskamp & Schultz, 1998) and for multiple negative experiences there, which reverse increased contact's positive effect and turn it more intensely negative (Barlow et al., 2012; Ilmarinen, Lönnqvist, & Paunonen, 2016; McKeown & Dixon, 2017; Richeson & Shelton, 2007).

13. The long quote describing the competitive nature of the typical American classroom (Aronson, 1975, pp. 44, 47), as well as evidence of the transformative impact of the jigsaw classroom program can be found in the work of Elliot Aronson and his collaborators (see Aronson et al., 1978, for a summary). Other versions of cooperative learning procedures in different school systems—and even different types of institutions such as business organizations (Blake & Mouton, 1979)—have produced similar outcomes (Johnson, 2003; Oskamp & Shultz, 1998; Roseth, Johnson, & Johnson, 2008).

14. The classic research of Sherif and coworkers (1961) has been supported by other researchers (Paolini et al., 2004; Wright et al., 1997), who confirmed that a shift from rivals to friends is made possible by the shift from competition to cooperation. The studies showing that beginning a negotiation with a handshake enhances the joint outcomes of the bargaining parties (Schroeder et al., 2019) makes me think the effect might be strengthened if, after a lunch break, the parties shook hands again. Although considerable evidence establishes the typical superiority of cooperative approaches to other forms of interpersonal orientations (Johnson, 2003; Roseth, Johnson, & Johnson, 2008; Stanne, Johnson, & Johnson, 1999), it would be naive to think that cooperative acts would be always best or even always effective. For instance, if a bargainer were to initiate a handshake every few minutes throughout a negotiation, my guess is that the tactic would foster suspicion and the effect would be toxic. As other research has indicated, installing cooperative-learning programs isn't universally successful (Rosenfeld & Stephan, 1981; Slavin, 1983), competition can sometimes prove useful (Murayama & Elliot, 2012), and invariant prescriptions for cooperation can backfire (Cikara & Paluck, 2013).

The conception of hell and heaven attributable to Rabbi Haim of Romshishok appears in analogous versions within Buddhist, Christian, and Hindu religious traditions. Although the details can change—for instance, instead of rigid elbow joints, inhabitants can be equipped with spoons or chopsticks too long to feed themselves—the lesson of cooperation as a heavenly solution to human problems surfaces in each.

15. It's remarkable how innocent the delivers of bad news were in studies showing resulting hostility toward them from recipients. In any rational view, they were not responsible for the distasteful news; they had just been assigned to

report it and gave no indication of enjoying doing so (Blunden, 2019; Manis, Cornell, & Moore, 1974). There's no doubt that such innocent associations apply to both negative and positive connections; for example, listening to liked or disliked music affects product preferences favorably or unfavorably, respectively (Gorn, 1982). For additional evidence of the two-way impact of mere associations, see Hofmann et al. (2010), Hughes et al. (2019), and Jones (2009). The evidence that observers assume we have the same traits as our friends (Miller et al., 1966) and that an attractive model in an automobile ad influences men to like the car more (Smith & Engel, 1968) has been long available.

The findings on the effects of credit cards on willingness to pay (Feinberg, 1986, 1990) have been extended by McCall & Belmont (1996) to the size of tips in restaurants and by Prelec & Simester (2001) to payments for tickets to a sports event; in the latter case, fans were willing to spend over 100 percent more to see a professional basketball game when paying by credit card versus cash.

16. The paragraph-long commentary on today's "natural-is-better bias" came from Meier, Dillard, & Lappas (2019). The Olympic Games aren't the only sports events that corporations spend big money to sponsor. For the 2018–19 season, corporate sponsorships of the National Football Association totaled $1.39 billion. When Papa John's Pizza ended its sponsorship as "Official Pizza of the NFL," Wall Street investors took note, and its stock price dropped by 8 percent immediately (https://thehustle.co/why-do-brands-want-to-sponsor-the-nfl). Journalists have documented the impact of popular cultural phenomena on purchases of incidentally related consumer products such as Mars candy bars (White, 1997) and the Nissan Rogue (Bomey, 2017). But it was researchers who uncovered the connection of Sale signs to purchasing rates above those warranted by financial savings (Naylor, Raghunathan, & Ramanathan, 2006).

17. Of course, Gregory Razran's (1938, 1940) "luncheon technique" research was preceded by Pavlov's (1927) discovery of classical conditioning on which the technique is based. Li et al. (2007) performed the work extending Razran's findings regarding smells to odors so faint that subjects could not knowingly sense them. The evidence is overwhelming that, like Pavlov's dogs, we can be susceptible to strategically fashioned pairings and clueless about our susceptibility. For instance, to the delight of advertisers, simply superimposing a brand of Belgian beer five times onto pictures of pleasant activities, such as sailing, waterskiing, and cuddling, increased observers' positive feeling toward the beer (Sweldens, van Osselaer, & Janiszewski, 2010); similarly superimposing a brand of mouthwash onto pictures of beautiful nature scenes six times led observers to feel more favorably toward the brand right away and *still* three weeks afterward (Till & Priluck, 2000); and subliminally exposing thirsty people eight times to pictures of happy (versus angry) faces just before having them taste a new soft drink caused them to consume more of the drink and to be willing to pay three times more for it in the store (Winkielman, Berridge, & Wilbarger, 2005). In none of these studies were the participants aware they'd been influenced by the pairings. Just because we are often surreptitiously influenced by mere associations doesn't mean we don't recognize how they work, as is evident from the research (Rosen & Tesser, 1970) on our strong proclivity to connect ourselves to good news and distance ourselves from bad news.

18.   Although my research team (Cialdini et al., 1976) conducted the original basking-in-reflected-glory research on American football fans, it has been replicated with French and English soccer fans (Bernache-Assolant, Lacassagne, & Braddock, 2007; Fan et al., 2019) and postelection voters in the Netherlands and the United States (Boen et al., 2002; Miller, 2009). Additional research indicates a reason for the practice: it works. Carter and Sanna (2006) found that individuals who were able to assert a connection to a successful sports team gained favorability in the eyes of observers; however, in keeping with the principle of association, this effect reversed if observers didn't view the successful team favorably. Tal-Or (2008) found that the basking-in-reflected-glory effect applied to a specific and desirable form of evaluation from others. Individuals who claimed a close association ("good friend") to a successful basketball player were rated by observers as more successful themselves.

Chapter 4: Social Proof

1.   As another measure of the strength and ease of implementation of the "most popular dishes" tactic, the Beijing restaurant chain (Mei Zhou Dong Po) has since incorporated it into *all* its locations (Cai, Chen, & Fang, 2009). The impact of the London brewery's bar sign was reported by advertising expert Richard Shotton, who designed the test (Shotton, 2018). Research on McFlurry choices was conducted by my InfluenceAtWork.com colleagues Steve J. Martin and Helen Mankin under the auspices of Dan Gertsacov, at the time the chief marketing officer of Arcos Dorados S.A., which owned the McDonald's locations in Latin America. For additional details on this and other McDonald's studies done by our team, go to www.influenceatwork.com/wp-content/uploads/2020/03/Persuasion-Pilots-McDonalds-Arcos-Dorados-INFLUENCE-AT-WORKpdf.pdf.

The lesson that popularity begets popularity also emerges from research into music-download choices. If, on a music site, a never-before-heard song was designated (at random by researchers) as popular, it became more popular (Salganik, Dodds, & Watts, 2006). Results like these fit with evidence that people believe, correctly, that the crowd is typically right (Surowiecki, 2004). For an extensive exploration of the rise of popularity in today's information environment, see Derek Thompson's (2017) engaging book on the topic, which confirms the tongue-in-cheek observation we could make that "Popularity these days is all the rage."

2.   The experiment showing the effect of social-proof information on estimates of morality was conducted by Aramovich, Lytle, & Skitka (2012). See Barnett, Sanborn, & Shane (2005) for the research showing that perceptions of the frequency of crimes by others are related to possible perpetrators' likelihood of performing the crimes themselves. Besides the bad news that when people perceive partner violence as frequent, they are more likely to engage in it (Mulla et al., 2019), there is the good news that when they get evidence that bad behavior is not the social norm, they refrain from it (Paluck, 2009). The data indicating that 98 percent of online shoppers prioritize authentic customer reviews most when making purchase decisions comes from a survey in *Search Engine Journal* (Nijjer, 2019). Marijn Stok and her associates (2014) did the research on Dutch teens' fruit consumption. The city of Louisville's success in getting parking-

ticket holders to pay on time was reported by the Behavioral Insights Team on p. 29 of *Behavioral Insights for Cities* (www.bi.team/wp-content/uploads/2016/10 /Behavioral-Insights-for-Cities-2.pdf). The research into face-mask wearing in Japan was conducted by Nakayachi et al. (2020). For reviews of the effectiveness of social-proof interventions on various forms of pro-environmental action, see Andor & Fels (2018), Bergquist, Nilsson, & Schultz (2019), and Farrow, Grolleau, & Ibanez (2017). Countries using social proof to reduce corporate pollution are Indonesia (Garcia, Sterner, & Afsah, 2007) and India (Powers et al., 2011). Albert Bandura and his coworkers performed the work on how to reduce children's fear of dogs via social proof in a pair of famous studies (Bandura, Grusec, & Menlove, 1967; Bandura & Menlove, 1968).

3.   Perhaps because of the quality of ragged desperation with which they approached their task, the believers were wholly unsuccessful at enlarging their number. According to Festinger, Riecken, & Schachter (1964), not a single convert was gained. At that point, in the face of the dual failures of physical and social proof, the cult quickly disintegrated. Less than three weeks after the date of the predicted flood, group members were scattered and maintained only sporadic communication with one another. In one final—and ironic—disconfirmation of prediction, it was the movement that perished in the flood.

Ruin has not always been the fate of doomsday groups whose predictions proved unsound, however. When such groups have been able to build social proof for their beliefs through effective recruitment efforts, they have grown and prospered. For example, when the Dutch Anabaptists saw their prophesied year of destruction, 1533, pass uneventfully, they became rabid seekers after converts, pouring unprecedented amounts of energy into the cause. One extraordinarily eloquent missionary, Jakob van Kampen, is reported to have baptized one hundred persons in a single day. So powerful was the snowballing social evidence in support of the Anabaptist position that it rapidly overwhelmed the disconfirming physical evidence and turned two-thirds of the population of Holland's great cities into adherents. More recent evidence supports the idea that when their central beliefs are undermined, people engage in efforts to persuade others to those beliefs as a way to restore their validity (Gal & Rucker, 2010).

4.   The scientific literature is clear that attention to the actions of others is intensified under conditions of uncertainty because those actions serve to reduce the uncertainty (Sechrist & Stangor, 2007; Sharps & Robinson, 2017; Wooten & Reed, 1998; Zitek & Hebl, 2007). For the Sylvan Goldman story, see Dauten (2004) and www.wired.com/2009/06/dayintech-0604.

Besides a lack of familiarity with a particular situation, another kind of uncertainty occurs when we don't have much confidence in our existing preferences on an issue. In that case, we are again especially influenced by social proof. Take as evidence the results of one more study done in Latin American McDonald's restaurants by my InfluenceAtWork.com colleagues Steve J. Martin and Helen Mankin. Most McDonald's customers don't purchase a dessert with their order; hence, they don't have confidence in their preferences toward the range of dessert selections there. Consequently, when given the social-proof information that a McFlurry was the favorite choice, their likely purchase of a McFlurry rose significantly. But most McDonald's customers *do* have a lot of experience with the burgers there. With that confidence of what they preferred already in place, when told the favorite burger selection at the restaurant, this information did not affect their burger choices. For additional details on this and other McDonald's studies done by our team, see www.influenceatwork.com/wp-content/uploads/2020/03/Persuasion-Pilots-McDonalds-Arcos-Dorados-INFLUENCE-AT-WORKpdf.pdf.

Finally, in one study, participants who were hooked up to brain-imaging equipment saw product reviews of consumer items available on Amazon. The participants with low levels of confidence in their own initial opinions of the products became especially likely to move in the direction of others' reviews as they saw more and more of them. This greater influence was registered in a sector of the brain associated with perceived value—the dorsomedial prefrontal cortex (De Martino et al., 2017).

5.   The famous, and now infamous, account of the Genovese neighbors' "apathy" was presented in detail first in a long, front-page *New York Times* article (Gansberg, 1964) and later in a book by the *Times* metropolitan editor A. M. Rosenthal (1964). Early work successfully challenging many of the central details of these accounts can be credited to Manning, Levine, & Collins (2007); see also Philpot et al. (2020). Evidence for the pluralistic-ignorance phenomenon was provided by Latané and Darley (1968), whereas evidence that it and bystander inaction are unlikely to occur when observers are confident that an emergency exists can be seen in Clark and Word (1972, 1974) as well as in Fischer et al. (2011). Shotland and Straw (1976) conducted the studies on what a woman should shout to get bystander assistance when in a physical confrontation with a man.

6.   The New York City study on looking up in a crowd (Milgram, Bickman, & Berkowitz, 1969) was replicated by investigators who found a similar pattern nearly a half-century later and in a different place, Oxford, England (Gallup et al., 2012). See Fein, Goethals, & Kugler (2007) and Stewart et al., (2018) for the work on the contagious effects of audience reactions at US presidential debates.

7.   Josef Adalian, "Please Chuckle Here," *New York Magazine*, November 23, 2011, http://nymag.com/arts/tv/features/laughtracks-2011-12/; "How Do Laugh Tracks Work?" www.youtube.com/watch?v=-suD4KbgTl4).

8.   Researchers from the Alfresco Labs performed the shopping-mall study; see www.campaignlive.co.uk/article/behavioural-economics-used-herd-shoppers/1348142. Freling & Dacin (2010) collected the data showing the greater and greater effectiveness of ads reporting higher and higher percentages of others' preference for the advertised brand. The fruit-fly research was done by Danchin et al. (2018). Doug Lansky (2002) reported his experience at the Royal Ascot Races in his newspaper travel column "Vagabond Roaming the World." Charles MacKay's account of the 1761 London earthquake panic appeared in his classic book, *Extraordinary Popular Delusions and the Madness of Crowds* (1841). For a detailed account of the consequences of the cascading white-van frenzy, see www.insider.com/suspicious-white-van-unfounded-facebook-stories-causing-mass-hysteria-2019-12.

Other evidence is available for the validation component of social proof. In one study, children six to eleven years old given information that the other kids in the study had chosen to eat a lot of carrots responded by eating more of their own carrots—*because* that information gave them confidence that eating carrots was a good choice (Sharps & Robinson, 2017). An online consumer-choice experiment showed a similar effect. Participants who learned that two-thirds of the bottles of a particular wine had already been sold were more willing to purchase that wine than if they learned that only one-third of the bottles had been sold. Why? Because they assigned greater quality to the wine if its sales were stronger (van Herpen, Pieters, & Zeelenberg, 2009).

9. The data on Italian residents' willingness to recycle household waste was collected in the cities of Rome, Cagliari, Terni, and Macomer by Fornara et al. (2011). My colleagues and I collected our data on household energy conservation in San Marcos, California, where, in addition to the effects I have described, we learned something else we found noteworthy. Our study included two control groups—one set of residents who received a message urging them to save energy but providing no stated reason for it and a second set of residents who received no message at all. Those two control groups were not different from one another in the subsequent energy they used (Nolan et al., 2008). In other words, simply exhorting people to conserve had the same impact as nothing. People want reasons to act. The important question is, of course, Which reasons are particularly mobilizing? In our study, easily the most persuasive reason to conserve energy in the home was that most of one's neighbors were doing so.

10. When people desire social approval, they are more likely to conform to the group mind on an issue; more perilously, they are also more likely to conform to the alcohol-consumption levels of the group (Cullum et al., 2013). Berns et al. (2005) collected the data showing greater conformity and greater psychological pain when people feel out of keeping with the opinions of other people (versus computers); see Ellemers & van Nunspeet (2020) for additional such evidence. For a description of cult "love bombing," see Hassan (2000).

11. Several research teams have confirmed that worried students' adjust better when informed that other students like them have overcome their similar concerns (Binning et al., 2020; Borman et al., 2019; Stephens et al., 2012; Wilson & Linville, 1985). The work on adolescent aggression was reviewed by Jung, Busching, & Krahé (2019). Boh & Wong (2015) did the study showing that coworkers use one another rather than managers to decide whether to share information. Studies demonstrating that physicians' prescribing practices conform to peer norms were reported by Fox, Linder, & Doctor (2016), Linder et al. (2017), and Sacarny et al. (2018). Robert Frank's review of the impact of peer behavior on environmental action is contained in his book, *Under the Influence: Putting Peer Pressure to Work* (2020). For additional evidence of the impact of peer-suasion on pro-environmental action, see Nolan et al. (2021), Schultz (1999), and Wolske, Gillingham, & Schultz (2020). Finally, college students' attitudes toward minority groups can be modified by information about their peers' attitudes (Murrar, Campbell, & Brauer, 2020).

12. It was Aune & Basil (1994) who hypothesized correctly that donations would rise after having an on-campus charity requester say, "I'm a student here, too." The studies showing the influence of same-age peers were done by Murray et al. (1984) within an antismoking program and Melamed et al. (1978) for dental anxieties. The success of Opower's Home Energy Reports containing peer consumption comparisons has been documented by Allcott (2011), Allcott & Rogers

(2014), and Ayres, Raseman, & Shih (2013); although Opower's reports have been delivered by mail, they work just as well when delivered electronically (Henry, Ferraro, & Kontoleon, 2019). Because of a corporate buyout, Opower's name has changed to Oracle Utilities/Opower.

13.   Phillips's sequence of investigations began with the Werther effect (Phillips, 1974, 1979)—the modern-day operation of which can be found in the study of the *13 Reasons Why* Netflix web series (Bridge et al., 2019)—and continued with his examination of the impact of widely publicized suicide stories on plane and automobile fatalities (Phillips, 1980). The story of contagious train suicides in a California high school was recounted by *Los Angeles Times* reporter Maria La Ganga (2009). Sumner, Burke, & Kooti (2020) provide a review of the role of the media in the contagiousness of suicide. A description of the infectious nature of product-tampering episodes is presented by Toufexis (1993). Mass murders in the United States are becoming more deadly and frequent over time—the largest total number of such deaths in recorded history, 224, occurred in 2017, whereas the largest number of incidents in recorded history, 41, occurred in 2019 (Pane, 2019). Evidence for the contagiousness of mass murder has been amassed by Towers et al. (2015) and reported on by Goode & Carey (2015) and Carey (2016).

Good accounts of the Jonestown massacre are provided by journalist J. Oliver Conroy in a 2018 retrospective (www.theguardian.com/world/2018/nov/17/an -apocalyptic-cult-900-dead-remembering-the-jonestown-massacre-40-years-on) and by survivor Tim Reiterman in his 2008 book on the matter. The analysis of factors affecting brands' market share was conducted by Bronnenberg, Dhar, & Dubé (2007), whose findings fit with research showing large personality and attitude differences between people who live in different regions (Rentfrow, 2010).

14.   The research on eating-disorder, suicide-prevention, and alcohol-deterrence programs was conducted by Mann et al. (1997), Shaffer et al. (1991), and Donaldson et al. (1995), respectively. In more recent research on programs designed to reduce stereotyping, informing participants that stereotyping was regrettably prevalent led them to exhibit more stereotyping (Duguid & Thomas-Hunt, 2015). The study my team and I performed in the Petrified Forest National Park is described more fully in Cialdini (2003).

Unfortunately, after we reported the outcomes of our study to park administrators, they decided not to change the relevant aspects of their signage. This decision was based on evidence from a survey they subsequently performed in which park personnel questioned several visitors, who said that information indicating the theft problem at the park was sizable would *not* increase their likelihood of stealing wood but would decrease it. We were disappointed—but, truth be told, not surprised—that in their signage decision, park officials weighted visitors' subjective responses to hypothetical questions more heavily than our experimentally based empirical evidence, as it confirms what appears to be a lack of understanding within the larger society of what constitutes confidence-worthy research results (Cialdini, 1997).

15.   The tendency for people to expect a trend to continue has been documented by Hubbard (2015), Maglio & Polman (2016), Markman & Guenther (2007), and Maus, Goh, & Lisi (2020). Our research into the effects of a trend on water conservation also included a study with similar results on willingness to com-

plete a survey without pay (Mortensen et al., 2017). In addition, researchers have demonstrated the positive impact of trends on other low-prevalence behaviors such as eating meatless meals (Sparkman & Walton, 2017), reducing sugar consumption (Sparkman & Walton, 2019), choosing reusable drinking cups in a cafeteria (Loschelder et al., 2019), and—among female high school and college students—intending to pursue STEM fields for future study (Cheng et al., 2020).

16. It is perhaps no accident that the events leading to the bank crash took place in Singapore (News, 1988), as research tells us that citizens of Far Eastern societies have a greater tendency to respond to social-proof information than do those from Western cultures (Bond & Smith, 1996). But any culture that values the group over the individual exhibits this greater susceptibility to information about peers' choices. A few years ago, some of my colleagues and I showed how this tendency operated in Poland, a country whose population is moving toward Western values but still retains a more communal orientation than do average Americans. We asked college students in Poland and the United States whether they would be willing to participate in a marketing survey. For the American students, the best predictor of their decision was information about how often they, themselves, had agreed to marketing-survey requests in the past; this is in keeping with the primarily individualistic point of reference of most Americans. For the Polish students, however, the best predictor of their decisions was information about how often their friends had agreed to marketing-survey requests in the past; this is in keeping with the more collectivistic values of their nation (Cialdini et al., 1999). Of course, as the evidence from this chapter shows, social proof also works forcefully in predominantly individualistic cultures, such as the United States. For instance, the data showing the deadly influence of social proof on the decisions of airplane pilots came from American flights (Facci & Kasarda, 2004).

Chapter 5: Authority

1. Additional reasons I think that "behavioral science is so hot now" are explicated in Cialdini (2018). The BIT charity study is described in *The Behavioural Insights Team Update, 2013–2015* report, www.bi.team/publications/the-behavioural -insights-team-update-report-2013-2015. For a history of the unit and a description of much the early work of the BIT as written by one of its founders, see Halpern (2016). Although in the BIT charity study combining two principles of influence had the greatest effect on donations, it would be a mistake to assume that inserting more than one principle into a persuasive message will always increase its impact. Shoehorning multiple tactics into the same communication can alert recipients to a heavy-handed effort to persuade them, which can have the opposite effect (Friestad & Wright, 1995; Law & Braun, 2000; Shu & Carlson, 2014).

2. The basic experiment, as well as his other variations on it, are presented in Milgram's highly readable *Obedience to Authority* (1974) as well as in Doliński & Grzyb's excellent *Social Psychology of Obedience toward Authority* (2020). A variety of reviews of subsequent research on obedience since the Milgram work concluded that the levels of obedience he found in his procedure in the United States in the 1960s are remarkably similar to those of more recent time periods

(Blass, 2004; Burger, 2009; Doliński et al., 2017; "Fake Torture TV 'Game Show' Reveals Willingness to Obey," www.france24.com/en/20100317-fake-torture-tv -game-show-reveals-willingness-obey) and similar to those in other countries.

In this latter respect, Milgram first began his investigations in an attempt to understand how the German citizenry could have participated in the concentration-camp destruction of millions of innocents during the years of Nazi ascendancy. After testing his experimental procedures in the United States, he had planned to take them to Germany, a country whose populace he was sure would provide enough obedience for a full-blown scientific analysis of the concept. The first eye-opening experiment in New Haven, Connecticut, however, made it clear that he could save his money and stay close to home. "I found so much obedience," he said, "I hardly saw the need of taking the experiment to Germany." But Americans have no monopoly on the need to obey authority. When Milgram's basic procedure was eventually repeated elsewhere (South Africa, the Netherlands, Germany, Austria, Spain, Italy, Australia, India, and Jordan), the results were on average similar (see Blass, 2012; and Meeus & Raaijmakers, 1986, for reviews).

The decades-long Milgram saga has something of a detective-story ending. The journalist Gina Perry was able to get access to the archive at Yale University where Milgram's papers are kept and where she discovered the procedures and findings of a study he never published. In it, each Teacher was instructed to deliver a shock to a Learner whom he thought was a friend or neighbor. Compliance with the experimenter's orders was drastically different as a consequence. Compared to the 65 percent of subjects who typically obeyed the experimenter to the end in Milgram's paradigm, only 15 percent did so under these circumstances. This outcome fits well with evidence we'll see in chapter 8 that compared to strangers or mere acquaintances, people are massively more likely to take the side of individuals with whom they feel a sense of unity, such as friends, neighbors, or kin. In addition to Perry's book-length account (2012), Rochat & Blass (2014) have authored an academic article describing Milgram's "secreted study."

3. The alarming statistics regarding the frequency and impact of medical errors come from analyses by Szabo (2007), Makary & Daniel (2016), and Wears & Sutcliffe (2020), respectively. Regrettably, the situation hasn't improved since "To Err Is Human," the first report on the magnitude of medical error in the United States by the Institute of Medicine over two decades ago. As the researcher Kathleen Sutcliffe (2019) points out, much of the problem is attributable not to how the human body works but, rather, to how human psychology works.

4. The research showing the physical "growth" of classroom lecturers, politicians, and task participants based on their perceived status was conducted by Wilson (1968), Higham & Carment (1992), Sorokowski (2010), and Duguid & Goncalo (2012). Additionally, politicians who are taller than their opponents typically receive more votes (McCann, 2001). For instance, since 1900, the US presidency has been won by the taller of the major-party candidates in nearly 90 percent of the elections. So, in people's minds, status doesn't just increase height; height increases status as well. Additional data collected in the Hofling et al. (1966) study of nurses suggest that nurses may not be conscious of the extent to which the title "doctor" sways their judgments and actions. A separate group of 33 nurses and student nurses was asked what they would have done in the

experimental situation. Contrary to the actual findings, only two predicted they would have given the medication as ordered.

More complete treatments of how hackers use psychology to breach elaborate security protections are available. One benefits from the coauthorship of Keven Mitnick, the acknowledged king of security hackers (Sagarin & Mitnick, 2012). The other offers a thoroughgoing, book-length description (Hadnagy & Schulman, 2020).

5. The studies of the compliance-enhancing effects of an authoritative uniform were done by Bickman (1974) and Bushman (1988); in a related update, Smith, Chandler, & Schwarz (2020) found that people who receive poor service from a company's employee are more likely to blame the organization rather than the employee if the employee was wearing a uniform while providing the service. The jaywalking study was done by Lefkowitz, Blake, & Mouton (1955); Doob & Gross (1968) performed the prestige-versus–economy car experiment. Nelissen & Meijers (2011) collected the data showing the positive impact of prestige clothing on survey participation, charity donations, and job-interview ratings, whereas Oh, Shafir, & Todorov (2020) conducted the research showing the practically instantaneous assignment of competence to wearers of higher- versus lower-quality clothing. These last authors commented on a troubling aspect of their results—individuals from poorer economic backgrounds who are unable to afford expensive clothing are put at definite, automatically occurring disadvantage in employment interviews.

6. Michel Strauss's account comes from his book, *Pictures, Passion, and Eye* (2011). For a thoroughgoing treatment of the increasingly valued role of the expert in modern life, see Stehr & Grundmann (2011). The research on the "halo effect" of expertise in a therapist's office is attributable to Devlin et al. (2009), whereas the large impact of a single Op-Ed piece by an expert on readers' opinions was documented by Coppock, Ekins, & Kirby (2018), who showed this effect for both ordinary readers and professional "elites," such as think-tank scholars, journalists, bankers, law professors, congressional staffers, and academics. The willingness to follow those who appear to know what they are doing starts young, showing itself in preschoolers (Keil, 2012) and infants (Poulin-Dubois, Brooker, & Polonia, 2011).

For confirmation that both expertise and trustworthiness lead to perceived credibility and dramatically greater influence, see Smith, De Houwer, & Nosek (2013). The effectiveness in legal contexts of the "be the one to disclose a weakness" tactic has been demonstrated repeatedly (e.g., Dolnik, Case, & Williams, 2003; Stanchi, 2008; Williams, Bourgeois, & Croyle, 1993); the same tactic has proved effective for corporations that revealed negative information about themselves (Fennis & Stroebe, 2014). The information that politicians can increase their trustworthiness as well as their vote-worthiness by seemingly arguing against self-interest was provided by Cavazza (2016) and Combs & Keller (2010); a related effect in the political arena is that politicians who frame a message in negative terms ("15% are unemployed") versus positive terms ("85% are employed") are more persuasive with it because they are viewed as more trustworthy (Koch & Peter, 2017). The advertising agency Doyle Dane Bernbach (now DDB) was the first to produce hugely successful ads admitting to a weakness that was then countered by a strength, such as the "Ugly is only skin deep" and "It's ugly but it gets you there" ads for the early Volkswagen Beetle, as well as the game-changing "We're #2. We try harder" campaign for Avis Rent A Car. Since then, similarly worded promotions for products, such as Buckley's cough syrup ("It Tastes Awful. And It Works"), have also been highly effective. Ward & Brenner (2006) confirmed that an acknowledge-a-negative strategy is effective only when the negative occurs first.

7.   The team that successfully trained people to disregard ads featuring bogus experts—by recognizing their vulnerability to such experts and distinguishing between relevant and irrelevant expertise—was led by my colleague Brad Sagarin (Sagarin et al., 2002). The tendency to resonate with the appeals of experts who seem impartial and resist the appeals of experts who have something to gain from our compliance has been demonstrated around the world (Eagly, Wood, & Chaiken, 1978; McGuinnies & Ward, 1980; Van Overwalle & Heylighen, 2006) and in young children (Mills & Keil, 2005).

Chapter 6: Scarcity

1.   Research into the psychological primacy of loss as demonstrated in a university cafeteria (West, 1975), multiple countries (Cortijos-Bernabeu et al., 2020), multiple domains (Hobfoll, 2001; Sokol-Hessner & Rutledge, 2019; Thaler et al., 1997; Walker et al., 2018), managerial decisions (Shelley, 1994), professional golfers' efforts (Pope & Schweitzer, 2011), college students' emotions (Ketelaar, 1995), energy-provider preferences (Shotton, 2018), task performers' cheating choices (Effron, Bryan, & Murnighan, 2015; Kern & Chung, 2009; Pettit et al., 2016), and individuals' physical reactions (Sheng et al., 2020; see Yechiam & Hochman, 2012, for a review) demonstrates the widespread applicability of prospect theory (Kahneman & Tversky, 1979). Evidence from a variety of contexts indicates that loss aversion is particularly strong when risk and/or uncertainty are great (De Dreu & McCusker, 1997; Kahneman, Slovic, & Tversky, 1982; Walker et al., 2018; Weller et al., 2007), including the health/medical context (Gerend & Maner, 2011; Meyerwitz & Chaiken, 1987; Rothman & Salovey, 1997; Rothman et al., 1999). When risk and uncertainty are low, however, a promotive (rather than protective) orientation becomes dominant, and people value gains over losses (Grant Halvorson & Higgins, 2013; Higgins, 2012; Higgins, Shah, & Friedman, 1997; Lee & Aaker, 2004). The influence of scarcity on the judgments of new car buyers and fair-price judges can be seen in the findings of Balancher, Liu, & Stock (2009) and Park, Lalwani, & Silvera (2020), respectively.

2.   The results of several experiments show that consumers are strongly attracted to products and experiences that possess unique elements (Burger & Caldwell, 2011; Keinan & Kivetz, 2011; Reich, Kupor, & Smith, 2018). The evidence that after a scarce item has been restored to good supply, people lose attraction for it comes from Schwarz (1984). A related point—that a rare object we think we like for its inherent qualities may surprise us and lose its appeal once it loses its scarcity—is made persuasively in a Reader's Report I received from a Minneapolis woman: "Although I am from the U.S., I always loved putting together jigsaw puzzles of London's Big Ben. They were rare finds in the U.S. and exciting when I came across one. But, once eBay came along and I could search

for these puzzles on eBay, I started to find a lot of them and buying each one. I lost interest in them after that. Your book helped me realize that the scarcity of the Big Ben puzzles was more of the reason I wanted them than my fascination with Big Ben. At that point, after 23 years of loving to put together Big Ben puzzles, I had no more desire to put together another one, once I could find many of them."

3. For the research showing that people assign greater worth to entities that are difficult to obtain and that they are normally correct in this presumption, see Lynn (1989) and McKenzie & Chase (2010). So ingrained is the belief that what's scarce is valuable that we have come to believe that if something is valuable, it must be scarce (Dai, Wertenbroch, & Brendel, 2008). Jack Brehm formulated reactance theory in the mid-1960s (J. W. Brehm, 1966), and subsequent work has provided considerable support for it (e.g., Burgoon et al., 2002; Bushman, 2006; Dillard, Kim, & Li, 2018; Koch & Peter, 2017; Koch & Zerback, 2013; Miller et al., 2006; Schumpe, Belanger, & Nisa, 2020; Zhang et al., 2011). The study revealing reactant tendencies toward physical barriers in two-year-old boys was performed by S. S. Brehm & Weintraub (1977). Two-year-old girls in their study did not show the same resistant response to the large barrier as did the boys. Another study suggested this to be the case *not* because girls don't oppose attempts to limit their freedoms. Instead, it appears that they are primarily reactant to restrictions that come from other persons rather than from physical obstacles (S. S. Brehm, 1981). For both sexes, however, children come to see themselves as separate individuals at around eighteen to twenty-four months of age, when they first recognize their "cognitive self" (Southgate, 2020; Howe, 2003).

Driscoll, Davis, & Lipetz (1972) performed the initial work identifying the Romeo and Juliet effect. The occurrence of the Romeo and Juliet effect should not be interpreted as a warning to parents to be always accepting of their teenagers' romantic choices. New players at this delicate game are likely to err often and, consequently, would benefit from the direction of an adult with greater perspective and experience. In providing such direction, parents should recognize that teenagers, who see themselves as young adults, will not respond well to control attempts that are typical of parent–child relationships. Especially in the adult arena of mating, adult tools of influence (preference and persuasion) will be more effective than traditional forms of parental control (prohibitions and punishments). Although the experience of the Montague and Capulet families is an extreme example, heavy-handed restrictions on a young romantic alliance may well turn it clandestine, torrid, and sad.

The reach of reactance into supermarket shoppers' petition-signing decisions was identified by Heilman (1976). Moore & Pierce (2016) collected the data indicating that officials were more likely to punish rule violators on their birthdays and especially when the birthday was made salient; among the researchers' six studies of the phenomenon, one examined 134,000 drunk-driving arrests in Washington State and found that police officers penalized drivers more harshly on the offender's birthday. The investigation of the effects of a ban on phosphate detergents was done by Michael Mazis and colleagues (Mazis, 1975; Mazis, Settle, & Leslie, 1973), whereas early research on banned information was done by a wider range of researchers (Ashmore, Ramchandra, & Jones, 1971; Lieberman &

Arndt, 2000; Wicklund & Brehm, 1974; Worchel, 1992; Worchel & Arnold, 1973; Worchel, Arnold, & Baker, 1975; Zellinger et al., 1974). The study of the effects of commodity scarcity plus information exclusivity was done as a doctoral dissertation by Amram Knishinsky (1982); for ethical reasons, the information provided to the customers was always true—there *was* an impending foreign-beef shortage, and this news had indeed come to the company through its exclusive sources.

4. See research by Thomas Koch (Koch & Peter, 2017; Koch & Zerback, 2013) for evidence that the perceived intent to persuade generates reactance and the resultant reactance weakens message effectiveness. Nicolas Guéguen and his colleagues are responsible for developing and testing the "But you are free" technique (Guéguen et al., 2013; Guéguen & Pascual, 2000). The meta-analysis of forty-two experiments was performed by Carpenter (2013). More recently, Guéguen has constructed another reactance-based compliance tactic. Rather than reducing reactance against saying *yes* to a request via words such as "But, you are free to refuse," he builds reactance against saying *no* with the words "You'll probably refuse, but . . ." Adding "You will probably refuse but" to a request for donations to a children's health-care organization increased the percentage of donors in one study from 25 percent to 39 percent (Guéguen, 2016).

5. Worchel, Lee, & Adewole (1975) are to be credited with the famous chocolate-chip-cookie study. For marketing-oriented descriptions of the New Coke, story see Benjamin (2015) and C. Klein (2020); for an academic account based on scarcity and reactance, see Ringold (1988).

The work identifying reimposed deprivation as an initiating factor in political revolutions can be found in Davies (1962, 1969) and Fleming (1997); Lance Morrow's commentary (1991) on how the people of the Soviet Union staged a coup against a coup still stands up to the test of history. Studies demonstrating that the inconsistent granting of freedoms by parents leads to generally rebellious children were done by Lytton (1979) and O'Leary (1995). To avoid this last form of insurgency, parents needn't be severe or unduly rigid rule-keepers. For example, a child who unavoidably misses lunch can be given a before-dinner snack because this would not violate the normal rule against such snacks and, consequently, would not establish a general freedom. The difficulty comes when the child is capriciously allowed a treat on some days but not on others and can see no good reason for the difference. It is this arbitrary approach that can build perceived freedoms and provoke insurrection.

6. Advertisers employ limited offers in their messages in either limited-number or limited-time form. By far, limited-time offers are the more frequent—in one study of 13,594 newspaper ads, nearly three times as often (Howard, Shu, & Kerin, 2007). Yet research indicates that if they had the choice, advertisers would be better off using limited-number offers, which are superior in outcome—because only limited-number arrangements include the (potentially crazy-making) factor of interpersonal competition (Aggarwal, Jun, & Huh, 2011; Häubl & Popkowski Leszczyc, 2019; Teuscher, 2005).

7. The idea that in situations with new romantic opportunities, individuals seek to differentiate themselves has been validated in studies of animals (Miller, 2000) and humans (Griskevicius, Cialdini, & Kenrick, 2006). In the latter re-

search, when placed in a romantic state of mind, college students displayed significantly more creativity. The effect among humans is hardly restricted to college students. For example, each of Pablo Picasso's highly generative artistic periods (Blue, Rose, Cubist, and Surrealist) reveals a constant. As Griskevicius and colleagues state, "Each new epoch blossoms with paintings of a new woman—not a sitter or model, but a lover—each of whom is touted to have served Picasso as an incandescent, albeit temporary, muse (Crespelle, 1969; MacGregor-Hastie, 1988)." The research on the ad for the San Francisco Museum of Art was also led by my colleague, Vladas Griskevicius (Griskevicius et al., 2009). The claim that, in matters of opinion, people like to be in the majority but, in matters of taste, they do not is supported by Spears, Ellemers, & Doosje (2009). See Chan, Berger, & Van Boven (2012) for a full description of the research showing how in-group members balance the desire to conform to group taste preferences with the desire to express their individuality. The best reporting of General Shinseki's rationale for his decision to provide black berets to the great majority all US Army personnel, as well as of the problem it produced and his resolution of it come from the official US Military newspaper, *Stars and Stripes*, October 20, 2000.

8. Data documenting the emotional arousal and narrowed focus that accompanies limitations are compelling (Shah et al., 2015; Zhu & Ratner, 2015; Zhu, Yang, & Hsee, 2018). Usually marketing schemes that use deceptive restrictions of a product (via "manufactured scarcity") are kept hidden (www.wired.com /2007/11/best-buy-lying; www.nbcnews.com/technolog/dont-blame-santa-xbox -playstation-supply-probably-wont-meet-demand-6C10765763), but Kellogg's chose to publicize one such scheme as evidence of the value of their Rice Krispies Treats (www.youtube.com/watch?v=LKcoGtt91Js).

Chapter 7: Commitment and Consistency

1. For an instructive article on Amazon's "Pay to Quit" program, see www .cnbc.com/2018/05/21/why-amazon-pays-employees-5000-to-quit.html. Evidence of the ability of a commitment, once made, to drive subsequent responding has been found at the horse track (Knox & Inkster, 1968), in political elections (Regan & Kilduff, 1988), and within resource-conservation efforts (Abrahamse & Steg, 2013; Andor & Fels, 2018; Pallak, Cook, & Sullivan, 1980). General support for the existence of consistency pressures has been obtained in a wide variety of studies (Briñol, Petty, & Wheeler, 2006; Bruneau, Kteily, & Urbiola, 2020; Harmon-Jones, Harmon-Jones, & Levy, 2015; Ku, 2008; Mather, Shafir, & Johnson, 2000; Meeker et al., 2014; Rusbult et al., 2000; Stone & Focella, 2011; Sweis et al., 2018).

2. Although he wasn't the first prominent theorist to give the need for consistency a central place in human behavior, easily the most famous was Leon Festinger, whose cognitive dissonance theory (1957) begins with the assumption that we are uncomfortable with our inconsistencies and will take steps to reduce or remove them, even if it requires fooling ourselves to do so (see Aronson & Tavris [2020] for a modern application of this powerful formulation to the COVID-19 pandemic). Moriarty (1975) conducted the radio-theft experiment. Not only is inconsistency a negatively viewed trait in ourselves; we also dislike it in others (Barden, Rucker, & Petty, 2005; Heinrich & Borkenau, 1998; Wagner, Lutz, &

Weitz, 2009; Weisbuch et al., 2010). There is good evidence that consistent responding can occur in automatic fashion (Fennis, Janssen, & Vohs, 2009) both to avoid the undesired conclusions that rational thought can bring (Woolley & Risen, 2018) and simply to avoid the rigors of thinking, which can, as Sir Joshua Reynolds said, be laborious (Ampel, Muraven, & McNay, 2018; Wilson et al., 2014). Besides those benefits of a mechanical tendency toward consistency, it's also the case that the propensity to stay consistent with an initial interpretation or choice very often leads to accurate decisions (Qiu, Luu, & Stocker, 2020). Siegal (2018) offers a highly critical look at the history and business model of TM.

3.   It is both remarkable and instructive that relatively minor verbal commitments can lead to much larger behavior changes in such arenas as auto sales (Rubinstein, 1985), charitable volunteering (Sherman, 1980), Election Day voting (Greenwald et al., 1987; Spangenberg & Greenwald, 2001), in-home purchases (Howard, 1990), self-presentation (Clifford & Jerit, 2016), health-care choices (Sprott et al., 2006), and sexual infidelity (Fincham, Lambert, & Beach, 2010).

4.   Information about the psychological indoctrination programs of the Korean War is available in the reports of Drs. Edgar Schein (1956) and Henry Segal (1954). It is important to note that the widespread collaboration Schein and Segal documented was not always intentional. The American investigators defined collaboration as "any kind of behavior which helped the enemy," and it thus included such diverse activities as signing peace petitions, running errands, making radio appeals, accepting special favors, making false confessions, informing on fellow prisoners, divulging military information, and more.

The "How are you doing today?" study conducted by Daniel Howard (1990) was one of three he reported that showed the same pattern. See Carducci et al. (1989) and Schwartz (1970) for studies demonstrating the "momentum of compliance" effect. The initial data documenting the foot-in-the-door technique were collected by Freedman & Fraser (1966), but a variety of subsequent studies have supported its effectiveness; Doliński (2016) provides a review. Burger and Caldwell (2003) show how even trivial commitments can lead to self-concept change.

5.   The reason active, public, effortful, and freely chosen commitments change our self-images is that each element gives us information about what we must truly believe. If you perceive yourself committing to a particular position by taking action regarding it, you are likely to attribute to yourself a stronger personal belief in the position. The same would be true if you see yourself taking the position for all to see, in a way that requires a lot of effort on your part, because of an entirely voluntary choice. The consequent impact on your self-concept would likely lead to resilient and enduring shifts (Chugani, Irwin, & Redden, 2015; Gneezy et al., 2012; Kettle & Häubl, 2011; Sharot, Velasquez, & Dolan, 2010; Sharot et al., 2012; Schrift & Parker, 2014).

The idea that people use their own actions as a primary source for deciding who they are was first rigorously tested by Bem (1972) and has since received good confirmation (e.g., Burger & Caldwell, 2003; Doliński, 2000). Poza (2016) posted the article describing the advantages of registration forms that limited their first page to two or three fields of requested information. The evidence for greater compliance from actively made commitments comes from Cioffi & Garner (1996), as well as from other experiments (Allison & Messick, 1988; Fazio,

Sherman, & Herr, 1982; Silver et al., 2020). The tendency of observers to believe that the author of a statement believes it unless there is strong evidence to the contrary appeared in research by Allison et al. (1993), Gawronski (2003), and Jones & Harris (1967). The effects of giving people a label to live up to in the context of charity requests, supermarket purchases, and international negotiations were described by Kraut (1973), Kristensson, Wästlund, & Söderlund (2017), and Kissinger (1982), respectively.

6.   The claim that public commitments tend to be lasting commitments has been well supported (e.g., Dellande & Nyer, 2007; Lokhorst et al., 2013; Matthies, Klöckner, & Preißner, 2006; Nyer & Dellande, 2010). An interesting form of this support comes from work showing consumers to be more loyal to brands they use publicly versus privately (Khamitov, Wang, & Thomson, 2019). Evidence that we want both to be consistent within ourselves and to appear consistent to others has been provided by Schlenker, Dlugolecki, & Doherty (1994) and Tedeschi, Schlenker, & Bonoma (1971). The stubbornness that public commitments confer on initial choices that Deutsch & Gerard (1955) observed can be seen in the hungjury findings of Kerr & MacCoun (1985).

One piece of research (Gollwitzer et al., 2009) stands in stark contrast to the conclusion we have drawn about public commitments by reporting data suggesting that making a goal commitment public actually *reduces* one's likelihood of reaching the goal. After reviewing the extant literature, one set of researchers (H. J. Klein et al., 2020) expressed frustration that even though this contradictory data set has been the only one to find its pattern, it is the one receiving the most media coverage outside of academic circles—in blogs, popular books, and a TED talk seen by millions. How might we account for its atypical pattern? I believe that psychological reactance (see chapter 6) may have played a role. Recall that reactance theory asserts that people become less likely to undertake an action if (1) deciding whether to take the action represents an important freedom for them and (2) they experience external pressure to take the action. In the Gollwitzer et al. (2009) work, participants were first asked to specify how they would take steps to further their educational goals. Next, in order to make these steps *public*, some participants were required to submit them to an external evaluator, the experimenter, who judged the steps before allowing the participants to continue. Other participants, in the *private* condition, did not have to gain the experimenter's approval before being allowed to continue; they simply submitted their planned steps without the constraints of the experimenter's permission to continue. These procedures led participants to become less likely to take the specified steps toward their goal only if both (1) the goal was important to them and (2) they experienced the external barrier of having the steps permitted by the experimenter—exactly what reactance theory would predict.

7.   The effortful-commitment data from Hangzhou were collected by Xu, Zhang, & Ling (2018). Additional research into the greater impact of difficultly made commitments has revealed that people who pay for goods and services by using more psychologically uncomfortable means of payment (cash or checks versus credit or debit cards) become more committed to the transaction and brand and thus more likely to make a repeat purchase (Shah et al., 2015).

Although Whiting, Kluckhohn, & Anthony reported on the initiation rites of

South Africa's Thonga in 1958, not much about their severity has changed in the decades since. In May of 2013, for example, the South African government had to call a temporary halt to the initiation ceremonies of various tribes, including the Thonga, after twenty-three young initiates died within a span of nine days (Makurdi, 2013). A similar conclusion could be drawn regarding school fraternity's hazing ceremonies, which were first recorded in the United States at Harvard in 1657 and have remained present, intractable, and deadly ever since. For a manageably-sized summary, see Reilly (2017); but for a comprehensive and continually updated record of school hazings, go to the website of college professor Hank Nuwer (www.hanknuwer.com) and his multiple books on the topic, from which I gleaned most of my information. The research on the effects of arduousness—either in the form of embarrassment (Aronson & Mills 1959) or pain (Gerard & Mathewson, 1966)—on an entrant's positive responses to an opportunity has been extended to a commercial context; consumers given access to an exclusive one-day-sale offer were more favorable to the deal if getting that access was made effortful rather than easy (Barone & Roy, 2010).

8. The idea that paying people to take a stand produces greater commitment to it if they are paid a small versus large amount for the commitment has received steady support since it was first predicted (Festinger & Carlsmith, 1959). For example, in a more recent experiment, participants who put themselves in the position of referring a friend to a brand became more favorable and loyal to the brand when the monetary reward for the referral was small (Kuester & Blankenstein, 2014). In a similar vein, since its early demonstrations (Cooper & Fazio, 1984; Deci et al., 1982; Zuckerman et al., 1978), the idea that giving people free choice produces greater commitment has also continued to receive support (e.g., Shi et al., 2020; Geers et al, 2013; Staats et al., 2017; Zhang et al., 2011), including among infants (Silver et al., 2020). One reason voluntary choices strengthen commitments is that they activate our brains' reward sectors (Leotti & Delgado, 2011). Evidence that commitments are undermined when they are made because of external pressures such as large monetary rewards or punishments can be seen in the work of Deci & Ryan (1985), Higgins et al. (1995), and Lepper & Greene (1978). Finally, when commitments are made for internal rather than external reasons, they lead to greater psychological well-being. Muslim women in Saudi Arabia and Iran who wear a veil have greater life-satisfaction scores if they do so for internal reasons, such as personal preferences or values, rather than for external reasons, such as government controls or social approval (Legate et al., 2020).

9. For examples of how people support their commitments with new justifying reasons, see Brockner & Rubin (1985) and Teger (1980). In addition to the Cialdini et al. (1978) study, several other experiments attest to the success of the lowball procedure in a variety of circumstances and with both sexes (Brownstein & Katzev, 1985; Burger & Petty, 1981; Guéguen & Pascual, 2014), and Joule, 1987. Burger & Caputo (2015) report a meta-analysis confirming the tactic's effectiveness, as do Pascual et al. (2016) who support a commitment-based explanation for it. A full description of the Iowa energy-users study is provided in Pallak, Cook, & Sullivan (1980).

10. The Grant & Hofmann (2011) study also evaluated the impact of two other

signs placed over soap and gel dispensers, neither of which was designed to remind doctors of their commitment to *patient* safety ("Gel in, Wash Out" and "Hand hygiene protects you from catching diseases") and neither of which had any effect on soap or gel usage. Meeker et al. (2014) conducted the study on prescription of antibiotics, whereas the work on reminders of prior pro-environmental commitments was performed by Cornelissen et al. (2008) and Van der Werff, Steg, & Keizer (2014).

11.   It is not altogether unusual for even some of our most familiar quotations to be truncated by time in ways that greatly modify their character. For example, it is not money the Bible claims as the root of all evil; it's the love of money. So as not to be guilty of the same sort of error myself, I should note that the Emerson quote is somewhat longer and substantially more textured than I have reported. In full, it reads, "A foolish consistency is the hobgoblin of little minds, adored by little statesmen and philosophers and divines."

Evidence that we are sensitive to our feelings on a topic earlier than our cognitions regarding it comes from Murphy & Zajonc (1993) and van den Berg et al. (2006). This is not to say that what we feel about an issue is always different from or always to be trusted more than what we think about it. However, the data are clear that our emotions and beliefs often do not point in the same direction. Therefore, in situations involving a commitment likely to have generated supporting rationalizations, feelings may well provide the truer counsel. This would be especially so when, as in the question of Sara's happiness, the issue at hand concerns an emotion (Wilson et al., 1989).

12.   My team's work on a preference for consistency scale and the relationship of age to the preference for consistency appears in Cialdini, Trost, & Newsom (1995) and Brown, Asher, & Cialdini (2005), respectively. The analysis of the tapes of scammers attempting to defraud the elderly is contained in Pratkanis and Shadel's informative book *Weapons of Fraud: A Sourcebook for Fraud Fighters* (2005). There is good evidence of the tendency of US residents to be individualistic (Santos, Varnum, & Grossmann, 2017; Vandello & Cohen, 1999) and that this tendency inclines them toward consistency with their prior choices (Cialdini et al., 1999; Petrova, Cialdini, & Stills, 2007).

Chapter 8: Unity

1.   This chapter incorporates and updates some material from my book *Pre-Suasion: A Revolutionary Way to Influence and Persuade* (2016), with permission of the publisher Simon & Schuster. Evidence for the multifaceted positive effects of in-group favoritism comes from Guadagno & Cialdini (2007) and Stallen, Smidts, & Sanfey (2013) for agreement; Foddy, Platow, & Yamagishi (2009) and Yuki et al. (2005) for trust; Cialdini et al., (1997), De Dreu, Dussel, & Ten Velden (2015), Gaesser, Shimura, & Cikara (2020), and Greenwald & Pettigrew (2014) for help and liking; Balliet, Wu, & De Dreu (2014) and Buchan et al. (2011) for cooperation; Westmaas & Silver (2006) for emotional support; Karremans & Aarts (2007) and Noor et al. (2008) for forgiveness; Adarves-Yorno, Haslam, & Postmes (2008) for judged creativity; Gino & Galinsky (2012) and Leach, Ellemers, & Barreto (2007) for judged morality; and Brandt & Reyna (2011), Haslam (2006), Smith (2020), and Markowitz & Slovic (2020) for judged humanness. Evidence

that in-group favoritism appears in other primates and among human infants is available in Buttleman & Bohm (2014), Mahajan et al. (2011), and Over & McCall (2018).

2.   The cognitive confusion that arises among the identities of in-group members can be seen in their tendencies to project their own traits onto those group members (Cadinu & Rothbart, 1996; DiDonato, Ulrich, & Krueger, 2011), to poorly remember whether they had previously rated traits belonging to themselves or fellow in-group members (Mashek, Aron, & Boncimino, 2003), and to take longer to identify differentiating traits between themselves and in-group members (Aron et al., 1991; Otten & Epstude, 2006; Smith, Coats, & Walling, 1999). The neuroscientific evidence for the blurring of self and close-other representations locates their common brain sectors and circuits in the prefrontal cortex (Ames et al., 2008; Kang, Hirsh, & Chasteen, 2010; Cikara & van Bavel, 2014; Mitchell, Banaji, & Macrae, 2005; and Volz, Kessler, & von Cramon, 2009). Pfaff (2007, 2015) introduced the concept of neuronal "cross-excitation."

Other kinds of cognitive confusions also seem to be due to the brain's use of the same structures and mechanisms for distinct undertakings (Anderson, 2014). For example, the tendency of individuals who repeatedly imagine doing something then coming to believe that they have actually done it can be partially explained by research showing that performing an action and imagining performing it involve some of the same brain components (Jabbi, Bastiaansen, & Keysers, 2008; Oosterhof, Tipper, & Downing, 2012). In another illustration, the hurt of social rejection is experienced in the same brain regions as physical pain, which allows Tylenol to reduce the discomfort of both (DeWall et al., 2010).

3.   Shayo (2020) provides a thoroughgoing presentation of the evidence that shared identities within in-groups are consistently linked to favorability toward and conformity with fellow members. The study showing team members' outsized favorability toward the robots on their team was done by Fraune (2020). Clark et al. (2019) offer strong support for their claim that "Tribalism is human nature," as does Greene (2014); and, along with Greene, Tomasello (2020) argues that human groups have sought to fortify such tribalism by making it a moral duty.

4.   Not surprisingly, supporters of Joe Girard have challenged Ali Reda's claim to superior sales production. However, Mr. Reda's sales manager, who has access to dealership records, stands by the claims. Informative articles on the similarities and differences between Girard and Reda can be found at www.auto news.com/article/20180225/RETAIL/180229862/who-s-the-world-s-best-car -salesman and www.foxnews.com/auto/the-worlds-best-car-salesman-broke-a-44 -year-old-record-and-someones-not-too-pleased. Scientific research confirms the favorable impact of shared "we"-ness on sales outcomes: prospects were significantly more willing to accept a sales appeal to join a personal-training program if they and their future trainer had been born in the same community. Similarly, a sales appeal for a package of dental services was more successful if prospects learned that they had the same birthplace as the dentist they would see (Jiang et al., 2010).

5.   Dimmock, Gerken, & Graham (2018) did the work demonstrating that financial advisors became more likely to commit financial misconduct if, in their

offices, they had contact with a fellow advisor of the same ethnicity who had done so. The study of auditors' financial misstatements was done by Du (2019). Fisman, Paravisini, & Vig (2017) analyzed the effects of Indian loan office-applicant religious similarities on loan approvals, terms, and repayments. Customers' greater willingness to forgive a service error if they shared the service provider's last name was observed by Wan & Wyer (2019). In the Polish study using "lost" letters (Dolińska, Jarząbek, & Doliński, 2020), the letters were dropped around a mid-sized city at one hundred sites, including bus stops, shopping malls, cash machines, and sidewalks that were at least 250 meters from the nearest visible mailbox. Kristin Michelitch (2015) performed the taxi fare–bargaining study in locations around a centrally located market in the city of Accra.

6.   The report summarizing the science of "blue" lies (Smith, 2017) appeared in *Scientific American Online*: https://blogs.scientificamerican.com/guest-blog /how-the-science-of-blue-lies-may-explain-trumps-support; in a similar finding, people were willing to follow the norms of a group, even when they knew the norms to be unconnected to reality, provided they felt a strong shared identity with the group (Pryor, Perfors, & Howe, 2019). The research showing that highly identified political-party members are willing to hide the tax fraud of a fellow member (Ashokkumar, Galaif, & Swann, 2019), delude themselves regarding their party's superior contributions to community welfare (Blanco, Gómez-Fortes, & Matute, 2018), prioritize the medical treatment of same-party individuals (Furnham, 1966), and accept the judgments of poorly skilled same-party followers (Marks et al., 2019) fits with emerging scholarship indicating that political-party adherents base many of their political decisions less on ideology than on loyalties to such identity-defining parties and their members (Achen & Bartels, 2017; Iyengar, Sood, & Lelkes, 2012; Jenke & Huettel, 2020; Kalmoe, 2019; Schmitt et al., 2019). This view of mornality as based in in-group loyalties has become a central feature of modern political persuasion efforts (Buttrick, Molder, & Oishi, 2020). Ellemers & van Nunspeet (2020) provide an instructive summary of the neuropsychological mechanisms through which such in-group biases emerge.

Political parties are hardly the only "we"-based frameworks in which members are willing to conceal the wrongdoings of their partners. When questioned, people (1) expressed a strong bias against reporting to police the harmful action of a close other, such as a good friend or family member; (2) were particularly unwilling to make such a report when the harmful action was severe versus minor (e.g., burglary or physical sexual harassment versus illegal music downloading or staring-based sexual harassment); and (3) admitted the reason for this reluctance was to protect their *own* reputations (Weidman et al., 2020; see also Hildreth & Anderson, 2018, and Waytz, Dungan, & Young, 2013). Once again, we see that the "we" implicates the "me."

7.   Biased calls by international football (soccer), Major League Baseball, and National Basketball Association officiators were uncovered in research by, in turn, Pope & Pope (2015), Parsons et al. (2011), and Price & Wolfers (2010). The Asimov (1975) quote appeared in a *TV Guide* magazine article, in which he commented on the over-the-top bias of each US state for its candidate in the Miss America pageant of that year.

8.　For research documenting declines in the health of romantic partners if ongoing problems are not resolved, see Shrout et al. (2019). Women's health complications stemmed mainly from the amount of time that relationship disagreements remained unresolved; whereas, for men, it was the sheer number of unsettled disagreements. For both sexes, the impact on health could be seen for as long as sixteen years. The partnership-raising study, one of my all-time favorites, was done by Oriña, Wood, & Simpson (2002). For a full examination of the grounds for my assertion that "the thing most likely to guide a person's behavioral decisions . . . is the one most prominent in consciousness at the time of decision," see Cialdini (2016).

9.　The study showing the link between friends' levels of physical activity (Priebe & Spink, 2011) also found that participants underestimated their friends' influence on their activity production, mistakenly assigning greater influence to factors associated with health and personal appearance. Bond et al. (2012) conducted the Facebook voter-mobilization study. The study of best friends' potent impact on college student's drinking demonstrated this effect for both White students and Native American students (Hagler et al., 2017). In general, friends see and actually possess higher levels of genetic overlap with one another than with nonfriends (Cunningham, 1986; Christakis & Fowler, 2014; Daly, Salmon, & Wilson, 1997).

10.　Norscia & Palagi (2011) collected the data revealing the proportional relationship between human contagious yawning and the degree of personal connection between the yawners; they found the same relationship when the yawns were transmitted only acoustically (Norscia et al., 2020). Demonstrations of contagious yawning intensified by social bonds in chimpanzees, baboons, bonobos, and wolves are provided by Campbell & de Waal (2011), Palagi et al. (2009), Demuru & Palagi (2012), and Romero et al. (2014), respectively. Romero, Konno, & Hasegawa (2013) performed the experiment on cross-species contagious yawning.

Cat lovers, don't despair. That I haven't provided data showing contagious yawning between feline pets and their owners may not mean the effect doesn't exist. The lack of evidence might just come from the fact that researchers haven't yet tested the possibility—probably because it's difficult to get cats to stay still and focused long enough. Nonetheless, anyone who really wants to believe can take heart from this article: https://docandphoebe.com/blogs/the-catvocate-blog/why-do-animals-yawn.

11.　Aside from business, politics, sports, and personal relationships, other important domains of human interaction show prejudicial effects of "we"-group identity, with equally striking levels of bias. In health, infant mortality at birth drops significantly when the attending physician is of the same race as that of the newborn (Greenwood et al., 2020). Within law enforcement, traffic stops by Boston police were less likely to result in a search of the driver's vehicle if the officer and the driver were of similar race (Antonovics & Knight, 2009). In Israeli small-claims courts, Arab and Israeli judges' decisions robustly favored members of their own ethnic group (Shayo & Zussman, 2011). Within education, teachers' grading practices show comparable effects: a teacher–student match on race, religion, gender, ethnicity, or nationality increases student class evaluations and examination grades (Dee, 2005). Particularly plain evidence of the favoritism comes from a study at a Dutch university (Maastricht) located near the border with Germany, which possesses large populations of students and teachers from both the Netherlands and Germany. When students' examination papers were randomly assigned to be graded by teachers with similar or dissimilar nationalities, higher scores were assigned to students with names that matched the grader's nationality (Feld, Salamanca, & Hamermesh, 2015).

12. The mainstay of evolutionary thinking—that individuals do not so much attempt to ensure their own survival as the survival of copies of their genes—flows from the concept of "inclusive fitness," initially specified by W. D. Hamilton (1964), which has continued to receive support against multiple challengers (Kay, Keller, & Lehmann, 2020). Evidence for the particularly strong pull of kinship in life-or-death situations is available in Borgida, Conner, & Mamteufal (1992), Burnstein, Crandall, & Kitayama (1994), and Chagnon & Bugos (1979). Furthermore, the closer the relative is in terms of genetic overlap (e.g., parent or sibling versus uncle or cousin), the greater the feelings of self–other overlap (Tan et al., 2015). Telzer et al. (2010) obtained the finding that teenagers experience brain-system rewards after helping family. Reviews of the impressively wrought "fictive families" research can be found in Swann & Buhrmester (2015) and Fredman et al. (2015); additional research offers an explanation for these group-advancing effects: making a group identity prominent in consciousness causes individuals to focus their attention intently on information that fits with that identity (Coleman & Williams, 2015), which causes them, in turn, to see that information as more important. A study by Elliot & Thrash (2004) showed that the almost-total amount of parents' support of their kids in my class was no fluke. These researchers offered a point of extra credit in a psychology class to students whose parents answered a questionnaire with forty-seven items; 96 percent of the questionnaires were returned completed. Joel Stein's "Mama Ann" column can be read it its entirety at http://content.time.com/time/magazine /article/0,9171,1830395,00.html. Preston (2013) provides a detailed analysis of offspring nurturance as the basis for much wider forms of helping.

Although biologists, economists, anthropologists, sociologists, and psychologists know it from their studies, one doesn't have to be a scientist to recognize the enormous pull that offspring have on their parents. For example, novelists have frequently depicted the strong emotional force of the pull. A story is told of a bet made by the novelist Ernest Hemingway, who was renowned for the emotive power his prose was able to create despite its spareness. While drinking in a bar with one of his editors, Hemingway wagered that in just six words, he could write an entire dramatic story that anyone would understand completely and experience deeply. If, after reading the story, the editor agreed, he would buy drinks for the house; if not, Hemingway would pay. With the terms set, Hemingway wrote the six words on the back of a drink napkin and showed them to the man, who then quietly rose, went to the bar, and bought a round of drinks for all present. The words were "For sale. Baby shoes. Never used."

13. A copy of Buffett's fiftieth-anniversary letter is available online at www .berkshirehathaway.com/letters/2014ltr.pdf as part of Berkshire Hathaway's 2014 Annual Report, which appeared in February of 2015. For an instructive treatment of how the messenger can become the message, see Martin and Marks's (2019)

highly readable book on the topic. Both inside and outside family boundaries, people use similarities to judge genetic overlap and to favor those high on the dimension (DeBruine, 2002, 2004; Hehman, Flake, & Freeman, 2018; Kaminski et al., 2010). Data supporting the phenomena of family members being more helpful toward and feeling more close to those who resemble them come from research by Leek & Smith (1989, 1991) and Heijkoop, Dubas, & van Aken (2009), respectively. The evidence that manipulated physical similarity influences votes was collected by Bailenson et al. (2008).

14. People use attitudinal similarities as a basis for assessing genetic relatedness and, consequently, as a basis for forming in-groups, which in turn affects their decisions about whom to help (Grey et al., 2014; Park & Schaller, 2005). That political and religious attitudes are most likely to be passed on through heredity and, therefore, to reflect the genetic "we" is well documented (Bouchard et al., 2003; Chambers, Schlenker, & Collisson, 2013; Hatemi & McDermott, 2012; Hufer et al., 2020; Kandler, Bleidorn, & Riemann, 2012; Lewis & Bates, 2010). These types of attitudes are also highly resistant to change (Bourgeois, 2002; Tesser, 1993).

15. A good review of the cues humans (and nonhumans) use to identify kinship was done by Park, Schaller, & Van Vugt (2008); one of those cues is commonality of residence (Lieberman & Smith, 2012). Strong evidence for the impact of coresidence and parents' observed care on their children's subsequent altruism can be found in Cosmides & Tooby (2013) and Lieberman, Tooby, & Cosmides (2007). As regards Chiune Sugihara, it is always risky to generalize from a single case to a broader conclusion, even one bolstered by Mother Teresa's account of her home environment. In this instance, however, we know he was not the only notable rescuer of the era whose early home life incorporated human diversity. Oliner & Oliner (1988) found such a history in a sizable sample of European Gentiles who harbored Jews from the Nazis. And as would be expected, while growing up, rescuers in Oliner & Oliner's sample felt a sense of commonality with a more varied group of people than did an otherwise comparable sample of nonrescuers at the time. Not only was this expanded sense of "we"-ness related to their subsequent decisions to aid people different from themselves during the Holocaust; when interviewed a half-century later, rescuers were still helping a greater variety of people and causes (Midlarsky & Nemeroff, 1995; Oliner & Oliner, 1988).

More recently, researchers have developed a personality scale assessing the degree to which an individual spontaneously identifies with all humanity. This important scale, which includes measures of the frequency of use of the pronoun *we*, the conception of others as *family*, and the perceived extent of *self–other overlap* with people in general, predicts willingness to help the needy in other countries by contributing to international humanitarian relief efforts (McFarland, Webb, & Brown, 2012; McFarland, 2017). Information on the situational and personal factors leading to Sugihara's helping action in the pre–World War II environment comes from histories of the circumstances in Japan and Europe at the time (Kranzler, 1976; Levine, 1997; Tokayer & Swartz, 1979) and from interviews with Sugihara (Craig, 1985; Watanabe, 1994).

16. Cohen's (1972) description of the concentration-camp incident came from a conversation with a former Nazi guard there who, in a bizarre association, was Cohen's roommate at the time he relayed the story. It's estimated that the people

of Le Chambon, led by André Trocmé and his wife, Magda, saved the lives of 3,500 people. As to the question of why he decided to help the first of those individuals—a Jewish woman he found freezing outside his home in December of 1940—it is difficult to answer with certainty. But when in custody near the end of the war and Vichy officials demanded the names of Jews he and his fellow residents had assisted, his response could easily have come straight from the mouth (but, more fundamentally, the heart and worldview) of Chiune Sugihara: "We do not know what a Jew is. We only know human beings" (Trocmé, 2007/1971). As regards the question of whether his relatives or neighbors were the more likely to accede to Trocmé's requests, evidence from other sources indicates that it would have been the former—individuals for whom certainty of kinship would be stronger (Curry, Roberts, & Dunbar, 2013; Rachlin & Jones, 2008). For example, when, during the Rwandan genocide of the mid-1990s, attacks against Tutsis by Hutus included neighbors, those agitating for the attacks did so on the basis of tribal membership; "Hutu Power" was both a rallying cry and a justification for the slaughter.

The statistical analysis of the effectiveness of the Obama local-field-office plan was performed by Masket (2009). For an overview of how Obama strategists employed other insights from behavioral science throughout the campaign, see Issenberg (2012). The finding that people are especially susceptible to local voices (e.g., Agerström et al., 2016) has been termed "the local dominance effect" (Zell & Alike, 2010) that, when translated into electoral politics, means citizens are more likely to comply with the voter-turnout requests of members of their own communities (Nickerson & Feller, 2008). By the way, this last recognition didn't emerge from an arm's-length reading of the behavioral-science literature; David Nickerson was embedded as a behavioral-science advisor within the Obama campaign.

Have you ever noticed how certain commercial organizations refer to their customers, subscribers, or followers as members of the "XYZ *community?*" I think it's for the same reason other such organizations cite membership in the "ZYX *family*" Each designation recruits a powerful, primordial sense of "we"-ness.

17. The evidence of willingness to answer a survey, follow the recommendation of an Amazon product reviewer, overestimate one's home state's role in history, oppose the war in Afghanistan, and desert one's military unit comes from Edwards, Dillman, & Smyth (2014), Forman, Ghose, & Wiesenfeld (2008), Putnam et al. (2018), Kriner & Shen (2012), and Costa & Kahn (2008), respectively. According to Levine (1997), Sugihara's visas salvaged the lives of up to ten thousand Jews, the majority of whom found asylum in Japanese territory. The events attendant to the Japanese decision to shelter them have been described by several historians (e.g., Kranzler, 1976, and Ross, 1994); but the most detailed account is provided by Marvin Tokayer, the former chief rabbi of Tokyo (Tokayer & Swartz, 1979). My own account is modified from a more academic version that appeared in a coauthored textbook (Kenrick et al., 2020).

Observant readers may have noticed that when describing the murderous policies of the Holocaust, I referred to them as Nazi, not German. That is the case because of my view that it is not accurate or fair to equate the Nazi regime in Germany with the culture or people of that country, as is sometimes done. After all, we don't equate the culture and people of Cambodia or Russia or China or Iberia or the United States with the brutal programs of the Khmer Rouge under Pol Pot, Stalin after World War II, the Gang of Four during the Cultural Revolution, the conquistadores after Columbus, or the Manifest Destiny enactors of adolescent America (the list could go on). Government regimes, which often arise from temporary and powerful situational circumstances, do not fairly characterize a people. Hence, I don't conflate the two in discussing the time of Nazi ascendency in Germany.

18. For a review of the various types of behavioral-science data supporting the role of response synchrony on feelings of unitization, including self–other identity confusion (e.g., Milward & Carpenter, 2018; Palidino et al., 2010), see Wheatley et al. (2012). The tendency to coordinate movements in time with rhythmic sounds appeared in our evolutionary past even earlier than the Neolithic and Chalcolithic eras; chimps sway together in response to acoustic beats, something that suggests the presence of the response in a common ancestor of approximately six million years ago (Hattori & Tomonaga, 2020). One researcher described the groupings resulting from coordinated movement among humans as temporary "neighborhoods," in which members exert high levels of influence over one another's direction (Warren, 2018). The case for societal mechanisms designed to foster collective solidarity is made particularly convincingly by Kesebir (2012) and Paez et al. (2015). Demonstrations of the effects of acting together on "we"-ness, as well as on video-game performance and brain-wave patterns, were provided by Koudenburg et al. (2015), von Zimmermann & Richardson (2016), and Dikker et al. (2017), respectively. Consistent with the idea that aspiring influencers might be able to benefit greatly from the unitizing effect of synchrony, consider the sweeping summary statement of renowned world historian William H. McNeill (1995, p. 152): "Moving rhythmically while giving voice together is the surest, most speedy, and efficacious way of creating and sustaining [meaningful] communities that our species has ever hit upon."

19. Studies of the homogenizing effects of coordinated movement via finger tapping, smiling, and body shifting were conducted by Hove & Risen (2009), Cappella (1997), and Bernieri (1988), respectively. The water-sipping experiment was done by Inzlicht, Gutsell, & Legault (2012), who also included a third procedure in the study, in which subjects were required to imitate the water-sipping actions of in-group (White) actors. That procedure produced the typical prejudice for Whites over Blacks to a somewhat exaggerated degree.

Interestingly, there is one form of synchronous activity that has an additional benefit: when directing attention to a piece of information, people do so with increased intensity (i.e., allot it greater cognitive resources) if they see that they are attending to it simultaneously with someone else. However, this will only be the case if they have a "we" relationship with the other person. It seems that the act of paying conjoint attention to something along with a closely related other is a signal that the thing warrants special focus (Shteynberg, 2015).

20. My statement that the gold standard of social influence is "supportive conduct" is not meant to dismiss the importance of altering another's feelings (or beliefs or perceptions or attitudes) within the influence process. At the same time, it does seem to me that efforts to create change in these factors are almost

always undertaken in the service of creating change in supportive conduct. The tapping study was performed by Valdesolo & DeSteno (2011), whereas the marching research was done by Wiltermuth & Heath (2009). Marching in unison is an interesting practice in that it is still employed in military training, even though its worth as a battlefield tactic disappeared long ago. In a pair of experiments, Wiltermuth provides one compelling reason. After marching together, marchers became more willing to comply with a fellow marcher's request to harm members of an out-group; and this was the case not only when the requester was an authority figure (Wiltermuth, 2012a) but also when the requester was a peer (Wiltermuth, 2012b).

21. As evidence for the idea grows, there is increasing acceptance of the conception of music as a socially unitizing mechanism that creates group solidarity and comes about via self–other merger (Bannan, 2012; Dunbar, 2012; Harvey, 2018; Loersch & Arbuckle, 2013; Oesch, 2019; Savage et al., 2020; Tarr, Launay, & Dunbar, 2014). Scholars aren't alone in recognizing the unitizing function of music, sometimes to comedic extents; it would be hard not to laugh at this one: www .youtube.com/watch?v=etEQz7NYSLg. The study of helping among four-year-olds was done by Kirschner & Tomasello (2010); conceptually similar results were obtained by Cirelli, Einarson, & Trainor (2014) among much younger children: fourteen-month-old infants. A study of adults offers an explanation for the helpfulness. Singing together leads to feelings of self-other merger with fellow singers (Bullack et al.,2020).

22. Kahneman's book, *Thinking, Fast and Slow* (2011) is the source for the most complete exposition of System 1 and System 2 thinking. Evidence for the validity of the distinction between the two systems is available there but also in less-fully-presented form from Epstein et al. (1992, 1999). The "I think" versus "I feel" evidence can be found in Clarkson, Tormala, & Rucker (2011) and Mayer & Tormala (2010). But, in general, the wisdom of having a good match between the emotional-versus-rational basis of an attitude and a persuasive argument can also be seen in Drolet & Aaker (2002) and Sinaceur, Heath, & Cole (2005).

23. Bonneville-Roussy et al. (2013) review and contribute data showing that young women view music as more important to them than clothing, films, books, magazines, computer games, TV, and sports—but not romance. There's solid scientific evidence that music and rhythm operate independently of rational processes (e.g., de la Rosa et al., 2012; Gold et al., 2013). The Elvis Costello quote comes from an interesting article by Elizabeth Hellmuth Margulis (2010), who added her own piece of evidence to the mix by showing that giving audience members prior structural information about musical pieces (excerpts from Beethoven string quartets) then reduced their enjoyment of experiencing them.

The study of popular song content over a recent span of forty years, found that 80 percent featured romantic and/or sexual themes (Madanika & Bartholomew, 2014). The French guitar-case experiment (Guéguen, Meineri, & Fischer-Lokou, 2014) recorded the following percentages of successful phone-number requests: guitar case = 31 percent, sports bag = 9 percent, nothing = 14 percent. Armstrong's description of the effects of music on advertising success is presented on pp. 271–72 of his 2010 book.

24. The Mandy Len Catron *New York Times* piece can be retrieved at www.ny
times.com/2015/01/11/fashion/modern-love-to-fall-in-love-with-anyone-do-this
.html, along with a link to the thirty-six questions. The interview with Elaine
Aron is available at www.huffingtonpost.com/elaine-aron-phd/36-questions-for
-intimacy_b_6472282.html. The scientific article that served as the basis for the
Catron essay is Aron et al. (1997). Evidence for the functional importance of the
reciprocal, turn-taking feature of the thirty-six-questions procedure is provided
by Sprecher et al. (2013). The procedure has been used in modified form to reduce prejudice between ethnic groups, even among individuals with highly prejudiced initial attitudes (Page-Gould, Mendoza-Denton, & Tropp, 2008).

25. Probably the most informed retelling of the Ernst Hess saga is that of historian Susanne Mauss (Mauss, 2012), who discovered Himmler's "letter of protection" in official Gestapo files and has verified it through other documents.
There is some debate among scholars as to whether Hitler personally instructed
Himmler to construct and send the letter or whether that was done by Hitler's
personal adjutant, Fritz Wiedemann, on Hitler's behalf. Although Hess's un-
touchable status lasted only a year (he was then placed in several forced-labor
stations during the war, including a work camp, a construction company, and a
plumbing firm), he was never sent to a death camp as were other members of his
family, such as his sister who was gassed at Auschwitz. After the war, he became
a railroad executive, eventually rising to the presidency of the German Federal
Railways Authority in Frankfurt, where he died in 1983.

The researchers who analyzed the effects of shared suffering on fused in-
group identity after the Boston Marathon bombings performed a similar analysis
on the effects of the prolonged conflict between Northern Irish Unionists and
Republicans and obtained similar results (Jong et al., 2015). The work showing
the impact of submerging one's hands in ice water also demonstrated its effects
when using other kinds of pain-producing procedures such as eating a hot chili
pepper and doing repeated leg squats together with group members (Bastian, Jetten, & Ferris, 2014). For additional research detailing the role of shared adversity
in bringing about fused identities and subsequent supportive and self-sacrificial
conduct, see Drury (2018) and Whitehouse et al. (2017). For reviews indicating
that the concept of collective emotion is different in nature from that of individual emotion, see Goldenberg et al. (2020) and Parkinson (2020).

More detail on the saga of Irish–Native American unity is available in various
news accounts (see, e.g., www.irishpost.com/news/irish-donate-native-american
-tribes-hit-covid-19-repay-173-year-old-favour-184706; and https://nowthisnews
.com/news/irish-repay-a-173-year-old-debt-to-native-community-hard-hit-by
-covid-19) and in an episode of the highly informative podcast *The Irish Passport*
(www.theirishpassport.com/podcast/irish-and-native-american-solidarity). The
extent of the wretchedness of the Trail of Tears ordeal is revealed in a little publicized fact. Its original label, gleaned from a portrayal by a Choctaw chieftain, was
"Trail of tears and death" (Faiman-Silva, 1997, p. 19).

26. Aldo Leopold's manifesto, *A Sand County Almanac*, which was first published
in 1949 and has since become a must-read primer for many wilderness groups,
is the source of my treatment of his birch-versus-pine musings (see pp. 68–70
of the 1989 paperback edition). His strong belief that wilderness management

is best accomplished through an ecology-centric rather than a human-centric approach is illustrated in his arguments against government predator-control policies in natural environments. Stunning evidence supports his position in the case of predator wolves. A visual presentation of that evidence is available at www.youtube.com/watch?v=ysa5OBhXz-Q; you'll be glad you watched it.

27. The IKEA-effect research was performed by Norton, Mochon, & Ariely (2012). The study of the evaluations of one's coworkers and cocreated products was conducted in collaboration with Jeffrey Pfeffer (Pfeffer & Cialdini, 1998)—one of the most impressive academic minds I know. The effects of collaboration on three-year-olds' sharing were demonstrated by Warneken et al. (2011). The positive results of cooperative-learning techniques are summarized in Paluck & Green (2009) and in Roseth, Johnson, & Johnson (2008); educators looking for information on how to implement one such approach ("The Jigsaw Classroom" as developed by Elliot Aronson and his associates) can find that information at www.jigsaw.org.

The survey study of the effects of asking for consumers' advice on subsequent consumer engagement was published by Liu & Gal (2011), who found, instructively, that paying consumers an unexpectedly high amount for their advice eliminated any increased favoritism toward the brand; although the researchers didn't investigate why this was the case, they speculated that the unexpected payment focused the participants away from the communal aspect of giving their advice and toward an individuating aspect of it—in this instance, their own economic outcomes associated with a financial exchange. For some examples of how various brands are employing cocreation practices to enhance customer engagement, see www.visioncritical.com/5-examples-how-brands-are-using-co-creation, and a pair of links within: www.visioncritical.com/cocreation-101 and www.greenbook blog.org/2013/10/01/co-creation-3-0. There's a good reason brands use techniques such as cocreation to bond consumers' identities with their brand. Consumers who have a strong feeling of shared identity with a brand (e.g., Apple) are more likely to ignore information about that brand's product failures in determining their attitudes and loyalties toward the brand (Lin & Sung, 2014).

28. The question of how kinship is determined by members of various species has been the subject of myriad scientific investigations (e.g., Holmes, 2004; Holmes & Sherman, 1983; Mateo, 2003). Although fewer in number, investigations of how humans go about the process have been particularly informative for our purposes (Gyuris et al., 2020; Mateo, 2015). For instance, Wells (1987) reported that the concept of "honorary kin"—unrelated individuals who are present in the home and who acquire family-like titles as a result—exists in *all* human cultures. Most instructively, see the landmark analysis of kin detection among humans by Lieberman and her associates (Lieberman, Tooby, & Cosmides, 2007; Sznycer et al., 2016), as well as its brief summary in Cosmides & Tooby (2013, pp. 219–22). My recommendation for parents to treat out-group visitors to the home as family rather than guests gains support from research showing that children pick up and follow adults' nonverbal signals toward social group members (Skinner, Olson, & Meltzoff, 2020).

29. Nai et al. (2018) collected the data showing the positive effects of living in a diverse neighborhood on benevolence toward strangers and on identification

with all humanity. Conceptually similar effects have been found in more ethnically diverse regions and countries (Bai, Ramos, & Fiske, 2020). Evidence of the favorable consequences of cross-group friendships on intergroup attitudes, expectations, and actions for both majority and minority group members comes from a variety of sources (Page-Gould et al., 2010; Pettigrew, 1997; Swart et al., 2011; Wright et al., 1997). For example, in South Africa, "Colored" junior high school students who had cross-group friendships with Whites held more trusting attitudes and less harmful intentions toward Whites in general (Stewart et al., 2011). The version of the thirty-six questions that reduced prejudice among individuals with hardened prejudicial attitudes was developed by Page-Gould et al. (2008). The significant role of self-disclosure in the beneficial effects of cross-group friendships appeared in work by Davies et al. (2011) and Turner et al. (2007).

30. The unitizing effect of an American identity was found by Riek et al. (2010) and Levendusky (2018), whereas a similar effect of genetic identity was confirmed by Kimel et al. (2016); Flade, Klar, & Imhoff (2019) uncovered the comparable impact of a mutual enemy; see also Shnabel, Halabi, & Noor (2013). The research on psychopaths' susceptibility to the effects of shared identity was conducted by Arbuckle & Cunningham (2012). McDonald et al. (2017) provided the evidence that the regrettable tendency of groups to dehumanize rival groups (Haslem, 2006; Haslam & Loughnan, 2014; Kteily et al., 2015; Markowitz & Slovic, 2020; Smith, 2020) could be countered through the shared experience of basic human emotions.

Evidence that perspective-taking can enhance the sense of self–other overlap with another is considerable (Ames et al., 2008; Čehajić & Brown, 2010; Davis et al., 1996; Galinsky & Moskowitz, 2000); the Ames et al. (2008) research offered particularly creative support by showing that individuals who used perspective-taking to think about another experienced greater activation of the brain sector (ventromedial prefrontal cortex) associated with thinking about oneself. The work implicating perspective-taking in approval of favorable political policies toward minority groups was conducted by Berndsen & McGarty (2012), Čehajić & Brown (2010), and Broockman & Kalla (2016). The finding that recognizing that another has taken our perspective prompts us to feel greater solidarity with that person was obtained in six separate experiments by Goldstein, Vezich, & Shapiro (2014).

31. Although the waves, leaves, and flowers quote is typically attributed to Seneca, he probably didn't author it. Most likely, it is from Bahá'u'lláh the founder of the Baha'i faith.

There is considerable evidence of the varying and often only temporary success of connections designed to reduce the dehumanization of rival groups or to build unity with them by highlighting common enemies or by finding some kind of shared identity or by undertaking perspective-taking (Catapano, Tormala, & Rucker, 2019; Dovidio, Gaertner, & Saguy, 2009; Goldenberg, Courtney, & Felig, 2020; Lai et al., 2016; Mousa, 2020; Over, 2020; Sasaki & Vorauer; 2013; Todd & Galinsky, 2014; Vorauer, Martens, & Sasaki, 2009). Evidence documenting the undercutting effects of perceived threat on unity-generating procedures is extensive (Gómez et al., 2013; Kauff et al., 2013; Morrison, Plaut, & Ybarra, 2010;

Pierce et al., 2013; Riek, Mania, & Gaertner, 2006; Sassenrath, Hodges, & Pfattheicher, 2016; Vorauer & Sasaki, 2011).

32.   For a review of evidence of likely greater genetic commonality among those
who share families, friendships, and locales, as well as political and religious attitudes, see research included in this chapter's endnotes 9, 12, 14, 16, and 17. The
initial research on which Kahneman based the focusing illusion was published
in Schkade & Kahneman (1998); for subsequent support, see Gilbert (2006),
Krizan & Suls (2008), Wilson et al. (2000), and Wilson & Gilbert (2008). Related
data come from a study investigating why items placed in the center of an array
of brands on store shelves tend to be purchased more often. The one in the center
gets more visual attention than those to the left or right. Furthermore, it is this
greater attention that predicts the purchase decision (Atalay, Bodur, & Rasolofoarison, 2012). As regards the general rationale for and the consequences of the
focusing illusion, there is evidence that what's important gains our attention and
what we attend to gains in importance. For instance, in the realm of attitudes,
researchers have shown that we are organized cognitively so that the attitudes
we can most readily access (focus upon) are the ones most important to us (Bizer
& Krosnick, 2001). As well, any attitude we can readily access comes to be seen
as more important (Roese & Olson, 1994). There is even evidence that concentrated visual attention to a consumer item increases the item's judged worth by
influencing sectors of the brain that govern perceived value (Lim, O'Doherty, &
Rangel, 2011; Krajbich et al., 2009). The studies demonstrating how attentional
focus from media coverage, landing-page imagery, and aged photos influenced
perceived importance were performed by Corning & Schuman (2013), Mandel &
Johnson (2002), and Hershfield et al. (2011).

Although not all methods have proved effective, considerable research indicates
that it is possible to be trained to shift attention away from threatening entities toward more positive or at least less frightening ones (Hakamata et al., 2010; Mogg,
Allison, & Bradley, 2017; Lazarov et al., 2017; Price et al., 2016). Besides training
ourselves to focus away from the sometimes threatening aspects of out-groups,
we can use focus in another way to defuse the resulting anxiety. It involves focusing away from the anxieties themselves and onto our strengths. When we
experience these sorts of threats, the key is to engage in "self-affirmations" that
channel attention to something about ourselves we value, such as a strong relationship with a family member, friend, or friendship network; it could also be to a
trait we prize—our creativity or sense of humor, perhaps. The effect is to reorient
our focus from threatened aspects of ourselves and the defensive responses that
accompany them (prejudice, combativeness, self-promotion) to valued aspects of
ourselves and the confident responses that follow (openness, equanimity, self-
control). Numerous studies have recorded the ability of timely self-affirmations
to reverse the negative impact of out-group threat (Čehajić-Clancy et al., 2011;
Cohen & Sherman, 2014; Shnabel et al., 2013; Sherman, Brookfield, & Ortosky,
2017; Stone et al., 2011).

33.   The studies documenting the greater dishonesty of employees of firms
with togetherness-emphasizing Code of Conduct statements were published by
Kouchaki, Gino, & Feldman (2019). The tendency to excuse such conduct from
members of a "we"-group isn't limited to humans. In another illustration, food

theft by young chimpanzees is much more tolerated by adult food-holders if the young thief is their kin (Fröhlich et al., 2020).

The wisdom of a no-tolerance policy for proven unethical conduct can be seen in evidence of the toxic economic consequences of allowing such behavior within an organization. My colleagues and I have labeled these consequences as "the triple-tumor structure of organizational dishonesty." We've argued that an organization that regularly allows the use of deceitful tactics by its personnel (against coworkers and also against customers, clients, stockholders, suppliers, distributors, and so on) will experience a trio of costly internal outcomes: declining employee performance, high employee turnover, and prevalent employee fraud and malfeasance. In addition, the outcomes will function like malignant tumors—growing, spreading, and eating progressively at the organization's health and vigor. In a set of studies, literature reviews, and analyses, we found support for our assertions (Cialdini, 2016, chap. 13; Cialdini et al., 2019; Cialdini, Petrova, & Goldstein, 2004).

A no-tolerance policy of dismissals following ethical infractions in organizations, especially togetherness-minded organizations, may seem ruthless, and I can't recall ever before advocating ruthlessness in human exchanges, yet, based on our findings, it seems justified. Of course, I recognize and am even generally sympathetic to counterarguments that stress forbearance, that say to err is human and people should be given a second chance, and that point to Shakespeare's lines in *The Merchant of Venice* regarding treatment of ethical abusers: "The quality of mercy is not strained. / It droppeth as the gentle rain from heaven / Upon the place beneath." But, pertaining specifically to unethical conduct in workforce units, I (unlike the Bard) have seen considerable research documenting a set of corrosive and contagious consequences that would be foolish to underestimate.

Chapter 9: Instant Influence

1.   Evidence of the perceptual and decisional narrowing produced by cognitive overload can be found in Albarracin & Wyer (2001); Bawden & Robinson (2009); Carr (2010); Chajut & Algom (2003); Conway & Cowan (2001); Dhami (2003); Easterbrook (1959); Hills (2019); Hills, Adelman, & Noguchi (2017); Sengupta & Johar (2001); and Tversky & Kahneman (1974).

BIBLIOGRAPHY

Aaker, D. A. (1991). *Managing brand equity*. New York: Free Press.

Abrahamse, W., & Steg, L. (2013). Social influence approaches to encourage resource conservation: A meta-analysis. *Global Environmental Change, 23*, 1773–1785.

Achen, C. H., & Bartels, L. M. (2017). *Democracy for realists: Why elections do not produce responsive government*. Princeton, NJ: Princeton University Press.

Adarves-Yorno, I., Haslam, S. A., & Postmes, T. (2008). And now for something completely different? The impact of group membership on perceptions of creativity. *Social Influence, 3*, 248–266.

Agerström, J., Carlsson, R., Nicklasson L., & Guntell L. (2016). Using descriptive social norms to increase charitable giving: The power of local norms. *Journal of Economic Psychology, 52*, 147–153, http://dx.doi.org/10.1016/j.joep.2015.12.007.

Aggarwal, P., Jun, S. Y., & Huh, J. H. (2011). Scarcity messages. *Journal of Advertising, 40*, 19–30. http://dx.doi.org/10.2753/JOA0091-3367400302.

Albarracin, D., & Wyer, R. S. (2001). Elaborative and nonelaborative processing of a behavior-related communication. *Personality and Social Psychology Bulletin, 27*, 691–705.

Alison, L., & Alison, E. (2017). Revenge versus rapport: Interrogation, terrorism, and torture. *American Psychologist, 72*, 266–277.

Algoe, S. B. (2012). Find, remind, and bind: The functions of gratitude in everyday relationships. *Social and Personality Psychology Compass, 6*, 455–469.

Algoe, S. B., Gable, S. L., & Maisel, N. (2010). It's the little things: Everyday gratitude as a booster shot for romantic relationships. *Personal Relationships, 17*, 217–233.

Algoe, S. B., & Zhaoyang, R. (2016). Positive psychology in context: Effects of expressing gratitude in ongoing relationships depend on perceptions of enactor responsiveness. *Journal of Positive Psychology, 11*, 399–415. http://dx.doi.org/10.1080/17439760.2015.1117131.

Allcott, H. (2011). Social norms and energy conservation. *Journal of Public Economics, 95*, 1082–1095. http://dx.doi.org/10.1016/j.jpubeco.2011.03.003.

Allcott, H., & Rogers, T. (2014). The short-run and long-run effects of behavioral interventions: Experimental evidence from energy conservation. *American Economic Review, 104*, 3003–37.

Allison, S. T., Mackie, D. M., Muller, M. M., & Worth, L. T. (1993). Sequential correspondence biases and perceptions of change. *Personality and Social Psychology Bulletin, 19*, 151–157.

Allison, S. T., & Messick, D. M. (1988). The feature-positive effect, attitude strength, and degree of perceived consensus. *Personality and Social Psychology Bulletin, 14*, 231–241.

Al Ramiah, A., & Hewstone, M. (2013). Intergroup contact as a tool for reducing, resolving, and preventing intergroup conflict: Evidence, limitations, and potential. *American Psychologist, 68*, 527–542. http://dx.doi.org/10.1037/a0032603.

Ames, D. L., Jenkins, A. C., Banaji, M. R., & Mitchell, J. P. (2008). Taking another person's perspective increases self-referential neural processing. *Psychological Science, 19*, 642–644. https://doi.org/10.1111/j.1467-9280.2008.02135.x.

Ampel, B. C., Muraven, M., & McNay, E. C. (2018). Mental work requires physical energy: Self-control is neither exception nor exceptional. *Frontiers in Psychology, 9*, 1005. https://doi.org/10.3389/fpsyg.2018.01005.

Anderson, M. (2014). *After Phrenology: Neural Reuse and the Interactive Brain.* Cambridge, MA: The MIT Press.

Anderson, E., & Simester, D. (2003). Mind your pricing cues. *Harvard Business Review, 81*, 103–134.

Anderson, S. M., & Zimbardo, P. G. (1984). On resisting social influence. *Cultic Studies Journal, 1*, 196–219.

Andor, M. A., & Fels, K. M. (2018). Behavioral economics and energy conservation—a systematic review of non-price interventions and their causal effects. *Ecological Economics, 148*, 178–210.

Antonovics, K., & Knight, B. G. (2009). A new look at racial profiling: Evidence from the Boston Police Department. *Review of Economics and Statistics, 91*, 163–177.

Aramovich, N. P., Lytle, B. L., & Skitka, L. J. (2012). Opposing torture: Moral conviction and resistance to majority influence. *Social Influence, 7*, 21–34.

Arbuckle, N. L, & Cunningham, W. A. (2012). Understanding everyday psychopathy: Shared group identity leads to increased concern for others among undergraduates higher in psychopathy. *Social Cognition, 30*, 564–583. https://doi.org/10.1521/soco.2012.30.5.564.

Arizona Republic (1999, March 7). For women, all's pheromones in love, war, E19.

Armstrong, J. S. (2010). *Persuasive advertising.* London: Palgrave Macmillan.

Arnocky, S., Bozek, E., Dufort, C., Rybka, S., & Herbert, R. (2018). Celebrity opinion influences public acceptance of human evolution. *Evolutionary Psychology,* https://doi.org/10.1177/1474704918800656.

Aron, A., Aron, E. N., Tudor, M., & Nelson, G. (1991). Self-relationships as including other in the self. *Journal of Personality and Social Psychology, 60*, 241–253.

Aron, A., Melinat, E., Aron, E. N., Vallone, R. D., & Bator, R. J. (1997). The experimental generation of interpersonal closeness: A procedure and some preliminary findings. *Personality and Social Psychology Bulletin, 23*, 363–377.

Aronson, E. (1975, February). The jigsaw route to learning and liking. *Psychology Today,* 43–50.

Aronson, E., & Mills, J. (1959). The effect of severity of initiation on liking for a group. *Journal of Abnormal and Social Psychology, 59*, 177–181.

Aronson, E., Stephan, C., Sikes, J., Blaney, N., & Snapp, M. (1978). *The jigsaw classroom.* Beverly Hills, CA: Sage.

Aronson, E., & Tavris, C. (2020, July 20). The role of cognitive dissonance in the pandemic. *The Atlantic.* www.theatlantic.com/ideas/archive/2020/07/role-cognitive-dissonance-pandemic/614074.

Ashmore, R. D., Ramchandra, V., & Jones, R. A. (1971, April). *Censorship as an attitude change induction*. Paper presented at the meeting of the Eastern Psychological Association, New York, NY.

Ashokkumar, A., Galaif, M., Swann, W. B. (2019). Tribalism can corrupt: Why people denounce or protect immoral group members. *Journal of Experimental Social Psychology, 85*. https://doi.org/10.1016/j.jesp.2019.103874.

Asimov, I. (1975, August 30). The Miss America pageant. *TV Guide.*

Atalay, A. S., Bodur, H. O., & Rasolofoarison, D. (2012). Shining in the center: Central gaze cascade effect on product choice. *Journal of Consumer Research, 39,* 848–856.

Aune, R. K., & Basil, M. C. (1994). A relational obligations approach to the foot-in-the-mouth effect. *Journal of Applied Social Psychology, 24,* 546–556.

Australian. (2009, December 11). Coin by coin, B14.

Ayres, I., Raseman, S., & Shih, A. (2013). Evidence from two large field experiments that peer comparison feedback can reduce residential energy usage. *Journal of Law, Economics, and Organization, 29,* 992–1022. http://dx.doi.org/10.1093/jleo/ews02056.

Bai, X., Ramos, M. R., & Fiske, S. T. (2020). As diversity increases, people paradoxically perceive social groups as more similar. *Proceedings of the National Academy of Sciences, 117,* 12741–12749. https://doi.org/10.1073/pnas.2000333117.

Bailenson, J. N., & Yee, N. (2005). Digital chameleons: Automatic assimilation of nonverbal gestures in immersive virtual environments. *Psychological Science, 16*(10), 814–819. https://doi.org/10.1111/j.1467-9280.2005.01619.x.

Bailenson, J. N., Iyengar, S., Yee, N., & Collins, N. A. (2008). Facial similarity between voters and candidates causes influence. *Public Opinion Quarterly, 72,* 935–961.

Balancher, S., Liu, Y., & Stock, A. (2009). An empirical analysis of scarcity strategies in the automobile industry. *Management Science, 10,* 1623–1637.

Balliet, D., Wu, J., & De Dreu, C. K. W. (2014). Ingroup favoritism in cooperation: A meta-analysis. *Psychological Bulletin, 140,* 1556–1581.

Bandura, A., Grusec, J. E., & Menlove, F. L. (1967). Vicarious extinction of avoidance behavior. *Journal of Personality and Social Psychology, 5,* 16–23.

Bandura, A., & Menlove, F. L. (1968). Factors determining vicarious extinction of avoidance behavior through symbolic modeling. *Journal of Personality and Social Psychology, 8,* 99–108.

Bannan, N. (ed.). (2012). *Music, language, and human evolution.* Oxford: Oxford University Press.

Barden, J., Rucker, D. D., & Petty, R. E. (2005). "Saying one thing and doing another": Examining the impact of event order on hypocrisy judgments of others. *Personality and Social Psychology Bulletin, 31,* 1463–1474. https://doi.org/10.1177/0146167205276430.

Bargh, J. A., & Williams, E. L. (2006). The automaticity of social life. *Current Directions in Psychological Science, 15,* 1–4.

Barlow, F. K., Paolini, S., Pedersen, A., Hornsey, M. J., Radke, H. R. M., Harwood, J., Rubin, M., & Sibley, C. G. (2012). The contact caveat: Negative contact predicts increased prejudice more than positive contact predicts reduced prejudice. *Personality and Social Psychology Bulletin, 38,* 1629–1643. https://doi.org/10.1177/0146167212457953.

Barnett, M. A., Sanborn, F. W., & Shane, A. C. (2005). Factors associated with individuals' likelihood of engaging in various minor moral and legal violations. *Basic and Applied Social Psychology, 27*, 77–84. http://doi.org/10.1207/s15324834 basp2701_8.

Barone, M. J., & Roy, T. (2010). The effect of deal exclusivity on consumer response to targeted price promotions: A social identification perspective. *Journal of Consumer Psychology, 20*, 78–89.

Bastardi, A., & Shafir, E. (2000). Nonconsequential reasoning and its consequences. *Current Directions in Psychological Science, 9*, 216–219.

Bastian, B., Jetten, J., & Ferris, L. J. (2014). Pain as social glue: shared pain increases cooperation. *Psychological Science, 25*, 2079–2085, https://doi.org/10.1177/095 6797614545886.

Bawden, D., & Robinson, L. (2009). The dark side of information: Overload, anxiety and other paradoxes and pathologies. *Journal of Information Science, 35*, 180–191.

Benjamin, J. (2015, June 22). Market research fail: How New Coke became the worst flub of all time. Business 2 Community (website). www.business2 community.com/consumer-marketing/market-research-fail-new-coke-became -worst-flub-time-01256904.

Benson, P. L., Karabenic, S. A., & Lerner, R. M. (1976). Pretty pleases: The effects of physical attractiveness on race, sex, and receiving help. *Journal of Experimental Social Psychology, 12*, 409–415.

Benton, A. A., Kelley, H. H., & Liebling, B. (1972). Effects of extremity of offers and concession rate on the outcomes of bargaining. *Journal of Personality and Social Psychology, 24*, 73–83.

Bergquist, M., Nilsson, A., & Schultz, W. P. (2019). A meta-analysis of field experiments using social norms to promote pro-environmental behaviors. *Global Environmental Change, 58*. doi.org/10.1016/j.gloenvcha.2019.101941.

Bernache-Assolant, I., Lacassagne, M-F., & Braddock, J. H. (2007). Basking in reflected glory and blasting: Differences in identity management strategies between two groups of highly identified soccer fans. *Journal of Language and Social Psychology, 26*, 381–388.

Berndsen, M., & McGarty, C. (2012). Perspective taking and opinions about forms of reparation for victims of historical harm. *Personality and Social Psychology Bulletin, 38*, 1316–1328. https://doi.org/10.1177/0146167212450322.

Bernieri, F. J. (1988). Coordinated movement and rapport in teacher-student interactions. *Journal of Nonverbal Behavior, 12*, 120–138.

Berns, G. S., Chappelow J., Zink, C. F., Pagnoni, G., Martin-Skuski, M. E., & Richards, J. (2005). Neurobiological correlates of social conformity and independence during mental rotation. *Biological Psychiatry, 58*, 245–253.

Bickman, L. (1974). The social power of a uniform. *Journal of Applied Social Psychology, 4*, 47–61.

Binning, K. R., Kaufmann, N., McGreevy, E. M., Fotuhi, O., Chen, S., Marshman, E., Kalender, Z. Y., Limeri, L., Betancur, L., & Singh, C. (2020). Changing social contexts to foster equity in college science courses: An ecological-belonging intervention. *Psychological Science, 31*, 1059–1070. https://doi.org/10.1177/0956797 620929984.

Bizer, G. Y., & Krosnick, J. A. (2001). Exploring the structure of strength-related attitude features: The relation between attitude importance and attitude accessibility. *Journal of Personality and Social Psychology, 81,* 566–586. https://doi.org/10.1037/0022-3514.81.4.566.

Blake, R., & Mouton, J. (1979). Intergroup problem solving in organizations: From theory to practice. In W. Austin and S. Worchel (eds.), *The social psychology of intergroup relations* (pp. 19–32). Monterey, CA: Brooks/Cole.

Blanco, F., Gómez-Fortes, B., & Matute, H. (2018). Causal illusions in the service of political attitudes in Spain and the United Kingdom. *Frontiers in Psychology, 28.* https//:doi.org/10.3389/fpsyg.2018.01033.

Blass, T. (2004). *The man who shocked the world: The life and legacy of Stanley Milgram.* New York: Basic Books.

Blass, T. (2012). A cross-cultural comparison of studies of obedience using the Milgram paradigm: A review. *Social and Personality Psychology Compass, 6,* 196–205.

Boen, F., Vanbeselaere, N., Pandelaere, M., Dewitte, S., Duriez, B., Snauwaert, B., Feys, J., Dierckx, V., & Van Avermaet, E. (2002). Politics and basking-in-reflected-glory. *Basic and Applied Social Psychology, 24,* 205–214.

Boh, W. F., & Wong, S-S. (2015). Managers versus co-workers as referents: Comparing social influence effects on within- and outside-subsidiary knowledge sharing. *Organizational Behavior and Human Decision Processes, 126,* 1–17.

Bollen, K. A., & Phillips, D. P (1982). Imitative suicides: A national study of the effects of television news stories. *American Sociological Review, 47,* 802–809.

Bomey, N. (2017, July 3). Nissan Rogue gets a galactic sales boost from "Star Wars." *Arizona Republic,* B4.

Bond, M. H., & Smith, P. B. (1996). Culture and conformity: A meta-analysis of studies using Asch's (1952b, 1956) line judgment task. *Psychological Bulletin, 119,* 111–137.

Bond, R., Fariss, C. J., Jones, J. J., Kramer, A. D. I., Marlow, C., Settle, J. E., & Fowler, J. H. (2012). A 61-million-person experiment in social influence and political mobilization. *Nature, 489,* 295–298. https://doi.org/10.1038/nature11421.

Bonneville-Roussy, A., Rentfrow, P. J., Potter, J., & Xu, M. K. (2013). Music through the ages: Trends in musical engagement and preferences from adolescence through middle adulthood. *Journal of Personality and Social Psychology, 105,* 703–717.

Boothby, E. J., & Bohns, V. K. (2020). Why a simple act of kindness is not as simple as it seems: Underestimating the positive impact of our compliments on others. *Personality and Social Psychology Bulletin.* https://doi.org/10.1177/0146167220949003.

Borgida, E., Conner, C., & Manteufal, L. (1992). Understanding living kidney donation: A behavioral decision-making perspective. In S. Spacapan and S. Oskamp (eds.), *Helping and being helped* (pp. 183–212). Newbury Park, CA: Sage.

Borman, G. D., Rozek, C. S., Pyne, J., & Hanselman, P. (2019). Reappraising academic and social adversity improves middle school students' academic achievement, behavior, and well-being. *Proceedings of the National Academy of Sciences, 116,* 16286–16291. https://doi.org/10.1073/pnas.1820317116.

Bornstein, R. F., Leone, D. R., & Galley, D. J. (1987). The generalizability of subliminal mere exposure effects. *Journal of Personality and Social Psychology, 53*, 1070–1079.

Bouchard, T. J., Segal, N. L., Tellegen, A., McGue, M., Keyes, M., & Krueger, R. (2003). Evidence for the construct validity and heritability of the Wilson-Paterson conservatism scale: A reared-apart twins study of social attitudes. *Personality and Individual Differences, 34*, 959–969.

Bourgeois, M. J. (2002). Heritability of attitudes constrains dynamic social impact. *Personality and Social Psychology Bulletin, 28*, 1063–1072.

Brandt, M. J., & Reyna, C. (2011). The chain of being: A hierarchy of morality. *Perspectives on Psychological Science, 6*, 428–446.

Brehm, J. W. (1966). *A theory of psychological reactance.* New York: Academic Press.

Brehm, S. S. (1981). Psychological reactance and the attractiveness of unattainable objects: Sex differences in children's responses to an elimination of freedom. *Sex Roles, 7*, 937–949.

Brehm, S. S., & Weintraub, M. (1977). Physical barriers and psychological reactance: Two-year-olds' responses to threats to freedom. *Journal of Personality and Social Psychology, 35*, 830–836.

Brendl, C. M., Chattopadhyay, A., Pelham, B. W., & Carvallo, M. (2005). Name letter branding: Valence transfers when product specific needs are active. *Journal of Consumer Research, 32*, 405–415. https://doi.org/10.1086/497552.

Bridge, J. A., Greenhouse, J. B., Ruch, D., Stevens, J., Ackerman, J., Sheftall, A. H., Horowitz, L. M., Kelleher, K. J., & Campo, J. V. (2019). Association between the release of Netflix's *13 Reasons Why* and suicide rates in the United States: An interrupted times series analysis. *Journal of the American Academy of Child and Adolescent Psychiatry.* https://doi.org/10.1016/j.jaac.2019.04.020.

Briñol, P., Petty, R. E., & Wheeler, S. C. (2006). Discrepancies between explicit and implicit self-concepts: Consequences for information processing. *Journal of Personality and Social Psychology, 91*, 154–170.

Brockner, J., & Rubin, J. Z. (1985). *Entrapment in escalating conflicts: A social psychological analysis.* New York: Springer-Verlag.

Bronnenberg, B. J., Dhar, S. K., & Dubé, J.-P. (2007). Consumer packaged goods in the United States: National brands, local branding. *Journal of Marketing Research, 44*, 4–13. https://doi.org/10.1509/jmkr.44.1.004.

Broockman, D. & Kalla, J. (2016). Durably reducing transphobia: A field experiment on door-to-door canvassing. *Science, 352*, 220–224.

Brown, J. L., Drake, K. D., & Wellman, L. (2015). The benefits of a relational approach to corporate political activity: Evidence from political contributions to tax policymakers. *Journal of the American Taxation Association, 37*, 69–102.

Brown, S. L., Asher, T., & Cialdini, R. B. (2005). Evidence of a positive relationship between age and preference for consistency. *Journal of Research in Personality, 39*, 517–533.

Browne, W., & Swarbrick-Jones, M. (2017). What works in e-commerce: A meta-analysis of 6700 online experiments. *Qubit Digital LTD.*

Brownstein, R., & Katzev, R. (1985). The relative effectiveness of three compliance techniques in eliciting donations to a cultural organization. *Journal of Applied Social Psychology, 15*, 564–574.

Bruneau, E. G., Kteily, N. S., & Urbiola, A. (2020). A collective blame hypocrisy intervention enduringly reduces hostility towards Muslims. *Nature Human Behaviour, 4,* 45–54. https://doi.org/10.1038/s41562-019-0747-7.

Buchan, N. R., Brewer, M. B., Grimalda, G., Wilson, R. K., Fatas, E., & Foddy, M. (2011). Global social identity and global cooperation. *Psychological Science, 22,* 821–828.

Budesheim, T. L., & DePaola, S. J. (1994). Beauty or the beast? The effects of appearance, personality, and issue information on evaluations of political candidates. *Personality and Social Psychology Bulletin, 20,* 339–348.

Bullack, A., Gass, C., Nater, U. M., & Kreutz, G. (2018). Psychobiological effects of choral singing on affective state, social connectedness, and stress: Influences of singing activity and time course. *Frontiers of Behavioral Neuroscience.* 12:223. https://doi.org/10.3389/fnbeh.2018.00223.

Burger, J. M. (2009). Replicating Milgram: Would people still obey today? *American Psychologist, 64,* 1–11.

Burger, J. M., & Caldwell, D. F. (2003). The effects of monetary incentives and labeling on the foot-in-the-door effect. *Basic and Applied Social Psychology, 25,* 235–241.

Burger, J. M., & Caldwell, D. F. (2011). When opportunity knocks: The effect of a perceived unique opportunity on compliance. *Group Processes & Intergroup Relations, 14,* 671–680.

Burger, J. M., & Caputo, D. (2015). The low-ball compliance procedure: a meta-analysis. *Social Influence, 10,* 214–220. DOI: 10.1080/15534510.2015.1049203.

Burger, J. M., Horita, M., Kinoshita, L., Roberts, K., & Vera, C. (1997). Effects of time on the norm of reciprocity. *Basic and Applied Social Psychology, 19,* 91–100.

Burger, J. M., Messian, N., Patel, S., del Prado, A., & Anderson, C. (2004). What a coincidence! The effects of incidental similarity on compliance. *Personality and Social Psychology Bulletin, 30,* 35–43.

Burger, J. M., & Petty, R. E. (1981). The low-ball compliance technique: Task or person commitment? *Journal of Personality and Social Psychology, 40,* 492–500.

Burgoon, M., Alvaro, E., Grandpre, J., & Voulodakis, M. (2002). Revisiting the theory of psychological reactance. In J. P. Dillard and M. Pfau (eds.), *The persuasion handbook: Theory and practice* (pp. 213–232). Thousand Oaks, CA: Sage.

Burnstein, E., Crandall, C., & Kitayama, S. (1994). Some neo-Darwin decision rules for altruism: Weighing cues for inclusive fitness as a function of the biological importance of the decision. *Journal of Personality and Social Psychology, 67,* 773–789.

Bushman, B. J. (1988). The effects of apparel on compliance. *Personality and Social Psychology Bulletin, 14,* 459–467.

Bushman, B. J. (2006). Effects of warning and information labels on attraction to television violence in viewers of different ages. *Journal of Applied Social Psychology, 36,* 2073–2078. https://doi.org/10.1111/j.0021-9029.2006.00094.x.

Buttleman, D., & Bohm, R. (2014). The ontogeny of the motivation that underlies in-group bias. *Psychological Science, 25,* 921–927.

Buttrick, N., Moulder, R., & Oishi, S. (2020). Historical change in the moral foundations of political persuasion. *Personality and Social Psychology Bulletin, 46,* 1523-1537. doi:10.1177/0146167220907467.

Cadinu, M. R., & Rothbart, M. (1996). Self-anchoring and differentiation processes in the minimal group setting. *Journal of Personality and Social Psychology, 70,* 666–677.

Cai, H., Chen, Y., & Fang, H. (2009). Observational learning: Evidence from a randomized natural field experiment. *American Economic Review, 99,* 864–882.

Campbell, M. W., & de Waal, F. B. M. (2010). Methodological problems in the study of contagious yawning. *Frontiers in Neurology and Neuroscience, 28,* 120–127.

Cappella, J. N. (1997). Behavioral and judged coordination in adult informal social interactions: Vocal and kinesic indicators. *Journal of Personality and Social Psychology, 72,* 119–131.

Carducci, B. J., Deuser, P. S., Bauer, A., Large, M., & Ramaekers, M. (1989). An application of the foot-in-the-door technique to organ donation. *Journal of Business and Psychology, 4,* 245–249.

Carey, B. (2016, July 26). Mass killings may have created contagion, feeding on itself. *New York Times,* A11.

Caro, R. A. (2012). *The passage of power.* Vol. 4 of *The years of Lyndon Johnson.* New York: Knopf.

Carpenter, C. J. (2013). A meta-analysis of the effectiveness of the "But You Are Free" compliance-gaining technique. *Communication Studies, 64,* 6–17. https://doi.org/10.1080/10510974.2012.727941.

Carr, N. (2010). *The shallows: What the internet is doing to our brains.* New York: W. W. Norton.

Carter, S. E., & Sanna, L. J. (2006). Are we as good as we think? Observers' perceptions of indirect self-presentation as a social influence tactic. *Social Influence, 1,* 185–207, https://doi.org/10.1080/15534510600937313.

Catapano, R., Tormala, Z. L., & Rucker, D. D. (2019). Perspective taking and self-persuasion: Why "putting yourself in their shoes" reduces openness to attitude change. *Psychological Science, 30,* 424–435. https://doi.org/10.1177/0956797976188 22697.

Cavazza, N. (2016). When political candidates "go positive": The effects of flattering the rival in political communication. *Social Influence, 11,* 166–176. https://doi.org/10.1080/15534510.2016.1206962.

Čehajić, S., & Brown, R. (2010). Silencing the past: Effects of intergroup contact on acknowledgment of in-group responsibility. *Social Psychological and Personality Science, 1,* 190–196. https://doi.org/10.1177/1948550609359088.

Čehajić-Clancy, S., Effron, D. A., Halperin, E., Liberman, V., & Ross, L. D. (2011). Affirmation, acknowledgment of in-group responsibility, group-based guilt, and support for reparative measures. *Journal of Personality and Social Psychology, 101,* 256–270.

Chagnon, N. A., & Bugos, P. E. (1979). Kin selection and conflict: An analysis of a Yanomano ax fight. In N. A. Chagnon and W. Irons (eds.), *Evolutionary biology and social behavior* (pp. 213–238). North Scituate, MA: Duxbury.

Chaiken, S. (1979). Communicator physical attractiveness and persuasion. *Journal of Personality and Social Psychology, 37,* 1387–1397.

Chaiken, S. (1986). Physical appearance and social influence. In C. P. Herman,

M. P. Zanna, and E. T. Higgins (eds.), *Physical appearance, stigma, and social behavior: The Ontario Symposium* (vol. 3, pp. 143–177). Hillsdale, NJ: Lawrence Erlbaum.

Chajut, E., & Algom, D. (2003). Selective attention improves under stress. *Journal of Personality and Social Psychology, 85*, 231–248.

Chambers, J. R., Schlenker, B. R., & Collisson, B. (2013). Ideology and prejudice: The role of value conflicts. *Psychological Science, 24*, 140–149.

Chan, C., Berger, J., & Van Boven, L. (2012). Identifiable but not identical: Combining social identity and uniqueness motives in choice. *Journal of Consumer Research, 39*, 561–573. https://doi.org/10.1086/664804.

Chan, E., & Sengupta, J. (2010). Insincere flattery actually works: A dual attitudes perspective. *Journal of Marketing Research, 47*, 122–133.

Cheng, L., Hao, M., Xiao, L., & Wang, F. (2020). Join us: Dynamic norms encourage women to pursue STEM. *Current Psychology.* https://doi.org/10.1007/s12144-020-01105-4.

Chernyak, N., Leimgruber, K. L., Dunham, Y. C., Hu, J., & Blake, P. R. (2019). Paying back people who harmed us but not people who helped us: Direct negative reciprocity precedes direct positive reciprocity in early development. *Psychological Science.* https://doi.org/10.1177/0956797619854975.

Christakis, N. A., & Fowler, J. H. (2014). Friendship and natural selection. *Proceedings of the National Academy of Sciences, 111*, 10796–10801. https://doi.org/10.1073/pnas.1400825111.

Chugani, S., Irwin, J. E., & Redden, J. P. (2015). Happily ever after: The effect of identity-consistency on product satiation. *Journal of Consumer Research, 42*, 564–577. https://doi.org/10.1093/jcr/ucv040.

Cialdini, R. B. (2003). Crafting normative messages to protect the environment. *Current Directions in Psychological Science, 12*, 105–109.

Cialdini, R. B. (1997). Professionally responsible communication with the public: Giving psychology away. *Personality and Social Psychology Bulletin, 23*, 675–683.

Cialdini, R. B. (2016). *Pre-Suasion: A revolutionary way to influence and persuade.* New York: Simon & Schuster.

Cialdini, R. B. (2018). Why the world is turning to behavioral science. In A. Samson (ed.), *The behavioral economics guide 2018* (pp. vii–xiii). www.behavioral economics.com/the-behavioral-economics-guide-2018.

Cialdini, R. B., & Ascani, K. (1976). Test of a concession procedure for inducing verbal, behavioral, and further compliance with a request to give blood. *Journal of Applied Psychology, 61*, 295–300.

Cialdini, R. B., Borden, R. J., Thorne, A., Walker, M. R. Freeman, S., & Sloan, L. R. (1976). Basking in reflected glory: Three (football) field studies. *Journal of Personality and Social Psychology, 34*, 366–375.

Cialdini, R. B., Brown, S. L., Lewis, B. P., Luce, C., & Neuberg, S. L. (1997). Reinterpreting the empathy-altruism relationship: When one into one equals oneness. *Journal of Personality and Social Psychology, 73*, 481–494.

Cialdini, R. B., Cacioppo, J. T., Bassett, R., & Miller, J. A. (1978). Low-ball procedure for producing compliance: Commitment then cost. *Journal of Personality and Social Psychology, 36*, 463–476.

Cialdini, R. B., Eisenberg, N., Green, B. L., Rhoads, K. v. L., & Bator, R. (1998).

Undermining the undermining effect of reward on sustained interest. *Journal of Applied Social Psychology, 28*, 249–263.

Cialdini, R. B., Li, J., Samper, A., & Wellman, E. (2019). How bad apples promote bad barrels: Unethical leader behavior and the selective attrition effect. *Journal of Business Ethics.* https://doi.org/10.1007/s10551-019-04252-2.

Cialdini, R. B., Petrova, P., & Goldstein, N. J. (2004). The hidden costs of organizational dishonesty. *MIT Sloan Management Review, 45*, 67–73.

Cialdini, R. B., Trost, M. R., & Newsom, J. T. (1995). Preference for consistency: The development of a valid measure and the discovery of surprising behavioral implications. *Journal of Personality and Social Psychology, 69*, 318–328.

Cialdini, R. B., Vincent, J. E., Lewis, S. K., Catalan, J., Wheeler, D., & Darby, B. L. (1975). Reciprocal concessions procedure for inducing compliance: The door-in-the-face technique. *Journal of Personality and Social Psychology, 31*, 206–215.

Cialdini, R. B., Wosinska, W., Barrett, D. W., Butner, J., & Gornik-Durose, M. (1999). Compliance with a request in two cultures: The differential influence of social proof and commitment/consistency on collectivists and individualists. *Personality and Social Psychology Bulletin 25*, 1242–1253.

Cikara, M., & Paluck, E. L. (2013), When going along gets you nowhere and the upside of conflict behaviors. *Social and Personality Psychology Compass, 7*, 559–571. https://doi.org/10.1111/spc3.12047.

Cikara, M., & van Bavel, J. (2014). The neuroscience of inter-group relations: An integrative review. *Perspectives on Psychological Science, 9*, 245–274.

Cioffi, D., & Garner, R. (1996). On doing the decision: The effects of active versus passive choice on commitment and self-perception. *Personality and Social Psychology Bulletin, 22*, 133–147.

Cirelli, L. K., Einarson, K. M., & Trainor, L. J. (2014). Interpersonal synchrony increases prosocial behavior in infants. *Developmental Science, 17*, 1003–1011. https://doi.org/10.1111/desc.12193.

Clark, C. J., Liu, B. S., Winegard, B. M., & Ditto, P. H. (2019). Tribalism is human nature. *Current Directions in Psychological Science, 28*, 587–592. https://doi.org/10.1177/0963721419862289.

Clark, M. S., Lemay, E. P., Graham, S. M., Pataki, S. P., & Finkel, E. J. (2010). Ways of giving benefits in marriage: Norn use, relationship satisfaction, and attachment-related variability. *Psychological Science, 21*, 944–951.

Clark, M. S., Mills, J. R., & Corcoran, D. M. (1989). Keeping track of needs and inputs of friends and strangers. *Personality and Social Psychology Bulletin, 15*, 533–542.

Clark, R. D., III, & Word, L. E. (1972). Why don't bystanders help? Because of ambiguity? *Journal of Personality and Social Psychology, 24*, 392–400.

Clark, R. D., III, & Word, L. E. (1974). Where is the apathetic bystander? Situational characteristics of the emergency. *Journal of Personality and Social Psychology, 29*, 279–287.

Clarkson, J. J., Tormala, Z. L., & Rucker, D. D. (2011). Cognitive and affective matching effects in persuasion: An amplification perspective. *Personality and Social Psychology Bulletin, 1415*–1427.

Clifford, S., & Jerit, J. (2016). Cheating on political knowledge questions in online surveys. *Public Opinion Quarterly, 80*, 858–887.

Coghlan, T. (2015, July 14). Weidenfeld's crusade to save Christians of Syria. *The Times* (London), A30.

Cohen, R. (1972). Altruism: Human, cultural, or what? *Journal of Social Issues, 28*, 39–57.

Cohen, A. (1999, May 31). Special report: Troubled kids. *Time*, 38.

Cohen, G. L., & Sherman, D. K. (2014). The psychology of change: Self-affirmation and social psychological intervention. *Annual Review of Psychology, 65*, 333–371.

Cohen, M., & Davis, N. (1981). *Medication errors: Causes and prevention.* Philadelphia: G. F. Stickley.

Coleman, N. V., & Williams, P. (2015). Looking for my self: Identity-driven attention allocation. *Journal of Consumer Psychology, 25*, 504–511.

Collins, J. (2018). Simple heuristics that make algorithms smart. http://behavioral scientist.org/simple-heuristics-that-make-algorithms-smart.

Combs, D. J. Y., & Keller, P. S. (2010). Politicians and trustworthiness: Acting contrary to self-interest enhances trustworthiness. *Basic and Applied Social Psychology, 32*, 328–339.

Converse, B. A., & Fishbach, A. (2012). Instrumentality boosts appreciation: Helpers are more appreciated while they are useful. *Psychological Science, 23*, 560–566.

Conway, A., & Cowan, N. (2001). The cocktail party phenomenon revisited: The importance of working memory capacity. *Psychonomic Bulletin & Review, 8*, 331–335.

Cooper, J., & Fazio, R. H. (1984). A new look at dissonance theory. In L. Berkowitz (ed.), *Advances in experimental social psychology* (vol. 17, pp. 229–266). New York: Academic Press.

Coppock, A., Ekins, E., & Kirby, D. (2018). The long-lasting effects of newspaper op-eds on public opinion. *Quarterly Journal of Political Science, 13*, 59–87.

Cornelissen, G., Pandelaere, M., Warlop, L., & Dewitte, S. (2008). Positive cueing: Promoting sustainable consumer behavior by cueing common environmental behaviors as environmental. *International Journal of Research in Marketing, 25*, 46–55. https://doi.org/10.1016/j.ijresmar.2007.06.002.

Corning, A., & Schuman, H. (2013). Commemoration matters: The anniversaries of 9/11 and Woodstock. *Public Opinion Quarterly, 77*, 433–454.

Cortijos-Bernabeu, A., Bjørndal, L. D., Ruggeri, K., Alí, S., Friedemann, M., Esteban-Serna, C., Khorrami, P. R., et al. (2020). Replicating patterns of prospect theory for decision under risk. *Nature Human Behaviour, 4*, 622–633.

Cosmides, L., & Tooby, J. (2013). Evolutionary psychology: New perspectives on cognition and motivation. *Annual Review of Psychology, 64*, 201–229.

Craig, B. (1985, July 30). A story of human kindness. *Pacific Stars and Stripes*, 13–16.

Crespelle, J. P. (1969). *Picasso and his women.* New York: Hodder & Stoughton.

Cronley, M., Posavac, S. S., Meyer, T., Kardes, F. R., & Kellaris, J. J. (2005). A selective hypothesis testing perspective on price-quality inference and inference-based choice. *Journal of Consumer Psychology, 15*, 159–169.

Cullum, J., O'Grady, M., Sandoval, P., Armeli, A., & Tennen, T. (2013). Ignoring norms with a little help from my friends: Social support reduces normative influence on drinking behavior. *Journal of Social and Clinical Psychology: 32*, 17–33. https://doi.org/10.1521/jscp.2013.32.1.17.

Cunningham, M. R. (1986). Levites and brother's keepers: A sociobiological perspective on prosocial behavior. *Humboldt Journal of Social Relations, 13*, 35–67.

Curry, O., Roberts, S. G. B., & Dunbar, R. I. M. (2013). Altruism in social networks: Evidence for a "kinship premium." *British Journal of Psychology, 104*, 283–295. https://doi.org/10.1111/j.2044-8295.2012.02119.x.

Dai, X., Wertenbroch, K., & Brendel, C. M. (2008). The value heuristic in judgments of relative frequency. *Psychological Science, 19*, 18–19.

Daly, M., Salmon, C. & Wilson, M. (1997). Kinship: The conceptual hole in psychological studies of social cognition and close relationships. In J. A. Simpson and D. T. Kendrick (eds.), *Evolutionary Social Psychology* (pp. 265–296). Mahwah, NJ: Erlbaum.

Danchin, E., Nöbel, S., Pocheville, A., Dagaeff, A-C., Demay, L., Alphand, M., Ranty-Roby, S., et al. (2018). Cultural flies: Conformist social learning in fruitflies predicts long-lasting mate-choice traditions. *Science, 362*, 1025–1030.

Darley, J. M., & Latané, B. (1968). Bystander intervention in emergencies: Diffusion of responsibility. *Journal of Personality and Social Psychology, 8*, 377–383.

Dauten, D. (2004, July 22). How to be a good waiter and other innovative ideas. *Arizona Republic*, D3.

Davies, J. C. (1962). Toward a theory of revolution. *American Sociological Review, 27*, 5–19.

Davies, J. C. (1969). The J-curve of rising and declining satisfactions as a cause of some great revolutions and a contained rebellion. In H. D. Graham and T. R. Gurr (eds.), *Violence in America* (pp. 547–644). New York: Signet.

Davies, K., Tropp, L. R., Aron, A., Pettigrew, T. F., & Wright, S. C. (2011). Cross-group friendships and intergroup attitudes: A meta-analytic review. *Personality and Social Psychology Review, 15*, 332–351. https://doi.org/10.1177/1088868311411103.

Davis, M. H., Conklin, L., Smith, A., & Luce, C. (1996). Effect of perspective taking on the cognitive representation of persons: A merging of self and other. *Journal of Personality and Social Psychology, 70*, 713–726. https://doi.org/10.1037/0022-3514.70.4.713.

DeBruine, L. M. (2002). Facial resemblance enhances trust. *Proceedings of the Royal Society, Series B, 269*, 1307–1312.

DeBruine, L. M. (2004). Resemblance to self increases the appeal of child faces to both men and women. *Evolution and Human Behavior, 25*, 142–154.

Dechêne, A., Stahl, C., Hansen, J., & Wänke, M. (2010). The truth about the truth: A meta-analytic review of the truth effect. *Personality and Social Psychology Review, 14*, 238–257. https://doi.org/10.1177/1088868309352251.

Deci, E. L., & Ryan, R. M. (1985). *Intrinsic motivation and self-determination in human behavior*. New York: Plenum.

Deci, E. L., Spiegel, N. H., Ryan, R. M., Koestner, R., & Kauffman, M. (1982). Effects of performance standards on teaching styles: Behavior of controlling teachers. *Journal of Educational Psychology, 74*, 852–859. https://doi.org/10.1037/0022-0663.74.6.852.

De Dreu, C. K. W., & McCusker, C. (1997). Gain-loss frames and cooperation in two-person social dilemmas: A transformational analysis. *Journal of Personality and Social Psychology, 72*, 1093–1106.

De Dreu, C. K. W., Dussel, D. B., & Ten Velden, F. S. (2015). In intergroup conflict, self-sacrifice is stronger among pro-social individuals and parochial altruism emerges especially among cognitively taxed individuals. *Frontiers in Psychology, 6*, 572. https://doi.org/10.3389/fpsyg.2015.00572.

DeJong, C., Aguilar, T., Tseng, C-W., Lin, G. A., Boscardin, W. J., & Dudley, R. A. (2016). Pharmaceutical industry–sponsored meals and physician prescribing patterns for Medicare beneficiaries. *Journal of the American Medical Association: Internal Medicine, 176*, 1114–1122.

de la Rosa, M. D., Sanabria, D., Capizzi, M., & Correa, A. (2012). Temporal preparation driven by rhythms is resistant to working memory interference. *Frontiers in Psychology, 3*. https://doi.org/10.3389/fpsyg.2012.00308.

Dellande, S., & Nyer, P. (2007). Using public commitments to gain customer compliance. *Advances in Consumer Research, 34*, 249–255.

De Martino, B., Bobadilla-Suarez, S., Nouguchi, T., Sharot, T., & Love, B. C. (2017). Social information is integrated into value and confidence judgments according to its reliability. *Journal of Neuroscience, 37*, 6066–6074. https://doi.org/10.1523/JNEUROSCI.3880-16.2017.

Demuru, E., & Palagi, E. (2012). In Bonobos yawn contagion is higher among kin and friends. *PLoS ONE, 7*. https://doi.org/10.1371/journal.pone.0049613.

DePaulo, B. M., Nadler, A., & Fisher, J. D. (eds.). (1983). *Help seeking*. Vol. 2 of *New directions in helping*. New York: Academic Press.

Deutsch, M., & Gerard, H. B. (1955). A study of normative and informational social influences upon individual judgment. *Journal of Abnormal and Social Psychology, 51*, 629–636.

Devlin, A. S., Donovan, S., Nicolov, A., Nold, O., Packard, A., & Zandan, G. (2009). "Impressive?" Credentials, family photographs, and the perception of therapist qualities. *Journal of Environmental Psychology, 29*, 503– 512. https://doi.org/10.1016/j.jenvp.2009.08.008.

DeWall, C. N., MacDonald, G., et al. (2010). Acetaminophen reduces social pain: Behavioral and neural evidence. *Psychological Science, 21*, 931–937.

Dhami, M. K. (2003). Psychological models of professional decision making. *Psychological Science, 14*, 175–180.

Dikker, S., Wan, L., Davidesco, I., Kaggen, L., Oostrik, M., McClintock, J., Rowland, J., et al. (2017). Brain-to-brain synchrony tracks real-world dynamic group interactions in the classroom. *Current Biology, 27*, 1375–1380. https://doi.org/10.1016/j.cub.2017.04.002.

Dillard, J. P., Kim, J., & Li, S. S. (2018). Anti-sugar-sweetened beverage messages elicit reactance: Effects on attitudes and policy preferences. *Journal of Health Communication, 23*, 703–711. https://doi.org/10.1080/10810730.2018 .1511012.

Dimmock, S. G., Gerken, W. C., & Graham, N. P. (2018). Is fraud contagious? Coworker influence on misconduct by financial advisors. *Journal of Finance, 73*, 1417–1450. https://doi.org/10.1111/jofi.12613.

Dion, K. K. (1972). Physical attractiveness and evaluation of children's transgressions. *Journal of Personality and Social Psychology, 24*, 207–213.

Dixon, J., Durrheim, K., & Tredoux, C. (2005). Beyond the optimal contact strategy: A reality check for the contact hypothesis. *American Psychologist, 60,* 697–711.

Dolińska, B., Jarząbek, J., & Doliński, D. (2020). I like you even less at Christmas dinner! *Basic and Applied Social Psychology, 42,* 88–97. https://doi.org/10.1080/01973533.2019.1695615.

Doliński, D. (2000). Inferring one's beliefs from one's attempt and consequences for subsequent compliance. *Journal of Personality and Social Psychology, 78,* 260–272.

Doliński, D. (2016). *Techniques of social influence: The psychology of compliance.* New York: Routledge.

Doliński, D., & Grzyb, T. (2020). *Social psychology of obedience toward authority: Empirical tribute to Stanley Milgram.* London: Routledge.

Doliński, D., Grzyb, T., Folwarczny, M., Grzybała, P., Krzyszycha, K., Martynowska, K., & Trojanowski, J. (2017). Would you deliver an electric shock in 2015? Obedience in the experimental paradigm developed by Stanley Milgram in the 50 years following the original studies. *Social Psychological and Personality Science, 8,* 927–933.

Dolnik, L., Case, T. I., & Williams, K. D. (2003). Stealing thunder as a courtroom tactic revisited: Processes and boundaries. *Law and Human Behavior, 27,* 267–287.

Donaldson, S. I., Graham, J. W., Piccinin, A. M., & Hansen, W. B. (1995). Resistance-skills training and onset of alcohol use. *Health Psychology, 14,* 291–300.

Doob, A. N., & Gross, A. E. (1968). Status of frustrator as an inhibitor of horn-honking response. *Journal of Social Psychology, 76,* 213–218.

Dovidio, J. F., Gaertner, S. L., & Saguy, T. (2009). Commonality and the complexity of "We": Social attitudes and social change. *Personality and Social Psychology Review, 13,* 3–20. https://doi.org/10.1177/1088868308326751.

Drachman, D., deCarufel, A., & Inkso, C. A. (1978). The extra credit effect in interpersonal attraction. *Journal of Experimental Social Psychology, 14,* 458–467.

Driscoll, R., Davis, K. E., & Lipetz, M. E. (1972). Parental interference and romantic love: The Romeo and Juliet effect. *Journal of Personality and Social Psychology, 24,* 1–10.

Drolet, A., & Aaker J. (2002). Off-target? Changing cognitive-based attitudes. *Journal of Consumer Psychology, 12,* 59–68.

Drury, J. (2018). The role of social identity processes in mass emergency behaviour: An integrative review. *European Review of Social Psychology, 29,* 38–81. https://doi.org/10.1080/10463283.2018.1471948.

Du, X. (2019). What's in a surname? The effect of auditor-CEO surname sharing on financial misstatement. *Journal of Business Ethics, 158,* 849–874. https://doi.org/10.1007/s10551-017-3762-5.

DuBois, D. L., Portillo, N., Rhodes, J. E., Silverthorn, N., & Valentine, J. C. (2011). How effective are mentoring programs for youth? A systematic assessment of the evidence. *Psychological Science in the Public Interest, 12,* 57–91. https://doi.org/10.1177/1529100611414806.

Duguid, M. M., & Goncalo, J. A. (2012). Living large: The powerful overestimate their own height. *Psychological Science, 23,* 36–40. https://doi.org/10.1177/0956797611422915.

Duguid, M. M., & Thomas-Hunt, M. C. (2015). Condoning stereotyping? How awareness of stereotyping prevalence impacts expression of stereotypes. *Journal of Applied Psychology, 100*, 343–359. https://doi.org/10.1037/a0037908.

Dunbar, R. I. M. (2012). On the evolutionary function of song and dance. In N. Bannan (ed.), *Music, language and human evolution* (pp. 201–214). Oxford: Oxford University Press.

Dunfield, K. A., & Kuhlmeier, V. A. (2010). Intention-mediated selective helping in infancy. *Psychological Science, 21*, 523–527.

Eagly, A. H., Wood, W., & Chaiken, S. (1978). Causal inferences about communicators and their effect on opinion change. *Journal of Personality and Social Psychology, 36*, 424–435.

Easterbrook, J. A. (1959). The effects of emotion on cue utilization and the organization of behavior. *Psychological Review, 66*, 183–201.

Edwards, M. L., Dillman, D. A., & Smyth, J. D. (2014). An experimental test of the effects of survey sponsorship on internet and mail survey response. *Public Opinion Quarterly, 78*, 734–750.

Effron, D. A., Bryan, C. J., & Murnighan, J. K. (2015). Cheating at the end to avoid regret. *Journal of Personality and Social Psychology, 109*, 395–414. https://doi.org/10.1037/pspa0000026.

Efran, M. G., & Patterson, E. W. J. (1976). The politics of appearance. Unpublished manuscript, University of Toronto.

Ellemers, N., & van Nunspeet, F. (2020, September). Neuroscience and the social origins of moral behavior: How neural underpinnings of social categorization and conformity affect everyday moral and immoral behavior. *Current Directions in Psychological Science.* https://doi.org/10.1177/0963721420951584.

Epley, N., & Gilovich, T. (2006). The anchoring-and-adjustment heuristic: Why adjustments are insufficient. *Psychological Science, 17*, 311–318.

Epstein, S., Lipson, A., Holstein, C., & Huh, E. (1992). Irrational reactions to negative outcomes: Evidence for two conceptual systems. *Journal of Personality and Social Psychology, 62*, 328–339.

Epstein, S., Donovan, S., & Denes-Raj, V. (1999). The missing link in the paradox of the Linda conjunction problem: Beyond knowing and thinking of the conjunction rule, the intrinsic appeal of heuristic processing. *Personality and Social Psychology Bulletin, 25*, 204–214.

Facci, E., L., & Kasarda, J. D. (2004). Revisiting wind-shear accidents: The social proof factor. Proceedings of the 49th Corporate Aviation Safety Seminar (pp. 205–232). Alexandrea, VA: Flight Safety Foundation.

Faiman-Silva, S. (1997). *Choctaws at the crossroads.* Lincoln: University of Nebraska Press.

Fan, M., Billings, A., Zhu, X., & Yu, P. (2019). Twitter-based BIRGing: Big data analysis of English National Team fans during the 2018 FIFA World Cup. *Communication & Sport.* https://doi.org/10.1177/2167479519834348.

Fang, X., Singh, S., & Ahulwailia, R. (2007). An examination of different explanations for the mere exposure effect. *Journal of Consumer Research, 34*, 97–103.

Farrow, K., Grolleau, G., & Ibanez, L. (2017). Social norms and pro-environmental behavior: A review of the evidence. *Ecological Economics, 140*, 1–13.

Fazio, L. K., Rand, D. G., & Pennycook, G. (2019). *Psychonomic Bulletin Review.* https://doi.org/10.3758/s13423-019-01651-4.

Fazio, R. H., Sherman, S. J., & Herr, P. M. (1982). The feature-positive effect in the self-perception process. *Journal of Personality and Social Psychology, 42,* 404–411.

Fein, S., Goethals, G. R., & Kugler, M. B. (2007). Social influence on political judgments: The case of presidential debates. *Political Psychology, 28,* 165–192. https://doi.org/10.1111/j.1467-9221.2007.00561.x.

Feinberg, R. A. (1986). Credit cards as spending facilitating stimuli. *Journal of Consumer Research, 13,* 348–356.

Feinberg, R. A. (1990). The social nature of the classical conditioning phenomena in people. *Psychological Reports, 67,* 331–334.

Feld, J., Salamanca, N., Hamermesh, D. S. (2015). Endophilia or exophobia: Beyond discrimination. *Economic Journal, 126,* 1503–1527.

Fennis, B. M., Janssen, L., & Vohs, K. D. (2008). Acts of benevolence: A limited-resource account of compliance with charitable requests. *Journal of Consumer Research, 35,* 906–924.

Fennis, B. M., & Stroebe, W. (2014). Softening the blow: Company self-disclosure of negative information lessens damaging effects on consumer judgment and decision making. *Journal of Business Ethics, 120,* 109–120.

Festinger, L. (1957). *A theory of cognitive dissonance.* Stanford, CA: Stanford University Press.

Festinger, L., & Carlsmith, J. M. (1959). Cognitive consequences of forced compliance. *Journal of Abnormal and Social Psychology, 58,* 203–210. https://doi.org/10.1037/h0041593.

Festinger, L., Riecken, H. W., & Schachter, S. (1964). *When prophecy fails.* New York: Harper & Row.

Fischer, P., Krueger, J. I., Greitemeyer, T., Vogrincic, C., Kastenmüller, A., Frey, D., Heene, M., et al. (2011). The bystander-effect: A meta-analytic review on bystander intervention in dangerous and non-dangerous emergencies. *Psychological Bulletin, 137,* 517–537. https://doi.org/10.1037/a0023304.

Fiske, S. T., & Neuberg, S. L. (1990). A continuum of impression formation: Influences of information and motivation on attention and interpretation. In M. P. Zanna (ed.), *Advances in experimental social psychology* (vol. 23, pp. 1–74). New York: Academic Press.

Fisman, R., Paravisini, D., & Vig, V. 2017. Cultural proximity and loan outcomes. *American Economic Review, 107,* 457–492.

Flade, F., Klar, Y., & Imhoff, R. (2019). Unite against: A common threat invokes spontaneous decategorization between social categories. *Journal of Experimental Social Psychology, 85.* https://doi.org/10.1016/j.jesp.2019.103890.

Fleming, T. (1997, November 23). 13 things you never knew about the American Revolution. *Parade,* 14–15.

Flynn, F. J. (2002). What have you done for me lately? Temporal adjustments to favor evaluations. *Organizational Behavior and Human Decision Processes, 91,* 38–50.

Foddy, M., Platow, M. J., & Yamagishi, T. (2009). Group-based trust in strangers. *Psychological Science, 20,* 419–422.

Foerster, M., Roser, K., Schoeni, A., & Röösli, M. (2015). Problematic mobile phone use in adolescents: Derivation of a short scale MPPUS-10. *International Journal of Public Health, 60*, 277–286, https://doi.org/10.1007/s00038-015-0660-4.

Fogg, B. J., & Nass, C. (1997a). How users reciprocate to computers: An experiment that demonstrates behavior change. In *Extended Abstracts of the CHI97 Conference of the ACM/SIGCHI*. New York: ACM.

Fogg, B. J., & Nass, C. (1997b). Silicon sycophants: The effects of computers that flatter. *International Journal of Human-Computer Studies, 46*(5), 551–561.

Fombelle, P., Gustafsson, A., Andreassen, T. W., & Witell, L. (2010). *Give and thou shall receive: Customer reciprocity in a retail setting*. Paper presented at the 19th Annual Frontiers In Service Conference, Karlstad, Sweden.

Forman, C., Ghose, A., & Wiesenfeld, B. (2008). Examining the relationship between reviews and sales: The role of reviewer identity disclosure in electronic markets. *Information Research Systems, 19*, 291–313. https://doi.org/10.1287/isre.1080.0193.

Fornara, F., Carrus, G., Passafaro, P., & Bonnes, M. (2011). Distinguishing the sources of normative influence on pro-environmental behaviors: The role of local norms in household waste recycling. *Group Processes & Intergroup Dynamics, 14*, 623–635.

Fox, C. R., Linder, J. A., & Doctor, J., N. (2016, March 27). How to stop overprescribing antibiotics. *New York Times*. www.nytimes.com/2016/03/27/opinion/sunday/how-to-stop-overprescribing-antibiotics.html.

Fox, M. W. (1974). *Concepts in ethology: Animal and human behavior*. Minneapolis: University of Minnesota Press.

Frank, R. H. (2020). *Under the Influence: Putting peer pressure to work*. Princeton, NJ: Princeton University Press.

Fraune, M. R. (2020). Our robots, our team: Robot anthropomorphism moderates group effects in human–robot teams. *Frontiers in Psychology, 11*, 1275. https://doi.org/10.3389/fpsyg.2020.01275.

Fredman, L. A., Buhrmester, M. D., Gomez, A., Fraser, W. T., Talaifar, S., Brannon, S. M., & Swann, Jr., W. B. (2015). Identity fusion, extreme pro-group behavior, and the path to defusion. *Social and Personality Psychology Compass, 9*, 468–480. https://doi.org/10.1111/spc3.12193.

Freedman, J. L. (1965). Long-term behavioral effects of cognitive dissonance. *Journal of Experimental Social Psychology, 1*, 145–155.

Freedman, J. L., & Fraser, S. C. (1966). Compliance without pressure: The foot-in-the-door technique. *Journal of Personality and Social Psychology, 4*, 195–203.

Freling, T. H., & Dacin, P. A. (2010). When consensus counts: Exploring the impact of consensus claims in advertising. *Journal of Consumer Psychology, 20*, 163–175.

Frenzen, J. R., & Davis, H. L. (1990). Purchasing behavior in embedded markets. *Journal of Consumer Research, 17*, 1–12.

Friedman, H. H., & Rahman, A. (2011). Gifts-upon-entry and appreciative comments: Reciprocity effects in retailing. *International Journal of Marketing Studies, 3*, 161–164.

Friestad, M., & Wright, P. (1995). Persuasion knowledge: Lay people's and researchers' beliefs about the psychology of persuasion. *Journal of Consumer Research, 22*, 62–74.

Fröhlich, M., Müller, G., Zeiträg, C., Wittig, R. M., & Pika, S. (2020). Begging and social tolerance: Food solicitation tactics in young chimpanzees (*Pan troglodytes*) in the wild. *Evolution and Human Behavior, 41*, 126–135. https://doi.org/10.1016/j.evolhumbehav.2019.11.002.

Furnham, A. (1996). Factors relating to the allocation of medical resources. *Journal of Social Behavior and Personality, 11*, 615–624.

Gaesser, B., Shimura, Y., & Cikara, M. (2020). Episodic simulation reduces intergroup bias in prosocial intentions and behavior. *Journal of Personality and Social Psychology, 118*, 683–705. https://doi.org/10.1037/pspi0000194.

Gal, D. & Rucker D. D. (2010). When in doubt, shout! Paradoxical influences of doubt on proselytizing. *Psychological Science, 21*, 1701–1707.

Galinsky, A. D., & Moskowitz, G. B. (2000). Perspective-taking: Decreasing stereotype expression, stereotype accessibility, and in-group favoritism. *Journal of Personality and Social Psychology, 78*, 708–724. https://doi.org/10.1037/0022-3514.78.4.708.

Gallup, A. C., Hale, J. J.,. Sumpter, D. J. T., Garnier, S., Kacelnik, A., Krebs, J. R., & Couzin, I. D. (2012). Visual attention and the acquisition of information in human crowds. *Proceedings of the National Academy of Sciences, 109*, 7245–7250. https://doi.org/10.1073/pnas.1116141109.

Gansberg, M. (1964, March 27). 37 who saw murder didn't call the police. *New York Times*, 1.

Garcia, D., & Rimé, B. (2019). Collective emotions and social resilience in the digital traces after a terrorist attack. *Psychological Science, 30*, 617–628. https://doi.org/10.1177/0956797619831964.

Garcia, J. H., Sterner, T., & Afsah, S. (2007). Public disclosure of industrial pollution: The PROPER approach in Indonesia. *Environmental and Developmental Economics, 12*, 739–756.

Garner, R. L. (2005). What's in a name? Persuasion perhaps? *Journal of Consumer Psychology, 15*, 108–116.

Gawronski, B. (2003). Implicational schemata and the correspondence bias: On the diagnostic value of situationally constrained behavior. *Journal of Personality and Social Psychology, 84*, 1154–1171.

Geers, A. L., Rose, J. P., Fowler, S. L., Rasinski, H. M., Brown, J. A., & Helfer, S. G. (2013). Why does choice enhance treatment effectiveness? Using placebo treatments to demonstrate the role of personal control. *Journal of Personality and Social Psychology, 105* (4), 549–566. https://doi.org/10.1037/a0034005.

Gehlbach, H., Brinkworth, M. E., King, A. M., Hsu, L. M., McIntyre, J., & Rogers, T. (2016). Creating birds of similar feathers: Leveraging similarity to improve teacher–student relationships and academic achievement. *Journal of Educational Psychology, 108*(3), 342–352. http://dx.doi.org/10.1037/edu0000042.

George, W. H., Gournic, S. J., & McAfee, M. P. (1988). Perceptions of postdrinking female sexuality. *Journal of Applied Social Psychology, 18*, 1295–1317.

Gerard, H. B., & Mathewson, G. C. (1966). The effects of severity of initiation on liking for a group: A replication. *Journal of Experimental Social Psychology, 2*, 278–287.

Gerend, M. A., & Maner, J. K. (2011). Fear, anger, fruits, and veggies: Interactive effects of emotion and message framing on health behavior. *Health Psychology, 30*, 420–423. https://doi.org/10.1037/a0021981.

Gergen, K., Ellsworth, P., Maslach, C., & Seipel, M. (1975). Obligation, donor resources, and reactions to aid in three cultures. *Journal of Personality and Social Psychology, 31*, 390–400.

Ghosh, B. (2009, June 8). How to make terrorists talk. *Time*, 40–43.

Gigerenzer, G., & Goldstein, D. G. (1996). Reasoning the fast and frugal way: Models of bounded rationality. *Psychological Review, 103*, 650–669.

Gilbert, D. T. (2006). *Stumbling on happiness*. New York: Knopf.

Gino, F., & Galinsky, A. D. (2012). Vicarious dishonesty: When psychological closeness creates distance from one's moral compass. *Organizational Behavior and Human Decision Processes, 119*, 15–26.

Gneezy, A., Imas, A., Brown, A., Nelson, L. D., & Norton, M. I. (2012). Paying to be nice: Consistency and costly prosocial behavior. *Management Science, 58*, 179–187.

Gold, B. P., Frank, M. J., Bogert, B., & Brattico, E. (2013). Pleasurable music affects reinforcement learning according to the listener. *Frontiers in Psychology, 4*. https://doi.org/10.3389/fpsyg.2013.00541.

Goldenberg, A., Garcia, D., Halperin, E., & Gross, J. J. (2020). Collective Emotions. *Current Directions in Psychological Science, 29*(2), 154–160. https://doi.org/10.1177/0963721420901574.

Goldenberg, J. L., Courtney, E. P., & Felig, R. N. (2020, April 29). Supporting the dehumanization hypothesis, but under what conditions? A commentary on "Over." *Perspectives on Psychological Science*. https://doi.org/10.1177/1745691620917659.

Goldstein, N. J., Griskevicius, V., & Cialdini, R. B. (2011). Reciprocity by proxy: A new influence strategy for motivating cooperation and prosocial behavior. *Administrative Science Quarterly, 56*, 441–473.

Goldstein, N. J., Mortensen, C. R., Griskevicius, V., & Cialdini, R. B. (2007, January 16). I'll scratch your back if you scratch my brother's: The extended self and extradyadic reciprocity norms. Poster presented at the meeting of the Society of Personality and Social Psychology, Memphis, TN.

Goldstein, N. J., Vezich, I. S., & Shapiro, J. R. (2014). Perceived perspective taking: When others walk in our shoes. *Journal of Personality and Social Psychology, 106*, 941–960. https://doi.org/10.1037/a0036395.

Gómez, Á., Dovidio, J. F., Gaertner, S. L., Fernández, S., & Vázquez, A. (2013). Responses to endorsement of commonality by in-group and outgroup members: The roles of group representation and threat. *Personality and Social Psychology Bulletin, 39*, 419–431. https://doi.org/10.1177/0146167213475366.

Gonzales, M. H., Davis, J. M., Loney, G. L., Lukens, C. K., & Junghans, C. M. (1983). Interactional approach to interpersonal attraction. *Journal of Personality and Social Psychology, 44*, 1192–1197.

Goode, E., & Carey, B. (2015, October 7). Mass killings are seen as a kind of contagion. *New York Times*, A21.

Goodenough, U. W. (1991). Deception by pathogens. *American Scientist, 79*, 344–355.

Goodman-Delahunty, J., Martschuk, N., & Dhami, M. K. (2014). Interviewing high value detainees: Securing cooperation and disclosures. *Applied Cognitive Psychology, 28,* 883–897.

Gorn, G. J. (1982). The effects of music in advertising on choice behavior: A classical conditioning approach. *Journal of Marketing, 46,* 94–101.

Gould, M. S., & Shaffer, D. (1986). The impact of suicide in television movies. *New England Journal of Medicine, 315,* 690–694.

Grant, A. (2013). *Give and take.* New York: Viking.

Grant, A. M., & Hofmann, D. A. (2011). It's not all about me: Motivating hand hygiene among health care professionals by focusing on patients. *Psychological Science, 22,* 1494–1499.

Grant Halvorson, H., & Higgins, E. T. (2013). *Focus: Use different ways of seeing the world for success and influence.* New York: Penguin.

Green, F. (1965). The "foot-in-the-door" technique. *American Salesmen, 10,* 14–16.

Greenberg, M. S., & Shapiro, S. P. (1971). Indebtedness: An adverse effect of asking for and receiving help. *Sociometry, 34,* 290–301.

Greene, J. (2014). *Moral tribes.* New York: Penguin.

Greenwald, A. F., Carnot, C. G., Beach, R., & Young, B. (1987). Increasing voting behavior by asking people if they expect to vote. *Journal of Applied Psychology, 72,* 315–318.

Greenwald, A. G., & Pettigrew, T. F. (2014). With malice toward none and charity for some. *American Psychologist, 69,* 669–684.

Greenwood, B. N., Hardeman, R. R., Huang, L., & Sojourner, A. (2020). Physician–patient racial concordance and disparities in birthing mortality for newborns. *Proceedings of the National Academy of Sciences, 117,* 21194–21200. https://doi.org/10.1073/pnas.1913405117.

Grey, K., Rand, D. G., Ert, E., Lewis, K., Hershman, S., & Norton, M. I. (2014). The emergence of "us and them" in 80 lines of code: Modeling group genesis in homogeneous populations. *Psychological Science, 25,* 982–990.

Griskevicius, V., Cialdini, R. B., & Kenrick, D. T. (2006). Peacocks, Picasso, and parental investment: The effects of romantic motives on creativity. *Journal of Personality and Social Psychology, 91,* 63–76.

Griskevicius, V., Goldstein, N. J., Mortensen, C. R., Sundie, J. M., Cialdini, R. C., & Kenrick, D. T. (2009). Fear and loving in Las Vegas: Evolution, emotion, and persuasion. *Journal of Marketing Research, 46,* 384–395.

Guadagno, R. E., & Cialdini, R. B. (2007). Persuade him by email, but see her in person: Online persuasion revisited. *Computers in Human Behavior, 23,* 999–1015.

Guéguen, N. (2009). Mimicry and seduction: An evaluation in a courtship context. *Social Influence, 4,* 249–255.

Guéguen, N. (2016). "You will probably refuse, but . . .": When activating reactance in a single sentence increases compliance with a request. *Polish Psychological Bulletin, 47,* 170–173.

Guéguen, N., Jacob, C., & Meineri, S. (2011). Effects of the door-in-the-face technique on restaurant customers' behavior. *International Journal of Hospitality Management, 30,* 759–761.

Guéguen, N., Joule, R. V., Halimi, S., Pascual, A., Fischer-Lokou, J., & Dufourcq-Brana, M. (2013). I'm free but I'll comply with your request: Generalization and multidimensional effects of the "evoking freedom" technique. *Journal of Applied Social Psychology, 43*, 116–137.

Guéguen, N., Meineri, S., & Fischer-Lokou, J. (2014). Men's music ability and attractiveness to women in a real-life courtship contest. *Psychology of Music, 42*, 545–549.

Guéguen, N., & Pascual, A. (2000). Evocation of freedom and compliance: The "But you are free of . . ." technique. *Current Research in Social Psychology, 5*, 264–270.

Guéguen, N., & Pascual, A. (2014). Low-ball and compliance: Commitment even if the request is a deviant one, *Social Influence, 9*, 162–171. https://doi.org/10.10 80/15534510.2013.798243.

Gyuris, P., Kozma L., Kisander Z., Láng A., Ferencz, T., & Kocsor, F. (2020). Sibling relations in patchwork families: Co-residence is more influential than genetic relatedness. *Frontiers of Psychology* 11:993. https://doi.org/10.3389/fpsyg .2020.00993.

Hadland, S. E., Cerda, M., Li, Y., Krieger, M. S., & Marshall, B. D. L. (2018). Association of pharmaceutical industry marketing with opioid products to physicians with subsequent opioid prescribing. *Journal of the American Medical Association: Internal Medicine, 178*, 861–863.

Hadnagy, C., & Schulman, S. (2020). *Human hacking: Win friends, influence people, and leave them better off for having met you.* New York: Harper Business.

Hagler, K. J, Pearson, M. R., Venner, B. L., & Greenfield, K. L. (2017). Descriptive drinking norms in Native American and non-Hispanic white college students. *Addictive Behaviors, 72*, 45–50. https://doi.org/10.1016/j.addbeh.2017.03.017.

Hakamata, Y., Lissek, S., Bar-Haim, Y., Britton, J. C., Fox, N. A., Leibenluft, E., Ernest, M., & Pine, D. S. (2010). Attention bias modification treatment: A meta-analysis toward the establishment of novel treatment for anxiety. *Biological Psychiatry, 68*, 982–990. https://doi.org/10.1016/j.biopsych.2010.07.021.

Halpern, D. (2016). *Inside the nudge unit: How small changes can make a big difference.* London: Elbury.

Hamermesh, D. (2011). *Beauty pays: Why attractive people are more successful.* Princeton, NJ: Princeton University Press.

Hamermesh, D., & Biddle, J. E. (1994). Beauty and the labor market. *American Economic Review, 84*, 1174–1194.

Hamilton, W. D. (1964). The genetic evolution of social behavior. *Journal of Theoretical Biology, 7*, 1–52.

Hamlin, J. K., Mahajan, N., Liberman, Z., & Wynn, K. (2013). Not like me = bad: Infants prefer those who harm dissimilar others. *Psychological Science, 24*, 589–594. https://doi.org/10.1177/0956797612457785.

Harmon-Jones, E., Harmon-Jones, C., & Levy, N. (2015). An action-based model of cognitive-dissonance processes. *Current Directions in Psychological Science, 24*, 184–189. https://doi.org/10.1177/0963721414566449.

Harvey, A. R. (2018). Music and the meeting of human minds. *Frontiers in Psychology, 9*, 762. https://doi.org/10.3389/fpsyg.2018.00762.

Haselton, M. G., & Nettle, D. (2006). The paranoid optimist: An integrated evolutionary model of cognitive biases. *Personality and Social Psychology Review, 10*, 47–66.

Haslam, N. (2006). Dehumanization: An integrative review. *Personality and Social Psychology Review, 10,* 252–264.

Haslam, N., & Loughnan, S. (2014). Dehumanization and infrahumanization. *Annual Review of Psychology, 65,* 399–423. https://doi.org/10.1146/annurev -psych-010213-115045.

Hassan, S. (2000). *Releasing the bonds: Empowering people to think for themselves.* Boston: Freedom of Mind Press.

Hatemi, P. K., & McDermott, R. (2012). The genetics of politics: Discovery, challenges, and progress. *Trends in Genetics, 28,* 525–533.

Hattori, Y., & Tomonaga, M. (2020). Rhythmic swaying induced by sound in chimpanzees (*Pan troglodytes*). *Proceedings of the National Academy of Sciences, 117,* 936–942. https://doi.org/10.1073/pnas.1910318116.

Häubl, G., & Popkowski Leszczyc, P. T. L. (2019). Bidding frenzy: Speed of competitor reaction and willingness to pay in auctions. *Journal of Consumer Research, 45,* 1294–1314. https://doi.org/10.1093/jcr/ucy056.

Hehman, E., Flake, J. K., & Freeman, J. B. (2018). The faces of group members share physical resemblance. *Personality and Social Psychology Bulletin, 44*(1), 3–15. https://doi.org/10.1177/0146167217722556.

Heijkoop, M., Dubas, J. S., & van Aken, M. A. G. (2009). Parent-child resemblance and kin investment. *European Journal of Developmental Psychology, 6,* 64–69.

Heilman, C. M., Nakamoto, K., & Rao, A. G. (2002). Pleasant surprises: Consumer response to unexpected in-store coupons. *Journal of Marketing Research, 39,* 242–252.

Heilman, M. E. (1976). Oppositional behavior as a function of influence attempt intensity and retaliation threat. *Journal of Personality and Social Psychology, 33,* 574–578.

Heinrich, C. U., & Borkenau , P. (1998). Deception and deception detection: The role of cross-modal inconsistency. *Journal of Personality, 66,* 687–712.

Henry, M. L., Ferraro, P. J., & Kontoleon, A. (2019). The behavioural effect of electronic home energy reports: Evidence from a randomised field trial in the United States. *Energy Policy, 132,* 1256–1261. https://doi.org/10.1016/j.enpol .2019.06.039.

Hershfield, H. E., Goldstein, D. G., Sharpe, W. F., Fox, J., Yeykelis, L., Carstensen, L. L., & Bailenson, J. N. (2011). Increasing saving behavior through age-progressed renderings of the future self. *Journal of Marketing Research, 48,* 23–37. https://doi.org/10.1509/jmkr.48.SPL.S23.

Higgins, C. A., & Judge, T. A. (2004). The effect of applicant influence tactics on recruiter perceptions of fit and hiring recommendations: A field study. *Journal of Applied Psychology, 89,* 622–632.

Higgins, E. T., (2012). *Beyond pleasure and pain: How motivation works.* New York: Oxford University Press.

Higgins, E. T., Lee, J., Kwon, J., & Trope, Y. (1995). When combining intrinsic motivations undermines interest. *Journal of Personality and Social Psychology, 68,* 749–767.

Higgins, E. T., Shah, J., & Friedman, R. (1997). Emotional responses to goal attainment: Strength of regulatory focus as moderator. *Journal of Personality and Social Psychology, 72,* 515–525. https://doi.org/10.1037/0022-3514.72.3.515.

Higham, P. A., & Carment, D. W. (1992). The rise and fall of politicians. *Canadian Journal of Behavioral Science*, 404–409.

Hildreth, J. A., & Anderson, C. (2018). Does loyalty trump honesty? Moral judgments of loyalty-driven deceit. *Journal of Experimental Social Psychology, 79*, 87–94.

Hills, T. T. (2019). The dark side of information proliferation. *Perspectives on Psychological Science, 14*, 323–330. https://doi.org/10.1177/1745691618803647.

Hills, T. T., Adelman, J. S., & Noguchi, T. (2017). Attention economies, information crowding, and language change. In M. N. Jones (ed.), *Big data in cognitive science* (pp. 270–293). New York: Routledge.

Hobfoll, S. E. (2001). The influence of culture, community, and the nested-self in the stress process. *Applied Psychology: An International Review, 50*, 337–421.

Hodson, G. (2011). Do ideologically intolerant people benefit from intergroup contact? *Current Directions in Psychological Science, 20*, 154–159. https://doi.org/10.1177/0963721411409025.

Hodson, G., Crisp, R. J., Meleady, R., & Earle, M. (2018). Intergroup contact as an agent of cognitive liberalization. *Perspectives on Psychological Science, 13*, 523–548. https://doi.org/10.1177/1745691617752324.

Hofling, C. K., Brotzman, E., Dalrymple, S., Graves, N., & Pierce, C. M. (1966). An experimental study of nurse–physician relationships. *Journal of Nervous and Mental Disease, 143*, 171–180.

Hofmann, W., De Houwer, J., Perugini, M., Baeyens, F., & Crombez, G. (2010). Evaluative conditioning in humans: A meta-analysis. *Psychological Bulletin, 136*, 390–421. http://dx.doi.org/10.1037/a0018916.

Holmes, W. (2004). The early history of Hamiltonian-based research on kin recognition. *Annales Zoologici Fennici, 41*, 691–711.

Holmes, W. G., & Sherman, P. W. (1983). Kin recognition in animals. *American Scientist, 71*, 46–55.

Hove, M. J., & Risen, J. L. (2009). It's all in the timing: Interpersonal synchrony increases affiliation. *Social Cognition, 27*, 949–961.

Howard, D. J. (1990). The influence of verbal responses to common greetings on compliance behavior: The foot-in-the-mouth effect. *Journal of Applied Social Psychology, 20*, 1185–1196.

Howard, D. J., Shu, S. B., & Kerin, R. A. (2007). Reference price and scarcity appeals and the use of multiple influence strategies in retail newspaper advertising. *Social Influence, 2*, 18–28.

Howe, L. C., Carr, P. B., & Walton, G. W. (in press). Normative appeals are more effective when they invite people to work together toward a common goal. *Journal of Personality and Social Psychology*.

Howe, M. L. (2003). Memories from the cradle. *Current Directions in Psychological Science, 12*, 62–65.

Hubbard, T. L. (2015). The varieties of momentum-like experience. *Psychological Bulletin, 141*, 1081–1119. https://doi.org/10.1037/ bul0000016.

Hufer, A., Kornadt, A. E., Kandler, C., & Riemann, R. (2020). Genetic and environmental variation in political orientation in adolescence and early adulthood: A Nuclear Twin Family analysis. *Journal of Personality and Social Psychology, 118*, 762–776. https://doi.org/10.1037/pspp0000258.

Hughes, S., Ye, Y., Van Dessel, P., & De Houwer, J. (2019). When people co-occur with good or bad events: Graded effects of relational qualifiers on evaluative conditioning. *Personality and Social Psychology Bulletin, 45,* 196–208. https:// doi.org/10.1177/0146167218781340.

Hugh-Jones, D., Ron, I., & Zultan, R. (2019). Humans discriminate by reciprocating against group peers. *Evolution and Human Behavior, 40,* 90–95.

Ilmarinen, V. J., Lönnqvist, J. E., & Paunonen, S. (2016). Similarity-attraction effects in friendship formation: Honest platoon-mates prefer each other but dishonest do not. *Personality and Individual Differences, 92,* 153–158. https://doi .org/10.1016/j.paid.2015.12.040.

Inzlicht, M., Gutsell, J. N., & Legault, L. (2012). Mimicry reduces racial prejudice. *Journal of Experimental Social Psychology, 48,* 361–365.

Iyengar, S., Sood, G., & Lelkes, Y. (2012). Affect, not ideology: A social identity perspective on polarization. *Public Opinion Quarterly, 76,* 405–431.

Jabbi, M., Bastiaansen, J., & Keysers, C. (2008). A common anterior insula representation of disgust observation, experience and imagination shows divergent functional connectivity pathways. *PLoS ONE, 3,* e2939. https://doi.org/10.1371 /journal.pone.0002939

Jackson, J. C., Gelfand, M. J., Ayub, N., & Wheeler, J. (2019). Together from afar: Introducing a diary contact technique for improving intergroup relations. *Behavioral Science & Policy, 5,* 15–33.

Jacob, C., Guéguen, N., Martin, A., & Boulbry, G. (2011). Retail salespeople's mimicry of customers: Effects on consumer behavior. *Journal of Retailing and Consumer Services, 18,* 381–388.

James, J. M., & Bolstein, R. (1992). Effect of monetary incentives and follow-up mailings on the response rate and response quality in mail surveys. *Public Opinion Quarterly, 54,* 442–453.

Jenke, L., & Huettel, S. A. (2020) Voter preferences reflect a competition between policy and identity. *Frontiers of Psycholology, 11:* 566020. https://doi.org /10.3389/fpsyg.2020.566020.

Jiang, L., Hoegg, J., Dahl, D. W., & Chattopadhyay, A. (2010). The persuasive role of incidental similarity on attitudes and purchase intentions in a sales context. *Journal of Consumer Research, 36,* 778–791.

John, L. K., Blunden, H., & Liu, H. (2019). Shooting the messenger. *Journal of Experimental Psychology: General, 148*(4), 644–666. http://dx.doi.org/10.1037 /xge0000586.

Johnson, D. W. (2003). Social interdependence: Interrelationships among theory, research, and practice. *American Psychologist, 58,* 934–945.

Jones, E. E., & Harris, V. E. (1967). The attribution of attitudes. *Journal of Experimental Social Psychology, 3,* 1–24.

Jones, J. T., Pelham, B. W., Carvallo, M., & Mirenberg, M. C. (2004). How do I love thee? Let me count the J's. Implicit egoism and interpersonal attraction. *Journal of Personality and Social Psychology, 87,* 665–683.

Jong, J., Whitehouse, H., Kavanagh, C., & Lane, J. (2015). Shared negative experiences lead to identity fusion via personal reflection. *PLoS ONE, 10.* https://doi .org/10.1371/journal.pone.0145611.

Joule, R. V. (1987). Tobacco deprivation: The foot-in-the-door technique versus the low-ball technique. *European Journal of Social Psychology, 17,* 361–365.

Judge, T. A., & Cable, D. M. (2004). The effect of physical height on workplace success and income. *Journal of Applied Psychology, 89*, 428–441.

Judge, T. A., Hurst, C., & Simon, L. S. (2009). Does it pay to be smart, attractive, or confident (or all three)? Relationships among general mental ability, physical attractiveness, core self-evaluations, and income. *Journal of Applied Psychology, 94*, 742–755.

Jung, J., Busching, R., & Krahé, B. (2019). Catching aggression from one's peers: A longitudinal and multilevel analysis. *Social and Personality Psychology Compass, 13*. https://doi.org/10.1111/spc3.12433.

Kahn, B. E., & Baron, J. (1995). An exploratory study of choice rules favored for high-stakes decisions. *Journal of Consumer Psychology, 4*, 305–328.

Kahneman, D. (2011). *Thinking, fast and slow*. New York: Farrar, Straus and Giroux.

Kahneman, D., Slovic, P., & Tversky, A. (eds.). (1982). *Judgment under uncertainty: Heuristics and biases*. New York: Cambridge University Press.

Kahneman, D., & Tversky, A. (1979). Prospect theory: An analysis of decision under risk. *Econometrica, 47*, 263–291.

Kalmoe, N. P. (2019). Dueling views in a canonical measure of sophistication. *Public Opinion Research, 83*, 68–90.

Kaminski, G., Ravary, F., Graff, C., & Gentaz, E. (2010). Firstborns' disadvantage in kinship detection. *Psychological Science, 21*, 1746–1750.

Kandler, C., Bleidorn, W., & Riemann, R. (2012). Left or right? Sources of political orientation: The roles of genetic factors, cultural transmission, assortative mating, and personality. *Journal of Personality and Social Psychology, 102*, 633–645.

Kang, S. K., Hirsh, J. B., Chasteen, A. L. (2010). Your mistakes are mine: Self-other overlap predicts neural response to observed errors. *Journal of Experimental Social Psychology, 46*, 229–232.

Kardes, F. R., Posavac, S. S., & Cronley, M. L. (2004). Consumer inference: A review of processes, bases, and judgment contexts. *Journal of Consumer Psychology, 14*, 230–256.

Karim, A. A., Lützenkirchen, B., Khedr, E., & Khalil, R. (2017). Why is 10 past 10 the default setting for clocks and watches in advertisements? A psychological experiment. *Frontiers of Psychology 8*:1410. https://doi.org/10.3389/fpsyg.2017.01410.

Karremans, J. C., & Aarts, H. (2007). The role of automaticity in determining the inclination to forgive close others. *Journal of Experimental Social Psychology, 43*, 902–917.

Kauff, M., Asbrock, F., Thörner, S., & Wagner, U. (2013). Side effects of multiculturalism: The interaction effect of a multicultural ideology and authoritarianism on prejudice and diversity beliefs. *Personality and Social Psychology Bulletin, 39*, 305–320. https://doi.org/10.1177/0146167212473160.

Kay, T., Keller, L., & Lehmann, L. (2020). The evolution of altruism and the serial rediscovery of the role of relatedness. *Proceedings of the National Academy of Sciences, 117*, 28894–28898; https://doi.org/10.1073/pnas.2013596117.

Keil, F. C. (2012). Running on empty? How folk science gets by with less. *Current Directions in Psychological Science, 21*, 329–334. https://doi.org/10.1177/0963721412453721.

Keinan, A., & Kivetz, R. (2011). Productivity orientation and the consumption of collectable experiences. *Journal of Consumer Research, 37*, 935–950.

Kende, J., Phalet, K., Van den Noortgate, W., Kara, A., & Fischer, R. (2018). Equality revisited: A cultural meta-analysis of intergroup contact and prejudice. *Social Psychological and Personality Science, 9*, 887–895. https://doi.org/10.1177/1948550617728993.

Kenrick, D. T. (2012). Evolutionary theory and human social behavior. In P. A. M. Van Lange, A. W. Kruglanski, and E. T. Higgins (eds.), *Handbook of Theories of Social Psychology* (pp. 11–31). Thousand Oaks, CA: Sage.

Kenrick, D. T. (2020). True friendships are communistic, not capitalist. http://spsp.org/news-center/blog/kenrick-true-friendships#gsc.tab=0.

Kenrick, D. T., Gutierres, S. E., & Goldberg, L. L. (1989). Influence of popular erotica on judgments of strangers and mates. *Journal of Experimental Social Psychology, 25*, 159–167.

Kenrick, D. T., Neuberg, S. L., Cialdini, R. B., & Lundberg-Kenrick, D. E. (2020). *Social Psychology: Goals in interaction.* 7th ed. Boston: Pearson Education.

Kerr, N. L., & MacCoun, R. J. (1985). The effects of jury size and polling method on the process and product of jury deliberation. *Journal of Personality and Social Psychology, 48*, 349–363.

Kesebir, S. (2012). The superorganism account of human sociality: How and when human groups are like beehives. *Personality and Social Psychology Review, 16*, 233–261.

Ketelaar, T. (1995, June). *Emotions as mental representations of gains and losses: Translating prospect theory into positive and negative affect.* Paper presented at the meeting of the American Psychological Society, New York, NY.

Kettle, K. I., & Häubl, G. (2011). The signature effect: Signing influences consumption-related behavior by priming self-identity. *Journal of Consumer Research. 38*, 474–489.

Keysar, B., Converse, B. A., Wang, J., & Epley, N. (2008). Reciprocity is not give and take: Asymmetric reciprocity to positive and negative acts. *Psychological Science, 19*, 1280–1286.

Khamitov, M., Wang, X., & Thomson, M. (2019). How well do consumer–brand relationships drive customer brand loyalty? Generalizations from a meta-analysis of brand relationship elasticities. *Journal of Consumer Research, 46*, 435–459. https://doi.org/10.1093/jcr/ucz006.

Kimel, S. Y., Huesmann, R., Kunst, J. R., & Halperin, E. (2016). Living in a genetic world: How learning about interethnic genetic similarities and differences affects peace and conflict. *Personality and Social Psychology Bulletin, 42*, 688–700. https://doi.org/10.1177/0146167216642196.

Kirschner, S., & Tomasello, M. (2010). Joint music making promotes prosocial behavior in 4-year-old children. *Evolution and Human Behavior, 31*, 354–364.

Kissinger, H. (1982). *Years of upheaval.* Boston: Little, Brown.

Klein, C. (2020, March 13). Why Coca-Cola's "New Coke" flopped. History (website). www.history.com/news/why-coca-cola-new-coke-flopped.

Klein, H. J., Lount, R. B., Jr., Park, H. M., & Linford, B. J. (2020). When goals are known: The effects of audience relative status on goal commitment and performance. *Journal of Applied Psychology, 105*, 372–389. https://doi.org/10.1037 /apl0000441.

Klein, N., & O'Brien, E. (2018). People use less information than they think to make up their minds. *Proceedings of the National Academy of Sciences*. https:// doi.org/10.1073/pnas.1805327115.

Knishinsky, A. (1982). The effects of scarcity of material and exclusivity of information on industrial buyer perceived risk in provoking a purchase decision. Unpublished PhD diss., Arizona State University, Tempe.

Knouse, S. B. (1983). The letter of recommendation: Specificity and favorability information. *Personal Psychology, 36*, 331–341.

Knox, R. E., & Inkster, J. A. (1968). Postdecisional dissonance at post time. *Journal of Personality and Social Psychology, 8*, 319–323.

Koch, T., & Peter, C. (2017). Effects of equivalence framing on the perceived truth of political messages and the trustworthiness of politicians. *Public Opinion Quarterly, 81*, 847–865. https://doi.org/10.1093/poq/nfx019.

Koch, T., & Zerback, T. (2013). Helpful or harmful? How frequent repetition affects perceived statement credibility. *Journal of Communication, 63*, 993–1010.

Kouchaki, M., Gino, F., & Feldman, Y. (2019). The ethical perils of personal, communal relations: A language perspective. *Psychological Science, 30*, 1745–1766. https://doi.org/10.1177/0956797619882917.

Koudenburg, N., Postmes, T., Gordijn, E. H., & van Mourik Broekman, A. (2015). Uniform and complementary social interaction: Distinct pathways to solidarity. *PloS ONE, 10*. https://doi.org/10.1371/journal.pone.0129061.

Krajbich, I., Camerer, C., Ledyard, J., & Rangel, A. (2009). Self-control in decision-making involves modulation of the vmPFC valuation system. *Science, 324*, 12315–12320.

Kranzler, D. (1976). *Japanese, Nazis, and Jews: The Jewish refugee community of Shanghai, 1938–1945.* New York: Yeshiva University Press.

Kraut, R. E. (1973). Effects of social labeling on giving to charity. *Journal of Experimental Social Psychology, 9*, 551–562.

Kriner, D. L., & Shen, F. X. (2012). How citizens respond to combat casualties: The differential impact of local casualties on support for the war in Afghanistan. *Public Opinion Quarterly, 76*, 761–770.

Kristensson, P., Wästlund, E., & Söderlund, M. (2017). Influencing consumers to choose environment friendly offerings: Evidence from field experiments. *Journal of Business Research, 76*, 89–97.

Krizan, Z., & Suls, J. (2008). Losing sight of oneself in the above average effect: When egocentrism, focalism, and group diffusiveness collide. *Journal of Experimental Social Psychology, 44*, 929–942.

Kteily, N., Bruneau, E., Waytz, A., & Cotterill, S. (2015). The ascent of man: Theoretical and empirical evidence for blatant dehumanization. *Journal of Personality and Social Psychology, 109*, 901–931. https://doi.org/10.1037/pspp000 0048.

Ku, G. (2008). Before escalation: Behavioral and affective forecasting in escalation of commitment. *Personality and Social Psychology Bulletin, 34*, 1477–1491. https://doi.org/10.1177/0146167208322559.

Kuester, M., & Benkenstein, M. (2014). Turning dissatisfied into satisfied customers: How referral reward programs affect the referrer's attitude and loyalty toward the recommended service provider. *Journal of Retailing and Consumer Services, 21*, 897–904.

Kunz, P. R., & Woolcott, M. (1976). Season's greetings: From my status to yours. *Social Science Research, 5*, 269–278.

Lack, D. (1943). *The life of the robin.* London: Cambridge University Press.

Lai, C. K., Skinner, A. L., Cooley, E., Murrar, S. Brauer, M., Devos, T., Calanchini, J., et al. (2016). Reducing implicit racial preferences: II. Intervention effectiveness across time. *Journal of Experimental Psychology: General, 145*, 1001–1016. https://doi.org/10.1037/xge0000179.

Lammers, H. B. (1991). The effect of free samples on immediate consumer purchase. *Journal of Consumer Marketing, 8*, 31–37.

Langer, E., Blank, A., & Chanowitz, B. (1978). The mindlessness of ostensibly thoughtful action: The role of "placebic" information in interpersonal interaction. *Journal of Personality and Social Psychology, 36*, 635–642.

Langer, E. J. (1989). Minding matters. In L. Berkowitz (ed.), *Advances in experimental social psychology* (vol. 22, pp. 137–173). New York: Academic Press.

Langlois, J. H., Kalakanis, A., Rubenstein, A. J., Larson, A., Hallam, M., & Smoot, M. (2000). Maxims or myths of beauty: A meta-analytic and theoretical review. *Psychological Bulletin, 126*, 390–423.

Lansky, D. (2002, March 31). A day for stiffupperlipps, other nags. *Arizona Republic*, T4.

LaPorte, N. (2018). In a major reversal, Netflix is about to reveal how many people watch its most popular shows. www.fastcompany.com/90335959/in-a-major-reversal-netflix-is-about-to-reveal-how-many-people-watch-its-most-popular-shows.

Latané, B., & Darley, J. M. (1968). Group inhibition of bystander intervention in emergencies. *Journal of Personality and Social Psychology, 10*, 215–221.

Law, S., & Braun, K., A. (2000). I'll have what she's having: Gauging the impact of product placements on viewers. *Psychology & Marketing, 17*, 1059–1075.

Lazarov, A., Abend, R., Seidner, S., Pine, D. S., & Bar-Haim, Y. (2017). The effects of training contingency awareness during attention bias modification on learning and stress reactivity. *Behavior Therapy, 48*, 638–650.

Leach, W. C., Ellemers, N., & Barreto M. (2007). Group virtue: The impact of morality (vs. competence and sociability) in the positive evaluation of in-groups. *Journal of Personality and Social Psychology, 93*, 234–249.

Leakey, R., & Lewin, R. (1978). *People of the lake.* New York: Anchor/Doubleday.

Lee, A. Y., & Aaker, J. L. (2004). Bringing the frame into focus: The influence of regulatory fit on processing fluency and persuasion. *Journal of Personality and Social Psychology, 86*, 205–218. https://doi.org/10.1037/0022-3514.86.2.205.

Lee, F., Peterson, C., & Tiedens, L. Z. (2004). Mea culpa: Predicting stock prices from organizational attributions. *Journal of Personality and Social Psychology, 30*, 1636–1649.

Lefkowitz, M., Blake, R. R., & Mouton, J. S. (1955). Status factors in pedestrian violation of traffic signals. *Journal of Abnormal and Social Psychology, 51*, 704–706.

Legate, N., Weinstein, N., Sendi, K., & Al-Khouja, M. (2020). Motives behind the veil: Women's affective experiences wearing a veil depend on their reasons for wearing one. *Journal of Research in Personality, 87*, 103969. https://doi.org /10.1016/j.jrp.2020.103969.

Leopold, A. (1989). *A Sand County almanac.* New York: Oxford University Press.

Leotti, L. A., & Delgado, M. R. (2011). The inherent reward of choice. *Psychological Science, 22*, 1310–1318. https://doi.org/10.1177/0956797611417005.

Lepper, M. R., & Greene, D. (eds.). (1978). *The hidden costs of reward.* Hillsdale, NJ: Lawrence Erlbaum.

Levendusky, M. S. (2018). Americans, not partisans: Can priming American national identity reduce affective polarization? *Journal of Politics, 80*, 59–70. https:// doi.org/10.1086/693987.

Levine, H. (1997). *In search of Sugihara.* New York: Free Press.

Levy J., Markell, D., & Cerf, M. (2019). Polar similars: Using massive mobile dating data to predict synchronization and similarity in dating preferences. *Frontiers of Psychology.* https://doi.org/10.3389/fpsyg.2019.02010.

Lewis, G. J., & Bates, T. C. (2010). Genetic evidence for multiple biological mechanisms underlying in-group favoritism. *Psychological Science, 21*, 1623–1628.

Li, W., Moallem, I., Paller, K. A., Gottfried, J. A. (2007). Subliminal smells can guide social preferences. *Psychological Science, 18*, 1044–1049.

Lieberman, J. D., & Arndt, J. (2000). Understanding the limits of limiting instructions. *Psychology, Public Policy, and Law, 6*, 677–711.

Lieberman, D., & Smith, A. (2012). It's all relative: Sexual aversions and moral judgments regarding sex among siblings. *Current Directions in Psychological Science, 21*, 243–247. https://doi.org/10.1177/0963721412447620.

Lieberman, D., Tooby, J., & Cosmides, L. (2007). The architecture of human kin detection. *Nature, 445*, 727–731. https://doi.org/10.1038/nature05510.

Lim, S., O'Doherty, J. P., & Rangel, A. (2011). The decision value computations in the vmPFC and striatum use a relative value code that is guided by visual attention. *Journal of Neuroscience, 31*, 13214–13223.

Lin, J. S., & Sung, Y. (2014). Nothing can tear us apart: The effect of brand identity fusion in consumer–brand relationships. *Psychology & Marketing., 31*, 54–69. https://doi.org/10.1002/mar.20675.

Linder, J. A., Meeker, D., Fox, C. R., Friedberg, M. W., Persell, S. D., Goldstein, N. J., & Doctor, J. N. (2017). Effects of behavioral interventions on inappropriate antibiotic prescribing in primary care 12 months after stopping interventions. *Journal of the American Medical Association, 318*, 1391–1392. https://doi .org/10.1001/jama.2017.11152.

Liu, W., & Gal, D. (2011). Bringing us together or driving us apart: The effect of soliciting consumer input on consumers' propensity to transact with an organization. *Journal of Consumer Research, 38*, 242–259.

Lloyd, J. E. (1965). Aggressive mimicry in *Photuris:* Firefly *femme fatales. Science, 149*, 653–654.

Loersch, C., & Arbuckle, N. L. (2013). Unraveling the mystery of music: Music as an evolved group process. *Journal of Personality and Social Psychology, 105*, 777–798.

Lokhorst, A. M., Werner, C., Staats, H., van Dijk, E., & Gale, J. L. (2013). Commitment and behavior change: A meta-analysis and critical review of commitment-making strategies in environmental research. *Environment and Behavior 45*, 3–34. https:// doi.org/10.1177/0013916511411477.

Loschelder, D. D, Siepelmeyer, H., Fischer, D., & Rubel, J. (2019). Dynamic norms drive sustainable consumption: Norm-based nudging helps café customers to avoid disposable to-go-cups. *Journal of Economic Psychology, 75*, 102146.

Lynn, M. (1989). Scarcity effect on value: Mediated by assumed expensiveness. *Journal of Economic Psychology, 10*, 257–274.

Lytton, J. (1979). Correlates of compliance and the rudiments of conscience in two-year-old boys. *Canadian Journal of Behavioral Science, 9*, 242–251.

MacGregor-Hastie, R. (1988). *Picasso's women*. London: Lennard.

Mack, D., & Rainey, D. (1990). Female applicants' grooming and personnel selection. *Journal of Social Behavior and Personality, 5*, 399–407.

MacKay, C. (1841/1932). *Extraordinary Popular Delusions and the Madness of Crowds*. New York: Farrar, Straus and Giroux.

MacKenzie, B. (1974, June 22). When sober executives went on a bidding binge. *TV Guide*.

Madanika, Y., & Bartholomew, K. (2014, August 14). Themes of lust and love in popular music from 1971 to 2011. *SAGE Open, 4*(3). https://doi.org/10.1177/2158 244014547179.

Maddux, W. W., Mullen, E., & Galinsky, A. (2008). Chameleons bake bigger pies and take bigger pieces: Strategic behavioral mimicry facilitates negotiation outcomes. *Journal of Experimental Social Psychology, 44*, 461–468.

Maestripieri, D., Henry, A., & Nickels, N. (2017). Explaining financial and prosocial biases in favor of attractive people: Interdisciplinary perspectives from economics, social psychology, and evolutionary psychology. *Behavioral and Brain Sciences, 40*, E19. https://doi.org/10.1017/S0140525X16000340.

Maglio, S. J., & Polman, E. (2016). Revising probability estimates: Why increasing likelihood means increasing impact. *Journal of Personality and Social Psychology, 111*, 141–158. https://doi.org/10.1037/pspa0000058.

Magruder, J. S. (1974). *An American life: One man's road to Watergate*. New York: Atheneum.

Mahajan, N., Martinez, M. A., Gutierrez, N. L., Diesendruck, G., Banaji, M. R., & Santos, L. R. (2011). *Journal of Personality and Social Psychology, 100*, 387–405.

Maheshwari, S. (2019, November 29). The online star rating system is flawed . . . and you never know if you can trust what you read. *New York Times*, B1, B4.

Main, K. J., Dahl, D. W., & Darke, P. R. (2007). Deliberative and automatic bases of suspicion: Empirical evidence of the sinister attribution error. *Journal of Consumer Psychology, 17*, 59–69. https://doi.org/10.1207/s15327663jcp1701_9.

Maisel, N. C, & Gable, S. L. (2009). The paradox of received social support: The importance of responsiveness. *Psychological Science, 20*, 928–932.

Makary, M. A., & Daniel, M. (2016). Medical error—the third leading cause of death in the US. *BMJ, 353*. https://doi.org/10.1136/bmj.i2139.

Makurdi, W. (2013, May 26). 23 youths dead in South Africa during adulthood initiation rites. *Arizona Republic*, A32.

Malinowski, B. (1922). *Argonauts of the Western Pacific: An account of native enterprise and adventure in the archipelagoes of Melanesian New Guinea*. www.guten berg.org/files/55822/55822-h/55822-h.htm.

Mallett, R. K., Wilson, T. D., & Gilbert, D. T. (2008). Expect the unexpected: Failure to anticipate similarities leads to an intergroup forecasting error. *Journal of Personality and Social Psychology, 94,* 265–277.

Mallon, B., Redies, C., & Hayn-Leichsenring, G. U. (2014). Beauty in abstract paintings: Perceptual contrast and statistical properties. *Frontiers of Human Neuroscience, 8,* 161. https://doi.org/10.3389/fnhum.2014.00161.

Mandel, N., & Johnson, E. J. (2002). When web pages influence choice: Effects of visual primes on experts and novices. *Journal of Consumer Research, 29,* 235–245.

Manis, M., Cornell, S. D., & Moore, J. C. (1974). Transmission of attitude relevant information through a communication chain. *Journal of Personality and Social Psychology, 30,* 81–94.

Mann, T., Nolen-Hoeksema, S. K., Burgard, D., Huang, K., Wright, A., & Hansen, K. (1997). Are two interventions worse than none? *Health Psychology, 16,* 215–225.

Mannes, A. E., Soll, J. B., & Larrick, R. P. (2014). The wisdom of select crowds. *Journal of Personality and Social Psychology, 107,* 276–299. https://doi.org/10.1037/a0036677.

Manning, R., Levine, M., & Collins, A. (2007). The Kitty Genovese murder and the social psychology of helping: The parable of the 38 witnesses. *American Psychologist, 62,* 555–562. https://doi.org/10.1037/0003-066X.62.6.555.

Marcoux, J-S. (2009). Escaping the gift economy. *Journal of Consumer Research, 36,* 671–685.

Margulis, E. H. (2010). When program notes don't help: Music descriptions and enjoyment. *Psychology of Music, 38,* 285–302.

Markman, K. D., & Guenther, C. L. (2007). Psychological momentum: Intuitive physics and naive beliefs. *Personality and Social Psychology Bulletin, 33,* 800–812. https://doi.org/10.1177/0146167207301026.

Markowitz, D. M., & Slovic, P. (2020). Social, psychological, and demographic characteristics of dehumanization toward immigrants. *Proceedings of the National Academy of Sciences, 117,* 9260–9269. https://doi.org/10.1073/pnas.1921790117.

Marks, J., Copland, E., Loh, E., Sunstein, C. R., Sharot, T. (2019). Epistemic spillovers: Learning others' political views reduces the ability to assess and use their expertise in nonpolitical domains. *Cognition, 188,* 74–84. https://doi.org/10.1016/j.cognition.2018.10.003.

Martin, S. J., Goldstein, N. J., & Cialdini, R. B. (2014). *The small BIG: Small changes that spark big influence.* New York: Grand Central Publishing.

Martin, S. J., & Marks, J. (2019). *Messengers: Who we listen to, who we don't, and why.* New York: Public Affairs.

Mashek, D. J., Aron, A., & Boncimino, M. (2003). Confusions of self with close others. *Personality and Social Psychology Bulletin, 29,* 382–392.

Masket, S. E. (2009). Did Obama's ground game matter? The influence of local field offices during the 2008 presidential election. *Public Opinion Quarterly, 73,* 1023–1039.

Mateo, J. M. (2003). Kin recognition in ground squirrels and other rodents. *Journal of Mammalogy. 84,* 1163–1181. https://doi.org/10.1644/BLe-011.

Mateo, J. M. (2015). Perspectives: Hamilton's legacy: mechanisms of kin recognition in humans. *Ethology 121*, 419–427. https://doi.org/10.1111/eth.12358.

Mather, M., Shafir, E., & Johnson, M. K. (2000). Misremembrance of options past: Source monitoring and choice. *Psychological Science, 11*, 132–138.

Matthies, E., Klöckner, C. A., Preißner, C. L. (2006). Applying a modified moral decision making model to change habitual car use: How can commitment be effective? *Applied Psychology 55*, 91–106. https://doi.org/10.1111/j.1464-0597 .2006.00237.x.

Maus, G. W., Goh, H. L., & Lisi, M. (2020). Perceiving locations of moving objects across eyeblinks. *Psychological Science*. https://doi.org/10.1177/09567976 20931365.

Mauss, M. (1990). *The gift: The form and reason for exchange in archaic societies.* Translated by W. D. Halls. Abingdon: Routledge.

Mauss, S. (December 4, 2012). "Hitler's Jewish Commander and Victim." *Jewish Voice from Germany.* http://jewish-voice-from-germany.de/cms/hitlers-jewish -commander-and-victim.

Mayer, N. D., & Tormala, Z. (2010). "Think" versus "feel" framing effects. *Personality and Social Psychology Bulletin, 36*, 443–454.

Mazis, M. B. (1975). Antipollution measures and psychological reactance theory: A field experiment. *Journal of Personality and Social Psychology, 31*, 654–666.

Mazis, M. B., Settle, R. B., & Leslie, D. C. (1973). Elimination of phosphate detergents and psychological reactance. *Journal of Marketing Research, 10*, 390–395.

McCall, M., & Belmont, H. J. (1996). Credit card insignia and restaurant tipping: Evidence for an associative link. *Journal of Applied Psychology, 81*, 609–613.

McDonald, M., Porat, R., Yarkoney, A., Reifen Tagar, M., Kimel, S., Saguy, T., & Halperin, E. (2017). Intergroup emotional similarity reduces dehumanization and promotes conciliatory attitudes in prolonged conflict. *Group Processes & Intergroup Relations, 20*, 125–136. https://doi.org/10.1177/1368430215595107.

McFarland, S. (2017). Identification with all humanity: The antithesis of prejudice, and more. In C. G. Sibley and F. K. Barlow (eds.), *The Cambridge handbook of the psychology of prejudice* (pp. 632–654). Cambridge: Cambridge University Press. https://doi.org/10.1017/9781316161579.028.

McFarland, S., Webb, M., & Brown D. (2012). All humanity is my in-group: A measure and studies of identification with all humanity. *Journal of Personality and Social Psychology, 103*, 830–853.

McGuinnies, E., & Ward, C. D. (1980). Better liked than right: Trustworthiness and expertise as factors in credibility. *Personality and Social Psychology Bulletin, 6*, 467–472.

McKenzie, C. R. M., & Chase, V. M. (2010). Why rare things are precious: The importance of rarity in lay inference. In P. M. Todd, G. Gigerenzer, and the ABC Research Group (eds.), *Ecological rationality: Intelligence in the world* (pp. 81–101). Oxford: Oxford University Press.

McKeown, S., & Dixson, J. (2017). The "contact hypothesis": Critical reflections and future directions. *Social & Personality Psychology Compass, 11*. https://doi .org/10.1111/spc3.12295.

McNeill, W. H. (1995). *Keeping together in time: Dance and drill in human history.* Cambridge, MA: Harvard University Press.

Meeker, D., Knight, T. K, Friedberg, M. W., Linder, J. A., Goldstein, N. J., Fox, C. R., Rothfeld, A., et al. (2014). Nudging guideline-concordant antibiotic prescribing: A randomized clinical trial. *JAMA Internal Medicine, 174*, 425–431. https://doi.org/10.1001/jamainternmed.2013.14191.

Meeus, W. H. J., & Raaijmakers, Q. A. W. (1986). Administrative obedience: Carrying out orders to use psychological-administrative violence. *European Journal of Social Psychology, 16*, 311–324.

Meier, B. P, Dillard, A. J, & Lappas, C. M. (2019). Naturally better? A review of the natural is better bias. *Social and Personality Psychology Compass*. https://doi.org/10.1111/spc3.12494.

Melamed, B. F., Yurcheson, E., Fleece, L., Hutcherson, S., & Hawes, R. (1978). Effects of film modeling on the reduction of anxiety-related behaviors in individuals varying in level of previous experience in the stress situation. *Journal of Consulting and Clinical Psychology, 46*, 1357–1374.

Melamed, D., Simpson, B., & Abernathy, J. (2020). The robustness of reciprocity: Experimental evidence that each form of reciprocity is robust to the presence of other forms of reciprocity. *Science Advances, 6*, https://doi.org/10.1126/sciadv.aba0504.

Mercer, A., Caporaso, A., Cantor, D., & Townsend, J. (2015). How much gets you how much? Monetary incentives and response rates in household surveys. *Public Opinion Quarterly, 79*, 105–129.

Meredith, J. (2020). Conversation analysis, cyberpsychology and online interaction. *Social and Personality Psychology Compass, 14*. https://doi.org/10.1111/spc3.12529.

Meyerwitz, B. E., & Chaiken, S. (1987). The effect of message framing on breast self-examination attitudes, intentions, and behavior. *Journal of Personality and Social Psychology, 52*, 500–510.

Michelitch, K. (2015). Does electoral competition exacerbate interethnic or interpartisan economic discrimination? Evidence from a field experiment in market price bargaining. *American Political Science Review, 109*, 43–61. https://doi.org/10.1017/S0003055414000628.

Midlarsky, E., & Nemeroff, R. (1995, July). Heroes of the holocaust: Predictors of their well-being in later life. Poster presented at the American Psychological Society meetings, New York, NY.

Milgram, S. (1970). The experience of living in cities: A psychological analysis. In F. F. Korten, S. W. Cook, & J. I. Lacey (eds.), *Psychology and the problems of society* (pp. 152–173). American Psychological Association. https://doi.org/10.1037/10042-011

Milgram, S. (1974). *Obedience to authority*. New York: Harper & Row.

Milgram, S., Bickman, L., & Berkowitz, O. (1969). Note on the drawing power of crowds of different size. *Journal of Personality and Social Psychology, 13*, 79–82.

Miller, C. B. (2009). Yes we did!: Basking in reflected glory and cutting off reflected failure in the 2008 presidential election. *Analyses of Social Issues and Public Policy, 9*, 283–296.

Miller, C. H., Burgoon, M., Grandpre, J. R., & Alvaro, E.M. (2006). Identifying principal risk factors for the initiation of adolescent smoking behaviors: The significance of psychological reactance. *Health Communication, 19*, 241–252. https://doi.org/10.1207/s15327027hci1903_6.

Miller, G. F. (2000). *The mating mind*. New York: Doubleday.

Miller, J. M., & Krosnick, J. A. (1998). The impact of candidate name order on election outcomes. *Public Opinion Quarterly, 62*, 291–330.

Miller, N., Campbell, D. T., Twedt, H., & O'Connell, E. J. (1966). Similarity, contrast, and complementarity in friendship choice. *Journal of Personality and Social Psychology, 3*, 3–12.

Miller, R. L., Brickman, P., & Bollen, D. (1975). Attribution versus persuasion as a means of modifying behavior. *Journal of Personality and Social Psychology, 31*, 430–441.

Miller, R. L., Seligman, C., Clark, N. T., & Bush, M. (1976). Perceptual contrast versus reciprocal concession as mediators of induced compliance. *Canadian Journal of Behavioral Science, 8*, 401–409.

Mills, C. M., & Keil, F. C. (2005). The development of cynicism. *Psychological Science, 16*, 385–390.

Mita, T. H., Dermer, M., & Knight, J. (1977). Reversed facial images and the mere exposure hypothesis. *Journal of Personality and Social Psychology, 35*, 597–601.

Mogg, K., Waters, A. M., & Bradley, B. P. (2017). Attention bias modification (ABM): Review of effects of multisession ABM training on anxiety and threat-related attention in high-anxious individuals. *Clinical Psychological Science, 5*, 698–717. https://doi.org/10.1177/2167702617696359.

Monahan, J. L., Murphy, S. T., & Zajonc, R. B. (2000). Subliminal mere exposure: Specific, general, and diffuse effects. *Psychological Science, 11*, 462–466.

Moons, W. G., Mackie, D. M., & Garcia-Marques, T. (2009). The impact of repetition-induced familiarity on agreement with weak and strong arguments. *Journal of Personality and Social Psychology, 96*, 32–44. http://dx.doi.org/10.1037/a0013461.

Moore, C., & Pierce, L. (2016). Reactance to transgressors: Why authorities deliver harsher penalties when the social context elicits expectations of leniency. *Frontiers in Psychology, 7*, 550. http://dx.doi.org/10.3389/fpsyg.2016.00550.

Moore, D. E., Kurtzberg, T. R., Thompson, L. L., & Morris, M. W. (1999). Long and short routes to success in electronically-mediated negotiations: Group affiliations and good vibrations. *Organizational Behavior and Human Decision Processes, 77*, 22–43.

Moreland, R. L., & Topolinski, S. (2010). The mere exposure phenomenon: A lingering melody by Robert Zajonc. *Emotion Review, 2*, 329–339. https://doi.org/10.1177/1754073910375479.

Moriarty, T. (1975). Crime, commitment, and the responsive bystander: Two field experiments. *Journal of Personality and Social Psychology, 31*, 370–376.

Morris, M., Nadler, J., Kurtzberg, T., & Thompson, L. (2002). Schmooze or lose: Social friction and lubrication in e-mail negotiations. *Group Dynamics: Theory, Research, and Practice, 6*, 89–100. http://dx.doi.org/10.1037/1089-2699.6.1.89.

Morrison, K. R., Plaut, V. C., & Ybarra, O. (2010). Predicting whether multiculturalism positively or negatively influences white Americans' intergroup attitudes: The role of ethnic identification. *Personality and Social Psychology Bulletin, 36*, 1648–1661. https://doi.org/10.1177/0146167210386118.

Morrow, L. (1991, September 2). The Russian revolution, *Time*, 20.

Mortensen, C. H., Neel, R., Cialdini, R. B., Jaeger, C. M., Jacobson, R. P., &

Ringel, M. M. (2017). Upward trends: A lever for encouraging behaviors performed by the minority. *Social Psychology and Personality Science.* https://doi.org/10.1177%2F1948550617734615.

Mousa, S. (2020). Building social cohesion between Christians and Muslims through soccer in post-ISIS Iraq, *Science, 369,* 866–870. https://doi.org/10.1126/science.abb3153.

Mrkva, K., & Van Boven, L. (2020). Salience theory of mere exposure: Relative exposure increases liking, extremity, and emotional intensity. *Journal of Personality and Social Psychology, 118,* 1118–1145. https://doi.org/10.1037/pspa0000184.

Mulla, M. M., Witte, T. H., Richardson, K., Hart, W., Kassing, F. L., Coffey, C. A., Hackman, C. L., & Sherwood, I. M. (2019). The causal influence of perceived social norms on intimate partner violence perpetration: Converging cross-sectional, longitudinal, and experimental support for a social disinhibition model. *Personality and Social Psychology Bulletin, 45,* 652–668. https://doi.org/10.1177/0146167218794641.

Murayama, K., & Elliot, A. J. (2012). The competition–performance relation: A meta-analytic review and test of the opposing processes model of competition and performance. *Psychological Bulletin, 138,* 1035–1070. http://dx.doi.org/10.1037/a0028324.

Murphy, S. T., & Zajonc, R. B. (1993). Affect, cognition and awareness. *Journal of Personality and Social Psychology, 64,* 723–739.

Murrar, S., Campbell, M. R., & Brauer, M. (2020). Exposure to peers' prodiversity attitudes increases inclusion and reduces the achievement gap. *Nature Human Behavior.* https://doi.org/10.1038/s41562-020-0899-5.

Murray, D. A., Leupker, R. V., Johnson, C. A., & Mittlemark, M. B. (1984). The prevention of cigarette smoking in children: A comparison of four strategies. *Journal of Applied Social Psychology, 14,* 274–288.

Nai, J., Narayanan, J., Hernandez, I., & Savani, K. (2018). People in more racially diverse neighborhoods are more prosocial. *Journal of Personality and Social Psychology, 114,* 497–515. https://doi.org/10.1037/pspa0000103.

Nakayachi, K., Ozaki, T., Shibata, Y., & Yokoi, R. (2020). Why do Japanese people use masks against COVID-19, even though masks are unlikely to offer protection from infection? *Frontiers in Psychology, 11.* https://doi.org/10.3389/fpsyg.2020.01918.

Naylor, R. W., Raghunathan, R., & Ramanathan, S. (2006). Promotions spontaneously induce a positive evaluative response. *Journal of Consumer Psychology, 16,* 295–305.

Nelissen, R. M. A., & Meijers, M. H. C. (2011). Social benefits of luxury brands as costly signals of wealth and status. *Evolution and Human Behavior, 32,* 343–355.

News. (1988). *Stanford Business School Magazine, 56,* 3.

Nijjer, R. (2019). 5 types of social proof to use on your website now. *Search Engine Journal.* www.searchenginejournal.com/social-proof-types/318667.

Nolan, J. M., Schultz, P. W., Cialdini, R. B., & Goldstein, N. J. (2021). The social norms approach: A wise intervention for solving social and environmental problems. In G. Walton and A. Crum (eds.) *Handbook of Wise Interventions.* (pp. 405–428). Guilford.

Nolan, J. M., Schultz, P. W., Cialdini, R. B., Goldstein, N. J., & Griskevicius, V. (2008). Normative social influence is underdetected. *Personality and Social Psychology Bulletin, 34,* 913–923.

Noor, M., Brown, R., Gonzalez, R., Manzi, Jorge, & Lewis, C. A. (2008). On positive psychological outcomes: What helps groups with a history of conflict to forgive and reconcile with each other? *Personality and Social Psychology Bulletin, 34,* 819–832.

Norscia, I., & Palagi, E. (2011). Yawn contagion and empathy in *Homo sapiens.* *PLoS ONE, 6.* https://doi.org/10.1371/journal.pone.0028472.

Norscia, I., Zanoli, A., Gamba, M., & Palagi, E. (2020). Auditory contagious yawning is highest between friends and family members: Support to the emotional bias hypothesis. *Frontiers of Psycholology, 11,* 442. https://doi.org/10.3389/fpsyg.2020.00442.

Norton, M. I., Mochon, D., & Ariely, D. (2012). The IKEA effect: When labor leads to love. *Journal of Consumer Psychology, 22,* 453–460. https://doi.org/10.1016/j.jcps.2011.08.002.

Oesch, N. (2019). Music and language in social interaction: Synchrony, antiphony, and functional origins. *Frontiers of Psychology, 10,* 1514. https://doi.org/10.3389/fpsyg.2019.01514.

Oh, D., Shafir, E., & Todorov, A. (2020). Economic status cues from clothes affect perceived competence from faces. *Nature Human Behaviour, 4*(3), 287–293. https://doi.org/10.1038/s41562-019-0782-4.

Ohadi, J., Brown, B., Trub, L., & Rosenthal, L. (2018). I just text to say I love you: Partner similarity in texting and relationship satisfaction. *Computers in Human Behavior, 78,* 126–132. https://doi.org/10.1016/j.chb.2017.08.048.

Oliver, A. (2019). *Reciprocity and the Art of Behavioural Public Policy.* Cambridge: Cambridge University Press. https://doi.org/10.1017/9781108647755.

O'Leary, S. G. (1995). Parental discipline mistakes. *Current Directions in Psychological Science, 4,* 11–13.

Oliner, S. P., & Oliner, P. M. (1988). *The altruistic personality: Rescuers of Jews in Nazi Europe.* New York: Free Press.

Olson, I. R., & Marshuetz, C. (2005). Facial attractiveness is appraised in a glance. *Emotion, 5,* 498–502.

Olson, J. M., & James, L. M. (2002). Vigilance for differences. *Personality and Social Psychology Bulletin, 28,* 1084–1093.

Onyeador, I. N., Wittlin, N. M., Burke, S. E., Dovidio, J. F., Perry, S. P., Hardeman, R. R., Dyrbye, L. N., et al. (2020). The value of interracial contact for reducing anti-Black bias among non-Black physicians: A cognitive habits and growth evaluation (CHANGE) study report. *Psychological Science, 31,* 18–30. https://doi.org/10.1177/0956797619879139.

Oosterhof, N. N., Tipper, S. P., & Downing, P. E. (2012). Visuo-motor imagery of specific manual actions: A multi-variate pattern analysis fMRI study, *NeuroImage, 63,* 262–271. https://doi.org/10.1016/j.neuroimage.2012.06.045.

Oriña, M. M., Wood, W., & Simpson, J. A. (2002). Strategies of influence in close relationships. *Journal of Experimental Social Psychology, 38,* 459–472.

Oskamp, S., & Schultz, P. W. (1998). *Applied Social Psychology.* Englewood Cliffs, NJ: Prentice-Hall.

Ott, M., Choi, Y., Cardie, C., & Hancock, J. T. (2011). Finding deceptive opinion spam by any stretch of the imagination. *Proceedings of the 49th Annual Meeting of the Association for Computer Linguistics*, 309–319. Portland, Oregon.Otten, S., & Epstude, K. (2006). Overlapping mental representations of self, ingroup, and outgroup: Unraveling self-stereotyping and self-anchoring. *Personality and Social Psychology Bulletin, 32,* 957–969. https://doi.org/10.1177/0146167206287254.

Over, H. (2020, April 29). Seven challenges for the dehumanization hypothesis. *Perspectives on Psychological Science.* https://doi.org/10.1177/1745691620902133.

Over, H., & McCall, C. (2018). Becoming us and them: Social learning and intergroup bias. *Social and Personality Compass.* https://doi.org/10.1111/spc3.12384.

Packard, V. (1957). *The hidden persuaders.* New York: D. McKay.

Paez, D., Rime, B., Basabe, N., Wlodarczyk, A., & Zumeta, L. (2015). Psychosocial effects of perceived emotional synchrony in collective gatherings. *Journal of Personality and Social Psychology, 108,* 711–729.

Paese, P. W., & Gilin, D. A. (2000). When an adversary is caught telling the truth. *Personality and Social Psychology Bulletin, 26,* 75–90.

Page-Gould, E., Mendoza-Denton, R., Alegre, J. M., & Siy, J. O. (2010). Understanding the impact of cross-group friendship on interactions with novel outgroup members. *Journal of Personality and Social Psychology, 98,* 775–793. https://doi.org/10.1037/a0017880.

Page-Gould, E., Mendoza-Denton, R., & Tropp, L. R. (2008). With a little help from my cross-group friend: Reducing anxiety in intergroup contexts through cross-group friendship. *Journal of Personality and Social Psychology, 95,* 1080–1094.

Palagi, E., Leone, A., Mancini, G., & Ferrari, P. F. (2009). Contagious yawning in gelada baboons as a possible expression of empathy. *Proceedings of the National Academy of Sciences 106,* 19262–19267.

Palidino, M-P., Mazzurega, M., Pavani, F., & Schubert, T. W. (2010). Synchronous multisensory stimulation blurs self-other boundaries. *Psychological Science, 21,* 1202–1207.

Pallak, M. S., Cook, D. A., & Sullivan, J. J. (1980). Commitment and energy conservation. *Applied Social Psychology Annual, 1,* 235–253.

Paluck, E. L. (2009). Reducing intergroup prejudice and conflict using the media: A field experiment in Rwanda. *Journal of Personality and Social Psychology, 96,* 574–587. http://dx.doi.org/10.1037/a0011989.

Paluck, E. L., & Green, D. P. (2009). Prejudice reduction: What works? A review and assessment of research and practice. *Annual Review of Psychology, 60,* 339–367.

Pane, L. M. (2019, December 29). Study: US mass killings reach new high in 2019. *Arizona Republic,* 8A.

Paolini, S., Hewstone, M., Cairns, E., & Voci, A. (2004). Effects of direct and indirect cross-group friendships on judgments of Catholics and Protestants in Northern Ireland. *Personality and Social Psychology Bulletin, 30,* 770–786.

Park, H., Lalwani, A. K., & Silvera, D. H. (2020). The impact of resource scarcity on price-quality judgments. *Journal of Consumer Research, 46,* 1110–1124. https://doi.org/10.1093/jcr/ucz031.

Park, J. H., & Schaller, M. (2005). Does attitude similarity serve as a heuristic cue for kinship? Evidence of an implicit cognitive association. *Evolution and Human Behavior, 26*, 158–170.

Park, J. H., Schaller, M., & Van Vugt, M. (2008). Psychology of human kin recognition: Heuristic cues, erroneous inferences, and their implications. *Review of General Psychology, 12*, 215–235.

Parkinson, B. (2020). Intragroup emotion convergence: Beyond contagion and social appraisal. *Personality and Social Psychology Review, 24*, 121–140. https://doi.org/10.1177/1088868319882596.

Parsons, C. A., Sulaeman, J., Yates, M. C., & Hamermesh, D. S. (2011). Strike three: Discrimination, incentives, and evaluation. *American Economic Review, 101*, 1410–1435.

Pavlov, I. P. (1927). *Conditioned reflexes.* Translated by G. V. Anrep. Oxford: Oxford University Press.

Peiponen, V. A. (1960). Verhaltensstudien am blaukehlchen [Behavior studies of the blue-throat]. *Ornis Fennica, 37*, 69–83.

Pennycook, G., Cannon, T. D., & Rand, D. G. (2018). Prior exposure increases perceived accuracy of fake news. *Journal of Experimental Psychology: General, 147*(12), 1865–1880. https://doi.org/10.1037/xge0000465.

Perry, G. (2012). *Behind the shock machine: The untold story of the notorious Milgram psychology experiments.* Melbourne: Scribe.

Pettigrew, T. F. (1997). Generalized intergroup contact effects on prejudice. *Personality and Social Psychology Bulletin, 23*, 173–185.

Pettigrew, T. F., & Tropp, L. R. (2006). A meta-analytic test of intergroup contact theory. *Journal of Personality and Social Psychology, 90*, 751–783. http://dx.doi.org/10.1037/0022-3514.90.5.751.

Petrova, P. K., Cialdini, R. B., & Sills, S. J. (2007). Personal consistency and compliance across cultures. *Journal of Experimental Social Psychology, 43*, 104–111.

Petty, R. E., Briñol, P., Fabrigar, L., & Wegener, D. T. (2019). Attitude structure and change. In R. Baumeister, and E. Finkel (eds.). *Advanced Social Psychology* (pp. 117–156). New York: Oxford University Press.

Petty, R. E., Cacioppo, J. T., & Goldman, R. (1981). Personal involvement as a determinant of argument-based persuasion. *Journal of Personality and Social Psychology, 41*, 847–855.

Pfeffer, J., & Cialdini, R. B. (1998). Illusions of influence. In R. M. Kramer & M. A. Neale (eds). *Power and Influence in Organizations* (pp. 1–20). Thousand Oaks, CA: Sage.

Phillips, D. P. (1974). The influence of suggestion on suicide: Substantive and theoretical implications of the Werther effect. *American Sociological Review, 39*, 340–354.

Phillips, D. P. (1979). Suicide, motor vehicle fatalities, and the mass media: Evidence toward a theory of suggestion. *American Journal of Sociology, 84*, 1150–1174.

Phillips, D. P. (1980). Airplane accidents, murder, and the mass media: Towards a theory of imitation and suggestion. *Social Forces, 58*, 1001–1024.

Phillips, D. P., & Cartensen, L. L. (1986). Clustering of teenage suicides after television news stories about suicide. *New England Journal of Medicine, 315*, 685–689.

Phillips, D. P., & Cartensen, L. L. (1988). The effect of suicide stories on various demographic groups, 1968–1985. *Suicide and Life-Threatening Behavior, 18,* 100–114.

Philpot, R., Liebst, L. S., Levine, M., Bernasco, W., & Lindegaard, M. R. (2020). Would I be helped? Cross national CCTV footage shows that intervention is the norm in public conflicts. *American Psychologist, 75,* 66–75.

Pierce, J. R., Kilduff, G. J., Galinsky, A. D., & Sivanathan, N. (2013). From glue to gasoline: How competition turns perspective takers unethical. *Psychological Science, 24,* 1986–1994. https://doi.org/10.1177/0956797613482144.

Pinsker, J. (2014, October 1). The psychology behind Costco's Free Samples: Mini pizza bagels? Now we're talking. *The Atlantic.* www.theatlantic.com/business /archive/2014/10/the-psychology-behind-costcos-free-samples/380969.

Plassmann, H., O'Doherty, J., Shiv, B., & Rangel, A. (2008). Marketing actions can modulate neural representations of experienced pleasantness. *Proceedings of the National Academy of Sciences, 105,* 1050–1054.

Pope, B. R., & Pope, N. G. (2015). Own-nationality bias: Evidence from UEFA Champions League football referees. *Economic Inquiry 53,* 1292–1304.

Pope, D. G., & Schweitzer, M. E. (2011). Is Tiger Woods loss averse?: Persistent bias in the face of experience, competition, and high stakes. *American Economic Review, 101.* 129–157. https://doi.org/10.1257/aer.101.1.129.

Poulin-Dubois, D., Brooker, I., & Polonia, A. (2011). Infants prefer to imitate a reliable person. *Infant Behavior and Development, 34,* 303–309. https://doi.org /10.1016/j.infbeh.2011.01.006.

Powers, N., Blackman, A., Lyon, T. P., & Narain, U. (2011). Does disclosure reduce pollution?: Evidence from India's Green Rating Project. *Environmental and Resource Economics, 50,* 131–155.

Poza, D. (2016). 7 simple hacks to supercharge your registration process. https:// auth0.com/blog/supercharge-your-registration-process.

Pratkanis, A. R. (2000). Altercasting as an influence tactic. In D. J. Terry and M. A. Hogg (eds.), *Attitudes, behavior, and social context* (pp. 201–226). Mahwah, NJ: Lawrence Erlbaum.

Pratkanis, A. R. (2007). Social influence analysis: An Index of tactics. In A. R. Pratkanis (ed.), *The science of social Influence: Advances and future progress* (pp. 17–82). Philadelphia, PA: Philadelphia Free Press.

Pratkanis, A., & Shadel, D. (2005). *Weapons of fraud: A sourcebook for fraud fighters.* Seattle, WA: AARP Washington.

Pratkanis, A. R., & Uriel, Y. (2011). The expert snare as an influence tactic: Surf, turf, and ballroom demonstrations of some compliance consequences of being altercast as an expert. *Current Psychology, 30,* 335–344. https://doi.org/10.1007 /s12144-011-9124-z.

Prelec, D., & Simester, D. (2001). Always leave home without it: A further investigation of the credit-card effect on willingness to pay. *Marketing Letters, 12,* 5–12.

Preston, S. D. (2013). The origins of altruism in offspring care. *Psychological Bulletin, 139,* 1305–1341.

Price, R. B., Wallace, M., Kuckertz, J. M., Amir, N., Graur, S., Cummings, L., Popa, P., et al. (2016). Pooled patient-level meta-analysis of children and adults completing a computer-based anxiety intervention targeting attentional bias. *Clinical Psychology Review, 50,* 37–49.

Price, J., & Wolfers, J. (2010). Racial discrimination among NBA referees. *Quarterly Journal of Economics 125*, 1859–1887.

Priebe, C. S., & Spink, K. S. (2011). When in Rome: Descriptive norms and physical activity. *Psychology of Sport and Exercise, 12*, 93–98. https://doi.org/10.1016/j .psychsport.2010.09.001.

Provine, R. (2000). *Laughter: A scientific investigation*. New York: Viking.

Pryor, C., Perfors, A., & Howe, P. D. L. (2019). Even arbitrary norms influence moral decision-making. *Nature Human Behaviour, 3*, 57–62. https://doi.org /10.1038/s41562-018-0489-y.

Putnam, A. L., Ross, M. Q., Soter, L. K., & Roediger, H. L. (2018). Collective narcissism: Americans exaggerate the role of their home state in appraising U.S. history. *Psychological Science, 29*, 1414–1422. https://doi.org/10.1177/0956 797618772504.

Qiu, C., Luu, L., & Stocker, A. A. (2020). Benefits of commitment in hierarchical inference. *Psychological Review, 127*, 622–639. https://doi.org/10.1037/rev0000193.

Rachlin, H., & Jones, B. A. (2008). Altruism among relatives and non relatives. *Behavioural Processes, 79*, 120–123. https://doi.org/10.1016/j.beproc.2008.06.002.

Rao, A. R., & Monroe, K. B. (1989). The effect of price, brand name, and store name on buyer's perceptions of product quality. *Journal of Marketing Research, 26*, 351–357. https://doi.org/10.1023/A:1008196717017.

Raue, M., & Scholl, S. G. (2018). The use of heuristics in decision-making under risk and uncertainty. In M. Raue, E. Lermer, and B. Streicher (eds.), *Psychological perspectives on risk and risk analysis: Theory, Models and Applications* (pp. 153–179). New York, NY: Springer.

Razran, G. H. S. (1938). Conditioning away social bias by the luncheon technique. *Psychological Bulletin, 35*, 693.

Razran, G. H. S. (1940). Conditional response changes in rating and appraising sociopolitical slogans. *Psychological Bulletin, 37*, 481.

Regan, D. T., & Kilduff, M. (1988). Optimism about elections: Dissonance reduction at the ballot box. *Political Psychology, 9*, 101–107.

Regan, R. T. (1971). Effects of a favor and liking on compliance. *Journal of Experimental Social Psychology, 7*, 627–639.

Reich, T., Kupor, D. M., & Smith, R. K. (2018). Made by mistake: When mistakes increase product preference. *Journal of Consumer Research, 44*, 1085–1103. https://doi.org/10.1093/jcr/ucx089.

Reich, T., & Maglio, S. J. (2020). Featuring mistakes: The persuasive impact of purchase mistakes in online reviews. *Journal of Marketing, 84*, 52–65. https:// doi.org/10.1177/0022242919882428.

Reilly, K. (2017, October 23). A deadly campus tradition. *Time*, 57–61.

Reis, H. T., Maniaci, M. R., Caprariello, P. A., Eastwick, P. W., & Finkel, E. J. (2011). Familiarity does promote attraction in live interaction. *Journal of Personality and Social Psychology, 101*, 557–570.

Reiterman, T. (2008). *Raven: The untold story of the Rev. Jim Jones and his people*. New York: Tarcher Perigee.

Rentfrow, P. J. (2010). Statewide differences in personality: Toward a psychological geography of the United States. *American Psychologist, 65*, 548–558. https:// doi.org/10.1037/a0018194.

Rice, B. (April 24, 2000). How plaintiff's lawyers pick their targets. *Medical Economics, 77*, 94–110.

Richeson, J. A., & Shelton, J. N. (2007). Negotiating interracial interactions. *Current Directions in Psychological Science, 16*, 316–320.

Riek, B. M., Mania, E. W., & Gaertner, S. L. (2006). Intergroup threat and outgroup attitudes: A meta-analytic review. *Personality and Social Psychology Review, 10*, 336–353. https://doi.org/10.1207/s15327957pspr1004_4.

Riek, B. M., Mania, E. W., Gaertner, S. L., McDonald, S. A., & Lamoreaux, M. J. (2010). Does a common in-group identity reduce intergroup threat? *Group Processes & Intergroup Relations, 13*, 403–423. https://doi.org/10.1177/1368430209346701.

Riley, D., & Eckenrode, J. (1986). Social ties: Subgroup differences in costs and benefits. *Journal of Personality and Social Psychology, 51*, 770–778.

Ritts, V., Patterson, M. L., & Tubbs, M. E. (1992). Expectations, impressions, and judgments of physically attractive students: A review. *Review of Educational Research, 62*, 413–426.

Rochat, F., & Blass, T. (2014). Milgram's unpublished obedience variation and its historical relevance. *Journal of Social Issues, 70*, 456–472.

Rodafinos, A., Vucevic, A., & Sideridis, G. D. (2005). The effectiveness of compliance techniques: Foot-in-the-door versus door-in-the-face. *Journal of Social Psychology, 145*, 237–240.

Roese, N. J., & Olson, M. J. (1994). Attitude importance as a function of repeated attitude expression. *Journal of Experimental Social Psychology, 30*, 39–51. http://dx.doi.org/10.1006/jesp.1994.1002.

Rollins, T. (2020). *The CEO formula*. McLean, VA: Rollins.

Romero, T., Ito, M., Saito, A., & Hasegawa, T. (2014). Social modulation of contagious yawning in wolves. *PLoS ONE, 9*. http://dx.doi.org/10.1371/journal.pone.0105963.

Romero, T., Konno, A., & Hasegawa, T. (2013). Familiarity bias and physiological responses in contagious yawning by dogs support link to empathy. *PLoS ONE, 8*. http://dx.doi.org/10.1371/journal.pone.0071365.

Rosen, S., & Tesser, A. (1970). On the reluctance to communicate undesirable information: The MUM effect. *Sociometry, 33*, 253–263.

Rosenthal, A. M. (1964). *Thirty-eight witnesses*. New York: McGraw-Hill.

Roseth, C. J., Johnson, D. W., & Johnson, R. T. (2008). Promoting early adolescents' achievement and peer relationships: The effects of cooperative, competitive, and individualistic goal structures. *Psychological Bulletin, 134*, 223–246. http://dx.doi.org/10.1037/0033-2909.134.2.223.

Ross, J. R. (1994). *Escape to Shanghai: A Jewish community in China*. New York: Free Press.

Rothman, A. J., Martino, S. C., Bedell, B. T., Detweiler, J. B., & Salovey, P. (1999). The systematic influence of gain- and loss-framed messages on interest in and use of different types of health behavior. *Personality and Social Psychology Bulletin, 25*, 1355–1369.

Rothman, A. J., & Salovey, P. (1997). Shaping perceptions to motivate healthy behavior: The role of message framing. *Psychological Bulletin, 121*, 3–19.

Rubinstein, S. (1985, January 30). What they teach used car salesmen. *San Francisco Chronicle*.

Rusbult, C. E., Van Lange, P. A. M., Wildschut, T., Yovetich, N. A., & Verette, J. (2000). Perceived superiority in close relationships: Why it exists and persists. *Journal of Personality and Social Psychology, 79,* 521–545.

Sabin, R. (1964). *The international cyclopedia of music and musicians.* New York: Dodd, Mead.

Sacarny, A., Barnett, M. L., Le, J., Tetkoski, F., Yokum, D., & Agrawal, S. (2018). Effect of peer comparison letters for high-volume primary care prescribers of quetiapine in older and disabled adults: A randomized clinical trial. *Journal of the American Medical Association Psychiatry, 75,* 1003–1011. https://doi.org/10.1001/jamapsychiatry.2018.1867.

Sagarin, B. J., Cialdini, R. B., Rice, W. E., & Serna, S. B. (2002). Dispelling the illusion of invulnerability: The motivations and mechanisms of resistance to persuasion. *Journal of Personality and Social Psychology, 83,* 526–541.

Sagarin, B. J., & Mitnick, K. D. (2012). The path of least resistance. In D. T. Kenrick, N. J. Goldstein, and S. L. Braver (eds.), *Six degrees of social influence: Science, application, and the psychology of Robert Cialdini* (pp. 27–38). New York: Oxford University Press.

Salant, J. D. (2003, July 20). Study links donations, vote patterns. *Arizona Republic,* A5.

Salganik, M. J., Dodds, P. S., & Watts, D. J. (2006). Experimental study of inequality and unpredictability in an artificial cultural market. *Science, 311,* February 10, 854–856.

Santos, H. C., Varnum, M. E. W., & Grossmann, I. (2017). Global increases in individualism. *Psychological Science, 28,* 1228–1239. https://doi.org/10.1177/0956797617700622.

Sasaki, S. J., & Vorauer, J. D. (2013). Ignoring versus exploring differences between groups: Effects of salient color-blindness and multiculturalism on intergroup attitudes and behavior. *Social and Personality Psychology Compass, 7,* 246–259. https://doi.org/10.1111/spc3.12021.

Sassenrath, C., Hodges, S. D., & Pfattheicher, S. (2016). It's all about the self: When perspective taking backfires. *Current Directions in Psychological Science, 25,* 405–410. https://doi.org/10.1177/0963721416659253.

Savage, P., Loui, P., Tarr, B., Schachner, A., Glowacki, L., Mithen, S., & Fitch, W. (2020). Music as a coevolved system for social bonding. *Behavioral and Brain Sciences,* 1–36. https://doi.org/10.1017/S0140525X20000333.

Schein, E. (1956). The Chinese indoctrination program for prisoners of war: A study of attempted "brainwashing." *Psychiatry, 19,* 149–172.

Schindler, R. M. (1998). Consequences of perceiving oneself as responsible for obtaining a discount. *Journal of Consumer Psychology, 7*(4), 371–392.

Schkade, D. A., & Kahneman, D. (1998). Does living in California make people happy? A focusing illusion in judgments of life satisfaction. *Psychological Science, 9,* 340–346.

Schlenker, B. R., Dlugolecki, D. W., & Doherty, K. (1994). The impact of self-presentations on self-appraisals and behavior. The power of public commitment. *Personality and Social Psychology Bulletin, 20,* 20–33.

Schmidtke, A., & Hafner, H. (1988). The Werther effect after television films: New evidence for an old hypothesis. *Psychological Medicine, 18,* 665–676.

Schmitt, M. T., Mackay, C. M. L., Droogendyk, L. M., & Payne, D. (2019). What predicts environmental activism? The roles of identification with nature and politicized environmental identity. *Journal of Environmental Psychology, 61*, 20–29. https://doi.org/10.1016/j.jenvp.2018.11.003.

Schrange, M. (2004, September). The opposite of perfect. *Sales and Marketing Management,* 26.

Schrift, R. Y., & Parker, J. R. (2014). Staying the course: The option of doing nothing and its impact on postchoice persistence. *Psychological Science, 25*, 772–780.

Schroeder, J., Risen, J. L., Gino, F., & Norton, M. I. (2019). Handshaking promotes deal-making by signaling cooperative intent. *Journal of Personality and Social Psychology, 116*, 743–768. http://dx.doi.org/10.1037/pspi0000157.

Schultz, P. W. (1999). Changing behavior with normative feedback interventions: A field experiment on curbside recycling. *Basic and Applied Social Psychology, 21*, 25–36.

Schumpe, B. M., Bélanger, J. J., & Nisa, C. F. (2020). The reactance decoy effect: How including an appeal before a target message increases persuasion. *Journal of Personality and Social Psychology, 119*, 272–292. https://doi.org/10.1037/pspa0000192.

Schwarz, N. (1984). When reactance effects persist despite restoration of freedom: Investigations of time delay and vicarious control. *European Journal of Social Psychology, 14*, 405–419.

Schwarzwald, D., Raz, M., & Zwibel, M. (1979). The applicability of the door-in-the-face technique when established behavior customs exit. *Journal of Applied Social Psychology, 9*, 576–586.

Sechrist, G. B., & Stangor, C. (2007). When are intergroup attitudes based on perceived consensus information? The role of group familiarity. *Social Influence, 2*, 211–235.

Segal, H. A. (1954). Initial psychiatric findings of recently repatriated prisoners of war. *American Journal of Psychiatry, III*, 358–363.

Seiter, J. S. (2007). Ingratiation and gratuity: The effect of complimenting customers on tipping behavior in restaurants. *Journal of Applied Social Psychology, 37*, 478–485.

Seiter, J. S., & Dutson, E. (2007). The effect of compliments on tipping behavior in hairstyling salons. *Journal of Applied Social Psychology, 37*, 1999–2007.

Sengupta, J., & Johar, G. V. (2001). Contingent effects of anxiety on message elaboration and persuasion. *Personality and Social Psychology Bulletin, 27*, 139–150.

Shadel, D. (2012). *Outsmarting the scam artists: How to protect yourself from the most clever cons.* Hoboken, NJ: Wiley & Sons.

Shaffer, D., Garland, A., Vieland. V., Underwood, M., & Busner, C. (1991). The impact of curriculum-based suicide prevention programs for teenagers. *Journal of the American Academy of Child and Adolescent Psychiatry, 30*, 588–596.

Shah, A. J., & Oppenheimer, D. M. (2008). Heuristics made easy: An effort reduction framework. *Psychological Bulletin, 134*, 207–222.

Shah, A. M., Eisenkraft, N., Bettman, J. R., & Chartrand, T. L. (2015). "Paper or plastic?": How we pay influences post-transaction connection. *Journal of Consumer Research, 42*, 688–708. https://doi.org/10.1093/jcr/ucv056.

Sharot, T., Fleming, S. M., Yu, X., Koster, R., & Dolan, R. J. (2012). Is choice-induced preference change long lasting? *Psychological Science, 23,* 1123–1129.

Sharot, T., Velasquez, C. M., & Dolan, R. J. (2010). Do decisions shape preference? Evidence from blind choice. *Psychological Science, 21,* 1231–1235.

Sharps, M., & Robinson, E. (2017). Perceived eating norms and children's eating behavior: An Informational social Influence account. *Appetite, 113,* 41–50.

Shayo, M. (2020). Social identity and economic policy. *Annual Review of Economics, 12,* 355–389.

Shayo, M., & Zussman, A. (2011). Judicial in-group bias in the shadow of terrorism. *Quarterly Journal of Economics, 126,* 1447–1484.

Shelley, M. K. (1994). Individual differences in lottery evaluation models. *Organizational Behavior and Human Decision Processes, 60,* 206–230.

Sheng, F., Ramakrishnan, A., Seok, D., Zhao, W. J., Thelaus, S., Cen, P., & Platt, M. L. (2020). Decomposing loss aversion from gaze allocation and pupil dilation. *Proceedings of the National Academy of Sciences, 117,* 11356-11363. https://doi.org/10.1073/pnas.1919670117.

Sherif, M., Harvey, O. J., White, B. J., Hood, W. R., & Sherif, C. W. (1961). *Intergroup conflict and cooperation: The Robbers' Cave experiment.* Norman, OK: University of Oklahoma Institute of Intergroup Relations.

Sherman, D. K., Brookfield, J., & Ortosky, L. (2017). Intergroup conflict and barriers to common ground: A self-affirmation perspective. *Social and Personality Psychology Compass, 11.* https://doi.org/10.1111/spc3.12364.

Sherman, L. E., Payton, A. A., Hernandez, L. M., Greenfield, P. M., & Dapretto, M. (2016). The power of the like in adolescence: Effects of peer influence on neural and behavioral responses to social media. *Psychological Science, 27,* 1027–1035. https://doi.org/10.1177/0956797616645673.

Sherman, S. J. (1980). On the self-erasing nature of errors of prediction. *Journal of Personality and Social Psychology, 39,* 211–221.

Shi, L., Romić, I., Ma, Y., Wang, Z., Podobnik, B., Stanley, H. E., Holme, P., & Jusup, M. (2020). Freedom of choice adds value to public goods. *Proceedings of the National Academy of Sciences, 117,* 17516–17521. https://doi.org/10.1073/pnas.1921806117.

Shiv, B., Carmon, Z., & Ariely, D. (2005). Placebo effects of marketing actions: Consumers may get what they pay for. *Journal of Marketing Research, 42,* 383–393. https://doi.org/10.1509/jmkr.2005.42.4.383.

Shnabel, N., Halabi, S., & Noor, M. (2013). Overcoming competitive victimhood and facilitating forgiveness through re-categorization into a common victim or perpetrator identity, *Journal of Experimental Social Psychology, 49,* 867–877.

Shnabel, N., Purdie-Vaughns, V., Cook, J. E., Garcia J., & Cohen G. L. (2013). Demystifying values-affirmation interventions: Writing about social belonging is a key to buffering against identity threat. *Personality and Social Psychology Bulletin.* 39, 663–676.

Shook, N. J., & Fazio, R. H. (2008). Interracial roommate relationships: An experimental field test of the contact hypothesis. *Psychological Science, 19,* 717–723. https://doi.org/10.1111/j.1467-9280.2008.02147.x.

Shotland, R. I., & Straw, M. (1976). Bystander response to an assault: When a man attacks a woman. *Journal of Personality and Social Psychology, 34,* 990–999.

Shrestha, K. (2018). 50 important stats you need to know about online reviews. www.vendasta.com/blog/50-stats-you-need-to-know-about-online-reviews.

Shrout, M. R., Brown, R. D., Orbuch, T. L., & Weigel, D. J. (2019). A multidimensional examination of marital conflict and health over 16 years. *Personal Relationships, 26*, 490–506. https://doi.org/10.1111/pere.12292.

Shteynberg, G. (2015). Shared attention. *Perspectives on Psychological Science, 10*, 579–590.

Shtulman, A. (2006). Qualitative differences between naïve and scientific theories of evolution. *Cognitive Psychology, 52*, 170–194.

Shu, S. B., & Carlson, K. A. (2014). When three charms but four alarms: Identifying the optimal number of claims in persuasion settings. *Journal of Marketing, 78*, 127–139. https://doi.org/10.1509/jm.11.0504.

Siegal, A. (2018). *Transcendental deception: Behind the TM curtain—bogus science, hidden agendas, and David Lynch's campaign to push a million public school kids into Transcendental Meditation while falsely claiming it is not a religion.* Los Angeles, CA: Janreg.

Silver, A. M., Stahl, A. E., Loiotile, R., Smith-Flores, A. S., & Feigenson, L. (2020). When not choosing leads to not liking: Choice-induced preference in infancy. *Psychological Science.* https://doi.org/10.1177/0956797620954491.

Sinaceur, M., & Heath, C., & Cole, S. (2005). Emotional and deliberative reaction to a public crisis: Mad cow disease in France. *Psychological Science, 16*, 247–254.

Skinner, A. L., Olson, K. R., & Meltzoff, A. N. (2020). Acquiring group bias: Observing other people's nonverbal signals can create social group biases. *Journal of Personality and Social Psychology, 119*, 824–838. https://doi.org/10.1037/pspi0000218.

Slavin, R. E. (1983). When does cooperative learning increase student achievement? *Psychological Bulletin, 94*, 429–445.

Smith, C. T., De Houwer, J., & Nosek, B. A. (2013). Consider the source: Persuasion of implicit evaluations is moderated by source credibility. *Personality and Social Psychology Bulletin, 39*, 193–205.

Smith, D. L. (2020). *On inhumanity: Dehumanization and how to resist it.* Oxford: Oxford University Press.

Smith, G. H., & Engel, R. (1968). Influence of a female model on perceived characteristics of an automobile. *Proceedings of the 76th Annual Convention of the American Psychological Association, 3*, 681–682.

Smith, R. W., Chandler, J. J., & Schwarz, N. (2020). Uniformity: The effects of organizational attire on judgments and attributions. *Journal of Applied Social Psychology, 50*, 299–312.

Sokol-Hessner, P., & Rutledge, R. B. (2019). The psychological and neural basis of loss aversion. *Current Directions in Psychological Science, 28*, 20–27. https://doi.org/10.1177/0963721418806510.

Sorokowski, P. (2010). Politicians' estimated height as an indicator of their popularity. *European Journal of Social Psychology, 40*, 1302–1309. https://doi.org/10.1002/ejsp.710.

Southgate, V. (2020). Are infants altercentric? The other and the self in early social cognition. *Psychological Review, 127*, 505–523. https://doi.org/10.1037/rev0000182.

Spangenberg, E. R., & Greenwald, A. G. (2001). Self-prophesy as a method for increasing participation in socially desirable behaviors. In W. Wosinska, R. B. Cialdini, D. W. Barrett, and J. Reykowski (eds.), *The practice of social influence in multiple cultures* (pp. 51–62). Mahwah, NJ: Lawrence Erlbaum.

Sparkman, G., & Walton, G. M. (2017). Dynamic norms promote sustainable behavior, even if it is counternormative. *Psychological Science, 28*, 1663–1674. https://doi.org/10.1177/0956797617719950.

Sparkman, G., & Walton, G. M. (2019). Witnessing change: Dynamic norms help resolve diverse barriers to personal change. *Journal of Experimental Social Psychology, 82*, 238–252.

Sprecher, S., Treger, S., Wondra, J. D., Hilaire, N., & Wallpe, K. (2013). Taking turns: Reciprocal self-disclosure promotes liking in initial interactions. *Journal of Experimental Social Psychology, 49*, 860–866.

Sprott, D. E., Spangenberg, E. R., Knuff, D. C., & Devezer, B. (2006). Self-prediction and patient health: Influencing health-related behaviors through self-prophecy. *Medical Science Monitor, 12*, RA85–91. http://www.medscimonit.com/fulltxt.php?IDMAN=8110.

Staats, B. R., Dai, H., Hofmann, D., & Milkman, K. L. (2017). Motivating process compliance through individual electronic monitoring: An empirical examination of hand hygiene in healthcare. *Management Science, 63*, 1563–1585.

Stallen, M., Smidts, A., & Sanfey, A. G. (2013). Peer influence: neural mechanisms underlying in-group conformity. *Frontiers in Human Neuroscience, 7*. https://doi.org/10.3389/fnhum.2013.00050.

Stanchi, K. M. (2008). Playing with fire: The science of confronting adverse material in legal advocacy. *Rutgers Law Review, 60*, 381–434.

Stanne, M. B., Johnson, D. W., & Johnson, R. T. (1999). Does competition enhance or inhibit motor performance: A meta-analysis. *Psychological Bulletin, 125*, 133–154.

Stehr, N., & Grundmann, R. (2011). *Experts: The knowledge and power of expertise.* London: Routledge.

Stelfox, H. T., Chua, G., O'Rourke, K., & Detsky, A. S. (1998). Conflict of interest in the debate over calcium-channel antagonists. *New England Journal of Medicine, 333*, 101–106.

Stephan, W. G. (1978). School desegregation: An evaluation of predictions made in *Brown vs. Board of Education. Psychological Bulletin, 85*, 217–238.

Stern, S. M. (2012). *The Cuban Missile Crisis in American memory: Myths versus reality.* Palo Alto, CA: Stanford University Press.

Stephens, N. M., Fryberg, S. A., Markus, H. R., Johnson, C., & Covarrubias, R. (2012). Unseen disadvantage: How American universities' focus on independence undermines the academic performance of first-generation college students. *Journal of Personality and Social Psychology, 102*, 1178–1197.

Stevens, M. (2016). *Cheats and deceits: How animals and plants exploit and mislead.* New York: Oxford University Press.

Stewart, P. A., Eubanks, A. D., Dye, R. G., Gong, Z. H., Bucy, E. P., Wicks, R. H., & Eidelman, S. (2018). Candidate performance and observable audience response: Laughter and applause-cheering during the first 2016 Clinton-Trump presidential debate. *Frontiers in Psychology, 9*, 1182. https://doi.org/10.3389/fpsyg .2018.01182.

Stirrat, M., & Perrett, D. I. (2010). Valid facial cues to cooperation and trust: Male facial width and trustworthiness. *Psychological Science, 21*, 349–354.

Strenta, A., & DeJong, W. (1981). The effect of a prosocial label on helping behavior. *Social Psychology Quarterly, 44*, 142–147.

Strohmetz, D. B., Rind, B., Fisher, R., & Lynn, M. (2002). Sweetening the till—the use of candy to increase restaurant tipping. *Journal of Applied Social Psychology, 32*, 300–309.

Stok, F. M., de Ridder, D. T., de Vet, E., & de Wit, J. F. (2014). Don't tell me what I should do, but what others do: The influence of descriptive and injunctive peer norms on fruit consumption in adolescents. *British Journal of Health Psychology 19*, 52–64.

Stone, J., & Focella, E. (2011). Hypocrisy, dissonance and the self-regulation processes that improve health, *Self and Identity, 10*, 295–303. https://doi.org/10.10 80/15298868.2010.538550.

Stone, J., Whitehead, J., Schmader, T., & Focella, E. (2011). Thanks for asking: Self-affirming questions reduce backlash when stigmatized targets confront prejudice. *Journal of Experimental Social Psychology, 47*, 589– 598.

Strauss, M. (2011). *Pictures, passions, and eye.* London: Halban.

Styron, W. (1977). A farewell to arms. *New York Review of Books, 24*, 3–4.

Suedfeld, P., Bochner, S., & Matas, C. (1971). Petitioner's attire and petition signing by peace demonstrators: A field experiment. *Journal of Applied Social Psychology, 1*, 278–283.

Sumner, S. A., Burke, M., & Kooti, F. (2020). Adherence to suicide reporting guidelines by news shared on a social networking platform. *Proceedings of the National Academy of Sciences, 117*, 16267–16272. https://doi.org/10.1073/pnas .2001230117.

Surowiecki, J. (2004). *The wisdom of crowds.* New York: Doubleday.

Sutcliffe, K. (2019, November 25). How to reduce medical errors. *Time*, 25–26.

Swaab, R. I., Maddux, W. W., & Sinaceur, M. (2011). Early words that work: When and how virtual linguistic mimicry facilitates negotiation outcomes. *Journal of Experimental Social Psychology, 47*, 616–621.

Swann, W. B., & Buhrmester, M. D. (2015). Identity fusion. *Current Directions in Psychological Science, 24*, 52–57.

Swart, H., Hewstone, M., Christ, O., & Voci, A. (2011). Affective mediators of intergroup contact: A three-wave longitudinal study in South Africa. *Journal of Personality and Social Psychology, 101*, 1221–1238. https://doi.org/10.1037/a002 4450.

Sweis, B. M., Abram, S. V., Schmidt, B. J., Seeland, K. D., MacDonald III, A. W., Thomas, M. J., & Redish, D. (2018). Sensitivity to "sunk costs" in mice, rats, and humans. *Science, 361*, 178–181.

Sweldens, S., van Osselar, S. M. J., & Janiszewski, C. (2010). Evaluative conditioning procedures and resilience of conditioned brand attitudes. *Journal of Consumer Research 37*, 473–489.

Szabo, L. (2007, February 5). Patient protect thyself. *USA Today*, 8D.

Sznycer, D., De Smet, D., Billingsley, J., & Lieberman, D. (2016). Coresidence duration and cues of maternal investment regulate sibling altruism across cultures. *Journal of Personality and Social Psychology, 111,* 159–177. https://doi.org /10.1037/pspi0000057.

Tadlock, B. L, Flores, A. R., Haider-Markel, D. P., Lewis, D.C., Miller, P. R., & Taylor, J. K. (2017). Testing contact theory and attitudes on transgender rights. *Public Opinion Quarterly, 81,* 956–972. https://doi.org/10.1093/poq/nfx021.

Tal-Or, N. (2008). Boasting, burnishing, and burying in the eyes of the perceivers. *Social Influence, 3,* 202–222. https://doi.org/10.1080/15534510802324427.

Tan, Q., Zhan, Y., Gao, S., Chen, J., & Zhong, Y. (2015). Closer the relatives are, more intimate and similar we are: Kinship effects on self-other overlap. *Personality and Individual Differences, 73,* 7–11.

Tarr, B., Launay, J., & Dunbar, R. I. (2014). Music and social bonding: "Self-other" merging and neurohormonal mechanisms. *Frontiers in psychology, 5.* https://doi.org/10.3389/fpsyg.2014.01096.

Taylor, R. (1978). Marilyn's friends and Rita's customers: A study of party selling as play and as work. *Sociological Review, 26,* 573–611.

Tedeschi, J. T., Schlenker, B. R., & Bonoma, T. V. (1971). Cognitive dissonance: Private ratiocination or public spectacle? *American Psychologist, 26,* 685–695.

Teger, A. I. (1980). *Too much invested to quit.* Elmsford, NY: Pergamon.

Telzer, E. H., Masten, C. L., Berkman, E. T., Lieberman, M. D., & Fuligni, A. J. (2010). Gaining while giving: An fMRI study of the rewards of family assistance among White and Latino youth. *Social Neuroscience, 5,* 508–518.

Tesser, A. (1993). The importance of heritability in psychological research: The case of attitudes. *Psychological Review, 100,* 129–142.

Teuscher, U. (2005, May). The effects of time limits and approaching endings on emotional intensity. Paper presented at the meetings of the American Psychological Society, Los Angeles, CA.

Thaler, R. H., Tversky, A., Kahneman, D., & Schwartz, A. (1997). The effect of myopia and loss aversion on risk taking: An experimental test. *The Quarterly Journal of Economics, 112,* 647–661, https://doi.org/10.1162/003355397555226.

Thompson, D. (2017). *Hit makers: The science of popularity in an age of distraction.* New York: Penguin.

Thompson, L. (1990). An examination of naive and experienced negotiators. *Journal of Personality and Social Psychology, 59,* 82–90.

Thompson, L., & Hrebec, D. (1996). Lose-lose agreements in interdependent decision making. *Psychological Bulletin, 120,* 396–409.

Tiger, L., & Fox, R. (1989). *The imperial animal.* New York: Holt.

Till, B. D., & Priluck, R. L. (2000). Stimulus generalization in classical conditioning: An initial investigation and extension. *Psychology & Marketing, 17,* 55–72.

Todd, A. R., & Galinsky, A. D. (2014). Perspective-taking as a strategy for improving intergroup relations: Evidence, mechanisms, and qualifications. *Social and Personality Psychology Compass, 8,* 374–387. https://doi.org/10.1111/spc3.12116.

Todd, P. M., & Gigerenzer, G. (2007). Environments that make us smart. *Current Directions in Psychological Science, 16,* 167–171.

Tokayer, M., & Swartz, M. (1979). *The Fugu Plan: The untold story of the Japanese and the Jews during World War II.* New York: Paddington.

Tomasello, M. (2020). The moral psychology of obligation. *Behavioral and Brain Sciences, 43*, E56. https://doi.org/10.1017/S0140525X19001742.

Tormala, Z. L., & Petty, R. E. (2007). Contextual contrast and perceived knowledge: Exploring the implications for persuasion. *Journal of Experimental Social Psychology, 43*, 17–30.

Toufexis, A. (1993, June 28). A weird case, baby? Uh huh! *Time*, 41.

Towers, S., Gomez-Lievano, A., Khan M., Mubayi, A., & Castillo-Chavez, C. (2015). Contagion in mass killings and school shootings. *PLoS ONE, 10*. https://doi.org/10.1371/journal.pone.0117259.

Trocmé, A. (2007/1971). *Jesus and the nonviolent revolution*. Farmington, PA: Plough Publishing House.

Turner, R. N., Hewstone, M., Voci, A., Paolini, S., & Christ, O. (2007). Reducing prejudice via direct and extended cross-group friendship. *European Review of Social Psychology, 18*, 212–255. https://doi.org/10.1080/10463280701680297.

Tversky, A., & Kahneman, D. (1974). Judgment under uncertainty: Heuristics and biases. *Science, 185*, 1124–1131.

Unkelbach, C., Koch, A., Silva, R. R., & Garcia-Marques, T. (2019). Truth by repetition: Explanations and implications. *Current Directions in Psychological Science, 28*, 247–253. https://doi.org/10.1177/0963721419827854.

Valdesolo, P., & DeSteno, D. (2011). Synchrony and the social tuning of compassion. *Emotion, 11*, 262–266.

van Baaren, R. B., Holland, R. W., Steenaert, B., & van Knippenberg, A. (2003). Mimicry for money: Behavioral consequences of imitation. *Journal of Experimental Social Psychology, 39*, 393–398.

Vandello, J. A., & Cohen D. (1999). Patterns of individualism and collectivism across the United States. *Journal of Personality and Social Psychology, 77*, 279–292.

van den Berg, H., Manstead, A. S. R., van der Pligt, J., & Wigboldus, D. H. J. (2006). The impact of affective and cognitive focus on attitude formation. *Journal of Experimental Social Psychology, 42*, 373–379.

Van der Werff, E., Steg, L., & Keizer, K. (2014). I am what I am, by looking past the present: The influence of biospheric values and past behavior on environmental self-identity. *Environment and Behavior, 46*, 626–657. https://doi.org/10.1177/0013916512475209.

van Herpen, E., Pieters, R., & Zeelenberg, M. (2009). When demand accelerates demand: Trailing the bandwagon. *Journal of Consumer Psychology, 19*, 302–312. https://doi.org/10.1016/j.jcps.2009.01.001.

Van Overwalle, F., & Heylighen, F. (2006). Talking nets: A multiagent connectionist approach to communication and trust between individuals. *Psychological Review, 113*, 606–627.

Verosky, S. C., & Todorov, A. (2010). Generalization of affective learning about faces to perceptually similar faces. *Psychological Science, 21*, 779–785. https://doi.org/10.1177/0956797610371965.

Vonk, R. (2002). Self-serving interpretations of flattery: Why ingratiation works. *Journal of Personality and Social Psychology, 82*, 515–526.

von Zimmermann, J., & Richardson, D. C. (2016). Verbal synchrony and action dynamics in large groups. *Frontiers of Psychology, 7*. https://doi.org/10.3389/fpsyg.2016.02034.

Vorauer, J. D., Martens, V., & Sasaki, S. J. (2009). When trying to understand detracts from trying to behave: Effects of perspective taking in intergroup interaction. *Journal of Personality and Social Psychology, 96*, 811– 827.

Vorauer, J. D., & Sasaki, S. J. (2011). In the worst rather than the best of times: Effects of salient intergroup ideology in threatening intergroup interactions. *Journal of Personality and Social Psychology, 101*(2), 307–320. https://doi.org/10.1037/a0023152.

Waber, R. L., Shiv, B., Carmon, Z., & Ariely, D. (2008). Commercial features of placebo and therapeutic efficacy. *Journal of the American Medical Association, 299*, 1016–1917.

Wagner, T., Lutz, R. J., & Weitz, B. A. (2009). Corporate hypocrisy: Overcoming the threat of inconsistent corporate social responsibility perceptions. *Journal of Marketing, 73*, 77–91. https://doi.org/10.1509/jmkg.73.6.77.

Walker, J., Risen, J. L., Gilovich, T., & Thaler, R. (2018). Sudden-death aversion: Avoiding superior options because they feel riskier. *Journal of Personality and Social Psychology, 115*, 363–378. https://doi.org/10.1037/pspa0000106.

Wall, L. L., & Brown, D. (2007). The high cost of free lunch. *Obstetrics & Gynecology, 110*, 169–173.

Wan, L. C., & Wyer, R. S. (2019). The influence of incidental similarity on observers' causal attributions and reactions to a service failure. *Journal of Consumer Research, 45*, 1350–1368. https://doi.org/10.1093/jcr/ucy050.

Ward, A., & Brenner, L. (2006). Accentuate the negative. The positive effects of negative acknowledgment. *Psychological Science, 17*, 959–965.

Warneken, F., Lohse, K., Melis, P. A., & Tomasello, M. (2011). Young children share the spoils after collaboration. *Psychological Science, 22*, 267–273.

Warren, W. H. (2018). Collective motion in human crowds. *Current Directions in Psychological Science, 27*, 232–240. https://doi.org/10.1177/0963721417746743.

Warrick, J. (2008, December 26). Afghan influence taxes CIA's credibility. *Washington Post*, A17.

Watanabe, T. (1994, March 20). An unsung "Schindler" from Japan. *Los Angeles Times*, 1.

Watson, T. J., Jr. (1990). *Father, son, & co.* New York: Bantam.

Waytz, A., Dungan, J., & Young, L. (2013). The whistleblower's dilemma and the fairness-loyalty tradeoff. *Journal of Experimental Social Psychology, 49*, 1027–1033.

Wears, R., & Sutcliffe, K. (2020). *Still not safe: Patient safety and the middle-management of American medicine.* New York: Oxford University Press.

Wedekind, C., & Milinski, M. (2000). Cooperation through image scoring in humans. *Science, 288*, 850–852.

Weidman, A. C., Sowden, W. J., Berg, M., & Kross, E. (2020). Punish or protect? How close relationships shape responses to moral violations. *Personality and Social Psychology Bulletin, 46*, 693–708. https://doi.org/10.1177/0146167219873485.

Weinstein, E. A., & Deutschberger, P. (1963). Some dimensions of altercasting. *Sociometry, 26*, 454–466.

Weisbuch, M., Ambady, N., Clarke, A. L., Achor, S., & Veenstra-Vander Weele, S. (2010). On being consistent: The role of verbal–nonverbal consistency in first impressions. *Basic and Applied Social Psychology, 32*, 261–268. https://doi.org/10.1080/01973533.2010.495659.

Weller, J. A., Levin, I. P., Shiv, B., & Bechara, A. (2007). Neural correlates of adaptive decision making for risky gains and losses. *Psychological Science, 18*, 958–964.

Wells, P. A. (1987). Kin recognition in humans. In D. J. C. Fletcher and C. D. Michener (eds.), *Kin recognition in animals* (pp. 395–416). New York: Wiley.

West, S. G. (1975). Increasing the attractiveness of college cafeteria food: A reactance theory perspective. *Journal of Applied Psychology, 60*, 656–658.

Westmaas, J. L., & Silver, R. C. (2006). The role of perceived similarity in supportive responses to victims of negative life events. *Personality and Social Psychology Bulletin, 32*, 1537–1546.

Wheatley, T., Kang, O., Parkinson, C., & Looser, C. E. (2012). From mind perception to mental connection: Synchrony as a mechanism for social understanding. *Social and Personality Psychology Compass, 6*, 589–606. https://doi.org/10.1111/j.1751-9004.2012.00450.x.

White, M. (1997, July 12). Toy rover sales soar into orbit. *Arizona Republic*, E1, E9.

Whitehouse, H., Jong, J., Buhrmester, M. D., Gómez, Á., Bastian, B., Kavanagh, C. M., Newson, M., et al. (2017). The evolution of extreme cooperation via shared dysphoric experiences. *Scientific Reports, 7*, 44292. https://doi.org/10.1038/srep44292.

Whiting, J. W. M., Kluckhohn, R., & Anthony A. (1958). The function of male initiation ceremonies at puberty. In E. E. Maccoby, T. M. Newcomb, and E. L. Hartley (eds.), *Readings in social psychology* (pp. 82–98). New York: Henry Holt.

Wicklund, R. A., & Brehm, J. C. (1974) cited in R. A. Wicklund, *Freedom and reactance*. Hillsdale, NJ: Lawrence Erlbaum.

Williams, K. D., Bourgeois, M. J., & Croyle, R. T. (1993). The effects of stealing thunder in criminal and civil trials. *Law and Human Behavior, 17*, 597–609.

Wilson, P. R. (1968). The perceptual distortion of height as a function of ascribed academic status. *Journal of Social Psychology, 74*, 97–102.

Wilson, T. D., Dunn, D. S., Kraft, D., & Lisle, D. J. (1989). Introspection, attitude change, and behavior consistency. In L. Berkowitz (ed.), *Advances in experimental social psychology* (vol. 22, pp. 287–343). San Diego, CA: Academic Press.

Wilson, T. D., & Gilbert, D. T. (2008). Affective forecasting: Knowing what to want. *Current Directions in Psychological Science, 14*, 131–134.

Wilson, T. D., & Linville, P. D. (1985). Improving the performance of college freshmen with attributional techniques. *Journal of Personality and Social Psychology, 49*, 287–293.

Wilson, T. D., Reinhard, D. A., Westgate, E. C., Gilbert, D. T., Ellerbeck, N., Hahn, C., Brown, C. L., & Shaked, A. (2014). Just think: The challenges of the disengaged mind. *Science, 345*, 75–77.

Wilson, T. D., Wheatley, T. P., Meyers, J. M., Gilbert, D. T., & Axsom, D. (2000). Focalism: A source of durability bias in affective forecasting. *Journal of Personality and Social Psychology, 78*, 821–836.

Wiltermuth, S. S. (2012a). Synchronous activity boosts compliance with requests to aggress. *Journal of Experimental Social Psychology, 48*, 453–456.

Wiltermuth, S. S. (2012b). Synchrony and destructive obedience. *Social Influence, 7*, 78–89.

Wiltermuth, S. S., & Heath, C. (2009). Synchrony and cooperation. *Psychological Science, 20*, 1–5.

Winkielman, P., Berridge, K. C., & Wilbarger, J. L. (2005). Unconscious affective reactions to masked happy versus angry faces influence consumption behavior and judgments of value. *Personality and Social Psychology Bulletin, 31*, 121–135.

Wölfer, R., Christ, O., Schmid, K., Tausch, N., Buchallik, F. M., Vertovec, S., & Hewstone, M. (2019). Indirect contact predicts direct contact: Longitudinal evidence and the mediating role of intergroup anxiety. *Journal of Personality and Social Psychology, 116*, 277–295. http://dx.doi.org/10.1037/pspi0000146.

Wolske, K. S., Gillingham, K. T., & Schultz, P. W. (2020). Peer influence on household energy behaviours. *Nature Energy 5*, 202–212. https://doi.org/10.1038/s41560-019-0541-9.

Woolley, K., & Risen, J. L. (2018). Closing your eyes to follow your heart: Avoiding information to protect a strong intuitive preference. *Journal of Personality and Social Psychology, 114*, 230–245. https://doi.org/10.1037/pspa0000100.

Wooten, D. B., & Reed, A. (1998). Informational influence and the ambiguity of product experience: Order effects on the weighting of evidence. *Journal of Consumer Research, 7*, 79–99.

Worchel, S. (1992). Beyond a commodity theory analysis of censorship: When abundance and personalism enhance scarcity effects. *Basic and Applied Social Psychology, 13*, 79–92. https://doi.org/10.1207/s15324834baspi301_7.

Worchel, S., & Arnold, S. E. (1973). The effects of censorship and the attractiveness of the censor on attitude change. *Journal of Experimental Social Psychology, 9*, 365–377.

Worchel, S., Arnold, S. E., & Baker, M. (1975). The effect of censorship on attitude change: The influence of censor and communicator characteristics. *Journal of Applied Social Psychology, 5*, 222–239.

Worchel, S., Lee, J., & Adewole, A. (1975). Effects of supply and demand on ratings of object value. *Journal of Personality and Social Psychology, 32*, 906–914.

Wright, S. C., Aron, A., McLaughlin-Volpe, T., & Ropp, S. A. (1997). The extended contact effect: Knowledge of cross-group friendships and prejudice. *Journal of Personality and Social Psychology, 73*, 73–90.

Xu, L., Zhang, X., & Ling, M. (2018). Spillover effects of household waste separation policy on electricity consumption: Evidence from Hangzhou, China. *Resources, Conservation, and Recycling. 129*, 219–231.

Yang, F., Choi, Y-U., Misch, A., Yang, X., & Dunham, Y. (2018). In defense of the commons: Young children negatively evaluate and sanction free riders. *Psychological Science, 29*, 1598–1611.

Yeh, J. S., Franklin, J. M., Avorn, J., Landon, J., & Kesselheim, A. S. (2016). Association of industry payments with the prescribing brand-name statins in Massachusetts. *Journal of the American Medical Association: Internal Medicine, 176*, 763–768.

Yu, S., & Sussman, S. (2020). Does smartphone addiction fall on a continuum of addictive behaviors? *International Journal of Environmental Research and Public Health, 17*, art. no. 422. www.mdpi.com/1660-4601/17/2/422/pdf doi: 10.3390/ijerph17020422.

Yuki, M., Maddox, W. M., Brewer, M. B., & Takemura, K. (2005). Cross-cultural differences in relationship- and group-based trust. *Personality and Social Psychology Bulletin, 31*, 48–62.

Zellinger, D. A., Fromkin, H. L., Speller, D. E., & Kohn, C. A. (1974). A commodity theory analysis of the effects of age restrictions on pornographic materials. (Paper no. 440). Lafayette, IN: Purdue University, Institute for Research in the Behavioral, Economic, and Management Sciences.

Żemła M., & Gladka, A., (2016). Effectiveness of reciprocal rule in tourism: Evidence from a city tourist restaurant. *European Journal of Service Management, 17,* 57–63.

Zhang, Y., Xu, J., Jiang, Z., & Huang, S-C. (2011). Been there, done that: The impact of effort investment on goal value and consumer motivation. *Journal of Consumer Research, 38,* 78–93. https://doi.org/10.1086/657605.

Zhao, X., & Epley, N. (2020). Kind words do not become tired words: Undervaluing the positive impact of frequent compliments. *Self and Identity.* https://doi.org/10.1080/15298868.2020.1761438.

Zitek, E. M., & Hebl, M. R. (2007). The role of social norm clarity in the influenced expression of prejudice over time. *Journal of Experimental Social Psychology, 43,* 867–876.

Zuckerman, M., Porac, J., Lathin, D., & Deci, E. L. (1978). On the importance of self-determination for intrinsically-motivated behavior. *Personality and Social Psychology Bulletin, 4,* 443–446. https://doi.org/10.1177/014616727800400317.

INDEX

Entries in *italics* refer to illustrations.

ABC TV, 280–81
Abraham, 209
Abrams, Robert, 256
abundance, 250
Academy Awards, 120–21
accidental deaths, 168–77
acting together, 398–409, 417, 423, 436
actors, 193, 214, 232, 443
Adams, Scott, 90, *215, 414*
adaptation, 25
adolescents, *164*, 465n
  helping family members, 481n
  psychological reactance and, 259–61, 289
  suicide and, 171–72, *171*
advertising, xvii, *8. See also specific advertisers; and types of ads*
  authority and, 212–14, *213*, 227
  celebrities, 112
  attractive models and, 109–10, 116
  average-person testimonials and, *164*, 192, *192*
  faked social proof and, 193
  familiarity and, 96
  liking and, 93
  moon landing and, 111–12
  music and, 403, 405
  naturalness and, 111
  Olympics and, 112
  scarcity and, 278
  social proof and, 130, 443
  "the many" and, 157
  trustworthiness and, 228, 469n
Advertising Age, 112
advice, 414–16, 487n
affinity schemes, 368–69

Afghanistan, 30, 393, 453n
age, consistency and, 358–59, 362, 477n
aggression, 84, 204, 216, 465n
Ahearn, Brian, 43
AIDS education, 315
"Ain't No Sunshine" (song), 403
Airbnb, 13
airlines
  aisle seat and, 30–31
  crashes and, 10, *11*, 168–70, 172–73, *175*, 195, 451n, 467n
  hijackings and, 174
  overbooked, 20–21
  social proof and, 195
Alawis, 26
alcohol and drug use, 131, 185, 187, 376, 465n, 466n
Algoe, Sara, 455n
Allen, Irwin, 280
All My Children (TV series), 212
altercasting, 93–94, 459n
Amazon
  online reviews, 13, 393, 464n, 483n
  "Pay to Quit" program, 291–93, 473n
American Association of Retired Persons (AARP), 359
American Cancer Society, 304
American Life, An (Magruder), 60
American Revolution, 272
American Salesman, 310
Amway, 40–41, 319–20
Amway Career Manual, 40–41
amygdala, 162
Anabaptists, 135, 463n
analysis, 402, 405, 450n–51n
  paralysis of, 442

Anderson, 454n
animals, 2–4, 438, 450n
Anthony, Albert, 328
anthropologists, 24, 45, 71, 453n
antibiotics, 349
antilittering signs, 185
antiphosphate ordinance, 262–63
antitheft signs, 184–86
antiwar marches, 84, 458n
Antony and Cleopatra (Shakespeare),
    107
Apple iPhones, 193, 243–45, *243*, 247
appliance stores, 250–51
Arab Americans, 367–68, *367*
Argonauts of the Western Pacific
    (Malinowski), 453n
Ariely, D., 449n
Arizona State University, 118
Armstrong, J. Scott, 405
Armstrong, Thomas, 135–42
Aron, Arthur, 406, 422
Aron, Elaine, 406–7, 422, 486n
Aronson, Elliot, 97–98, 101, 333–34,
    460n
art appreciation, 28–29, 452n
art auctions, 226
Asimov, Isaac, 372, 479n
Associated Press, 35, 358
association, 122, 125
    bad odors and, 114
    bad vs. good news and, 116–17
    celebrities and, 112–13
    fundraising meals and, 114–16
    liking and, 107–17, 461n–62n
    naturalness and, 111
    negative, 107–9, 114
    Olympics and, 112
    Pavlov's dogs and, 115–16, *115*
    positive, 109–11
    reflected glory and, 119–21
    space and, 111–12
    sports and, 117–20
    success and, 117–21
Astrogen, 217
athletes, 112
attentional focus, 247, 426–29, 436,
    484n, 489n
attitudinal similarities, 385
Auden, W. H., 453n
Austin, Texas, schools, 97–98

Australia, 51, 379–80
    Indigenous groups and, 424
Australia-France mutual aid, 453n
authority, xvii, 199–240, 467n–70n
    automaticity and, 9, 439, 446
    blind obedience and, 208–13,
        467n–68n
    credentials and, 232–33, 430
    credibility and, 225–31, 239
    defenses vs., 231–40
    eboxes on, 218–19, 229–31, 253
    expertise and, 226, 231–33, 238, 239
    faking symbols of, 216, 231, 430
    medicine and, 216–18
    Milgram experiments and,
        200–207, *202*, 238–39
    perceptions of size and, 215
    protesters and, 207–8
    Reader's Reports on, 211, 222–25,
        237–38
    scarcity and, 267
    sly sincerity and, 233–34
    social proof and, 188
    status and, 222–23
    titles, clothing, and trappings of,
        213–27, 239
    trustworthiness and, 226–32,
        237–39
    Tupperware parties and, 75
    uncertainty and, xviii, xix
    underestimating influence of, 224,
        231, 239
automaticity (automatic behavior;
    click, run responding), 3–5, 21.
    See also influence levers; *and
    specific levers*
    bad weather and, 107
    Christmas cards and, 23
    efficiency of, 7–9
    exploiters of, 15–16, 22
    humans and, 4, 21–22, 450n
    modern, 439–40, 442–43, 446
    personal stakes and, 9–10
    primitive or animal, 438–39
    recognizing, 11–12
    small favors and, 32
automatic writing, 136, 140
automobile accidents
    aid in towing and, 31–32
    emergencies and, 151

fatalities and, 168–74, *175*
hit-and-run violations, 131, 424
jump starting and, 48
automobiles
   attractive models in ads and,
      109–10, 461n
   electric cars and, 163
   limited production and, 246
   as status symbol, 223–24, 469n
automobile salesmen
   "combat" vs. boss and, 104
   commitment and, 341
   contrast and, 19–20
   deadline tactic, 254
   liking and, 73, 81–82, *81*, 85,
      90–91, 104, 122–24, 478n
   "low-ball" tactic and, 341–43
   recruitment of, 133–34
   Systems thinking and, 402
   used, 285–87, 303–4
   unity and, 365–68, 478n
autopilots, 190–91, 193, 195
average-person-on-the-street ads,
   192–93, *192*, 443
aviation-safety researchers, 195
Avis, 234, 470n
Awareness, 376
axe fights, 379

bacteria, 12
bad news, 107–8
Bahá'u'lláh, 488n
Baltimore white van panic, 159
"band of brothers" speech, 407–9
Bandura, Albert, 132, 463n
bank examiner scheme, 221–22
bank guard uniform, 221–22
banks, 369
   charitable donations and, 24,
      199–200
   refer-a-friend program, 79
   runs on, 194–95, 467n
   security-system hackers and,
      218–19
bargain-basement sales, 278–80, *279*
Bargh, 450n
Bar-Ilan University, 56
Barnyard Bingo, 116
bartenders, 130
baseball teams, 250, 385

basking-in-reflected-glory effect,
   119–21, 462n
Bassett, Rod, 343
beach-theft experiment, 294–95,
   473n
"because" experiment, 5
behavioral science, 199
Behavioural Insights Team (BIT),
   199, 467n
Beijing, China, 127, 144, 462n
Belgium, 119
Bell, Mr., 158–59
Bellow, Saul, 416
bereavement, 169–70
Bergman, Peter, 212
Berkshire Hathaway, 228–29, 382–84
Bernstein, Elizabeth, 459n
Best Buy, 445
Bezos, Jeff, 293
Bhanji, Vartan, 452n
Bhimbetka, India, *397*
Bible, 477n
Bible sales, 166–68, 190
Bickman, Leonard, 220
bill paying, 131
birthdays, 23, 261, 471n
birthplace, 409
Bizzarocomics, *441*
Black-White relations, 89, 97, 102,
   272–74, 399, 423, 465n, 484n,
   488n. *See also* cross-group
   interactions; race relations
blood donations, 63
Bloomberg, 224
bluethroat, 4, 450n
Bobbs, Pat, xiii
Bock, Hartnut, xiii
body posture, 87
boiler-room operations, 255–56
Booking.com, 249
Bookman's resale shop, 249–50
boot camp, 334–35
Bose, 227
Boston, 455n, 480n
Boston Marathon bombings, 409,
   486n
Boyle, James, xi, 449n
Boy Scouts, 52, 54, 59
brain activation, 247, 398, 458n,
   464n, 478n, 488n

brands, 475n
   co-creation and, 415
   geography and, 183, 466n
   initial letters and, 85
   liking and, 461n
   referrals, 476n, 487n
   "the many" and, 157
breast cancer self-exams, 248
Brehm, Jack, 257, 471n
Breitling watches, 113
Brendl, C., 458n
Bronner, Frederick, 330
Buffett, Warren, 228–30, 234, 382–85,
   395, 481n–82n
BUGs, 40–41
bull markets, 188
Burkin, Alice, 75, 456n
business suits, 220–21, 232
Butler, Samuel, 340
"but you are free" technique, 268
bystanders, emergencies and, 145–53,
   152, 197, 464n

Cabbage Patch Kids, 302–3
Caciopo, John, 343
calcium-channel blockers, 35
calories, estimating, 16, 452n
Cambridge University, 215
camps, summer, 99–101
Canada, 62, 83
candy
   Boy Scouts sales of, 52, 54
   food server tips and, 32, 49
   Mars landing and, 112
   store offering free, 38, 454n
Captainitis, 10, 11, 451n
Carmon, 449n
Caro, Robert, 34
Carter, S., 462n
Carter, Jimmy, 34
Carto, Annie, xiii
Castro, Fidel, 316–17
Catron, Mandy Len, 405–6, 486n
cave painting, 397
CBS TV, 280, 284
celebrities, 112–14, 113, 199–200,
   456n–57n
cell phones, 440
censorship, 263–68, 290
Chalcolithic era, 396, 484n

chants, 396
charitable donations, xvi, xvii, 24
   bankers and, 199–200
   before-the-act, 454n
   commitment and, 304–5, 309–10
   clothing and, 223
   credit cards and, 110
   dinners and, 114
   "freedom to say no" and, 268
   liking and, 93, 200
   loss aversion and, 248
   opinions of others and, 317
   peer-suasion and, 164–65
   personalization and, 200
   petition signatures and, 312
   reciprocity and, 200, 248
   social proof and, 197, 465n
   unsolicited gifts and, 44–46
Charles, Prince of Wales, 158
cheating, 247
Chernev, Alexander, 452n
Chesterton, G. K., 241
Chevrolets, 81
Chicago Art Institute, 146
children
   authority and, 469n
   because response and, 450n
   Catholic priests and, 431
   collaborative effort and, 415
   cross-group unity and, 419–20
   inner choice and, 337–40
   loss of freedoms and, 275, 471n
   music and, 401, 485n
   obligation and, 453n
   peer-suasion and, 165
   portrait photography and, 254
   psychological reactance and,
      258–59
   social proof and, 197, 463n
China
   auditors and, 369
   Cultural Revolution, 484n
   Jews escape Holocaust to, 387–90,
      393
   Korean War POWs and, 307–9,
      314–19, 321–22, 335–36
   trash separation in, 328
Chivas Regal Scotch Whiskey, 450n
Choctaw Nation, Irish and, 410,
      486n

choices
  poor, and low-ball tactic, 344
  too many, 440
Christian-Jewish reciprocity, 26, 453n
Christmas cards, 23
Christmas toy sales, 299–303
church collection baskets, 130
CIA, 30
Cialdini, Richard, 285–86
civil-rights movement, 273
Civil War, 272, 393
Clark, Laura, xiii
Clinton, Bill, 34
Clooney, George, 74–75, 456n, 457n
clothing
  authority and, 213–14, 219–20,
    222–23, 239, 469n
  liking and, 84, 458n
clothing stores, 18–19, 84, 452n
CNBC, 224
CO_2 emissions, 165
Coca-Cola, 269–71, 351, 472n
co-creation, 412–15, 414, 436
Code of Conduct, 429, 431, 435,
    489n–90n
coercive approach, 374
cognitive overload, 446
Cohen, Michael, 210
Cohen, Ronald, 363, 391, 408–9,
    482n
Cold War, 36
collaborative tasks, 420
collectors, 246
college students. See also fraternities
  Black-White relations and, 89,
    465n
  cafeteria evaluations, 242
  coed dorms and, 264
  grades and contrast principle, 17–18
  grades and loss aversion, 247
Colombia, 117
color, as trigger, 4
command-and-control leadership, 225
commitment, xvii, 291–362, 446,
    473n–77n. See also consistency
  active, 315–17, 361
  age and, 358–59
  automaticity and, 439
  defenses vs., 350–60
  effort and, 327–35, 361

  escalating, 309–13, 309
  financial advice and, 225
  growing legs and, 340–44, 361
  hearts and minds and, 313–49
  individualism and, 360
  inner change and, 340–44
  inner choice and, 335–40, 361
  job interviews and, 307
  as key to consistency, 303–13
  Korean War POWs and, 307–9,
    316–19
  "low-ball" tactics and, 341–47
  public, 322–27, 361
  public good and, 344–47
  Reader's Reports on, 306–7,
    321–22, 326, 333–34
  reminders and, 347–49, 361
  self-image and, 317–18, 323, 361
  self-imposed imprisonments and,
    307–8
  small, 313–15, 323
  special vulnerabilities and, 357–61
  TM course and, 296–99
  toy sales and, 299–303
  Tupperware parties and, 76
  used car sales and, 303–4
  written declarations and, 316–22,
    320
Committee to Re-elect the President
    (CREEP), 58
commonalities, contrived, 87–88
common enemies, 424–26
common goals, 100–101
communities, unity and, 417
community service, 340
competition
  scarcity and, 277–78, 277, 285–87,
    290
  school integration and, 98–99,
    103–4, 460n
  summer camps and, 99–100
compliance devices. See also specific
    levers of influence
  categories of, xvii
  human triggers and, 22
  momentum of, 309–10
  psychology of, xv-xvi
  profiteers and, 16
  rejection-then-retreat technique,
    53–66

compliance practitioners, xvi. *See also* con artists; *and specific levers of influence*
  as allies, vs. falsifiers, 442–44
  associations and, 109–10, 116
  authority and, 214–15
  blind obedience exploited by, 212
  commitment and, 303, 341
  liking and, 104, 121–24
  observing techniques of, xvi-xvii
  perceptual contrast and, 22
  scarcity and, 257
  self-interest rule and, 449n
  use of influence levers by, 13–15
compliance process, defined, 22
compliments, 89–95, 90, 123, 125, 458n–59n
  altercasting and, 93–95
  behind person's back, 92–93
  counterfeit, 91–92
  job interviewees and, 90
  public, 92
  sincere, 91–92
  to live up to, 93–95
con artists (swindlers)
  age of victims and, 359–50
  authority and, 213–22
  lifts in shoes of, 216
  petitions and, *312*
  urgency and, 255–56
concessions
  e-commerce and, 253
  escalating commitment and, 316
  initial, 53–56, 72
  reciprocity and, 52–53
  rejection-then-retreat technique and, 53–64
  rejecting, 72
conditioning, 107–20
conformity, 143–44
Conroy, J. Oliver, 466n
Conroy, Michael, xiii
consistency, xvii, 473n–77n
  See also commitment
  attraction of, 295–96
  avoiding foolish, 350–57
  commitment as key to, 303–13, 318
  commitments that grow own legs and, 341

defenses vs., and heart-of-heart signs, 355–57, 362
defenses vs., and stomach signs, 352–55, 362
exploitation of, 299–303, 352–57
job interviews and, 307
motivating action and, xviii, xix
principle, 294–95
Reader's Report on, 351
reminders and, 347–49
social value of, 295
special vulnerabilities and, 357–61
troubling realizations and, 296–99
consumer demand, 133–34
consumer-protection agencies, xvi
Consumer Reports, 80
contact approach, 98–100, 460n
contagion effects, 158, 184
contagious yawning, 377–78, *378*, 480n
contrast, perceptual, 16–22, *20*, 57–61, *61*, 106, 452n
Conyers, Georgia, school shootings, 176
cookies, 268–69, 271, 275–77, 284–85, 289, 305, 472n
"cooling off" laws, 319–20
Cooper, William, xiii
cooperation, 123, 125, 460n
  compliance professionals and, 104
  Good Cop/Bad Cop and, 106
  intergroup hostility reduced by, 100–104
  leadership and, 225–26
  negotiators' handshakes and, 103
  suffering and, *408*
  unitizing experiences and, 417
cooperative learning, 99–104, *102*, 415, 460n, 487n
Core Motives Model of Social Influence, xvii–xviii
co-residence, by nonrelatives, 418
Cornell University, 13–14, 451n
corporations
  authority and, 231
  campaign contributions, 36
  price negotiations and, 38
Costco, 39, 454n
Costello, Elvis, 402–3, 485n
Costner, Kevin, 120–21

Coué, Émile, 437
counterfeit social evidence, 191, 198, 216
courtship or mating rituals, 3, 12, 45n. *See also* romance
COVID-19, 131–32, 379–80, 410, 422, 473n
Cox Communications, 80
creative accounting, *414*
credentials, 232–33
credibility
    expertise and, 226
    online reviews and, 230
    outsourced, *227*
    scarcity and, 268
credit cards, 110–11, 461n
crime, 105–6, 131, 174–75, 462n, 479n
cross-group interactions, 419–29, 460n
    attentional focus and, 426–29
    diverse neighborhoods and, 420–21, 425–26, 487n–88n
    family-like experiences and, 419–20, 426, 487n
    friendships and, 421–22, 425–26
    mutual enemy and, 424–25
    reciprocal exchanges and, 422
Cruise, Tom, 384
Cuban missile crisis, 36–37, *37*, 454n
cults
    doomsday, 134–43, 463n
    mass suicide and, 178–82
    social acceptance and, 162–63
    social proof and, 134–36, 463n
culture, reciprocity and, 45
customers, unity and, 416–17
Czechoslovakia, *389*

Dade County, Florida, 262–63
damned if you do, damned if you don't, 61–62
dances, 396–97, *397*, 484n
Dances with Wolves, 120–21
Dansk, *8*
Darwin, 73, 425, 426. *See also* evolutionary theory
Davenport, Iowa, 121
Davies, James C., 271–73
Davis, Neil, 210
deadline tactic, 254, 289
dealer, liking deal vs., 124

Dean, John, 59
Dearborn, Michigan, 367–68
DeLuca, Fred, 321–22
Democratic Party, 58–59, 423
dental anxieties, 165, 465n
detail, online reviews and, 14, 191
Deutsch, Morton, 324
Deutschberger, Paul, 459n
Dexter Shoe, 229
Dilbert, *90*, *215*, *414*
Diller, Barry, 280–81
Disabled American Veterans, 44
discount coupons, 276
disease, common fear of, 423
distinctiveness, 281–83
divorce, 241–45
dogs, fear of, 132–33, 463n
Domino's pizza, 228
Doonesbury, *235*
Dorr's Rebellion, 272
Drubeck, Sid and Harry, 452n
Druz, 26
Dylan, Bob, 85

eating habits, 131, 163, 188, 464n–65n, 466n, 467n
eBay, 250
eboxes, xiii, 13–14, 33, 40, 87–88, 128–29, 159, 191, 218–19, 229–30, 253–54, 323, 326–27, 375–76, 411
Ecclesiasticus, 23
e-commerce sites, xiii, 87–88, 253–54. *See also* eboxes
Ecuador, 156
effort, 327–36, 361, 475n
Egyptian Revolution, 272
elections. *See* political campaigns
electronics sales
    scarcity and, 444–45
    service contracts and, 65–66
    similarity and, 87
Elizabeth II, Queen of England, 158
email, 88
emergency aid, 147–56, *148*, *152*, 194, 197
Emerson, Ralph Waldo, 350, 477n
emotion
    joint experience of, 436
    music and, 402–4
    scarcity and, 288, 290

employees. *See also* job candidates
    ethics and, 429, 431, 435
    loyalty and, 27
    peer-suasion and, 163
employers, authority of, 209
endless chain method, 78–79
energy conservation
    commitment and, 293–94, 328
    feasibility and, 160–61
    loss aversion and, 247
    low-ball tactic and, 345–47, *346*
    peer-suasion and, 165
    social proof and, 132, 465n
energy-drink prices, 1, 7, 449n, 450n
Ent, Uzal Girard, 451n
entertainment club membership,
    352–55
environmental action. *See also* energy
        conservation; water conservation
    effort and, 328
    Leopold and red birches and, 412
    littering and, 185
    peer-suasion and, 163–64, 465n
    reminders and, 349
    social proof and, 132, 185, 463n
    trash separation and disposal, 328
Epps, Jake, xiii
Escobar, Andres, 117
Essex, England, 156–57
Etches, Melanie, 291, 293
ethics, 429–33, 490n
Ethiopia-Mexico aid reciprocity,
    25–26, 453n
ethnicity. *See also* cross-group
        interactions
    affinity groups and, 368–70
    diverse neighborhoods and, 420–21
    liking and, 89
    schools and, 101–3, *102*
    suffering and, 410
    unity and, 418, 435
ethology, 2–4, 12, 21
Evangelical preachers, 130
evolutionary theory, 73–75, 245,
    425–26, 435, 456n–57n, 481n,
    484n
Exodus, 42
expensive items
    contrast and, 18–19
    as "good," 2–3, 5–9, *8*, 15, 450n–52n

experts, 226–27, 231, 469n
    authority and, 231, 239, 469n
    credible, 225–27, 239
    distinguishing true, 232–33, 239,
        470n
    evaluating relevance of, 232–33
    impartiality of, 234
    trustworthiness of, 225–26, 234,
        239–40
    as witnesses, 432–34
exploitation
    authority and, 212
    characteristics of, 71–72
    consistency and, 299–303
    heart-of-hearts signals and, 355–57
    reciprocity rule and, 67–72
    social proof and, 191–96
    stomach signals and, 352–55
    unity and, 430
*Extraordinary Popular Delusions and
    the Madness of Crowds* (MacKay),
    158, 464n

face, mirror image of, 96, 459n
Facebook, 159, 376, 480n
false information, 442–46. *See also*
    lies
    familiarity and, 96–97, 459n
    social proof and, 191–94, *192*, 198
familiarity, 122, 125
    cooperation and, 104
    liking and, 96–98, 459n
    school integration and, 97–98
    uncertainty and, 144–45, 196
family, 395
    aid to, 379, 481n–82n
    fictive, 382
    unity and, 435
family-like relationships, 425
Faraday, Michael, 295
FBI, 174–75
feasibility, 160–61, 197
Federal Aviation Administration, 10
Federal Trade Commission, 191, 451n
feeding frenzy, 278–79
Feinberg, Richard, 110–11
Festinger, Leon, 135, 138, 473n
filling station, 356–57
financial investments
    authorities and, 224–25, 452n

boiler-room sales operations,
255–56
experts and, 224–25
family and, 382–83, 384
trustworthiness and, 229
"we" group unity and, 368–70,
478n–79n
fingerprint-pattern partner, 85, 458n
finger tapping, 398, 400, 484n, 485n
fire
inspectors and, 219
rescues from, 379
safety proposal, 69
fireflies, 12
First Amendment, 264
first-person pronouns, 14, 191
fishermen, 278–79
fixed-action patterns, 3–5, 7, 21
flattery, 91, 318, 459n. *See also*
compliments
Fleming, Thomas, 272
Florida, transgender individuals and,
424
Florida State University, 242
flowers, gift of, at school open house,
67–68
focusing illusion, 426–27, 489n
food, 123
free gifts of, 43
free samples and, 39
Pavlov's dogs and, 115–16, *115*
political campaigns and, 114
food court posters, 156–57, 160
food servers, 369
candy with bill and, 32, 454n
compliments and, 90, 95
rejection-then-retreat technique,
456n
similarity and, 87, 458n
tricks by, to increase tips, 235–38
foot-in-the-door technique, 310–13,
359, 360, 433–34
fossil theft, 184–86, *186*
Foundation Fighting Blindness, 248
Fox, M. W., 450n
Fox, Robin, 24–25
Fox Television Network, 280
Foxtrot, *302*
France, 392, 404, *404*, 456n, 485n
France-Australia mutual aid, 453n

Frank, Robert, 163–64, 465n
Franklin, Ben, 414
Frantz, Sue, *312*
Fraser, Scott, 310–13
fraternities
hazing and, 329–36, 476n
similar looks and, 385
Freedman, Jonathan, 310–13, 337–39
freedom-establishing wording, 268
freedom of speech, 264
freedoms, loss of, 273–76, 289
scarcity and, 257–60, 262–63, 267,
471n
freedom to say no, 268, 472n
free-information-and-inspection
gambit, 69–70
freeloaders, 28
free samples, 38–42, *39*, 49
French Revolution, 272
Friedman, Alicia, xiii
friends
advice and, 416
best, 376
close, 375–76, 480n
cross-group or diverse, 421–22,
425–26, 436
endless chain of, 78–79
f-commerce and, 376
home party sales and, 73–78, 457n
referrals by, 79–80, 457n
similar-looking, 385
strategic, 80–81
fruit consumption, 131, 462n
fruit flies, 157, 464n
fundraising. *See* charitable donations
funerals, hiring criers for, 156
furniture, online store, 427–28

gambling, 188
betting the odds and, 7–8, 10
racetrack commitment and, 293
racetrack odds and, 195–96
Garcia, David, 411
Garfinkle, Yosef, *397*
General Foods, 321
General Hospital (TV drama), 212
genetic relatedness, 385, 480n–82n,
488n–89n
Genovese, Kitty, 145–46, 464n
geography, 183

Gerard, Harold, 324
Gerber baby foods, 174
Gertsacov, Daniel, 454n, 462n
Gestapo, 407
Ghana, 369
Gift, The (Mauss), 455n
gifts. *See also* small favors
    charitable donations and, 24, 200
    employee loyalty and, 27
    free samples and, 38–42, *39*, 49
    future span and, 25
    memorable, 25
    obligation and, 25, 45–46
    personalized, 42
    personalized service and, 44
    refusing, 41–42, 50
    social pressures and, 45
    small, 24–25
    Tupperware parties and, 75
    uninvited, 45–46
    women's obligation to men giving, 50
Girard, Joe, 73, 81, 90–91, 123,
    366–68, 478n
Goebbels, Joseph, 97
Goethe, Johann Wolfgang von, 170
GoFundMe, 410
Goldberg, L., 452n
Goldman, Sylvan, 144
Goldstein, Noah, 27, 47
golfers, 188, 244
Gollwitzer, 475n
Gomez, Juan, xiii
Good Cop/Bad Cop, 105–6
"goosing 'em off the fence" tactic,
    278
Gorbachev, Mikhail, 274, 275
Gordon's restaurant, 326
Gouldner, Alvin, 24, 452n
government leaders, 209
government safety monitors, 219
Grammer, Karl, 451n
Grand Canyon, 184
grandparental favoritism, 381–82
Grant, Adam, 348–49
gratitude, 455n
Graziano, William, xiii
Greece, 456n
Green, Donna, 262
Green Bay Packers, 373
Greer, Robert, 85

greeting cards, 23, 452n
    car salesmen and, 91
    fundraisers and gift of, 46
Griskevicius, Vladas, 473n
group-bonding, 397. *See also* cross-
    group interactions
group dynamics, 162
group video games, 398
Guardians, 136–43, 463n
Guéguen, Nicolas, 472n
guilt by association, 109
Guinness Book of World Records, 73,
    82, 366
guitar, attractiveness and, 404–5, *404*,
    485n
Gulban, Daniel, 255, 256
guns, 261–62

Haim, Rabbi, of Romshishok, 103,
    460n
hair stylists, 90
halo effects, 82, 108, 124, 226, 457n,
    469n
Hamermesh, Daniel, 83
Hamilton, W. D., 481n
handicapped zones, 131
hand sanitizer, 379–80
Hangzhou, China, 328
Harries, Jonathan, xiii
Harris, James, 316–17
Hasting, Mark, xiii
Hastings, Reed, 129
health-care management, 348
health-care staffs, 210. *See also* nurses;
    physicians
health club memberships, 254
heart disease, 35
heart-of-heart signs, 355–57, 362
height, 215–16, *215*, 468n
help, calling for, 149–50
Help a Capital Child, 199
Hemingway, Ernest, 481n
Henry V (Shakespeare), 407, 409
Hess, Ernst, 407–8, 486n
Hidden Persuaders, The (Packard), 39
high school students, college and, 323
Himmler, Heinrich, 407–8, 486n
Hippocratic oath, 348
Hitler, Adolf, 387–88, 393–94, 408–9
Hobbes, Thomas, 208

Hoffer, Eric, 127
Hofmann, David, 348–49, 461n
Holland, 135, 462n, 481n
Holocaust, 386–95, *389, 395,* 407, 423, 482n–84n, 486n
home
    unity and, 386–87, 390, 435
    unifying practices and, 418–19, 426, 436, 482n, 487n
    waste separation and, 328
Home Fire Safety Association, 69
homeowners
    billboard experiment and, 310–13, 433–34
    charity solicitors and, 223
hometown teams, 372–73
Hong Kong, 369
horns effect, 108
hostage negotiations, 86
hotels, 454n
    bookings and, 249
    fake reviews and, 14
    personalized service and, 43–44, 455n
Howard, Daniel, 305, 474n
human family, getting together, as species, 417–29, 436, 482n–83n
Hyer, Michelle, 283

IBM, 111, 451n
ice-cream toppings, 128
ice water, putting hand in, 409, 486n
identity
    blurring of, 365, 478n
    shared, xiii, 426, 488n
"if expert said so" rule, 9–10
IKEA effect, 412, 487n
Inclusion of Other in the Self Scale, *365*
inclusive fitness, 481n
indebtedness, 455n
    free gifts and, 44–47
    free samples and, 38
    people who gain from, 28
    power of, 29
    reciprocation and, 24
    unequal exchanges and, 47–48
    web of, 24
independence, pain of, 162
India, 369, 452n, 463n, 479n

individualism, 360, 362, 477n
individuality, 282, 289, 473n
Indonesia, 463n
"inexpensive = bad" rule, 6
influence levers. *See also* authority; commitment and consistency; liking; reciprocation; scarcity; social proof; unity
    defined, 1–22
    instant, 437–46
    power of, 52–53
    triggers for, 13
    use of, 13–15, 22 (*see also* compliance practitioners; con artists; profiteers)
information
    avalanche of, 440–42, 446, 490n
    exclusive, 290, 472n
information-systems salespersons, 228
in-group, 477n–79n, 482n. *See also* family; kinship; "we"-groups
    acting in unison and, 398–99
    favoritism and, 364, 369
    Japanese and Jews and, 394–95
    lies by, vs. out-group, 370
    politics and, 370–71
    similar looks and, 385
    sports and, 371–73
initiation ceremonies, 328–34, 475n–76n
inner choice, 335–40, 361, 476n
Institute of Medicine, 210
insurance agents, 93, 306–7
intelligence, attractiveness and, 84
international relations, 36, 317–18, 417–18, 453n
internet, xiii. *See also* eboxes
    bots and, 96
    refer-a-friend promotions, 80
    social proof-fueled panics, 159
intimate partner violence, 131
invoices, gifts sent with, 42
Iowa, 121, 345–46, *346*
Ireland–Native American reciprocity, 410, 486n
ISIS, 26
Islamic terrorism, 423
Israeli-Palestinian relations, 423–24, 480n
Italian canned tomatoes, 211

Italy
  Cuban missile crisis and, 36–37
  Ethiopia and, 26
  recycling and, 465n
Izmir, 135

Janis, Irving, 162
Japan, 379, 455n
  COVID-19 and, 132, 463n
  Holocaust and, 387–95, 395, 483n
  obligation and, 24
  pets and, 377
  proverbs and, 49
jaywalking, 221, 232, 469n
Jerry Maguire (film), 384
jewelry-store customers, 2–3, 5–7, 15
Jews
  Arabs and, 423
  Christian reciprocity and, 26
  Holocaust and, 26, 386–95, 389,
    395, 407–9, 423, 482n–83n
  Madoff and, 368–69
jigsaw classroom, 101–3, 102, 487n
job candidates
  attractiveness and, 83
  clothing and, 223
  compliments and, 90
  recommendations, 235
  salary offer and, 223
  weaknesses and, 228
Johnson, Lyndon, 34
Johnston, Cynthia, 85
Johnston, Phillip, xiii
Jones, Edward, 316–17
Jones, Rev. Jim, 42, 178–84, 198
Jones, Steve, 417–18
Jonesboro, Arkansas, school
    shootings, 178
Jonestown, Guyana, massacre, 42,
    178–84, 182, 198, 454n, 466n
Joyce, James, 291
judges, authority of, 209, 231
judgmental heuristics, 9
Jupiter missiles, 36
Jütte, Astrid, 451n
juvenile delinquents, 55, 456n

Kahan, Dan, 456n
Kahneman, Daniel, 244, 402, 426,
    485n, 489n

Kalisch, Rabbi Shimon, 394–95, 423
Kalogris, Michael, 330
Kampen, Jakob van, 463n
Kappa Sigma fraternity, 330
Keech, Marian, 135–43
Kendie, Endayehu, xiii
Kennedy, John F., 36–37, 37
Kennesaw, Georgia, 262
Kenrick, 452n, 456n
Keough, Donald, 269
Kerr, Peter, 255
key rings, gift of, 46, 455n
KGB, 274
Khmer Rouge, 484n
Khrushchev, Nikita, 36, 37
kidney disease, 371, 379
Kindertransport, 26
kinship, 378–85, 381, 435, 481n, 487n,
    490n
  acting together and, 398
  co-residence and, 418
  honorary, 487n
  similarity and, 385
Kirkman & Scott, 277
Kissinger, Henry, 318
Klawer, Karen, xiii
Kluckhohn, Richard, 328
Knishinsky, Amram, 472n
knowledge, 71, 440–42
Kobe, Japan, Jews in, 387, 393
Koch, Thomas, 472n
Korean War POWs, 307–9, 314–22,
    335–36, 474n
Kunz, Jenifer, 452n
Kunz, Phillip, 452n

labor negotiators, 55
labor unions, 430
La Ganga, Maria, 466n
Lakota Sioux, 120
Lampedusa, Giuseppe Tomasi di,
    449n
Langer, Ellen, 4–5
language styles, 86
Lansky, Doug, 158, 464n
LaPorte, Nicole, 128–29
larger-then-smaller requests, 57–58
LaRue, Frederick, 58, 60
laugh-trackers, 156, 191, 443
laundry detergents, 262–63, 471n

Leakey, Richard, 24, 453n
Le Chambon, France, 392, 483n
Leopold, Aldo, 412–13, 486n–87n
Levi's, 376
Lewin, R., 453n
Lewis, C. S., 313
Liddy, G. Gordon, 58–60, *61*
lies. *See also* false information
   political in-groups and, 370–71
   repeated, 97
liking, xvii, xviii, 73–125, 456n–62n
   acting in unison and, 398–401
   association and, 107–20
   attractiveness and, 82–84
   automaticity and, 439, 446
   bearers of bad news and, 107–8, 117
   beliefs and, 73–75
   charitable donations and, 200
   compliance and, 29–30
   compliments and, 89–95
   contact and cooperation and,
     96–106
   defense vs., 121–24
   ebox on, 253
   malpractice suits and, 75
   online persuaders and, 87–88
   profit and, 75–80
   Reader's Report on, 211
   reciprocity and, 29–32, 44
   scarcity and, 267
   sensitivity to undue, 125
   similarity and, 84–89
   social proof and, 188
   strategic friendship and, 80–81
   Tupperware parties and, 75–78, *78*
Lil Wayne, 373
limited-number tactic, 249–50, 253,
   254, 289, 472n, 473n
limited-time tactic, 252–56, 472n
line-length estimates, 324–25
Lithuania, 387–89
Littleton, Colorado, school shootings,
   176, *178*
local-field-office strategy, 392
locality, 183, 386–87, 390–93, 435
logical/factual approach, 374
London
   brewery pub, 128, 462n
   earthquakes of 1761, 158, 464n
L'Oréal, 234

loss aversion, 244–48, 247–48, 289,
   470n
Louie, Diane, 42, 454n
Louis-Dreyfus, Julia, *381*
Louisville, Kentucky, 131, 462n
love bombing, 163, 465n
low-balling tactic, 341–47, *346*, 359,
   361, 476n
Lubnicka, Danuta, xiii
luncheon technique, 114–16, 461n
lynching, 273

MacKay, Charles, 158–59, 464n
MacKenzie, Bob, 281
macular degeneration, *248*
Macy's, 376
Madoff, Bernard, 368
magazine sales, 254
Magna Carta (1215), 24
Magruder, Jeb Stuart, 58–60
mail and mail appeals
   investment bankers and, 199
   liking and response rate, 85
   lost letters experiment, 369–70,
     479n
   unsolicited gifts with, 32, 44, 46
mail-order catalogues, 110
Major League Baseball, 372
Malinowski, Bronislaw, 453n
managers, 215, 413–14
Mankin, Helen, 32, 454n, 462n
"many, the," 143, 156–63, 197
marching in step, 396, 400–401,
   485n
Mars candy bars, 112, 461n
Mars landing, 112
Martin, Steve J., 27, 32, 454n, 462n
mask wearing, 131–32, 463n
mass shootings, 176–77, 466n
mass suicide, 177–84
MasterCard, 110
Mauss, Marcel, 45, 455n
Mauss, Susanne, 486n
McConaughey, Matthew, 112
McDonald's, 32, 128, 454n, 462n,
   463n–64n
McGovern, George, 58
MCI Friends and Family Calling
   Circle, 79–80
McLuhan, Marshall, 384–85

McNeill, William H., 484n
medical errors, 468n
medical tests, 248. *See also*
    physicians
Medication Errors (Cohen and Davis),
    210
Meisinger, Josef, 394
Meningitis Research UK, 199
Merchant of Venice, The (Shakespeare),
    490n
Mesa, Arizona, 252–53
Mexico-Ethiopia mutual aid, 25–26,
    453n
Michaels, James, xiii
Mihaly, Orestes J., 256
Milgram, Stanley, 200–209, 202, 224,
    238, 467n–68n
military, 207–8, 334–35, 400, 417,
    485n
Mill, John Stuart, 439
Miller, John, 343
Millerites, 135
Mills, Judson, 333–34
mimics, 12–15
mistake
    Big, 188, 198
    precious, 246
Mitchell, John, 58–60
Mitnick, Keven, 469n
mononucleosis, 12
Montanists, 135
moon landing, 111–12
morality, 462n
Morga, Alicia, 323
Mormon temple, 252–53
Morrow, Lance, 274, 472n
Moysey, Steven, xiii
Mud Run race, 408
Mueller, Katie, xiii
Mullins, Gay, 269
Multiple Sclerosis Association, 317
Munger, Charlie, 228, 382, 383
music, 401–5, 404, 436, 462n, 484n,
    485n
Muskie, Edmund, 58
mutual aid, 26, 410
mutual concession, 53
mutual enemy, 423, 436
mutual identity, 423
MyFitness Pal, 323

Nail, Paul, xiii
name-droppers, 120
name resemblance, 85, 458n
National Auto Dealers Association,
    303–4
National Basketball Association, 372
National Football League, 373, 461n
national identity, 435–36, 488n
Native Americans, 1–2, 5–7, 120–21,
    410, 486n
natural-gas users, 345–46, 346
naturalness, 461n
Navajo-Ireland mutual aid, 410
Naval Weapons Station (Concord,
    California), 207
Nazi Germany, 97, 363, 387–95, 389,
    395, 407–8, 468n, 482n–84n,
    486n
NBC TV, 280
negotiations
    deadlock near end of, 241–45
    handshakes and, 103, 460n
    rejection-then-retreat technique,
        64–66
    similarity and, 86–88, 458n, 479n
    unsolicited favors, 455n
Neidert, Gregory, xvii
neighborhood diversity, 420–21,
    425–26, 436, 487n–88n
Neolithic era, 396, 397, 484n
Netflix, 128–29, 171
news, 466n
    delivering bad, 116–17, 459n,
        460n–61n
    fake, 459n
    suicide stories and, 171
newspaper ads, 285–86
newspaper carrier, 94–95
New Yorker, 20
New York Times, 145, 255–56, 323, 405,
    464n, 486n
Nicaragua, 207
Nickerson, David, 483n
Nicklaus, Jack, 358–60
Nielsen Company, 79, 457n
nightclubs, 130, 443–44
9/11/2001 attacks, 427–28
Nissan "Rogue" SUV, 112, 461n
Nixon, Richard, 58
Norris, Dan, xiii

North Carolina, 91
Northern Illinois University shooting, 176
Northern Ireland, 486n
Northwestern University, 229–30
no-tolerance clause, 435, 490n
nuclear missiles, 36–37, 37
nurses, 216–18, 222, 224, 468n–69n
Nuwer, Hank, 476n

Obama, Barack, 34, 392, 483n
obedience, blind, 208–13, 467n–468n
obligation, 453n, 455n
    exploitation through, 45
    human network of, 24
    liking and, 29–30
    limited span of, 25
    reciprocity and, 24–26
    refusing gifts to avoid, 41–42
    unequal exchanges and, 47
    uninvited debts and, 44–47
O'Brien, Lawrence, 59–60
Ohio State University, 330
Old Cola Drinker of America, 269
Old Testament, 208–9
Olympics, 112, 461n
Omar, Sam, xiii
Omega Gamma Delta fraternity, 330
Omega watches, 111
online dating, 84, 458n
online marketing
    customer ratings and, 131, 462n
    fake or paid reviews, 13–14, 130, 191, 192, 444, 451n
    familiarity and, 96
    f-commerce and, 376
    negative reviews, 230
    similarity and, 87–88
    social proof and, 157
    trustworthiness and, 229–31
    verified buyers and, 230
    visitor registration forms and, 315, 474n
Op-Eds, 226, 469n
Operation Safe Haven, 26
opinion statements, 96
Opower, 165, 465n–66n
Oregon, 27
out-group threat, 489n

Packard, Vance, 39
Paese, 455n
Pakistan, 452n
Pallak, Michael, 345
Papa John's Pizza, 461n
Paramount Pictures, 280
parents
    adolescent rebellion vs., 259–60, 275
    authority of, 209
    bad kids in neighborhood and, 108–9
    caring for unrelated individual and, 418–19
    survey participation by, and student grades, 380–81, 417, 481n
    unitizing experiences provided by, 417
parking-meter experiment, 220
parking tickets, 131, 462n–63n
partnership-raising approach, 374–75
party invitations, 23
Pathfinder rocket, 112
Patriot, The (film), 192
Patton (film), 280
Pavlov, Ivan, 115–16, 115, 461n
Paws, 309
Pearl Harbor attacks, 393
peer-suasion, 163–68, 465n
    public commitment and, 323–24
    suicide and, 174, 177, 197–98
People's Temple, 178–84
Perry, Gina, 468n
Persian messengers, 107–8, 116
personalization, 42–44, 200
perspective taking, 426, 436, 488n
Persuasive Advertising (Armstrong), 405
pest-control experts, 219
Peters, Greg, 129
petitions, 261, 310–13, 312, 471n
Petrified Forest National Park, 184–87, 186, 466n
pets, unity and, 377–78, 378, 480n
pet-supply warehouse, 38, 456n
PGA tour, 244
pharmaceutical companies, 35, 454n
Phillips, David, 170, 172–77, 197, 466n
phobias, 132–33, 197

phones
  addiction to, *441*
  fraud by callers, 359–60
  friends' accounts and, 79–80
  in-person conversation vs., 246–47
physical attractiveness
  contrast and, 16, 452n
  copulins and, 451n
  halo effect and, 108, 457n
  liking and, 82–84, 122, 124
physicians
  appointments and, 327
  authority and, 210–12, 216–18, 231
  blind obedience to, 210–11, 216–18,
    468n–69n
  claimed title of, 217–18
  clothes and trappings of, 214
  drug companies and, 454n
  errors of, 210
  hand washing and, 348, 477n
  overprescribing and, 163, 349, 465n
  reminders and, 348–49
  TV ads and, 212–13, *213*, 233
  white coat and, 222–23
physiological arousal, 247, 284
Picasso, Pablo, 473n
Player, Gary, 358
"please no theft" sign, 184–85
pluralistic ignorance, 145–46, 151, 182,
    194, 464n
Poland, 193, 369–70, 396, 467n, 479n
polecat, turkey and, 2–3, 5
police, xvi, 104–6, 480n
political attitudes, 385, 435
  in-group unity, 370–71, 480n
political campaigns (elections)
  attractiveness and, 83
  celebrities and, 113–14
  contributions and, 34–35
  exchange of favors and, 33, 454n
  familiarity and, 96–97
  field-office volunteers and, 392,
    483n
  food and, 114
  height of candidates and, 215, 468n
  lawn signs and, 119
  odors and, 114
  reciprocity and, 33–38
  similarity and, 86, 385

trustworthiness and, 228, 469n
  unity and, 417, 479n
  voting commitment and, 304
political revolutions, 271–75, 472n
polluting firms, 132
Ponzi, Charles, 368–69
popularity. *See also* social proof
  brewery pub beer choices, 128,
    462n
  McDonald's McFlurry and, 128,
    462n, 463n
  menu choices and, 127–28, 144
  music downloads, 462n
  Netflix and, 128–29
  trends and, 190
Portuguese language, 24
Poseidon Adventure, The (film),
    280–81, 284
post office shootings, 176–77
Poza, Diego, 315
Pratkanis, Anthony, 359, 459n
prayer, 306, 396
prehistoric art, *397*
prejudice. *See also* cross-group
    relations; ethnic groups; race
  school desegregation and, 97–99
  unifying practices to combat,
    419–29, 486n, 487n–488n
prescriptions, 210–11, 217, 349
presidential elections, 381–82, 392
presidents, legislators and, 34
Pre-Suasion (Cialdini), 477n
prices
  contrast and, 18–20
  controls petition, 261
  value and, 1–2, 5–6, 450n, 452n
prison sentences, 212
Procter & Gamble, 276, 321
product tampering, 174, 466n
professor, title of, 214
profiteers. *See also* con artists
  influence levers and, 15–16
  reciprocal rule and, 68–71
  social proof and, 193, 196
  triggers and, 12–13, 15–16, 22
  unity and, 430, 435
prospect theory, 244
psychological reactance theory,
    257–68, 289, 475n

Psychology for Marketers, 87
psychopaths, 423, 488n
psychophysics, 16
public good, 344–45
public commitment, 322–27, 345, 361,
    475n
Purdue University, 265
Pyne, Joe, 437–38

rabies, 12
race relations. *See also* cross-group
    interactions
  acting together and, 398–99
  contact approach and, 97
  diverse neighborhoods and,
    420–21, 487n–488n
  jigsaw classroom and, 102
  liking and similarity and, 89
  school integration and, 101–4, 102
  segregation and, 272–73
  sports and, 372
  unitizing experiences and, 417–29,
    435
radio call-letters jingles, 116
raffle tickets, 28–29, 45, 48
rationality, 403, 405
Razran, Gregory, 114–16, 461n
Reader's Reports, xii–xiii, 6,
    20–21, 27, 31–32, 46–47, 51,
    56–57, 65–66, 70–71, 79–80, 95,
    120–21, 133–34, 144–45, 150–51,
    195–96, 211, 222–25, 237–38,
    245, 249–50, 261, 276, 287–88,
    306–7, 321–22, 326, 333–34, 351,
    379–80, 444–45, 470n–71n
real-estate sales, 19, 22, 188, 278
reciprocation, xvii, xviii, 23–72,
    452n–56n
  advantages of, 28, 45
  authority and, 236–38
  automaticity and, 439, 446
  breaking rule of, 455n
  charitable donations and, 200, 248
  communal relationships and, 50
  compliance devices and, 71–72
  concessions and, 51–66, 68
  cross-group friendships and, 422
  defenses against 66–72
  defined, 23–24

exploitation of, 28, 45, 47
failing to conform to, 49–50
gifts and, 24–25
Good Cop/Bad Cop and, 106
group obligations and, 47
initial favors, redefined as tricks, 72
international negotiations and,
    36–37, 37
international relations and, 25–26,
    410
LBJ and, 34
liking and, 29–32
marriage and, 456n
not-so-free sample and, 38–42
obligation and, 24–26, 45, 47
online vouchers and, 33
personalization and, 42–44
pervasiveness of, 24
politics and, 33–38, 114
power of, 29–32, 38, 71–72
rejecting, 67–69
rejection-then-retreat technique
    and, 53–64, 72
repeated exchange and, 405–7, 436
scarcity and, 267
Tupperware parties and, 75
unequal exchanges triggered by,
    47–50, 72
uninvited debts and, 44–47, 72
victims' reactions and, 62–64
Watergate and, 57–60, 61
women and gifts from men, 50
recruiters, xvi, 93, 133–34
rectal earache case, 210–11
recycling, 132, 160, 328, 465n
Reda, Ali, 366–68, 367, 478n
Regan, Dennis, 28–29, 32, 45, 48, 453n
Reiterman, Tim, 466n
rejection-then-retreat technique,
    53–66, 61, 72, 456n
relationships, xviii–xviii
  number of, 440
  similarity and, 87
relief aid, 25
religion, 73–74, 208–9, 369–70, 385,
    417, 435, 456n
reminders, 347–49
Republican Party, 58–59, 423
request-plus-reason experiment, 4–5

Resnik, Alan J., xiii
restaurants. *See also* food servers
   advice from consumers on, 415–16
   candy with bill, 32, 49
   credit card logos on tip trays and, 110
   early lunch sign, 156–57
   gifts and fast-food, 42–43
   menu choice popularity and,
     127–28, 144, 190, 462n
   no-show reservations and, 326–27
   rejection-then-retreat technique,
     456n
résumés, 238
retailers
   attractive staff and, 84
   bargain-basement sales, 278–80,
     279
   contrast and, 18–19
   price reductions and, 451n–52n
   scarcity and, 247
   theft and, 131
   waiting lines outside shops, 193,
     243–44
Retzlaff, Daryl, xiii
revenge, 47
revolutions, 271–72
Reynolds, Sir Joshua, 296, 474n
Rice, Berkeley, 456n
Riecken, Henry, 135, 138
Rimé, Bernard, 411
risk
   loss aversion and, 247
   of failing, 244
rituals, 396, 452n
Robert, Cavett, 131
robins, 4, 450n
Robinson, Chris, 212
robot toy, 337–39
rock-music groupies, 120
Rogue One (film), 112
Rolling Stone, 85
Rolling Stones, 85
Roman Catholic clergy, 430–31
romance
   commitment and, 292–93, 305–6,
     355–56
   competition and, 278
   distinctiveness and, 281–82,
     472n–73n
   health and, 480n

   infidelity and, 305–6
   in-groups and, 374–75
   loss aversion and, 247
   low-ball tactic and, 344
   music and, 403–4
   parental interference on teenagers,
     259–61
   physical attraction and, 457n
   repeated reciprocal exchange and,
     405–7, 417
   Romeo and Juliet effect and,
     260–61, 471n
   similar language and, 86
   speed-dating and, 87
Romeo and Juliet effect and, 261, 471n
Rosenberger, Geofrey, xiii
Rosenthal, A. M., 464n
Ross, Lee, 37–38
Rosten, Leo, 452n
Rothman, Alexander, 248
Royal Ascot Races, 158, 464n
"rule of the bagel," 453n
Russian Revolution, 272
Rwandan genocide, 483n
Ryan, Leo R., 179

Sabbataists, 135
Sadat, Anwar, 317–18
sale signs, 112, 461n
salespeople, xvi, xvii. *See also*
    automobile salesmen
   boiler-room investment swindles
    and, 255–56
   competition and, 278
   contrast principle and, 18–19
   deadline tactic and, 254–55
   escalating commitment and, 310
   free samples and, 40
   grooming and, 84
   liking and, 93
   magazine, door-to-door, 254
   peer-suasion and, 166–68
   scarcity and limited-number tactic,
    250–51
   similarity and, 87
   social proof and, 131, 190
   supermarket buyers and limited
    information, 266–67
   "we" groups and, 366–67
   written commitments and, 319–20

Salovey, Peter, 248
Sand County Almanac, A (Leopold), 412, 486n
San Francisco Museum of Art, 282, 473n
Sanna, L. J., 462n
Sarandros, Ted, 129
scarcity, xvii–xix, 241–90, 470n–73n
  automaticity and, 439, 446
  boiler-room swindles and, 255–56
  charitable donations and, *248*
  competition and, 277–81, 290
  cookie taste tests and, 271
  defenses vs., 283–90
  distinctiveness and, 281–83
  ebox on, 253–54
  free online vouchers and, 33
  information and, 265–67
  iPhone waiting line and, 243–45
  limited-numbers tactic and, 249–52
  limited-time tactic and, 252–56
  loss aversion and, 246–56, *247, 248*
  New Coke and, 269–71
  newly scarce items and, 290
  political turmoil and, 271–75
  psychological reactance and, 257–68
  Reader's Reports and, 245, 249–50, 276, 287–88, 444–45
  social proof and, 188
  thoughtful decisions and, 284–85
  Tupperware parties and, 76
  used car sales and, 285–87
  value and, 289
Scarry, Richard, 249
Schacter, Stanley, 135, 138
Schein, Edgar, 308–9, 316, 474n
Schiele, Egon, 226
Schindler, Oskar, 386, 387
Schindler, Robert, 456n
schools
  basketball games, 121
  competitiveness within, 98, 460n
  cooperative learning and, 101–4, 415, 460n, 487n
  desegregation and, 273
  integration of, 97–98
  jigsaw classroom, 101–3, *102*
  peer-suasion and, 163

shootings at, 176–77, *178*
  unitizing experiences and, 417
Schrange, Michael, 455n
Schwartz, Benjamin, 454n
Schwarzenegger, Arnold, 233
science and scientists
  communicators and, 73–74
  COVID-19 and, 131–32
  pharmaceuticals and, 35, 454n
security guard uniform, 220, 224
security systems, hackers and, 219, 469n
Segal, Henry, 314, 474n
Self, William, 280
self-affirmations, 489n
self-disclosure, 422, 488n
self-image, 313–14, 317–18, 323, 335, 361, 474n–75n
self-interest, 449n
self-other merging, 401, 484n, 485n
"Self-Reliance" (Emerson), 350
self-sacrifice, 397, 399–402
Seneca, 425, 488n
Serbia, 390, 424
service contract sales, 65–66
sex-discussion group, 333
sexual attitudes, 385
sexual material, censorship of, 264–65
Shadel, Doug, 359, 451n
Shakespeare, William, 107, 260, 407, 409, 490n
Shaklee Corporation, 78–79
Shanghai, China, 387–90, 393
shareholders, 417
Shatzkes, Rabbi Moses, 394
Shayo, 478n
Sherif, Carolyn Wood, 99
Sherif, Muzafer, 99, 101, 460n
Sherman, Steven J., 304
Shinseki, Eric, 282, 283, 473n
shopping cart, 144
shortcuts, 7–10. *See also specific influence levers*
  consistency and, 361
  efficiency and, 22, 438, 442
  falsifiers and, 443
  information overload and, 442, 446
  scarcity and, 257
Shotton, Richard, 462n
Shtulman, Andrew, 456n

similarity, 122, 124–25, 446
  contrived, 87–88
  liking and, 84–89, 458n
  peer-suasion and, 163–68
  physical, 385
  social proof and, 143, 197–98
  uncertainty and, 198
sincerity, sly, 233–34, 237
Sinclair, Gordon, 326
Singapore, 194–95, 467n
Small Big, The (Martin, Goldstein, &
    Cialdini), 27
small favors. See also gifts
  donation request and, 70–71
  importance of not minimizing,
    30–31
  McDonald's and, 32, 454n
  obligation and, 25, 32
  purchases after, 32
  questionnaires and, 32
  reciprocity and, 30, 455n
  tips in restaurants and, 32, 454n
  unequal exchanges and, 48–50
  women's obligation to men
    offering, 50
smiling, synchronized, 398, 484n
smoking cessation, 162, 165, 325–26,
    465n
smoking referendum, 113–14
soccer, 117, 372–73, 462n, 479n
social acceptance, 161–63, 197
social conditions, 170, 176–77
social media, xiii, 376
  likes and, 89–90
  online marketing and, 88
  rumors and, 159–60
social proof, xvii, 127–98, 197,
    462n–67n
  automaticity and, 439, 443
  average-person ads and, 192, 443
  Big Mistake and, 184–89, 198
  bystanders in emergency and,
    145–52
  car salesmen and, 133–34
  commitment and, 323–24
  copycat crimes and, 174–75
  COVID-19 and, 131–32
  crowds mistakenly acting on,
    194–95
  defenses vs., 190–95, 198

defined, 13, 129–30
doomsday cults and, 134–43
ebox on, 253
environmental action and, 132
false and, 130, 156, 191, 430,
    443–44
feasibility and, 160–61, 197
incorrect data and, 191–92
"the many" and, 143, 156–63, 197
mass shootings and, 176–77
mass suicide and, 177–82
mimics and, 13–15
never trusting fully, 195, 198
optimizers of, 143–44
peer-suasion and, 163–68, 197
people power and, 131–34
pluralistic-ignorance and, 194
popularity and, 127–29
Reader's Reports on, 195–96
scarcity and, 267, 278
similarity and, 143, 197
social media and, 159–60
suicide and accidental deaths and,
    168–77
trends and, 187–90, 198
Tupperware parties and, 76
TV sitcoms and, 156
uncertainty and, xviii, xix, 143–46,
    181, 197, 463n
validity, 197
solar panels, 163
Solomon, Thomas "TJ," 178
Somme offensive, 407
songs, 396
Sony Pictures, 192–93
Sorrows of Young Werther, The
    (Goethe), 170
South Africa, 488n
South Korea, 199
Soviet Union, 36–37, 274, 275, 396,
    472n
space program, 111–12
Spain, 382
Spiegel Research Center, 229–30
Splash! restaurant survey, 415–16
sports, 244, 461n
  fans and, 117–20, 119, 125, 372–73,
    462n
  referees and, 371–73, 479n
Spychala, Joanna, xiii

Stalin, Joseph, 274, 484n
stamp collectors, 246
Stanford University, 453n
Stanko, Jack, 303–4
Starbucks, 33
Star Wars, 112, 426
status, 215–16, 223–24, 468n
Stauth, Robert, xiii
Stein, Joel, 381
stereotypes, 8–9
stereotyping, 466n
Stern, Sheldon, 454n
Stevenson, McLean, 89
Stickley, Jim, 219
Stillman, Jessica, 13
St. John, Joe, xiii
Stoke, Marijn, 462n
stomach signs, 352–55, 362
Storke, Bill, 280
story, reading together, 397
Strathewen, Australia, 453n
Strauss, Michel, 226, 469n
strongest argument, place for, 230–31
Styron, William, 334–35
Subway restaurants, 321–22
suffering, 407–11, *408*, 436, 486n
Sugihara, Chiune, 387–90, *389*,
    418–19, 482n, 483n
suicide
    accidental deaths and, 168–77, *171*,
        175
    mass, at Jonestown, 177–84, *182*
    prevention programs, 186–87
    social proof and, 197–98, 466n
suicide-murder stories, 170, 173
Sunday Riley Skincare, 191
supermarkets, 471n
    ecologically grown bananas and,
        317
    free samples and, 38–39
    gifts and, 454n, 455n
    tastings at, 288
supportive conduct, 484n–85n
surveys, 188, 223, 268, 393
Sutcliffe, Kathleen, 468n
Swanson, Richard, 331
Sweden, 455n
Swift, Dan, xiii
Swift, Jonathan, 74, 89
swimming lessons, 165–66

Sydney, Australia, 379–80
synchrony, 484n
System 1 vs. System 2 thinking,
    402–5, 485n

Taber, Alberta, school shootings, 176,
    178
Taliban, 30
Tamraz, Roger, 34
Target, 77
taste, 282, 473n
taxi drivers, 369, 479n
tax policy, 35–36
Taylor, 457n
teachers and teaching
    acting in unison with students, 398
    authority of, 209
    competitiveness in schools and,
        98–99
    cooperative learning and, 99, 101–3
    similarity of, to students, 85–86,
        480n–81n
Teacher's Scotch, 320
technology, 440, 442, 446
Teresa, Mother, 363, 390, 418–19, 482n
terrible twos, 258–59, 289
territorial defense, 3–4
terrorism, 411, 427–28
Tesla owners, 80
texting styles, 86
therapists, 226
thinking-processes experiment, 343–44
13 Reasons Why (web series), 171, 466n
Thomas, Carol, xiii
Thomas, Owen, 323
Thompson, Derek, 462n
Thompson, Leigh, 88
Thonga tribe, 328–31, 334, 476n
Thorne, Avril, 118
threat, 425, 489n
Tiger, Lionel, 24–25
Timberlake, Justin, 373
Time, 269, 274
timing, liking and, 122
tipping. *See* food servers
titles
    authority and, 213–18, 239
    counterfeit, 216–18
    recognizing empty, 232
Tokayer, Marvin, 483n

Tolstoy, Leo, 457n
toothpaste-preference test, 189
torture, 131, 453n
toys
    forbidden, 337–39
    postholiday sales and, 299–303, 302
Trabolt, Jens, xiii
Trail of Tears, 410, 486n
Transcendental Meditation, 296–99
"Trashing Arizona" series, 185
travel, 440
Trebek, Alex, 233
trends, 188–89, 198, 466n
trials
    expert witnesses, 432–34
    inadmissible evidence and, 265–66
    jury commitment and, 304, 325
    trustworthiness and, 228
tribalism, 478n
tribal societies
    dancing and, 397
    initiations and, 328–31, 334
trick-or-treat problem, 67
triggers, 3–5, 8, 10, 12–13, 21–22
Trobriand Islanders, 453n
Trocmé, André, 392, 483n
Trocmé, Magda, 483n
Trudeau, G. B., 235
Trump, Donald, 34
trustworthiness
    experts and, 226, 227, 227–28, 231,
        233–34, 237, 239, 469n
    online reviews and, 229–31
truth by repetition, 459n
Tully, Vanessa, 410
Tupperware, 75–78, 78, 80, 116, 457n
Turkey, 36–37, 135
turkeys, 2–5, 438, 450n
TV ads, 214, 405
TV news, 171
TV sitcoms, 156, 191, 443
20th Century Fox, 280
Twitter, 411
Tylenol, 174

Uber, 455n
UCLA, 64, 180
uncertainty, xix, xviii, 197
    aid in emergency and, 145–52, 148,
        197

loss aversion and, 244, 247
Jonestown suicides and, 198
social proof and, 143–47, 181, 196,
    463n
woman attacked by man and,
    151–52
unequal exchanges, 47–50
uniforms, 219–20, 469n
unifying practices, 418–29
United Kingdom, 24, 247
unity, xiii, xvii, xviii, 363–436,
    477n–90n
    acting together and, 396–415, 436
    advice and, 414–16
    attentional focus and, 426–28, 436
    automaticity and, 439, 446
    business and, 366–69, 367
    close friendships and, 375–76
    co-creation and, 412–14, 436
    Code of Conduct and, 429
    dealing with big problems and,
        417–18
    defense and, 429–35
    diversity and, 420–22, 488n
    ebox on, 375–76, 411
    evolution and, 425–26
    exploitation and, 430
    favorable consequence of, 416–17
    financial investment and, 368–69,
        382–84
    finger tapping and, 400
    home and, 386–90, 419–20
    human family and, 416–29
    in-group effects, 365–70
    kinship and, 378–85
    liking, 398–99
    locality and, 386–87, 390–96
    marching in step and, 400
    merger of identities and, 385
    Milgram study and, 468n
    music and, 401–5, 436
    personal relationships and, 374–75
    pets and, 377–78
    politics and, 370–71
    Reader's Report on, 379–80
    reciprocal exchange and, 405–7,
        436
    romantic partnerships and, 374–75
    speaking-in-unison and, 398
    sports and, 371–73

suffering and, 407–10, *408*, 436
support and, 399–401
Tupperware parties and, 76
unity-building techniques, 400
"we"-groups and, 364–66
University of California, Los Angeles
    (UCLA), 456n
University of Chicago, 20
University of Georgia, 116–17, *119*
University of Minnesota, 135
University of North Carolina, 264
University of Southern California,
    330–32
University of Virginia, 451n
University of Washington, 332, 335
University of Wisconsin, 412
unwanted behavior, decrying
    frequency of, 184–87, 198
UPI, 146
urban riots, 272
urgency, 253, 255–56
US Army Rangers, 282–83, 473n
US Congress, 34, 210
US Constitution, 264
US Forest Service, 185
US history, 393
US Marines, 335
US military intelligence, 30
US Senate, 256
US Supreme Court, 273

vacuum-cleaner sales, 255
validity, the many and, 157–59, 197
value
    price and, 1–2, 5–7
    scarcity and, 246–47, 250, 471n
Vaska, Karla, xiii
Veep (TV series), *381*
Venezuela, 379
verbal style, 87
    online reviews, 14, 191
verified buyers, 230
Viagra, 30
Vicks Formula 44, 212–13, 232–33
Vietnam War, 207–8, 458n
Villers-Bretonneux, France, 453n
Vinci, Leonardo da, 1
Virgil, 199
Virginia Tech massacre, 176
Voltaire, 403

waiting lines, 130, 193, 243–45, 443–44
Wallenberg, Raoul, 386
Wall Street Journal, 276
Wannsee Conference, 393
Warrick, Joby, 453n
watches, smile and, *113*
water conservation, 188–89, 466n–67n
    commitment and, 294
    social proof and, 132
Watergate break-in, 58–60, *61*
water-glass sipping, 399, 484n
water temperature, contrast principle,
    16–17, 19
Watson, Emma, 75, 456n, 457n
Watson, Thomas, Jr., 451n
weaknesses, admitting, 469n
    career and, 237–38
    dishonest, 234–35
    job candidates and, *235*
    placement of, 230–31
    trustworthiness and, 228–30, 240,
    469n–70n
"We Are the World" position, 425
weatherman, 107–8, *109*
"we"-groups, 364–76, 397, 480n–84n
    business and, 366–69
    car sales and, 366–68, *367*, 478n
    Catholic priests, 431
    close friendships and, 375–76
    Code of Conduct and, 429,
    489n–90n
    collectives and, 382, 397
    cross-group connections and,
    423–29
    ethics and, 432–34, *434*–35
    evolution and, 435
    expert witness and, 432–34
    exploiters and, 429–32
    fellow members favored by, 365–66
    financial investment and, 368–69,
    479n
    home and place and, 386–95, *395*
    human family as, 418
    labor unions and, 429
    pets and, 377–78
    politics and, 370–71, 479n
    romantic partners and, 374–75
    shared identities and, 435
    sports and, 371–73
    suffering and, 409–10

Weidenfeld, Lord Arthur George, 26,
    453n
weight loss, 323–25
weight of objects, judging, 16
Weimann, Lucas, xiii
Weinstein, Eugene, 459n
Werther effect, 170–73, 466n
West, Dr. Louis Jolyon, 180
When Prophesy Fails (Festinger,
    Riecken, and Schacter), 135
White-Black relations, 89, 97, 102,
    272–74, 399, 423, 465n, 484n,
    488n. *See also* cross-group
    interactions; race
Whitehead, Alfred North, 1
White House, legislators and, 114
white pine, red birch vs., 412–13
white van abduction fears, 159
Whiting, John W. M., 328
wildlife management, 412, 486n–87n
Willson, S. Brian, 207–8
Wilson, Lee Alexis, 146
Withers, Bill, 403
women
    getting help, during attack by man,
        151–56, 152, 464n
    intimate partner violence and, 131
    male judges of attractiveness of, 451n

obligation to men offering favors,
    50, 455n
white vans abducting, 159
young, and musicians, 403–4,
    485n
Wood, Robert, 280–81, 284
Worchel, Stephen, 268
World Cup, 117
World War I, 407, 453n
World War II, 272, 308, 372–73, 451n
Wosinska, Wilhelmina, xii, 396
Wright, Frank Lloyd, 121
written commitment, 316–27, 320,
    336, 349, 431–32, 434
Wroblewski, Anna, xiii

Yadav, Agrima, xiii
Yale University, 204, 468n
Yazidis, 26
"you get what you pay for" rule, 7
Young, Bernard, 159
youth mentoring, 85–86

Zappa, Frank, 437–38
Zellweger, Renee, 384
Zeta Beta Tau fraternity, 331
Zimbardo, 454n
zoo-trip experiment, 55, 456n